Combat Operations

STEMMING THE TIDE
May 1965 to October 1966

NORTH
VIETNAM

DEMARCATION LINE

QUANG TRI

LAOS

THAILAND

THUA THIEN

Hue

I CTZ

SOUTH CHINA SEA

Da Nang

QUANG NAM

QUANG TIN

QUANG NGAI

KONTUM

BINH DINH

SOUTH
VIETNAM

PLEIKU

CAMBODIA

Tonle
Sap

PHU BON

PHU YEN

DARLAC

II CTZ

KHANH
HOA

QUANG DUC

TUYEN DUC

Da Lat

PHUOC
LONG

Cam Ranh

NINH
THUAN

BINH
LONG

LAM DONG

TAY NINH

III CTZ

BINH THUAN

BINH
DUONG

LONG
KHANH

BINH
TUY

HAU
NGHIA

BIEN
HOA

KIEN TUONG

SAIGON

CHAU
DOC

KIEN PHONG

LONG AN

GIA
DINH

PHUOC TUY

SOUTH
CHINA
SEA

DINH TUONG

GO CONG

AN
GIANG

VINH LONG

KIEN HOA

Vung Tau

KIEN GIANG

PHONG
DINH

VINH BINH

GULF OF
THAILAND

IV CTZ

CHUONG
THIEN

BA XUYEN

BAC LIEU

AN XUYEN

SOUTH VIETNAM

1965–1966

Corps Tactical Zone Boundary

Administrative Boundary

Hue   Autonomous Municipality

0   150 Miles

0   150 Kilometers

United States Army in Vietnam

Combat Operations

STEMMING THE TIDE
MAY 1965 to October 1966

by

John M. Carland

MILITARY INSTRVCTION

Center of Military History
United States Army
Washington, D.C., 2000

Library of Congress Cataloging-in-Publication Data

Carland, John M., 1942–
    Combat operations : stemming the tide, May 1965 to October
1966 / by John M. Carland.
        p.   cm. — (United States Army in Vietnam)
    Includes bibliographical references and index.
    1. Vietnamese Conflict, 1961–1975—United States. 2. Vietnamese
Conflict, 1961–1975—Campaigns. 3. United States. Army—
History—Vietnamese Conflict, 1961–1975.
I. Title.   II. Series.
DS558.C37   2000
959.704'3373—dc21   99–16962
                                                            CIP

CMH Pub 91–5–1

First Printing

For sale by the U.S. Government Printing Office
Superintendent of Documents, Mail Stop: SSOP, Washington, DC 20402-9328
ISBN 0-16-050198-9

United States Army in Vietnam

Jeffrey J. Clarke, General Editor

Advisory Committee
(As of October 1999)

Gerhard L. Weinberg
University of North Carolina

Lawrence R. Atkinson IV
The *Washington Post*

Linda S. Frey
University of Montana

Michael J. Kurtz
National Archives and
Records Administration

Brig. Gen. Fletcher M. Lamkin, Jr.
U.S. Military Academy

Peter Maslowski
University of Nebraska–Lincoln

Col. Charles C. Ware
U.S. Army War College

John H. Morrow, Jr.
University of Georgia

Lt. Gen. David H. Ohle
Deputy Chief of Staff for Personnel

Carol A. Reardon
Pennsylvania State University

Mark A. Stoler
University of Vermont

Maj. Gen. Charles W. Thomas
U.S. Army Training and
Doctrine Command

Brig. Gen. John R. Wood
U.S. Army Command and General Staff College

U.S. Army Center of Military History

Brig. Gen. John S. Brown, Chief of Military History

Chief Historian
Chief, Histories Division
Editor in Chief

Jeffrey J. Clarke
Richard W. Stewart
John W. Elsberg

. . . to Those Who Served

Foreword

*S*temming the Tide chronicles a critical chapter in the Vietnam War, the first eighteen months of combat by the U.S. Army's ground forces. When American ground troops entered the theater in March 1965, Communist forces were on the verge of military victory. Reversing the tide, the Army's brigades and divisions swept out of their bridgeheads into dangerous enemy base areas, blunted the Communist offensive, and shifted to a series of high-tempo operations to keep the enemy off balance until more U.S. fighting units arrived in late 1966.

Combat was grueling. The enemy could be anywhere and everywhere, and was often indistinguishable from the rural population. Battles seemed to flow without order or logic over paddies and hilltops, and victory was hard to measure when villages, once taken, were rarely held. Little by little, however, improvements in communications and intelligence, the helicopter's capacity to extend the battlefield, and the enormous firepower available to commanders crystallized into an attrition and area-denial approach to the fighting which brought an increasing measure of security to key towns and installations. If the war was far from over when the period covered by this volume came to a close, commanders nevertheless believed that the ingredients for ultimate victory were present, chief among them the courage and perseverance of the American soldier in a ferocious war and the inventiveness of the U.S. Army in harnessing the latest in technology to project expeditionary force into a distant theater.

Stemming the Tide is the eighth volume published in the United States Army in Vietnam series. The volume's appearance constitutes partial fulfillment of the Center of Military History's commitment to produce an authoritative history of Army participation in the Vietnam War. Still to come are two additional battle histories, a study examining the war from the perspective of the headquarters that oversaw operations, a work that discusses logistics, another that examines the engineer effort, and a study of U.S. advice and support to the South Vietnamese between 1960 and 1965.

Washington, D.C.
10 March 2000

JOHN S. BROWN
Brigadier General, USA
Chief of Military History

The Author

John M. Carland graduated from the University of Arkansas at Little Rock with a degree in history and political science and spent a year in India at the University of Madras on a Rotary International Fellowship. Later, he received his M.A. in political science from the City College of New York and his Ph.D. in history from the University of Toronto. After teaching history at the University of Kentucky, he joined the U.S. Army Center of Military History in 1985. In recent years he has also taught Vietnam War history at George Mason University. Dr. Carland is the author of *The Colonial Office and Nigeria, 1898–1914,* and is currently involved in the writing of the third combat volume in the United States Army in Vietnam series. He has also contributed numerous articles and reviews in American and Canadian journals.

Preface

Stemming the Tide describes the combat experiences of U.S. Army ground forces in a distant theater. In early 1965 a Communist insurgency seemed close to toppling the South Vietnamese government. Refusing to accept the loss of its Asian ally, the United States committed combat units to the field of battle. In the spring and summer the first Army brigades arrived, established bridgeheads, and began to conduct operations. During the second half of 1965 divisions deployed, and in November and December the Army fought its first big battles. As a result of these battles, and earlier ones fought by the marines, the American commander, General William C. Westmoreland, believed that he had halted the Communist offensive. In 1966, because promised reinforcements arrived in a gradual and piecemeal fashion, Westmoreland could not create the large and experienced force he deemed necessary to take the war to the enemy. Throughout the year, therefore, U.S. troops carried out spoiling operations, denying the initiative to the Communists and buying time to prepare for a later American offensive. By the fall of 1966 Westmoreland and his senior subordinates were optimistic, convinced that American mobility and firepower, knowledge and courage, would eventually defeat the Viet Cong and the North Vietnamese.

In researching and writing this book I received guidance, assistance, and support from a great many people. At the Center of Military History my colleagues in Histories Division take center stage. George L. MacGarrigle, who retired in 1997, answered questions too numerous to count about tactics and operations and about his own service in the Army in Vietnam. And over the years I came to rely on Vincent H. Demma's generosity and his encyclopedic knowledge of Vietnam War sources. For assisting me in crafting the manuscript into its final form, I am deeply indebted to Dr. Joel D. Meyerson and a group of my colleagues—Charles R. Anderson, Dale W. Andrade, Dr. Andrew J. Birtle, Dr. Graham A. Cosmas, Dr. William M. Hammond, Dr. David W. Hogan, Dr. Richard A. Hunt, and Adrian G. Traas. The narrative is a better one for their contributions.

Others at the Center of Military History contributed to this book. In Production Services Joanne M. Brignolo edited the text with unflagging dedication and attention to detail; Sherry L. Dowdy worked magic transforming rough maps into vivid ones; Arthur S. Hardyman, Chief of the Graphics Branch, helped in many ways, especially in the development of the map plan and in the selection and procurement of photographs;

Catherine A. Heerin, Chief of the Editorial Branch, assisted at just the right time; and Teresa K. Jameson, the desktop publisher, demonstrated her proficiency in design. I should acknowledge too the assistance of the Historical Resources Branch in making material in its custody readily available; James B. Knight deserves special mention for his tenacity in locating dozens of documents and books. The Organizational History Branch repeatedly provided sound information on a variety of questions concerning the personnel, organization, and equipment of Army units during the Vietnam War.

Those in the Center's chain of command should also be recognized. I appreciate the efforts of a succession of branch chiefs—Drs. John Schlight, Joel Meyerson, and Graham Cosmas—on my behalf. My thanks also extend to the division chiefs—Lt. Col. Richard O. Perry; Cols. Robert H. Sholly, William T. Bowers, and Clyde L. Jonas; and Dr. Richard W. Stewart. I am grateful for the support of several Chiefs of Military History—Brig. Gens. William A. Stofft, Harold W. Nelson, John W. Mountcastle, and the present chief, John S. Brown.

Useful recommendations came from the review panel convened by Dr. Jeffrey J. Clarke, the Center's Chief Historian and panel chair. I wish to thank the members—Lt. Gens. Sidney B. Berry, Jr., and John Norton; Col. Clyde Jonas; Drs. Graham Cosmas, George C. Herring, Joel Meyerson, Jack Shulimson, and James H. Willbanks; and Joanne Brignolo. Eric M. Bergerud acted as a panel reader.

A number of people outside the Center provided advice and information, including Jack Shulimson, now retired but formerly of the History and Museums Division, U.S. Marine Corps; Dr. David C. Humphrey, presently at the Office of the Historian, Department of State, but previously at the Lyndon Baines Johnson Library, and Regina B. Greenwell, also at the Johnson Library; Richard L. Boylan of the National Archives and Records Administration; Dr. Wayne W. Thompson of the Office of Air Force History; Dr. Edward J. Marolda of the U.S. Naval Historical Center; and Dr. Richard J. Sommers, David A. Keogh, and John J. Slonaker of the U.S. Army Military History Institute. Finally, I owe a special debt of gratitude to George Herring, a good friend who generously shared his insights into the origin, nature, and consequences of the American involvement in Vietnam.

Many who experienced the war firsthand during 1965–66 have assisted me through their knowledge of events and personalities. A few should be highlighted. General William B. Rosson explained in detail General William E. DePuy's role in the formation and evolution of American military strategy in Vietnam, and General Tran Van Tra of the People's Army of Vietnam made clear to me how the Communist leadership came to grips with the American intervention. Robert J. Destatte, a gifted translator of Vietnamese and an expert on the ways of the Communist forces, also became a helpful consultant. I benefited greatly from Joseph L. Galloway's and Lt. Gen. Harold G. Moore's remarkable knowledge of the 1st Cavalry Division's experiences in the Central Highlands. And if my account of the 173d Airborne Brigade is thorough and accurate, it is because Maj. Gen. Ellis W. Williamson, the unit's first commander, took the time to explain the brigade's story to me.

Finally, I would like to thank my wife, Maria, and my sons, Blaise and Raphael, for their understanding, patience, and humor during the years this volume was in the making. They are grateful, I suspect, that the long slog is over.

It remains only to note that the conclusions and interpretations expressed in this book are mine alone and that I am solely responsible for any errors.

Washington, D.C. JOHN M. CARLAND
10 March 2000

Contents

PART ONE
The U.S. Army Enters the War

PART TWO
First Battles

PART FOUR

The Tempo Quickens

Table

Maps

Illustrations

Illustrations courtesy of the following sources: pp. 12 and 100, United Press International; pp. 48 and 156, Lyndon Baines Johnson Library, Austin, Texas; p. 66, U.S. Cavalry Museum, Fort Riley, Kansas; pp. 67, 75, 121, 133, 153, 232, 251, 272, 273, and 315, U.S. Army Center of Military History, Washington, D.C.; p. 105, *1st Air Cavalry Division: Memoirs of the First Team, Vietnam, August 1965–December 1969*; pp. 108, 144, and 323, Wide World Photos; p. 127, Joseph L. Galloway; p. 234, *The 25th's 25th . . . in Combat: "Tropic Lightning," 1 October 1941–1 October 1966*; and p. 335, Col. Leonard L. Lewane. All other illustrations are from the National Archives and Records Administration, Washington, D.C.

PART ONE

The U.S. Army Enters the War

At the Crossroads

The U.S. government regarded the conflict in Southeast Asia with frustration and growing dismay as 1965 began. The American people had committed hundreds of millions of dollars and almost twenty-five thousand military advisers and support troops to South Vietnam's conflict against the North Vietnamese–supported Communist insurgency, but all to no avail. The enemy seemed to be growing stronger by the day, and South Vietnam's rural population was just as impoverished and insecure as when the war began. The U.S. commander in South Vietnam, General William C. Westmoreland, predicted that the next six months would be decisive, for the enemy was moving from guerrilla and small unit combat to a new phase of warfare featuring attacks by large units that stood and fought when challenged. Unless a change occurred, the Communists would consolidate their gains in the countryside, reducing South Vietnamese military units to "a series of islands of strength clustered around district and province capitals . . . clogged with . . . refugees." In that case, Westmoreland warned, the government of South Vietnam might resort to a negotiated settlement on terms unfavorable to the United States. "We are headed toward a . . . [Communist] take-over . . . sooner or later," he added, "if we continue down the present road at the present level of effort."[1]

The Path to War

The path the United States had followed to that point had taken many turns. It began shortly after World War II, when President Harry S. Truman decided to support France in Indochina as a means of gaining leverage against the Soviet Union and its allies in the Cold War. When

[1] COMUSMACV's (Commander, U.S. Military Assistance Command, Vietnam) Military Estimate of the Situation in Vietnam, pp. B1, B4 (first quotation), B5 (second quotation), Tab B of Report on Survey of the Military Situation in Vietnam, [5–12 March 1965], Incl to Memo, Gen Harold K. Johnson, Chief of Staff, U.S. Army, for Secretary of Defense et al., 14 Mar 65, box 5A, Harold K. Johnson Papers, U.S. Army Military History Institute (MHI), Carlisle Barracks, Pa.

France lost heart and agreed in 1954 to split Vietnam into Communist and non-Communist zones at the 17th Parallel, the United States moved to shore up the non-Communist side in the South by providing increasing levels of advice and assistance. With the success of the new country's president, Ngo Dinh Diem, in neutralizing the warlords and religious sects that formed his only opposition, American policymakers decided that Diem represented their best choice for the future. Siding with him, they concentrated on equipping and training his army to provide security for the fledgling state.[2]

The Communists, for their part, had no intention of allowing the Republic of Vietnam to go its own way. When Diem decided against holding elections mandated by the Geneva Accords of 1954 to reunify the country, the leaders of the Democratic Republic of Vietnam in the North resolved to overthrow him. Combining Mao Tse-tung's concept of revolutionary warfare with their own experience fighting the French, they laid out a three-part plan of action. During the first phase, they would concentrate upon base building and political organizing. In the second, they would attempt to destabilize the Diem regime by conducting small unit guerrilla attacks but would deliver larger, more conventional military assaults when the opportunity arose. In the third, large-scale military operations and offensives would seal their victory.[3]

In general, Hanoi's strategy served as a guide to action rather than as a definitive blueprint. Movement from one stage to the next was not automatic but dependent upon progress in the field, however defined at any particular moment. Since the war itself would be fought in many areas at once rather than along contiguous lines of advance and withdrawal, and since different populations, terrains, and weather conditions would prevail in each, Communist forces might find themselves preoccupied with one stage of warfare in one area but with another elsewhere. If they suffered reverses, they could abandon an advanced stage to regroup in an earlier one before resuming their march to victory. In short, Hanoi's strategy was no neat, tidy, mechanical formula. Battlefield reality was key, leaving room, as North Vietnam's defense minister, General Vo Nguyen Giap, observed, for final victory to unfold in a "lively and complicated manner."[4]

Following that outline, the insurgents spent much of the interval between 1956 and 1960 recruiting among South Vietnam's populace and

---

[2] James S. Olson and Randy Roberts, *Where the Dominos Fell: America and Vietnam, 1945–1995* (New York: St. Martin's Press, 1996), pp. 61–63.

[3] For the Chinese Communist approach to revolutionary warfare, see Mao Tse-tung, *On Protracted War* (Peking: Foreign Languages Press, 1967). For an American view of North Vietnamese theory, see Study 67–039, Combined Intelligence Center, Vietnam (CICV), 29 Jun 67, sub: Strategy Since 1954, Historians files, U.S. Army Center of Military History (CMH), Washington, D.C.

[4] Vo Nguyen Giap, *People's War, People's Army* (New York: Frederick A. Praeger, 1962), p. 101.

developing bases in remote areas. When Diem's American-advised armed forces reacted and began to make inroads, the Communists responded by infiltrating men and materiel into the South to further their organizing. They also increased the tempo of their military operations. As they did, they allowed the Communist Party to assume an open role in the conduct of the insurgency's political and military affairs, leading Diem to dub his opponents *Viet Cong*, a derogatory term broadly meaning "Vietnamese Communists."

The Viet Cong divided their combat forces into three ranks. From lowest to highest, they consisted of a part-time guerrilla militia, organized into platoons and squads that served mainly to provide security at the hamlet level; the local forces, or full-time guerrilla units, organized into companies under district or provincial control; and the main force regular units, organized into battalions, regiments, and divisions that answered ultimately to the senior leadership of the entire Communist movement in South Vietnam. According to American estimates at the time, the enemy force totaled only four thousand men in April 1960, but three years later that number had soared to thirty-five thousand.[5]

During January 1961, to improve coordination of the expanding effort in the South, Hanoi established two organizations: the *Central Office for South Vietnam* (*COSVN*) and the *People's Liberation Armed Forces*. *COSVN*, located somewhere in the jungles northwest of Saigon, was to be the politico-military headquarters that directed the war in the South; the *People's Liberation Armed Forces* contained all of the Viet Cong guerrillas and main force units. Within six months Communist Party leaders in Hanoi would split *COSVN*'s responsibilities by establishing a new administrative entity, *Region 5*. Reporting directly to Hanoi, *Region 5* would manage enemy military efforts in the northernmost portions of South Vietnam. Hanoi called the military headquarters under *Region 5* the *B1 Front* and the military headquarters under *COSVN* the *B2 Front*. Other changes took place in the years that followed. The most important occurred in January 1964, when Hanoi separated the southern section from the *B1 Front* to create the *Southern Sector*. Then, in May, it included the highlands provinces in a new B3, or *Western Highlands, Front*. As with the *B1 Front*, the new departments were subordinate to *Region 5* (*see Map 1*).[6]

By late 1961, as the enemy intensified and expanded his effort, the South Vietnamese armed forces had seemed less and less capable, even though on the surface they made a good appearance. Organized along American lines, the South Vietnamese Army consisted of ten infantry

---

[5] Admiral U. S. G. Sharp and General William C. Westmoreland, *Report on the War in Vietnam (as of 30 June 1968)* (Washington, D.C.: Government Printing Office, 1969), p. 77.

[6] Memo, Robert J. Destatte, Senior Analyst, Defense Prisoner of War and Missing Personnel Office, for Dale Andrade and author, 1 Nov 96, sub: Region Five and Military Region Five Defined, pp. A2–A3, Historians files, CMH.

MAP 1

A U.S. Army adviser instructs South Vietnamese infantrymen on helicopter boarding procedures.

divisions serving under four corps headquarters—the I Corps Tactical Zone at Da Nang in the north; the II Corps Tactical Zone at Pleiku City in the western highlands; the III Corps Tactical Zone at Bien Hoa near Saigon, the country's capital; and the IV Corps Tactical Zone at Can Tho in the Mekong Delta. Each of the divisions contained three regiments, as well as artillery and engineer battalions and smaller supporting units. Although the number of troops in an individual division might vary, the authorized total in each was 10,500. In addition, the South Vietnamese order of battle contained eight separate battalions of artillery, five battalions of airborne troops, and four battalion-size armored cavalry regiments. These came under either Saigon's immediate control or that of the corps commanders. Despite the size of these forces, however, and the equipment the Americans had provided, the South Vietnamese made little headway as the war progressed.

Hoping for more positive results, President John F. Kennedy sent his military adviser, General Maxwell D. Taylor, and a national security assistant, Walt W. Rostow, to Vietnam to propose additional measures of support for President Diem. Besides calling for an expansion of advisory and assistance programs, General Taylor recommended dispatching an 8,000-man task force composed mainly of logistical units. He justified his proposal by arguing that the introduction of U.S. forces into

South Vietnam would serve to reassure America's allies around the world by underscoring its "seriousness of purpose" in the region.[7]

But Kennedy held back. Seeking to halt the military and political deterioration of South Vietnam, he approved Taylor's recommendations to increase the volume of U.S. assistance and the number of advisers, but he declined to send all the men the general had sought. Even so, the measures he did approve constituted a major augmentation in U.S. assistance to South Vietnam. They included not only the provision of more sophisticated weaponry but also the commitment of two helicopter companies, a squadron of fighter aircraft, communications, intelligence, and other U.S. elements to the war effort. Equally important, the president more than quadrupled the number of advisers assisting Diem's troops from seven hundred to thirty-two hundred men, and he liberalized the rules of engagement that defined their role in combat. To handle the augmentation, he established in February 1962 a new operational headquarters in Saigon, the U.S. Military Assistance Command, Vietnam (MACV), and appointed General Paul D. Harkins to head it.[8]

The gradual growth of the American military mission in South Vietnam took place within the context of routine contingency planning. As early as 1954 the Office of the Commander in Chief, Pacific, had developed the OPLAN (Operational Plan) 32 series to guide commanders on positioning their forces, establishing logistical systems, and determining the role their troops would play if a Communist threat arose in Southeast Asia. Under the two most likely scenarios for South Vietnam, the planners sought to anticipate either an increasingly successful Communist insurgency about to overwhelm the South Vietnamese government or a North Vietnamese invasion. To defeat an insurgency, the 1964 version of the plan envisioned part of a Marine expeditionary force going to Da Nang and two Army brigades to the Saigon area. It assumed that these forces would play a defensive role, shielding vital areas and installations against attack in order to buy time for the South Vietnamese to launch a counteroffensive. If an invasion occurred, however, a full Marine expeditionary force would go to Da Nang while the bulk of the American force—an Army division and a corps headquarters—would deploy along the Pleiku–Qui Nhon axis in the center of the country. These forces would assume an aggressive posture, mounting offensive operations to reunite the two Vietnams under a government friendly to the United States.[9]

---

[7] Msg, Gen Maxwell D. Taylor, President's Special Military Representative, to the President, [1 Nov 61], in *The Pentagon Papers: The Defense Department History of United States Decisionmaking on Vietnam*, Senator Gravel ed., 4 vols. (Boston: Beacon Press, 1971), 2:90–91 (quoted words, p. 90).

[8] George C. Herring, *America's Longest War: The United States and Vietnam, 1950–1975*, 3d rev. ed. (New York: McGraw-Hill, 1996), pp. 88–93. See also *Pentagon Papers* (Gravel), 2:73–127.

[9] Alexander S. Cochran, Jr., "American Planning for Ground Combat in Vietnam, 1952–1965," *Parameters* 14 (Summer 1984): 66; *A Study of Strategic Lessons Learned in Vietnam*, vol. 5, *Planning the War* (McLean, Va.: BDM Corp., 1980), pp. 3–7, copy in CMH.

Although American planners concentrated on military options, they understood that U.S. assistance to South Vietnam could not be limited to military advice and support. Since the Communists depended on popular dissatisfaction with Diem to fuel their insurgency, the South Vietnamese government needed to establish institutions responsive to its people. The policies that resulted, known collectively as the pacification program, were to parallel military measures. They were designed not only to provide security for South Vietnam's rural inhabitants but also to involve them in social, economic, and political programs that would win their allegiance to the government.

The Diem regime inaugurated the strategic hamlet program in 1961 as part of that effort. The idea was to congregate the inhabitants of threatened outlying areas into fortified villages, where trained and armed members of the community could provide security. Laudable on the surface, the program rapidly turned counterproductive by degenerating into a means for Diem and his increasingly influential brother, Ngo Dinh Nhu, to bolster their own personal power while appearing to produce the quick results that American officials wanted. In the end, the South Vietnamese people came to resent what they saw as forced relocation from their homes and the graves of their ancestors to areas where even rudimentary public services—not to mention the improvements promised by government spokesmen—were virtually nonexistent. In addition, the training and weaponry provided to the local force defenders of the hamlets were almost never sufficient to fend off concerted enemy attacks.

Other pacification programs, initiated with American prodding, encouragement, and assistance, suffered similar fates. The best known was the *Chieu Hoi*, or "Open Arms," program. Offering clemency to insurgents who came over to the government, it achieved modest success and continued in one form or another until the end of the war. But pacification never reached the root of South Vietnam's weakness—the corruption and incompetence of Saigon's political leaders and their failure to create a broadly based, multiparty system capable of winning the loyalty of the people.[10]

Until the end of 1963 the American effort in South Vietnam followed a simple premise. Although President Kennedy increased the level of U.S. assistance and allowed American advisers to take an active role in the fighting, the central idea remained that the United States would support rather than supplant the indigenous government's efforts. That began to change when Diem fell in a 1963 coup d'etat clearly sanctioned by the United States. Prior to the event, Kennedy seems to have entertained the

---

[10] Richard A. Hunt, *Pacification: The American Struggle for Vietnam's Hearts and Minds* (Boulder, Colo.: Westview Press, 1995), pp. 24–30; Brig. Gen. Tranh Dinh Tho, *Pacification*, Indochina Monographs (Washington, D.C.: U.S. Army Center of Military History, 1980), p. v; Record of Conversation, Sec Def Robert S. McNamara with Monsignor Salvatore Asta, Papal Delegate to South Vietnam, 30 Sep 63, Historians files, CMH; Memo, McNamara for the President, 21 Dec 63, sub: Vietnam Situation, in *Pentagon Papers* (Gravel), 3:494.

idea that the United States might be able to withdraw from the war without suffering a substantial loss of face. After the coup that option was gone. American consent to the coup constituted a de facto pledge of continued and even enhanced support for the war. At first, the overthrow of Diem and the rise of a triumvirate, led by Maj. Gen. Duong Van Minh, produced rising expectations in the United States, but within weeks the mood dissipated as power struggles roiled the new administration. On 30 January 1964 Maj. Gen. Nguyen Khanh added to the confusion by overthrowing Minh in a bloodless coup. Although ambitious and vigorous, Khanh lacked a political following in the country at large, and his standing with the army itself seemed uncertain.[11]

In the meantime, Kennedy fell to an assassin's bullet, and was succeeded by his vice president, Lyndon B. Johnson. The new president fully supported the pledges that earlier administrations had made to South Vietnam, but at the same time he was quite aware of the fact that most Americans paid little attention to events in Southeast Asia. Convinced that the public and Congress would not accept the projected casualty totals associated with any decision to fight, he set out to prepare a strong political and military case for future action against North Vietnam while preserving his options by drawing no more attention to the war than necessary.[12]

Although certain of America's ultimate objective in South Vietnam, President Johnson seemed unsure of how to achieve it. On 17 March 1964 he issued his first statement of policy on Vietnam, National Security Action Memorandum 288. He avowed that the United States was working for "an independent non-Communist South Vietnam" but blandly added, "We do not require that [South Vietnam] serve as a Western base or as a member of a Western alliance." Johnson likewise told a press conference during June that if he was prepared to uphold South Vietnam's independence, he intended "no rashness" and sought "no wider war."[13]

At the same time, some of his actions seemed to belie the cautious statements, suggesting that he would take military action if that was the only way to halt Communist advances in Southeast Asia. American pilots were flying officially unacknowledged bombing raids in Laos, low-profile statements to the press indicated that the U.S. Air Force was upgrading the air base at Da Nang, and unconfirmed but authoritative

---

[11] Leslie H. Gelb and Richard K. Betts, *The Irony of Vietnam: The System Worked* (Washington, D.C.: Brookings Institution, 1979), pp. 92–93; Robert S. McNamara, with Brian VanDeMark, *In Retrospect: The Tragedy and Lessons of Vietnam* (New York: Times Books, Random House, 1995), pp. 86–87, 95–96; *Pentagon Papers* (Gravel), 3:494–96.

[12] "The Gallup Poll: Less Than 40% of People Follow Vietnam Events," *Washington Post*, 27 May 64.

[13] National Security Action Memorandum (NSAM) 288, 17 Mar 64, in *Pentagon Papers* (Gravel), 3:50; Presidential Press Conference, 23 Jun 64, in *Public Papers of the Presidents of the United States: Lyndon B. Johnson, Containing the Public Messages, Speeches, and Statements of the President, 1963–64*, 2 vols. (Washington, D.C.: Government Printing Office, 1965), 1:804.

leaks to reporters revealed that American logisticians were building contingency stockpiles in neighboring Thailand.[14]

The enemy, for his part, remained steadfast in his goals. Convinced that the United States would give way in the end, North Vietnam's prime minister, Pham Van Dong, in contrast to Johnson, left no doubt about his nation's objectives during an interview in July, when he used a powerful metaphor to state them clearly. There was, he said, "no light at the end of the tunnel" for the United States.[15]

Decisions To Escalate

The war began to take on momentum for the United States in mid-summer 1964. On 2 August North Vietnamese torpedo boats attacked the U.S. destroyer *Maddox* in the Gulf of Tonkin and, a few days later, appeared to engage the *Maddox* and another destroyer, the *Turner Joy*. Terming the assaults "open aggression on the high seas," President Johnson retaliated by launching air strikes against the North Vietnamese naval bases harboring the enemy vessels.[16] If Johnson adopted an aggressive stance in public, however, he remained cautious in private. When General Westmoreland, the MACV commander since June, requested U.S. Marine units to guard Da Nang Air Base, a starting point for strikes against North Vietnam but also an inviting target, the president held off on any decision. Three days later, on an assumption that the enemy attacks were unprovoked, Congress ratified what became known as the Gulf of Tonkin Resolution. Authorizing Johnson to take whatever action he needed to protect American forces in South Vietnam, the act was so comprehensive in the administration's eyes that it made a more formal declaration of war superfluous.[17]

The final months of 1964 brought no end to the chaos in South Vietnam. Buddhist demonstrators took to the streets in the nation's cities, and dissident officers launched an abortive coup against the government. All the while, the enemy exploited these events by expanding his influence in the countryside. As the situation deteriorated, American

[14] William M. Hammond, *Public Affairs: The Military and the Media, 1962–1968*, United States Army in Vietnam (Washington, D.C.: U.S. Army Center of Military History, 1988), p. 96.

[15] Msg, State 74 to Saigon, 11 Jul 64, U.S. Department of State, Foreign Affairs Information Management, Bureau of Intelligence and Research, Record Group (RG) 59, National Archives and Records Administration (NARA), Washington, D.C.

[16] For accounts of the real and alleged attacks, see Herring, *America's Longest War*, pp. 134–37, and Edward J. Marolda and Oscar P. Fitzgerald, *From Military Assistance to Combat, 1959–1965*, United States Navy and the Vietnam Conflict (Washington, D.C.: Naval Historical Center, Department of the Navy, 1986), pp. 410–19, 426–44. Johnson is quoted in Daniel Hallin, *The Uncensored War: The Media and Vietnam* (New York: Oxford University Press, 1986), p. 70.

[17] Graham A. Cosmas, "MACV, the Joint Command," ch. 5, CMH.

Viet Cong plan an attack on a government outpost northwest of Saigon.

policymakers began to wonder whether the Saigon government might lose all ability to rule. Remaining dedicated to the policy of providing advice and support, they wasted little time considering a commitment of American ground forces. Instead, they concluded that a program of gradually increasing air attacks against the North, starting fairly soon, had the best chance for success.[18]

Time was nonetheless running out. The enemy's strength in South Vietnam had grown steadily throughout 1964 because of greater infiltration from the North and accelerated recruitment in the South. Communist main forces numbered about twenty-three thousand in January and about thirty-three thousand in December—an increase of almost 50 percent. Organized into five regiments, forty-six battalions, and one hundred thirty-four separate companies, they were better armed and equipped than before, drawing on North Vietnam for supplies and modern weaponry—particularly Chinese copies of the Soviet assault rifle, the AK47. As their numbers grew, their will to action increased as well, with government casualties rising from 1,900 in January to 3,000 in December.[19]

As the year ended the Viet Cong took to the offensive by launching an attack on government forces at Binh Gia, southeast of Saigon, while

[18] Gelb and Betts, *Irony of Vietnam*, pp. 100–104.
[19] Sharp and Westmoreland, *Report*, p. 117; Cosmas, "MACV, the Joint Command," ch. 6.

12

North Vietnamese Army units began moving southward to the western highlands. The enemy hoped to destroy "a large section of the puppet regular army" and to control more territory in the South.[20] With South Vietnam's leaders more concerned with political intrigue than with fighting the war, and with enemy control of the nation's territory growing, Assistant Secretary of State William P. Bundy concluded that the country was in imminent danger of collapse. Westmoreland was similarly pessimistic. He believed that the enemy was about to begin the third stage of revolutionary warfare, the general offensive.[21]

As the battle raged at Binh Gia, President Johnson on 30 December sent Taylor, now the U.S. ambassador in Saigon, a wide-ranging dispatch, the purpose of which was "to show you the state of my thinking and to ask for your frankest comments and responses." Johnson noted that despite initially approving bombing reprisal raids over the North, "I have never felt that this war will be won from the air." Therefore, he continued, "what is much more needed and would be more effective is a larger and stronger use of [American] Rangers and Special Forces and Marines, or other appropriate military strength on the ground and on the scene." He already had substantial combat elements in the country. Over thirteen hundred members of the U.S. Army Special Forces manned surveillance camps all along the inland border. Also present were four battalions of Army aircraft, including recent vintage UH–1 Iroquois, or Huey, helicopters, providing transport, gunships, and resupply for the South Vietnamese. So in talking of increasing the strength on the ground, Johnson was not yet ready to concede that American ground forces would inevitably take a leading role. To him, the focus of the U.S. effort had to remain advice and support. Any new troops were to stiffen South Vietnamese aggressiveness up and down the line rather than risk taking control of the war. Even so, by sending his message, Johnson had dramatically extended the range of what could be considered and what might be done, and he had shown that he, the person with the authority to make such far-reaching decisions, was favorably disposed to doing so. "I myself am ready to substantially increase the number of Americans in Vietnam," he declared to Ambassador Taylor, "if it is necessary to provide this kind of fighting force against the Viet Cong."[22]

As 1965 began, the Departments of State and Defense were still reluctant to commit U.S. troops to the war, believing that reprisal bomb-

---

[20] *Su Doan 9* [*9th Division*] (Hanoi: Nha Xuat Ban Quan Doi Nhan Dan [People's Army Publishing House], 1990), pp. 27–28 (quotation, p. 27), copy in CMH (hereafter cited as *9th Division*).

[21] *Pentagon Papers* (Gravel), 3:293; William C. Westmoreland, *A Soldier Reports* (Garden City, N.Y.: Doubleday and Co., 1976), p. 126. See also Sharp and Westmoreland, *Report*, pp. 84, 95.

[22] Msg, White House CAP 64375 to Saigon, 30 Dec 64, tab 1, box 40, National Security Council (NSC) History "Deployment of Major U.S. Forces to Vietnam, July 1965," National Security Files (NSF), Lyndon Baines Johnson Library (LBJL), Austin, Tex.

ing raids against the North would constitute the best response to any form of aggression. The Joint Chiefs of Staff drew up a list of likely targets in North Vietnam and named the proposed mission Operation FLAMING DART. President Johnson declined at first to approve the attacks, but he understood that the loss of South Vietnam would result in a destructive debate in the United States that might well destroy not only his domestic program but also his effectiveness as president. Temporizing, he ordered his national security adviser, McGeorge Bundy, to travel to Saigon with a team of military and civilian experts to take "a hard look at the situation." Arriving on 3 February, the group began discussions on the whole range of U.S.-Vietnam policy options, particularly future pressures on the North. Bundy rapidly concluded that the situation was about as bad as everyone had thought.[23]

On 7 February the enemy provided an excuse to activate FLAMING DART. In a morning attack on a U.S. barracks and airfield at Pleiku enemy sappers, backed by mortars, killed 9 Americans and wounded 108 while destroying twenty-one fixed-wing aircraft and helicopters. Bundy was appalled. Joining Westmoreland, Taylor, and all of the senior American officials in Saigon, he recommended immediate reprisal raids against the North. In response, President Johnson authorized air strikes against the targets proposed by the Joint Chiefs and ordered all American dependents to leave the South. "We have no choice now but to clear the decks," he told the American public, "and make absolutely clear our determination to back South Vietnam in its fight to maintain its independence."[24]

Thereafter, events moved rapidly. "The situation in Vietnam is deteriorating," Bundy reported to the president on 7 February, "and without new U.S. action defeat appears inevitable—probably not in a matter of weeks or perhaps even months, but within the next year or so. . . . There is still time to turn it around, but not much."[25] Two days later Secretary of Defense Robert S. McNamara asked the Joint Chiefs for their recommendations on an eight-week air campaign against infiltration-related targets in the lower segment of North Vietnam. The very next day the enemy underscored the urgency of the request by killing 23

[23] Herring, *America's Longest War*, pp. 142–43; Memo, William P. Bundy, Assistant Secretary of State, Far Eastern Affairs, for Dean Rusk, Sec State, 6 Jan 65, sub: Notes on South Vietnamese Situation and Alternatives, in *Pentagon Papers* (Gravel), 3:684; Msg, Saigon 2052 to State, 6 Jan 65, Westmoreland History files, CMH; Msg, State 1419 to Saigon, 8 Jan 65, Historians files, CMH; Lyndon Baines Johnson, *The Vantage Point: Perspectives of the Presidency, 1963–1969* (New York: Holt, Rinehart and Winston, 1971), pp. 120–32 (quoted words, p. 123).

[24] Westmoreland, *A Soldier Reports*, p. 116; Memo, Gen William C. Westmoreland, COMUSMACV J00, for Ambassador Maxwell D. Taylor, 8 Feb 65, sub: Weekly Assessment of Military Activity, 31 Jan–7 Feb 65, Westmoreland History files, CMH; "United States and South Vietnamese Forces Launch Retaliatory Attacks Against North Viet-Nam," *Department of State Bulletin*, 22 Feb 65, p. 238; Johnson, *Vantage Point*, p. 126 (quotation).

[25] *Pentagon Papers* (Gravel), 3:309.

14

Army officers at Pleiku assess the damage from the sapper attack.

Americans and wounding 21 in an attack on an enlisted men's billet at Qui Nhon on the II Corps coast. Johnson again responded with air strikes, this time pegging them not to any specific event but to North Vietnam's continued assaults against the South. Three days later he authorized the commencement of Operation ROLLING THUNDER, a program of sustained, gradually increasing air attacks on North Vietnam. Then, on the twenty-sixth, he approved Westmoreland's request for U.S. Marine battalions to guard Da Nang Air Base. But the troops were to have a limited defensive role, and few officials saw them as harbingers of an American-controlled ground war.[26]

The graduated nature of ROLLING THUNDER disturbed some within the military, particularly the air power advocates in the Air Force. They urged Johnson to begin an all-out campaign targeting airfields, power plants, fuel storage facilities, and other strategic sites so that North Vietnam would understand the seriousness of the message the United States was sending. Johnson's civilian advisers disagreed. Besides stimulating

[26] Phillip B. Davidson, *Vietnam at War: The History, 1946–1975* (Novato, Calif.: Presidio Press, 1988), pp. 343–44.

15

antiwar sentiment at home and abroad, the all-out approach might prompt North Vietnam's allies, the Soviet Union and Communist China, to take a more active hand in the war. Seeking to preserve his own options while giving the North Vietnamese president, Ho Chi Minh, every chance to bargain, Johnson sided with the civilians. The first ROLLING THUNDER attacks, which began on 2 March, hit only minor targets in the southernmost third of North Vietnam.[27]

Simultaneous with the bombing, Secretary McNamara set a new tone to policy deliberations, declaring in a 1 March memorandum to Secretary of the Army Stephen Ailes: "I want it clearly understood that there is an unlimited appropriation available for the financing of aid to Vietnam. Under no circumstances is lack of money to stand in the way of aid to that nation."[28] President Johnson also dispatched the chief of staff of the Army, General Harold K. Johnson, to the war zone to evaluate the American effort and to determine what might shift the balance in South Vietnam's favor. On the day of his departure for Saigon he had breakfast with the president. "Coming down in the elevator," General Johnson later recalled, the president "bored his finger into my chest and . . . said 'get things bubbling.'"[29]

The general and his entourage spent 5–12 March in South Vietnam, meeting with Taylor and Westmoreland, with various members of their staffs, and with South Vietnamese leaders. Early on, when speaking to senior American military officers in Saigon, he told everyone below the rank of general to leave and then informed those who remained: "I don't come as the Army Chief of Staff. I am here as a representative of the President of the United States. Mr. Johnson asked me to come and to tell you that I come with a blank check." He then asked, "What do you need to win the war?"[30]

Over the days that followed, the general reviewed an array of new military options, all prepared without regard to how much they would cost or what personnel and equipment they would require. MACV already was exploring the possibility of enclosing heavily populated areas and regions that contained important military or administrative complexes in enclaves cleared of the enemy, and a number of the options dealt with the use of American units as reserve and rapid-reaction forces to provide security for those zones. Consideration also went

---

[27] John Schlight, *The War in South Vietnam: The Years of the Offensive, 1965–1968*, United States Air Force in Southeast Asia (Washington, D.C.: Office of Air Force History, United States Air Force, 1988), p. 23. See also Westmoreland, *A Soldier Reports*, p. 119.

[28] Memo, Sec Def for Sec Army et al., 1 Mar 65, box 44, 70A/3717, RG 319, NARA.

[29] Interv, Charles B. MacDonald and Charles von Luttichau with Gen Harold K. Johnson, 20 Nov 70, p. 8, Historians files, CMH.

[30] Memo, Gen Johnson for Sec Def et al., 14 Mar 65; Interv, Col Glenn A. Smith and Lt Col August M. Cianciolo with Maj Gen Delk M. Oden, former Commanding General (CG), U.S. Army Support Command, Vietnam, 27 May 77, p. 20 (Johnson quotations), Senior Officer Oral History Program, MHI.

to the feasibility of the contingency plans MACV had drafted to position blocking forces across enemy infiltration routes in South Vietnam and Laos. When Westmoreland suggested the deployment of a U.S. Army division to western II Corps to relieve enemy pressure in the highlands, Johnson volunteered that a new airmobile division might be available.[31]

General Johnson left South Vietnam convinced that the situation had deteriorated so drastically that quick remedial action was necessary. "Time is running out swiftly in Vietnam," he wrote, "and temporizing or expedient measures will not suffice."[32] His report to the president laid out three categories of recommendations. The first proposed a series of refinements to the ongoing effort to provide advice and support to the South Vietnamese. The second involved the dispatch of combat units, the equivalent of a tailored division force, to South Vietnam to defend important towns and installations and to free South Vietnamese troops to concentrate on critical coastal regions, where much of the nation's population lived. The third proposed stationing four or more American divisions across South Vietnam and Laos at the point where the two nations joined North Vietnam. Such a force would help to restrict enemy infiltration into the South while enhancing the American position in any future negotiations.[33]

Proposals from the Joint Chiefs and Westmoreland soon followed. On 20 March the Joint Chiefs called for the dispatch of additional marines to Da Nang; a U.S. Army division to the Central Highlands; and a South Korean division, if obtainable, to some other location. They reasoned that if the United States wanted to turn the tide in Vietnam it would have to make destruction of the enemy its objective. To accomplish this end, U.S. forces in strengths sufficient to achieve an effective margin of power would have to assume a ground combat role.[34]

On 26 March Westmoreland submitted his "Commander's Estimate of the Military Situation in South Vietnam." He focused on the need for

---

[31] Memo, Sec Def for Sec Army et al., 1 Mar 65; Headquarters, United States Military Assistance Command, Vietnam, "Command History, 1965" (Saigon, Vietnam: Military History Branch, Office of the Secretary, MACV, 1966), pp. 106, 421–22, CMH (hereafter cited as MACV History, date); Msgs, Westmoreland MAC 1228 to Gen John K. Waters, CG, U.S. Army, Pacific (USARPAC), 8 Mar 65, and Westmoreland MAC 1463 to Gen Earle G. Wheeler, Chairman, Joint Chiefs of Staff (CJCS), 17 Mar 65, both in Westmoreland Message files, CMH. See also Cosmas, "MACV, the Joint Command," ch. 6.

[32] Report on Survey of the Military Situation in Vietnam, [5–12 Mar 65], p. 15, Incl to Memo, Gen Johnson for Sec Def et al., 14 Mar 65.

[33] Ibid., pp. 6–12.

[34] Memo, CJCS JCSM–204–65 for Sec Def, 20 Mar 65, sub: Deployment of US/Allied Combat Forces to Vietnam, in *Foreign Relations of the United States, 1964–1968*, vol. 2, *Vietnam, January–June 1965* (Washington, D.C.: Government Printing Office, 1996), pp. 465–67 (hereafter cited as *FRUS, 1964–1968, Vietnam*). See also "The Joint Chiefs of Staff and the War in Vietnam, 1960–1968," Part 2, "1965–1966" (Historical Division, Joint Secretariat, Joint Chiefs of Staff, 1970), ch. 19, pp. 13–14, CMH (hereafter cited as JCS History).

American forces to stabilize the situation until either a planned South Vietnamese military buildup was completed or ROLLING THUNDER persuaded the North Vietnamese to halt their attacks. An Army division, preferably the new airmobile division General Johnson had mentioned, should go either to the region between Qui Nhon and Pleiku or to enclaves along the coast in the same area. In addition, a separate Army brigade was needed to secure the airfields at Bien Hoa and Vung Tau near Saigon and to conduct mobile operations in support of efforts to provide security for the local inhabitants. Finally, a Marine battalion landing team should reinforce the marines already at Da Nang, and a Marine infantry battalion should go to Phu Bai north of Da Nang to secure the airfield where an Army intelligence unit was stationed. Westmoreland warned that additional deployments would have to be considered after the middle of the year if ROLLING THUNDER failed. He judged General Johnson's idea of blocking enemy infiltration through Laos to be impractical because it would take nine months or more to amass enough troops and equipment to begin the effort. In addition, he said, the introduction of American troops into Laos would spark heated debate in the United States and around the world.[35]

In the end, President Johnson settled on an approach that promised to postpone political problems while preparing for possible large American commitments in the future. On 6 April, in National Security Action Memorandum 328, he approved most of General Johnson's proposals, particularly the suggestions for broadening air and naval operations, but he declined to commit the larger number of combat troops the general, the Joint Chiefs, and Westmoreland had recommended. In fact, he ordered only two additional Marine battalions and a Marine air squadron to South Vietnam. However, he did allow an 18,000- to 20,000-man increase in logistical forces to lay the base for any additional actions he might later decide to take. The press guidance that accompanied the decision avowed cryptically that "we do not desire [to] give [the] impression [of a] rapid massive buildup." Other than the marines, who were to move as soon as possible, the deployments were to be spaced out, with publicity "kept at the lowest possible key."[36]

In keeping with those instructions, the Defense Department announced that the marines at Da Nang would continue in a defensive role; but, after a little over a month in position, as a result of decisions reached by President Johnson and his advisers, the marines started searching for the enemy throughout their area of operations. The term used to describe the new mission—*counterinsurgency combat operations*—

---

[35] MACV Commander's Estimate of the Military Situation in South Vietnam, 26 Mar 65, pp. 5–6, 25–26, Westmoreland History files, CMH; Msg, Westmoreland MAC 1463 to Wheeler, 17 Mar 65.

[36] NSAM 328, 6 Apr 65, in *Pentagon Papers* (Gravel), 3:702–03; Msg (quotations), State 2184 to Saigon, 3 Apr 65, in *FRUS, 1964–1968, Vietnam*, 2:532.

was designed to be vague in order to give Westmoreland maximum flexibility as his forces moved step by step toward the offensive.[37]

In the meantime, enemy military activity had diminished in South Vietnam, but the lull had little long-term meaning in the eyes of military analysts. With the enemy clearly resolved to press ahead despite ROLLING THUNDER, President Johnson decided on 15 April that the time had come to use "all practicable means" to strengthen the American position in South Vietnam.[38] On the twentieth, as a result, Secretary McNamara and a number of senior military and civilian officials met in Honolulu to weigh further ground force deployments to Vietnam. The group advised the president to approve a substantial increase in the number of American troops and combat units, including two Army brigades, a Marine regiment, and a regiment from the Republic of Korea.[39]

Johnson approved some of the recommendations almost immediately and the rest by 15 May. At the time, there were thirty-three thousand American and two thousand Korean troops in South Vietnam. Once all the forces approved for deployment had arrived, the number of American military personnel in South Vietnam would stand at eighty-two thousand and that of third-country troops, mainly Australians and Koreans, at seventy-two hundred.[40]

With American forces assuming an increasing role in ground combat, the Pentagon launched a step-by-step revision of its rules governing the employment of American jet aircraft in South Vietnam. Beginning in late January, the Joint Chiefs authorized Westmoreland to use the planes—chiefly B–57 Canberras and F–100 Super Sabres—in support of South Vietnamese combat operations in emergency situations. A month later Westmoreland's immediate superior, Admiral Ulysses S. G. Sharp, Commander in Chief, Pacific, suggested that the greatest single action the United States could take to improve the security of South Vietnam would be to provide for the full use of American air power. When McNamara and the Joint Chiefs agreed, Sharp and Westmoreland in early March

[37] Msg, CINCPAC (Commander in Chief, Pacific) to COMUSMACV, 14 Apr 65; Memorandum for the Record (MFR), H. Freeman Matthews, Political Section, American Embassy, Saigon, 3 Apr 65, sub: Meeting Between Rusk, Taylor, McGeorge Bundy, et al. Both in Westmoreland History files, CMH. See also Jack Shulimson and Maj. Charles M. Johnson, *U.S. Marines in Vietnam: The Landing and the Buildup, 1965* (Washington, D.C.: History and Museums Division, Headquarters, U.S. Marine Corps, 1978), pp. 27–28.

[38] Msg (quoted words), McGeorge Bundy, President's Assistant for National Security Affairs, Deptel 2332 to Taylor, 15 Apr 65, Westmoreland History files, CMH; MACV History, 1965, p. 5; Memo, Brig Gen William E. DePuy, Asst CofS, J–3 [Opns], MACV, for Lt Gen John L. Throckmorton, Deputy COMUSMACV, 28 May 65, sub: How Goes the War, file D (65), 1956–1965, William E. DePuy Papers, MHI.

[39] *Pentagon Papers* (Gravel), 3:410; MFR, John T. McNaughton, Asst Sec Def, International Security Affairs, 23 Apr 65, sub: Minutes of the 20 April 1965 Honolulu Meeting, Historians files, CMH.

[40] Johnson, *Vantage Point*, p. 142; JCS History, pt. 2, ch. 21, p. 19; Memo, McGeorge Bundy for the President, 24 Jul 65, sub: The History of Recommendations for Increased US Forces in Vietnam, tab 417, box 43, NSC History, NSF, LBJL.

A B–57 Canberra returns from a bombing run.

received authority to employ American aircraft in support of ground operations as necessary. Then, on 23 April, anticipating a growing need for close air support as more and more American troops arrived, McNamara authorized Sharp and Westmoreland to make the provision of that support the first priority for all American air units in South Vietnam.[41]

As preparations for an expanded war continued, General Westmoreland developed a plan that he hoped would transform the incoming battalions and brigades from green arrivals to seasoned troops. At first, each new unit would concentrate on securing an area around its base out to the range of light artillery. Having gained a measure of experience, it would then begin to conduct deeper patrols into the countryside to seek out the enemy. Finally, always prepared to strike on the spur of a moment, it would begin sweeping operations that ranged over broad regions.[42] He envisioned for this stage of the intervention, in short, a rapid climb up the ladder of combat to the traditional attack mission of the infantry.

[41] JCS History, pt. 2, ch. 24, pp. 12–14. See also Schlight, *Years of the Offensive*, pp. 15–21; Westmoreland, *A Soldier Reports*, pp. 86, 110–11.

[42] Msg, COMUSMACV to CINCPAC, 8 May 65, tab 224, box 41, NSC History, NSF, LBJL.

Establishing the Bridgeheads

One month after the marines first landed in I Corps, President Johnson gave the go-ahead for the Army to deploy forces of its own. Between May and late July the 1st Brigade, 101st Airborne Division, took up station in II Corps and both the 173d Airborne Brigade and the 2d Brigade, 1st Infantry Division, moved into III Corps. Like the marines, the brigades had a limited mission. They were to protect essential airfields and other installations and to act, in the last resort, as a reaction force to obstruct an enemy takeover. As such, they were manifestations of General Westmoreland's assertion in March that what the United States now needed to do most was to put its own "fingers in the dike."[1]

An Airborne Brigade for III Corps

The first of the Army brigades to reach III Corps was the two-battalion 173d Airborne Brigade (Separate) under the command of Brig. Gen. Ellis W. Williamson. Organized on Okinawa in mid-1963 from the 1st and 2d Airborne Battle Groups, 503d Infantry, the 173d had been serving as the Pacific area's "fire brigade," prepared to move at a moment's notice to any point in the region where American interests came under threat. For two years General Williamson, who had learned his craft as a battalion commander during World War II, had emphasized speed, flexibility, and innovation in all operations, with airborne techniques, jungle tactics, and physical fitness receiving emphasis in his conditioning program. To bring training as close as possible to the real thing, field maneuvers had been conducted in the jungles of not only Okinawa but also the Philippines, Thailand, and Taiwan.[2]

[1] Msg, Westmoreland MAC 1463 to Wheeler, 17 Mar 65, Westmoreland Message files, CMH.

[2] Interv, author with Maj Gen Ellis W. Williamson, 2 Jun 98, Historians files, CMH; Bob Breen, *First To Fight: Australian Diggers, N.Z. Kiwis and U.S. Paratroopers in Vietnam, 1965–66* (Sydney, Australia: Allen and Unwin, 1988), p. 19; Annual Hist Supp, 1965, 173d Abn Bde (Sep), n.d., pp. x and 3, box 48, 73A/3330, RG 338, NARA.

Starting in 1965, the 173d initiated contingency planning on the chance that it might deploy to Vietnam. In January a team visited the theater to lay the groundwork for any future move. In February, with Communist fortunes clearly on the rise, the Army put Williamson's unit on increased alert, a status that placed its high-priority requisitions ahead of those of other units. The notice to deploy arrived in April, by which time the 173d was as well prepared as it could be and in "the best possible equipment posture."[3]

Although a battalion of the 173d would deploy to Vung Tau, Westmoreland's primary objective for the paratroopers was the air base at Bien Hoa. Some twenty kilometers northeast of Saigon, Bien Hoa, with about sixty thousand inhabitants, was the site of III Corps headquarters and was served by two strategic roads: Highway 1, which ran southwest to Saigon and east to the coast; and Highway 15, which ran south to Vung Tau, about ninety kilometers away. Highway 1 was especially important. It represented an avenue of approach to the air base and the capital city.[4]

General Williamson moved almost the entire unit to its new duty station in a matter of days. A planning group, commanded by the unit's logistics officer, flew from Okinawa to Vietnam on 15 April to establish liaison with American and South Vietnamese authorities, to determine the brigade's possible new roles and missions, and to conduct initial surveys of the unit's likely area of responsibility. On 3 May an advance party landed at Bien Hoa Air Base to begin establishing the base camp, lay down initial security, and prepare for the arrival of the brigade's individual components. Between the fifth and seventh the bulk of the brigade arrived on military air transports, employing one hundred fifty C–130 Hercules and eleven C–124 Globemaster flights. The first contingent (856 men)—the command and combat-oriented elements of the Headquarters and Headquarters Company; the 2d Battalion (Airborne), 503d Infantry; Troop E, 17th Cavalry, with jeep-mounted machine guns and recoilless rifles; an aviation platoon; an engineer detachment; and a medical detachment—deployed to Bien Hoa Air Base. The next group (1,056 men)—the 1st Battalion (Airborne), 503d Infantry; an engineer detachment; and a medical detachment—took up station at Vung Tau airfield. The final elements—the 3d Battalion, 319th Artillery, equipped with 105-mm. towed howitzers; the 173d Support Battalion (-); Company D, 16th Armor, armed with 90-mm. M56 Scorpion antitank guns; the 173d Engineer Company (-); and the remainder of the Headquarters and Headquarters Company—departed Okinawa aboard the Navy transport *General W. A. Mann* on the seventh, landed five days later at Vung

---

[3] Annual Hist Supp, 1965, 173d Abn Bde, p. 26.

[4] Ian McNeill, *To Long Tan: The Australian Army and the Vietnam War, 1950–1966* (St. Leonards, New South Wales, Australia: Allen and Unwin in association with the Australian War Memorial, 1993), pp. 81–82.

Soldiers of the 173d Airborne Brigade disembark at Saigon.

Tau, and moved immediately to Bien Hoa. Three ocean freighters carrying the brigade's heavy equipment reached Saigon port on the thirteenth. After unloading, the equipment moved by motor convoy to Bien Hoa. At this juncture, the 173d Airborne Brigade's strength in Vietnam stood at 161 officers and 2,816 enlisted men out of an authorized strength of a little over 3,300. For the time being, the brigade would be supplied by a daily C–130 flight from Okinawa.[5]

Because of the brigade's training, little time was needed to settle in. At Bien Hoa the base camp was established northeast of the airfield so that the men could occupy the local high ground facing enemy War Zone D, from where Viet Cong attacks were likely to come. The paratroopers quickly went to work building bunkers for protection against mortars, digging trenches, clearing fields of fire, and erecting barbed wire barriers. From the bunkers and trenches the soldiers could see about two hundred meters of open area, which then gave way to thick brush and, ultimately, to jungle farther north. At first, the soldiers lived in pup tents. These were gradually replaced by larger tents and then by more permanent structures. Regarding fire support, Williamson dispersed his artillery throughout the base, believing that this made it more difficult for the Viet Cong to destroy all of the howitzers at one time.[6]

[5] Annual Hist Supp, 1965, 173d Abn Bde, pp. 26–30.
[6] Interv, author with Maj Gen Ellis W. Williamson, 17 Jul 98, Historians files, CMH.

The brigade's aviation platoon contributed little to the defense of the airfield. On Okinawa it had had but six helicopters, only two of which were recent vintage UH–1B Hueys. The Hueys had been disassembled for shipment to Vietnam, and the other four had been left behind. Within a week of the brigade's arrival, the two Hueys had been reassembled and the brigade had received a third one. But because the paratroopers had deployed with little practical training in airmobile warfare, Williamson had to use the three helicopters to make up for the deficiency. The heart of the training regimen, which he called "Helicopter 101," was simplicity itself: making his men drill again and again on getting in and out of the Huey as a unit until they could do so quickly "without someone sticking a rifle barrel into someone else's eye."[7]

General Williamson at a field briefing

Assigned to mount a mobile defense of Bien Hoa and Vung Tau and to conduct offensive counterinsurgency operations as the need arose, the 173d assumed its mission quickly. By the end of the second day in country initial defenses around each base were in place, and commanders were pushing aggressively beyond their perimeters to disrupt Viet Cong plans for future attacks. Although South Vietnamese Army units were stationed nearby, they were neither involved nor consulted as the patrols began.

From the beginning, the brigade operated under a number of constraints that troubled Williamson and his officers. For example, the soldiers could fire at anyone who fired at them or when an obviously hostile act was in progress or about to be committed, but American forces could neither enter nor fire upon hamlets. The question thus arose: Could the men of the brigade return fire when fired upon from a hamlet or were they simply to collect their casualties and leave the area? As time went by, MACV would develop new rules of engagement to guide its

---

[7] Ibid.; Annual Hist Supp, 1965, 173d Abn Bde, pp. 44–45; Ellis W. Williamson, "Forty Years of Fun in the Army," ch. 21, p. [5] (quotation), copy in Historians files, CMH.

24

commanders during battle. Even so, as long as U.S. troops remained in Vietnam, commanders would face the dilemma of waging war with civilians nearby.[8]

Combat operations commenced around mid-May. On the twelfth brigade elements conducted platoon-size patrols a short distance from the Bien Hoa base camp. The men were under orders to be extremely cautious. Before starting out, the units involved received routes, times of departure and return, and key phase lines. Because the brigade's artillery had not yet arrived, the units used battalion mortars for fire support and were accompanied by a forward air controller and a Vietnamese interpreter. The operation was to be completed before dark.

On 15 May the brigade carried out its first airmobile assault (*see Map 2*). Early that morning eighteen helicopters, flying in two lifts, transported two companies of the 2d of the 503d Infantry to landing zones northeast of the base camp. The men worked their way back to preselected target areas before being picked up in the afternoon by their helicopters. A more complicated mission followed on the nineteenth and twentieth. During Operation 9–65 portions of the 2d Battalion entered a sector stretching ten to twenty-five kilometers north of Bien Hoa in search of enemy troops who might pose a threat to the air base. Although none of the mid-May operations resulted in major contact with the enemy, the men involved gained valuable experience.[9]

The battalion task force at Vung Tau mounted its first large operation on 26 and 27 May. Intelligence reports indicated that Viet Cong units might be in an area fifteen to twenty kilometers northwest of the base. A battery of the 3d Battalion, 319th Artillery, moved by motor convoy to firing positions within range of a landing zone in the area. In a procedure that was already standard practice in Vietnam, the unit registered its artillery on the landing zone and then fired a barrage from 0820 to 0835 to soften it. An air strike followed from 0835 to 0855, accompanied by helicopter gunship fire between 0855 and 0900 to suppress any resistance that remained. The procedure, which the men called "prepping the landing zone," sacrificed the chance to surprise the Viet Cong in exchange for a safe landing by American soldiers. After the preparation three companies from the 1st Battalion, 503d Infantry, landed unopposed and then maneuvered toward a preselected objective. Over the next two days the troops met the enemy on eleven occasions. Each of these short, sometimes violent, encounters ended with an enemy withdrawal in the face of superior American firepower. The brigade commander estimated that his men had killed or wounded 7 of the enemy. The Americans suffered 8 casualties, none fatal.[10]

---

[8] Quarterly Cmd Rpt, 1 May–31 Jul 65, 173d Abn Bde (Sep), 15 Aug 65, pp. 3–4, box 49, 73A/3330, RG 338, NARA.

[9] Ibid., pp. 4–10.

[10] Ibid., pp. 10–11.

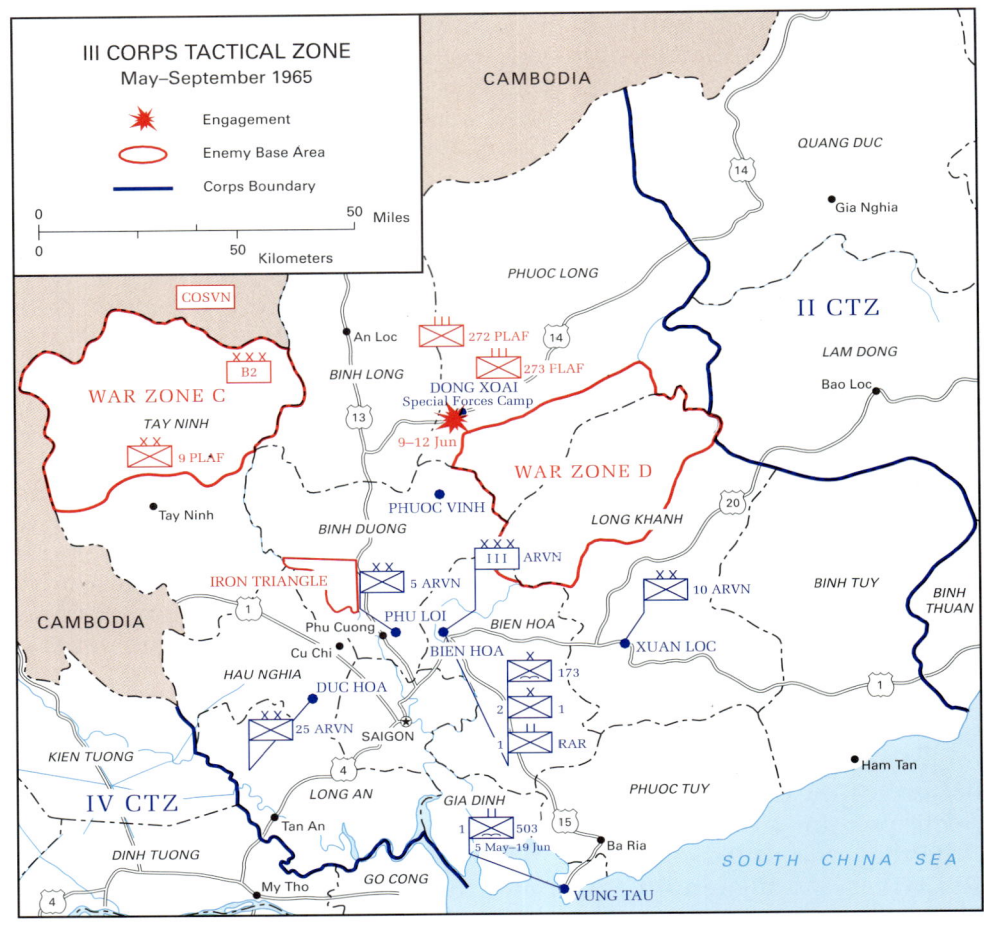

III CORPS TACTICAL ZONE
May–September 1965

★ Engagement
⬭ Enemy Base Area
━ Corps Boundary

0 _____ 50 Miles
0 _____ 50 Kilometers

CAMBODIA

QUANG DUC

Gia Nghia

PHUOC LONG

II CTZ

LAM DONG

Bao Loc

COSVN

An Loc

272 PLAF

273 FLAF

BINH LONG

WAR ZONE C
XXX
B2

TAY NINH

9 PLAF

Tay Ninh

DONG XOAI
Special Forces Camp

9–12 Jun

WAR ZONE D

PHUOC VINH

LONG KHANH

BINH DUONG

ARVN

IRON TRIANGLE

5 ARVN

BINH TUY

BINH THUAN

10 ARVN

CAMBODIA

Phu Cuong

PHU LOI

Cu Chi

BIEN HOA

BIEN HOA

173

XUAN LOC

HAU NGHIA

DUC HOA

2   1

25 ARVN

SAIGON

1   RAR

KIEN TUONG

LONG AN

GIA DINH

PHUOC TUY

Ham Tan

IV CTZ

Tan An

1   503

15

DINH TUONG

5 May–19 Jun

Ba Ria

SOUTH CHINA SEA

My Tho

GO CONG

VUNG TAU

MAP 2

In early June the 173d Airborne Brigade received a third maneuver element—the 1st Battalion, Royal Australian Regiment, which remained with the brigade for about a year. The presence of this unit, which included the 161 Battery, New Zealand Artillery, gave the brigade its full complement of infantry battalions. It also satisfied an already stated goal of the Johnson administration of bringing more allies into the war. But though the arrival of the Australian element in III Corps was welcome news indeed, differences in style and approach from the Americans soon became evident to all. Years of fighting in Malaya had convinced the Australians of the importance of jungle warfare tactics, and, as a result, they were critical of the 173d. As a member of the Australian battalion observed, "Our patrols do not fire off ammo or shoot up flares like the Yanks—they listen and move quietly, we haven't fired a shot or sent up a flare yet. The Americans think we are mad. It seems to me though, that all they're doing is letting the Viet Cong know where they are. I guess we have a bit to teach them." Another Australian later admitted, however, that his nation's forces had much to learn from the Americans about "large scale command, control, and communications, artillery and close air support, armoured, APC [armored personnel carrier] and infantry operations, rapid 'on the march' orders . . . and helicopter resupply."[11]

The 173d came close to exercising a fire brigade, or rapid-reaction, function at the time of the Australians' arrival. Shortly before midnight on 9 June elements of the *272d* and *273d People's Liberation Armed Forces (PLAF) Regiments* attacked a U.S. Special Forces–advised Civilian Irregular Defense Group (CIDG) camp and district headquarters located immediately west of Dong Xoai in Phuoc Long Province, some eighty-five kilometers north of Saigon. During the fighting the Viet Cong forced the camp's defenders, some four hundred Cambodians and South Vietnamese and twenty Americans, to abandon one position after another. By noon the next day the attackers had overrun much of the camp. Two South Vietnamese battalions—one infantry, the other ranger—moved up to recapture the position. Landing by helicopter, they bumped into the insurgents and were badly mauled. Another South Vietnamese battalion arrived on the eleventh. The Viet Cong waited until the twelfth to attack, and this battalion took heavy casualties as well.[12]

Unwilling to leave the enemy with a hold on a position that might allow him to dominate all of Phuoc Long Province, General Westmoreland told Admiral Sharp that "unless directed otherwise, I intend if necessary to commit the 173d to this action." Sharp agreed but warned that more than military issues rode on the decision: "I'm sure you realize that there would be grave political implications involved if sizable U.S. forces are committed for the first time and suffer a defeat."[13]

Sharp's concerns on the record, General Westmoreland ordered in the paratroopers. On 13 June General Williamson established a battalion task force, using 738 men from the 1st of the 503d Infantry, and moved it by air to Phuoc Vinh some forty kilometers north of Bien Hoa. That evening Battery A, 3d Battalion, 319th Artillery, followed. The task force waited for five days, but it soon became apparent that the enemy had no intention of holding territory and had left the area. On the eighteenth the task

[11] Breen, *First To Fight*, pp. 30 (first quotation) and 34 (second quotation).

[12] Battle of Dong Xoai (also known as Don Luan), p. 1, Historians files, CMH. See also *9th Division*, pp. 36–44, 46–48, copy in CMH; Quarterly Cmd Rpt, 1 Apr–30 Jun 65, 5th Special Forces (SF) Gp (Abn), 1st SF, 15 Jul 65, incl. 14, pp. 1–2, box 14, 73A/3330, RG 338, NARA.

[13] Msgs, Westmoreland MAC 3072 to Sharp and Sharp to Westmoreland and Wheeler, both 13 Jun 65, Westmoreland Message files, CMH.

Paratroopers patrol the jungle near War Zone D.

force returned to base. It had done all that could be expected and proved that its elements could respond quickly in an actual emergency.[14]

The next day the brigade elements at Vung Tau began moving to Bien Hoa. The first unit to arrive, the 1st of the 503d Infantry, assumed the task of guarding the western edge of the base camp. By the middle of the following week, for the first time since arriving in Vietnam, the entire brigade was assembled in one place.[15]

On 27 June General Westmoreland directed the 173d to join South Vietnamese units in a combined incursion into War Zone D, the vast enemy redoubt that began just beyond the curves of the Dong Nai River some ten kilometers north of Bien Hoa. The plan General Williamson devised required that his two U.S. battalions conduct an airmobile assault onto Landing Zone NORTH, some twenty-five kilometers north of Bien Hoa. Then moving southward, the force would conduct a four-day search of the area. At the same time, two battalions from the South Vietnamese Airborne Brigade would move by helicopter to Landing Zone SOUTH, about five kilometers to the south-

---

[14] Cmd Rpt, 13–18 Jun 65, 173d Abn Bde (Sep), 4 Jul 65, pp. 1–3, Historians files, CMH.
[15] Quarterly Cmd Rpt, 1 May–31 Jul 65, 173d Abn Bde, p. 2.

west of Landing Zone NORTH, and remain in the field for about twenty-four hours to seek out enemy forces. Fire support would come from the 173d's artillery, located less than ten kilometers west of the two landing zones. The command element for the operation would be stationed with the artillery, which would be covered by the 173d's armored company and cavalry troop. Elements of the South Vietnamese 48th Regiment, 10th Infantry Division, would escort the artillery and command post units to their positions. Remaining at Bien Hoa, the Australians would serve as a reserve, ready to move at an hour's notice.[16]

Following artillery and air preparations, the American and South Vietnamese units deployed to their landing zones during the late morning and early afternoon of 28 June. For the next two days they, soon joined by the Australians, combed their assigned areas, uncovering enemy caches that contained an estimated two hundred tons of rice and quantities of dried milk, tea, corn, barley, and tobacco. Except for scattered sniping incidents and firing a few mortar rounds, the enemy kept his distance. Consequently, on the thirtieth, the operation ended early and the troops returned to base.

Although short on contacts with the enemy, the mission represented a number of firsts for U.S. forces. Involving over one hundred forty UH–1s flying several sorties each to transport the two American and two South Vietnamese battalions to their targets, the attack was not only the largest troop helicopter lift to date but also the first major ground combat operation conducted by U.S. forces in the Vietnam War. And, as a test of cooperation and coordination between American and South Vietnamese forces, it seemed a success. But as a test of combat it proved little. As later reported by an Australian who believed that a significant number of Viet Cong units in the area had refused to give battle, "The first major foray [into War Zone D] had been successful but not contested."[17]

Over the next several weeks the 173d entered War Zone D again and also conducted an interdiction operation. Between 6 and 9 July its battalions searched for the enemy just south of the area they had covered earlier. A larger than usual firefight occurred on the seventh, when Company A, 1st Battalion, 503d Infantry, walked into an L-shaped ambush. The troops fought their way out, killing an estimated 50 Viet Cong. Then, from 28 July through 2 August brigade elements mounted an operation designed to sever a suspected Viet Cong supply route. The route was believed to run from the Rung Sat Special Zone, located in the mangrove swamps southeast of Saigon, through Phuoc Tuy Province to vari-

---

[16] Ibid., incl. 15, pp. 1–5; Westmoreland, *A Soldier Reports*, p. 141.

[17] Commander's Combat Note no. 66, 173d Abn Bde (Sep), 7 Jul 65, pp. 1–4, Incl to Cmd Rpt, 27–30 Jun 65, 173d Abn Bde (Sep), 11 Jul 65, box 6, 82/1474, RG 338, NARA; Breen, *First To Fight*, p. 50 (quotation).

ous sections of III Corps. The brigade searched the area but, as Williamson noted, met "no opposition other than . . . extremely thick vegetation."[18]

The Australian battalion was not involved in the Rung Sat mission. Concerned lest heavy casualties turn the Australian people against the war, the Canberra government had requested that Westmoreland use the unit only on operations in defense of Bien Hoa Air Base. Westmoreland acquiesced, but was unhappy with the restriction. A short time later, less sensitive by then to the vulnerability of its force in Vietnam, the Australian government relaxed the ban by permitting its troops to operate in any province contiguous to Bien Hoa Province. It remained impossible, however, for the Australians to participate as a part of Westmoreland's reserve, which was to be available for employment anywhere in South Vietnam.[19]

As the summer progressed, the 173d's rapid-reaction function seemed less important. Although Westmoreland retained it as one of the unit's missions, there appeared to be little need for it. That was about to change. In the highlands of II Corps the Special Forces camp at Duc Co, some forty-five kilometers southwest of Pleiku City near the Cambodian border, had been under siege since June by the enemy's local forces and possibly a contingent of North Vietnamese. In early August intelligence sources indicated that an attack on the base by a North Vietnamese unit, the *32d People's Army of Vietnam (PAVN) Regiment*, was imminent. Westmoreland believed that the siege was part of a larger enemy campaign in the highlands to seize district towns, put pressure on province seats, and cut routes of communication in an attempt not only to break the morale of the people but also to bring about economic strangulation. In response, the South Vietnamese II Corps commander, Lt. Gen. Vinh Loc, directed two task forces—each roughly two battalions strong—to relieve the camp. On 3 August one moved by air directly to Duc Co. The other, an armored group, would take Highway 19 to the hamlet of Thanh Binh, about halfway between Pleiku and Duc Co. After securing the town, it would continue westward, clearing the road to the camp.[20]

From 4 to 9 August the two task forces implemented Vinh Loc's plan. The one operating near Duc Co clashed intermittently with an unidentified North Vietnamese unit, but the other en route to Thanh Binh ran into an ambush. Although gunships and fighter-bombers

[18] Msgs, Westmoreland MAC 3886 and 4087 to Sharp, 30 Jul and 12 Aug 65, Westmoreland Message files, CMH; Commander's Combat Note nos. 67 and 73, 173d Abn Bde (Sep), 14 Jul 65, p. 3, and 5 Aug 65, p. 2 (quotation), Historians files, CMH.

[19] McNeill, *To Long Tan*, pp. 117–22; Msgs, Westmoreland MAC 3886 and MAC 4087 to Sharp, 30 Jul and 12 Aug 65.

[20] MFR, Westmoreland, 2 Jul 65, sub: Meeting by Ambassador Taylor, Ambassador Johnson, and Myself With Generals Thieu, Ky, and Co, 2 Jul 65, Westmoreland History

responded quickly, the situation appeared bleak. Vinh Loc had only two marine battalions in reserve. If he committed them to the relief of Duc Co, Pleiku City would stand unguarded. Asserting that no troops were available, the South Vietnamese high command turned to Westmoreland for assistance. The general immediately agreed to move the 173d Airborne Brigade to Thanh Binh. If the enemy lingered near Duc Co, the brigade would join the fight. By deploying the brigade Westmoreland hoped to "eliminate any and all excuses" for why the South Vietnamese should not seek out and destroy the enemy.[21]

The brigade's move to the highlands was swift. By 11 August the 1st and 2d Battalions, 503d Infantry, had reached Pleiku and moved into the field. For this offensive they would be under the operational control of Maj. Gen. Stanley R. Larsen's newly activated tactical command in II Corps, Task Force ALPHA, at Nha Trang. The 1st Infantry Division's 2d Battalion, 18th Infantry, having recently arrived in Vietnam, would take responsibility for local defense while the remainder of the American force moved to Thanh Binh. With American forces nearby, Vinh Loc could attack toward Duc Co.

Once in position, brigade elements conducted patrols and airmobile assaults to hold open a mountain pass near Thanh Binh, but they hardly saw the enemy, who had again chosen to withdraw in the face of a superior force. On 17 August, with no one left to fight, Vinh Loc's units began to pull back to Pleiku via Highway 19. The next day the last of their trucks passed into safe territory east of the Thanh Binh pass.[22]

Remaining in the highlands for the rest of August and into early September, the 173d operated mainly around the city of Pleiku, except for a detachment that searched north into Kontum Province in late August. When the patrols produced no significant contact with the enemy, the brigade returned to Bien Hoa, where it once again assumed responsibility for defending the air base. The foray into II Corps had cost the unit 1 killed and 8 wounded.[23]

Both Williamson and Westmoreland considered the operation a success, demonstrating, according to the former, the brigade's "ability to react immediately, move rapidly for great distances, and arrive to perform a difficult mission in an outstanding manner." Westmoreland saw the operation as serving both a political and training function. "The

---

Backup files, CMH; Vietnam War Fact Sheets, Enemy Buildup, 1965, William C. Westmoreland Papers, CMH; George L. MacGarrigle, "Arrival of U.S. Army Combat Units in the Central Highlands," pp. 1–6, Historians files, CMH.

[21] MFR, Westmoreland, 2 Jul 65, sub: Meeting by Ambassador Taylor, Ambassador Johnson, and Myself With Generals Thieu, Ky, and Co, 2 Jul 65; MACV History, 1965, p. 167, CMH; MacGarrigle, "Army Combat Units in the Highlands," p. 7 (quoted words).

[22] MACV History, 1965, p. 361.

[23] After Action Rpt (AAR), Opn at Thanh Binh Pass, Pleiku, and Kontum, 173d Abn Bde (Sep), 13 Sep 65, p. 14, Historians files, CMH.

major purpose of this deployment," he said, "was to bolster the military posture of the Vietnamese forces and their morale." He added that he hoped the operation boded well for the future "as we gain the capability of routinely backing up and reinforcing the Vietnamese with U.S. troops."[24]

During the rest of September and into October the 173d Airborne Brigade provided security for units of the 1st Infantry Division while they moved into base camps near Saigon. Two operations were representative of the role it played. On 12 September the brigade received instructions to enter an enemy base area known as the Long Nguyen Secret Zone, which straddled an east–west Viet Cong infiltration and supply corridor between War Zones C and D. The objective was to disrupt any plans the enemy might have had north and northwest of Ben Cat, where the 1st Division's new base camps would be located. A regiment belonging to the South Vietnamese 5th Infantry Division would conduct operations with the same purpose in an adjacent area to the east.[25]

The Americans moved into position by truck and helicopter on 14 September to begin patrolling near Ben Cat. They had no sustained contact with the enemy during the two weeks the operation lasted, but special units from the brigade did conduct a civic action campaign, in which they provided food, supplies, and medical care to the region's inhabitants. The object of that effort, soon to become a routine feature of American combat operations, was to persuade the people that the government represented their best hope for the future while generating intelligence about the Viet Cong. On the twenty-seventh and twenty-eighth the brigade returned to Bien Hoa. In addition to 40 wounded, 3 Americans, 2 New Zealanders, and 1 Australian lost their lives during the operation. The brigade claimed 46 enemy dead by body count, another 69 estimated dead, and large quantities of ammunition and equipment captured.[26]

During the second week of October the 173d Airborne Brigade carried out Operation 25–65 in what was known as the Iron Triangle, a notorious enemy stronghold just north of Saigon. The brigade's purpose remained the provision of security for 1st Division units arriving in Vietnam. A South Vietnamese force outside of Williamson's command participated by coordinating its actions with those of his brigade. Once again, despite aggressive patrolling, little action occurred. At the time Williamson was ebullient, declaring that "we have completed a successful operation right in the back yard of the enemy," that "the Iron Triangle has been . . . for all practical purposes destroyed," and that Ameri-

---

[24] Ibid., p. 16 (first quotation); Msg (remaining quotations), Westmoreland MAC 4124 to Sharp, 14 Aug 65, Westmoreland Message files, CMH.

[25] AAR, Opn 24–65, 173d Abn Bde (Sep), 29 Oct 65, pp. 1–2, Historians files, CMH.

[26] Ibid., pp. 20–21.

can forces had proved they could "go and stay anywhere and anytime in Vietnam."[27] Years later, the general would concede that he had overstated the case: "I should have said that the mystery [of the Iron Triangle] was no more," because "it was no longer the psychological bogeyman that it had been for so long."[28]

Reinforcing Bien Hoa

If the deployment of the 173d Airborne Brigade was fairly predictable given its place in the theater's contingency plans, that of the second unit committed was rather less. In fact, the unit's orders, when they came, arrived most abruptly. On 14 April the commander of the 1st Infantry Division, Maj. Gen. Jonathan O. Seaman, received a top secret message from U.S. Continental Army Command instructing him to ready, for planning purposes, a brigade for deployment to Vietnam within a month. General Seaman informed his 2d Brigade, the division's rapid-deployment force, four days later. Then, on the twenty-second, he visited the Pentagon in hopes of obtaining more information from the Army chief of staff, General Johnson. "Jack," Johnson told him, "the situation is getting real serious. And you better be prepared to send your division, or a part of it, to Vietnam by 15 June." Seaman received specific confirmation of the Army's intentions on 13 May, when planners notified him that he should consider 30 June as the brigade's personnel readiness date. Over the next two weeks he and his staff worked out the brigade's force structure for Vietnam. Then, toward the end of the month formal notification arrived that the brigade was indeed Vietnam bound.[29]

Seeking to make the 2d "the best possible brigade out of my own resources," Seaman replaced those commissioned and noncommissioned officers considered to be substandard with high-performing individuals from his two other brigades. He also filled out shortages in vehicles, armaments, and ammunition with requisitions from the other two. He understood that by cannibalizing his division for the benefit of the 2d Brigade he would make it more difficult to prepare his remaining brigades for any future deployment. Once in Vietnam, however, the 2d would face a multitude of perils and needed the best it could get. Therefore, as he recalled later, "I really tore that division apart."[30]

---

[27] Commander's Combat Note no. 80, 173d Abn Bde (Sep), 15 Oct 65, p. 1 (first two quotations), and Critique, Opn 25–65, 173d Abn Bde (Sep), 25 Oct 65, p. 20 (third quotation). Both in Historians files, CMH. For more details on the operation, see, in same files, Commander's Combat Note no. 82, 173d Abn Bde (Sep), 16 Oct 65.

[28] Interv, author with Maj Gen Ellis W. Williamson, 22 Jan 93, Historians files, CMH.

[29] Interv, John Albright with Lt Gen Jonathan O. Seaman, 10 Sep 70, pp. 6–9 (quotation, p. 8), Historians files, CMH; [Unit History, 1965], 2d Bde, 1st Inf Div, n.d. pp. [1–3], box 1, 81/748, RG 338, NARA.

[30] Interv, Albright with Seaman, 10 Sep 70, pp. 6–10 (quotations, p. 9).

Preparations for the deployment proceeded apace. At the end of May the 2d Brigade's executive officer, Lt. Col. Edgar N. Glotzbach, made a liaison trip to Vietnam. Upon his return in the middle of June he briefed General Seaman and the brigade's commanders and their staffs on the conditions that he had observed. Then on the twentieth the 2d Brigade commander, Col. James E. Simmons, and the advance party flew to Vietnam to make arrangements for the arrival of the brigade.

In the meantime, the deploying units completed their preparations for departure. The units included the 2d Battalion, 16th Infantry; the 1st and 2d Battalions, 18th Infantry; the 1st Battalion, 7th Artillery, equipped with 105-mm. towed howitzers; Battery C, 8th Battalion, 6th Artillery, armed with 155-mm. towed howitzers; and various support elements, including engineer, medical, and maintenance companies, police and military intelligence elements, and a radio research (or signal intercept) unit. During the first two weeks of June the brigade loaded its equipment on trains for shipment to California, the first train leaving Fort Riley, Kansas, on the fourteenth. Between the twenty-first and twenty-fourth the rest of the unit went by rail and air to the Oakland Army Terminal. The troops then embarked on the Navy transport *General W. H. Gordon*, with three other ships moving the brigade's equipment. The *Gordon* departed on the twenty-fifth. Once under way the men were officially informed of what they had long suspected: They were en route to Vietnam.[31]

The brigade's destination and mission in Vietnam changed a week before its arrival. Instead of establishing and maintaining defenses for port and supply facilities under construction at Qui Nhon in northern II Corps, two of the unit's infantry battalions, the 2d of the 16th and the 2d of the 18th, were to go to Bien Hoa to assist in securing the air base, while the third battalion, the 1st of the 18th, and an artillery battery proceeded to Cam Ranh Bay, about two hundred kilometers south of Qui Nhon, to provide security for the new port being built there. The *Gordon* reached Cam Ranh on 12 July, stopping just long enough for the infantry and artillery to disembark. Continuing south, the ship arrived at Vung Tau on the fourteenth. Over the next two days the troops made their way to the Vung Tau airfield, where they enplaned for Bien Hoa Air Base. Upon arrival, they moved by truck to their prospective base camp, about three kilometers southeast of the airfield, a site chosen because it lay astride a line of approach into the air base. There, for the first few days in Vietnam, Colonel Simmons' force came under the command of MACV, but on the nineteenth the 173d Airborne Brigade assumed operational control. The arrangement lasted until the 1st Division headquarters reached Vietnam in October.[32]

---

[31] [Unit History, 1965], 2d Bde, 1st Inf Div, pp. [2–3].

[32] Quarterly Cmd Rpt, 1 Jul–30 Sep 65, 2d Bde, 1st Inf Div, 16 Oct 65, pp. 2–3, box 1, 68A/1507, RG 334, NARA; McNeill, *To Long Tan*, pp. 96–97.

Bien Hoa encampment of the 2d Brigade, 1st Infantry Division

The change of station from Qui Nhon to Bien Hoa created supply problems. Food stores and ammunition earmarked for the brigade and prepositioned at Qui Nhon were now unavailable, and could not be easily replaced out of the Army warehouses scattered about Saigon, which were having trouble supporting the American buildup. For the rest of the summer Simmons' brigade lived hand to mouth, and only the presence of a Navy commissary not far from downtown Saigon kept the men from subsisting on field rations for weeks at a time. Even then, ammunition became so scarce at one point during the summer's operations that the brigade had to borrow artillery rounds from the South Vietnamese.[33]

On 17 July the brigade's men began work on their first priority, construction of a base camp. Clearing the jungle and thick brush that clogged the encampment site, with some of the second-growth underbrush so dense that visibility was limited to a few feet only, they quickly slashed fields of fire so that they could lay down an adequate defense in case of an attack. On the night of the eighteenth-nineteenth the enemy mortared the area and probed the perimeter—an action that produced the brigade's first battle-related casualty. By the end of month, sometimes working around the clock and despite daily downpours and nightly sniper fire, the brigade had completed the job.[34]

---

[33] Joel D. Meyerson, "Logistics in the Vietnam Conflict," ch. 4, CMH; Quarterly Cmd Rpt, 1 Jul–30 Sep 65, 2d Bde, 1st Inf Div, p. 9.

[34] [Unit History, 1965], 2d Bde, 1st Inf Div, p. [3]; Quarterly Cmd Rpt, 1 Jul–30 Sep 65, 2d Bde, 1st Inf Div, p. 2.

An event occurred on 22 July that graphically illustrated the kind of battle injuries awaiting soldiers in Vietnam. On that day a bulldozer clearing an area near the base camp turned up a sniper position. In the ensuing attempt to capture the fleeing Viet Cong, Lt. Col. Lloyd L. Burke, the 2d of the 16th Infantry commander flying overhead in his helicopter, was shot down. As a result of injuries, Burke had to be evacuated and, eventually, returned to the United States. A later inventory by Burke himself bore sober witness to the cost of combat:

A rundown of my wounds reveals a hole in my right ankle, [a] hole in my left foot, a chunk of meat out of the left calf about as big as your fist and a compound fracture of the left tibia. Moving up the body my left index finger is gone, [there is] a big gash in my left thumb, [and] a badly bruised left hand. A hole in my right cheek about as big as your thumb and about 1 inch deep. That piece severed the nerve in my cheek causing the right part of my upper lip to be dead. [I have] superficial shrapnel holes in the face, head, arms, and chest. I'm told the flax [flak] jacket saved my life. It's pretty well chewed up.[35]

But he was alive!

On 8 September the 2d of the 16th Infantry embarked on the brigade's first battalion-size operation. Lasting two days, the mission provided logistical and organizational experience for the battalion but produced no contact with the enemy. On the sixteenth the unit conducted a second operation, about fifteen kilometers north of Bien Hoa. Although it again failed to find the Viet Cong, it found sufficient signs of their activity in the area to warrant the involvement of a larger force. As a result, on the twenty-third, with the 2d of the 18th Infantry back from the Central Highlands, Colonel Simmons mounted a two-battalion operation, the brigade's largest since arriving in Vietnam. While carrying out this four-day mission, the force had its first encounter with the enemy. Although precise numbers are unknown, it killed or wounded a number of Viet Cong while destroying well-defended, dug-in positions. On the twenty-ninth the 1st of the 18th ceded its mission at Cam Ranh to the recently arrived 1st Brigade, 101st Airborne Division, and rejoined the 2d Brigade. For the first time since reaching Vietnam, the brigade's battalions were together at one location.[36]

The next month the 2d Brigade left the control of 173d Airborne Brigade to rejoin the rest of the 1st Infantry Division, which deployed to Vietnam at that time. Appropriately enough, the 2d Brigade's last operation before rejoining its parent organization involved providing security for the arrival of a sister divisional unit, the 1st Brigade, 1st In-

---

[35] Ltr, Lt Col Lloyd L. Burke to Maj Gen Jonathan O. Seaman, 28 Jul 65, Personal Corresp (1965), Jonathan O. Seaman Papers, MHI.

[36] [Unit History, 1965], 2d Bde, 1st Inf Div, p. [4]; Quarterly Cmd Rpt, 1 Jul–30 Sep 65, 2d Bde, 1st Inf Div, p. 3.

fantry Division, at Phuoc Vinh. Two battalions, backed by artillery, began to patrol the area on 4 October, securing and clearing the site of the 1st Brigade's base camp. The newly arrived brigade moved into its future home between the twenty-second and twenty-fourth. During the operation the Americans encountered no opposition, and the 2d Brigade returned to Bien Hoa on the twenty-fifth.[37]

A Brigade for Coastal II Corps

With installations and enclaves in I and III Corps secured by American units, priorities shifted to coastal II Corps, where the strategically important area between Qui Nhon and Cam Ranh Bay was still wide open and at risk. Initially, the 1st Brigade, 101st Airborne Brigade, had been slated to relieve the 173d Airborne Brigade at Bien Hoa so that the 173d could return to Okinawa. But when the Viet Cong rainy season offensive began, the Army reassigned the 173d to a permanent station in South Vietnam. With the 1st Brigade suddenly free for duty, General Westmoreland decided to use it in II Corps. Commanded by Col. James S. Timothy, a Distinguished Service Cross winner in France during World War II and a graduate of the French war college *Ecole Superieure de Guerre*, the brigade had a twofold mission: establishing itself at Cam Ranh Bay to guard the port and logistical complex under construction; and, thereafter, standing prepared to conduct rapid-reaction operations anywhere in South Vietnam.

The brigade's deployment from the United States followed the pattern laid down by earlier arrivals. A liaison party visited Vietnam from 3 to 12 June to make arrangements for expediting the move and to obtain whatever advice it could from officers already at the scene. Next, an advance party under the brigade commander flew to Nha Trang. Following that, on 6 and 7 July the bulk of the brigade flew from Fort Campbell, Kentucky, to the Oakland Army Terminal. The troops then embarked on the Navy transport *General LeRoy Eltinge*—in the words of one enlisted wag, "five hundred and ten feet of rusting gray steel." The accommodations it provided seemed so bleak that, as the men boarded, one wit among them was heard to remark loudly that its namesake must have lost a major battle.[38]

On 29 July the brigade reached Cam Ranh Bay, where General Westmoreland and Ambassador Taylor, former commanders of the 101st

---

[37] [Unit History, 1965], 2d Bde, 1st Div, p. [5]. See also Hist Study, 1st Inf Div, n.d., sub: Deployment of the 1st Infantry Division to Vietnam, p. 17, box 8, 67A/5293, RG 319, NARA.

[38] *Pentagon Papers* (Gravel), 3:461–62; Quarterly Cmd Rpt, 1 Jul–30 Sep 65, 1st Bde, 101st Abn Div, 18 Oct 65, p. 1, Historians files, CMH; Robert H. McKenzie, "The First Brigade in the Republic of Vietnam, July 1965–January 1966," pp. 14–15, in Pratt Museum files, Fort Campbell, Ky., and copy in Historians files, CMH; Michael Clodfelter, *Mad Minutes and Vietnam Months: A Soldier's Memoir* (New York: Zebra Books, 1988), p. 25 (quoted words).

Airborne Division, were on hand to greet the men. What they found was a unit much stronger than the 173d Airborne Brigade had been upon its arrival. Unlike its predecessor, the 1st Brigade came with its full complement of maneuver battalions—the 1st Battalion (Airborne), 327th Infantry; the 2d Battalion (Airborne), 327th Infantry; and the 2d Battalion (Airborne), 502d Infantry—plus the 2d Battalion, 320th Artillery, equipped with 105-mm. towed howitzers; Troop A, 2d Squadron, 17th Cavalry, with jeep-mounted machine guns and recoilless rifles; a support battalion; an engineer company; a signal platoon; a military police platoon; a military intelligence detachment; and a radio research unit. All it lacked was an aviation unit.[39]

For Westmoreland, the arrival of the 1st Brigade, 101st Airborne Division, meant a welcome addition of American power. In conjunction with the 173d Airborne Brigade, he finally had the two highly mobile airborne units that he had requested for reserve and rapid-reaction duty anywhere in the theater. Ultimately, Westmoreland hoped to place both brigades under a single task force headquarters to give them flexibility of command and the capability to respond quickly in order to deliver "the heavy mobile punch" he wanted.[40] Such an organization never came into being, but the concept illustrated Westmoreland's early thinking on how to structure an effective force for Vietnam.

By the time the last soldier and the last piece of cargo had emerged from the *Eltinge*, the 1st Brigade had set out upon its mission. The troops moved just across the bay from the Cam Ranh peninsula to establish their base camp near the hamlet of Dong Ba Thin along Highway 1 (*Map 3*). Although visibly tired from their twenty-one-day sea journey and entry into their encampment, "they seemed to realize that they were in an area where they could conceivably be hit by an attack from insurgent forces. Foxholes and guard duty no longer appeared as an unnecessary evil to be tolerated only during field problems." And so, the soldiers dug in "with an air of urgency and expectancy." Unlike the sandy shore at Cam Ranh, some of the ground in the camp area near Dong Ba Thin was so hard that holes had to be blown with explosives before digging could commence.[41]

Over the days that followed, after establishing a rough-and-ready base camp and defensive perimeter, the soldiers turned to their first order of business: on-the-job training. Beginning with squad-size patrols, they graduated to platoon, company, and battalion missions and, finally,

---

[39] Robert H. McKenzie and David A. Bagwell, "Movement of a Brigade to a Foreign Theater: Some Lessons from the 1965 Experience of the 1st Brigade, 101st Airborne Division" (Fort Campbell, Ky.: 322d Military History Detachment, 1973), p. 1, copy in Historians files, CMH; McKenzie, "First Brigade," p. 14.

[40] Msg (quoted words), Westmoreland MAC 3240 to Wheeler and Sharp, 24 Jun 65, Westmoreland Message files, CMH. See also MACV History, 1965, p. 41; Admiral U. S. G. Sharp and General William C. Westmoreland, "Report on the War in Vietnam (as of 30 June 1968)," p. 139, copy in CMH.

[41] Unit History, May–Dec 1965, Support Bn, 1st Bde, 101st Abn Div, n.d., p. 6, box 1, 82/1253, RG 338, NARA.

LAOS

CAMBODIA

QUANG TIN

I CTZ

QUANG NGAI

KONTUM

Kontum

XX 3 PAVN

BINH DINH

XX 1 CAV

X 173
11 Aug–5 Sep

PLEIKU

19

18 Sep

XX 502
2

XXX II ARVN

AN KHE

XX 22 ARVN

XX CAP ROK(-)

2 7
7 Jul–4 Nov

3 7
1–8 Jul

XXX B3

32 PAVN

33 PAVN

PLEIKU

66 PAVN

2 PLAF

QUI NHON

Cheo Reo

PHU BON

14

PHU YEN

1

Tuy Hoa

SOUTH

CHINA

SEA

DARLAC

21

BAN ME THUOT

XX 23 ARVN

95 PAVN

XXX TF ALPHA

X 2 ROK

X 101
29 Jul–10 Nov

X 18
12 Jul–29 Sep

Ninh Hoa

KHANH HOA

NHA TRANG

QUANG DUC

14

Gia Nghia

TUYEN DUC

Da Lat

NINH THUAN

CAM RANH

1
101
10 Nov–

PHUOC LONG

LAM DONG

Bao Loc

20

Tung Nghia

11

1

PHAN RANG

LONG KHANH

BINH THUAN

III CTZ

BINH TUY

1

Phan Thiet

PHUOC TUY

Dao Phu Qui

II CORPS TACTICAL ZONE
July—November 1965

✸ Engagement

—— Corps Boundary

0 _____ 50 Miles

0 _____ 50 Kilometers

MAP 3

Troops of the 1st Brigade, 101st Airborne Division, during HIGHLAND, *with Highway 19 in the background*

to a brigade-size operation code-named ANVIL. On 16 and 17 August two battalions, an artillery battery, and the cavalry troop sought to find and destroy Viet Cong forces west of Nha Trang. No contact and no casualties occurred, but their performance did indicate that the brigade was capable of conducting large operations.[42]

During these early weeks the 1st Brigade began to sort out its supply problems. Similar to the other two Army brigades in Vietnam, Colonel Timothy's unit encountered shortages of repair parts and munitions and had particular trouble replacing worn-out boots, clothing, and organizational equipment. Part of the difficulty was that some materiel sent from Fort Campbell took longer to arrive than expected, not least because the brigade was soon on the move, far from its base camp. Delay in receiving medical supplies meant that for several weeks soldiers ill from anything more serious than heat rash or diarrhea had to be evacuated to the 8th Field Hospital at Nha Trang. In addition, a number of items the brigade had brought to Vietnam proved unnecessary, while others that had been left behind, such as water trucks, were sorely missed. Although the combat necessities were provided for, the brigade's first several months in country found it living on a shoestring.[43]

---

[42] McKenzie, "First Brigade," pp. 15–16; Table, U.S. Army Major Unit Opns, 1st Bde, 101st Abn Div, 29 Jul–29 Sep 65, n.d., Historians files, CMH.

[43] Quarterly Cmd Rpt, 1 Jul–30 Sep 65, 1st Bde, 101st Abn Div, p. 6; McKenzie, "First Brigade," p. 27; Unit History, May–Dec 1965, Support Bn, 1st Bde, 101st Abn Div, pp. 7–8.

As the soldiers gained experience and developed skills, it became increasingly evident that they were deficient in airmobile tactics. To remedy the problem, Timothy called upon Company A of the 502d Aviation Battalion to familiarize his brigade with the procedures involved. The company, in Vietnam since December 1964, took the brigade through intensive training in the transportation and landing of units by helicopter, the concepts of aerial resupply, the use of command and control helicopters, the employment of airborne radio relay stations, and the exercise of close air support using gunships. When the brigade moved to An Khe in Binh Dinh Province to provide security for the arrival of the 1st Cavalry Division (Airmobile), the aviation company accompanied and supported it throughout the operation.[44]

The mission to An Khe was the brigade's first important undertaking in Vietnam. Code-named Operation HIGHLAND, it involved some risk because Binh Dinh Province contained a heavy enemy presence that would render the 1st Cavalry Division vulnerable during its move inland. South Vietnamese troops, assisted by a U.S. Marine battalion, protected Qui Nhon, the port of entry for the cavalry division. A single battalion from the 1st Brigade would initially handle security for the base area at An Khe itself, to be joined by a second battalion as soon as Highway 19, the route from Qui Nhon to An Khe, had been cleared. At that point the remainder of the brigade, involved in monitoring likely ambush sites along the road and providing protection for supply convoys, would make its way up to An Khe.[45]

The brigade executed the operation in phases. In Phase I (22–25 August) elements moved by road, air, and sea from Dong Ba Thin to the area of operation. The 2d of the 327th Infantry flew to An Khe and established a defensive perimeter around the base's airstrip on the twenty-second. Over the next two days the rest of the brigade, including the 1st of the 327th Infantry and the 2d of the 502d Infantry, and its heavy equipment arrived by sea at Qui Nhon and moved to An Khe via Highway 19. Supported by air and artillery strikes, these units carried out Phase II on the twenty-sixth, clearing Highway 19 through to An Khe so that convoys could begin to bring cavalry division supplies and soldiers to their new base camp.

With both Highway 19 and the base camp in hand, Phase III began— an aggressive campaign to keep the highway open for convoys and protect the force building the division's base. Between 27 August and 1 October the brigade carried out twenty-three company-size or larger operations, eight of them airmobile assaults, against known or suspected Communist concentrations. Although the patrols and sweeps generated

---

[44] Quarterly Cmd Rpt, 1 Jul–30 Sep 65, 1st Bde, 101st Abn Div, pp. 2, 7; Unit History, 14 Dec 64–31 Dec 65, Co A, 502d Avn Bn (Ambl Light), n.d., p. 16, box 8, 75/1000, RG 338, NARA.

[45] Quarterly Cmd Rpt, 1 Jul–30 Sep 65, Field Force, Vietnam (FFV), 15 Oct 65, pp. 1, 6, Historians files, CMH.

only fleeting engagements, the object of the operation was achieved. The 1st Cavalry Division arrived at its destination unharmed.[46]

One instance of intense combat did occur, however, when a 620-man strike force conducting Operation GIBRALTAR, one of a series of attacks under the HIGHLAND umbrella, engaged a Viet Cong main force battalion and elements of another. The 2d of the 502d Infantry and a South Vietnamese ranger company had deployed by helicopter shortly after 0700 on 18 September into an area near An Ninh, a hamlet thirty kilometers east of An Khe and about fourteen kilometers north of Highway 19. Intelligence sources suggested the presence of an enemy unit in the mountains nearby. To the Americans' surprise they set down on a training base that harbored the *95th Battalion* and elements of the *94th Battalion*, both battalions belonging to the *2d PLAF Regiment* of the recently formed *3d PAVN Division*. The Viet Cong did nothing to contest the first American lift, but when the second arrived, fire from small arms, automatic weapons, and mortars became so intense that the American commander on the scene, Lt. Col. Wilfrid K. G. Smith, had to wave off the rest of the Hueys before all the men could land. As a result, only 224 men were actually on the ground. After some initial confusion, the troops organized a defensive perimeter and began to return fire.[47]

Over the next few hours the enemy pressed his attack, throwing the survival of the force into question. Complicating the situation, the Americans had neglected to bring along mortars and recoilless rifles; the battalion commander never considered the possibility that his men could use them in mountain country. Artillery support was unavailable because recent rains had rendered a critical ford impassable, and helicopters capable of carrying artillery within range of the battle were flying other missions. Although A–1E Skyraiders had struck the landing zone prior to the insertion, none were available from shortly after 0730 until 0900 as the fuel at Bien Hoa Air Base had somehow become contaminated. The force on the ground was thus on its own for almost two hours, encountering enemy fire so intense that it brought down or damaged twenty-six helicopters during the course of the day. Shortly after 0900 F–100s finally arrived. Fifty more air strikes followed as the day lengthened. Colonel Smith called in some of the strikes to within one hundred meters of his position, and two of his men died in the bombing. But air power did the job and reversed the situation.[48]

---

[46] AAR, Opn HIGHLAND, 1st Bde, 101st Abn Div, 5 Dec 65, p. 2, box 1, 82/1263, RG 338, NARA. See also McKenzie, "First Brigade," pp. 14–16.

[47] AAR, Opn GIBRALTAR, 2d Bn, 502d Inf, 8 Oct 65, pp. 1–8, box 1, 82/1263, RG 338, NARA; AAR, Opn GIBRALTAR, 2d Bn, 327th Inf, 4 Oct 65, pp. [1–6], Historians files, CMH; David H. Hackworth and Julie Sherman, *About Face: The Odyssey of an American Soldier* (New York: Simon and Schuster, 1989), pp. 468–75.

[48] AAR, Opn GIBRALTAR, 2d Bn, 502d Inf, pp. 1–3; Hackworth and Sherman, *About Face*, p. 470.

A U.S.–South Vietnamese relief force began moving into the area by helicopter during the late afternoon. But by the time it had landed and reorganized, night had fallen, making it impossible to travel the final distance overland to assist the beleaguered troops. Setting out early the next day, the group reached the American perimeter by midmorning. By then the fighting had ended. In all, 13 Americans died in the encounter and 28 were wounded. Enemy losses reportedly ranged from 226 to 257 by body count, most killed by air strikes. Joined on 20 September by other units approaching from the west, the relief force searched the area but found little. The brigade shut down GIBRALTAR on the twenty-first.[49]

Although soon overshadowed by other events, the battle produced contradictory interpretations. Colonel Timothy, the brigade commander, considered the engagement "particularly significant because it marked the first conquest of a VC Main Force unit by any U.S. Army element in Vietnam."[50] General Westmoreland agreed, terming the operation a "spectacular success."[51] On the other hand, Timothy's operations officer, Maj. David H. Hackworth, writing years later, characterized the battle as "most definitely . . . *not* . . . a great victory."[52] Looking back, the operations officer of the 2d of the 327th Infantry, Maj. Charles W. Dyke, scored it a "disaster" and the product of a "shoddy, ill-conceived plan." In particular, according to Dyke, the number of helicopters assigned to the operation was insufficient, leading to a slow buildup of combat power at the landing zone when speed was essential.[53]

With the conclusion of GIBRALTAR, the 1st Brigade's work for the 1st Cavalry Division came to an end. Now the paratroopers moved to other missions: screening the arrival of Korean units at Qui Nhon and Cam Ranh; keeping Cam Ranh secure; and working to create a new base camp at Phan Rang, some forty kilometers south of Cam Ranh port. In just two months the men of the 1st Brigade, 101st Airborne Division, had completed their pathfinder assignment, opening up the II Corps coast to follow-on units—the reinforcements the administration had promised to the theater command. The first step was done. The war was about to change, but in ways few could have guessed or hoped to manage.

---

[49] Table, Unit Opns, 1st Bde, 101st Abn Div, 29 Jul–29 Sep 65; AARs, Opn GIBRALTAR, 2d Bn, 502d Inf, p. 7, and 2d Bn, 327th Inf, p. [5].

[50] MFR, Col James S. Timothy, Commanding Officer (CO), 1st Bde, 101st Abn Div, 12 Jan 66, sub: After Action Report, Operation GIBRALTAR, Historians files, CMH.

[51] Msg, COMUSMACV to CINCPAC, 21 Sep 65, document 77, vol. 40, box 22, Vietnam Country File, NSF, LBJL.

[52] Hackworth and Sherman, *About Face*, p. 474.

[53] Lt Gen Charles W. Dyke, Letter to Editor, *Army* 39 (September 1989): 5–6.

3

Divisions Deploy

Now elements in the war's equation modified its shape in the summer of 1965. Concerned by the continuing inability of the South Vietnamese to handle the Communist threat, a threat punctuated by Viet Cong successes in May and June, the Johnson administration committed two Army divisions and promised more as needed. With that commitment, and a matching enemy escalation, the conflict broadened out, forcing General Westmoreland to search for a new approach to operations that he hoped would bring the allies eventual victory.

The Decision To Reinforce

In May the Viet Cong launched offensives in two areas of South Vietnam, breaking a two-month lull in operations. In III Corps the Viet Cong opened their Dong Xoai campaign, seeking "to annihilate a large portion of the puppet main-force [South Vietnamese] Army, intensify guerrilla warfare, assist the masses in destroying 'strategic hamlets,' expand the liberated areas, [and] connect the eastern Nam Bo [III Corps] bases with the southern part of the Central Highlands." The offensive began on the eleventh north of Saigon, with an attack on the capital of Phuoc Long Province, Song Be, by up to four Viet Cong battalions. Overrunning most of the town, the attackers held their ground into the next day. When the South Vietnamese dispatched two relief forces, both were ambushed. On the twenty-ninth the offensive expanded into southern I Corps. A Viet Cong force, probably in regimental strength, attacked a South Vietnamese Army company on a road-clearing operation near the hamlet of Ba Gia, west of Quang Ngai City. The battalion commander committed his other two companies, but the Viet Cong ambushed both as they neared the battle site. The following day three more battalions entered the fray, and all took a beating. At the end of the fighting it was clear that the South Vietnamese had suffered a major defeat, losing 107 killed, 123 wounded, and 367 missing, as well as 384 individual weapons.[1] The en-

---

[1] *9th Division*, p. 37 (quotation), copy in CMH; MACV History, 1965, pp. 221–22, CMH.

emy had used a favorite tactic: attacking and pinning down a South Vietnamese element, and then ambushing the inevitable relief force.

American officials feared the worst. The South Vietnamese seemed whipped. As General Larsen recalled, "We had to do something and very fast."[2] An analysis prepared on 5 June by the U.S. Embassy's Mission Intelligence Committee and transmitted to Washington in Ambassador Taylor's name, with General Westmoreland's concurrence, reached a similar conclusion. The growing American military commitment had persuaded the enemy to commit more troops of his own. Although suffering heavy losses, the Communists remained capable of continuing their attacks, and soon U.S. combat troops would have to move out of their enclaves and go into battle.[3]

Two days later, on 7 June, General Westmoreland informed Admiral Sharp and the chairman of the Joint Chiefs of Staff, General Earle G. Wheeler, that Viet Cong main forces and the increasing number of North Vietnamese units in the South could mount regimental-size operations in all of the corps tactical zones and battalion-size ones in all of the provinces. Furthermore, he believed that in the near future the enemy would initiate attacks in several strategic areas. The South Vietnamese Army, with its high desertion rate and higher than expected losses in recent battles, might not be able to hold. Therefore, the United States had few options if it wanted to reverse the trend. "I see no course of action open," wrote Westmoreland, "except to reinforce our efforts in SVN [South Vietnam] with additional U.S. or third country forces as rapidly as is practical during the critical weeks ahead." As his only recourse, he requested the commitment of additional maneuver elements. Counting these units plus the brigades already in country or on the way, the number of U.S. and third-country (Australian and South Korean) battalions would total forty-four, and the U.S. expeditionary force would increase to some 175,000 officers and enlisted men by the end of 1965. The maneuver elements would establish "a substantial and hard hitting offensive capability on the ground to convince the V.C. that they cannot win."[4] Planning also had to begin for the deployment of even greater forces, if and when required, to defeat the Communists.

Another major South Vietnamese setback soon punctuated the need for American troops. Shortly after General Westmoreland made his request, the South Vietnamese at Dong Xoai suffered their worst defeat since 1964. When the fighting ended on 12 June, they had lost 416 killed, 174 wounded, and 233 missing. For a time, the 173d Airborne Brigade was poised to intervene, but the enemy's withdrawal eliminated the

---

[2] Interv, Allan W. Sandstrum with Lt Gen Stanley R. Larsen, 11 Mar 70, p. 7B, Historians files, CMH.

[3] Msg, Saigon 4074 to State, 5 Jun 65, tab 263, box 41, NSC History, NSF, LBJL.

[4] Msg, COMUSMACV MAC 19118 to CINCPAC and JCS, 7 Jun 65, tab 269, box 41, NSC History, NSF, LBJL.

need. MACV termed the engagement "a tactical and psychological victory for the VC."[5]

Given the almost certain likelihood that incidents like Dong Xoai would recur, Westmoreland sought confirmation of his authority to commit his troops for offensive operations. On 13 June Admiral Sharp informed him that he could use his troops in support of South Vietnamese forces facing aggressive attack when other reserves were unavailable and when the military situation warranted it. Less than two weeks later, in an even clearer message approved by the Department of Defense, Secretary of State Dean Rusk added unequivocally that Westmoreland could commit U.S. troops to combat "independently of or in conjunction with GVN [government of Vietnam] forces in any situation in which the use of such troops is requested by an appropriate GVN commander and when, in COMUSMACV's judgment, their use is necessary to strengthen the relative position of GVN forces."[6] The formula gave Westmoreland about as free a hand in managing his troops as he was ever likely to receive.

Meanwhile, on 11 June the Joint Chiefs of Staff had seconded Westmoreland's reinforcement request by calling for additional troops, particularly the men of the 1st Cavalry Division. President Johnson, however, temporized. On the nineteenth he approved preparatory steps necessary for major deployments, but he held back on sending the troops themselves. Frustrated, General Wheeler on the twenty-fifth asserted that "we need more troops [in Vietnam]. . . . Everything else aside, this is the heart of the problem." As the president deliberated, discussion within the administration began to shift from what was necessary to prevent a South Vietnamese collapse to what would be required to win the struggle. Four days later, at Johnson's request, Secretary of Defense McNamara asked Westmoreland to specify the forces that would be necessary beyond the forty-four battalions to convince the enemy he could not prevail. In response, the general recommended twenty-four more battalions plus the support and air units necessary to sustain them, an additional 100,000 men. Under the plan he developed, the forty-four battalions would arrive as soon as possible to contain the Communist offensive and to prevent a South Vietnamese collapse. The second wave of troops would reach Vietnam in 1966 to consolidate earlier gains by attacking the enemy's main forces in their strongholds and by assisting with the pacification of politically important areas.[7]

---

[5] MACV History, 1965, p. 223.

[6] Msg, CINCPAC to JCS, 12 Jun 65, sub: Concept of Counterinsurgency Operations in South Vietnam, tab 293, box 42, NSC History, NSF, LBJL; Msg, Sharp to Westmoreland, 13 Jun 65, Westmoreland Message files, CMH; Msg (quotation), State 3057 to Saigon, 26 Jun 65, Historians files, CMH.

[7] Msg (quotation), Wheeler to Sharp, 25 Jun 65, Westmoreland Message files, CMH; Cosmas, "MACV, the Joint Command," ch. 7, CMH; Memo, McGeorge Bundy for the President, 24 Jul 65, sub: The History of Recommendations for Increased US Forces in Vietnam, tab 417, and Msg, Defense 5319 to U.S. Embassy Saigon, 7 Jul 65, tab 378, both box 43, NSC History, NSF, LBJL; Westmoreland, *A Soldier Reports*, pp. 141–42.

Secretary McNamara briefs President Johnson on the additional troop deployments, with Secretary Rusk and General Wheeler looking on.

Throughout the month of July senior officials in the Johnson administration pondered the additional deployments. The Saigon-Honolulu-Washington cable traffic hummed during these weeks, and McNamara made yet another trip to Saigon for consultations with Westmoreland and Taylor. After McNamara returned, President Johnson and his most senior national security advisers met several times to arrive at a decision on Vietnam. On the twenty-seventh Johnson approved Westmoreland's original request of forty-four battalions, but with two significant reservations: He declined to declare a national emergency, and he postponed any decision on calling up reservists for service in Southeast Asia.

President Johnson announced the decision the next day, 28 July, at a news conference. After highlighting the importance of convincing "the Communists that we cannot be defeated by force of arms" and also his request that Westmoreland specify what more was needed to curb the North, he added that he intended to meet the general's requirements. By ordering the 1st Cavalry Division and other units to Vietnam, he continued, American fighting strength in the theater would rise from 75,000 to 125,000 men, but additional forces would be necessary later and would be sent as requested. Realizing the significance of the president's statement, a reporter asked if the existing policy of relying on the South Vietnamese to carry out offensive operations while American forces protected American installations and were available only as an emergency backup had changed. Johnson responded that the decision "does not imply any change in policy whatever. It does not imply any change of objective."[8] But it did, and dramatically so. In the words of one historian, the president's decree became "the closest thing to a formal decision for war in Vietnam."[9]

The July deliberations solidified America's military objective in Vietnam, with new combat units and logistical systems now identified and tagged for deployment. But much remained to be determined. Where, for example, was the enemy's military center? What strategy would afford the best approach to it? And what concept of operations would ensure its destruction? Westmoreland was ready with preliminary answers. The United States had no alternative, he told Sharp on 11 June, but to prepare for the long haul by assembling enough forces to wear the enemy down. The struggle would become, he added two weeks later in a message to his superiors, primarily "a war of attrition."[10]

Command and Operational Concepts

While President Johnson shaped the nature and size of the military commitment, General Westmoreland pondered issues related to the conduct of the war—how to command and employ the combat units, how to structure the U.S.–South Vietnamese command relationship, how to build a responsive logistical apparatus, and how to improve the intelligence-gathering system.

The issue of an intermediate tactical command between MACV and the field arose quickly. Existing theater plans assumed the formation of a corps headquarters when U.S. divisions arrived in country. Following the plans, Westmoreland in early August established the field headquarters Task Force ALPHA at Nha Trang in II Corps, complementing the Marine Corps tactical command—III Marine Amphibious Force—in I Corps. Despite being modeled on a corps, the new Army headquarters was an area command with a fixed location. Later in the year, to reflect its expanded mission of directing battalion-, brigade-, and division-

---

[8] *Public Papers of the Presidents of the United States: Lyndon B. Johnson, Containing the Public Messages, Speeches, and Statements of the President, 1965*, 2 vols. (Washington, D.C.: Government Printing Office, 1966), 2:795 (first quotation) and 2:801 (second quotation). See also Summary Notes of 553d NSC Meeting, 27 Jul 65, 5:40 p.m.–6:20 p.m., sub: Deployment of Additional U.S. Troops to Vietnam, tab 426, box 43, NSC History, NSF, LBJL.

[9] Herring, *America's Longest War*, p. 157.

[10] Msg, Westmoreland to Sharp, 11 Jun 65, Westmoreland History Backup files, CMH; Msg (quoted words), Westmoreland MAC 3240 to Wheeler and Sharp, 24 Jun 65, Westmoreland Message files, CMH.

level operations throughout central South Vietnam, Task Force ALPHA became Field Force, Vietnam. Its principal objectives were to assume control of designated units in the zone under its responsibility; to defend critical installations throughout the II Corps area; and, most significant to its commander, to search out and destroy the enemy's marauding main force units.[11]

When General Larsen assumed command on 4 August, Task Force ALPHA had only one permanent maneuver unit assigned, the 1st Brigade, 101st Airborne Division. To compensate for this shortage, MACV attached the following units to the command for short periods during August and September: the 173d Airborne Brigade; the 1st Infantry Division's 1st Battalion, 18th Infantry; and the 2d Battalion, 7th Marines. Shortly thereafter, two other units joined the field force—the 1st Cavalry Division in September and the 3d Brigade, 25th Infantry Division, in December. The South Korean Capital Division and the South Korean 2d Marine Corps Brigade also were present by year's end. Although the Koreans answered to a separate command structure, Larsen could usually depend on their commanders to follow his recommendations.[12]

When General Seaman's 1st Infantry Division began to arrive in October, Westmoreland placed it directly under MACV. Since the division would operate in the region around Saigon, the MACV commander wanted closer control over the unit than General Larsen's Field Force, Vietnam, could provide from faraway Nha Trang. In addition, because of Larsen's duties as both field force commander and senior adviser to the South Vietnamese Army's II Corps commander, he believed that Larsen would find it difficult to take on the III Corps responsibilities as well.[13] Accordingly, on 1 November, Westmoreland gave the 1st Division operational control over all Army forces in III Corps, making the command, in Seaman's words, a "super division." One month later Seaman became the senior American adviser to the South Vietnamese III Corps commander. Virtually duplicating Larsen's role, he had command of a field force in the making.[14]

As for relations with the South Vietnamese armed forces, Westmoreland inclined at first toward a combined command and staff arrange-

[11] Quarterly Cmd Rpt, 1 Jul–30 Sep 65, FFV, 10 Oct 65, pp. 1, 5; Msg, COMUSMACV MAC 22005 to CINCPAC, 27 Jun 65. Both in Historians files, CMH. See also Maj. Gen. George S. Eckhardt, *Command and Control, 1950–1969*, Vietnam Studies (Washington, D.C.: Department of the Army, 1974), pp. 52–54.

[12] Quarterly Cmd Rpt, 1 Jul–30 Sep 65, FFV, incl. 8, p. 1; Debriefing, Lt Gen Stanley R. Larsen, 31 Jul 67, p. 27, Senior Officer Debriefing Program, Department of the Army (DA), Historians files, CMH; Interv, Col Robert S. Holmes with Lt Gen Stanley R. Larsen, 26 Oct 76, sec. 5, p. 3, Senior Officer Oral History Program, MHI.

[13] Msgs, Westmoreland MAC 4052 and 4217 to Gen Johnson, 9 and 20 Aug 65, and Westmoreland MAC 4749 to Sharp, 23 Sep 65, Westmoreland Message files, CMH.

[14] Interv, Albright with Seaman, 10 Sep 70, p. 23 (quoted words), Historians files, CMH; MACV History, 1965, p. 99; Quarterly Cmd Rpt, 1 Oct–31 Dec 65, 1st Inf Div, n.d., p. 12, Historians files, CMH.

ment similar to the one the United States had employed with the South Korean Army during the Korean War. The approach would have given Americans a prominent role in the direction of South Vietnamese operations. Planning for the system had hardly begun, however, when Saigon's receptive civilian leaders were ousted and a less pliant military council assumed control. Shortly thereafter, the nation's new rulers notified the MACV commander that they would never accept any system that implied South Vietnamese military subordination to a foreign power. In the end, Westmoreland backed off, retreating to the tried-and-tested advisory relationship. Cooperation and coordination, not command and control, would be his bywords.[15]

In developing concepts for using U.S. troops, Westmoreland drew on methods that had either been applied during the advisory period or were in general circulation in the U.S. armed forces. The tactical employment of the troops, for example, would follow a plan that he had laid down in 1964 for the South Vietnamese. At the time, his staff had developed terms to describe three types of military operations. In a clearing operation, the objective was to drive Viet Cong main force units out of a populated area so that pacification efforts could proceed. A securing operation would follow, directed at eliminating local guerrillas and the Viet Cong underground. Meanwhile, South Vietnamese units would conduct what were called search and destroy missions—seeking, attacking, and destroying enemy units, base areas, and supply caches. To the extent that the search and destroy operations succeeded, they kept the Viet Cong focused on defending themselves and their bases and thus unable to disrupt pacification.[16]

As the number of U.S. combat troops in Vietnam grew larger, the MACV commander adapted the three types of operations to his own needs. Relegating the clearing and securing mostly to the South Vietnamese, Westmoreland assumed the search and destroy mission for his own forces because it seemed a logical response to the enemy's big unit buildup and because it fit in with the spirit of the offensive in the U.S. Army.[17] The MACV operations officer, Brig. Gen. William E. DePuy, later described such operations in blunt terms: "You go out and look for the bastards and try to destroy them, right?"[18] The search and destroy operation was to be the chief means by which the Americans intended to turn the war around.

---

[15] MACV History, 1965, pp. 100–102; Memo, Col James L. Collins, Jr., Senior Adviser, Regional Forces and Popular Forces, MACV, for CofS, MACV, 14 Apr 65, sub: Development of Combined Staff Organization, Westmoreland History files, CMH.

[16] Sharp and Westmoreland, *Report*, p. 91.

[17] MACV History, 1965, p. 161.

[18] Remarks of DePuy in *Operation Cedar Falls: I Corps Battle Analysis Conference, 13– 14 September 1988* (Fort Lewis, Wash.: History Office, 1988), p. 36, copy in Historians files, CMH. In Ltr, Gen William B. Rosson to author, 28 Feb 93, Historians files, CMH, the former MACV chief of staff stated that "DePuy . . . was the father of search and destroy, with General Westmoreland serving as senior proponent."

Building the Support Base

General Westmoreland had to cope with a system of supply that seemed in continual danger of collapsing under the demands of escalation. With the establishment of the 1st Logistical Command on 1 April, MACV had a framework within which to build and augment the necessary supply, storage, and transportation systems. Given the crescent shape of South Vietnam, a single logistical depot would not work. MACV thus adopted a logistical islands concept, whereby regional headquarters would be established in cities along the coast, with ports and depots to support the troops in the area either created or improved. Once the decision had been made that the U.S. Marines would operate in I Corps, logistical responsibility for them shifted to the Naval Support Activity, Da Nang. Army troops in II, III, and IV Corps were taken care of by the 1st Logistical Command's three regional support commands—at Qui Nhon, at Cam Ranh Bay, and at Saigon. Because of the halting nature of the buildup decisions, the process of developing the ports and depots and deploying the logistical units progressed by fits and starts. Despite the uneven development, however, which lasted through 1966 and put a premium on improvisation, the soldiers rarely lacked the necessities for waging war: food, fuel, and ammunition.[19]

To wage a prolonged American-style war in Vietnam, MACV planned and implemented a massive construction program to expand existing or to build new ports, depots, hospitals, and base camps; communications and transportation systems; and airfields. Because the airfields were so critical as the Americans arrived and took over much of the fighting, Westmoreland accelerated their development. Beginning in the spring, the three jet-capable air bases at Tan Son Nhut, Bien Hoa, and Da Nang were upgraded, and new ones were constructed—at Chu Lai, Cam Ranh Bay, and Phan Rang. Aircraft stationed at them could conduct retaliatory raids against the North and also carry out close air support missions in the South. Transport aircraft, vital for moving troops and supplies, could operate from shorter runways, so scores of smaller airfields were built across South Vietnam to accommodate the Army CV–2 Caribous and the Air Force C–123 Providers and C–130 Hercules.[20]

Once American tactical units began deploying to South Vietnam, the problem of cantonments became apparent. American military engineer units had yet to arrive, and only a few civilian contractors were in country. A good deal of the early base-building efforts revolved around ad hoc arrangements carried out by the incoming tactical unit, a few engi-

---

[19] Douglas Kinnard, *The War Managers* (Hanover, N.H.: University Press of New England, 1977), pp. 117–19. See also Joel D. Meyerson, "War Plans and Politics: Origins of the American Base of Supply in Vietnam," in *Feeding Mars: Logistics in Western Warfare From the Middle Ages to the Present*, ed. John A. Lynn (Boulder, Colo.: Westview Press, 1993), pp. 271–87.

[20] MACV History, 1965, pp. 126–27; Sharp and Westmoreland, *Report*, pp. 260–61.

neer planners, and South Vietnamese laborers. The process became more systematic with the arrival of engineer units. For example, the 70th Engineer Battalion (Combat), working at An Khe in conjunction with the advance party of the 1st Cavalry Division and a large number of South Vietnamese, played a pivotal role in the construction of the division's base camp; it built bridges, roads, helipads, guard towers, ammunition storage areas, administration buildings, a hospital, and a 20,000-man cantonment for the division's personnel.[21] Other engineer units would organize, supervise, and carry out similar work as additional American forces arrived. The military base camps, in effect, were the staging grounds from which units moved to the field to undertake combat. At the same time, they had to function as places where the troops lived, thus making the provision of food, fresh water, quarters, and sanitary facilities essential.

Toward the end of the year Westmoreland decided that the service component commands would control development of their own bases. In I Corps the U.S. Naval Forces, Vietnam, had responsibility for base construction. In II, III, and IV Corps the Air Force and Army divided the responsibility, with the Air Force component—the 2d Air Division—overseeing the construction of air bases and the Army component—U.S. Army, Vietnam—supervising the construction of base camps. In September the deputy commander of the Army component, Brig. Gen. John Norton, made the newly arrived 18th Engineer Brigade the umbrella organization in charge of operational planning and supervision of all Army projects in the country.[22]

Initially, Westmoreland had believed that it was unnecessary to create a planning board for base development at the MACV level. If need be, the work could be informally coordinated. However, late in 1965, as the buildup progressed, he judged that "the enormous size of our future construction effort became manifest and management by coordination was no longer feasible." He would establish a Directorate of Construction in early 1966 to provide the centralized control that was vital. MACV's principal staff officer for base development and construction matters would head the new directorate and, consequently, would exercise control over all construction resources in South Vietnam, including men, materiel, and funds.[23]

A key element in the success or failure of Westmoreland's concept of operations became and remained the quality of intelligence on the enemy's capabilities and intentions. At this stage of the war such intelligence was all too frequently neither timely nor accurate. The MACV

---

[21] Maj. Gen. Robert R. Ploger, *U.S. Army Engineers, 1965–1970*, Vietnam Studies (Washington, D.C.: Department of the Army, 1974), pp. 78–79.

[22] Ibid., p. 65.

[23] Sharp and Westmoreland, "Report," pp. 300–301 (quotation), copy in CMH; MACV History, 1965, p. 127.

intelligence organization, which during its early years had focused on advising the South Vietnamese military, began functioning as a provider of combat intelligence to an active U.S. fighting force only in mid-1965. Responding to Secretary McNamara's authorization, Westmoreland's new intelligence officer, Brig. Gen. Joseph A. McChristian, started to assemble a large and sophisticated organization in South Vietnam. Although McChristian threw "the maximum amount of manpower, machines, buildings, and money at the intelligence problem," it took time to build collection, analytical, and distribution systems staffed by trained and knowledgeable personnel while simultaneously expanding intelligence relationships with the South Vietnamese. As a result, McChristian's organization did not become "even minimally effective" in 1965.[24]

1st Cavalry Division

As the brigades adjusted to conditions in South Vietnam and as base development and construction got under way, two U.S. Army divisions began preparations to deploy to the war zone. Of the two, the airmobile 1st Cavalry Division received the most attention from policymakers. In both organization and tactical capabilities, it represented a marked departure from the combat divisions of the past.

The formation of the airmobile division had been in the planning for some time but was given the highest priority in June 1965, when Defense Secretary McNamara approved the concept. To bring the concept to reality, the Army immediately undertook a series of administrative changes involving three units. It switched—on paper only—the designation of the 2d Infantry Division at Fort Benning, Georgia, for that of the 1st Cavalry Division in Korea, moving neither personnel nor equipment but only the flags of the two units. Then it inactivated Maj. Gen. Harry W. O. Kinnard's 11th Air Assault Division (Test), which was also at Fort Benning testing the feasibility of fielding large forces transported and almost totally supported by helicopters. Those elements of the 11th Division essential to an airmobile division were assigned to the new Fort Benning–based unit, while those portions that were no longer consistent with its mission were inactivated. On 1 July the newly configured 1st Cavalry Division, under the command of General Kinnard, became the first airmobile unit in the Army's force structure.[25]

---

[24] Maj. Gen. Joseph A. McChristian, *The Role of Military Intelligence, 1965–1967*, Vietnam Studies (Washington, D.C.: Department of the Army, 1974), pp. 4–6; Phillip B. Davidson, *Secrets of the Vietnam War* (Novato, Calif.: Presidio Press, 1990), p. 6 (quotations).

[25] Memo, H. W. Caldwell, Adj Gen Office, DA, for CG, USARPAC, et al., 22 Jul 65, sub: Reorganization of 1st Cavalry Division (Airmobile), p. 2, Historians files, CMH; Annual Hist Rpt, 1 Jul 65–30 Jun 66, U.S. Continental Army Command (USCONARC), Jun 67, pp. 196–97, copy in CMH. The Army chief of staff, General Johnson, chose the

Concurrent with his decision to activate an airmobile division, McNamara directed the Army to bring the new unit to a combat-ready deployable status as quickly as possible. General Johnson delegated the task to his vice chief of staff, General Creighton W. Abrams, who formed a team to assist him from the Department of the Army, the U.S. Army Combat Developments Command, the Continental Army Command, the Third Army, the 2d Infantry Division, the Infantry Center, the 10th Air Transport Brigade, and the 11th Air Assault Division. The target date for completion of the project was 28 July. At a 17 June meeting Abrams told members of the team that they should keep in mind a future deployment to South Vietnam.[26]

In two days of consultation between 17 and 19 June at Fort Benning, the group cataloged various problems and devised possible solutions. The airmobile division would need an infusion of about 3,200 soldiers, mainly from such thinly populated but critical specialties as helicopter pilots and aviation mechanics, to fill out its 16,000-man roster. Since making up that shortage would become impossible if the Army proceeded with General Kinnard's plan to require all troops in the three maneuver brigades to be airborne qualified, the team rejected the idea but agreed to include three battalions of qualified paratroopers. To find the 2,500 men for those battalions, the division would have to train some of its own personnel to fill the spaces and also rely on fillers from the Airborne School. Complicating matters, many current members of the new division had just finished tours of duty overseas. Although they could volunteer for Vietnam, they could not be ordered to go under the Army's personnel rules.[27]

Problems with personnel were only the beginning. The new division had to submit requisitions for some twenty thousand items of supply necessary for operations. In addition, its CH–47 and UH–1 helicopters needed to have radios and electronic navigational devices installed, and its soldiers had to be equipped with the new lightweight 5.56-mm. M16 rifle in time to train with it before departing for the war zone. The issue of spare parts took on special urgency. Since helicopters required high maintenance, the unit's logisticians were going to have to supply huge numbers of items. Yet the CH–47 Chinook and the UH–1

---

name of the new division. See Intervs, Col Glenn A. Smith with Lt Gen Harry W. O. Kinnard, 31 Mar 77, p. 19, and Lt Col Jacob B. Couch, Jr., with Kinnard, 20 Jan 83, p. 87, Senior Officer Oral History Program, MHI. See also J. D. Coleman, *Pleiku: The Dawn of Helicopter Warfare in Vietnam* (New York: St. Martin's Press, 1988), app. 1.

[26] Memos, Col John C. Honea, Jr., Team Chief, DA, for Acting Asst CofS, Force Development, 21 Jun 65, sub: Trip Report, p. 1 and incl. 2, pp. 1–3, and Gen Creighton W. Abrams, Vice CofS, Army, for Dep CofS, Mil Opns, et al., 17 Jun 65, sub: Organization of the 1st Cavalry Division (Airmobile), p. 1, Historians files, CMH.

[27] Memo, Honea for Acting Asst CofS, Force Development, 21 Jun 65, sub: Trip Report, p. 1 and incl. 3, p. 1; Remarks of Gen Johnson at Army Commanders' Conference, 29 Nov–1 Dec 65, p. 2, copy in Historians files, CMH; Quarterly Cmd Rpt, 1 Jul–30 Sep 65, 1st Cav Div (Ambl), 1 Dec 65, p. 3, Historians files, CMH.

Huey were still relatively new. Parts for them were at times difficult to find in Army inventories, and they would undoubtedly become even more of a problem when the division went overseas into combat.[28]

Preparations for deployment moved quickly following the planning conference, with personnel issues becoming a far larger problem than anyone had imagined. By 1 July the 1st Cavalry Division was short over 6,000 men rather than the 3,200 initially projected. Included were requirements for some 400 officers and 400 warrant officers, many of the latter slots for helicopter pilots. The Army filled the gaps with selective personnel drafts, principally from the 82d and 101st Airborne Divisions, as well as stepped-up instruction in parachute techniques and accelerated pilot training. The quick-step pace of preparations still left some helicopter pilots short of experience in certain aspects of their specialty. When the 1st Cavalry Division departed for Vietnam, 35 of the 350 pilots it had acquired had yet to finish general training, some 300 were untrained in unit flying techniques specific to airmobile warfare, and about 325 needed aerial gunnery instruction.[29]

The logistical situation was more tractable, but only to a degree. Diligent searching by Army agencies located most of the twenty thousand supply items that the division needed. The unit was also able to complete 2,475 of 2,750 work actions, modifying its helicopters and installing radios, navigational aids, and other equipment prior to its departure for Vietnam. Even so, as the date for deployment neared, somewhat less than 50 percent of the spare parts it needed for its aircraft were on hand. The commander of the Continental Army Command, General Paul L. Freeman, worried that the lack might have "a significant impact" on the unit's operational capabilities once the force arrived in Vietnam.[30]

Freeman's concerns included much more than spare parts. Acutely aware of the division's deficiencies in other areas, he questioned its overall readiness for service in Southeast Asia. "As you know," he pointed out to General Johnson, "this is a special type division, unique to the Army, which has demonstrated the potential of bold and imaginative tactical concepts. It would be unfortunate if this division were employed in combat prematurely."[31] He strongly recommended that a special Army briefing team, headed by a general officer, be dispatched to South Vietnam to acquaint General Westmoreland and his staff with the character-

---

[28] Meyerson, "Logistics in the Vietnam Conflict," ch. 4, CMH.

[29] Ltr, Gen Paul L. Freeman, CG, USCONARC, to Gen Harold K. Johnson, 26 Jul 65, Harold K. Johnson Papers, MHI; Headquarters, USCONARC, "The Role of USCONARC in the Army Buildup, FY 1966," p. 112, copy in CMH; Walter G. Hermes, "Department of the Army: The Buildup, 1965–1967," ch. 5, CMH.

[30] Ltr (quoted words), Freeman to Gen Johnson, 26 Jul 65; Rpt, Ben J. Gilleas, Director of Investigations, to Preparedness Investigating Subcommittee, Senate Committee on Armed Services, 12 Jan 66, sub: Highlights of Visit to 1st Cavalry Division (Airmobile) at An Khe, 21 Oct 65, p. 2, Historians files, CMH.

[31] Ltr, Freeman to Gen Johnson, 26 Jul 65.

istics of the division and its special requirements for training and support, also adding Kinnard's recommendation that the division have twenty-eight days for preparation and acclimatization before beginning operations. The chief of staff declined Freeman's suggestions, but he did summon Kinnard to Washington to discuss Freeman's concerns and to underscore the extra responsibilities that the leaders of untried units assumed when they took their men into combat for the first time. The meeting apparently satisfied Johnson that the cavalry division was in capable hands and ready for war.[32]

Over and above Freeman's concerns, other questions lingered. Had the division's rapid formation allowed enough time for its men to bond with their officers and one another? If not, would they come together as a fighting unit or fragment under the stresses of combat? Would it be wise to delay longer for unit cohesion to solidify or to take other steps to speed the process? As General Larsen recalled, "The First Cavalry Division had been marvelously prepared . . . for combat, but they also had a lot of inexperienced troops, troops that had been pulled together to make units, other units that had been pulled in and changed their nomenclatures so that they became First Cav units late in the game before they left the States and still had to be tried really as part of a big team."[33] There were no clear answers to the questions. Only time would tell.

The 1st Cavalry Division moved to South Vietnam in three stages during the period 2 August to 3 October. Under the assistant division commander for support, Brig. Gen. John M. Wright, Jr., a small advance liaison party of 32 officers and enlisted men departed by commercial airline on the second. Wright and his men had three missions: to acquaint the MACV and U.S. Army, Vietnam, staffs with the unique capabilities of the airmobile division, to allow the pilots in the group to familiarize themselves with flying conditions in the highlands and with the tactics employed by aviation units already fighting there, and to develop a construction plan for the division's base of operations. Between the fourteenth and twenty-eighth a larger contingent of 1,030 officers and enlisted men, accompanied by one hundred fifty-two tons of cargo, followed on military air transports. Its mission was to assist General Wright in building a base camp. The men and equipment of the division itself went by sea, the first ship leaving the United States on the eighth and the last on the eighteenth. Shortly afterward, General Kinnard himself flew to Vietnam to ensure that all arrangements were in place and to meet his troops when they finally disembarked at their destination.[34]

---

[32] Gen Harold K. Johnson's Critique of "Department of the Army: The Buildup, 1965–1967," Historians files, CMH; Interv, Couch with Kinnard, 20 Jan 83, p. 93.

[33] Interv, Sandstrum with Larsen, 11 Mar 70, p. 14.

[34] Quarterly Cmd Rpt, 1 Jul–30 Sep 65, 1st Cav Div, pp. 11–14; Intervs, Lt Col David M. Fishback with Lt Gen John M. Wright, Jr., 1 Mar 83, 2:382–400, Senior Officer Oral History Program, MHI; Charles S. Sykes, comp., *Interim Report of Operations: First Cavalry Division, July 1965 to December 1966* (Albuquerque, N.Mex.: 1st Cavalry Division

CH–47 Chinooks of the 1st Cavalry Division arrive at Qui Nhon on the USS Boxer.

Ten cargo ships, six troopships, and four small aircraft carriers—sailing respectively from New Orleans, Louisiana; Charleston, South Carolina, and Savannah, Georgia; and Mobile, Alabama, and Jacksonville, Florida—transported the division's soldiers, aircraft, and equipment to Vietnam. On the Navy transport *Geiger* the officers of the 1st Battalion (Airborne), 8th Cavalry, commanded by Lt. Col. Kenneth D. Mertel, created programs in physical training, counterguerrilla tactics, patrol techniques, jungle navigation skills, the infantry role in airmobile warfare, weapons training, combined arms, and Vietnamese language and history. Such activities did not seem a high priority on other vessels. The trip itself took nearly a month, with the flotilla carrying troops arriving at Qui Nhon between 6 and 22 September. Since the port had no deep-water piers, the ships anchored offshore and discharged across the beach. It was a time-consuming process, but by the twenty-ninth the men and their equipment were all ashore.[35]

While unloading continued, most troops made the final leg of the trip to the encampment at An Khe in the unit's CH–47 helicopters, which ex-

---

Association, n.d.), p. 3; Rpt, 14th Mil Hist Det, 1st Cav Div (Ambl), 9 Jun 67, sub: Seven Month History and Briefing Data (September 1965–March 1966), p. 15, box 16, 74/053, RG 319, NARA.

[35] Interv, Couch with Kinnard, 20 Jan 83, p. 95; Kenneth D. Mertel, *Year of the Horse—Vietnam: 1st Air Cavalry in the Highlands* (New York: Exposition Press, 1968), p. 36.

pended more than eleven hundred hours of flying time. Many of the remaining helicopters flew directly from the carriers' decks, arriving between 15 and 29 September after a brief stop in Qui Nhon to refuel. Helicopter pilot WO1 Robert C. Mason felt vulnerable during the trip. "I conjured up," he later wrote, "grinning VC who sighted along the barrels of their guns as they stood concealed under the green canopy. It suddenly became obvious to me that I was completely exposed to any fire that came from the front." The division's supplies and equipment were moved by convoy on Highway 19 throughout the period 5 September to 3 October.[36]

The location of the cavalry's base was the subject of much debate. General Westmoreland wanted to station the division deep in the highlands, preferably near Pleiku, where it could dominate the region by launching operations in every direction. Both Generals Wheeler and Johnson agreed with him. Admiral Sharp, however, argued emphatically for a base at Qui Nhon. If the division were located at Pleiku and the enemy gained control of Highway 19, Sharp maintained that all ground supply from the coast would cease. With airfields limited in the highlands, it might become exceedingly difficult to provide the six to eight hundred tons of supplies a day needed by the division. Other senior officers also opposed Westmoreland's plan. General Johnson later reported that the commandant of the Marine Corps, General Wallace M. Greene, wanted the cavalry "down on the beach with one foot in the water."[37] The Air Force chief of staff, General John P. McConnell, also considered Pleiku a poor choice. If it were selected and the enemy attacked, he believed that an Air Force effort at resupply would be short-lived because the base would not last.[38]

Generals Westmoreland and DePuy considered the opposition ill-founded. DePuy later observed that "Admiral Sharp had a deep fear of the dangers associated with land warfare." Referring to the catastrophic defeat suffered by the French in 1954, DePuy noted that Sharp "had a Dien Bien Phu syndrome. He didn't want to put the 1st Cavalry Division very far inland. [He believed that] . . . we would have another Dien BienPhu."[39] In the end, Westmoreland compromised by placing the camp near An Khe in western Binh Dinh Province, roughly halfway between

[36] Sykes, comp., *First Cavalry Division*, p. 4; Robert C. Mason, *Chickenhawk* (New York: Viking Press, 1983), p. 42 (quotation); Rpt, 14th Mil Hist Det, 1st Cav Div, 9 Jun 67, sub: Seven Month History and Briefing Data (September 1965–March 1966), p. 15.

[37] MACV Commander's Estimate of the Military Situation in South Vietnam, 26 Mar 65, an. G, Westmoreland History files, CMH; Westmoreland, *A Soldier Reports*, p. 175; Interv, MacDonald and von Luttichau with Gen Johnson, 20 Nov 70, p. 6, Historians files, CMH; U. S. Grant Sharp, *Strategy for Defeat: Vietnam in Retrospect* (San Rafael, Calif.: Presidio Press, 1978), pp. 90–91; Interv, D. Clayton James with Gen Harold K. Johnson, 7 Jul 71, p. 39 (quotation), box 134, Johnson Papers, MHI.

[38] Schlight, *Years of the Offensive*, pp. 61–62.

[39] General William E. DePuy, *Changing an Army: An Oral History of General William E. DePuy, USA Retired*, interv. Romie L. Brownlee and William J. Mullen III ([Carlisle Barracks], Pa., and Washington, D.C.: U.S. Army Military History Institute and U.S.

Qui Nhon and Pleiku. Those concerned about a possible Dien Bien Phu and about difficult supply problems in the highlands would feel more secure with the division closer to the sea, while those who wanted the unit to fight in the highlands would be nearer that goal. Although not able to dominate the high plateau, the division could now operate in both the highlands and on the coast.[40]

To establish the base camp, General Wright first set up an office in Saigon, where he gathered information and sought suggestions from senior officers. He also visited the base camps of the 173d Airborne Brigade and 1st Brigade, 101st Airborne Division, to observe layouts and security arrangements. In developing a plan for An Khe, Wright sought to create a camp that required the least number of men to defend it so that the maximum number could serve in the field. In addition, since the division's four hundred plus helicopters were vulnerable to almost any kind of attack, the provision of physical security for the expensive aircraft was crucial. In the end, Wright's proposal required that the division secure all of its helicopters in a two-by-three-kilometer rectangle. To guard against an attack on the heliport, he would place the division's infantry and artillery battalions close to one another around the rectangle.[41]

General Kinnard, still in the United States, reacted negatively to the plan because it violated the principle that the dispersion of resources offered fewer targets. He ordered Wright to do nothing more until he arrived. A few days later Wright met him "with blackboards and plenty of chalk." Eventually recognizing that Wright's plan had the advantage of reducing the perimeter the troops would have to defend, Kinnard gave Wright the go ahead to proceed.[42]

With the plan approved, the 1,030 officers and men tasked with building the camp began their work. Wright directed that they plant grass on the ground they had cleared for the heliport. He believed that "each blade of grass was going to help in keeping down the dust, thus minimizing the maintenance problems that we would have on the helicopters as well as the wear on the rotor blades." He even ordered those working on the field to avoid scuffing the area with their boots, going so far as to declare that anyone who did would have to work in his bare feet. His exhortations to make the area "look exactly like a fine golf course" gave the heliport its nickname—"the Golf Course." On 21 February 1966 the base itself was formally named Camp Radcliff in honor of one of the division's first fatalities in Vietnam, Maj. Donald G. Radcliff.[43]

Army Center of Military History, 1988), pp. 134–35 (quotations); Westmoreland, *A Soldier Reports*, p. 144.

[40] Cosmas, "MACV, the Joint Command," ch. 5; Interv, Holmes with Larsen, 26 Oct 76, sec. 5, p. 5.

[41] Interv, Fishback with Wright, 1 Mar 83, 2:384–88.

[42] Ibid., 2:389.

[43] Ibid., 2:391 (quoted words); Rpt, 14th Mil Hist Det, 1st Cav Div, 9 Jun 67, sub: Seven Month History and Briefing Data (September 1965–March 1966), p. 26.

1st Cavalry Division troops clear the ground at An Khe.

When the 1st Cavalry Division became operational in Vietnam on 1 October 1965, it had 15,995 men—105 more than authorized. Overstrength by 98 officers and 245 enlisted men, it still lacked 238 warrant officers, mostly helicopter pilots. Despite its having elements specific to an airmobile unit, the division was organized along the lines of a standard Army division in the mid-1960s, with a headquarters, three brigades, and organic and attached supporting units. Its brigades—designated the 1st, 2d, and 3d—were task organized, had no fixed number of maneuver elements, and could contain from two to five battalions. Each had a headquarters element to provide command and control for its attached units. In contrast to the regiments and regimental combat teams of World War II and the Korean War, the formation had more flexibility to meet the requirements of a particular operation, with divisional and nondivisional elements arriving and departing as the need arose.[44]

For administrative purposes, a brigade was assumed to have three battalions. As a result, when the Army approved Kinnard's suggestion that the 1st Cavalry Division include an airborne brigade, it tacitly agreed that the division would contain three maneuver battalions of airborne-qualified soldiers. Kinnard assigned those units—the 1st and 2d Battalions (Airborne), 8th Cavalry, and the 1st Battalion (Airborne), 12th Cav-

---

[44] Operational Report–Lessons Learned (ORLL), 1 Oct–31 Dec 65, 1st Cav Div (Ambl), 10 Jan 66, p. 4, Historians files, CMH; Shelby L. Stanton, *Vietnam Order of Battle* (New York: Galahad Books, 1986), p. 7.

alry—to his 1st Brigade. The division's other five battalions were par-
celed to its two remaining brigades. The 2d Brigade took command of
the 1st and 2d Battalions (Airmobile), 5th Cavalry, and the 2d Battalion
(Airmobile), 12th Cavalry. The 3d Brigade had control of the 1st and 2d
Battalions (Airmobile), 7th Cavalry, with its third element, the 5th Battalion (Airmobile), 7th Cavalry, arriving in August 1966. On the surface,
the practice of attaching specific battalions to specific brigades seemed
to undercut the notion of the brigade as a flexible tactical headquarters,
but that was not the case. A strict line was drawn within the division
between the administrative and the tactical so that individual battalions could serve in the field with the brigade that needed them most.
The majority of the division's support units—such as the military police company, the engineer battalion, and the signal battalion—differed
little from the more conventional configurations.

The division's maneuver battalions and the reconnaissance squadron were smaller than their counterparts in a standard infantry division
because of the need to stay as lean and light as possible. Each battalion,
trained in airmobile tactics and techniques, had an authorized strength
of 767 officers and men, significantly fewer than the 849 in a standard
infantry battalion, and consisted of three rifle companies, a headquarters company, and a combat-support company. The aerial reconnaissance
element, the 1st Squadron, 9th Cavalry, had eighty-eight helicopters and
an authorized strength of 770—compared to an infantry division's
ground reconnaissance cavalry squadron with its various armored vehicles, twenty-six helicopters, and 905 men. Consisting of three airmobile cavalry troops and one ground-based troop, the squadron provided
reconnaissance and security for the division and its subordinate combat
elements, along with limited air and ground antitank defenses. It could
also patrol roads and keep ground supply lines open.

The nature of its artillery and aviation components further distinguished the 1st Cavalry Division from standard infantry divisions. Like
most divisions, the unit had three direct-support 105-mm. howitzer battalions—the 2d Battalion, 19th Artillery; the 1st Battalion, 21st Artillery;
and the 1st Battalion, 77th Artillery. But general support was provided by
an aerial rocket artillery unit—the 2d Battalion, 20th Artillery. It had thirty-
nine UH–1B helicopters, each equipped with two 24-tube 2.75-inch rocket
launchers (one on each side) and machine guns, that extended the range
of the division's firepower. Another component was the 11th Aviation
Group, equipped with two hundred twenty-one helicopters—nearly six
times that found in the aviation battalion of a typical infantry division—
and six fixed-wing OV–1 Mohawks for electronic surveillance. The 11th
Group's two assault helicopter units, the 227th and 229th Aviation Battalions, outfitted mainly with UH–1s, transported the division's infantry for
airmobile operations. Its one assault support helicopter unit, the 228th
Aviation Battalion, with CH–47s, moved troops and artillery and maintained supply. Rounding out the division's resources were two attached

units: the 478th Aviation Company, equipped with four CH–54 Tarhes, or Flying Cranes, to provide heavy cargo helilift; and the 17th Aviation Company, whose eighteen Caribous flew longer-range airlift missions.[45]

When added up, the 1st Cavalry Division's special capabilities gave the unit broad flexibility. As one 1965 analysis noted, the division could conduct operations in all types of terrain, respond immediately and maneuver rapidly over large areas, reconnoiter and screen wide fronts, conduct raids in the enemy's rear, and transport combat forces for immediate use in other areas by vertical entry into and from the battlefield. Additionally, "in an unsophisticated or semi-sophisticated environment," the division could project its influence rapidly by using its increased mobility and firepower to gain and maintain control over land areas.[46]

1st Infantry Division

A different set of issues confronted the other large combat unit tagged for deployment. When the 1st Infantry Division received orders to deploy to Vietnam on or before 1 September, its commander, General Seaman, had just finished stripping his 1st and 3d Brigades in order to send the 2d Brigade to Vietnam in the best possible condition. Thus, officers, noncommissioned officers, and certain specialists were in short supply, whereas nondeployable soldiers were plentiful. The division also needed to reorganize to comply with instructions from General Johnson and to meet other pressing needs.[47]

As in the 1st Cavalry Division, the problems with personnel were the most difficult. The extent of the 1st Infantry Division's shortage in July was hard to establish but appears to have been approximately 250 officers and a little over 3,000 enlisted men. Helicopter pilots, in particular, were scarce, for many had been pulled for service with forces already in Vietnam. To remedy the situation, Seaman drew some replacements from the Fifth Army and others from 1st Division units that were not then scheduled for deployment. Processing those men complicated matters, but by 1 September the division had located enough troops and pilots—2,900 enlisted men and 170 officers—to reach 97 percent of its deployable strength.[48]

---

[45] Information in this and above two paragraphs based on Rpt, 14th Mil Hist Det, 1st Cav Div, 9 Jun 67, sub: Seven Month History and Briefing Data (September 1965–March 1966), p. 2.

[46] *Airmobile Division Supplement to Infantry Reference Data* (Fort Benning, Ga.: U.S. Army Infantry School, 1965), p. 2.

[47] Interv, Albright with Seaman, 10 Sep 70, pp. 8–11.

[48] Lt. Gen. Jonathan O. Seaman, "Elements of Command" (Lecture given at Army War College Seminar, Carlisle Barracks, Pa., February 4, 1970), pt. 1, p. 14, Incl to Interv, Col Clyde H. Patterson, Jr., with Lt Gen Jonathan O. Seaman, 1971–72, Senior Officer Oral History Program, MHI; Quarterly Cmd Rpt, 1 Oct–31 Dec 65, 1st Inf Div, pp. 1–3.

Prior to their September deployment, 1st Division troops received training that was, to a degree, Vietnam specific. Beginning on 25 July, some 140 soldiers spent a week on the 25th Infantry Division's special jungle warfare training course in Hawaii. Upon rejoining the division, they shared the lessons they had learned with the other members of their units. Meanwhile, everyone participated in a mandatory four-week course, called the Intensified Combat Training Program, that began on 2 August. The course emphasized day, night, and long-range patrolling, map reading, perimeter defense, radio/telephone procedures, counterguerrilla tactics, individual and crew-served weapons, codes of conduct, and physical training. Beyond its obvious benefits, the training facilitated the quick integration of new soldiers into the division.[49]

As of 1 July the division itself had—exclusive of the three infantry battalions already in Vietnam—two infantry, two mechanized, and two tank battalions. General Johnson was adamant about not deploying the armor battalions, explaining that during the Korean War the enemy had demonstrated an ability "to employ relatively primitive but extremely effective box mines" against American tanks.[50] If the United States introduced tanks into Vietnam, he felt certain that this would happen again. He also argued that the division's planned sector of operations north of Saigon contained few areas that were accessible to tanks and that the South Vietnamese armed forces did not appear to be using the tanks already available. General Seaman disagreed, stressing his need for at least one tank battalion in the division, but Johnson's views carried the day. Westmoreland backed his superior but went further, stating that he wanted only dismounted infantry battalions in the 1st Division.[51]

Once that decision had been made, the Army moved to replace the 1st Division's tank battalions and to reorganize its mechanized battalions. Two elements from the 5th Infantry Division (Mechanized) at Fort Devens, Massachusetts, the 1st and 2d Battalions, 2d Infantry, replaced the two tank battalions, with both units remaining at Fort Devens until they deployed. To complete the transition to an all-infantry unit, the 1st Division's two mechanized battalions were reorganized as standard infantry units, becoming the 1st Battalion, 26th Infantry, and the 1st Battalion, 28th Infantry. Its 1st Battalion, 16th Infantry, and the 2d Battalion, 28th Infantry, remained unchanged.[52]

The appearance of a study on force structure in South Vietnam further complicated the move, if only momentarily. The deputy assistant chief of staff for force development, Brig. Gen. Arthur L. West, had chaired a group assembled for the purpose of defining the organiza-

---

[49] Quarterly Cmd Rpt, 1 Oct–31 Dec 65, 1st Inf Div, pp. 5–10.

[50] Msg, Gen Johnson WDC 05078 to Westmoreland, 3 Jul 65, Westmoreland Message files, CMH.

[51] Interv, Albright with Seaman, 10 Sep 70, pp. 20–21; Msgs, Westmoreland MAC 3407 and 3444 to Gen Johnson, 5 and 7 Jul 65, Westmoreland Message files, CMH.

[52] Quarterly Cmd Rpt, 1 Oct–31 Dec 65, 1st Inf Div, pp. 1–3.

tions and equipment best suited for the requirements of the war. General West's group recommended that the Army reconfigure the 1st Division as a light infantry division, giving General Seaman three possible options: reorganizing under the light infantry concept, if that could be done without interfering with preparations for deployment; evaluating the proposed equipment deletions to eliminate those items, mainly vehicles, that would not affect the deployment; or taking the unit to South Vietnam as it was and reorganize there. These options seemed too radical to General Johnson. "Changing horses completely at this late stage," he said, "could cause serious turbulence within the division that I am not prepared to cause right now." He wanted the division to arrive in Vietnam "with all of its heart and spirit just as it is." He also stated that the unit could arrange for substitutions later and eliminate as many of the unnecessary vehicles as possible prior to departure.[53] Following the chief of staff's lead, Seaman chose the second option.

Although wanting his division to deploy with the latest equipment, Seaman encountered difficulties and found himself embroiled in disputes over certain items. His 1st Division troops reached Vietnam equipped with the M14 rifle, instead of the newer M16 that had been issued to the 1st Cavalry Division and the 173d Airborne Brigade. Seaman had also planned for the division's 1st Squadron, 4th Cavalry, to deploy with its M114 armored reconnaissance vehicles; however, after learning that they lacked adequate cross-country mobility and had trouble entering and leaving waterways, he sought permission to replace the M114 with the M113 armored personnel carrier, which had better overall reliability and mobility. After considerable give-and-take, senior Army officials backed Seaman, and the division deployed with M113s. Finally, a controversy also arose over whether to include the 8-inch self-propelled howitzer battery with the division's general-support 8th Battalion, 6th Artillery. Seaman wanted the 8-inch howitzer because of its 2,200-meter range advantage over the battalion's other weapon, the 155-mm. towed howitzer, "and its greater lethality." Westmoreland wanted to leave the battery behind because it would limit mobility, but General Johnson supported Seaman, and the battery deployed with the battalion.[54]

Deployment occurred in stages, commencing in August and continuing into the next two months. A small liaison party under the assistant division commander for support, Brig. Gen. Charles M. Mount, Jr., flew to Vietnam in early August to find a site for the division headquarters

---

[53] Ibid., p. 3; Msg (quotations), Gen Johnson WDC 06510 to Westmoreland, 31 Jul 65, Westmoreland Message files, CMH.

[54] General Donn A. Starry, *Mounted Combat in Vietnam*, Vietnam Studies (Washington, D.C.: Department of the Army, 1978), p. 38; Quarterly Cmd Rpt, 1 Oct–31 Dec 65, 1st Inf Div, pp. 6–7; Msgs, Gen Johnson WDC 06810 to Westmoreland, 10 Aug 65 (quoted words), and Westmoreland MAC 4099 to Gen Johnson, 12 Aug 65, Westmoreland Message files, CMH.

1st Division equipment ready for departure from Fort Riley

and to identify any possible problems. Toward the end of the month a planning group of 9 officers and 1 enlisted man followed to lay the groundwork for the selection and procurement of the five base camp areas around Saigon. Then at the end of September 320 officers and enlisted men joined the others, to confirm that the proposed locations were indeed suitable as base areas and to coordinate the support necessary to move divisional units into the country.[55]

Meanwhile, the actual order to deploy had arrived on 2 September, and the bulk of the division completed the final preparations for deployment. Thereafter, the troops, equipment, and supplies moved by air and rail to various ports, mostly on the West Coast. During the period 16 September to 9 October the men and most of the materiel departed from the Oakland Army Terminal in twelve ships, with eight others leaving from Long Beach and Alameda, California; Tacoma, Washington; and Boston, Massachusetts. The vessels reached Vietnam between 1 and 30 October. The men disembarked at Vung Tau; supplies and equipment came through Vung Tau and the port of Saigon.[56] When the first troops arrived, Generals Westmoreland, Seaman, and Norton were at Vung Tau to greet them. Echoing the unit's motto, "No Mission Too Difficult, No Sacrifice Too Great—Duty First," Seaman pledged that "whether this fight will be long

[55] Interv, Albright with Seaman, 10 Sep 70, p. 17; Quarterly Cmd Rpt, 1 Oct–31 Dec 65, 1st Inf Div, p. 7; Seaman, "Elements of Command," pt. 1, p. 10, Incl to Interv, Patterson with Seaman, 1971–72.

[56] Quarterly Cmd Rpt, 1 Oct–31 Dec 65, 1st Inf Div, pp. 9, 12. See also [Annual Hist Rpt, 1965], 1st Bn, 26th Inf, 29 Mar 66; Annual Supp to Unit History, [1965], 1st Bn, 2d Inf, 25 Mar 66; Annual Hist Supp, [1965], 2d Bn, 33d Arty, 17 Mar 66. All in box 3, 81/469, RG 338, NARA.

Generals Seaman, Norton, and Westmoreland await the arrival of the 1st Division at Vung Tau.

or short, we of the 'Fighting First' will carry out every mission to a successful completion whatever the cost or sacrifice."[57]

Code-named Operation BIG RED after the unit's nickname, the Big Red One, the process of unloading the division's troops and supplies and transporting them to the field started on 5 October and lasted until 2 November. Coordinated and supervised by the U.S. Army, Vietnam, the operation involved the 1st Logistical Command, the 2d Signal Group, the 12th Aviation Group, the 716th Military Police Battalion, and the 173d Airborne Brigade. The troops moved to the Vung Tau airfield and then took C–130s to Bien Hoa, from where they went by truck to a staging area about halfway between Saigon and Bien Hoa near Saigon University and thence to their base camps. In the meantime, the small amount of cargo that had accompanied the troopships was loaded onto an LST (landing ship, tank) for transshipment to Saigon. From there, the cargo moved by truck to the staging area. The equipment on the cargo ships followed much the same route.[58]

At the direction of MACV, the 173d Airborne Brigade assumed responsibility for providing security for the 1st Division so that it could

[57] Rpt, 1st Inf Div, n.d., sub: Historical Study on the Deployment of the 1st Infantry Division to Vietnam, incl. 5, p. 1, box 8, 67A/5293, RG 319, NARA.
[58] Ibid., pp. 15, 22.

concentrate on the move and on the establishment of its base camps. The 173d already had conducted a two-week operation in the vicinity of Lai Khe to thwart any disruptions insurgent forces might have planned for that area. Next, with the assistance of the 2d Brigade, 1st Infantry Division, which by then had been in country for nearly three months, it secured the divisional staging area and began sweeping the division's various base camp locations and the routes to them. By the end of October the 173d had seen the 3d Brigade, 1st Infantry Division, safely to its base area near Lai Khe, and the 2d Brigade had escorted its sister unit, the 1st Brigade, 1st Infantry Division, safely to a site near Phuoc Vinh. A few days later the 173d secured an area near Di An, which would become the base camp for the division's headquarters and support elements. Toward the end of the month the 2d Brigade guarded the movement of division artillery and aviation elements to a base area near Phu Loi. These base camps—none more than forty-five kilometers from another—were positioned both to guard the approaches to Saigon from the northwest, north, and northeast, and, from Lai Khe and Phuoc Vinh, to block enemy movement between War Zones C and D. In all, Operation BIG RED had succeeded in moving over 9,600 troops and their equipment and supplies to their destinations in III Corps without loss of life or serious injury to anyone. Upon completion of the operation, the 2d Brigade returned to the command of its parent unit, and Seaman's 1st Infantry Division was in place, ready to go.[59]

The Coming Campaign

As the 1st Cavalry and 1st Infantry Divisions moved into position in II and III Corps, General Westmoreland began developing his plan for the coming campaign. McNamara gave impetus to the process in July, when during a fact-finding trip to Saigon he asked how the commander proposed to use both the forty-four battalions he had requested during June and any other forces that might be approved out to January 1966 and beyond. In response, over the next few months, Westmoreland outlined a three-phase campaign, whose earliest stage was already in effect. At the heart of the concept was the notion that U.S. forces would assume an active role, serving as the vanguard of the allied expansion into enemy-controlled or -contested territory.[60]

In Phase I, which had begun with the arrival of the marines and the Army combat units, American and other allied forces were to take emergency action to halt the enemy's gains on the battlefield and to buy time

---

[59] Ibid., incl. 11, pp. 1–4; Seaman, "Elements of Command," pt. 1, p. 10, Incl to Interv, Patterson with Seaman, 1971–72; Interv, Albright with Seaman, 10 Sep 70, p. 17.

[60] MACV History, 1965, p. 137; *Pentagon Papers* (Gravel), 3:475; Sharp and Westmoreland, *Report*, p. 100.

for themselves and the South Vietnamese. Containing the North Vietnamese invasion and the Viet Cong insurgency while building up operational and logistical bases for sustained operations, they would secure the ports, airfields, base camps, and communications hubs; defend important political and population centers; conduct offensive operations against major enemy base areas in order to divert and destroy main force units; and provide rapid-reaction forces to prevent the loss of formerly secure areas under threat. Westmoreland believed that his troops would achieve the objective of this phase by the end of 1965.[61]

The transition from Phase I to Phase II would be gradual, a shift of emphasis rather than a radical change of direction. Coming in early 1966, it would nonetheless be different in spirit and aim from Phase I. Retaining the tactical initiative gained during the earlier period, U.S. forces would "shift, in a strategic sense, into a sustained offensive" and start winning the war.[62] Gaining the initiative and taking the war to North Vietnamese and Viet Cong strongholds, American and allied forces would penetrate the enemy's hitherto inviolate bases and sanctuaries in the South, forcing Communist units to fight or withdraw.[63] Phase II would end, as the MACV commander wrote later, when "the enemy had been worn down, thrown on the defensive, and driven well back from the major populated areas."[64]

A successful Phase II would obviate proceeding with Phase III. Should a third stage become necessary, however, it would involve the destruction of whatever North Vietnamese and Viet Cong forces and base areas remained and would require additional American and third-country troops. Virtually indistinguishable from its predecessor, Phase III, in effect, would be an effort to do more of the same deeper in the base areas. Westmoreland estimated that Phase III would need from twelve to eighteen months to complete; but, since the length of Phase II remained indeterminate, his calculation contributed little toward projecting how long success would take. The plan notwithstanding, the only conclusion he would offer thus far was that the war in Vietnam would be long.[65]

---

[61] MACV Directive 525–4, 17 Sep 65, sub: Tactics and Techniques for Employment of US Forces in the Republic of Vietnam, p. 2, Westmoreland History files, CMH. See also USMACV Concept of Operations in the Republic of Vietnam, 1 Sep 65, p. 2, Historians files, CMH; MACV History, 1965, p. 142.

[62] Commander in Chief, Pacific, "Command History, 1965," 2 vols. (Honolulu, May 1966), 2:296, CMH.

[63] William C. Westmoreland, "A Military War of Attrition," in *The Lessons of Vietnam*, eds. W. Scott Thompson and Donaldson D. Frizzell (New York: Crane, Russak and Co., 1977), p. 62.

[64] Sharp and Westmoreland, "Report," p. 137.

[65] USMACV Concept of Operations, 1 Sep 65, p. 2.

PART TWO

First Battles

4

Pressing Out From Saigon

O f all the regions in the theater of operations vying for General Westmoreland's attention, the one containing Saigon was the most important. The political heart of the nation and the rapidly expanding hub of the allied war effort, the area was the site of South Vietnam's largest and most modern seaport, two of its main air bases, a variety of critical supply depots, and virtually all of the high-level headquarters directing the war against the insurgents and regulars. It was with reason, therefore, that General Seaman, having settled his 1st Infantry Division into laagers north of the city, began an aggressive push to weaken the Communists' hold around the capital by bleeding their forces dry.

Seaman was able to take the battle to the Viet Cong because of the infusion of resources in the latter months of 1965. The number of infantry battalions alone had doubled with the arrival of the rest of the 1st Division. Seaman now had a total of twelve to fight with, plus the division's 1st Squadron, 4th Cavalry, to provide an armored punch. The increase in artillery was even more dramatic. At the end of September only two and one-third battalions were in III Corps supporting the two brigades stationed at Bien Hoa. At the end of November the number had grown to eight battalions, two of them general-support units of heavy guns organized in the 23d Artillery Group based at Phu Loi. Helicopter resources also had risen sharply, as the nondivisional 12th Aviation Group, activated in August at Tan Son Nhut, received two more battalions in the fall.[1]

Seaman's formations would operate in a fan-shaped area opening northward from Saigon over a distance of some fifty-five kilometers. The land surface favored combat and varied from grasslands to rolling forested hills, few over seventy meters high. The road network thinned out rapidly to the north, but Highway 13—III Corps' main north–south

[1] Remarks of Maj Gen Robert H. Schellman, Asst CofS, G–3 [Opns], USARPAC, at USARPAC Commanders' Conference, 1–3 March 1966, p. 19, and Quarterly Cmd Rpt, 1 Oct–31 Dec 65, 1st Inf Div, n.d., p. 12, Historians files, CMH; *Infantry Reference Data* (Fort Benning, Ga.: Brigade and Battalion Operations Department, U.S. Army Infantry School, 1965), p. 22; and Stanton, *Vietnam Order of Battle*, pp. 49–50, 110, 112–13, 115, 125.

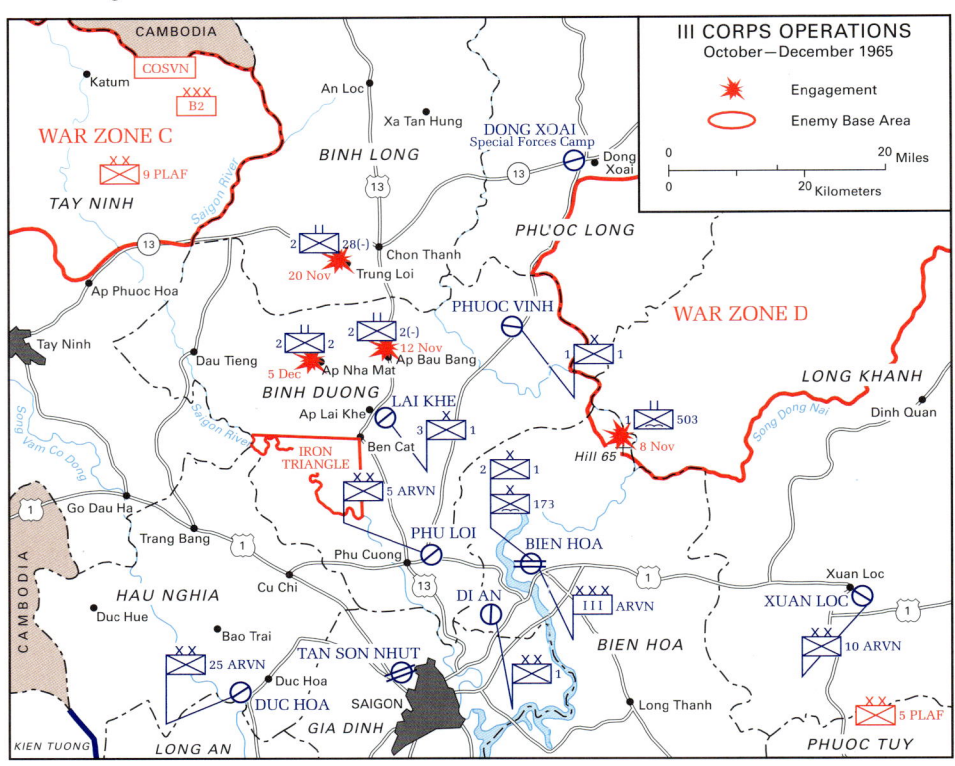

MAP 4

artery—ran through and beyond the security zone that Seaman hoped to establish. Because it also coursed between the two well-entrenched enemy strongholds to the north, War Zones C and D, securing it was one of Seaman's top priorities (*Map 4*).[2]

To assist the Americans, the South Vietnamese Joint General Staff had stationed a variety of forces, both regular and paramilitary, in the III Corps area. The 5th Infantry Division was in Binh Duong Province, north of Saigon; the 25th Infantry Division was in Hau Nghia Province, to the west; and the newly formed 10th Infantry Division was in Long Khanh Province, to the east. The III Corps commander, Lt. Gen. Nguyen Bao Tri, also controlled a number of separate units—including various ranger, armored cavalry, airborne, and marine units—and the territorial Regional and Popular Forces that were scattered throughout the region to provide local defense. Although more experienced than most U.S. formations in the capital sector, the South Vietnamese units displayed low morale since suf-

---

[2] Intel Estimate on III CTZ, Asst CofS, J–2 [Intel], MACV, 23 May 66, pp. 1–3, box 13, 69A/702, RG 334, NARA; Intel Estimate no. 2, II FFV, 30 Nov 66, pp. 1–3, box 2, 69A/729, RG 338, NARA.

fering spectacular setbacks earlier in the year.[3]

As his forces gained experience, General Seaman could envision extending allied influence beyond Phuoc Vinh, his northernmost laager, to the Cambodian border, one hundred thirty kilometers from Saigon. Along the way his battalions and brigades would link up with the seventeen Special Forces camps in III Corps, seven of which were near the border.[4] General Westmoreland endorsed the new possibilities open to the 1st Division and 173d Airborne Brigade by giving Seaman free rein to operate as he wished. Westmoreland stipulated only that Seaman keep uppermost in mind the need to defend Saigon.

Waiting for Seaman's and Tri's forces were just under sixteen

General Tra

thousand regulars of the *B2 Front*. General Nguyen Chi Thanh commanded both the *B2 Front* and *COSVN*, but Thanh's deputy, Maj. Gen. Tran Van Tra, ran day-to-day military operations in III Corps.[5] Tra's regulars manned five regiments, organized into two divisions. The *9th PLAF Division*, composed of the *271st*, *272d*, and *273d PLAF Regiments*, was activated on North Vietnam's national day, 2 September 1965, and generally operated in Binh Duong, Binh Long, and Tay Ninh Provinces. The *5th PLAF Division*, constituted in November, consisted of the *274th* and *275th PLAF Regiments*, and worked mostly in Bien Hoa, Long Khanh, and Phuoc Tuy Provinces, serving as the eastern arm of the *B2 Front*'s long-term campaign against Saigon. Additional regulars, although in unknown strength, manned the *165th PLAF Regiment* operating close to Saigon, several separate main force battalions, and the five artillery and one mortar battalions of the *U80 PLAF Artillery Regiment*. In their movements and operations, Tra's regulars could count on the support of more

[3] "Command Histories and Historical Sketches of RVNAF Divisions," January 1974 [1973], pp. 22–23, 26–27, 33–34, Incl to Airgram 23, State EO 11652 to Saigon, 6 Feb 73, Historians files, CMH.

[4] Operational Summary (Op Sum), 1–30 Nov 65, 5th SF Gp (Abn), 1st SF, 15 Dec 65, pp. 26–27, Historians files, CMH.

[5] Quarterly Cmd Rpt, 1 Oct–31 Dec 65, 1st Inf Div, pp. 13–14; Intel Sum on Lao Dong Central Committee Membership of *COSVN*, n.d., item 208, p. 3, Captured Documents and Interrogation Rpts, State Dept Collection, copy in Historians files, CMH.

than fourteen thousand local force troops and guerrillas.[6] Whatever Seaman's plans, he would be dogged by an experienced enemy determined to retain freedom of movement in the III Corps area.

Hill 65

In October, with some of his combat and support units still settling into their base camps, General Seaman went looking for the Viet Cong. Over the next three months the 173d Airborne Brigade, working east and northeast of Saigon, conducted fourteen company-size or larger operations and nearly two hundred smaller ones, with one turning into a major fight. The 1st Infantry Division conducted fifty-nine battalion-size or larger operations, mostly north of the capital city, of which at least forty-four resulted in contacts with the enemy, two of them significant. Nearly three thousand smaller operations took place, with over eight hundred producing some result.[7]

The 173d's big encounter with the Viet Cong happened during Operation HUMP. On 5 November intelligence received at the brigade indicated that a regimental headquarters, mistakenly reported as belonging to the *272d* instead of the *271st*, its three battalions, and the *274th Regiment*'s *D800 Battalion* were massed near the confluence of the Dong Nai and Song Be rivers in War Zone D. About twenty-two kilometers northeast of Bien Hoa Air Base, the area had been entered by the Americans several times before. The information provided an almost textbook opportunity to bring American power to bear. Wasting no time, the brigade commander, General Williamson, organized a force of three battalions: the 1st Battalion, 503d Infantry, commanded by Lt. Col. John E. Tyler; the 1st Battalion, Royal Australian Regiment, led by Lt. Col. I. R. W. Brumfield; and the 3d Battalion, 319th Artillery, under Lt. Col. Lee E. Surut. The brigade's third maneuver element—the 2d Battalion, 503d Infantry, commanded by Lt. Col. George E. Dexter—remained in reserve at Bien Hoa. The plan required the artillery to establish a firebase near the area of operation. Once the small fortification was in place, Williamson's infantry would helicopter into the countryside to see what it could find. The only requirement, long standard in Vietnam, was that the maneuver elements remain within range of the firebase's guns.[8]

---

[6] Rpt, U.S. Army, Vietnam (USARV), 5 Feb 70, sub: History of the 273 VC Regiment, July 1964–December 1969, p. 6; Periodic Intel Rpt no. 45, 5–11 Nov 67, II FFV, 12 Nov 67, an. F, p. 1; Intel Estimate no. 3, II FFV, 31 Jan 67, pp. 15–16. All in Historians files, CMH. See also *Lich Su Quan Doi Nhan Dan Viet Nam* [*History of the People's Army of Vietnam*], 2 vols. (Hanoi: Nha Xuat Ban Quan Doi Nhan Dan [People's Army Publishing House], 1974–90), 2(bk.I,ch.3):6, copy in CMH (hereafter cited as *People's Army of Vietnam*), and Quarterly Cmd Rpt, 1 Oct–31 Dec 65, 1st Inf Div, p. 14.

[7] Monthly Eval Rpts, MACV, Oct 65, pp. A16–A17, Nov 65, pp. A13–A14, and Dec 65, pp. A17–A18, MHI.

[8] AAR, Opn HUMP, 173d Abn Bde (Sep), 19 Dec 65, pp. 1–2, Historians files, CMH.

Early on the morning of 5 November the artillery battalion, accompanied by Troop E, 17th Cavalry, and Company D, 16th Armor, went into Position ACE, east of the Dong Nai and about eight kilometers southwest of its junction with the Song Be. Brumfield's Australians then moved by helicopter to Landing Zone JACK—also east of the Dong Nai but closer to the Song Be by about five kilometers. Following an artillery preparation and tactical air strikes, the Australian battalion was on the ground by midmorning. Shortly afterward, helicopters delivered a battery of four 105-mm. lightweight Italian howitzers belonging to the 105 Field Battery, Royal Australian Artillery. Colonel Tyler's battalion followed in the afternoon at Landing Zone KING, about one and a half kilometers southwest of the Dong Nai–Song Be junction.

The two infantry battalions devoted the rest of the day to settling in and clearing fields of fire. The soldiers of the 173d Airborne Brigade were all armed with the M16 rifle, a good match for the enemy's highly efficient AK47. The American soldiers had trained with the M16 before coming to Vietnam and were well versed in its maintenance, while the Australians had received the weapon only in September. The Australians set up very close to their landing zone, which was located near a paddy field that stretched east and south toward small hill masses ranging up to twenty-five meters in height. The hills had many open areas but also contained jungle in some places. There the trees could reach up to forty meters in height and the undergrowth was tangled thick with vines and underbrush. Observation out from the laager for about fifty meters was good, and cover and concealment were excellent, but fields of fire on the approach favored the enemy. Tyler's battalion was in similar terrain north and west of the Australians.[9]

Units from the two battalions began working outward to the south and east of their bases on 6 and 7 November, employing company- and platoon-size patrols. Except for two fleeting exchanges in which the Australians killed 3 Viet Cong, neither force found the enemy. Both did, however, uncover empty camps complete with supplies and equipment, bunker and tunnel complexes, and a number of booby-trapped huts. They destroyed everything they could.

On 7 November Colonel Tyler's 1st of the 503d Infantry continued probing west of the Dong Nai, a few kilometers north of the original landing zone. Late that afternoon camp was established near the bottom of Hill 65, an important objective to Tyler because the hill provided excellent observation and because intelligence had pinpointed a Viet Cong unit about two kilometers to its west. The information on the enemy's position seemed promising, for the message in which it was identified had included the words *Sour Apples*. During briefings prior to the operation Tyler and his operations officer had been instructed to

[9] Ibid., p. 3.

keep a special watch for the phrase and to make certain that the area it signified was searched.[10]

Just before dark on the seventh Tyler sent patrols to check the area in question. What happened next remains unclear. The commander of Tyler's Company A, Capt. Walter B. Daniel, recalled that when the patrols returned they had nothing to report. The Protestant chaplain accompanying the battalion, Capt. James M. Hutchens, subsequently wrote that one of the patrols found fresh footprints less than one kilometer from the unit's camp and also heard the "occasional muffled cackling of chickens," which enemy soldiers carried for food. Whatever the troops found, the enemy's historians would confirm later that the *271st's 3d Battalion* was in the area and that it received orders on the morning of the eighth to attack Tyler and his men. The unit commander hoped to ambush the Americans after they emerged from their encampment to sweep around the base of the hill.[11]

As the Viet Cong expected, Company C, under Capt. Henry B. Tucker, and Company B, under Capt. Lowell D. Bittrich, began moving west on the morning of 8 November, while Captain Daniel's Company A remained at the battalion patrol base. Tucker took the lead, his men moving in three files about thirty meters apart. Bittrich's unit followed to the right. As Tucker's men moved through an open area into the jungle, they found a recently vacated hamlet. Making their way through the area with care because of possible mines and booby traps, they continued on west. Suddenly, around 0800, one of the platoons took fire from a camouflaged enemy force well entrenched some fifteen to thirty meters away. Claymore mines exploded, and sheets of fire from carefully positioned .30- and .50-caliber machine guns engulfed the troopers. "The whole earth," Chaplain Hutchens later exclaimed, "seemed to erupt furiously before our eyes." Despite casualties and some initial confusion, the Americans responded well. When the enemy adopted hugging tactics, fighting at such close quarters that artillery and air strikes could not be called, the troopers unleashed heavy fire, holding for the moment.[12]

As the fight developed, concern arose at brigade headquarters. Absent that morning in Saigon to brief U.S. officials on a fact-finding visit, General Williamson returned to his headquarters to find one of his battalions in serious trouble. Believing he should be on the spot, he flew over the battle site in his helicopter but could find no place to land. On returning to Bien Hoa, he started to make arrangements to parachute into the action and then reconsidered upon realizing that he could do

---

[10] Ibid., pp. 2–5; Al J. Conetto, "The Hump: A Soldier's Search for Peace" (M.A. thesis, San Jose State University, 1993), p. 57; Ltr, Col Walter B. Daniel to Al J. Conetto, 19 Mar 93, copy in Historians files, CMH.

[11] James M. Hutchens, *Beyond Combat* (Chicago: Moody Press, 1968), p. 100 (quoted words); Breen, *First To Fight*, p. 114; *9th Division*, p. 55, copy in CMH.

[12] Hutchens, *Beyond Combat*, p. 100 (quotation); Critique, Opn Hump, 173d Abn Bde (Sep), 19 Nov 65, p. 9, Historians files, CMH; AAR, Opn Hump, 173d Abn Bde, p. 5.

little that the commander on the spot could not do and that such a move would have been, as he later stated, "completely inappropriate."[13] Furthermore, if he landed outside the American perimeter or in a tree or both, troops might have taken casualties getting him to safety.

The Viet Cong attempted three times during the day to encircle Colonel Tyler's men. First, they tried to envelop Company C from the right, causing Tyler to commit Captain Bittrich's company to secure that flank. In the fighting that followed, Bittrich's men moved into the breach from the northeast to break the envelopment. Later in the morning, following a second unsuccessful effort, the enemy attempted a wide envelopment of both Companies B and C, by then clustered in a single position. Tyler thwarted the move by committing his reserve force, Captain Daniel's Company A. But he instructed Daniel to avoid becoming decisively engaged because the 173d lacked enough helicopters to bring up reinforcements quickly. Daniel's company, in other words, was Tyler's only backup.

So completely focused on overrunning Tucker and Bittrich, the Viet Cong apparently overlooked Company A's advance through the thick underbrush. Captain Daniel and his men, coming upon them as they rushed the American position, opened fire and stopped the assault. Regrouping, the insurgents turned on Daniel, who had to fight off three attacks in quick succession while pulling back to the east. As Company A continued its fighting withdrawal, Tyler came up on the radio to warn Daniel against leading the enemy to the battalion base. The order proved unnecessary, because the Viet Cong had abandoned the pursuit. Toward midafternoon they also discontinued their attack against Tucker and Bittrich and pulled back.

Although the fighting was over, Tyler's battalion remained for the night near Hill 65. The following day, 9 November, it continued its search of the area but found no enemy. After that, with the insurgents clearly gone and American dead and wounded attended to, there seemed little reason to stay. General Williamson terminated HUMP, and the brigade returned to base.[14]

Official reports would later claim that the 173d had killed about 400 Viet Cong by body count and another 200 by estimate while putting American casualties at 49 killed and 83 wounded. The figure of 400 turned out to be a guess, however, which Williamson made in the immediate aftermath of the battle under pressure from MACV headquarters. Later appraisals would raise the count to 700, but they are suspect as well. Since the enemy unit involved was the *271st's 3d Battalion*, a body count of 700 would have meant that the 1st of the 503d Infantry had killed twice as many of the enemy as were present during battle. Whatever the case, Tyler's men had killed enough insurgents to claim

[13] Interv, author with Williamson, 22 Jan 93, Historians files, CMH.
[14] Ltr, Daniel to Conetto, 19 Mar 93; AAR, Opn HUMP, 173d Abn Bde, pp. 5–6.

the battlefield for themselves. Williamson later observed that they had "beat the living hell" out of the Viet Cong. By so doing, they had achieved the sort of success that President Johnson, General Westmoreland, and others hoped would convince the leadership in Hanoi to pull back and negotiate. At the same time, how the battle had originated bothered Williamson, and he eventually concluded that "it was not the smartest fight. The enemy had set a trap." In the hope of destroying an American unit, "he had lured us into a battle in an area of his choosing."[15]

Bau Bang

The enemy chose the next battleground shortly after the fight at Hill 65. On 4 November Maj. Gen. Pham Quoc Thuan, the South Vietnamese 5th Division commander, requested that General Seaman's 1st Division secure Highway 13 from Lai Khe north to the Bau Long Pond, a distance of about thirteen kilometers. The objective of the operation was to ensure the safe passage of the 5th Division's 7th Regiment over a dangerous stretch of the road on the first leg of its move to the Michelin Rubber Plantation, where the allied unit would conduct a series of search and destroy operations. Seaman gave the mission to the 3d Brigade and its commander, Col. William D. Brodbeck, who in turn passed the job to Lt. Col. George M. Shuffer, Jr.'s 2d Battalion, 2d Infantry. Shuffer's men would find themselves operating farther north along Highway 13 than any Americans had previously. Unlike the men of the 173d Airborne Brigade, they had yet to convert to the M16 rifle and were still armed with the slower firing, heavier, but still highly effective M14.[16]

Colonel Shuffer constructed his task force out of his own unit, plus Troop A, 1st Squadron, 4th Cavalry, and Battery C, 2d Battalion, 33d Artillery. Under his plan the thirteen-kilometer stretch of road was divided into three sectors, each assigned company-size units. The command group, the battalion's reconnaissance platoon, the 105-mm. towed artillery battery, the cavalry troop, and Company A went into the middle sector. The other two sectors, one to the north, the other to the south, went to the remaining two companies. Shuffer planned for each unit to sweep its sector during the day. Toward nightfall the three forces would pull into perimeters, located at intervals along the highway. The Americans followed this procedure on 10 and 11 November, but other than the uneventful passage of the 7th Regiment little occurred. The most notable events of the two days were visits by the battalion's civil affairs

---

[15] AAR, Opn Hump, 173d Abn Bde, p. 9; Interv, author with Williamson, 22 Jan 93; *9th Division*, p. 55; *People's Army of Vietnam*, 2(bk.I,ch.3):11; Williamson, "Forty Years of Fun," ch. 21, p. [37] (quotations), copy in Historians files, CMH.

[16] MACV History, 1965, p. 171, CMH; AAR, Opn Bushmaster I, 3d Bde, 1st Inf Div, 31 Dec 65, p. 3, box 1, 81/756, RG 338, NARA.

teams to the hamlets of Ben Dong So and Bau Bang to hand out rice, beans, dry milk, candy, bundles of used clothing, and CARE packages.[17]

Following the passage of the South Vietnamese regiment, Colonel Shuffer on the afternoon of the eleventh ordered his middle units to establish night defensive positions. The armored cavalry and artillery set up north of Bau Bang and Company A to the south. As the troops began to settle in, however, Shuffer changed his mind. Judging the artillery's position to be vulnerable, he ordered the units there to move south of Bau Bang and Company A slightly north. In that way the two groups could create a single large perimeter, measuring three hundred by four hundred meters. To clear the area and create better fields of fire, an armored personnel carrier dragged a destroyed vehicle of the same type around the perimeter, knocking down bushes and young rubber trees. Shuffer's other two task forces likewise established laagers. At all three positions the Americans installed concertina wire, dug foxholes, and, after sunset, sent ambush patrols out a short distance. During the night Shuffer's middle force received two mortar rounds, and one of its ambushes killed two Viet Cong, but most of the time passed in "sluggish quiet."[18]

Having learned on the tenth of the arrival of Shuffer's unit, the *9th Division* commander, Senior Col. Hoang Cam, seized the chance to fight Americans. Shuffer's command post would be his objective. Backed by division mortars and augmented by battalions from the *271st* and *273d Regiments,* the *272d Regiment* would lead the way. The *273d's 9th Battalion* would block any attempt by the Americans south of Bau Bang to assist and its *7th Battalion* would stand in reserve.

On the afternoon of the eleventh Colonel Cam's forces began to gather for the attack, some of them marching for up to seven hours to reach Bau Bang. At 2200 Cam learned that Shuffer had pulled the task force north of the hamlet southward to a strongpoint located only two hundred meters from the perimeter of the second element in the American middle. Assuming the risk, the Viet Cong colonel decided to expand his plan and to stage an assault that would destroy both troop concentrations. Under the new scenario, the *272d Regiment* would attack the relocated task force and the *273d Regiment* would engage the unit just to its south.

Colonel Cam's forces prepared for the assault throughout the night. While signalmen laid wire for field telephones around the Americans, other troops entered Bau Bang. They positioned mortars within the hamlet itself and dug machine gun and recoilless rifle emplacements into a berm located just to its south near the new American perimeter. To the west and south of the target, hidden by chest-high grass that extended out for about six hundred meters, the Viet Cong crouched among rub-

---

[17] AAR, Opn BUSHMASTER I, 3d Bde, 1st Inf Div, an. B, p. 1.

[18] Ibid. (see also map); Starry, *Mounted Combat*, p. 62; Press Release, Info Office, 1st Inf Div, 20 Feb 67, sub: The Battle of Ap Bau Bang, 12 November 1965, p. 2 (quoted words), in Vietnam Interview (VNI) 139, CMH.

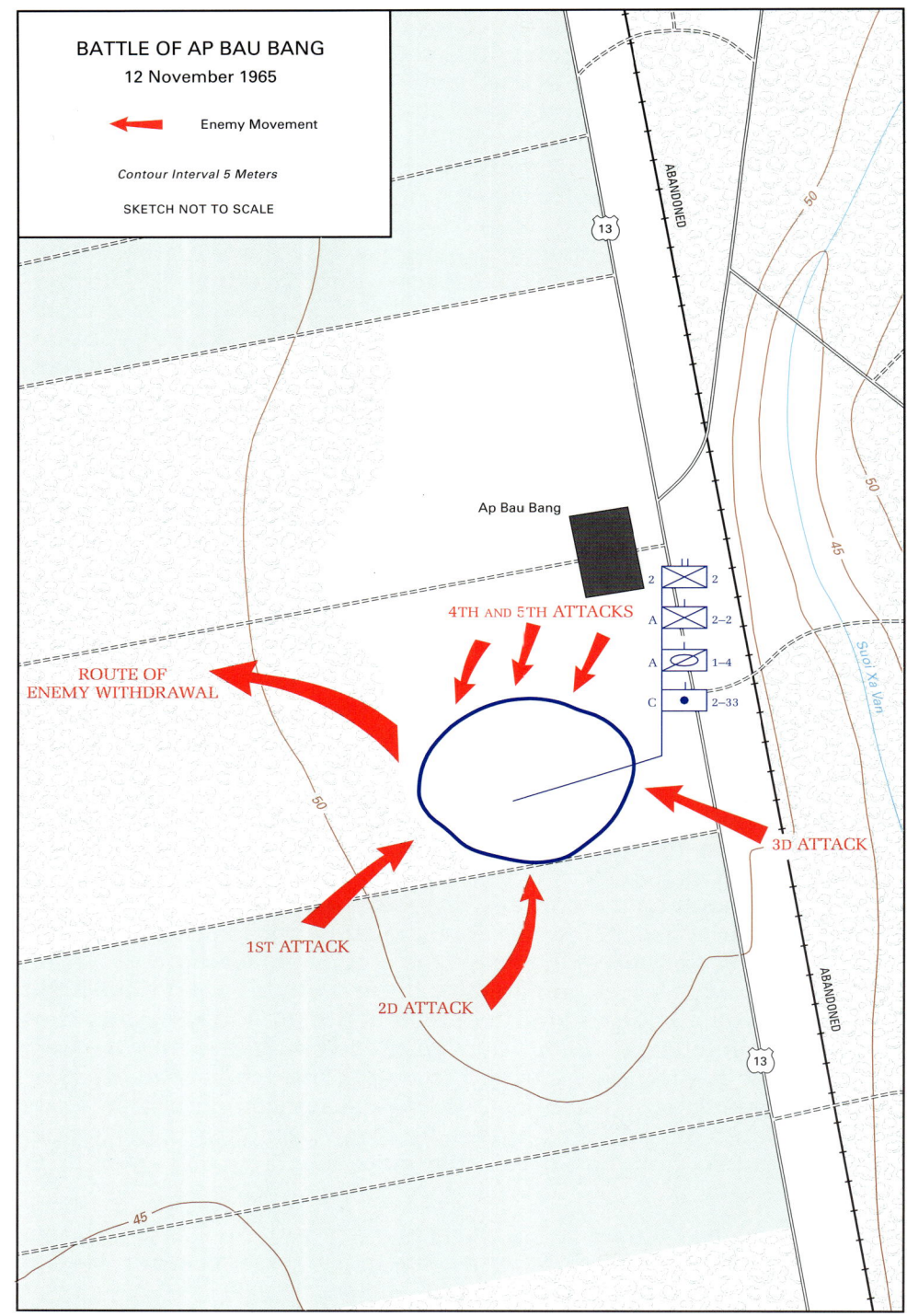

BATTLE OF AP BAU BANG

12 November 1965

Enemy Movement

Contour Interval 5 Meters

SKETCH NOT TO SCALE

Ap Bau Bang

4TH AND 5TH ATTACKS

ROUTE OF
ENEMY WITHDRAWAL

3D ATTACK

1ST ATTACK

2D ATTACK

ABANDONED

ABANDONED

Suoi Xa Van

MAP 5

ber trees awaiting the order to attack. To the southeast of the target, more of them assembled near the edge of Highway 13, which ran less than a hundred meters to the east of the American perimeter along a level grassy field.[19]

The next morning Shuffer's men began preparations to move out on the road, slating departure for just after 0600. Cam launched his attack at 0605. Although he had laid wire, his communications were still so primitive that he had direct contact with only one of his battalions. Cam had to hope that when he signaled that battalion to attack, the others would coordinate their actions with the sound of its guns. For all its flaws, the system worked. Over the first ten minutes of the assault, Cam's troops fired some fifty mortar rounds into their targets and then added automatic weapons and small-arms fire. Meanwhile, the soldiers who had been in among the rubber trees made their way through the tall grass to within forty meters of the American perimeter and charged (*Map 5*).[20]

Up and alert, Shuffer's men responded with deadly effect. Troop A's 3d Platoon quickly boarded M113s that roared out to meet the enemy. Mounting a .50-caliber machine gun and two 7.62-mm. M60 machine guns, the armored personnel carriers blazed away; the troops aboard fired from open cargo hatches. The onslaught broke the assault. The Viet Cong had little more success in the two attacks that followed. In the first, as they crept close to the American position through high bushes and then dashed toward the concertina wire, they met fire from troopers in stationary armored personnel carriers and from infantrymen in foxholes and retreated. In the second, a number of them rushed the American line from the southeast across Highway 13, but Shuffer's men were again ready and beat them back.[21]

A fourth attack came at 0700, when the Viet Cong, in what probably represented Colonel Cam's main effort, poured south across the berm at Bau Bang and out of a wooded area near the hamlet. Backed by mortar, recoilless rifle, and automatic weapons fire, they caused some difficult moments for the Americans, especially when a suicide squad penetrated the perimeter and threw a grenade into a howitzer position, killing 2 crewmen and wounding 4. In the end, however, these attackers were no more successful than their predecessors. Reaching the wire, they fell back under the combined weight of the defenders' artillery, machine guns, and rifles. Especially effective were fifty-five rounds from Battery

---

[19] Rpt, Combined Documents Exploitation Center, 3 Aug 67, sub: Translation Report Entitled "Review of the Signal and Communication Operations in the Raid Conducted by the 2nd and 3rd Regiments, Cong Truong 9, Against the 3rd Brigade, 1st US Infantry Division at Bau Bang on 12 November 1965," pp. 3–5, Historians files, CMH; *9th Division*, p. 57.

[20] Memo, Lt Col Dan H. Williamson, Jr., M113 Project Officer, for Chief, Army Concept Team in Vietnam (ACTIV), 16 Nov 65, sub: Report of Visit to 3d Brigade, 1st Infantry Division, pp. 1–2, Historians files, CMH.

[21] Ibid.; AAR, Opn BUSHMASTER I, 3d Bde, 1st Inf Div, an. B, p. 2.

C's howitzers, using two-second time fuses and fired level to the ground at point-blank range.[22]

Close air support and artillery played a critical role in the battle. Just prior to the 0700 attack, a flight of Air Force A–1H Skyraiders hit the wooded area to the northwest. Initially reluctant to fire into Bau Bang itself for fear of killing civilians, Colonel Shuffer's men changed their minds when they realized that the enemy had placed mortars in the hamlet and recoilless rifles on the berm. Soon Shuffer's howitzers were dropping high explosives right on target. A flight of Navy carrier-based A–4 Skyhawks and another of Skyraiders also arrived, delivering iron bombs, napalm, and cluster bombs that spewed high-velocity pellets upon detonation.[23]

For awhile the hamlet was quiet. Then, at 0900, the Viet Cong who survived launched a final attack. Once again the artillery responded, as did a flight of F–100s. As high explosives pounded enemy emplacements and Shuffer's other two companies arrived, the Viet Cong withdrew. By 1330 all American positions were secure and the enemy was gone.[24]

The men of the 2d Battalion, 2d Infantry, had performed well in their first major encounter with a main force unit. According to Colonel Shuffer and the acting commander of Troop A, 2d Lt. John L. Garcia, the defenders had killed 146 Viet Cong by body count and possibly another 50 whose bodies had been removed. Given the size of the attacking force, the vigor of the attack, and the weight of the American response, those numbers were credible, particularly in light of the large quantities of equipment that the enemy had left behind, an array that included rifles, machine guns, mortars, recoilless rifles, a rocket launcher, a flamethrower, and a radio. The Americans took losses as well, with 20 soldiers killed and 103 wounded. No one recorded the civilian casualties in the hamlet, whether inflicted by the Americans or the Viet Cong. Clearly, however, the people of the area had suffered greatly. The site of civic action efforts just twenty-four hours before, Bau Bang "lay barren, a smoldering, lifeless ruin."[25]

Trung Loi

The 1st Division had a second encounter with a unit from the *9th Division* a little over a week later, during Operation BUSHMASTER I. Act-

---

[22] AAR, Opn BUSHMASTER I, 3d Bde, 1st Inf Div, an. B, p. 2.

[23] Ibid.

[24] Memo, Lt Col Williamson for Chief, ACTIV, 16 Nov 65, sub: Report of Visit to 3d Brigade, 1st Infantry Division, pp. 1–2.

[25] Ibid., p. 2; AAR, Opn BUSHMASTER I, 3d Bde, 1st Inf Div, an. B, p. 2 (quoted words). The enemy claimed to have inflicted about 2,000 American casualties while suffering 109 killed and 200 wounded. See *9th Division*, p. 58.

1st Division soldiers pause before entering the Michelin Plantation.

ing on information that Viet Cong had been seen in the Michelin Plantation, South Vietnamese and American commanders ordered a search of the area. On the American side, Colonel Brodbeck of the 3d Brigade planned to use the 1st Battalion, 16th Infantry, the 1st and 2d Battalions, 28th Infantry, and the 2d Battalion, 33d Artillery, even though General Seaman as late as 13 November remained undecided about proceeding. Work on a crucial bridge that carried Route 239 across Bot Creek near the eastern fringe of the plantation had been slated for completion by the thirteenth but remained unfinished. When the South Vietnamese 5th Division assured the general that the span would be repaired by the following morning, he decided to go ahead.[26]

Under Seaman's plan, heavy air strikes would take place south of the plantation on 14 November. A short time later the 2d of the 28th Infantry and the 2d of the 33d Artillery would move by convoy from Lai Khe on Highway 13 to Chon Thanh and turn west toward the plantation on Route 239. Meanwhile, the 1st of the 16th Infantry and the 1st of the 28th Infantry would air-assault southeast of the plantation. Initially, on the fourteenth, these two battalions would search east to west from phase line to phase line, while the 2d of the 28th would function as a blocking force. On the third day all three infantry battalions would

---

[26] AAR, Opn BUSHMASTER I, 3d Bde, 1st Inf Div, an. B, p. 6; Unit History, 1965, 2d Bn, 28th Inf, 29 Mar 66, p. 4, box 3, 81/469, RG 338, NARA.

maneuver to the northwest toward a final phase line near the airfield at Dau Tieng.[27]

The operation fell behind schedule almost from the start, but the troops stuck doggedly to a modified version of the original plan and covered the area assigned. For all of their searching, they turned up little. By 20 November they were done, and plans were afoot to return them to base. The 1st of the 16th Infantry would move to Lai Khe by air, but the other units, including the 2d of the 28th Infantry, commanded by Lt. Col. George S. Eyster, would travel by motor convoy.[28]

Colonel Eyster's men left the area company by company. The first to depart was Company B, which escorted one of the artillery batteries to a spot from where it could support the troops that would move down Highway 13 to Chon Thanh. It would stay with the battery to provide security. Next came Company A. Mounting armored personnel carriers supplied by the 1st Squadron, 4th Cavalry, the unit was to move east on Route 239 to Chon Thanh and south on Highway 13 to Lai Khe. Company C was last, accompanied by the command group except for Eyster who had flown to Lai Khe on business. Also present were Battery B, 2d Battalion, 33d Artillery, and the artillery battalion's commander, Lt. Col. Frank R. Tims, who was in charge of the convoy. Unfortunately for Colonel Tims and the men under him, the late-season heavy monsoon rains had begun to fall and soon rendered Route 239 all but impassable. Before long, the column was deep in mud and moving at a rate that rarely exceeded one hundred meters an hour. Realizing that the force could never reach Chon Thanh in daylight, Tims considered setting up a perimeter and pulling in for the night. When he failed to find a suitable site, he decided to press on toward his destination despite the rain and mud.[29]

Almost three kilometers in length, the convoy approached the hamlet of Trung Loi, about eight kilometers short of Highway 13, at 1820. Two Company C rifle platoons, accompanied by Colonel Tims, led the formation. Noticing an armed enemy soldier running away from the road, a sergeant in one of the lead platoons shot and killed the man. From then on, the lead elements in the column began to receive small-arms fire from both sides of the road. At Tims' direction, the two forward platoons dismounted, formed a perimeter, and began to return fire. Over the next twenty minutes, the attack spread to the middle of the column. With machine gun and small-arms fire raking the road from both sides and with grenades going off, some of the infantrymen were pinned down. In response, Company C's mortar platoon set up and began to fire at maximum elevation, allowing its rounds to fall within

---

[27] AAR, Opn BUSHMASTER I, 3d Bde, 1st Inf Div, pp. 4, 6.

[28] Ibid., an. C, p. 1; Press Release, Info Office, 1st Inf Div, 20 Nov 65, sub: The Battle of Trung Loi, p. 1, in VNI 99, CMH.

[29] Unit History, 1965, 2d Bn, 28th Inf, p. 5; Interv, Albright with Seaman, 10 Sep 70, p. 26, Historians files, CMH; AAR, Opn BUSHMASTER I, 3d Bde, 1st Inf Div, p. 7.

twenty to thirty meters of each side of the road. When a recoilless rifle from the attacking force, later identified as the *272d Regiment's 4th Battalion*, began firing from the east side of the road toward the mortars and Company C's command group, the Americans returned fire, killing the original gun crew and a team that came forward to take its place. Then the Americans ran out of ammunition. In the meantime, a third gun crew took over and resumed firing. The Viet Cong also began to shower the Americans with mortar rounds and grenades.[30]

At that point American firepower provided relief. Huey gunships arrived and made firing passes from west to east on the southeast side of the road, where most of the enemy seemed to be. Next, the gunships made a series of sweeps to drive the ambushers out of their positions onto the roadway, where fire from the convoy killed some of them. The helicopters departed after ten minutes, but by then Air Force fighter-bombers were on the scene and dropping napalm along the southeast side of the road. American and South Vietnamese artillery also zeroed in, bringing the opposite side of the roadway under fire.[31]

By 1900 the vigor of the American response had broken the ambush, and by 2000 Tims and his men were moving again. At 2115 they passed out of the ambush site, arriving at Chon Thanh forty-five minutes later. Over the next two days, 21 and 22 November, Colonel Eyster's battalion proceeded to Lai Khe and Operation BUSHMASTER ended. In all, the Viet Cong had killed 6 Americans, wounded 38 more, and so damaged 6 vehicles that they could not be moved. Estimates of enemy killed ranged from 40 to 142.[32]

From one standpoint, as General Seaman observed years later, except for the ambush at Trung Loi, the results of BUSHMASTER I "didn't amount to a hill of beans." From another, however, a valuable operational idea had emerged from the action. According to Seaman, the employment of simultaneous artillery, gunships, and air strikes in support of ground combat had always been a source of trouble. Following procedures developed in Vietnam between 1962 and 1965, ground-control radar guided strike aircraft to the vicinity of a target. When they arrived, Air Force officers at the scene took over. A forward air controller flying a Cessna O–1 Bird Dog over the battlefield would describe the target, issue an attack heading, and provide whatever facts he had on artillery fire in the area. With that information, a second controller stationed with the unit on the ground would mark friendly positions by popping smoke grenades. With the allies identified, the air controller

---

[30] Press Release, Info Office, 1st Inf Div, 20 Nov 65, sub: The Battle of Trung Loi, p. 2.

[31] AAR, Opn BUSHMASTER I, 3d Bde, 1st Inf Div, an. C, p. 1; Unit History, 1965, 2d Bn, 28th Inf, p. 5.

[32] For the various totals of enemy killed, see Quarterly Cmd Rpt, 1 Oct–31 Dec 65, 1st Inf Div, p. 15; Interv, Albright with Seaman, 10 Sep 70, p. 26; AAR, Opn BUSHMASTER I, 3d Bde, 1st Inf Div, an. C, p. 2. The Viet Cong estimated that they killed nearly 100 Americans. See *9th Division*, p. 59.

would tag the enemy's positions with smoke rockets and instruct the fighters to begin the attack.[33]

Unless everything was well aligned, however, the bombing runs could easily intersect the paths of helicopters—medevac, transport, or gunships—supporting the operation. Premature bomb releases by startled pilots might then occur, endangering the lives of friendly troops and civilians. Similarly, falling artillery shells and the shrapnel from their explosions might damage gunships and strike aircraft or even bring some down. Building upon the experience at Trung Loi, the 1st Division's fire support officers developed a procedure to do away with those problems. From then on, they eliminated conflicts by assigning artillery, fighter-bombers, and gunships to clearly demarcated sectors on the battlefield. The procedure, Seaman later remarked, "worked like a charm."[34]

Nha Mat

American operations along Highway 13 and west to the Michelin Plantation continued into December, at which time the month's most notable fight in all of III Corps occurred—the battle at Nha Mat. As at Bau Bang, it originated in American support of a South Vietnamese operation. In the early hours of 27 November the *271st* and *273d Regiments* attacked elements of the 5th Division's 7th Regiment near the plantation. The Viet Cong attackers, according to General Seaman, "practically wiped the 7th Regiment out." In response, Seaman ordered Colonel Brodbeck's 3d Brigade, with two battalions and artillery, to move in and protect the regiment as it regrouped. On the third day of the operation Seaman changed Brodbeck's mission. Intelligence indicated that elements of the attacking Viet Cong regiments and, perhaps, the *Phu Loi Local Force Battalion* might be found southeast of the plantation. In addition, late word had arrived that the *9th Division*'s third regiment, the *272d*, might also be in the area. The Americans were to move aggressively to exploit the intelligence. To increase the odds, Seaman assigned a third battalion to Brodbeck's task force to provide security for the brigade command group, releasing the other two battalions for the chase.[35]

---

[33] Interv, Albright with Seaman, 10 Sep 70, p. 26 (quoted words); John J. Sbrega, "Southeast Asia," in *Case Studies in the Development of Close Air Support*, ed. Benjamin Franklin Cooling (Washington, D.C.: Office of Air Force History, United States Air Force, 1990), pp. 432–33; Schlight, *Years of the Offensive*, pp. 130–31.

[34] Interv, Albright with Seaman, 10 Sep 70, p. 26.

[35] Seaman, "Elements of Command," pt. 1, p. 18 (quoted words), Incl to Interv, Patterson with Seaman, 1971–72, Senior Officer Oral History Program, MHI; Rpt, USARV, 5 Feb 70, sub: History of the 273 VC Regiment, July 1964–December 1969, pp. 8–9; *9th Division*, pp. 59–60. See also Op Sum, Opn XAY DUNG 12 (Michelin Plantation, 27 Nov 65), pp. 1–2; AAR, Opn BLOODHOUND/BUSHMASTER II, 3d Bde, 1st Inf Div, 30 Dec 65, pp. 1–4. Both in Historians files, CMH.

On 1 December Operation BLOODHOUND (later renamed BUSHMASTER II) began. The two infantry battalions—one of them Colonel Shuffer's 2d of the 2d Infantry—moved to DALLAS, a landing zone inside the Michelin Plantation. The site would function as a staging base for the two battalions and as a command post for the brigade command group.[36]

Between 2 and 5 December Brodbeck's task force searched to the southeast of DALLAS in a rectangle of jungle and heavy undergrowth that extended about eight kilometers west to east and twenty kilometers north to south. The search area was within the Long Nguyen Secret Zone, which recent intelligence suggested was being used by the *272d Regiment* as a safe haven. Following Brodbeck's plan, the two infantry battalions maneuvered methodically over several days from phase line to phase line but failed to find the Viet Cong.[37]

Then on 5 December Shuffer's 2d of the 2d Infantry finally made contact. The battalion had begun the day searching along a jungle road in a southerly direction. Companies B and C moved abreast of one another on the east and west sides of the road, while Company A and Shuffer's command group followed C. Toward midday, just north of the hamlet of Nha Mat and about nine kilometers west of Bau Bang, Shuffer's lead companies came under small-arms, mortar, machine gun, and recoilless rifle fire from bunkers and small-arms fire from the surrounding trees (*see Map 6*).[38]

The encounter soon developed into a major firefight. Colonel Shuffer sent Company A around the enemy's left, or western, flank because it seemed the weaker, but the Viet Cong unit, later identified as the *272d*, stopped the Americans cold. Meanwhile, its largest contingent attempted to outflank and attack the Americans on the east side of the road, forcing Company B across the road to the west. In response, Shuffer deployed his command group along the northern boundary of the emerging U.S. position, establishing what he considered to be the best perimeter defense under the circumstances. It contained the command group on the northern side of the perimeter, Company C to the south, Company B on the east, and Company A on the west and southwest.[39]

Although pinned down and surrounded by dense jungle, Shuffer had the advantage of firepower. Responding to his requests for support, Colonel Brodbeck gave him priority on all available air and artillery and also alerted an infantry company to reinforce. In short order, a battery each from the 1st Division's 8th Battalion, 6th Artillery, and the

---

[36] AAR, Opn BLOODHOUND/BUSHMASTER II, 3d Bde, 1st Inf Div, pp. 2–4; Rpt, USARV, 5 Feb 70, sub: History of the 273 VC Regiment, July 1964–December 1969, p. 9; Seaman, "Elements of Command," pt. 1, p. 18, Incl to Interv, Patterson with Seaman, 1971–72.

[37] George M. Shuffer, Jr., "Finish Them With Firepower," *Military Review* 47 (December 1967): 11–12.

[38] Ibid., p. 13; Press Release, Info Office, 1st Inf Div, 20 Feb 67, sub: The Battle of Ap Nha Mat, p. 3, in VNI 137, CMH.

[39] Shuffer, "Finish Them With Firepower," p. 13.

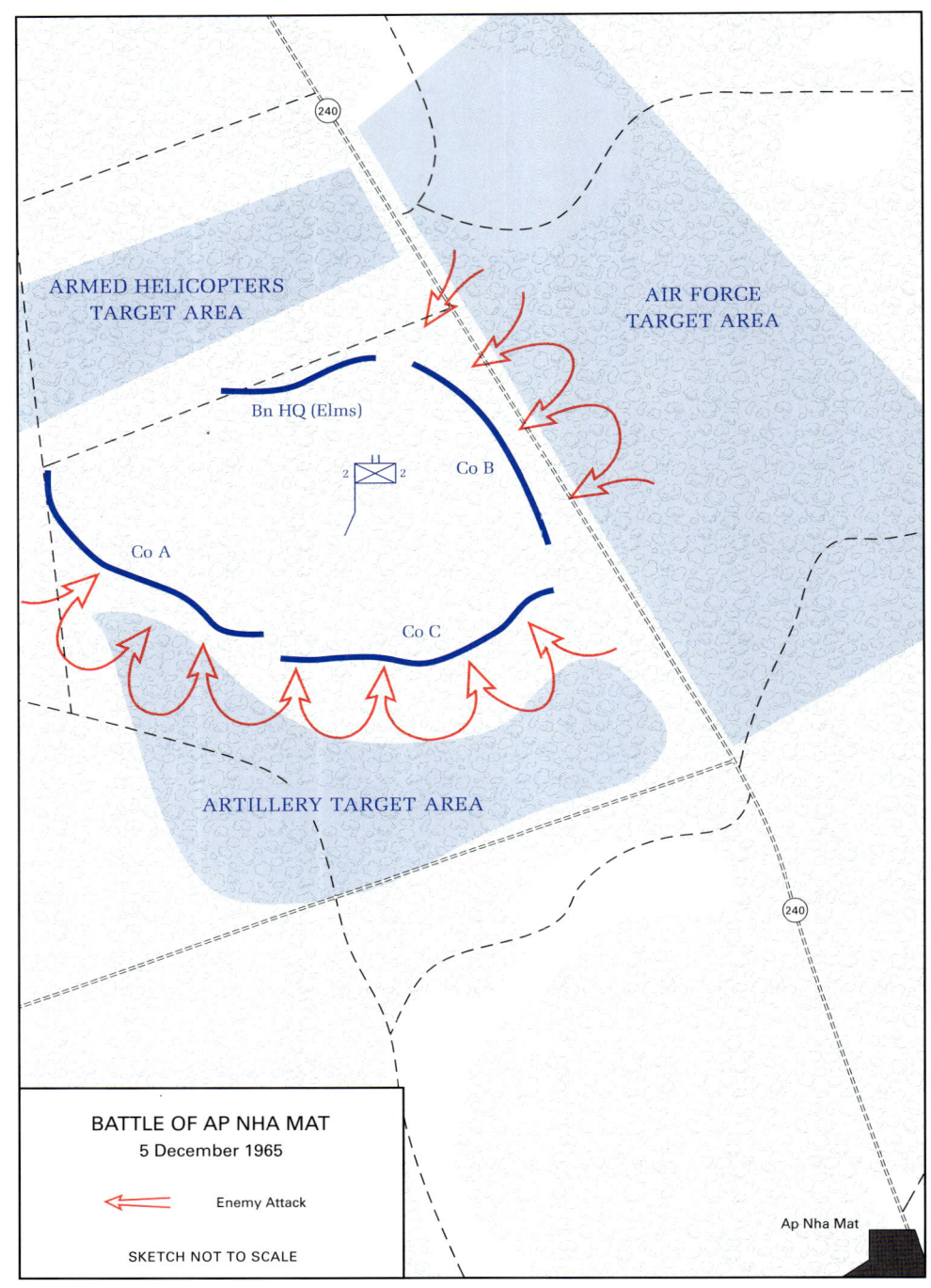

ARMED HELICOPTERS
TARGET AREA

AIR FORCE
TARGET AREA

Bn HQ (Elms)

2 ⊠ 2

Co B

Co A

Co C

ARTILLERY TARGET AREA

BATTLE OF AP NHA MAT
5 December 1965

Enemy Attack

SKETCH NOT TO SCALE

Ap Nha Mat

MAP 6

A 175-mm. gun from the 23d Artillery Group provides support north of Saigon.

23d Artillery Group's 2d Battalion, 32d Artillery, mounting 175-mm. self-propelled guns, began to lay down heavy fires. Shuffer also had three helicopter gun teams, made up of two Huey gunships each, at his disposal. In fact, he was so rich in firepower that it posed an organizational challenge. Although believing that the simultaneous employment of his resources would produce the best results, Shuffer had to do it in a way that avoided casualties among his own men. Recalling Trung Loi, he solved the problem by assigning each category of fire support to a clearly designated area. The sector east of the jungle road went to the Air Force, the area south and southwest to the artillery, and the northern flank of his perimeter to the helicopters. The Viet Cong tried to force a postponement of additional fires by moving in close to the Americans, but Shuffer's troops maintained a volume of fire that kept the insurgents at a distance.[40]

The air strikes and artillery bursts that followed laid down a curtain of fire for almost four hours. That protection allowed Company B to hold firm against an assault from the east. Meanwhile, Companies A and C attacked south into the heart of the enemy bunkers, keeping pace with artillery bursts marching just ahead of them. By 1430 the Ameri-

[40] Ibid., pp. 13–15; Unit History, [1965–66], 2d Bn, 33d Arty, n.d., p. 55, box 2, 81/725, RG 338, NARA; AAR, Opn BLOODHOUND/BUSHMASTER II, 3d Bde, 1st Inf Div, pp. 5, 8–9; Interv, author with Brig Gen George M. Shuffer, Jr., 25 Jun 98, Historians files, CMH.

cans had penetrated so deeply into the position that the defenders began to lose heart. Running to the rear, the Viet Cong left behind not only their dead but also their weapons and equipment. Shuffer decided against a pursuit; it was late in the day, the size of the enemy force was unknown, and the Viet Cong knew the region and its trails and hiding places much better than the Americans. Instead, somewhat before sunset, he withdrew his men to the protection of a perimeter. A relief company joined them that night.[41]

Along with artillery and air support, Shuffer's men killed some 300 Viet Cong. American intelligence analysts concluded that the operation severely damaged the *272d Regiment* because the unit failed to enter combat for the next four months and appeared to have gone into seclusion to rest, refit, and retrain. The Americans lost 39 killed. They spent the next several days destroying as much of the bunker system as they could and continuing to look for the enemy. When the search came up empty, Colonel Brodbeck ruled that the damage done had been sufficient and ended BUSHMASTER II.[42]

Winding Down

Three other operations in December extended the reach of American forces in III Corps, but this time the action came east of Saigon. Since the mid-1950s the La Nga Valley in Long Khanh and Binh Tuy Provinces had been a major rice-producing area. Until the early 1960s hamlets in the valley had supported the central government, but in 1963 the Viet Cong arrived in force, seizing about one-half of the rice crop that year and all of it the next. Between 21 November and 17 December 1965 the 173d Airborne Brigade launched Operation NEW LIFE. The effort had three objectives: to destroy local Viet Cong units, to ensure that the farmers could harvest and sell their rice, and to help restore government to the valley.

At the beginning of NEW LIFE the 173d established a centrally located base camp in the La Nga Valley and began road-clearing operations, air assaults, night patrols, and other actions to secure the sector and provide protection for the harvest. In addition, U.S. Army and Filipino medical, dental, psychological operations, and civil affairs teams worked among the villagers, attempting to break their ties to the Viet Cong and to promote a modicum of interest in the Saigon authorities. In the end, the farmers harvested their crops without interference and officials returned district-level government to the thirty

---

[41] Press Release, Info Office, 1st Inf Div, 20 Feb 67, sub: The Battle of Ap Nha Mat, p. 3; Interv, author with Shuffer, 25 Jun 98.

[42] AAR, Opn BLOODHOUND/BUSHMASTER II, 3d Bde, 1st Inf Div, pp. 2, 5, 7; Rpt, III Corps Order of Battle (OB) Section, CICV, 30 Jan 70, sub: The *272d Regiment*, p. 3, Historians files, CMH.

Paratroopers flush Viet Cong from a tunnel during New Life.

thousand residents of La Nga. The results of the operation, if isolated, seemed encouraging.[43]

Purely military operations also took place off to the east, in this case between Highway 15 and Route 2 as far north as the town of Xuan Loc. When intelligence uncovered intimations that the Viet Cong might be planning a major assault there during the Christmas holiday period, U.S. commanders decided to begin spoiling operations to throw the plans off balance. Accordingly, the 173d Airborne Brigade launched Operation Smash I, while General Seaman's 2d Brigade began Operation Smash II. The two efforts were to be loosely coordinated, with the 173d's battalions patrolling west of Route 2 and the 2d Brigade working east of Highway 15.[44]

Smash I started on 17 December, when the 173d moved into position. Colonel Dexter's 2d of the 503d Infantry soon found the enemy. On the eighteenth, operating from the battalion's base southwest of the Courtenay Plantation area, about nine kilometers west of Route 2, the 2d of the 503d carried out company-size search and destroy missions,

[43] AAR, Opn New Life 65, 173d Abn Bde (Sep), 26 Jan 66, p. 23, Historians files, CMH.

[44] AAR, Opn Smash I, 173d Abn Bde (Sep), 26 Jan 66, p. 1, Historians files, CMH; [Unit History, 1965], 2d Bde, 1st Inf Div, n.d., p. [6], box 1, 81/748, RG 338, NARA.

one each to the north, the east, and the west. Shortly after 1030, about a half kilometer from the base camp, the company operating to the east encountered dug-in Viet Cong. When the Viet Cong opened up with machine guns and antitank weapons, Dexter's men returned fire and called in artillery and air support. Meanwhile, the company operating to the west pushed to assist, with Dexter's third company returning to secure the battalion base and, if necessary, to reinforce. Although the Air Force flew fourteen sorties and artillery fired over a thousand rounds during the afternoon, the enemy fought on. Finally, just before dark, when the reinforcing company arrived, Dexter decided to finish the affair and launched an all-out attack. With that, the insurgents withdrew and the battle ended. The Viet Cong lost 62 killed, plus a large quantity of arms and ammunition. Six of Dexter's men died. Although the search for the enemy continued in the days that followed, combat was over. General Williamson ended the operation on the twenty-first.[45]

During SMASH II, which ran from 18 to 23 December, the 2d Brigade saw no Viet Cong at all but found their bases and destroyed their supply caches. While the effect of the operations on enemy plans could not be immediately determined, U.S. commanders believed that they had prevented the holiday offensive. More importantly, the presence of their units at this distance from the capital had served notice that the Americans were now here to stay in these contested parts of III Corps.

[45] Commander's Combat Note no. 89, 173d Abn Bde (Sep), 28 Dec 65, p. 2, Historians files, CMH.

5

Into the Highlands

If III Corps with the nation's seat of government was crucial to both the allies and the Communists, II Corps with the Central Highlands was more immediately pressing. For as General Westmoreland had long understood, an enemy force that held the plateau controlled the high ground in the middle of the country. From there, it could attack north or south at will or move eastward toward the lowlands and the coast, possibly, the general feared, cutting the country in two. His forebodings proved to be real. No sooner had the airmobile 1st Cavalry Division encamped in Binh Dinh Province when North Vietnamese troop movements were detected off to the west near the border with Cambodia.[1]

The Campaign Takes Shape

Hanoi had been planning a campaign in the highlands since mid-1964, when it had established the *B3 Front* and had begun moving the *325th PAVN Division* south for service on the plateau. Although the division was subsequently broken up, with each of its regiments going to other battlefronts in South Vietnam, Hanoi's plans remained unchanged. Three new North Vietnamese regiments soon arrived in the highlands: the *32d PAVN Regiment* in late 1964 and early 1965, the *33d PAVN Regiment* by October 1965, and the *66th PAVN Regiment* by early November. With these units and the *H15 Local Force Battalion*, the *B3 Front* commander, Maj. Gen. Chu Huy Man, and his deputy, Lt. Col. Nguyen Huu An, planned a push that would begin in September 1965 and last until the following spring. Their targets would be not only Special Forces camps and other staging areas in Kontum and Pleiku Provinces but also Pleiku City itself, the province capital and the site of II Corps headquar-

---

[1] Westmoreland, *A Soldier Reports*, p. 156; Sharp and Westmoreland, *Report*, p. 98; *Luc Luong Vu Trang Nhan Dan Tay Nguyen Trong Khang Chien Chong My Cuu Nuoc* [*The People's Armed Forces of the Western Highlands During the War of National Salvation Against the Americans*] (Hanoi: Nha Xuat Ban Quan Doi Nhan Dan [People's Army Publishing House], 1980), pp. 3–4, copy in CMH (hereafter cited as *Western Highlands*).

ters. In the process, General Man hoped to "annihilate" an American force.[2]

The effort would not go unopposed. The South Vietnamese had long recognized the importance of the highlands and had stationed substantial forces there. General Vinh Loc, the II Corps commander, directly controlled four battalions of South Vietnamese rangers, three of airborne troops, and two of marines. The two-regiment 23d Infantry Division at Ban Me Thuot in Darlac Province also operated on the plateau, while the independent 42d Regiment defended a special tactical zone in Kontum Province opposite Cambodia. When the 1st Cavalry Division reached An Khe in September, ready to operate either on the coast or in the highlands, the prospects for the allies in western II Corps improved dramatically.[3]

But fighting there would not be easy. Defined by the Annamite Chain, which formed a crescent-shaped plateau some four hundred kilometers long by one hundred sixty wide, the Central Highlands had only two roads of any consequence: the north–south Highway 14, which connected the cities of Kontum, Pleiku, and Ban Me Thuot; and Highway 19, which climbed westward from the coast through Pleiku to the Cambodian border and the enemy sanctuaries beyond. The rugged terrain also posed tremendous physical challenges, enough to test any troops, even those with helicopters. The steep mountains, with jagged crests and deep narrow valleys, had dense tropical forests on their slopes, broken here and there by clearings and stands of small trees. The plateau was easier to traverse but still difficult. Heavy forests, with trees that sometimes reached a hundred feet in height, covered much of it, and even in areas where the jungle thinned, bushes and shoulder-high elephant grass impeded movement. A huge irregularly shaped mountain, the Chu Pong Massif, with peaks rising to over seven hundred meters, dominated the area southwest of Pleiku. Straddling the border with Cambodia, the mountain extended for thirteen kilometers east to west at its base and almost the same distance north to south. A river, the Ia Drang, flowed along its northern edge, generally to the northwest.

Other than the fourteen Special Forces camps strung out along the II Corps border from Kontum to Darlac and the province capitals and their

[2] Maj Andrew Boyle and Maj Robert Samabria, "The Lure and the Ambush: An Account of the Opening Battle of Phase Three in the Struggle for the Highlands, 19 October 1965–26 November 1965," [December 1965], box 16, 74/053, RG 319, NARA; Robert W. Pringle, "NVA Strategy in the South," an. A, pp. 9–10, Historians files, CMH; William S. Turley, "Order of Battle of PAVN and PLAF," in *Encyclopedia of the Vietnam War*, ed. Stanley I. Kutler (New York: Charles Scribner's Sons, 1996), p. 389; MFR, Col Curtis F. Livingston, Asst CofS, G–2 [Intel], I FFV, 1 Aug 70, sub: Enemy Order of Battle Holdings for II Corps Tactical Zone, p. 24, Historians files, CMH; *Western Highlands*, p. 29 (quoted word).

[3] Jeffrey J. Clarke, *Advice and Support: The Final Years, 1965–1973*, United States Army in Vietnam (Washington, D.C.: U.S. Army Center of Military History, 1988), pp. 33–34, 114.

Highway 19, the gateway to the Central Highlands

district satellites, friendly outposts in the western highlands were few and far between. Given the circumstances, a question loomed large for the allies—especially, the 1st Cavalry Division—now looking expectantly toward the border: What sort of staying power was possible in such an inhospitable and uninhabitable land?[4]

These were the challenges for the future, the preoccupation of the military planners. The immediate task for the 1st Cavalry Division was to secure its base at An Khe. And to do so, it had to take control of the adjacent Vinh Thanh Valley. A Viet Cong–dominated rice-growing area located about twenty kilometers east of An Khe, the valley was approximately twenty kilometers long from north to south and from two to five kilometers wide. The Song Con river flowed through it.[5]

Launching Operation HAPPY VALLEY on 6 October, the division deployed elements of the 2d Brigade and then replaced them with units of the 3d Brigade. Under orders to find the enemy, uproot him, and then aid in the establishment of a government presence in the valley, the division conducted several one or two company-size air assaults into roughly five- by one-kilometer tracts of land each day. Once on the

---

[4] Op Sum, 1–30 Nov 65, 5th SF Gp (Abn), 1st SF, 15 Dec 65, pp. 9–10, Historians files, CMH.

[5] Harry W. O. Kinnard, "A Victory in the Ia Drang: The Triumph of a Concept," *Army* 17 (September 1967): 73.

ground the men spent the next twenty-four to seventy-two hours patrolling rice paddies, hamlets, grazing land, and foothills. Although they captured some Viet Cong and Viet Cong suspects, they had little contact with the enemy, who appeared prepared to sacrifice supplies and facilities and, for the moment, even the valley itself rather than fight on American terms.[6]

The effect of the operation on the people of the region was dramatic. Initially, the sight of an American helicopter had sent the local Vietnamese into hiding. By late October they came to see the American troops more as protectors and thus returned to the central portion of the valley and to the safe areas near the brigade command post and a local militia camp. The airmobile assaults continued through October, as did small unit saturation patrolling. The number of night ambushes increased.[7]

As HAPPY VALLEY progressed, so did the pacification activities of the American troops and South Vietnamese police. While the police went after the insurgent underground, the Americans focused on civic action. The climax of the division's efforts came on 31 October and 1 November, when the 1st Battalion, 5th Cavalry, initiated Operation FRIENDSHIP as an adjunct to HAPPY VALLEY. The venture began with a concert by the 1st Cavalry Division's band and speeches by the battalion commander, Lt. Col. Frederic Ackerson, and local officials. The soldiers then handed out clothing, candy, milk, orange juice, soft drinks, salt, C-rations, sewing kits, and gifts. Following the festivities, the division continued its small unit patrolling and its civic action projects. When the operation ended on 19 November, life in the area appeared to revert to normal. With the South Vietnamese government reestablished in the valley, American commanders thought that the Viet Cong had left permanently.[8]

While continuing HAPPY VALLEY, the 1st Cavalry Division also conducted more straightforward combat operations. In SHINY BAYONET, which began on 10 October, the 3d Brigade sought to find and destroy two battalions of the *2d PLAF Regiment*, which were supposed to be operating about thirty-two kilometers northeast of An Khe in the mountains immediately to the east of the Suoi Ca Valley. The size of the American force suggested that U.S. commanders anticipated substantial combat, but no major battles occurred—only several small firefights over a four-day period, during which the troopers killed 49 enemy soldiers and possibly another 122. When later assessing SHINY BAYONET and the rest of the HAPPY VALLEY campaign, General Larsen concluded that the cavalry division had done "a little pooping and snooping in the Binh Dinh

---

[6] Op Sum, Opn HAPPY VALLEY, 1st Bn, 5th Cav, 11 Nov 65, p. 1, and Quarterly Cmd Rpt, 1 Oct–31 Dec 65, 1st Cav Div (Ambl), 10 Jan 66, pp. 13–14, Historians files, CMH; Rpt, 14th Mil Hist Det, 1st Cav Div (Ambl), 9 Jun 67, sub: Seven Month History and Briefing Data (September 1965–March 1966), p. 31, box 16, 74/053, RG 319, NARA.

[7] Op Sum, Opn HAPPY VALLEY, 1st Bn, 5th Cav, incl. 1, p. 2; Quarterly Cmd Rpt, 1 Oct–31 Dec 65, 1st Cav Div, p. 14.

[8] Op Sum, Opn HAPPY VALLEY, 1st Bn, 5th Cav, incl. 3, pp. 1–2.

area, . . . teeth cutting operations" that would be a prelude to affairs to come. He assumed that the next operations would happen in Binh Dinh Province as well. But when the *B3 Front* launched its Central Highlands campaign, the 1st Cavalry Division found itself increasingly oriented to the west.[9]

Plei Me Under Siege

As a first step in his highlands campaign, General Man targeted the Special Forces camp at Plei Me, some forty-five kilometers southwest of Pleiku City, certain that his enemies would fight to protect a facility critical to the defense of the province capital. Using two North Vietnamese regiments, Man devised a three-part plan. In the first phase the *33d Regiment* would surround and assault the camp, applying enough pressure to compel the South Vietnamese to send reinforcements. In the second phase the *32d Regiment*, positioning itself on the only road a relief column could take, Route 6C, would ambush and destroy that force. In the third phase the *32d* would join the *33d* in a final overwhelming push against the camp. Man's troops began preparations for the operation in mid-September. One month later, at sunset on 19 October, the time set for the Plei Me attack, they were ready.[10]

The Plei Me garrison was a varied group, consisting of twelve American advisers, fourteen South Vietnamese Special Forces troops, and a CIDG unit of over four hundred Montagnard tribesmen. Of these, eighty-five Montagnards and two Americans were on a mission fifteen kilometers northwest of the camp. Another forty Montagnards were conducting security ambush patrols in its immediate vicinity, and forty more were manning two listening posts located about two kilometers to the north and southwest of the facility. The remaining members of the garrison were inside the camp.[11]

The *33d Regiment* began its attack at approximately 1900, when some of its troops opened fire on a Montagnard patrol. At 2200 a company of the *33d's 1st Battalion* overran the outpost southwest of the camp. At the same time, the camp itself came under mortar and recoilless rifle fire. Shortly after midnight the North Vietnamese attacked from the north and northwest. Around 0100 they began a second push from the south and east, penetrating the camp's wire barriers before being turned back. These initial assaults set the pattern for the next several days. Keeping

[9] Intervs, Holmes with Larsen, 26 Oct 76, sec. 5, p. 6 (quotation), Senior Officer Oral History Program, MHI, and Sandstrum with Larsen, 11 Mar 70, p. 11, Historians files, CMH.

[10] *Western Highlands*, pp. 23–24; Boyle and Samabria, "Lure and Ambush," p. 4; Vinh Loc, *Why Plei Me?* (Pleiku, 1966), p. 59.

[11] Quarterly Cmd Rpt, 1 Oct–31 Dec 65, 5th SF Gp (Abn), 1st SF, incl. 1, p. [1], Historians files, CMH.

Plei Me Special Forces camp under attack

one battalion in reserve, the *33d Regiment* poured small-arms, mortar, and recoilless rifle fire into the camp while carrying out intermittent probes and larger attacks to maintain the pressure. In response, the advisers called in fighter-bombers, and the South Vietnamese commander, as Man had expected, requested reinforcements.[12]

The first air strikes arrived around 0400 on 20 October, followed by more than a hundred others over the next twenty-six hours, along with airdrops of food and ammunition. During the late evening hours of the twentieth Vinh Loc authorized the creation of a relief force, consisting of elements from an armored cavalry squadron, a ranger battalion, and a few other units. The contingent was to take Highway 14 south to Route 6C and then to turn southwest toward Plei Me. Since the assembly of the task force might take several days, the dispatch of interim reinforcements seemed imperative. The commander of the 5th Special Forces Group (Airborne), Col. William A. McKean, who was responsible for organizing the relief effort, proposed a parachute drop into the camp, but Vinh Loc's American adviser, Col. Theodore D. Mataxis, rejected the idea. After some discussion, all concerned agreed that it would be

---

[12] Ibid., pp. [1–2]; AAR, Pleiku Campaign, 1st Cav Div (Ambl), 4 Mar 66, p. 18, box 10, 67A/5216, RG 319, NARA; *Western Highlands*, p. 32; Contemporary Historical Evaluation of Combat Operations (CHECO) Rpt, Pacific Air Forces (PACAF), 24 Feb 66, sub: The Siege at Plei Me, pp. 2–3, copy in Historians files, CMH.

safer and quicker to land a force by helicopter near the camp and send it overland to Plei Me. One hundred and seventy-five men, the majority South Vietnamese rangers, received the assignment. Colonel McKean selected Maj. Charles A. Beckwith, an expert in long-range reconnaissance, to lead them.[13]

Beckwith's men landed about five kilometers northeast of Plei Me on the morning of 21 October. They had worked their way to a point near the camp by nightfall, but Major Beckwith decided to delay the final leg of the journey until the following morning because of the likelihood that the facility's defenders might mistake his men for the enemy in the darkness and open fire. Shortly after sunrise on the twenty-second Beckwith instructed his men to "run like hell . . . to the gates."[14] Surprising the enemy, the move succeeded. Once inside the camp, Beckwith became the senior officer present and took command.

Meanwhile, dispatch of the main relief force had been delayed by a disagreement between Vinh Loc and Colonel Mataxis. Mataxis wanted a larger relief force to counter the ambush everyone expected. Vinh Loc, however, considered the attack at Plei Me a possible ruse to lure South Vietnamese forces away from Pleiku, thus leaving the city unprotected. He wanted to do nothing until the situation at Plei Me became clear. On 22 October General Larsen broke the stalemate by promising Vinh Loc that American troops would ensure the safety of Pleiku if he would commit his reserves to Plei Me's defense. A short while later the South Vietnamese general increased the size of the relief force by two battalions. Larsen reciprocated by ordering General Kinnard to dispatch a battalion task force, including an artillery battery, to Pleiku. Kinnard sent his division's 2d Battalion, 12th Cavalry, under the command of Lt. Col. Earl Ingram (*see Map 7*).[15]

Then, seeing an opportunity for combat, Kinnard obtained permission on 23 October to transfer his entire 1st Brigade to Pleiku. Under acting commander Lt. Col. Harlow G. Clark, elements of the brigade began the move that day by Caribou transport. By evening Colonel Clark's headquarters, the 2d Battalion, 8th Cavalry, and two artillery batteries had joined Colonel Ingram's force at the province capital. Clark's unit had two missions: to provide artillery support for the relief column and to prepare a reaction force for commitment to the camp. In the meantime, Vinh Loc added one of his two reserve battalions to the relief force, increasing its size to some fourteen hundred men. Following the column's departure for Plei Me, he moved his other reserve bat-

---

[13] Charlie A. Beckwith and Donald Knox, *Delta Force* (New York: Harcourt Brace Jovanovich, 1983), pp. 62–72. See also Quarterly Cmd Rpt, 1 Oct–31 Dec 65, 5th SF Gp, 1st SF, incl. 1, p. [2].

[14] Beckwith and Knox, *Delta Force*, p. 67.

[15] Coleman, *Pleiku*, p. 76; AAR, Pleiku Campaign, 1st Cav Div, p. 18; Interv, Sandstrum with Larsen, 11 Mar 70, p. 13; Vinh Loc, *Why Plei Me?*, p. 61; Kinnard, "Victory in the Ia Drang," p. 73.

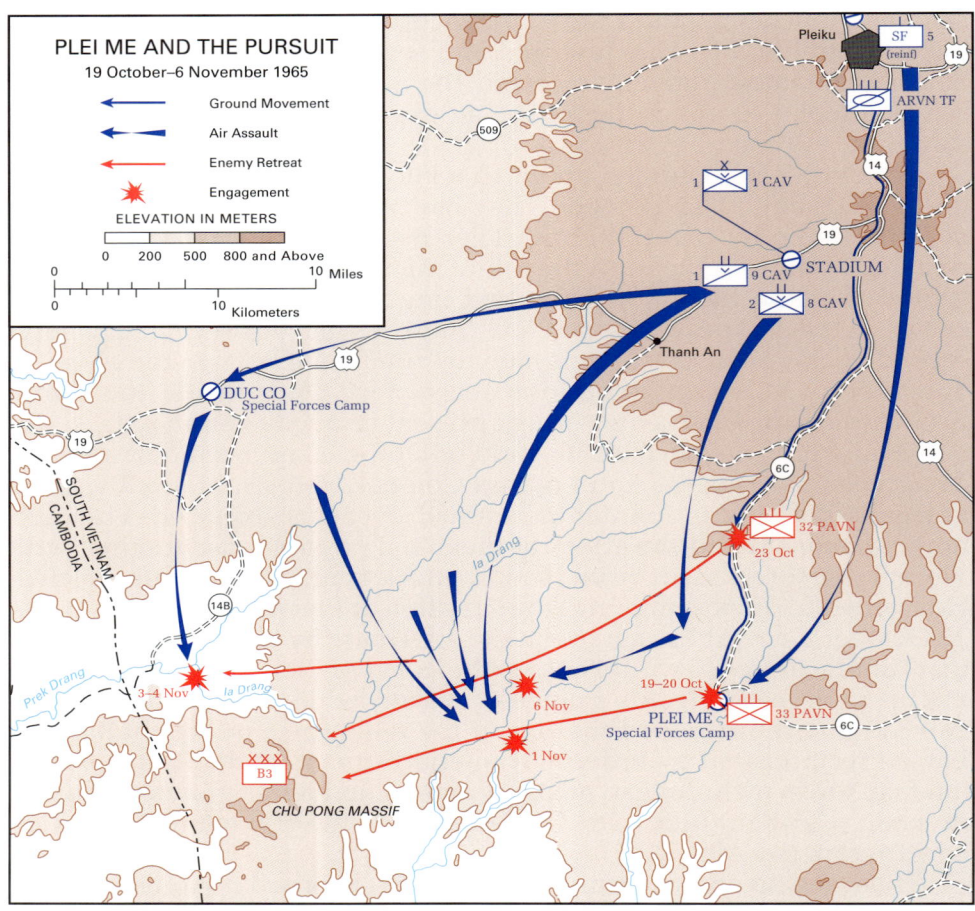

MAP 7

talion, a ranger unit, by helicopter several kilometers west of what he suspected would be the ambush site. It had orders to sweep toward the highway on command.[16]

On the twenty-third the relief column made its way cautiously, approaching the edge of the suspected ambush zone around 1700. Armored personnel carriers and M41 tanks headed up the column, with infantry on the flanks and with supply trucks and a small infantry force trailing about two kilometers behind. Around 1800 small-arms, recoilless rifle, and mortar fire tore into the leading elements of the task force. The tanks and armored personnel carriers wheeled to the right and left of the road,

[16] AAR, Pleiku Campaign, 1st Cav Div, p. 18; Kinnard, "Victory in the Ia Drang," p. 75.

102

fanning out and laying down heavy cannon and machine gun fire. Soon afterwards F–100s arrived on station, dispensing rockets, cannon fire, and napalm. Huey gunships also joined in. After two hours of battering, the attacking force withdrew.

The rest of the column did not fare so well. Under attack by a battalion-size force, the South Vietnamese took heavy casualties in the first moments of the encounter, and many of the trucks, loaded with ammunition and fuel, exploded and burned. After the initial assault, however, air strikes kept the enemy at bay, enabling the survivors to form a perimeter. The night passed quietly, except for an unsuccessful attack on the armored group. By morning there could be no doubt that the ambush had failed and that the *32d Regiment* had suffered heavy casualties. Confronted by the likelihood of continued massive American fire support, the unit's commander ordered a withdrawal toward the regimental base, located north of the Ia Drang near the Cambodian border.[17]

Although the enemy seemed beaten, the commander of the South Vietnamese task force, Lt. Col. Nguyen Trong Luat, kept his unit in place at the ambush site on the twenty-third and twenty-fourth, refusing to move until resupplied because he feared another attack. In fact, Colonel Luat wanted to return to Pleiku rather than proceed to Plei Me, and could be persuaded to continue only by a promise of U.S. artillery support. With that in hand, he finally started his men toward Plei Me at 1300 on the twenty-fifth. Experiencing only harassing small-arms fire, he and his men reached their destination at dusk.[18]

While the fighting raged on the road, the force at Plei Me hung on. On 22 October, shortly after Beckwith's men entered the camp, Colonel McKean ordered the major to "get outside the camp, rummage around, [and] clear the enemy out of there." Despite strong misgivings, Beckwith complied, dispatching two South Vietnamese companies and their American advisers. In short order, the North Vietnamese killed 14 friendly troops, including one of the advisers. As Beckwith recalled, "We were all beginning to realize that we would be damn fortunate to get out of this camp alive."[19]

Pulling back, Beckwith tightened the camp's defenses, fully expecting the *33d Regiment* to mount another assault. To discourage this action, the 1st Cavalry Division's artillery fired on suspected enemy targets, and Air Force and Navy aircraft attacked the *33d*'s positions and gun emplacements throughout the day.[20]

Over the next two days the North Vietnamese continued to lay down mortar and recoilless rifle fire, but they failed to mount a ground assault. By the twenty-fifth, according to later comments by enemy

---

[17] Coleman, *Pleiku*, p. 83; Boyle and Samabria, "Lure and Ambush," p. 9; AAR, Pleiku Campaign, 1st Cav Div, p. 28; Kinnard, "Victory in the Ia Drang," p. 76.

[18] Coleman, *Pleiku*, pp. 85–87; AAR, Pleiku Campaign, 1st Cav Div, p. 24.

[19] Beckwith and Knox, *Delta Force*, pp. 69 (first quotation) and 68 (second quotation).

[20] Boyle and Samabria, "Lure and Ambush," pp. 9–10.

prisoners, the *33d* had taken more punishment than it could stand. Two of the regiment's battalion commanders were dead; the *2d Battalion* had lost nearly 250 men, about half its strength; and the *1st* and *3d Battalions* had suffered heavily. Late that evening the *33d*'s commander began preparations to withdraw. The unit moved at dawn toward a staging area about eight kilometers southwest of Plei Me. General Man also decided to reposition the tactical headquarters overseeing the assault to a spot on the north bank of the Ia Drang close to Cambodia. All was not lost for him, however. For even as his troops pulled back, a new regiment, the *66th*, was arriving from North Vietnam.[21]

Decision and Action

On 24 October General Westmoreland met with General Larsen at the Field Force, Vietnam, headquarters at Nha Trang to consider what the 1st Cavalry Division should do once the siege at Plei Me had ended. Should General Kinnard consider his job in the highlands done and concentrate on the coastal lowlands and Binh Dinh Province? Or should he attempt to bring to battle the North Vietnamese regiments that had turned up in Pleiku Province? Kinnard, who had begun his warfighting at Normandy on D–Day, wanted not only to go after the enemy but also the freedom to do the job his own way; he greatly disliked the division's early operations that were subject to time constraints imposed by General Larsen, especially those hindering thorough searches in areas that showed promise of containing main forces. What Kinnard preferred was "a mission-type order." After a four-day wait, on the twenty-eighth, Westmoreland decided that Kinnard could have his way and ordered him to seize the initiative in Pleiku Province. The order marked a turning point for the 1st Cavalry Division. Rather than continue to serve as a reaction force in the Pleiku campaign, the unit would begin to wage an "unlimited offense."[22]

With Westmoreland's authorization in hand, Kinnard laid his plans. Using a brigade task force, initially Colonel Clark's 1st Brigade, which was already on the spot, the 1st Cavalry Division would conduct an intensive search for the enemy, looking everywhere—in the hamlets, in the jungles, and along the streambeds. Employing helicopters from the division reconnaissance squadron and dispersing battalions into company-size sweeps, the force would range systematically over large areas. After locating enemy soldiers, a rapid-reaction force moving by helicopter

---

[21] Ibid., p. 10; Kinnard, "Victory in the Ia Drang," p. 76; AAR, Pleiku Campaign, 1st Cav Div, p. 28.

[22] Interv, Couch with Kinnard, 20 Jan 83, pp. 96–97 (first quoted words), Senior Officer Oral History Program, MHI; Kinnard, "Victory in the Ia Drang," p. 76; AAR, Pleiku Campaign, 1st Cav Div, pp. 15, 29 (second quoted words), 30.

would finish them off. The helicopter made all the difference in the approach, Kinnard would later say. With it, "you could respond faster than anyone in history."[23]

Colonel Clark set his initial air assaults to the immediate north and west of Plei Me. He had at his disposal the 2d Battalion, 8th Cavalry; the 2d Battalion, 12th Cavalry; Company B, 1st Battalion, 8th Cavalry; the 105-mm. towed howitzers of the 2d Battalion, 19th Artillery, and of Battery B, 2d Battalion, 17th Artillery; and the gunships of Battery A, 2d Battalion, 20th Artillery. Hueys of the 1st Squadron, 9th Cavalry, provided reconnaissance. The 1st Battalion, 12th Cavalry, acted initially as brigade reserve.[24]

General Kinnard

Clark's men achieved little at first. On 27 October the 2d of the 8th Cavalry searched an area three to four kilometers north of Plei Me, while the 1st of the 9th Cavalry screened to the west. Neither unit found any North Vietnamese. The pattern held for the next four days, as the number of air assaults and artillery moves rapidly climbed.[25]

This rise in the use of helicopters put huge demands on aviation fuel, or JP–4. The division's inability to meet that demand almost ended the Pleiku campaign before it began. On 27 October Kinnard requested resupply assistance from the Air Force, but by the following evening the situation had not improved. Instead, Larsen's headquarters informed MACV that the fuel situation in the highlands was "critical."[26]

On 28 October Kinnard put the matter in the hands of his assistant division commander for operations, Brig. Gen. Richard T. Knowles, who was now running the campaign from the division's forward command post in Pleiku City. Knowles contacted General Norton, the deputy commander of U.S. Army, Vietnam, to inform him that the cavalry division had only enough fuel to return the troops in the field to base and that, unless given firm

---

[23] AAR, Pleiku Campaign, 1st Cav Div, p. 29; Alexander S. Cochran, Jr., with Harry W. O. Kinnard, "First Strike at River Drang," *Military History* 1 (October 1984): 48 (quotation).

[24] AAR, Pleiku Campaign, 1st Cav Div, pp. 30, 33.

[25] Ibid., pp. 30–44.

[26] Ray L. Bowers, *Tactical Airlift*, United States Air Force in Southeast Asia (Washington, D.C: Office of Air Force History, United States Air Force, 1983), p. 213.

assurances of immediate resupply, he would have to terminate the campaign. In response, with MACV's approval, Norton arranged for the Air Force to make the delivery of JP–4 to the highlands its first priority. That night, Air Force C–130s began to shuttle empty 500-gallon collapsible fuel containers from Pleiku to Tan Son Nhut for refilling and return the next day. Even so, consumption continued to outpace supply, with the result that by the evening of the twenty-ninth there was again no fuel at Pleiku. Over the next three days, however, a continuous stream of C–130s was ferrying fuel both to Pleiku and to the airfield serving as the 1st Brigade's forward command post, which by then was located at STADIUM some fifteen kilometers southwest of Pleiku near the Catecka Tea Plantation. By 1 November fuel deliveries were running at about three-quarters of the amount Kinnard thought necessary for the division, hardly as much as he wanted but enough to keep things going.[27]

While the cavalry division secured its supply lines, the enemy continued to leave Plei Me. Between 24 and 28 October the *32d Regiment*, undetected by the Americans, pulled back toward the *B3 Front* headquarters near Cambodia. The *33d Regiment*'s withdrawal began on the morning of the twenty-sixth. Its move was more troubled than its sister regiment's and its cohesion more difficult to maintain, because by then Kinnard had begun positioning his troops in the general area of the unit's retreat. By 1 November, nevertheless, the *33d*'s headquarters group had reached its destination on the eastern edge of the Chu Pong Massif.

During the early segments of the enemy's withdrawal, Colonel Clark's force made little progress in finding large bodies of North Vietnamese. That began to change on 1 November, when Maj. Robert B. Zion's Troop B, 1st of the 9th Cavalry, conducted a reconnaissance and screening mission along the southern boundary of the 1st Cavalry Division's area of operations. Just before 0800, about eleven kilometers southwest of Plei Me, the unit's scout helicopters spotted several enemy soldiers. Major Zion sent his rifle platoon to investigate; his men took a small group under fire, killing 5 and capturing 4. Continuing on, they encountered a larger group near a streambed and in the firefight that followed killed 15 and captured 15. The North Vietnamese had apparently decided to stand and fight because they were guarding the *33d Regiment*'s medical aid station. With no more enemy in sight, the commander of the 1st of the 9th Cavalry, Lt. Col. John B. Stockton, directed Troop B to secure the area so that he could evacuate the prisoners, weapons, and medical equipment taken in the raid. These tasks occupied his helicopters for the rest of the morning and the early afternoon, during which time a number of senior officers—including Colonel Mataxis and Generals Vinh Loc, Larsen, and Knowles—visited the battle site.[28]

---

[27] Ibid., p. 214; Coleman, *Pleiku*, pp. 107–08.
[28] Daily Jnl, 1st Sqdn, 9th Cav, 1 Nov 65, Historians files, CMH; AAR, Pleiku Campaign, 1st Cav Div, p. 45; Kinnard, "Victory in the Ia Drang," p. 78.

Meanwhile, scout helicopters continued to search for the North Vietnamese. At 1410 they observed a large group of enemy soldiers, possibly all or part of the *33d Regiment*'s rearguard battalion, advancing from the northeast toward the aid station. Assuming that they intended to recapture the position, Colonel Stockton requested assistance from Colonel Clark, who at the moment had none to give. Moving quickly, Stockton ordered the two rifle platoons from Troops A and C to reinforce the area under threat. Helicopter gunships stopped the enemy's advance for a time, but the North Vietnamese soon recovered, launching an attack and flanking movement. "All we could do," one American infantryman said, "was dig in and shoot back." Then the rifle platoons arrived. Troop A's put down near the aid station, while Troop C's came in some fifteen hundred meters to the southwest. In the end, however, gunships firing on the enemy troops attempting to flank the American position made all the difference. Relieving some of the pressure on Troop B, they gave the troopers the space they needed to repel the direct assault.[29]

Around 1500 the first of Clark's brigade reinforcements, a platoon from the 2d Battalion, 8th Cavalry, reached the aid station, followed by the reconnaissance platoon of the 1st Battalion, 12th Cavalry, and a platoon from the 2d Battalion, 12th Cavalry. With six platoons at his command Stockton divided his force into two parts, one containing the units from the cavalry squadron and the other the three infantry platoons. He ordered the infantry to counterattack, a move that left the North Vietnamese with no choice but to pull back since anything else would have exposed a flank. In withdrawing, they moved north to bypass the Americans and then west toward their destination near the border. When Colonel Ingram, the 2d of the 12th Cavalry commander, reached the aid station that afternoon, he assumed control of the units there, now including two more companies. He immediately allowed Stockton and his three platoons to return to base. Ingram and the remainder of the task force spent the night in the area, but when they attempted to renew contact with the enemy the next morning, they found no one.[30]

During the battle the North Vietnamese had suffered 99 killed and another 183 estimated killed. In addition, they had lost not only the aid station, with all of its equipment, medicine, and supplies, but also a trove of documents that included a map revealing their march and supply routes. The cavalry, for its part, had sustained 11 killed and 47 wounded. Seven helicopters were damaged.[31]

---

[29] Matthew Brennan, ed., *Headhunters: Stories From the 1st Squadron, 9th Cavalry, in Vietnam, 1965–1971* (Novato, Calif.: Presidio Press, 1987), p. 17 (quoted words); AAR, Pleiku Campaign, 1st Cav Div, p. 46; Coleman, *Pleiku*, pp. 117–29.

[30] AAR, Pleiku Campaign, 1st Cav Div, p. 45; Kinnard, "Victory in the Ia Drang," p. 78.

[31] AAR, Pleiku Campaign, 1st Cav Div, p. 46; Coleman, *Pleiku*, p. 129.

Men of the 1st Cavalry Division sweep the high ground after the action at Plei Me.

New Targets

Despite the violence, the fight at the aid station hardly represented the major encounter Kinnard sought. Continuing to probe near Plei Me, the cavalry division's officers began to look for other possible targets and turned to the captured documents for suggestions. When an analysis of the map showed that a search of the region to the west toward Cambodia might bring results, Kinnard decided, as he put it, to "get something going close to the . . . border."[32]

The general soon had what he wanted. His 1st Squadron, 9th Cavalry, established night ambushes along trails, footpaths, and other locations that the North Vietnamese would probably use as they withdrew from Plei Me. On the night of 3–4 November the rifle platoons of Troops A, B, and C, under the command of Major Zion, and a CIDG team moved by helicopter to Landing Zone MARY just north of the Chu Pong Massif. There they established a base and laid three ambushes—to the northwest of MARY, manned by the CIDG team; and to the north and south, manned by troops from the reconnaissance squadron. Company A, 1st Battalion, 8th Cavalry, part of the division reserves, held at Duc Co, ready to bolster the force if General Knowles thought it necessary.[33]

[32] AAR, Pleiku Campaign, 1st Cav Div, p. 48.

[33] Ibid., p. 58; MFR, Lt Col John B. Stockton, 6 Nov 65, sub: Drang River Ambush, and Intervs, author with Lt Gen Richard T. Knowles, 20 Aug 96, and with Maj Gen John

At 1930, to the surprise of the Americans, a North Vietnamese column moving east instead of west approached the kill zone of the southernmost ambush site. About a company in strength, the troops chattered among themselves and made no effort to move quietly because they apparently believed that they were on a safe trail. Given their direction of march, they were most likely recent infiltrators from North Vietnam rather than part of the force withdrawing from Plei Me. About a hundred meters before reaching the ambush, they stopped to eat. After the break, they resumed their march. The American commander, Capt. Charles S. Knowlen, triggered the ambush after about ninety of them had passed by. Claymore mines, set along a hundred-meter kill zone, "belched fire and steel and troopers blazed away with M16's for two minutes."[34] Many of the enemy were killed or wounded. Realizing that the force he had attacked was larger than his own, Captain Knowlen quickly returned to Landing Zone MARY. Major Zion also ordered the troops at the northern ambush site to return to base, but he directed the CIDG team to hold in place temporarily, lest his own men fire accidentally on the mostly Vietnamese group.[35]

By 2200 Major Zion had his entire force back within the confines of MARY. They arrived just ahead of the North Vietnamese, who launched an immediate attack with two or three companies. Firepower provided by gunships helped repel the assault, but when the enemy came on a second time, Zion found his unit hard pressed. At 2315 he informed Colonel Stockton that if he was not "immediately reinforced his force would be over-run."[36]

Considering the situation an emergency, Colonel Stockton took it upon himself to order the reserves at Duc Co to deploy, contrary to an order from General Knowles that the force was not to be committed without his permission.[37] The first platoon to reach MARY was in combat by 0040 and the rest of the company by 0245. The new men turned the tide. With the perimeter of the base strengthened, Zion's troops turned back third and fourth assaults, prompting the North Vietnamese to withdraw. By first light, all enemy fire had ceased except for occasional sniping from the trees. Although Zion's men would search the area for the next half day, they would find nothing. The enemy had gone.[38]

A. Hemphill, 23 Aug 96, Historians files, CMH. Hemphill was the operations officer at the 1st Cavalry Division's forward command post at Pleiku.

[34] AAR, Pleiku Campaign, 1st Cav Div, p. 51.

[35] Account by Capt Theodore S. Danielson, CO, Co A, 1st Bn, 8th Cav, in Mertel, *1st Air Cavalry in the Highlands*, pp. 124–25.

[36] AAR, Pleiku Campaign, 1st Cav Div, p. 51; MFR (quotation), Stockton, 6 Nov 65, sub: Drang River Ambush.

[37] Interv, author with Knowles, 20 Aug 96; Daily Jnl, 1st Sqdn, 9th Cav, 4 Nov 65; MFR, Stockton, 6 Nov 65, sub: Drang River Ambush.

[38] Account by Danielson, in Mertel, *1st Air Cavalry in the Highlands*, pp. 126, 128–30.

The action on the night of 3–4 November revealed a number of important developments. The reconnaissance squadron had set and sprung a deadly ambush. Then, when the enemy had counterattacked, U.S. forces had reinforced under heavy fire at night, a difficult task previously done only in training. The movement of reinforcements by helicopter across twenty kilometers of roadless jungle demonstrated that the division was not bound by, in Kinnard's phrase, the "tyranny of terrain."[39] Four Americans had died and 25 were wounded in the encounter, but the Americans had killed 72 North Vietnamese and believed they had accounted for another 24. Those killed belonged to the *66th's 8th Battalion*, confirming that North Vietnamese main force units were in the area and that a new regiment—the *66th*—was operating near the Chu Pong Massif. Although the badly bloodied unit made a tempting target for pursuit, Colonel Clark decided against it. There was ample evidence, he told General Knowles, that North Vietnamese units were present in force near the aid station. A move far to the west would risk overextending the 1st Brigade. Knowles reluctantly accepted Clark's reasoning.[40]

Events on 6 November appear to have justified the colonel's caution. Early that morning Company B, 2d Battalion, 8th Cavalry, began searching an area about ten kilometers west of Plei Me. The unit split into three platoon-size forces. The first patrolled to the west and then the southwest, the second searched to the south and southwest, and the third remained at the company base. The first encountered enemy fire around 1000, but as the Americans advanced, their opponents withdrew. A short while later the second also received fire, and once more the enemy broke contact. Over the next two hours intermittent firing occurred between the two forces, growing in intensity as the American units attempted to move toward one another in hopes of catching the North Vietnamese in between. As the day progressed, however, the Americans realized that their quarry was but the flanking element of a larger force occupying well-prepared positions on nearby high ground. Under increasing fire from above, they began to fear encirclement themselves.[41]

Shortly after the noon hour the commander of the 2d of the 8th Cavalry, Lt. Col. James H. Nix, ordered Company C, operating several kilometers west of Company B, to reinforce its sister unit. Reaching the battle area on foot around 1300 and intending to attack the enemy's left rear, Company C charged across a stream and then up a ridge. The

---

[39] As quoted in Harry Maurer, comp., *Strange Ground: An Oral History of Americans in Vietnam, 1945–1975* (New York: Avon Books, 1989), p. 139.

[40] MFR, Stockton, 6 Nov 65, sub: Drang River Ambush; Interv, author with Knowles, 20 Aug 96; AAR, Pleiku Campaign, 1st Cav Div, pp. 52, 55; Coleman, *Pleiku,* pp. 152, 154.

[41] Coleman, *Pleiku,* p. 164.

North Vietnamese waited until the Americans were within range and then opened up with deadly fire, killing 17 riflemen. Despite the heavy casualties, the attack served its purpose. The pressure on Company B eased.[42]

As the afternoon lengthened, the clash settled into an odd stalemate. Instead of disappearing as usual, the enemy stayed and kept the Americans under fire. Neither side seemed able to maneuver against the other. Upon approach of darkness the North Vietnamese departed, leaving behind a covering force to harass the Americans. By 1900 the fighting had died down enough for Companies B and C to establish a common perimeter. Two platoons from Company A then arrived, along with helicopters to remove the dead and wounded. In all, 26 had been killed and another 53 wounded, the heaviest American toll thus far in the campaign. The unit those troops had fought was later identified as part of the *33d Regiment*. It, too, had suffered heavily—77 dead by body count and another 121 estimated killed.[43]

With Colonel Clark's brigade all but spent, General Kinnard decided to replace it with Col. Thomas W. Brown's 3d Brigade. The 1st Brigade yielded formal control of its mission at 1100 on 9 November, but the actual changeover occurred between the seventh and twelfth, when units in the field left for An Khe while fresh troops took their place. The 1st Battalion, 8th Cavalry, returned first, on the seventh. The 2d Battalion, 8th Cavalry, followed on the eighth, passing its responsibilities to Lt. Col. Harold G. Moore's 1st Battalion, 7th Cavalry, which moved directly to a search area east of Plei Me. When the 2d Battalion, 12th Cavalry, pulled back on the eleventh, Lt. Col. Robert B. Tully's 2d Battalion, 5th Cavalry, helicoptered to a search area due north of Colonel Moore's. Finally, on the twelfth, the 1st Battalion, 12th Cavalry, and the 2d Battalion, 19th Artillery, both returned to An Khe, while Lt. Col. Robert A. McDade's 2d Battalion, 7th Cavalry, moved to a search area south of Plei Me. On the same day the 1st Battalion, 21st Artillery, commanded by Lt. Col. Robert M. Short, flew in to provide support.[44] With fresh troops in place, the 1st Cavalry Division was ready for anything. It did not have long to wait.

[42] Ibid., p. 169; AAR, Pleiku Campaign, 1st Cav Div, p. 68.
[43] AAR, Pleiku Campaign, 1st Cav Div, pp. 60–63.
[44] Ibid., pp. 63–78; Kinnard, "Victory in the Ia Drang," p. 84.

6

The Pleiku Campaign

On 12 November General Larsen visited General Knowles at the 1st Cavalry Division's forward command post at Pleiku City. The division's primary task, Larsen reminded Knowles, was to find and destroy enemy main forces, which Knowles took to mean that his units should be searching in new areas. A short while later, meeting in the field with two of his commanders, Colonel Brown of the 3d Brigade and Colonel Moore of the 1st of the 7th Cavalry, Knowles told them to look west toward the Ia Drang Valley, a rugged notch north of the Chu Pong Massif near Cambodia. Fresh intelligence suggested that an enemy base camp might be concealed in the thick jungle there.[1]

With Knowles' instructions in hand, the 3d Brigade's Operations Section, under Maj. Henri G. Mallet, established three new search areas— Maroon, Bronze, and Lime—to the west of Plei Me, extending progressively toward the Cambodian border. The last one, Lime, jutted into the Chu Pong Massif itself. Each of Brown's three battalions would be responsible for one area, with Moore's 1st of the 7th Cavalry taking the lead. The rest of the brigade, at least initially, would supply firepower to back the troops on the ground, screen the firebases supporting the operation, or stand by in reserve.[2]

On the afternoon of 13 November Colonel Moore received orders at his Plei Me bivouac to prepare his battalion for an air assault into Lime on the fourteenth, followed by a two-day search of the Ia Drang Valley. Fire support would come from two 105-mm. howitzer batteries. During the next several hours the battalion staff planned the operation. Moore, however, postponed selecting a site for the assault until the morning of the fourteenth, Sunday, when he intended to conduct an air reconnais-

---

[1] Coleman, *Pleiku*, p. 181; Harold G. Moore and Joseph L. Galloway, *We Were Soldiers Once . . . and Young. Ia Drang: The Battle That Changed the War in Vietnam* (New York: Random House, 1992), p. 33; Ltrs, Col Thomas W. Brown and Maj Henri G. Mallet to Capt John A. Cash, 8 and 25 Aug 67, box 16, 74/053, RG 319, NARA; Interv, author with Knowles, 20 Aug 96, and AAR, Ia Drang Valley Opn, 1st Bn, 7th Cav, 9 Dec 65, p. 1, Historians files, CMH.

[2] Coleman, *Pleiku*, pp. 183–84.

sance of possible landing zones. Only then would he make his choice and issue orders.[3]

Before retiring, Moore pondered the next day's prospects. Convinced that North Vietnamese main force units were in the Chu Pong area and that combat was a distinct possibility, he tallied both his assets and the liabilities weighing against his battalion. On the positive side were the men—well trained, well motivated, and well armed. Most soldiers would carry the M16 rifle, although some would be armed with 40-mm. M79 grenade launchers, and each platoon would be equipped with at least two M60 machine guns. In addition to weapons, the individual soldier carried a single meal, a poncho, two canteens of water, salt tablets, and "plenty of ammunition." To Moore, ammunition and water were the critical items; anything else could be supplied by helicopters as needed. What constituted "plenty of ammunition" would broaden as the war went on, but under Moore each trooper would land with two twenty-round magazines, one in his rifle and one in reserve, plus an ammunition bag with a minimum of two hundred sixty rounds. Moore was determined that the troopers go into battle as light as possible, for an unburdened soldier could more easily and effectively pursue and fight than one carrying the traditional combat load of sixty-five pounds or more.[4]

Although the men of the 1st Cavalry Division had trained long and hard, most had never seen combat. In addition, Colonel Moore had only 431 of a possible 633 men available. The rest were sick with malaria, away on some administrative or guard detail at the base camp, or unavailable because their enlistments were about to expire. Even more troubling was the limited number of helicopters assigned to ferry his men into the valley—only sixteen out of the division's inventory of over four hundred. Their higher-than-anticipated use during the division's first weeks in Vietnam had exacerbated an already extant spare parts shortage, and many were grounded. The disturbing implication for air assaults was that American commanders would have to shuttle troops to battle rather than moving them in a single lift.

As for the aircraft themselves, the very latest UH–1D Hueys, they could technically carry eight infantrymen with combat loads. But because the thin air of the highlands reduced engine efficiency, no more than five could be accommodated during the operation in the Ia Drang Valley. This meant that no more than eighty men would be on the landing zone after the first flight. Given the turnaround time of up to thirty minutes between landings, these men would be on their own for at least half an hour.[5]

[3] AAR, Ia Drang Valley Opn, 1st Bn, 7th Cav, pp. 1–2; Ltr, Brown to Cash, 8 Aug 67.

[4] AAR, Ia Drang Valley Opn, 1st Bn, 7th Cav, pp. 16–17; Moore and Galloway, *We Were Soldiers Once*, p. 57; Interv (quoted words), author with Lt Gen Harold G. Moore, 7 Jul 98, Historians files, CMH; Shelby L. Stanton, *Anatomy of a Division: The 1st Cav in Vietnam* (Novato, Calif.: Presidio Press, 1987), pp. 197–98.

[5] Meyerson, "Logistics in the Vietnam Conflict," ch. 4, CMH; Moore and Galloway, *We Were Soldiers Once*, p. 39.

Realizing that he could do little about either the shortfall in troops or the lack of helicopters, Moore directed his energies to dealing with the dangers before his men. To minimize the perils confronting the first troops to reach the landing zone, he decided to ride in the first helicopter himself and land with the initial wave, affording him a final opportunity to abort the mission. He also planned to station his command helicopter, with his operations officer and fire-support team on board, directly above the landing zone so that if an emergency arose artillery, gunships, and fighter-bombers could be called in without delay. Finally, he selected an unorthodox procedure for securing the landing zone. The standard approach called for the lead assault elements to secure 360 degrees of the zone's perimeter, a sensible course of action provided the rest of a battalion arrived right behind the initial lift or if the turnaround time for the second lift was considerably less than thirty minutes. Since neither of these conditions would be the case in the Ia Drang Valley, Moore arranged for the troops in the first lift to fan out into the surrounding terrain, while those immediately following would remain on the landing zone in reserve. If one of the squads scouting the area encountered opposition, Moore later wrote, "I could then shift the rest of the company in that direction and carry the fight to the enemy well off the landing zone." Colonel Brown approved the plan.[6]

While planning continued, the units of the 3d Brigade carried out their missions. On 13 November Moore's 1st of the 7th Cavalry helicoptered to positions south and southwest of Plei Me, set up patrol bases, and searched the area. At the same time, Colonel Tully's 2d Battalion, 5th Cavalry, deployed to BRONZE, where it established an artillery base for the 1st Battalion, 21st Artillery, at Landing Zone FALCON. Colonel McDade's 2d Battalion, 7th Cavalry, continued without success its probe for the enemy south of Plei Me, and the division reconnaissance squadron, the 1st of the 9th Cavalry, maintained its screen to the northwest on the brigade's flanks.[7]

Before the Assault

Aerial reconnaissance began shortly after first light on the morning of 14 November. Colonel Moore and six key officers were aboard two Hueys, flying over the Ia Drang Valley at a height of forty-five hundred feet. Two gunships were close by. To conceal the flight's purpose from enemy observers, the four helicopters flew southwest from Plei Me to a point south of the Chu Pong Massif and then overflew the valley by turning north and heading for the Special Forces camp at Duc Co. After

---

[6] Moore and Galloway, *We Were Soldiers Once*, p. 41 (quotation); Ltr, Brown to Cash, 8 Aug 67.

[7] AAR, Pleiku Campaign, 1st Cav Div (Ambl), 4 Mar 66, p. 81, box 10, 67A/5216, RG 319, NARA.

loitering around Duc Co for five minutes, they reversed their route for a second look at the target zone and then returned to Plei Me.

Moore's reconnaissance turned up three potential landing zones: TANGO, X-RAY, and YANKEE. Initially, YANKEE appeared to be the best, although it was a short distance south of LIME's boundary. TANGO had the advantage of being in the middle of the Ia Drang Valley, but the area was so small that only four helicopters could land at a time and the surrounding trees were so tall that rapid descent would be impossible, making the helicopters easy targets. In contrast, X-RAY was flat, was surrounded by only short trees, and could accommodate at least eight helicopters at once. Moore tentatively decided on X-RAY, but he wanted one more look. Sending observers in OH–13 Sioux scout helicopters on a fast close-to-the-earth reconnaissance of both YANKEE and X-RAY, he learned that old tree stumps covered YANKEE and that X-RAY could in fact take as many as ten helicopters. In addition, the scouts observed a wire running east to west on a trail just north of X-RAY. Presumably a communications line, it was strong evidence that the enemy was nearby. X-RAY's landing capacity and proximity to the enemy made it Moore's logical choice (*see Map 8*).[8]

At 0845 Colonel Moore issued his operations order and briefed his commanders. According to intelligence, a North Vietnamese battalion might be operating along the lower reaches of the Chu Pong Massif about four kilometers northwest of X-RAY. A second might be in the immediate vicinity of the landing zone, and an enemy base might be less than three kilometers to the northeast.[9]

Moore went on to explain how he expected events to unfold. A half hour before touchdown, artillery at Landing Zone FALCON, about nine kilometers east of X-RAY, would pound Landing Zones YANKEE and TANGO for eight minutes to create a diversion. Then for the next twenty minutes the guns would turn on X-RAY. In a carefully timed sequence beginning just one minute before the first wave of troops arrived, helicopter gunships would fire into the area surrounding the landing zone. The sixteen troop-carrying helicopters would descend on X-RAY, with the battalion command group riding the lead helicopter. The assault element, Capt. John D. Herren's Company B (-), would follow directly behind. Once on the ground Captain Herren would send out four patrols while the rest of his men assembled at the landing zone in a strike formation. The remainder of Company B and part of Capt. Ramon A. Nadal II's Company A would arrive in the second lift. Taking up station along the northern and northeastern segments of X-RAY's perimeter, they would move to the east and northeast. In subsequent

---

[8] AAR, Ia Drang Valley Opn, 1st Bn, 7th Cav, pp. 2–3; Moore and Galloway, *We Were Soldiers Once*, pp. 56–57.

[9] AAR, Ia Drang Valley Opn, 1st Bn, 7th Cav, tab C, p. [1]; Interv, author with Lt Gen Harold G. Moore, 19 Aug 96, Historians files, CMH.

lifts the rest of Company A and then Companies C and D, in sequence, would land. Capt. Robert H. Edwards' Company C would not only assume the role of battalion reserve but also prepare to move west and northwest to search portions of the Chu Pong Massif. Capt. Louis R. Lefebvre's Company D would arrive last, assume C's reserve role, and take charge of providing mortar support if a fight developed. Moore finished his briefing at 0915 and set 1030 as the arrival time for the first helicopter at X-Ray.[10]

The Fight at X-Ray

Bright sun and clear skies greeted the men of the 1st Battalion, 7th Cavalry, as they climbed aboard their Hueys on 14 November. The next two days would be the same. The northeast monsoon was in full swing, dropping rain on the coast, but leaving the highlands dry. Daytime temperatures would range from the mid-seventies to mid-eighties Fahrenheit. The moon each night would be bright.[11]

The terrain at X-Ray was less encouraging. The immediate landing zone was about one hundred meters long, east to west, and roughly funnel-shaped. The ninety-meter-wide mouth of the funnel lay to the west near a dry creek bed that ran along the clearing's western edge. Colonel Moore would establish his command post in a grove of trees toward the middle of the open area, near a ten-foot-tall termite mound. The trees and grass were especially thick along the western edge of X-Ray, where they extended off into the jungle-clad foothills that led toward the Chu Pong Massif. For men in foxholes, the grass severely limited observation. Additionally, the vegetation at the base of the massif and the high grass near X-Ray would allow the enemy to approach undetected.[12]

Unknown to Colonel Moore, the *7th* and *9th Battalions, 66th PAVN Regiment*, and a composite battalion of the *33d PAVN Regiment* had massed in the vicinity of the Chu Pong and were on a ridge above X-Ray. Although some of these units had been bloodied in the fighting around Plei Me and had fled westward with the 1st Cavalry Division in pursuit, they still constituted a substantial force—up to sixteen hundred troops—and were well positioned to attack. In addition, the *32d PAVN Regiment*, the *H15 Local Force Battalion*, and the *66th Regiment's 8th Battalion* stood nearby. Far from

[10] AAR, Ia Drang Valley Opn, 1st Bn, 7th Cav, p. 3.

[11] Ibid., pp. 2–3; Coleman, *Pleiku*, p. 193; Moore and Galloway, *We Were Soldiers Once*, p. 61.

[12] AAR, Ia Drang Valley Opn, 1st Bn, 7th Cav, p. 3; Capt Robert H. Edwards, "Operations of the 1st Battalion, 7th Cavalry, 1st Cavalry Division (Airmobile), in the Airmobile Assault of Landing Zone X-Ray, Ia Drang Valley, Republic of Vietnam, 14–16 November 1965: [The] Personal Experience of a Company Commander" (Fort Benning, Ga.: United States Army Infantry School, 1967), p. 7, copy in Historians files, CMH; Ltr, Capt Ramon A. Nadal II to Capt John A. Cash, 3 Oct 67, box 16, 74/053, RG 319, NARA.

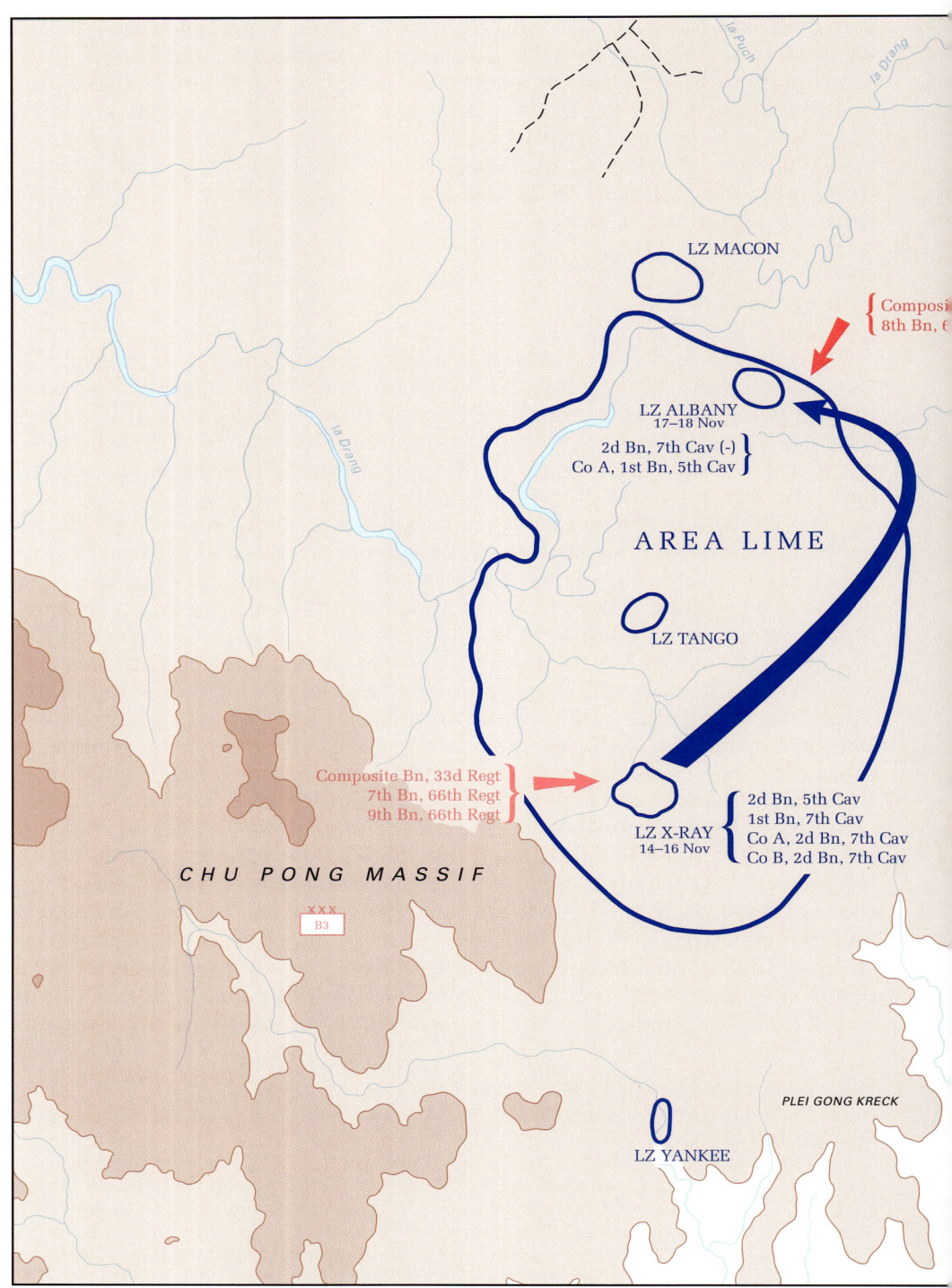

LZ MACON

Composi{
8th Bn, 6

LZ ALBANY
17–18 Nov

2d Bn, 7th Cav (-)}
Co A, 1st Bn, 5th Cav

AREA LIME

LZ TANGO

Composite Bn, 33d Regt}
7th Bn, 66th Regt
9th Bn, 66th Regt

2d Bn, 5th Cav
1st Bn, 7th Cav
Co A, 2d Bn, 7th Cav
Co B, 2d Bn, 7th Cav

LZ X-RAY
14–16 Nov

CHU PONG MASSIF

x x x
B3

PLEI GONG KRECK

LZ YANKEE

Ia Puch

Ia Drang

Ia Drang

MAP 8

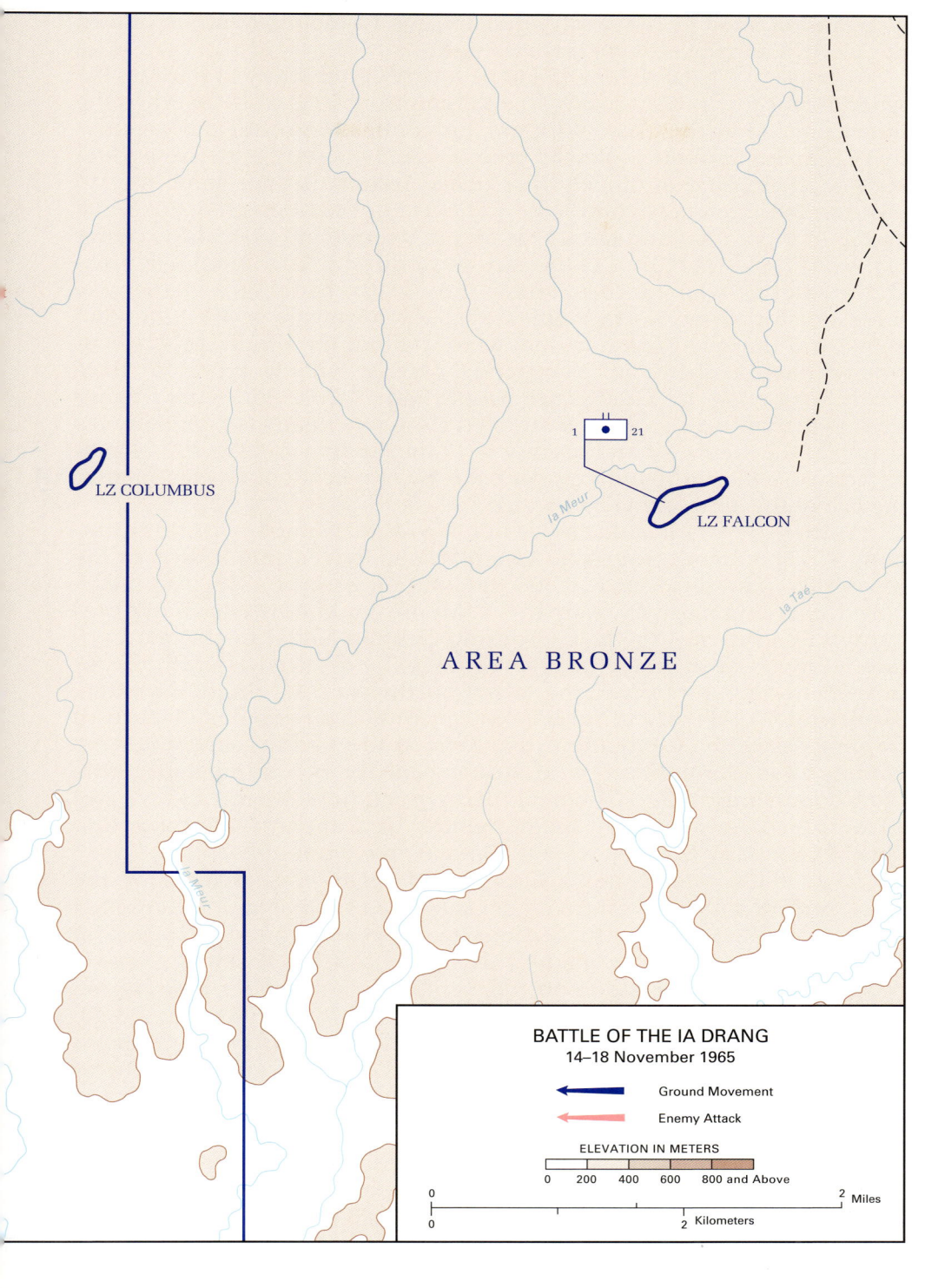

LZ COLUMBUS

1 [ ] 21

la Meur

LZ FALCON

la Tae

AREA BRONZE

la Meur

BATTLE OF THE IA DRANG
14–18 November 1965

Ground Movement

Enemy Attack

ELEVATION IN METERS

0   200   400   600   800 and Above

0   2 Miles

0   2 Kilometers

being intimidated by the cavalry division and its mobility and firepower, the North Vietnamese were ready to fight.

Because of a brief delay in placing an artillery battery at FALCON, the schedule for the first lift into X-RAY slipped from 1030 to 1048. When the time came, however, Colonel Moore, his command group, and seventy-five Company B troopers flew to their target. Swooping onto the landing zone, Captain Herren quickly dispatched reconnaissance some fifty to one hundred meters beyond X-RAY. The rest of the troops remained in a clump of high grass and trees near Moore's command post at the center of the position. At 1120 one of the patrols captured an enemy soldier, probably a deserter, who informed Moore through the battalion's Vietnamese translator that three North Vietnamese battalions were on the mountain above and that their commanders were spoiling for a fight. Moore considered the prisoner to be "a godsend," because what he reported "fit in neatly with what our intelligence people had told us." Since the circumstances demanded action, he instructed Herren to intensify Company B's search of the area west and northwest of the landing zone and to be prepared to use the entire unit to search the lower reaches of the massif after the last of the air assaults had ended.[13]

As these developments played out, the rest of Company B, plus Company A's command group and one platoon, arrived unopposed in the second lift. The third lift reached the landing zone at 1210, also unopposed, carrying more of Company A. Moore could now use all of Company B in a full-scale search. Ordering Captain Nadal to assume Captain Herren's mission as the reserve force, he directed Herren to continue his searching by moving to the northwest up a fingerlike ridge. Meanwhile, Company A soldiers began probes as soon as enough of Captain Edwards' Company C had arrived to provide security for the landing zone. Throughout the afternoon helicopters continued to shuttle the troopers into X-RAY. The next lift, arriving in two parts at 1332 and 1338, respectively, brought the remainder of Company A and the first part of Company C. They were the last to arrive unopposed.[14]

At 1230 Captain Herren's Company B began its search. Using the creek bed on X-RAY's western edge as its line of departure, it deployed with two platoons forward and one to the rear. Around 1245 the 1st Platoon, the lead unit on the left, was pinned down by sniper fire on both flanks. The 2d Platoon on the right also came under fire. Herren wanted the 2d Platoon to assist the other, but its commander, 2d Lt. Henry T. Herrick, had just spotted enemy soldiers to his front and wanted to chase them down. Captain Herren approved, but warned the officer to "be careful because I don't want you to get pinned down or sucked into anything." As Lieutenant Herrick's men gave chase, however, they

---

[13] AARs, Pleiku Campaign, 1st Cav Div, p. 85, and Ia Drang Valley Opn, 1st Bn, 7th Cav, p. 4; Moore and Galloway, *We Were Soldiers Once*, pp. 51, 63 (quotation).

[14] AAR, Ia Drang Valley Opn, 1st Bn, 7th Cav, p. 4.

Soldiers advance through the elephant grass at X-RAY.

drew away from the rest of the company. Running into heavy fire, they were soon cut off. By 1330 Herren's Company B was fully engaged. He radioed Colonel Moore and then tried to organize his men so that they would not be overrun.[15]

Moore realized that his battalion was in danger. He believed that the North Vietnamese would try to push through to his command post by attacking Company B's left flank as its remaining two platoons turned to the northwest in an effort to save Herrick. To foreclose that possibility, he committed the landing zone strike force, Captain Nadal's Company A, to the fight. The original plan was "out the window," he told Nadal. Company A had to get close to Company B and protect its left, as well as to send a platoon to help Herrick. Moore also decided to use newly arrived portions of Captain Edwards' Company C that had just landed to the south and southwest of X-RAY to block any attempt to flank Nadal and overrun the landing zone.[16]

Now came the most critical period of the afternoon. With an estimated seventy-five to one hundred enemy soldiers assailing Herrick's 2d Platoon, Captain Herren's other two platoons moved in to break the attack. Two hundred meters behind, Nadal's 2d Platoon, commanded by 2d Lt. Walter J. Marm, moved off the landing zone to join them. By

[15] Interv (quotation), Capt John A. Cash with Capt John D. Herren, 21 Aug 67, box 16, 74/053, RG 319, NARA; Moore and Galloway, *We Were Soldiers Once*, p. 72.

[16] Moore and Galloway, *We Were Soldiers Once*, p. 64 (quoted words); AAR, Ia Drang Valley Opn, 1st Bn, 7th Cav, p. 4.

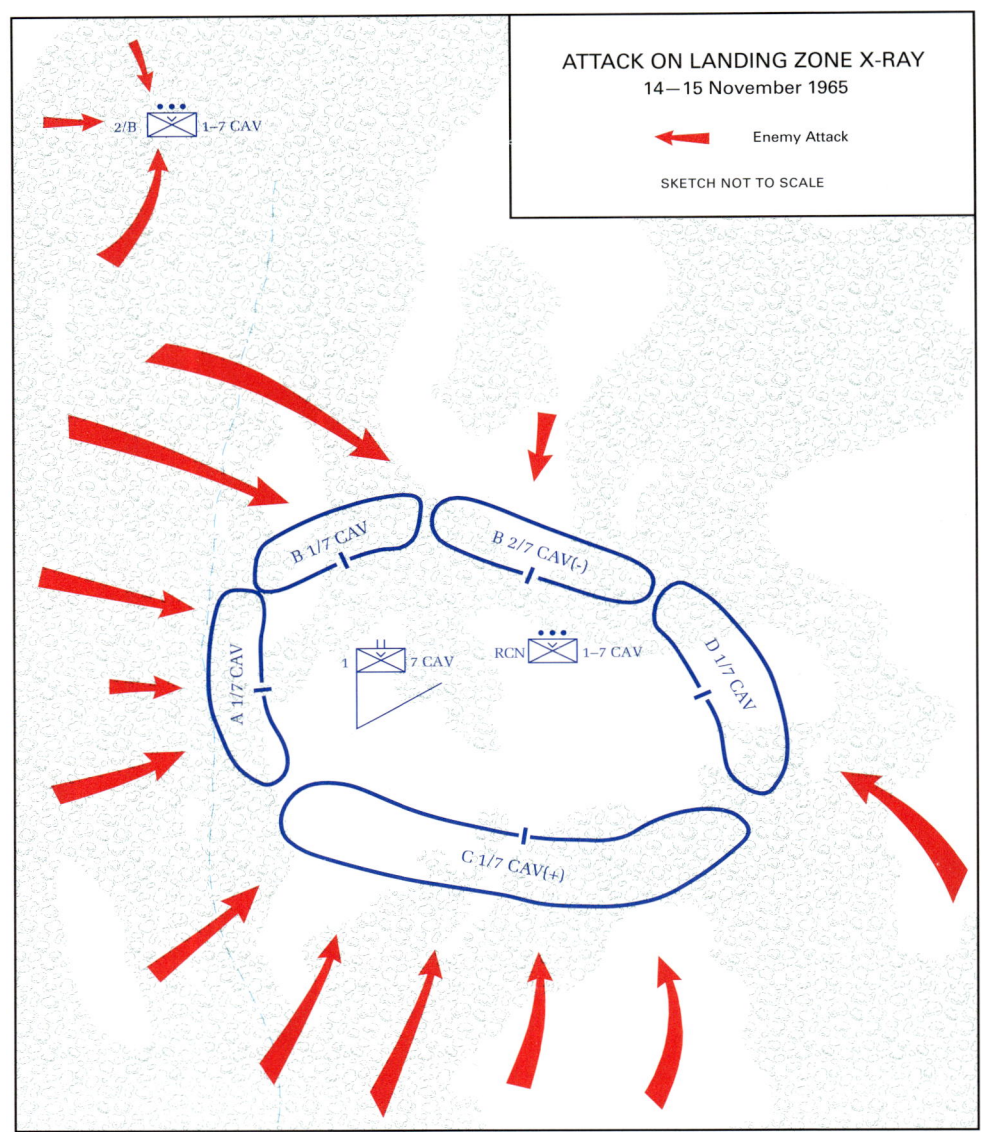

ATTACK ON LANDING ZONE X-RAY
14—15 November 1965

← Enemy Attack

SKETCH NOT TO SCALE

2/B ⊠ 1–7 CAV

B 1/7 CAV

B 2/7 CAV(-)

A 1/7 CAV

1 ⊠ 7 CAV

RCN ⊠ 1–7 CAV

D 1/7 CAV

C 1/7 CAV(+)

MAP 9

then, however, the North Vietnamese had enveloped Herrick's unit. Intending also to encircle Company B's approaching platoons, they apparently failed to notice Lieutenant Marm's men, who decimated them
as they charged past. Hard hit but undeterred, the North Vietnamese
used the nearby creek bed as a footpath to continue their advance upon
Company B's rear. But they were now close to Company A's other two

platoons, which were hunkered down in positions just east of the creek bed. Nadal's men picked off the lead soldiers as they came within range. Although they were in a strong position to delay the enemy, the firefight made it impossible for Marm's platoon to link up with Company B. To make matters worse, Company B's two platoons were unable to reach Herrick. They were a mere seventy-five meters from the beleaguered platoon, but Moore had no choice but to order them back because the remainder of Company B had taken so many casualties. Herren and his men drifted back toward the creek bed, where they took up position on Company A's right. The time was roughly 1430 (*Map 9*).[17]

From the moment he had landed at X-Ray Colonel Moore believed that if an enemy attack occurred, it would come from the west, the southwest, or both. Thus, as a precaution, after ordering Company B to rescue Herrick's platoon and Company A (-) to move off the clearing to protect B's left flank, he also instructed Captain Edwards and part of his Company C, just then arriving in the fourth lift, to deploy directly to positions south and southwest of the landing zone. There, they could protect both Nadal's left flank and the clearing itself from any assault coming off the massif. As Edwards moved his men into position, the North Vietnamese peppered them with machine gun fire and rocket-propelled grenades. It was a calculated risk for Moore. In ordering the move, he left his battalion without reserves and abandoned any attempt for the time being to guard the northern and eastern approaches to X-Ray.[18]

The fifth lift of sixteen helicopters arrived at 1442. Eight managed to reach X-Ray, dropping off most of the remainder of Company C before enemy gunfire forced Moore to wave off the remaining eight. Edwards pulled the new arrivals into his sector, and none too soon. Five minutes later, just as Moore had expected, a North Vietnamese force estimated to be around two hundred men attacked from the southwest. The Americans laid down a barrage of small-arms and machine gun fire and called in artillery and air support, inflicting heavy casualties. Edwards informed Moore that his company was locked in a heavy fight but was still in good shape, which was not the case for the enemy. Around 1615, withered by the onslaught, the North Vietnamese withdrew in disarray.[19]

One of the eight helicopters, carrying the lead elements of Captain Lefebvre's Company D, arrived just as the North Vietnamese attempted to puncture the perimeter that Nadal's and Edwards' companies had formed. With two of Nadal's machine gun crews providing cover, Lefebvre and four other men jumped from the helicopter and ran west

---

[17] AAR, Ia Drang Valley Opn, 1st Bn, 7th Cav, p. 5; Ltr, Nadal to Cash, 3 Oct 67; Interv, Cash with Herren, 21 Aug 67.

[18] Moore and Galloway, *We Were Soldiers Once*, pp. 61, 72–73; Interv, Capt John A. Cash with Capt Robert H. Edwards, n.d., box 16, 74/053, RG 319, NARA.

[19] Edwards, "Personal Experience of a Company Commander," p. 16; AAR, Ia Drang Valley Opn, 1st Bn, 7th Cav, p. 5; Moore and Galloway, *We Were Soldiers Once*, p. 103.

toward a fold in the ground directly in the path of the attack. Moments later they were joined by Herren and his radio operators, who had become separated from the rest of Company B while trying to find Colonel Moore. Although few in number, the group was in the right place at the right time. In the short fierce firefight that followed, one of Herren's men was killed and Captain Lefebvre wounded, but the Americans fought off the attack. If the enemy's advance had succeeded, it might very well have split Moore's already hard-pressed force.[20]

Shortly thereafter, around 1520, the rest of Company D and the battalion reconnaissance platoon arrived. Captain Edwards asked Moore to position Company D on his left to close his open flank. Moore agreed, ordering the company's acting commander, S. Sgt. George Gonzales, to move to the southern and southeastern edges of the open area. Moore also put the battalion reconnaissance platoon on the northern and eastern fringes of the clearing as a reserve. For the first time, he had the semblance of a complete perimeter and could begin to look beyond immediate survival.[21]

The first priority was to rescue Herrick's platoon. The unit's surviving members had established a small perimeter, twenty-five meters wide, in the middle of which they had placed their dead and wounded. By midafternoon Lieutenant Herrick was dead, as was the next in line to command, S. Sgt. Carl L. Palmer. 3d Squad leader S. Sgt. Clyde E. Savage was in charge. Although the platoon remained under almost constant fire, Sergeant Savage kept the enemy at bay by ringing his position with artillery fire, some shells bursting as close as twenty meters.

Moore prepared a coordinated assault, casting two companies against an estimated enemy force of over two hundred. Company A and portions of Company B would carry out the mission, while Company C stayed at X-Ray to guard it from attack. Before starting, Moore had both assault companies withdraw to the landing zone under covering artillery fire. After bringing out their casualties for evacuation, the two would then have a chance to reorganize themselves before undertaking the rescue, which would commence around 1620.[22]

Supported by both tube and aerial rocket artillery fire, the assault began on schedule. Company A advanced on the left and Company B (-) on the right. Some fifty meters beyond the creek bed, which again formed a line of departure, the rescuers ran into well-entrenched enemy firing from concealed positions and from trees. The North Vietnamese worked

---

[20] Moore and Galloway, *We Were Soldiers Once*, p. 98; Ltr, Capt Louis R. Lefebvre to Capt John A. Cash, n.d., box 16, 74/053, RG 319, NARA; Interv, Cash with Herren, 21 Aug 67. See also AAR, Ia Drang Valley Opn, 1st Bn, 7th Cav, p. 5.

[21] Moore and Galloway, *We Were Soldiers Once*, pp. 114–15; Interv, author with Moore, 19 Aug 96.

[22] John A. Cash, "Fight at Ia Drang, 14–16 November 1965," in *Seven Firefights in Vietnam* by John A. Cash, John Albright, and Allan W. Sandstrum (Washington, D.C.: Office of the Chief of Military History, United States Army, 1970), p. 22.

their way inside the wall of artillery fire, closing with the advancing Americans.[23]

The rescuers were hit hard. Company B suffered 30 casualties while gaining less than one hundred meters. Company A surpassed B by fifty meters, but also suffered losses. Lieutenant Marm was one of the casualties. Finding his platoon's forward motion stopped by machine gun fire, he stood up and fired an M72 light antitank weapon, or LAW, to destroy the position. Machine gun bullets continued to fly, so Marm charged across the thirty meters that separated his platoon from the North Vietnamese, threw a hand grenade, and then shot those who ran from the blast. But Marm did not escape unscathed: He was shot in the face during his one-man charge and had to be evacuated. As the casualties mounted, Moore realized that he would have to suspend the rescue. At 1740 he ordered Herren and Nadal to pull back; they might be able to make another attempt during the night or the next morning. In the meantime, Moore made certain that Sergeant Savage had as much artillery support as he needed.[24]

Other pressing matters vied for Moore's attention. Heavy casualties and the unexpected size of the enemy force had prompted him to request an additional rifle company. It would arrive that evening, allowing the Americans to tighten their defenses and prepare for a night in hostile territory. Moore also needed more fire support and asked for almost continuous artillery and air strikes along the lower part of the massif, concentrating on the approaches to X-RAY.[25]

Colonel Brown, the brigade commander, knew that Moore would need even more reinforcements. He believed that the North Vietnamese would settle for nothing less than the utter destruction of Moore's force and that they had enough troops to do it. So he arranged to bring in the security element at STADIUM—Capt. Myron F. Diduryk's Company B, 2d Battalion, 7th Cavalry. Lacking helicopters to dispatch a larger force before nightfall, Brown never gave any consideration to sending one. He nonetheless anticipated a need for further reinforcements the next day by ordering Colonel Tully's 2d Battalion, 5th Cavalry, to assemble at Landing Zone VICTOR about three kilometers southeast of X-RAY. Meanwhile, the rest of Colonel McDade's 2d Battalion, 7th Cavalry, was to gather at Landing Zone MACON about four kilometers north of X-RAY. Brown also requested that General Kinnard assign another battalion to the brigade. The selected unit, Colonel Ackerson's 1st Battalion,

---

[23] Moore and Galloway, *We Were Soldiers Once*, p. 121; Boyle and Samabria, "Lure and Ambush," p. 13, box 16, 74/053, RG 319, NARA.

[24] Albert N. Garland, ed., *Infantry in Vietnam* (Fort Benning, Ga.: Infantry Magazine, 1967), p. 333; AAR, Ia Drang Valley Opn, 1st Bn, 7th Cav, p. 7; Edwards, "Personal Experience of a Company Commander," p. 19. For his actions that day Lieutenant Marm received the Medal of Honor. See Cash, "Fight at Ia Drang," pp. 23–24.

[25] Moore and Galloway, *We Were Soldiers Once*, p. 105; AAR, Ia Drang Valley Opn, 1st Bn, 7th Cav, pp. 13–15.

5th Cavalry, would begin arriving at STADIUM on the morning of the fifteenth.[26]

By 1700 the enemy's attacks on X-RAY had ceased, and the situation was calm enough to allow one hundred twenty men from Captain Diduryk's Company B to begin landing. Colonel Moore made the unit X-RAY's reserve. For the next two hours Moore organized his ragged line of defense into a more standard circular perimeter. Deciding that he had no need to keep an entire company in reserve at his command post, he assigned the job to the battalion reconnaissance platoon and moved Diduryk's men forward. He gave one of Diduryk's platoons to Captain Edwards to reinforce Company C's position in the southern and southeastern sectors—the largest share of the perimeter. Edwards placed the unit on his right flank, where it abutted Nadal's Company A positioned on a relatively small part of the line facing mostly west. Even farther to the right was the remainder of Herren's Company B, occupying a small portion of the perimeter's northern and northwestern sides. Diduryk's remaining two platoons came next, in positions on the north and somewhat to the northeast. Their left flank touched Herren's company, while their right flank adjoined Company D, now commanded by 1st Lt. James L. Litton. Lieutenant Litton's unit was the smallest of the companies present, but it had responsibility for a large portion of X-RAY's eastern perimeter.[27]

While the units guarding Moore's landing zone settled in for the night, helicopters delivered water, medical supplies, rations, and ammunition, and evacuated the dead and wounded. Water posed a special problem because the nearby streambed was dry, making the Americans totally dependent on what they could bring in. With no water to drink by midafternoon, some of the soldiers had eaten C-ration jam for its moisture content, while others had made their thirst even worse by drinking the salty water of their C-ration ham and lima beans. The water brought in that evening temporarily satisfied the Americans' need and was quickly consumed. By 1915 Moore's battalion seemed in reasonably good shape, having been reinforced to a strength of five companies. The afternoon's fighting had been the first taste of heavy combat for most of the troops present. Although tired, the men were satisfied that they had done well.[28]

During the night the North Vietnamese probed X-RAY but launched no major attacks. Consisting of five to ten soldiers each, the probes sought to locate American strongpoints by drawing automatic weapons fire,

[26] Ltrs, Brown and Mallet to Cash, 8 and 25 Aug 67.

[27] Capt Myron F. Diduryk, "[An Account of the Activities of Company B, 2d Battalion, 7th Cavalry, at Landing Zone X-RAY, 14–16 November 1965]," box 16, 74/053, RG 319, NARA; Cash, "Fight at Ia Drang," pp. 25–26; AAR, Ia Drang Valley Opn, 1st Bn, 7th Cav, maps.

[28] Interv, author with Moore, 7 Jul 98; Interv, author with Joseph L. Galloway, 7 Jul 98, Historians files, CMH. See also Meyerson, "Logistics in the Vietnam Conflict," ch. 4; Edwards, "Personal Experience of a Company Commander," p. 24.

Its load of supplies on the ground, a UH–1 Huey prepares to evacuate casualties of the X-RAY fighting.

but the men on the line maintained fire discipline, responding only with rifles and grenade launchers. To disrupt nighttime assaults before they began, the artillery batteries at FALCON pounded suspected enemy concentrations around the perimeter and on the mountain above, firing more than four thousand rounds of high explosives. The Air Force also bombed the area. A nighttime flight of A–1E Skyraiders, scrambled from Pleiku, hit the area beyond Captain Herren's sector, where a particularly strong probe was taking place. Meanwhile, a C–123 flare ship remained on station to illuminate the battlefield if necessary.

About three hundred meters northwest of the perimeter, Sergeant Savage's isolated platoon turned back three enemy attempts to overrun it. In support of the platoon, an Air Force AC–47 Spooky gunship expended twelve thousand rounds against the high ground just west of Savage.[29]

Still determined to rescue the platoon, Colonel Moore devised a new plan during the night. This time he would use all three companies. Herren's Company B would spearhead the assault at daybreak, followed by Moore and his command group; behind and to the right and left, Nadal's and Edwards' Companies A and C would protect the flanks and assist the main effort. Moore's operations officer, Capt. Gregory P. Dillon, who had landed at X-RAY that evening, would be in charge at the

---

[29] Edwards, "Personal Experience of a Company Commander," p. 24; AAR, Pleiku Campaign, 1st Cav Div, p. 84; CHECO Rpt, PACAF, 28 Feb 66, sub: SILVER BAYONET, pp. 2–3, copy in Historians files, CMH. See also Ltr, Nadal to Cash, 3 Oct 67.

landing zone, where Litton's Company D and Diduryk's Company B would hold the perimeter and stand in reserve.[30]

On 15 November, before setting the plan in motion, Moore at 0640 ordered his company commanders to send reconnaissance patrols out to approximately two hundred meters. Around 0650 two of Company C's patrols on the left began receiving fire and taking casualties. The patrols withdrew rapidly into X-RAY, followed by well-camouflaged North Vietnamese soldiers who had been crawling toward the camp through the tall grass, probably to position themselves for an assault.[31]

Two to three companies in strength, they struck X-RAY's southern perimeter, hitting hardest at Edwards' command post and his center and left flank. Concerned that the attack would overwhelm Company C, Captain Edwards asked Colonel Moore to commit the battalion reserve. Unconvinced that the assault represented the main attack, Moore declined. Company C's problems deepened when enemy soldiers reached the foxholes. As his men fought hand-to-hand with the North Vietnamese, Edwards saw another group moving toward his command post. He hurled a grenade, only to be cut down by a bullet in the back. "It felt like a real hard slap," he recalled. Still conscious but no longer able to stand, he radioed Moore to request that the battalion's executive officer, 1st Lt. John W. Arrington, take his place. Lieutenant Arrington hurried to take charge, but was wounded himself while Edwards briefed him. Hanging on, Edwards had no choice but to remain in command.[32]

With enemy soldiers in grenade range, Edwards again requested help. If the North Vietnamese could exploit the opening, they might be able to overrun the landing zone. Although Moore again refused to release the battalion reserve, he instructed Nadal to send a platoon. Seventeen men moved out at 0715, but heavy fire bogged them down. Almost an hour later they reached Company C, suffering 2 killed and 2 wounded. The survivors took up a position about fifteen meters behind the center right of Edwards' sector, providing a defense in depth against any attempt to overrun the battalion command post.[33]

Meanwhile, the fighting spread. At 0715 an enemy force charged Company D in the northeast sector. After thirty minutes of escalating combat Moore decided to commit his reserve, the battalion reconnaissance platoon, to the juncture between Company D's right flank and Company C's left. He also ordered Diduryk to shift his remaining platoon and the company command group to the interior of X-Ray, where

[30] Cash, "Fight at Ia Drang," pp. 28–30.

[31] Ibid., p. 30; AAR, Ia Drang Valley Opn, 1st Bn, 7th Cav, p. 9; AAR, Pleiku Campaign, 1st Cav Div, p. 87.

[32] Edwards, "Personal Experience of a Company Commander," p. 26 (quotation); Cash, "Fight at Ia Drang," pp. 30–31; AAR, Pleiku Campaign, 1st Cav Div, p. 87; Interv, Cash with Edwards, n.d.

[33] Interv, Cash with Edwards, n.d.; Cash, "Fight at Ia Drang," pp. 31–32; Edwards, "Personal Experience of a Company Commander," p. 27.

it would serve as the new reserve. By then, enemy fire was so intense that any movement inside the American position was dangerous. Striking from the south, southeast, and northeast in less than half an hour, the North Vietnamese commander had committed a thousand men to a full-scale attempt to overrun X-RAY.[34]

Beset from three sides, with the heaviest assault coming against Companies C and D, Moore's men held out. Shortly before 0800 Moore requested reinforcements but received only the promise of another rifle company from McDade's battalion as soon as firing at the landing zone diminished enough to allow helicopters to land. At the same time, on Colonel Brown's order, Tully's battalion prepared to march from Landing Zone VICTOR to X-RAY. Assured that reinforcements were coming, Moore ordered all of his units to outline his perimeter's boundaries by popping smoke grenades. That would allow fire support to be brought close to the American position. The fires that followed—from gunships, artillery, and aircraft, and from Moore's organic weapons—reduced the intensity of the assault. Three F–100s arrived on station at 0805. After dropping six napalm canisters and six iron bombs on enemy positions, they strafed the area, firing twenty-four hundred 20-mm. cannon rounds to within one hundred meters of X-RAY.[35]

Shortly after 0900 the first of Moore's reinforcements arrived: Company A, 2d of the 7th Cavalry, commanded by Capt. Joel E. Sugdinis. Moore dispatched the unit to Edwards' southern sector because the troops there had suffered the most. At 0941 the enemy's attack in the Company C and D sectors stopped, and the North Vietnamese, except for a few snipers, began to withdraw.[36]

Of Company C's one hundred fifty-three men who had landed at X-RAY on the previous day, 42 were dead and 62 wounded. Moore decided that Edwards' unit should become the battalion reserve and that Diduryk's Company B should take its place on the line. Supplemented by one platoon from Captain Sugdinis' Company A, Diduryk's men took responsibility for what had been Company C's sector. The two remaining platoons of Sugdinis' unit assumed their position on the northern perimeter.[37]

While Moore reorganized his command, Colonel Tully's 2d of the 5th Cavalry began its cross-country trip to X-RAY. Colonel Brown had ordered the ground approach because, as he later stated, "I didn't relish the idea of moving a steady stream of helicopters into an LZ as hot

---

[34] Edwards, "Personal Experience of a Company Commander," p. 27; Moore and Galloway, *We Were Soldiers Once*, pp. 150, 152.

[35] AAR, Ia Drang Valley Opn, 1st Bn, 7th Cav, p. 10; Cash, "Fight at Ia Drang," pp. 32–33; CHECO Rpt, PACAF, 28 Feb 66, sub: SILVER BAYONET, pp. 3–4.

[36] Diduryk, "[Co B, 2d Bn, 7th Cav, at X-RAY]"; AAR, Ia Drang Valley Opn, 1st Bn, 7th Cav, p. 10.

[37] Moore and Galloway, *We Were Soldiers Once*, p. 165; Edwards, "Personal Experience of a Company Commander," p. 28.

as X-RAY." He also believed that the men on the ground had a chance of advancing unobserved. During the subsequent march the soldiers moved in columns, with Company A on the left and Company B on the right. Company C followed directly to A's rear. If the enemy attacked, Tully reasoned, he would probably do so from the direction of the Chu Pong Massif on the left. But Tully's force met no resistance. The lead elements reached X-RAY shortly after noon. As the man on the spot as well as the senior officer in rank, Colonel Moore automatically became commander of all American forces at the landing zone, including Colonel Tully's.[38]

With reinforcements in hand, Moore made the rescue of Savage's platoon his first priority. A battalion-size task force, consisting of his own Company B and Tully's Companies A and C, would conduct the mission. Employing the two-up, one-back formation Tully had used on the way into X-RAY, the three companies began their move at 1315. Artillery and aerial rocket bursts marched alongside the force, which reached its objective around 1520. Again there was no resistance. The rescuers gathered up the living and the dead and returned to X-RAY quickly, taking less than an hour to make the move back. Since the platoon had suffered no additional casualties on 15 November, its losses were those it had incurred on the first day of its ordeal—8 dead and 12 wounded. The survivors owed their lives to Sergeant Savage and the accuracy of the American artillerymen who had, upon his instructions, zeroed their fire to within feet of the platoon's position.[39]

During the midafternoon U.S. forces unleashed another powerful weapon. At 1600 eighteen Air Force B–52 Stratofortress heavy bombers struck the Chu Pong Massif, the first time they had been used in support of an ongoing tactical operation. Although the damage they caused was difficult to assess, General Westmoreland believed that the raid was effective. He therefore requested and received permission to conduct additional attacks over the next several days. By the time the B–52, or ARC LIGHT, raids ended on the twenty-second, ninety-six sorties had dropped almost five thousand bombs on enemy positions and supply routes. Interrogation of captured North Vietnamese soldiers during and after the campaign testified to the fear that those strikes instilled in enemy ranks.[40]

---

[38] Ltr (quotation), Brown to Cash, 8 Aug 67; Ltrs, Lt Col Robert B. Tully and Capt Edward A. Boyt (CO, Co C, 2d Bn, 5th Cav) to Capt John A. Cash, 5 Sep and 20 Nov 67, box 16, 74/053, RG 319, NARA; AAR, Opn SILVER BAYONET, 2d Bn, 5th Cav, 5 Dec 65, p. 2, and Intervs, author with Lt Gen Harold G. Moore and Col Robert B. Tully, 1 and 19 Jun 95, Historians files, CMH; AARs, Pleiku Campaign, 1st Cav Div, p. 87, and Ia Drang Valley Opn, 1st Bn, 7th Cav, p. 11.

[39] Ltr, Tully to Cash, 5 Sep 67; AAR, Ia Drang Valley Opn, 1st Bn, 7th Cav, p. 11; Moore and Galloway, *We Were Soldiers Once*, p. 175; Interv, author with Col John D. Herren, 6 Jul 95, Historians files, CMH.

[40] Schlight, *Years of the Offensive*, pp. 104–05; Boyle and Samabria, "Lure and Ambush," p. 14.

The early evening of 15 November was quiet. Moore used the time to tighten his perimeter. Pulling Litton's Company D from the line to join Company C in reserve, he replaced it with Tully's battalion, facing the unit north and east. With his line strengthened by the new battalion, he could leave his remaining units in place but now responsible for covering narrower segments of the perimeter.[41]

During the night and into the early morning artillery fired continuously on X-RAY's perimeter and on the nearby mountainsides, setting off a series of secondary explosions. As morning approached, the Americans were in considerably better condition than they had been twenty-four hours earlier. Besides the force at X-RAY, four artillery batteries stood nearby, and tactical air and aerial rocket artillery were available.[42]

Despite the firepower, the North Vietnamese again attacked—four times in the early morning hours of 16 November. They were first detected around 0400, when movement to the south of Diduryk triggered flares and trip-wire alarms, some as far as three hundred meters out. The Americans also heard high-pitched whistles, used by the enemy to assemble and move troops. Twenty-two minutes later the platoon leader on Diduryk's left flank opened fire on some three hundred regulars approaching from the southeast. The attackers retreated. Less than ten minutes later another force, or perhaps the same force reduced by casualties, charged across Diduryk's entire sector. To repel the attack, forward observers directed the supporting 105-mm. artillery batteries to fire different defensive concentrations and to shift their fires laterally and in one-hundred-meter depth adjustments. This attack also failed, with apparently heavy North Vietnamese losses. The enemy made two more assaults on Diduryk's southern position, one from the southwest at 0503 and another on his right flank around 0630. Neither accomplished much (*see Map 10*).[43]

At 0655, to guard against new assaults and to gain a general sense of the situation, Moore ordered all of his men to fire into the woods surrounding X-RAY. The so-called mad minute, which actually lasted two minutes, brought down six concealed snipers, one of whom dropped out of a tree directly in front of Herren's command post, and triggered the last push against the landing zone. As it turned out, North Vietnamese soldiers had been creeping toward Sugdinis' northern sector, using high grass, bushes, and anthills to conceal their movement. When the firing began, they were still one hundred fifty meters away; but, believing either that the attack had begun or that their positions had been betrayed, they sprang to their feet and opened fire. American small-arms fire and artillery cut many of them down and forced the rest to retreat.[44]

---

[41] Cash, "Fight at Ia Drang," p. 36; Moore and Galloway, *We Were Soldiers Once*, p. 180.

[42] AAR, Ia Drang Valley Opn, 1st Bn, 7th Cav, p. 11.

[43] Ibid., pp. 11–12; Diduryk, "[Co B, 2d Bn, 7th Cav, at X-RAY]."

[44] Edwards, "Personal Experience of a Company Commander," p. 31. Moore discusses the mad minute in AAR, Ia Drang Valley Opn, 1st Bn, 7th Cav, p. 12. See also Cash, "Fight at Ia Drang," pp. 38–39.

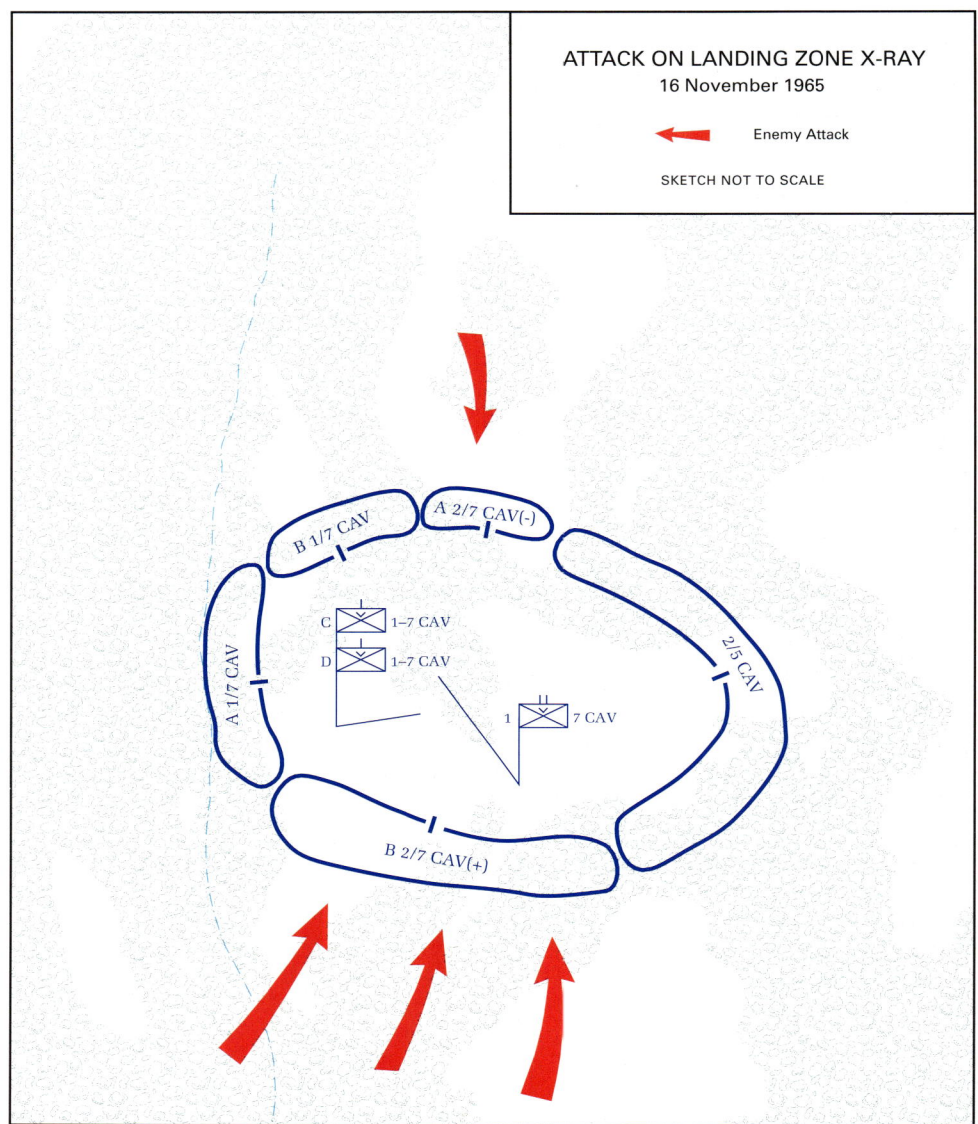

ATTACK ON LANDING ZONE X-RAY
16 November 1965

Enemy Attack

SKETCH NOT TO SCALE

MAP 10

When over an hour passed without further enemy action, Moore ordered all units on the perimeter to patrol to a distance of three hundred to five hundred meters. Beginning at 0955, the only company to make significant contact was Diduryk's, which lost 1 trooper in a clash with a small but well-armed group of wounded North Vietnamese. The

Colonel Moore examines the body of a North Vietnamese soldier.

sweep continued, tallying a total of 27 more enemy soldiers killed before returning to the perimeter.[45]

Colonel Moore surveyed the field of battle. It was, he later wrote, "a sobering sight": enemy dead "sprawled by ones and twos and heaps across a torn and gouged land" that was littered with body fragments, torn and bloody uniforms, and shattered weapons. Those North Vietnamese who had survived were moving away from the battle area, heading north and west along the base of the Chu Pong Massif.[46]

The clash between American and North Vietnamese forces at X-Ray represented the largest single action of the war so far. By body count the Americans had killed 634 of the enemy and by estimate another 1,215. American casualties were 79 killed, with 121 wounded. The toll on the enemy was clearly substantial. At the least, the battle at X-Ray had diminished the fighting capacity of the key North Vietnamese units in the area. The *B3 Front* would have to obtain, train, and

[45] AAR, Ia Drang Valley Opn, 1st Bn, 7th Cav, p. 12.
[46] Moore and Galloway, *We Were Soldiers Once*, pp. 194–95 (quoted words); AAR, Pleiku Campaign, 1st Cav Div, p. 21.

integrate new soldiers into them before they would again become fully operational.[47]

With the fighting at X-Ray over, all that remained was to relieve the weary soldiers who had spent the better part of two days under enemy fire. In the late morning of 16 November Colonel McDade's 2d of the 7th Cavalry, less Companies A and B, which were already at X-Ray, and Company A of Colonel Ackerson's 1st of the 5th Cavalry marched from Landing Zone Columbus to X-Ray, completing the five-kilometer trek around noon. At that time, Ackerson's remaining two companies, which had become available to Colonel Brown on the fifteenth, moved to Columbus, ready to reinforce if necessary.

At 1155 Moore began to withdraw his troops from X-Ray. By 1500 all of them, along with Captain Diduryk's Company B and a platoon from Captain Sugdinis' Company A, had flown to Landing Zone Falcon. From there they would fly to Camp Holloway, an Army base near Pleiku City, where the last of them would arrive at 1830. The rest of McDade's battalion and Tully's troops remained at X-Ray, but only for the night.[48]

The March to Albany

At 0900 the following morning, 17 November, Colonel Tully's 2d of the 5th Cavalry and Colonel McDade's 2d of the 7th Cavalry marched out of X-Ray together. Tully's battalion took the lead, moving northeast toward Landing Zone Columbus about five kilometers away. Accompanied by marching artillery fire, it left X-Ray as it had arrived—two companies moving abreast and one behind. McDade's battalion, its destination an open area to the north named Landing Zone Albany, departed in column. Capt. George G. Forrest's Company A, 1st of the 5th Cavalry, substituted for the two McDade units that had returned to Camp Holloway.[49]

Around 1100, after traveling about three kilometers together, the 2d of the 5th Cavalry broke off on its own to head east toward Columbus. It arrived forty minutes later, in time for a hot lunch. The 2d of the 7th Cavalry veered off to the north and then to the northwest toward Albany, still two kilometers away. When the two units parted, Tully offered to hand McDade the marching fire that had sheltered his unit.

[47] AAR, Ia Drang Valley Opn, 1st Bn, 7th Cav, p. 13; AAR, Opn Silver Bayonet, 3d Bde, 1st Cav Div (Ambl), 4 Dec 65, p. 3, Historians files, CMH.

[48] Ltr, Brown to Cash, 8 Aug 67; AARs, Pleiku Campaign, 1st Cav Div, pp. 90, 93, and Ia Drang Valley Opn, 1st Bn, 7th Cav, pp. 12–13.

[49] AAR, Opn Silver Bayonet, 2d Bn, 5th Cav, p. 2; ibid., 2d Bn, 7th Cav, 24 Nov 65, p. 3, and Daily Jnl, 1st Cav Div (Ambl), 17 Nov 65, Historians files, CMH; William Triplett, "Chaos in the Ia Drang," *Veteran* 6 (October 1968): 20; Ltr, Mallet to Cash, 25 Aug 67; Kinnard, "Victory in the Ia Drang," p. 88; S. Lawrence Gwin, "A Day at Albany," p. 1, box 16, 74/053, RG 319, NARA; and Moore and Galloway, *We Were Soldiers Once*, pp. 215–16.

McDade declined, believing that the firing might betray his location to the enemy.[50]

In command for only three weeks, Colonel McDade left up to his officers decisions that a more experienced battalion commander might have taken upon himself. Although he expected his officers and enlisted men to stay alert, he did not require his commanders to arrange their units in tactical march formation during the move to ALBANY. Inevitably, some of them were more careful than others. The commander of the lead unit in the column, Captain Sugdinis of Company A, placed his two rifle platoons abreast and to the rear of a Company D reconnaissance platoon over which he had temporary operational control. Inside the wedge formed by the three platoons he placed himself and his command group and then closed the wedge by aligning his mortar platoon to the rear. According to his executive officer, 1st Lt. S. Lawrence Gwin, the company moved out slowly and cautiously in an orderly formation— "dispersion was excellent. We were all looking to the trees for snipers." Bringing up the rear of the column, Captain Forrest of Company A, 1st of the 5th Cavalry, also took precautions, making separate arrangements for artillery support, placing his company in a wedge formation, and sending out flankers before moving out.[51]

The commanders of Companies C and D, located in the interior of the column, were less vigilant. Capt. John A. Fesmire started his Company C in tactical formation, but as the temperature rose and the tall grass made control of the march difficult, he ordered his platoons into a column. Company D appears to have been even less alert. The unit's commander, Capt. Henry B. Thorpe, would recall that the march had seemed a mere "walk in the sun" to him and that "nobody knew what was going on." In other words, major portions of McDade's force were crossing an enemy-infested area in a formation that invited trouble. McDade explained years later that his only instructions were "to go to a place called ALBANY and establish a landing zone." He had intended, he stated, to plow through to that destination, not to "creep" or feel his way.[52]

Shortly before noon, with the lead Company A somewhere between two hundred and five hundred meters from its destination, the Company D reconnaissance platoon under 2d Lt. David P. Payne captured two North Vietnamese soldiers. The platoon brought the prisoners to Captain Sugdinis, who informed McDade. The colonel came forward with his staff and an interpreter to interrogate the men. The two told him that they were sick with malaria and terrified of the B–52s. Having no further desire to fight, they had deserted. Learning no useful tactical

---

[50] AAR, Opn SILVER BAYONET, 2d Bn, 7th Cav, p. 3; Coleman, *Pleiku*, p. 231.

[51] S. Lawrence Gwin, "Narrative [of Events at Landing Zone ALBANY]," p. 1 (quotation), box 16, 74/053, RG 319, NARA; Moore and Galloway, *We Were Soldiers Once*, pp. 219–22.

[52] Moore and Galloway, *We Were Soldiers Once*, p. 219 (Thorpe's words, p. 219; McDade's, p. 217).

information, McDade sent the men under guard down the column. According to one estimate, the interrogation lasted about thirty minutes. Combined with the time it took for McDade and the others to come forward, the episode appears to have cost the battalion nearly an hour. In the interim, having spent three hours pushing through the jungle, McDade's men sat back on their packs and rested. Some went to sleep.[53]

Following the questioning, Colonel McDade and his staff stayed with Captain Sugdinis at the head of the column. The battalion began to move again, approaching ALBANY from the east-southeast. An irregular square from three hundred to four hundred meters in length and width, the landing zone had a grove at its center measuring about one hundred fifty meters west to east and one hundred meters north to south. Just to its north lay a clearing suitable for helicopters. Fairly open and about the size of a football field, it sloped gently upward toward another wooded area, beyond which lay a second open field.[54]

At 1307 Lieutenant Payne's reconnaissance platoon reached ALBANY, followed by the two platoons of Captain Sugdinis' Company A, the battalion command group, and the mortar platoon. Intent upon securing the area for the safe entry of the rest of the battalion, Payne's unit quickly moved to the western edge of the landing zone. The two rifle platoons positioned themselves, respectively, on the northeast and south sides of AL-BANY, while the mortar platoon set up in the wooded area in the center.[55]

As Sugdinis' men began to enter ALBANY, Colonel McDade halted the column and ordered his company commanders and their radio operators to come forward for instructions on placing their troops in the landing zone. Captains Forrest, Thorpe, and Fesmire made their way to the head of the column. Commanding the trail company, Forrest had the farthest to go, between five hundred and six hundred meters. As he moved forward through the dense jungle and tall grass, Forrest noted that most of the men he passed had "just stopped, sitting on their packs. It was a Sunday walk, and now we're taking a break." He ordered his second in command to spread the men out and keep them alert.[56]

The Ambush

The fight at X-RAY had been costly for the North Vietnamese, but their losses had not dampened their desire to bloody the 1st Cavalry

[53] AARs, Opn SILVER BAYONET, 2d Bn, 7th Cav, p. 3, and Pleiku Campaign, 1st Cav Div, p. 93; Gwin, "[Landing Zone ALBANY]," pp. 4–5; Triplett, "Chaos in the Ia Drang," p. 21; Harold G. Moore and Joseph L. Galloway, "Death in the Tall Grass," *U.S. News & World Report*, 12 Oct 92, pp. 50–52.

[54] Moore and Galloway, "Death in the Tall Grass," p. 52; Triplett, "Chaos in the Ia Drang," p. 21; Gwin, "[Landing Zone ALBANY]," pp. 5–6.

[55] Gwin, "[Landing Zone ALBANY]," p. 6.

[56] AAR, Opn SILVER BAYONET, 2d Bn, 7th Cav, p. 3; Moore and Galloway, *We Were Soldiers Once*, p. 227 (Forrest's words).

Division. Well aware that American units remained in the area, General Man intended to continue pressing them. He still had several effective *B3 Front* units available for combat: the *66th Regiment*'s *8th Battalion*, a company formed out of the *33d Regiment*'s *1st Battalion*, and the headquarters unit of the *33d*'s *3d Battalion*. On the morning of the seventeenth Man ordered the *8th Battalion* to rejoin its regiment and prepare for a possible large-scale battle with the Americans. Toward midday the battalion commander, Le Xuan Phoi, bivouacked his unit in the woods northeast of ALBANY.[57]

Around this time Man's deputy, Colonel An, who had received definitive intelligence that the Americans were approaching, ordered Phoi's *8th Battalion* to attack. Within the hour Phoi laid out an L-shaped ambush just outside of the clearing that appeared to be the Americans' destination. The soldiers already northeast of ALBANY formed the long stem of the L, which ran parallel to the American column's line of advance; the *1st Battalion*'s company formed the base of the L. They waited along the upper edge of ALBANY's first clearing, across the point where the head of McDade's column would enter the landing zone. Phoi augmented the force occupying the stem of the L by moving cooks and clerks from the *3d Battalion* headquarters to attack positions. He also pulled in troops on outpost duty and several porters (rice and ammunition carriers) to strengthen the formation's shorter base.[58]

Phoi's plan was simple but deadly. All units would hold their fire until McDade's lead elements entered the landing zone and reached its far edge. When the soldiers in that area began to fire, nearby mortar teams would lob rounds into the Americans, signaling the rest of the force along the length of the ambush to open fire. Then the attackers would charge into the column, cutting it to pieces.

The ambush exploded at 1315. Phoi's men waited until the Americans were about forty meters from their position before opening fire. The first shots seemed ragged and uncoordinated, as though they were fired by a scattering of stragglers. Then, as Lieutenant Gwin remembered, "everything just opened up. The firing just crescendoed." Farther down the column the battalion surgeon, Capt. William A. Shucart, smelled Vietnamese cigarettes just prior to the attack. He was still trying to figure out what that meant when the firing began in earnest. Soon, he said, "mortars were dropping all around us, then a lot of small arms fire, and . . . everything dissolved into confusion." At that moment Captains Forrest, Thorpe, and Fesmire had just reached the head of the column to meet with Colonel McDade. Fesmire and Thorpe never made it back to their units; they spent the rest of the battle in the clearing with McDade. Forrest,

[57] *Western Highlands*, p. 37, copy in CMH; Moore and Galloway, *We Were Soldiers Once*, p. 229.

[58] AAR, Opn SILVER BAYONET, 2d Bn, 7th Cav, p. 3; Interv, Lt Col Edward S. Broderick with Lt Col John A. Fesmire, 1982, ch. 2, pp. 45–46, Company Commanders in Vietnam, MHI; Moore and Galloway, "Death in the Tall Grass," p. 53.

however, sprinted back to his unit with his radiomen as soon as the first mortar rounds exploded, without waiting for a dismissal from McDade. Enemy fire killed both radio operators during the dash, but Forrest got through to his men unscathed. The head and the tail of the American column had commanders, but the units in the middle—the most unprepared for an attack—had to make do with alternates (*Map 11*).[59]

As soon as the attackers around the landing zone fired, Phoi's mortars opened up, and then his *8th Battalion* troops on the American right charged into the column. Surprise was total. The American line reeled under the shock and began to break. Chaos reigned. Few of the men had any idea of where they were in relation to other American units or even of the direction from which the enemy had attacked. A platoon of Sugdinis' Company A radioed that it was surrounded and had suffered heavy casualties. The men attempted to return to their company's position but did not know where that was. Captain Sugdinis soon concluded that they were all dead or wounded or overrun.[60]

The situation was grave, particularly at the center of the column. North Vietnamese soldiers were everywhere. The tall grass obscured the battlefield and made it difficult to maintain formations. Men milled about and bunched up, making themselves inviting targets. Within moments, platoons and companies ceased to exist as fighting units, and the encounter disintegrated into a frenzied hand-to-hand melee. At that point the group no longer mattered: Every man was on his own.

A clerk with Fesmire's Company C, Sp4c. Jack P. Smith, was smoking a cigarette when the attack occurred. He threw himself to the ground and reached for his M16. He could hear the sound of shooting close to his position. It seemed to be coming from snipers in the trees. As he later wrote, "Then a few shots were fired right behind me, [and] . . . I was getting scared." The enemy's fire intensified, becoming "a continuous roar." American soldiers all around him began to drop. "We were even being fired at by our own guys. . . . Some were in shock and were blazing away at everything they saw or imagined they saw."[61]

Although sorely pressed and lacking company commanders, the troops in the middle followed their training and tried to consolidate their positions and increase the effectiveness of their fire. Watching from the landing zone, Fesmire saw that Thorpe's Company D was under assault on its right flank and receiving heavy mortar fire. He ordered his own Company C, under the control of his executive officer, 1st Lt. Donald C. Cornett, to relieve the pressure and help Thorpe's men move

[59] Moore and Galloway, "Death in the Tall Grass," p. 53 (Gwin's and Shucart's words), and *We Were Soldiers Once*, p. 238; Kinnard, "Victory in the Ia Drang," p. 88; Daily Jnl, 1st Cav Div, 18 Nov 65; AAR, Pleiku Campaign, 1st Cav Div, p. 94; *Western Highlands*, p. 37; Triplett, "Chaos in the Ia Drang," p. 22.

[60] Gwin, "[Landing Zone ALBANY]," pp. 6–8.

[61] Jack P. Smith, "Death in the Ia Drang Valley," *Saturday Evening Post*, 28 Jan 67, pp. 81–82.

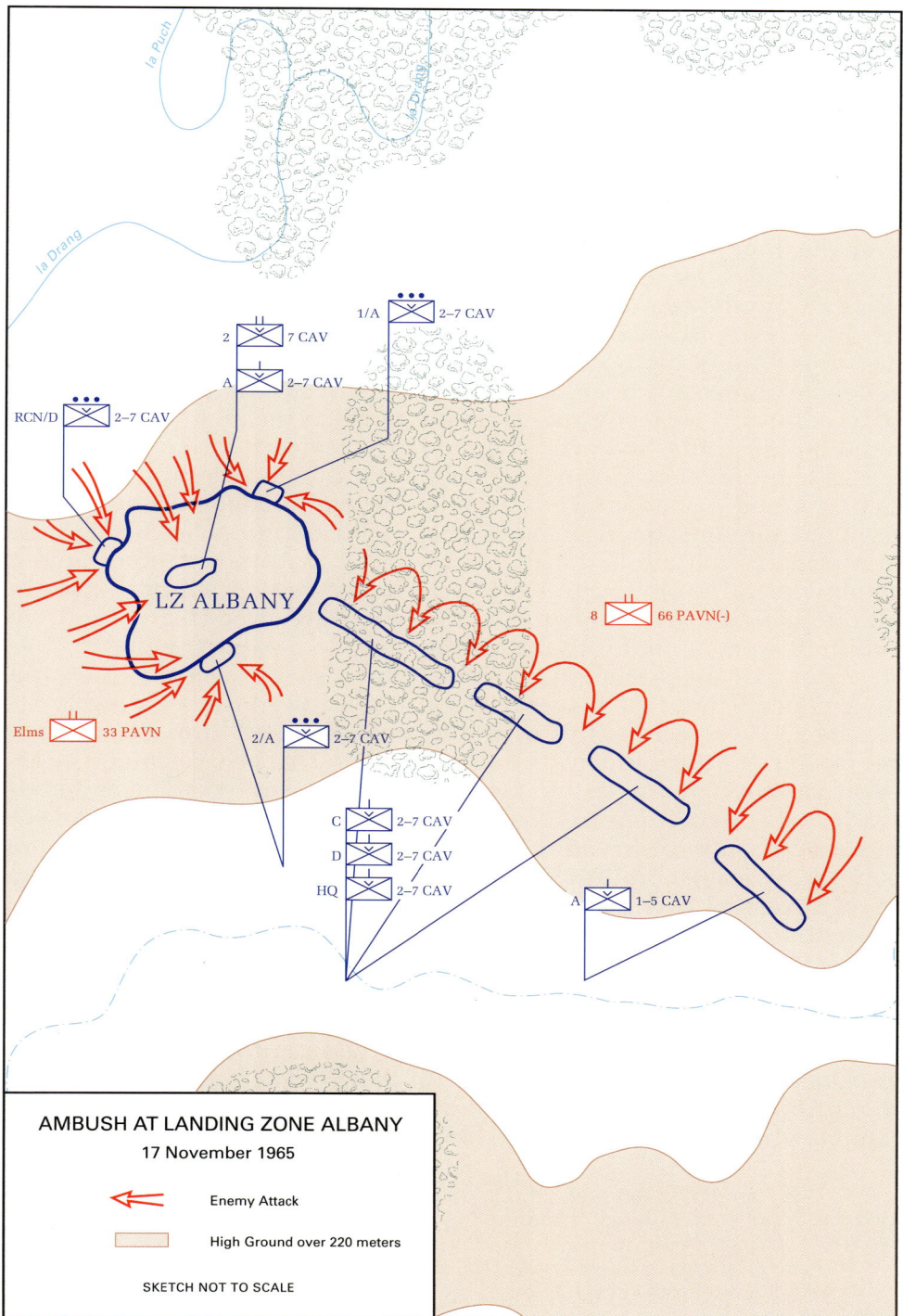

la Puch

la Drang

la Drang

la Drang

1/A • • • 2–7 CAV

2 ⊠ 7 CAV

A ⊠ 2–7 CAV

RCN/D • • • ⊠ 2–7 CAV

LZ ALBANY

8 ⊠ 66 PAVN(-)

Elms ⊠ 33 PAVN

2/A • • • ⊠ 2–7 CAV

C ⊠ 2–7 CAV

D ⊠ 2–7 CAV

HQ ⊠ 2–7 CAV

A ⊠ 1–5 CAV

AMBUSH AT LANDING ZONE ALBANY

17 November 1965

Enemy Attack

High Ground over 220 meters

SKETCH NOT TO SCALE

MAP 11

away from the mortars' killing zone. Lieutenant Cornett did as instructed, but he and his men ran into heavy opposition and never reached Company D. Cornett was killed.

About a dozen soldiers in Company D tried to form a twenty-meter-long battle line in hopes of creating the beginnings of a defensible perimeter. Before they could do so, however, the enemy outflanked them. The position crumbled, and most of the men fled. Fesmire's Company C also attempted to resist. Disoriented by the shock of the attack, however, the troops fired into Sugdinis' position, where his unfortunate men found themselves receiving friendly fire from the rear and enemy mortar fire from the front.[62]

To survive, those infantrymen who came through the first minutes had to get out of the way of the *8th Battalion*'s assault and then, if possible, move forward toward the lead troops securing the landing zone or back toward Forrest's trail company. Some of the men from the shattered middle units, however, were too disoriented to go anywhere.

As the confusion spread, Colonel Brown and his fire support officer, Capt. Dudley L. Tademy, crisscrossed the battle zone in a helicopter, trying to pinpoint American units. They could not find where the middle of McDade's column had been, and without that information Captain Tademy could not bring in effective artillery and air support. "So we just kept flying back and forth," Tademy later remarked, "and we couldn't see a damn thing, and we couldn't do a damn thing."[63]

After a delay of over an hour the first air strikes went in, followed by artillery. They struck enemy troop concentrations preparing to attack McDade's position in the landing zone, but had little effect where the middle of the column was concerned. There, the men remained hopelessly intermingled with the North Vietnamese. In the end, commanders leveled their firepower on that area as well, in order to prevent attacks on the two surviving perimeters at the top and bottom of the column. Specialist Smith would later assert that the effort, despite the friendly casualties it caused, saved his life.[64]

As the afternoon lengthened into evening and darkened into night, the middle area bustled with activity. There, some twenty thirsty and wounded Americans had formed a small perimeter. During the night a patrol from Forrest's company that was checking on calls from wounded soldiers came upon them. The troops placed the four worst cases on stretchers and encouraged about ten of those who seemed able to walk to return with them. Smith was present and sought to go along, but he fainted when he stood up. When he came to, the patrol had gone. It left

---

[62] AAR, Opn Silver Bayonet, 2d Bn, 7th Cav, p. 3; Interv, Broderick with Fesmire, 1982, ch. 2, pp. 41–42; Gwin, "[Landing Zone Albany]," pp. 7–8; Moore and Galloway, *We Were Soldiers Once*, pp. 241–42.

[63] Triplett, "Chaos in the Ia Drang," p. 21.

[64] AAR, Pleiku Campaign, 1st Cav Div, p. 93; Smith, "Death in the Ia Drang Valley," pp. 83–84.

behind a medic, however, who remained with the men for the rest of the night. The officers at the head of the column also considered sending patrols into the middle zone, but they were more cautious than Forrest and rejected the idea. The effort, they believed, might diminish the forces available at ALBANY if the men became lost in the confusion, blundered into the North Vietnamese, or fell victim to the fire of wounded Americans who could not tell friend from foe in the dark. As for the wounded, moving them would achieve little unless they could be evacuated immediately, and there was little chance of that. "Wait until dawn" became the watchword at the head of the column.[65]

Meanwhile, a few individuals and small groups made their way from the middle area to the safety of the two surviving perimeters, but many of the troops, disoriented or wounded, had no choice but to remain where they were. A number of them were executed by the North Vietnamese.[66]

Throughout the night artillery pounded the zone between the two perimeters and other likely areas of enemy concentration. Occasionally, the artillery came so close to the isolated groups of Americans that, between the deafening explosions, they could hear shrapnel striking nearby trees or humming by a few inches overhead. The shelling stopped around dawn, at which time Smith and those of his comrades who remained began to hear small-arms fire. Friendly troops were moving into the area and firing at snipers in the trees.

If the fighting at the middle of the American column was one long agony, conditions at its head were touch and go. Concealed North Vietnamese soldiers had ambushed Sugdinis' Company A as soon as it entered the clearing at ALBANY, opening fire with small arms and mortars from the southwest, west, and north. Immediately afterward, those along the stem of the L had cut off the company and had overrun its 1st Platoon, which had been advancing on its northeastern flank. Receiving small-arms and mortar fire from the enemy, as well as friendly fire from Fesmire's Company C, the 2d Platoon also suffered heavy casualties. Surrounding and isolating the unit, the North Vietnamese then overran it, killing or wounding all but a few of its members.

Elsewhere on the landing zone Payne's reconnaissance platoon, composed of some of the battalion's best men, successfully defended itself and fell back to a termite hill on the north side of the wooded area. Sugdinis and his command group did the same at a similar hill to the south, while McDade and his group bunched at a third hill some fifty meters to the east.

Having survived the initial onslaught, Captain Sugdinis needed to establish a defensive perimeter capable of accommodating helicopters

---

[65] AAR, Opn SILVER BAYONET, 2d Bn, 7th Cav, p. 4; AAR, Opn HITCHHIKE, 1st Bn, 5th Cav, 5 Dec 65, p. 4, Historians files, CMH; Smith, "Death in the Ia Drang Valley," p. 84; Moore and Galloway, *We Were Soldiers Once*, p. 284 (quoted words).

[66] Smith, "Death in the Ia Drang Valley," p. 85; Moore and Galloway, *We Were Soldiers Once*, pp. 257, 268–76; AAR, Opn SILVER BAYONET, 2d Bn, 7th Cav, p. 4.

while constituting a nucleus around which all of the Americans in the clearing could rally. Lieutenant Gwin suggested that he use the triangle formed by the three termite hills as the basis for a defense. Over the next thirty minutes they managed to hammer a cohesive tactical force out of the battalion and company command elements, the reconnaissance force, survivors from Company A's two rifle platoons, and a few men from the middle of the column who had made their way into Sugdinis' area. The perimeter, however, was too small for helicopters to land. They would have to set down a short distance to the north when the enemy pulled back and the firing diminished.[67]

Sugdinis' men could see scores of North Vietnamese soldiers roaming about in the open outside their new perimeter. They were well within M16 range, and over the next half hour, between 1345 and 1415, the Americans picked off dozens of them; Gwin himself shot 10 to 15. Later, it became clear to Gwin and his comrades that these troops had been searching for wounded Americans to kill.[68]

More important than sharpshooting was the need to arrange for fire support before the enemy made an all-out assault. McDade's executive officer, Maj. Frank L. Henry, and Captain Fesmire requested close air support, which came in the form of A–1E Skyraiders from Pleiku. As they approached, McDade's operations officer, Capt. James W. Spires, consulted with Sugdinis and his officers on possible targets for the planes. Concerned about the 2d Platoon, the group discussed whether the strike should go near the unit's last reported position but in the end decided that the platoon no longer existed and that its men were beyond help. All agreed that the incoming pilots could consider the area outside the perimeter a free fire zone.[69]

The Skyraiders arrived at 1415, while an enemy force of between fifty and one hundred men was concentrating to the east of ALBANY for an assault. The planes started with a strafing attack. Cheers rang out from the Americans as the Skyraiders repeatedly struck the North Vietnamese, firing cannon and then dropping napalm. "We could see the . . . canisters break on the tree tops," Gwin recalled, "and spread burning napalm all over large groups of the enemy." About thirty North Vietnamese soldiers turned to run, but they were engulfed in flames. For about two hours the strikes rained down, spoiling the attack and allowing the men on ALBANY's perimeter time to reorganize and consolidate. Sniping, probes, and small-scale firefights continued until about 1800, but then the firing died down.[70]

---

[67] Moore and Galloway, *We Were Soldiers Once*, pp. 232–33; Gwin, "[Landing Zone ALBANY]," p. 13.

[68] Gwin, "[Landing Zone ALBANY]," pp. 16–17.

[69] AAR, Opn SILVER BAYONET, 2d Bn, 7th Cav, p. 3; Gwin, "[Landing Zone ALBANY]," p. 16.

[70] AAR, Opn SILVER BAYONET, 2d Bn, 7th Cav, p. 3; Schlight, *Years of the Offensive*, p. 105; Moore and Galloway, *We Were Soldiers Once*, p. 260; Gwin, "[Landing Zone ALBANY]," pp. 19–21 (quotation, pp. 19–20).

To that point, it had been an exceedingly bad day for Colonel McDade. The enemy had almost overrun Company A; his headquarters had been cut off both physically and by radio from the companies behind it, all the way back to Captain Forrest's group; and then for over an hour the fighting had been so fluid that he had been forced to operate more as a platoon leader than as a battalion commander. Unable to determine what was happening or how bad the situation truly was, but in constant radio contact with his brigade commander, McDade decided to play the situation in a matter-of-fact manner. "I wasn't going to scream that the sky was falling," he later reported, "especially in a situation where nobody could do anything about it anyway."[71]

Colonel Brown, however, was concerned, and in midafternoon he started to organize reinforcements for McDade's battalion. He ordered Captain Diduryk's Company B, with an effective strength of only eighty-three men, to depart Camp Holloway for the perimeter at ALBANY itself. As the troops entered the fifteen waiting helicopters, Diduryk issued a succinct three-sentence order: "We'll be landing from the southeast. Open fire at anything on your left. Run to your right." But the helicopters took the men in so quickly that they arrived unopposed around 1830. By nightfall the position at ALBANY seemed more secure than it had been all day. Wounded soldiers had been removed, reinforcements had arrived, and artillery and air strikes would provide continuous fire support throughout the night. Whatever the enemy planned for the morning, McDade and his men were as ready as they could be.[72]

The third American group in the widely dispersed battle—Captain Forrest's rear company—endured less combat than the others, perhaps because it was farthest down the American column, where the North Vietnamese had spread themselves thin. The fact that Forrest himself had managed to return to his unit after his desperate sprint through enemy fire probably also helped. As soon as he reached his men, he ordered them to pull back and to form a perimeter. Soon under attack, they laid down such a stout defense that the North Vietnamese withdrew. This constituted the only major attack that Forrest and his men would face. Even so, lacking any knowledge of the size of the enemy force arrayed against them and of the locations of the remaining American positions closer to ALBANY, they could do little to assist the rest of the battalion. They had to wait for help to arrive.[73]

Relief was on the way. Shortly after 1400 Colonel Brown ordered Company B, 1st of the 5th Cavalry, at Landing Zone COLUMBUS to join with Forrest's Company A and to move together to reinforce McDade. At 1442 Company B, under Capt. Walter B. Tully, who was Colonel Tully's cousin,

---

[71] Moore and Galloway, *We Were Soldiers Once*, p. 248.

[72] Ibid., p. 266 (Diduryk's words); Coleman, *Pleiku*, pp. 241–42; Gwin, "[Landing Zone ALBANY]," pp. 22–23; AAR, Opn SILVER BAYONET, 2d Bn, 7th Cav, p. 3.

[73] Coleman, *Pleiku*, p. 238.

Americans killed in action at ALBANY

began marching west toward ALBANY. At 1640 Captain Tully linked up with Forrest, and the two companies continued west, with Tully's company in the lead. After going no more than four hundred meters, they started taking heavy fire from their right. Tully ordered a counterattack. The charge succeeded, but the North Vietnamese kept on firing, prompting Tully to radio his commander, Colonel Ackerson, for instructions. With darkness approaching, Ackerson ordered him to organize a two-company perimeter with Forrest and to link up with McDade the next morning. The enemy withdrew during the night. The two companies reached AL-BANY without incident the following morning.[74]

With the North Vietnamese gone, the task of recovering American casualties and equipment and of computing enemy losses began. The job fell initially to the two freshest units at ALBANY—Diduryk's and Tully's. One soldier described the area as "the devil's butcher shop." The task had yet to be completed at 1400, when Forrest's and Tully's companies received orders to proceed to COLUMBUS to provide base security. The remnants of McDade's battalion took over the job, finishing it a day later. On the afternoon of 19 November they helicoptered to Landing Zone CROOKS, about eleven kilometers to the northwest. They

[74] Walter B. Tully, "Company B," *Armor* 76 (September/October 1967): 15–16; Kinnard, "Victory in the Ia Drang," p. 88; AARs, Opn SILVER BAYONET, 2d Bn, 7th Cav, p. 4, and Opn HITCHHIKE, 1st Bn, 5th Cav, p. 4.

remained there a day before moving on to Camp Holloway on the twentieth and to the division base camp at An Khe a day later.[75]

Forrest's and Tully's companies reached Columbus at 1700 on 18 November. Within an hour they were in combat, beating back an enemy foray against the landing zone. The attack appears to have been a parting shot, for it was the last North Vietnamese assault of any consequence during the Pleiku campaign.[76]

The American force at Albany—some four hundred strong prior to the ambush—had experienced a terrible bloodletting. Initial estimates reported 151 killed, 121 wounded, and 5 missing. The Albany force had lost nearly 40 percent of its men killed and, when taking into consideration the wounded, had sustained casualties of almost 70 percent. Fesmire's Company C suffered the most, with 45 killed and 50 wounded out of 112.[77]

According to the 1st Cavalry Division's after action report, the enemy lost 403 by body count and another 100 by estimate, for a total of 503 killed. However, these totals are probably inaccurate. Lieutenant Gwin later asserted that he had overheard Colonel McDade in a radio conversation with brigade headquarters reporting 300 enemy dead. McDade himself denied the incident: "We never saw 300 [bodies] at Albany. Or 200. I don't remember reporting *any* figure. Certainly not a round one like 300." Whatever the case, North Vietnamese losses were significant. The *8th Battalion* lost its commander, Le Xuan Phoi, at Albany, and following the battle some—if not all—of the enemy units involved withdrew into Cambodia to refit and reorganize.[78]

In later years the fight at Albany tended to disappear from official discussions of the Pleiku battles, in part because the battalion's daily journal for the period 16 through 22 November had itself vanished. That key piece of evidence, missing at least since September 1967, would have allowed a more accurate and authoritative understanding of the tragic events to emerge and would have answered many of the questions raised. In addition, official reports prepared in the aftermath of Albany either dissembled the facts or avoided the battle altogether. The 1st Cavalry Division's final report intimated that the fight had sorely depleted the enemy's ability to continue combat in the region. The 3d Brigade's summary stated that "superior firepower made the difference" and saved

[75] Smith, "Death in the Ia Drang Valley," p. 85 (quoted words); Gwin, "[Landing Zone Albany]," p. 25; AAR, Opn Silver Bayonet, 2d Bn, 7th Cav, p. 5.

[76] Tully, "Company B," pp. 18–19; *Western Highlands*, p. 38; AAR, Pleiku Campaign, 1st Cav Div, p. 97.

[77] AAR, Pleiku Campaign, 1st Cav Div, p. 94; Moore and Galloway, *We Were Soldiers Once*, pp. 320–21; Gwin, "[Landing Zone Albany]," p. 26; Triplett, "Chaos in the Ia Drang," p. 22. In April 1966 Moore, then commanding the 3d Brigade, led a search into the area and located the remains of the five missing soldiers.

[78] Triplett, "Chaos in the Ia Drang," p. 22 (Gwin's and McDade's words); AAR, Pleiku Campaign, 1st Cav Div, p. 94; *Western Highlands*, pp. 37–38; Msg, Westmoreland MAC 0592 to Arthur Sylvester, Asst Sec Def for Public Affairs, 22 Jan 66, sub: PAVN Actions Following Tet, Westmoreland Message files, CMH.

McDade's battalion.[79] The battalion's account merely related the story, making no judgments beyond those narrowly focused on the way Americans could have done better.

Personal recollections do not clarify the event. General Kinnard claimed in 1967 that the 2d of the 7th Cavalry had "won the day" at ALBANY. Captain Sugdinis and Colonel McDade, the two officers most involved in the battle, were much more measured in their assessments. Sugdinis believed that neither side had won or lost, for both had been battered and each "was grateful to still resemble a military organization when it was over." McDade commented that "I never thought of [ALBANY] . . . as a victory. We got into a scrap. We gave a good account of ourselves and proved to the men that we didn't have to be afraid of [the enemy]."[80] Overall, no one seemed willing to concede that the fight had been fraught with failures of leadership, particularly at the battalion level.

Following ALBANY, General Knowles recommended that the 3d Brigade return to An Khe for a "richly deserved breather" and that Col. William R. Lynch's 2d Brigade, thus far unused in the campaign, take its place. General Kinnard agreed, directing that the changeover occur at noon on 20 November. Accordingly, Colonel Brown's 1st and 2d Battalions, 7th Cavalry, and his 3d Brigade headquarters returned to An Khe. At the same time, the 1st and 2d Battalions, 5th Cavalry, were removed from the 3d Brigade and given to Colonel Lynch. The fresh brigade also brought into the operation two units regularly assigned to it, the 2d Battalion, 12th Cavalry, and the 1st Battalion, 8th Cavalry. Lynch changed the brigade's forward command post from STADIUM at Catecka Plantation to the Special Forces Camp at Duc Co, about twenty kilometers north of the Ia Drang.[81]

Lynch's mission differed from that of the 1st and 3d Brigades in one respect. In addition to conducting search and destroy operations in the area north of the Chu Pong Massif and south of Duc Co, he was expected to work with the South Vietnamese Airborne Brigade, which had its forward command post at Duc Co. In the days that followed, Lynch and the commanders of the South Vietnamese unit drew a rough line south from Duc Co. The South Vietnamese became responsible for the sector west of the line toward Cambodia, while the Americans took the area immediately to the east. In practical terms, cooperation between the two meant that U.S. forces supplied fire support. On 20 November,

---

[79] AAR, Pleiku Campaign, 1st Cav Div, p. 94; Ltr, Lt Col Hames L. Quinn, Asst Adj Gen, U.S. Army, Ryukyu Islands, to Brig Gen Hal C. Pattison, Chief of Mil Hist, U.S. Army, 8 Sep 67, box 16, 74/053, RG 319, NARA; AARs, Opn SILVER BAYONET, 2d Bn, 7th Cav, pp. 3–6, and 3d Bde, 1st Cav Div, p. 2 (quoted words).

[80] Kinnard, "Victory in the Ia Drang," p. 88 (Kinnard's words); Moore and Galloway, *We Were Soldiers Once*, pp. 316–17 (Sugdinis' and McDade's words). See also Annual Hist Sum, 1 Jul–31 Dec 65, 2d Bn, 7th Cav, n.d., Historians files, CMH.

[81] Kinnard, "Victory in the Ia Drang," p. 89 (Knowles' words); AAR, Pleiku Campaign, 1st Cav Div, pp. 99–103.

searching near Cambodia, two South Vietnamese battalions discovered a North Vietnamese battalion and called in American artillery. During the ensuing clash the South Vietnamese claimed to have killed 200 enemy soldiers, with artillery accounting for 130. The 2d Brigade, for its part, conducted methodical searches between the Ia Drang and Duc Co for almost a week but came up empty handed.[82]

The question of sanctuary versus the right of hot pursuit came alive at this juncture. Immediately following the fights at X-Ray and ALBANY, General Kinnard and his commanders wanted to pursue the North Vietnamese across the border. Although Kinnard later admitted that he probably should have initiated action immediately, he refrained from doing so because his troops were exhausted. "By the time we got ourselves ready and chased them" with the South Vietnamese, he recalled, "they had gone out of the X-Ray area. We pushed them the final distance over the border." Kinnard sought permission either to change or waive temporarily the rules of engagement that put Cambodia off limits to American forces so that he could finish off the North Vietnamese units. He wanted them "totally out of the war," emphasizing that he "didn't want to just rough them up."[83]

Westmoreland approved Kinnard's request, as did the new U.S. ambassador to Saigon, Henry Cabot Lodge, but authorities in Washington rejected it. President Johnson had decided that the United States sought no wider war and would fight the ground war solely within the borders of South Vietnam. Unable to pursue the enemy into Cambodia, American efforts west of Pleiku quickly petered out. On 26 November Kinnard ended the campaign.[84]

Westmoreland had no choice but to accept Washington's ruling. Even so, the debate over the issue led to a modification of the rules of engagement in December. Thereafter, ground combat units could maneuver temporarily into Cambodia as necessary for self-defense, provided such action did nothing to widen the conflict.[85]

An Assessment

Following the Pleiku campaign, General Kinnard made three claims of success. First, he believed that the 1st Cavalry Division and its airmobile concept had been tested in combat and had passed "with flying colors." Second, the division had prevented North Vietnamese forces from splitting the country along the Pleiku–Qui Nhon axis. Finally, while thwarting

[82] AAR, Pleiku Campaign, 1st Cav Div, pp. 102, 104, 107, 110, 113, 116; AAR, Opn SILVER BAYONET II, 2d Bde, 1st Cav Div (Ambl), 4 Dec 65, p. 2, Historians files, CMH; Vinh Loc, *Why Plei Me?*, p. 103; Kinnard, "Victory in the Ia Drang," p. 89.

[83] Maurer, comp., *Strange Ground*, p. 145 (Kinnard's words).

[84] AAR, Pleiku Campaign, 1st Cav Div, p. 120.

[85] MACV History, 1966, p. 359, CMH.

the enemy's strategic aims, the division had destroyed the better part of three North Vietnamese regiments. Westmoreland agreed, saying at a news conference that the Pleiku campaign had been an "unprecedented victory."[86]

The efficacy of airmobility was, in fact, proved during the campaign. Because of the helicopter, Moore's 1st of the 7th Cavalry had dropped suddenly and unexpectedly out of the sky on 14 November, achieving surprise. And once the battle began, helicopters sustained the effort, bringing in supplies and reinforcements and evacuating the wounded.

The achievement at X-Ray and the survival of McDade's force at Albany also owed a great deal to firepower. Air strikes and artillery broke up enemy assaults and concentrations and probably killed as many or more North Vietnamese than did American troops on the ground. Here, too, the helicopter played a major role. Because no roads existed near the Chu Pong Massif, artillery and ammunition had to be lifted by helicopter to firebases within range of the battlefield. In addition, helicopter gunships were a constant element in the campaign.

But if helicopters were decisive, they also had weaknesses. Once Kinnard's combat elements became dependent on them for mobility and firepower, wear and tear on flying equipment, spare parts shortages, pilot fatigue, and massive fuel consumption became factors in the battle. Kinnard pointed out that his maintenance troops put more helicopters into operation than were removed during the campaign, but he had to admit that if the campaign had continued with the same intensity much longer, his ground crews would have fallen behind.

More fundamentally, however, the campaign raised questions about the airmobile division's staying power. The division had been hard put to sustain a single brigade in the western highlands at an acceptable level of activity, relying heavily on the Air Force to keep the troops supplied and the helicopters fueled. The Air Force's 2d Air Division in Saigon reported that during November, at the height of the campaign, it delivered a daily average of one hundred eighty-six tons of supplies to Kinnard's command, with 58 percent of the total being fuel. The effort represented 16 percent of the entire airlift work load expended in South Vietnam during the period and one-fourth of the flying time. While the effort continued, the backlog of cargo awaiting delivery to commands other than Kinnard's increased by 50 percent.[87]

Beyond maintenance and logistics, questions also remained about the 1st Cavalry Division's performance in combat. If the presence of helicopters gave the unit outstanding mobility at the beginning of the

---

[86] AAR, Pleiku Campaign, 1st Cav Div, p. 132 (Kinnard's words); Interv, Couch with Kinnard, 20 Jan 83, p. 72, Senior Officer Oral History Program, MHI; Kinnard, "Victory in the Ia Drang," p. 91; *New York Times*, 20 Nov 65 (Westmoreland's words).

[87] George C. Herring, "The 1st Cavalry and the Ia Drang Valley, 18 October–24 November 1965," in *America's First Battles, 1776–1965*, eds. Charles E. Heller and William A. Stofft (Lawrence: University Press of Kansas, 1986), p. 325; Bowers, *Tactical Airlift*, pp. 212–16; Meyerson, "Logistics in the Vietnam Conflict," ch. 4.

A Chinook delivers troops of the 1st Cavalry Division to a rugged mountaintop.

operation, the circumstances changed at X-RAY and ALBANY once battle was joined. When heavy incoming fire kept helicopters from bringing in reinforcements or from moving troops to more defensible positions, the men in the Ia Drang Valley were on their own. Lacking the tanks, trucks, and other heavy equipment that made the job of infantrymen in standard divisions so much easier and safer, they lost many of the advantages U.S. forces usually had over the enemy and were essentially on par with the North Vietnamese, fighting as light infantry. The presence of massive air support and artillery was the only real edge they had, providing the margin between life and death. In this light, the future for airmobile operations was clear. As Kinnard stressed in his final assessment of the campaign, the support of the Air Force would be essential in almost every large operation that the 1st Cavalry Division undertook.[88]

Firepower was indeed a crucial factor, but the fight at ALBANY demonstrated that the enemy was capable of countering even that advantage. When McDade declined Tully's offer of marching artillery support on his way into ALBANY, he appears to have assumed that fire would be available if needed. It was, but the enemy's tactics at ALBANY—staying close to the Americans—partially nullified its effect. At this juncture, the North Vietnamese had the advantage because they were fighting on

[88] Bowers, *Tactical Airlift*, pp. 212–16.

their own terms in a place of their own choosing. Circumstances changed when the Americans solidified their positions, allowing commanders to use their fires to good effect. But it was a very near thing.

The strategic implications of the campaign were less clear. There was no evidence, then or later, that Hanoi had a plan to cut South Vietnam in two. However, it is likely that Kinnard's division slowed and then halted a North Vietnamese effort to dominate the highlands by overrunning Special Forces camps and, perhaps, even Pleiku City.

Attrition was another goal—on both sides. The North Vietnamese clearly hoped to take a heavy toll of Americans, while the 1st Cavalry Division wanted to find, fix, and destroy as many enemy units as possible. Overall, Kinnard's forces suffered 305 killed and 524 wounded during the campaign while killing, according to official records, 1,519 of the enemy by body count and another 2,042 by estimate. The figures for the enemy's losses in four of the five major engagements—at the enemy hospital on 1 November, at the ambush north of the Chu Pong on 3–4 November, at X-Ray, and at Albany—are nonetheless open to doubt. At X-Ray Colonel Moore recognized that estimates were almost never accurate and reduced the total of 834 killed submitted by his men to 634 because the former figure seemed too high.[89] At Albany nothing resembling an organized and accurate body count took place. Anecdotal evidence obtained from Americans who participated in the battle strongly suggested that the enemy had suffered substantial losses, but that hardly justified the numbers General Kinnard cited for the action.

All in all, little time was spent on the ambiguities dogging the campaign. For MACV, the main conclusion seemed clear: American forces had killed hundreds of enemy and had won a victory in their first major fight against North Vietnamese regulars. If Albany had been a near disaster, X-Ray was the model of what a successful engagement should be in Vietnam. Whether or not President Johnson would allow hot pursuit into Cambodia, the way still seemed open to winning the war.

---

[89] Moore and Galloway, *We Were Soldiers Once*, p. 199; Memo, Col Harold G. Moore for Maj Gen Harry W. O. Kinnard, 16 Nov 66, sub: The Battle at X-Ray, p. 2, Historians files, CMH. For body counts of separate battles, see Coleman, *Pleiku*, p. 129, and Account by Danielson, in Mertel, *1st Air Cavalry in the Highlands*, p. 124.

7

Patterns of Perseverance

The Ia Drang campaign came at a sober moment for American policymakers. They understood that U.S. firepower and mobility had taken a heavy toll of the enemy during recent operations. They were also well aware that Hanoi's efforts showed no sign of abating, that infiltration into the South was increasing, and that much more would have to be done to achieve American ends. As General Westmoreland pointed out to General Larsen in a brutally frank memorandum on 10 December, "We are not engaging the VC with sufficient frequency or effectiveness to win the war in Vietnam." To remedy the problem, Westmoreland outlined a number of essential actions to be taken by his commanders: keeping their troops in the field for longer periods of time; developing imaginative, aggressive tactics for bringing Communist forces to bay on American terms; improving the acquisition of intelligence; and, above all, becoming more flexible and more willing than ever before to adapt their plans to fit fast-breaking developments.[1]

Plans and Troops

Although deeply concerned about improving his command's tactics, General Westmoreland never doubted that his forces would prevail and that his concept of how to fight the war was sound. For him, the evidence was compelling. Earlier in 1965, before the arrival of the combat units, both he and Ambassador Taylor had informed officials in Washington that South Vietnam would never survive another year without drastic steps to avert collapse. In the ensuing months he oversaw the introduction of the first U.S. brigades and divisions into Vietnam and watched those units stabilize the situation by their very presence. The battles of November and December followed, producing lopsided kill ratios in favor of the United States and putting an abrupt end to all thought of collapse. By January 1966 he believed that Phase I of his three-

---

[1] Memo, COMUSMACV for CG, FFV, 10 Dec 65, sub: Tactical Employment of US Forces and Defensive Action, p. 1, box 5, 69A/702, RG 334, NARA.

part campaign plan was complete and that Phase II could begin—a relentless effort that would subvert the enemy's ambitions and, once and for all, secure the future of South Vietnam.[2]

Like Westmoreland, enemy commanders were also critical of their tactics and just as confident. The *B2 Front*'s General Tra understood that the direction of the war had changed because of the introduction of American forces. As he later remarked, "We were forced at the beginning to think and discuss at length the U.S. intervention. At the time we were strong enough to counter the Saigon Army, but when U.S. forces came we were very concerned about whether we were able to counter the U.S. Army. That army was a modern army with sophisticated weapons." But after studying various battles, such as the U.S. Marines' Operation STARLITE in southern I Corps and those at Hill 65 and Bau Bang in III Corps, Tra and his colleagues decided they could cope. Although U.S. forces were superior "logistically, in weapons, in all things," Tra was convinced that his men could develop tactical counters to the largely conventional methods used by the Americans, ultimately causing so many casualties that U.S. policymakers would realize that the freedom fighters of the North and South would never retreat and that the United States was waging war "against a whole nation." At that point, the United States would understand that the war was unwinnable and would leave. "Strategically, it was a war of attrition. Tactically, we tried to destroy U.S. units."[3]

Attrition also figured prominently in Westmoreland's plans, along with the well-established theme of pacification. In the Combined Campaign Plan for 1966, which the Joint General Staff and MACV issued in December 1965, the allies declared their "basic objective" for the year to be clearing, securing, and developing the heavily populated regions around Saigon, in the Mekong Delta, and in selected portions of the I and II Corps coastal plain. "Coincident" with this effort, they would defend significant outlying government and population centers and conduct search and destroy operations against "major VC/PAVN forces." In pursuit of these objectives, South Vietnam's army would concentrate on defending, clearing, and securing the designated strategic areas. American and third-country forces, besides securing their own bases and helping to protect rice-producing areas, were to "conduct operations outside of the secure areas against VC forces and bases." Implicit in these words was the *de facto* division of labor between the South Vietnamese and Americans that had been in effect since the summer.[4]

---

[2] Maj Gen William E. DePuy, "Vietnam" (Address delivered at National War College, Washington, D.C., March 20, 1967), pp. 46, 48, Historians files, CMH; Sharp and Westmoreland, "Report," p. 151, copy in CMH.

[3] Interv, author with Lt Gen Tran Van Tra, 23 Nov 90, Historians files, CMH.

[4] Joint General Staff and MACV, "Combined Campaign Plan for Military Operations in the Republic of Vietnam, 1966," 31 Dec 65, AB 141, an. G, pp. 153–54, Historians files, CMH.

Viet Cong strength kept pace with American escalation.

By the time the Combined Campaign Plan was issued, General Westmoreland knew that during the coming year he would have increasing resources with which to carry it out. But he also knew that the enemy was expanding his own forces. Earlier in the year the Joint Chiefs of Staff had estimated that the North Vietnamese would introduce the equivalent of one or two additional divisions into South Vietnam by the end of 1965. During November, however, it became clear that a huge buildup was under way, with at least six and possibly as many as nine North Vietnamese regiments having infiltrated during the previous months. Similarly, the Viet Cong had added seven main force regiments to the five present in July. As a result, the total strength of the combined North Vietnamese and Viet Cong force stood at some 99,600 in combat units, 16,900 in combat-support units, and 103,600 in the militia. On 23 November Westmoreland addressed the issue, noting that the trend showed no signs of diminishing. While the United States planned to add an average of seven maneuver battalions per quarter over the coming year, the enemy would add fifteen. In Westmoreland's opinion, the United States had no alternative but to commit more forces just to counter the immediate threat and, more importantly, agree to much larger troop deployments in the future to ensure the success of Phase II operations.[5]

[5] Periodic Intel Rpt, 1 Jan–30 Jun 66, MACV, 20 Aug 66, p. 9, MHI; *Pentagon Papers* (Gravel), 4:295, 306–07.

The White House, the Departments of State and Defense, and MACV had begun to weigh Westmoreland's troop requirements for 1966 in July 1965. By September the participants unanimously agreed that Westmoreland needed two more infantry divisions, an armored cavalry regiment, a second field force headquarters, and another battalion for the 173d Airborne Brigade. With support units, the total came to some 117,000 men. In November, just as planners were beginning to identify the forces to be assigned, word arrived about the increase in enemy infiltration. When Westmoreland requested a doubling of the Phase II reinforcement, all concerned recognized that more forces than those already agreed to might be necessary. Returning from a fact-finding mission to Vietnam during December, General Johnson asserted that "the U.S. would be well advised to make a sizeable increase in the shortest time possible in additional forces . . . in order to create a favorable power balance suddenly and achieve a maximum destruction of the increased enemy presence." For the Army, those add-ons included an infantry division, a separate brigade, two air cavalry squadrons, one airmobile infantry battalion, and support units. If all of the troops designated arrived in Vietnam by the end of 1966, the U.S. Army's strength in country at that time would amount to some 268,000 men.[6]

Following a trip to Saigon with General Wheeler, Secretary McNamara endorsed the expanded Phase II in early December, at which time he instructed his staff to begin planning for the doubled deployment and to work toward a conference in Honolulu during January to establish troop lists, movement schedules, and final goals. In the meantime, General Westmoreland and his superior, Admiral Sharp, developed their own comprehensive plan, combining the approved buildup of forty-four battalions in 1965 with the additional troops under consideration for 1966. Under the scenario Sharp and Westmoreland envisioned, more than 440,000 U.S. and third-country troops—including one hundred two maneuver battalions, seventy-nine of them American—would be present in Vietnam by the end of 1966.[7]

With further major deployments in the offing, the magnitude of what was happening bore heavily upon President Johnson. Doggedly determined to meet the Communist threat in Vietnam, he began to seek some way to solidify support at home for what he knew had to be done. His problem was clear. As Assistant Secretary of State Bundy observed in a cable to the U.S. Embassy in Saigon, the size of the escalation in the war in prospect would "hit Congress and the U.S. public hard and could trigger prolonged and difficult debate." Unless some sort of dramatic move for peace preceded the announcement of the move, the "noise level

---

[6] MFR, Gen Harold K. Johnson, 29 Dec 65, sub: Random Thoughts To Be Sorted Out Later, p. 3 (quotation), box 37, Harold K. Johnson Papers, MHI; MACV History, 1965, pp. 43–45, CMH. For a general discussion of these issues, see Cosmas, "MACV, the Joint Command," ch. 7, CMH.

[7] Cosmas, "MACV, the Joint Command," ch. 7.

could reach [a] point that would seriously damage our basic posture of firmness and determination."[8]

Deciding that a pause in the bombing of North Vietnam would suffice to assuage public opinion, President Johnson moved on 27 December to extend indefinitely a brief bombing halt that had begun on the twenty-fourth as part of a Christmas truce. Prominent American emissaries then began highly visible diplomatic missions to governments around the world in search of some opening to Hanoi that would spark negotiations. Johnson and his advisers were well aware that they had little to lose from this course of action, for bad weather over North Vietnam precluded most air strikes during January.[9]

The effort appeared to have achieved Johnson's ends. When the North Vietnamese failed to respond and the bombing resumed on 30 January, few Americans were dismayed. Instead, Harris polls indicated that 61 percent of them were ready to accept all-out bombing of North Vietnam if the peace initiative failed. Another 60 percent declared that they would also support a deployment of up to 500,000 men if that would shorten the war.[10]

The Honolulu Conference

The Honolulu Conference convened on 17 January 1966, while the bombing halt was still in effect. Operating on a commission from President Johnson to come up with "a better military program, a better pacification program . . . , and a better peace program," the conference was organized in two sessions, running through 9 February. The first, which involved some four hundred fifty civilian and military staff members from MACV, the Office of the Joint Chiefs of Staff, the U.S. Pacific Command, and the other concerned commands, dealt with planning and deployments for the coming year. The second, with President Johnson, South Vietnam's chief of state, Lt. Gen. Nguyen Van Thieu, and the nation's premier, Air Vice Marshal Nguyen Cao Ky, in attendance, covered political questions. A multitude of civilian and military dignitaries also participated: National Security Adviser McGeorge Bundy, Secretary of Defense McNamara, Secretary of State Rusk, Secretary of Agriculture Orville L. Freeman, Ambassador Lodge, former Ambassador Taylor, General Wheeler, Admiral Sharp, and General Westmoreland.[11]

---

[8] Ibid.; Msg (quotations), State to Saigon, 11 Dec 65, Historians files, CMH.

[9] Msg, McNamara Defense 5038 to Westmoreland, 28 Dec 65, Miles Policy/Strategy files, Paul L. Miles Papers, MHI.

[10] Louis Harris, *The Anguish of Change* (New York: W. W. Norton, 1973), p. 59.

[11] *United States–Vietnam Relations, 1945–1967: Study Prepared by the Department of Defense*, 12 vols. (Washington, D.C.: Government Printing Office, 1971), 6:IV.C.8:38 (quotation) (hereafter cited as *U.S.-Vietnam Relations*); Johnson, *Vantage Point*, pp. 242–45.

Marshal Ky (left) *and General Thieu* (right) *with President Johnson at Honolulu*

The staff meetings concentrated on three alternatives for meeting Sharp's and Westmoreland's request for one hundred two battalions. Case I provided all the troops but called for a mobilization of reserves and an extension of enlistments in order to fill the requirement. Case II also authorized the full complement of battalions. Responding, however, to President Johnson's growing concern that a reserve call-up would serve only to divide the American people, it avoided both the call-up and the enlistment extension but compensated by postponing the deployment of nine battalions until early 1967. Case III was the most conservative of the alternatives. Seeking to satisfy Johnson's political concerns while meeting objections from the Joint Chiefs of Staff that a large deployment without a reserve call-up would deplete U.S. forces around the world, it abstained from the call-up and reduced the number of battalions to eighty-four. Because of projected shortages in aviation and logistical forces, none of the alternatives provided full helicopter, artillery, and supply support for the units involved.[12]

During the working session the head of the MACV delegation, General DePuy, pushed for Case I but expressed his willingness to abide by Case II. Case III, he stated, would sorely restrict MACV's ability to sap

[12] *U.S.-Vietnam Relations*, 5:IV.C.6(a):19–28, 34–38.

156

the enemy's offensive power and would diminish the command's ability to guarantee the security of some province and district capitals, particularly in I and II Corps. Admiral Sharp sided with DePuy.[13]

During the formal session and in the conference communique President Johnson, General Thieu, and Marshal Ky mainly focused on the human dimension of the war, especially pacification and the need for political and social reform in South Vietnam. They also made important decisions on strategy and troop commitments. The goals they sought included increases in the percentage of the nation's people living in government-controlled areas, an enlargement of the proportion of road and rail networks under full government control, and the pacification of selected territories. They also wanted Westmoreland to penetrate an increasing number of enemy base areas and to inflict enough casualties on the Viet Cong and North Vietnamese to offset their gains in strength through recruitment and infiltration. Both Johnson and McNamara assured Westmoreland that he would receive all of the battalions he had requested, but they cautioned that a reserve call-up would be politically impossible. McNamara advised the MACV commander to anticipate logistical shortages by reducing requirements, employing civilian contractors, and promoting exchanges of resources and personnel among the military services.[14]

Although the size of future deployments for the war seemed settled, the question of a reserve call-up gave rise to considerable haggling between the civilian leadership of the Defense Department and the Joint Chiefs of Staff during the months following the conference. The Joint Chiefs pointed out that, without a mobilization, an unacceptably large number of troops would have to be withdrawn from stations in Europe, the United States, and elsewhere. This, in turn, would undermine America's capacity to meet its international obligations. Should North Vietnam's Communist allies cause problems in central Europe or on the Korean peninsula, U.S. forces might find themselves hard pressed to mount an effective response. Since President Johnson declined to authorize a reserve call-up to remedy the shortfall, the Joint Chiefs recommended extending the buildup into 1967, which would "preserve critical worldwide skills and allow more time for [the] buildup of a training base" in the United States. In the end, McNamara delayed fewer units than the Joint Chiefs had proposed but nonetheless approved a lengthened schedule that came close to resembling the Case II option discussed at Honolulu.[15]

[13] MACV History, 1965, pp. 66–67; Cosmas, "MACV, the Joint Command," ch. 7.

[14] Sharp and Westmoreland, *Report*, pp. 113–14; Cosmas, "MACV, the Joint Command," ch. 7; Paper, 8 Feb 66, sub: 1966 Program To Increase the Effectiveness of Military Operations and Anticipated Results Thereof, Westmoreland History files, CMH. See also Andrew F. Krepinevich, Jr., *The Army and Vietnam* (Baltimore: Johns Hopkins University Press, 1986), p. 179.

[15] JCS History, ch. 32, pp. 1–5, CMH; MACV History, 1966, p. 68 (quotation).

The objectives enunciated at the conference were nothing new to General Westmoreland. They conformed, he later observed, to "the broad outline of how the war was to be fought as I had worked it out over months of consultation with South Vietnamese officials, Admiral Sharp, and the Joint Chiefs of Staff. Indeed, in setting the goals for 1966, senior civilian authorities acting for the President formally directed that I proceed as I had planned." Although pacification remained a major concern of MACV and the U.S. mission as a whole, Brig. Gen. Phillip B. Davidson, who replaced General McChristian as Westmoreland's intelligence chief in 1967, later stated that attrition of the enemy became "the first priority" of U.S. forces.[16]

At first, the changes in deployment schedules made little difference to Westmoreland. His immediate needs were filled. But the new schedule contained a serious strategic flaw. By extending the troop deployments well into 1967, the sudden powerful surge in forces that General Johnson had sought would never become a reality. As a result, Westmoreland during most of 1966 would not have in hand the troops—both maneuver battalions and support units—that he required to implement the second, or offensive, phase of his campaign, forcing him to spend some months buying time while the buildup proceeded. More importantly, the stretch-out also meant that the enemy would be able to nullify the U.S. buildup by expanding his own forces at the same or even faster pace than the Americans.[17]

Preparing for New Battles

As the fighting verged on a new phase, General Westmoreland moved to solidify MACV's war role. At the beginning of 1965 the command had functioned, in essence, as an overseer, responsible for coordinating American military advice and assistance to the government of South Vietnam. By the beginning of 1966 its role had changed. While continuing its advisory functions, MACV had become a major operational headquarters controlling air, naval, and ground combat forces in what was now a full-scale war. To that end, Westmoreland expanded his joint headquarters staff and added new agencies, including a large combat operations center with a Marine brigadier general as director. Extending his reach into the field, he maintained control of units in contact with the enemy through what, in essence, were corps commands—Field Force, Vietnam; the 1st Infantry Division; and the III Marine Amphibious Force.[18]

[16] Westmoreland, *A Soldier Reports*, p. 161; Davidson, *Vietnam at War*, p. 401.

[17] MACV History, 1965, pp. 36–37, 44–45; Cosmas, "MACV, the Joint Command," ch. 7.

[18] Eckhardt, *Command and Control*, pp. 44–46, 61–62; Cosmas, "MACV, the Joint Command," chs. 8 and 9; Sharp and Westmoreland, *Report*, p. 100.

With the increasing U.S. role in combat and the buildup of American forces, Westmoreland, in conjunction with Admiral Sharp and the Joint Chiefs of Staff, upgraded his service component commands. Early in 1966 he established the U. S. Naval Forces, Vietnam, to direct the naval advisory effort and command the task forces that patrolled South Vietnam's coast and rivers. At the same time, MACV's Air Force component, the 2d Air Division, became the Seventh Air Force. Separated from Naval Forces, Vietnam, the III Marine Amphibious Force functioned, in effect, as a service component command as well as a corps-level field headquarters.[19]

Given the size of the Army buildup, Westmoreland paid special attention to his Army component command. In mid-1965 he transformed the existing organization, U.S. Army Support Command, Vietnam, into a much larger headquarters, the U.S. Army, Vietnam. Unlike the other component commands, U.S. Army, Vietnam, did not direct Army combat operations or the advisory effort, which remained under MACV headquarters. But for all other purposes it commanded and administered the Army units assigned to MACV and furnished them with supply and combat-service support. It also provided common item supply to all U.S. forces in II, III, and IV Corps, as well as much of the logistical and combat assistance to the Free World allies and the South Vietnamese. Even though Westmoreland retained his second hat as the Army component commander, he secured a three-star deputy to run the organization. He gave Lt. Gen. Jean E. Engler, a logistics expert who replaced General Norton as deputy commander in January 1966, a mandate to clear up the supply logjams that were hindering the buildup. General Engler set to work at once to unclog the ports, get depots up and running, and solve the spare parts crisis epitomized by the 1st Cavalry Division's problems during the Pleiku campaign.[20]

The majority of soldiers in U.S. Army, Vietnam, were in support rather than maneuver units. The distance at which U.S. forces were operating from the United States—not to mention American tactics, which habitually attempted to expend firepower and materiel in place of men—dictated this preponderance of service troops. These soldiers repaired vehicles and aircraft, transported and distributed supplies, and filled the myriad other jobs that kept the American military machine well greased and rolling. Out of a total of 82,300 U.S. soldiers and marines in South Vietnam in August 1965, no more than 20,000 served in maneuver battalions. By the end of the year 155,000 soldiers

---

[19] Cosmas, "MACV, the Joint Command," ch. 9; "USAF Management Summary: Southeast Asia," January 1966, copy in Air Force History Support Office, Bolling Air Force Base, Washington, D.C.

[20] Sharp and Westmoreland, *Report*, p. 100; MACV History, 1965, pp. 96–97; Cosmas, "MACV, the Joint Command," ch. 9.

and marines had arrived, but only about 31,000 were in maneuver units.[21]

As 1966 began, Westmoreland, having achieved his Phase I objective and being well on the way to organizing his command to his satisfaction, started to work on Phase II, looking toward taking the offensive in due course and expanding pacification. The task before him was daunting. He had to keep the enemy at bay while laying the foundations for the effort to come. Of the two goals, the first was the more immediate. Applying the military principle of economy of force, he assigned the highest operational priority to the populated areas in III Corps around Saigon and then to those of the coastal lowlands in I and II Corps. In other areas, such as the Central Highlands, he planned to respond to enemy initiatives when they occurred but otherwise maintain no more of a U.S. presence than necessary.[22]

Looking forward to the fighting, Westmoreland spent considerable time analyzing the tactical employment of American forces.[23] A successful search and destroy operation had to contain several elements to achieve maximum effect. Timely, reliable intelligence was essential. Commanders had to be able to discern the presence of enemy forces in a general area and then to pinpoint the precise locations of individual units within that area before an attack could proceed. Once the assault began, they then had to be able to hold the enemy in place long enough to defeat him.

Westmoreland felt reasonably confident about MACV's intelligence operations. By the end of 1965 the technical means for collecting information were so well advanced that U.S. forces could often locate major Communist formations, such as battalions and regiments, within a ten- by thirty-kilometer area. But much remained to be done. Commanders had to have a fairly precise appreciation of the size, location, and dispositions of an enemy force before they could launch an assault. Since only aggressive long-range ground reconnaissance could provide this information and since few of the units in South Vietnam were trained in this military specialty, Westmoreland had no choice but to make each division and brigade responsible for establishing its own reconnaissance units, an approach that put heavy reliance on the resourcefulness of individual commanders.

As for fixing the enemy in place, the attempt was difficult in any war but particularly so when dealing with the Viet Cong, who had accumulated years of experience and were fighting on their own ground. "We have learned through long and unhappy experience," Westmoreland wrote, "that preplanned schemes of maneuver . . . by a force moving in one direction will nearly always fail to make significant contact

---

[21] MACV History, 1965, p. 269.

[22] Sharp and Westmoreland, *Report*, pp. 113–14.

[23] This and the remaining paragraphs, including quotations, based on Memo, COMUSMACV for CG, FFV, 10 Dec 65, sub: Tactical Employment of US Forces and Defensive Action, p. 1.

unless that contact is at the choosing of the VC . . . when he thinks he has all the advantage." It would not be enough, he continued, to attempt to catch the enemy between an attacking and a blocking force because the Viet Cong had long before demonstrated that they could elude such tactics. Friendly forces had not only to position themselves on all four sides of their quarry but also to find and guard potential withdrawal routes, even the most unlikely. It was a labor-intensive approach that might require the requisition of troops from other operations or, on occasion, even justify the delay of one operation in favor of another. In the end, Westmoreland believed that American commanders would have to respond to any indication that the enemy was attempting to escape by shifting position with great speed either around him, behind him, or to his flanks. Bold and skillful commanders were required at every echelon, individuals who could make speed and deception the watchwords of their tactical maneuvers.

Whatever Westmoreland's intentions, however, too few American and allied maneuver battalions were present in Vietnam at the beginning of 1966 to conduct the aggressive and sustained operations he envisioned. Neither was the U.S. logistical base adequate to support such actions on a large scale. The move into Phase II would have to be gradual, therefore, and most of 1966 would be a period of transition.

PART THREE

The Theater Buys Time

8

The Saigon Corridors

By the start of 1966 General Westmoreland, having received the promise of additional soldiers, was ready for Phase II operations. Rather than change tactics, however, he planned to consolidate his hold on Saigon while pushing his units deeper into I, II, and III Corps. Adopting a cautious approach because the steady inflow of new infantry battalions would not resume until late summer, he would husband his resources until all of the means were at hand to wage the relentless campaign that he had always wanted.

Two New Brigades for III Corps

While high-level discussions continued on troop lists and deployment schedules, Westmoreland counted on the 25th Infantry Division to fill part of the gap in his combat power that loomed ahead. Stationed in Hawaii as the Pacific Command's contingency force, the division had trained for years in jungle warfare and counterguerrilla tactics. When its troops were ready to deploy in late December, Westmoreland had no qualms about sending its 3d Brigade to Pleiku Province, a point of continuing concern in the highlands, and its 2d Brigade to Cu Chi, northwest of Saigon, where the approaches to the capital city appeared particularly vulnerable. Its 1st Brigade, when it arrived in April, also went to Cu Chi, giving the commander of the division, Maj. Gen. Frederick C. Weyand, six battalions and three cavalry troops (two armored and one airmobile) to hold part of the defensive arc facing out from Saigon.[1]

The deployment of the 25th Division, which added a second divisional headquarters to the Saigon area, precipitated administrative changes. On 15 March Westmoreland established II Field Force, Vietnam, at Bien Hoa, a corps-level headquarters responsible for coordinating the U.S. ground war throughout III Corps. For the sake of consistency, General Larsen's

---

[1] Quarterly Cmd Rpt, 1 Oct–31 Dec 65, 25th Inf Div, n.d., pp. 2–3, Historians files, CMH; ORLL, 1 Jan–30 Apr 66, 25th Inf Div, n.d., pp. 1–3, box 8A, 67A/5293, RG 319, NARA; Westmoreland Jnl, 9 Dec 65, Westmoreland History files, CMH.

Field Force, Vietnam, at Nha Trang, which filled the same function in II Corps, received a new name, becoming I Field Force, Vietnam. Westmoreland selected General Seaman to be in charge of the new headquarters, which within a month moved to new buildings at nearby Long Binh. General DePuy took Seaman's place as commander of the 1st Division and was promoted to major general on 1 April.[2]

By the end of April the 25th Division's two brigades, entering the line beside the 1st Division, increased the size of the American contingent in III Corps to 36,000 men. This seemed impressive, particularly when combined with the 39,000 South Vietnamese and Australian troops also present. Yet the odds against the enemy were hardly as long as they seemed. According to intelligence estimates, the insurgent forces in the Saigon area as of 1 January had totaled about 61,000, including some 21,000 regulars serving with various Viet Cong units. When three North Vietnamese regiments reached III Corps between January and April, the number increased to some 66,000, bringing the two sides to a rough parity.[3]

Westmoreland intended to counter the enemy threat over the long term by ringing the capital with base camps. For the time being, however, he had to content himself with guarding the most likely avenues of attack. He had already located the 1st Division's 1st and 3d Brigades north of Saigon and its 2d Brigade to the northeast at Bien Hoa, where the 173d Airborne Brigade was stationed. During March the 2d Brigade would leave Bien Hoa and move to Bearcat, a newly constructed base due east of Saigon off Highway 15. By then the 25th Division's 2d Brigade would be well established at Cu Chi along Highway 1 (*Map 12*).

The move to Cu Chi entailed considerable preparation. While various portions of the 2d Brigade dribbled into the area in late January, the 1st Division's 3d Brigade under Colonel Brodbeck conducted Operation BUCKSKIN to clear out the enemy. After establishing a forward command post at Trung Lap, thirteen kilometers northwest of Cu Chi, Brodbeck sent three battalions and a cavalry troop to sweep the flat, open terrain. One patrol located and destroyed an enemy camp. Another uncovered an extensive tunnel network, more than two kilometers long. Nearly every day of the operation the Americans found ample signs of the Viet Cong's presence—booby traps, mines, weapons, ammunition, supplies, bunkers, and more tunnel systems—but few soldiers.

On 24 January, certain that no large Viet Cong units were in the area, Colonel Brodbeck moved his brigade to Cu Chi proper to establish a perimeter around what was to become the 25th Division's new home. Almost immediately, his troops turned up a series of trenches and

---

[2] ORLLs, 1 Jan–30 Apr 66, II FFV, 1 Jun 66, pp. 1–2, box 5, 67A/5216, RG 319, and 1st Inf Div, n.d., box 1, 81/472, RG 338, NARA; Eckhardt, *Command and Control*, pp. 54, 64.

[3] ORLL, 1 Jan–30 Apr 66, 1st Inf Div, pp. 1–2; MACV History, 1965, p. 237, CMH; MACV, "Working Paper on ARVN: OB Recap," 10 Jan 66, Historians files, CMH; Periodic Intel Rpt, 1 Jan–30 Jun 66, MACV, 20 Aug 66, pp. 11–13, MHI.

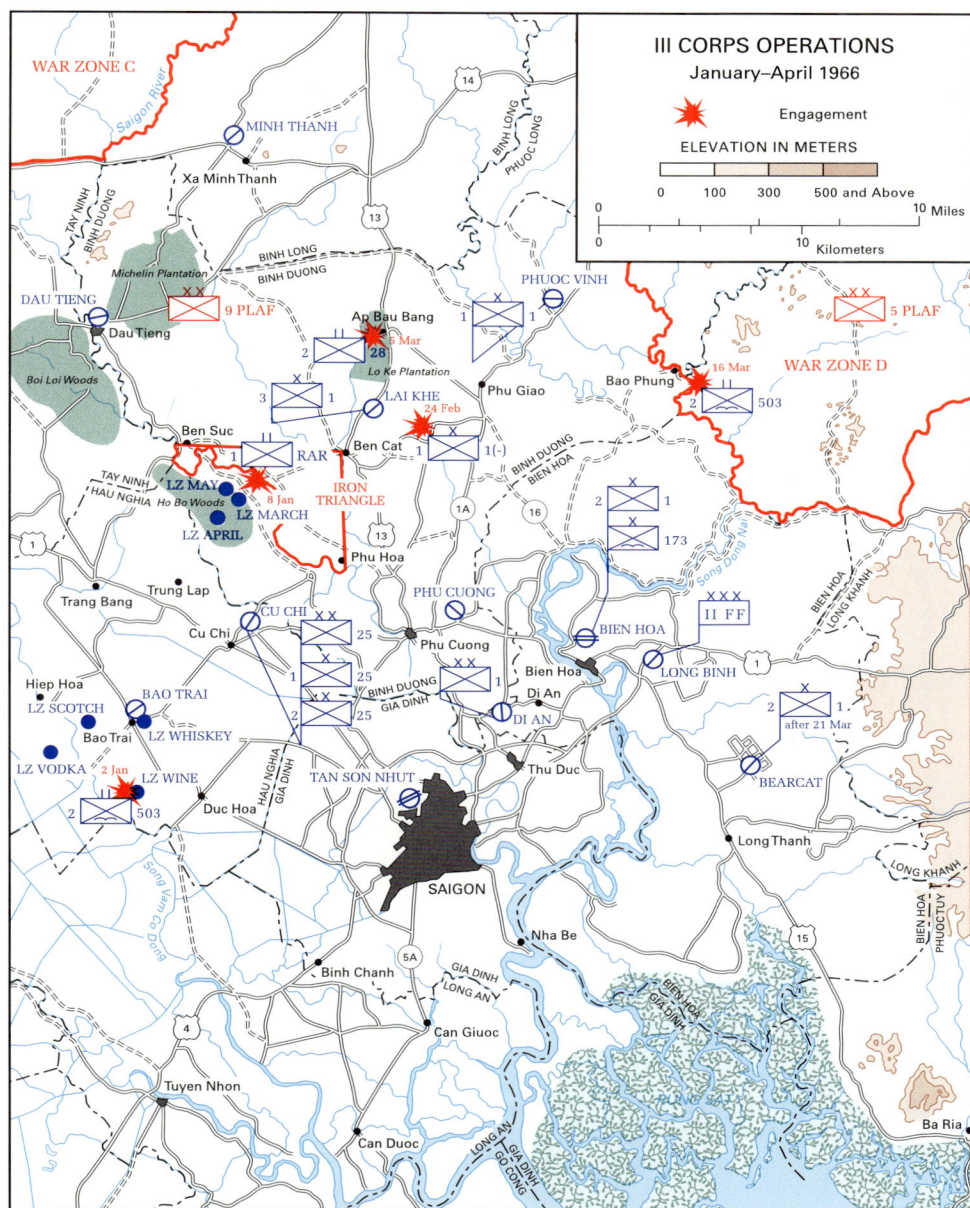

III CORPS OPERATIONS
January–April 1966

Engagement

ELEVATION IN METERS

0   100   300   500 and Above

0 _____ 10 Miles

0 _____ 10 Kilometers

WAR ZONE C

MINH THANH

Xa Minh Thanh

Michelin Plantation

DAU TIENG

Dau Tieng

9 PLAF

Boi Loi Woods

Ben Suc

TAY NINH
HAU NGHIA

LZ MAY

8 Jan

Ho Bo Woods

LZ MARCH

LZ APRIL

Trung Lap

Trang Bang

Cu Chi

CU CHI

25

25

25

Hiep Hoa

BAO TRAI

LZ SCOTCH

Bao Trai

LZ WHISKEY

BINH DUONG
GIA DINH

LZ VODKA

2 Jan

LZ WINE

503

Duc Hoa

HAU NGHIA
GIA DINH

TAN SON NHUT

SAIGON

BINH LONG
BINH DUONG

BINH LONG
BINH DUONG

An Bau Bang

5 Mar

28

Lo Ke Plantation

LAI KHE

24 Feb

Phu Giao

RAR

Ben Cat

1(-)

IRON
TRIANGLE

Phu Hoa

PHU CUONG

Phu Cuong

Di An

DI AN

Thu Duc

BINH DUONG
BIEN HOA

PHUOC VINH

1   1

Bao Phung   16 Mar

2   503

5 PLAF

WAR ZONE D

2   1

173

II FF

BIEN HOA

Bien Hoa

LONG BINH

2   1

after 21 Mar

BEARCAT

Long Thanh

LONG KHANH

BIEN HOA
LONG KHANH

Nha Be

Binh Chanh

GIA DINH
LONG AN

Can Giuoc

Tuyen Nhon

Can Duoc

LONG AN
GIA DINH
GO CONG

BIEN HOA
GIA DINH

BIEN HOA
PHUOC TUY

Ba Ria

MAP 12

tunnels that seemed to permeate the site in every direction. Recognizing the threat, Brodbeck ordered all tunnel systems at the base seeded with riot control agents and then destroyed. The demolition effort proved only partially successful, and before long his men were routinely exploring the tunnels; they would emerge hundreds of meters from their starting points, often after discovering large stores of enemy weapons and documents. Some Americans were killed, but others routed Viet Cong suspects and took prisoners. On the morning of 30 January, with the 25th's 2d Brigade largely in place, Brodbeck turned over control of Cu Chi to the brigade commander, Col. Lynnwood M. Johnson, and returned to Lai Khe.[4]

But the job had just begun, and Colonel Johnson's troops spent much of the next few months trying to clear the 25th Division's base camp of the maze of tunnels that lay beneath it. In one month alone the 2d Brigade lost 50 men killed and 350 wounded. The tunnels of Cu Chi would torment the 25th Division for years to come.[5]

Northwest of the City

While the 25th Division was slowly settling in at Cu Chi, Phase II operations in III Corps began with a series of spoiling attacks. On 1 January General Williamson's 173d Airborne Brigade launched Operation MARAUDER I, an assault on the *506th Local Force Battalion* operating along the Vam Co Dong River in Hau Nghia Province northwest of Saigon—new terrain for the Americans. Westmoreland's orders to Williamson were matter of fact: locate and destroy the enemy unit and establish a measure of control over the hostile area near the river.

By the afternoon Williamson's brigade had deployed without incident to Landing Zones VODKA and SCOTCH on the west and east sides of the Vam Co Dong. Colonel Tyler's 1st Battalion, 503d Infantry, was at VODKA and Lt. Col. Alec E. Preece's 1st Battalion, Royal Australian Regiment, was at SCOTCH. The third maneuver element, Colonel Dexter's 2d Battalion, 503d Infantry, helicoptered to Landing Zone WHISKEY near Bao Trai, the province capital, where it spent the night with Williamson's command post and the brigade artillery.

The next morning Dexter's troops found the enemy. As the 2d of the 503d Infantry reached Landing Zone WINE, seven kilometers south of Bao Trai and just one kilometer from the east bank of the Vam Co Dong, Communist infantry peppered the helicopters at the moment of touchdown. The first Americans on the ground managed to lay down enough

[4] AAR, Opn BUCKSKIN, 3d Bde, 1st Inf Div, 3 Mar 66, pp. 7–11, box 1, 81/472, RG 338, NARA.

[5] Debriefing, Lt Gen Frederick C. Weyand, 15 Jul 68, pp. 1–2, Senior Officer Debriefing Program, DA, Historians files, CMH; Tom Mangold and John Penygate, *The Tunnels of Cu Chi* (New York: Random House, 1985), pp. 202–13, 263–64.

fire to force the attackers back into the forest. Once the rest of the battalion landed safely, the troops attacked. The Viet Cong withdrew toward the river.

The chase was on. But as Colonel Dexter's men closed on the Vam Co Dong, they ran into a well-entrenched force, later identified as the *267th Battalion, Dong Thap II PLAF Regiment.* Dexter halted, calling in artillery fire and air strikes, but the insurgents held fast. Although General Williamson dispatched M113s, the vehicles bogged down in mud and failed to arrive. With no sign of reinforcements in sight, Dexter requested more artillery fire and then attacked. Advancing behind a curtain of exploding shells, two companies made a frontal assault while a third tried a flank. The artillery then shifted fire to the Viet Cong's rear, hoping to destroy them as they fled, but they stood firm, forcing Dexter into yet another assault. This time the defense crumbled, and by late afternoon the Americans were in pursuit. U.S. artillery, air strikes, and small-arms fire had killed 111 enemy soldiers.[6]

MARAUDER I failed to instigate any other major fights, but American forces did make an important intelligence find. While patrolling southwest of Bao Trai near the east bank of the Vam Co Dong on 6 January, elements of Colonel Dexter's force discovered what had been the headquarters of the operation's target, the *506th Battalion.* The enemy unit had abandoned the site in such haste that it left behind not only a sizeable quantity of supplies, weapons, and ammunition but also a cache of documents. Among them were personnel rosters for the battalion, lists of area Communist Party members, and tactical maps. Dexter's men removed the documents and everything else of value before turning the base over to a demolitions team for destruction. The operation ended formally on the morning of 8 January.[7]

On the day before MARAUDER I ended, General Westmoreland launched Operation CRIMP with both the 173d Airborne Brigade and elements of the 1st Division. Although General Seaman was technically in charge, Westmoreland had granted General Williamson specific responsibility for formulating and implementing plans involving the 173d's sector, so the exercise became, in effect, two separate operations running side by side.

CRIMP took place in the Ho Bo Woods in southwestern Binh Duong and northeastern Hau Nghia Provinces. This enemy base area abutted the west bank of the Saigon River opposite the Iron Triangle. Much of the terrain was open, except near the river, which was choked with thick jungle and overgrown rubber plantations. Seaman directed Colonel Brodbeck's 3d Brigade to operate in the southern portion of the sector while Williamson's 173d covered the area to the north. Although both

---

[6] AAR, Opn MARAUDER I, 173d Abn Bde (Sep), n.d., p. 5, and Commander's Combat Note no. 90, 173d Abn Bde (Sep), 18 Jan 66, p. 2, Historians files, CMH.

[7] AAR, Opn MARAUDER I, 173d Abn Bde, p. 17.

A 1st Division soldier enters a tunnel during Crimp.

brigades were to hunt down and destroy enemy units, Williamson had the special task of finding and assaulting the headquarters of *Military Region 4*, also known as the *Saigon-Cholon-Gia Dinh Special Sector Committee*. Directly subordinate to the *B2 Front*, the group controlled Communist military and political activities in the Saigon area.[8]

Colonel Brodbeck's portion of the operation began on the morning of 8 January. While a massive B–52 strike softened the Ho Bo Woods, the 3d Brigade command group and other support elements departed Di An by convoy, reaching Trung Lap, on the western edge of the area of operations, by midday. Meanwhile, two of the three maneuver battalions involved deployed by helicopter to the southwest corner of the objective; one blocked off the south side of the woods, and the other searched for the enemy. The third battalion moved by truck from Di An to Trung Lap and then on foot to its assigned sector of the sweep.

At first there was no contact. On 9 January the Americans found and destroyed a cache of medical supplies, two tons of rice, and a small hos-

---

[8] AAR, Opn Crimp, 3d Bde, 1st Inf Div, 15 Feb 66, p. 4, box 1, 81/472, RG 338, NARA; AAR, Opn Crimp, 173d Abn Bde (Sep), 23 Feb 66, p. 1, Historians files, CMH.

pital, capturing some thirty Viet Cong as well. The next day the blocking battalion discovered a small enemy base camp, which it demolished, and one of the attack battalions captured ten tons of rice and fifteen bales of cotton after a brief firefight. On the eleventh it was more of the same. The Americans found and destroyed bunkers, houses, sampans, supplies, and food. In one tunnel complex they found a collection of maps, charts, and documents but met little resistance. As the units carried out their missions, they lost more men to booby traps than to enemy fire. By dusk of the eleventh the battalions had completed searching their assigned areas, and the following morning Colonel Brodbeck ended the 3d Brigade's participation in CRIMP.[9]

The brigade's meager accomplishments had not been totally unexpected. An analysis completed by Brodbeck before the operation had indicated that the Viet Cong would probably not stand and fight a large American force, but instead would use hit-and-run and ambush techniques to inflict casualties. An enemy combat officer, Lt. Nguyen Thanh Linh, later confirmed Brodbeck's conclusion in an interview:

We waited until they [the Americans] were very close. We were in our spider-hole firing positions—the Americans never saw us at all. I ordered my men to fire, one GI fell down, the others just stood around looking at him. . . . They did not even know where the bullets had come from. We kept on shooting. Although their fellows kept falling down, they kept on advancing. Then they called for artillery. When the first shells landed we simply went into the . . . tunnels and went on to another place.

Using such methods, the Viet Cong killed 6 and wounded 45 3d Brigade soldiers during CRIMP at a cost of 22 confirmed dead and an unknown number of additional casualties.[10]

The 173d Airborne Brigade began its portion of CRIMP at about the same time as Brodbeck's unit. General Williamson had hoped to achieve tactical surprise by deliberately withholding from South Vietnamese III Corps headquarters any information about his force's role in the operation until the American helicopters were in the air. Despite the precaution, there may have been a security breach. An American electronic intelligence unit would note later that a radio transmission went from III Corps headquarters to the enemy early on the morning of 8 January, just prior to the start of CRIMP.[11]

The operation began at 0930, following a forty-five-minute preparation by fighter-bombers, artillery, and helicopter gunships. Behind the barrage Colonel Preece's 1st Battalion, Royal Australian Regiment, flew

---

[9] AARs, Opn CRIMP, 3d Bde, 1st Inf Div, pp. 5–7, and 173d Abn Bde, pp. 4–7.

[10] AAR, Opn CRIMP, 3d Bde, 1st Inf Div, pp. 3, 7–8; Mangold and Penygate, *Tunnels of Cu Chi*, p. 50 (quotation).

[11] Breen, *First To Fight*, p. 179.

A 105-mm. howitzer provides firepower to the 173d Airborne Brigade on the last day of CRIMP.

into Landing Zone MARCH, located inside an old rubber plantation just to the west of Route 15 and then maneuvered to the east across the road to its designated blocking position. The Australians met only light resistance at first, but shortly after noon, as the battalion's companies moved through an area thick with booby traps and mines, they suddenly ran into determined fire from small arms, recoilless rifles, and mortars. The fighting intensified and continued into the late afternoon, with the Australians overrunning successive enemy positions until nightfall. The Viet Cong fought tenaciously, according to a report, "obviously in defense of something of great value to them."[12]

The 173d's other two infantry battalions landed southwest and west of the Australians. Colonel Tyler's 1st of the 503d Infantry touched down at Landing Zone APRIL at 1200; Colonel Dexter's 2d of the 503d Infantry arrived at MAY around 1430. Advancing to the east and southeast of the suspected site of *Military Region 4* headquarters, the two converged on the target, but a thorough search turned up no sign of enemy soldiers. It appeared that the Australians had chased them away earlier that day.[13]

The brigade's battalions established defensive perimeters at dusk. During the night the Australians heard sounds of scuffling and digging,

[12] AAR, Opn CRIMP, 173d Abn Bde, p. 5.
[13] Ibid.

172

and saw shadowy figures emerge from the undergrowth and slip away. It seemed to them that they might be sitting atop a major enemy complex, perhaps the very one they had targeted. But, unable to distinguish friend from foe in the darkness, they held their fire.[14]

The next morning the Australians found a network of tunnels leading to a deserted headquarters. Inside were some seventy-five hundred documents—the working files of a major political and military command, very likely *Military Region 4*. Included were lists of Communist Party members living nearby and data on the command's organization and staff. Perhaps more important, the records conveyed a sense of what Viet Cong and North Vietnamese commanders in the area knew about American efforts in III Corps. There were detailed maps of friendly installations, lists of the units manning them, and even extensive rosters of Americans living in metropolitan Saigon. One valuable find was the notebook of a high-level political officer that contained a history of the insurgency from the mid-1950s through early 1963. It became known as the "CRIMP Document." In all, as one intelligence analyst later remarked, the discovery was a "real treasure."[15]

To the south, the rest of the 173d Airborne Brigade had less luck. Tyler's and Dexter's battalions began the second day of CRIMP by searching eastward toward the Saigon River. They continued to find supply caches and abandoned positions, but reported only light skirmishes. Consequently, on 10 January, General Williamson ordered Tyler's 1st of the 503d to advance in a new direction, a move that quickly generated a clash with a company-size force. Supported by artillery and air strikes, Tyler's men killed 29 Viet Cong before the enemy withdrew. Subsequent searches failed to generate significant contacts, and on the fourteenth Williamson terminated CRIMP and the brigade returned to Bien Hoa.[16]

Although *Military Region 4* headquarters troops had escaped the 173d's dragnet and although the enemy threat remained, the U.S.-Australian team had killed 128 Viet Cong regulars, and possibly 190 more, at a cost of 23 killed and 102 wounded. Besides cutting into Viet Cong battle strength, the allied team had limited enemy operations in other ways by capturing large stocks of food and munitions. In addition, the huge haul of headquarters documents would force the Communists to adjust their planning for some time to come.[17]

A little over a month after CRIMP ended, General Seaman conducted another spoiling attack north of Saigon—Operation MASTIFF. Planning

---

[14] Breen, *First To Fight*, p. 189.

[15] AAR, Opn CRIMP, 173d Abn Bde, pp. 3–4, 18; U.S. Department of State, "Working Paper on the North Vietnamese Role in the War in South Viet-Nam," March 1968, item 301 ("CRIMP Document"), Historians files, CMH; Sedgewick D. Tourison, Jr., *Talking With Victor Charlie: An Interrogator's Story* (New York: Ivy Books, 1991), p. 160 (quoted words).

[16] AAR, Opn CRIMP, 173d Abn Bde, p. 8.

[17] Ibid., p. 18.

Infantrymen during MASTIFF search for the bodies of Americans missing since December.

for MASTIFF began after American intelligence revealed that the *9th PLAF Division* intended to attack the South Vietnamese 5th Infantry Division's 8th Regiment at Dau Tieng. Informed that the enemy was massing his forces in the Boi Loi Woods twelve kilometers south of Dau Tieng, Westmoreland ordered Seaman to launch a preemptive strike.[18]

In planning the strike Seaman was determined to prevent the South Vietnamese from leaking details of the operation. He prepared a false attack plan that targeted the Michelin Plantation east of Dau Tieng and the Saigon River, making sure it was seen by the III Corps staff. To lend authenticity to the ruse, he increased aerial surveillance south of the plantation and sent B–52s against decoy targets. If all went well, the Viet Cong would withdraw their forces to the west bank of the river, where they would be caught unaware when the real attack began.

After the deception plan had been in place for a week, Seaman launched a large-scale encirclement. On the morning of 21 February one hundred forty-two helicopters began a series of lifts that deployed the

---

[18] AAR, Opn MASTIFF, 1st Inf Div, n.d., pp. 2, 4, box 1, 81/472, RG 338, NARA.

1st Division's 2d and 3d Brigades along three sides of a hundred-square-kilometer area bordering the west bank of the Saigon River. The three battalions of Col. Albert E. Milloy's 2d Brigade took up positions to the north and west of the target area; two battalions of Colonel Brodbeck's 3d Brigade and the division's armored cavalry squadron deployed to the south and southeast. A sixth battalion, in reserve, flew to the southwest. Once the seal was formed, two of Milloy's battalions attacked south while Brodbeck's infantry pushed north, with the remaining units holding their positions to prevent escape. But the Viet Cong had not taken the bait. Although the Americans uncovered base camps, small hospitals stocked with medical supplies, training areas, rice storage caches, and small munitions factories, they met little organized resistance, killing only 61 soldiers, 40 of them in a single air strike. Without any big battle payoff Seaman terminated MASTIFF on the morning of 25 February, but it took another two days for the operation to wind down completely. American casualties totaled 17 killed and 94 wounded, mostly by mines and booby traps. MASTIFF proved to be a major disappointment for the American high command.[19]

Operations CRIMP and MASTIFF gave U.S. commanders a frustrating reminder of the enemy's skill at avoiding battle with large formations. Colonel Brodbeck thought the key to changing that pattern lay in reducing the size of the U.S. units sent into the field—creating, in effect, tempting targets for the Viet Cong. To test that theory, his 3d Brigade launched Operation BOSTON/COCOA BEACH.

Under Brodbeck's plan, the brigade would conduct a series of battalion-size operations north of Lai Khe and immediately to the west of Highway 13 near the hamlet of Bau Bang. American intelligence believed that the *9th Division's 272d Regiment* was lurking there. Brodbeck envisioned his battalions rotating one at a time through a specified sector, each conducting company-size sweeps. If no contact occurred after a few days, the battalion would move to another location, but a second would arrive to carry out the same mission in a different segment of the area. After two more days, the first battalion would return to the brigade's base camp at Lai Khe and a third battalion would arrive to continue the search. Each mission would take place within range of the 105-mm. howitzers at Lai Khe. For the complex operation to work, a premium would be placed on leadership and staff work at the brigade command post.[20]

Lt. Col. Kyle W. Bowie's 2d Battalion, 28th Infantry, initiated BOSTON/COCOA BEACH at 0800 on 3 March, moving on foot to the Lo Ke Rubber Plantation just west of Bau Bang. Colonel Bowie established a

---

[19] Ibid., pp. 16, 18; AARs, Opn MASTIFF, 2d Bde, 1st Inf Div, 31 Mar 66, p. 5, box 1, 81/471, and 3d Bde, 1st Inf Div, 25 Mar 66, pp. 7–8, box 1, 81/472, RG 338, NARA.

[20] AAR, Opn COCOA BEACH, 3d Bde, 1st Inf Div, 3 Apr 66, pp. 4, 7, box 1, 81/471, RG 338, NARA; ORLL, 1 Jan–30 Apr 66, 1st Inf Div, incl. 13, p. 1.

patrol base, and as his troops dug foxholes and fighting positions, helicopters brought extra ammunition and supplies. By sundown the 2d of the 28th Infantry was ready. As darkness fell, Bowie sent out squad ambushes along the approaches to his perimeter. The next morning he deployed two company patrols, one to the west and the other to the north. Later in the day the northern company came upon a kilometer-long trench that clearly had been occupied by a large enemy force as recently as two days before. Bowie believed the trench could be used as a jumping-off point for an assault on his base camp, so that evening he sent out three fifteen-man patrols—one each to the south, north, and east. He also dispatched a four-man listening post to the west. All would act as the battalion's eyes and ears overnight. Shortly after midnight Bowie's concern grew when his intelligence section reported a large, perhaps regimental-size, Viet Cong force only four kilometers northeast of his position. The night, however, passed without incident.[21]

Early in the morning of 5 March, as Bowie's troops prepared for the day, the company patrol to the north of the perimeter heard noises. Led by Company B's 2d Lt. Robert J. Hibbs, the unit went on the alert and kept low. Although it was still dark, Lieutenant Hibbs could see well enough through his Starlight scope, a night-imaging device that intensified the existing light. Half an hour later, shortly before daybreak, Hibbs' men spotted an enemy supply column of about one hundred women and children moving slowly from the east along a road that lay on the northwest corner of the Lo Ke Plantation. The women were carrying weapons, while the children bore ammunition. The file stopped fifty to one hundred meters short of the patrol's position, meeting up with about a company of Viet Cong coming in from the north. Hibbs noticed that they were breathing hard, "as if they had been running for some distance." As Hibbs watched through the wavy green hues of the Starlight scope, the commander appeared to issue instructions to his men and then moved a short distance down the road to meet with the women. Hibbs slipped quietly from concealment and repositioned two of his claymore mines.[22]

The Viet Cong commander returned to his column. Accompanied by some of the women and children, the insurgents continued south toward Bowie's perimeter. As they passed Hibbs, he detonated the two claymores. A blast of steel flechettes tore through the column, killing almost everyone in their path. One small boy miraculously survived, but was stunned and ran around in circles. Hibbs' men extended the killing zone by hurling grenades onto and beyond the road. After the volley of grenades exploded the Viet Cong began to return fire, and the

[21] Resumé of Comments of the Commanding Officer of the 2d Battalion, 28th Infantry, on the Battle of Lo Ke on 5 March 1966, p. 1, Historians files, CMH (hereafter cited as Bowie's Comments).

[22] Ibid., p. 2 (quoted words); Annual Hist Sum, 1966, 2d Bn, 28th Inf, n.d., app. B, p. ii, box 6, 81/469, RG 338, NARA.

Americans withdrew toward the battalion perimeter. They were a mere hundred meters from safety when they ran into another enemy force, which was probably preparing to attack Bowie's position. At first, Hibbs thought they were Americans, but when he realized his mistake, his men opened fire and tossed grenades to clear the way back to the battalion.[23]

Lieutenant Hibbs did not make it to safety. One soldier was wounded in the hail of gunfire, and Hibbs and his sergeant stopped to help him. But as they reached their fallen comrade, two machine guns ripped into them. Hibbs ordered the others to keep going and then, armed only with his M16 and a pistol, charged the gun crews. He fell, mortally wounded, in a hail of bullets. As he lay dying, he smashed his Starlight scope to keep it from falling into enemy hands.[24]

As soon as the Americans were back inside the perimeter, the Viet Cong commenced their assault. The attackers of Hibbs' patrol charged first, running into concentrated fire from the dug-in Americans. They fell back and regrouped. Next came a series of overlapping attacks from different directions. The first, launched from a tangle of tall grass northeast of the perimeter, came at 0645. Ten minutes later a second one targeted the east side, followed at 0715 by a larger assault from the southwest. At the same time, concealed enemy troops poured fire into the Americans. Although greatly outnumbered, Bowie's men turned the tide by calling in air strikes. F–100s swooped in on the southwest side of the perimeter, dropping 500-pound bombs on the advancing forces. Explosions and shrapnel sent them reeling. Aircraft also dropped cluster bombs on those who had taken cover in a trench north of the perimeter, killing many. By midmorning the Viet Cong had had enough and were filtering away from the battlefield.[25]

Their withdrawal did not end the operation. Earlier, Colonel Brodbeck had placed Lt. Col. William S. Lober's 1st Battalion, 16th Infantry, on alert to assist Colonel Bowie. Since the largest and most persistent of the attacks had come from the northeast, Brodbeck assumed that the enemy would retreat in that direction and ordered Lober's battalion to a landing zone about two kilometers northeast of Bowie. With a little luck, the Viet Cong would be trapped between the two battalions.

By 1050 the 1st of the 16th was on the ground and moving west and then south toward the 2d of the 28th. Brushing aside a small force dressed in the light khaki of North Vietnamese regulars, Lober's battalion reached Bowie's around 1430. About two hours earlier one of Bowie's patrols had sighted a company of troops facing away from the American position, as if planning to ambush an expected relief force from Lai Khe. The patrol called in artillery, but did not search the impact zone. The

[23] ORLL, 1 Jan–30 Apr 66, 1st Inf Div, incl. 13, p. 3.

[24] Bowie's Comments, p. 2. Lieutenant Hibbs received the Medal of Honor posthumously. See Annual Hist Sum, 1966, 2d Bn, 28th Inf, app. A.

[25] Annual Hist Sum, 1966, 2d Bn, 28th Inf, app. B, p. iii; Interv, author with Col Kyle W. Bowie, 11 Mar 99, Historians files, CMH.

following morning, 6 March, Brodbeck committed a third battalion to the operation, Colonel Shuffer's 2d of the 2d Infantry. Throughout the day the three battalions searched the battle area but found only enemy dead and discarded equipment. That evening Bowie's men ended their part in the operation with a sweep through Bau Bang and then returned to Lai Khe. Lober's and Shuffer's men remained in the field for another two unproductive days before Brodbeck terminated the operation.[26]

The battle had cost the *272d Regiment* dearly. According to MACV figures, 199 Viet Cong died in the fighting. The Americans suffered 15 killed, 6 of whom died on 5 March when a resupply helicopter crashed near the battalion perimeter. General Westmoreland was pleased with the outcome at Lo Ke, calling it a "complete rout of the enemy." Colonel Brodbeck also believed that it was "a complete success" and argued that its results more than justified his earlier contention that battalion searches rather than brigade- and division-size operations were more likely to produce fruitful contact with main force Viet Cong units.[27]

North and East

To the north and east of Saigon the pace of operations was slower. Enemy units there lacked the luxury of Cambodian sanctuaries, and, except for War Zone D, they had few safe havens to retreat to when they found themselves in trouble on the battlefield. Also, the population was less sympathetic to the Communist cause, especially in the clusters of villages made up of Catholic refugees from the North. Still, together with the few main force units nearby, the local forces were in sufficient number to keep the Americans busy. During the winter and early spring U.S. forces launched three major operations in the area to harry the Viet Cong.

The first was Operation MALLET, aimed at enemy forces between Bien Hoa and Ba Ria, the capital of Phuoc Tuy Province. General Seaman gave the job to Colonel Milloy's 2d Brigade, dividing the operation into two phases. During Phase I Milloy would operate in Nhon Trach District west of Highway 15; during Phase II he would shift his forces to Long Thanh District east of the road. For the most part Milloy would be operating blind, since the Americans had only superficial knowledge of the Viet Cong order of battle. The equivalent of six battalions—half of them main force units—were thought to be operating in Nhon Trach District, while Long Thanh District was suspected of harboring the *D800 Battalion*.

On the first day of Phase I, 28 January, Colonel Milloy took an infantry and artillery battalion, a cavalry troop, and civil affairs and psychological operations teams south from Bien Hoa to a point about four kilo-

---

[26] AAR, Opn COCOA BEACH, 3d Bde, 1st Inf Div, p. 3 and incl. 5, p. 3; ORLL, 1 Jan–30 Apr 66, 1st Inf Div, incl. 13, p. 4.

[27] AAR, Opn COCOA BEACH, 3d Bde, 1st Inf Div, pp. 2, 7; Monthly Eval Rpt, MACV, Mar 66, p. A14 (quoted words), MHI.

meters below the town of Long Thanh. They conducted sweeps to the south, while the brigade's other two infantry battalions made unopposed air assaults several kilometers south and began maneuvering north. The patrols continued through 2 February, but turned up only a handful of base camps and supply caches. The following day Milloy, using his three infantry battalions, launched an attack on an unnamed enemy-dominated hamlet in the northern part of Nhon Trach District. Two of the infantry battalions, supported by helicopter gunships and a Regional Forces company, sealed off the hamlet; the third, using helicopters, attacked from the west. A thorough search flushed only a few enemy soldiers, a far cry from the major battle Colonel Milloy had hoped to provoke.[28]

Phase II began on 7 February. Two battalions traveled by truck to the hamlet of Binh Son, about ten kilometers east of Long Thanh, and then patrolled to the southeast; the third moved by truck some seven kilometers south of Binh Son and struck out to the east. Over the next eight days they discovered rice caches and base camps, one of which was big enough to accommodate a regiment, but the insurgents once again proved elusive. Disappointed with the lack of action, Milloy ended MALLET on 15 February and returned his units to Bien Hoa.

During the operation the Viet Cong lost 47 killed; the Americans, 10. Milloy assumed that the enemy had more casualties not found by his men. His suspicion proved to be correct; a few days later a South Vietnamese unit discovered the bodies of 94 Viet Cong, killed in an air strike. More important than the body count, MALLET also opened Highway 15 and established an allied presence in the area, permitting government officials to enter a number of hamlets that had long been controlled by the Viet Cong. It was now up to the South Vietnamese to maintain their hold after the American troops departed.[29]

MALLET had not quite wound down when the 1st Division launched Operation ROLLING STONE on 11 February. The purpose of the operation was to provide security for the 1st Engineer Battalion as it built an all-weather road linking Highway 13 with Route 16 north of Saigon in Binh Duong Province. The new thoroughfare would improve communications between the 1st Division's bases at Phuoc Vinh and Lai Khe and allow the South Vietnamese government to extend its authority over the intervening territory. Since the proposed road lay astride a major enemy supply and infiltration route linking War Zones C and D, successful completion of the project and associated pacification measures threatened further to isolate War Zone D from Communist bases to the west. General Seaman anticipated a violent response.

Seaman gave the job of securing the road-building detail to Col. Edgar N. Glotzbach's 1st Brigade. Colonel Glotzbach, in turn, assigned

---

[28] AAR, Opn MALLET, 2d Bde, 1st Inf Div, 7 Mar 66, p. 5, box 1, 81/472, RG 338, NARA.
[29] Ibid.

one of his three battalions to guard the engineers on a rotating basis, while the other two probed nearby to keep the enemy off balance. At first all went smoothly, as the only adversary the Americans had to fight was the dry season's oppressive heat. Then, nearly two weeks into the operation, the Viet Cong struck, massing nearly eighteen hundred soldiers from the *9th Division's 271st* and *273d Regiments,* the *D800 Battalion,* and possibly two other units, for what they hoped would be a decisive blow.[30]

On 23 February Colonel Glotzbach established his command post outside of Tan Binh, a hamlet just north of the new roadway and less than five kilometers west of Route 16. Early on the morning of the twenty-fourth American soldiers at listening posts outside the perimeter detected small groups of Viet Cong moving about. One outpost opened fire, killing 2 enemy soldiers. The action alerted those inside the camp—elements of the 1st Battalion, 26th Infantry, two batteries from the 1st Battalion, 5th Artillery, as well as Troop B, 1st Squadron, 4th Cavalry, and Company B, 1st Battalion, 28th Infantry. The Viet Cong, however, receded into the night, and for the next forty-five minutes the Americans waited nervously in position, straining eye and ear to penetrate the dark silence that enveloped them. Then, at 0145, a barrage of mortar and small-arms fire shattered the stillness. Over the next hour the firing gradually intensified until, at 0300, the enemy shifted fires, now augmented by recoilless rifles, to the northwest side of the perimeter. Glotzbach feared a ground assault, but the Viet Cong held back, intimidated by the American response. Glotzbach's two 105-mm. batteries were particularly effective, lowering their tubes and firing one hundred sixty-six high explosive rounds directly into enemy positions, while the heavy 6th Battalion, 27th Artillery, firing from Phuoc Vinh, added depth to the kill zone.[31]

As daybreak neared, the Viet Cong seemed confused, unwilling either to attack or to withdraw. Then at 0530 they made their move. But there was no mass assault, only a series of disjointed attacks, none of which contained more than forty soldiers. The Americans repelled them all without difficulty, and by 0645 the insurgents began to withdraw.[32]

The battle at Tan Binh cost Glotzbach 11 dead and 74 wounded. One tank and two trucks had been destroyed, and two tanks and four armored personnel carriers had been damaged. The cost to the Viet Cong was much higher. At least 142 insurgents died in the assault, and blood trails along their evacuation route, interviews with local Vietnamese, and reports from government agents indicated that the toll was probably far higher. The Americans also captured and destroyed a good deal

[30] AAR, Opn ROLLING STONE, 1st Bde, 1st Inf Div, 28 Mar 66, incl. 1., pp. 1–2, box 1, 81/472, RG 338, NARA; *9th Division*, p. 64, copy in CMH.

[31] AAR, Opn ROLLING STONE, 1st Bde, 1st Inf Div, incl. 1, pp. 1–2.

[32] Annual Hist Sum, 1966, 1st Sqdn, 4th Cav, 7 May 67, p. 2, box 5, 81/469, RG 338, NARA.

of equipment, including small arms and ammunition, crew-served weapons, and grenades.[33]

After their bloody repulse at Tan Binh, the Viet Cong avoided battle, choosing instead to harass the work parties with occasional mortar and sniper fire. Although they killed 3 Americans and wounded 29, they were unable to stop the engineers, and by 2 March the road was complete. In the meantime, Colonel Glotzbach tried to solidify his gains by waging an aggressive civic action campaign. His civil affairs and psychological operations teams distributed over 250,000 posters, safe conduct passes, and leaflets with such themes as "Inevitable Victory," "Don't Let the VC Use Your Property To Shoot at Us, for We Must Shoot Back," and "You Help the Army, the Army Helps You." While loudspeaker teams broadcast anti-Communist messages, soldiers repaired damaged houses and distributed food, American MEDCAP teams treated seven hundred fifty-four civilians, and South Vietnamese health workers inoculated four hundred children. Indicative of the new level of security, two district chiefs visited nearby hamlets for the first time in years. Glotzbach was optimistic that the combination of military security and goodwill would soon convert the population into supporters of the central government, but only if the authorities followed up aggressively by permanently stationing South Vietnamese Army regulars in the area to protect against a return of the Viet Cong. Without such protection, he doubted that ROLLING STONE would have any long-term effect in Binh Duong Province.[34]

Five days after wrapping up ROLLING STONE , Colonel Glotzbach's 1st Brigade joined the 173d Airborne Brigade in Operation SILVER CITY, a sweep of the southwestern sector of War Zone D. The goal of the operation was to destroy the headquarters of the *B2 Front's Military Region 1*, a five-province expanse east and north of Saigon, and to bring to battle the five major units currently under its command—the *9th PLAF Division's 271st* and *273d Regiments*; the *5th PLAF Division's 274th* and *275th Regiments*; and the *308th Main Force Battalion*—a total of almost nine thousand men. Intelligence analysts hoped that enemy commanders would rise to the challenge offered by the two brigades. If they did not, they risked the destruction of their supply routes and depots in War Zone D.

On 7 March Colonel Glotzbach's units moved southeast of Phuoc Vinh to their area of operations, called NEVADA. At the same time, the 173d Airborne Brigade, now commanded by Brig. Gen. Paul F. Smith, moved into its own area, code-named ARIZONA, which extended eastward from the Song Be into War Zone D. By the morning of the ninth all was ready. The first of Smith's battalions helicoptered to the west

[33] AAR, Opn ROLLING STONE, 1st Bde, 1st Inf Div, p. 16.

[34] Ibid. and incl. 2, pp. 1–4. Consisting mainly of U.S. Army medical personnel, MEDCAP (or Medical Civic Action Program) teams joined with South Vietnamese medical workers to establish temporary health clinics in hamlets, treating civilians on an outpatient basis. See Maj. Gen. Spurgeon Neel, *Medical Support of the U.S. Army in Vietnam, 1965–1970*, Vietnam Studies (Washington, D.C.: Department of the Army, 1973), pp. 164–65.

bank of the Song Be. The lead unit was followed by a second battalion, which crossed over to the Song Be's eastern bank. Meanwhile, the 173d's artillery and command group reached a landing zone east of the river, near the hamlet of Bao Phung, and set up there. The 173d's third battalion was in position by the eleventh.[35]

Paratroopers hunt along the Song Be near War Zone D.

In the days that followed, both brigades sent out patrols to search the territory's low rolling hills. Although the ground was dry this time of year, the going was tough, as thick triple-canopied jungle covered much of the area. From time to time there were a few scattered firefights, but generally the Viet Cong remained hidden. The Americans discovered and destroyed a number of installations, but for the most part the search was unproductive.

There was one exception. On the fourteenth the 173d's Company C, 2d Battalion, 503d Infantry, found an enemy force east of the Song Be. Hunkered down in trenches and machine gun nests and protected by command-detonated mines, the Viet Cong refused to budge. Lt. Col. John J. Walsh, who had assumed command of the 2d of the 503d Infantry after a sniper had wounded Colonel Dexter just prior to SILVER CITY, called in artillery and air strikes. When the smoke cleared, the Americans rushed the position, killing at least 9 enemy soldiers. As it turned out, the Viet Cong were defending a headquarters complex that included offices, a hospital, even a tailor's shop. General Smith believed that his men had overrun the headquarters of *Military Region 1*, the central target of the operation, or at least some part of a major political headquarters.[36]

The next day, the fifteenth, Colonel Walsh's battalion conducted a detailed search of the complex. The troops discovered caches containing rice and other food, medical supplies, documents, mines, and a printing press, and destroyed them all. They then settled in for the night about six kilometers east of the brigade command post at Bao Phung.

---

[35] Msg, MACJ–2 07474 to CG, 1st Inf Div, 9 Mar 66, sub: Opn SILVER CITY, box 6, 69A/702, RG 334, NARA.

[36] Breen, *First To Fight*, p. 215; Commander's Combat Note no. 1, 173d Abn Bde (Sep), 14 May 66, pp. 7–8, box 6, 82/1474, RG 338, NARA.

Although the Americans set out the standard night watch and listening posts, the commander of the *271st Regiment* managed to deploy nearly two thousand soldiers around Colonel Walsh's perimeter, some as close as three hundred meters. The next morning Walsh inadvertently assisted his adversary's preparations when he neglected to send out patrols to check the surrounding terrain. The Americans were quite surprised when at 0730 a burst of machine gun fire greeted an incoming resupply helicopter. The soldiers watched in horror as the stricken Huey "dropped out of the sky like a rock." Fortunately for the Americans, the incident also seemed to have distracted the Viet Cong; some interpreted the fusillade as the signal to attack, while others hesitated. The resulting confusion gave Walsh's troops the chance to man every defensive position.[37]

Throughout the morning the Viet Cong launched assaults on all sides of the American laager. At times, the Communists surged to as close as fifteen meters before being driven back. The Americans soon began to run short of ammunition, but at 0930 helicopters swooped in with crates of bullets and grenades. Meanwhile, the Air Force flew ground-support missions all morning, aiming mainly at Viet Cong formations in reserve behind the attackers. American and Australian artillery also battered the enemy with over three thousand rounds, sometimes coming as close as thirty meters to the perimeter.[38]

Reinforcements for Walsh arrived shortly before 1000, but by that time the enemy was in retreat. General DePuy, now commanding the 1st Division, deployed two battalions south of Walsh in hopes of cutting off the Viet Cong, but they escaped anyway. The insurgents left 303 dead behind and carried off as many as 150 more. The Americans suffered 7 killed and 162 wounded.[39]

Operation SILVER CITY went on for another week without contact. On 22 March the 173d Airborne Brigade pulled back, followed the next day by the 1st Division's 1st Brigade. In all, the two units had killed 353 Viet Cong soldiers and estimated an additional 218 killed. American losses came to 11 killed and 228 wounded. The two brigades had found and destroyed some three hundred seventy tons of rice, had interdicted the enemy's lines of communication, and had disrupted one of the major Viet Cong sanctuaries in III Corps. In this case at least, a spoiling operation on the approaches to Saigon had brought some good results.[40]

---

[37] Breen, *First To Fight*, p. 231 (quoted words); Commander's Combat Note no. 1, 173d Abn Bde, pp. 4–5, 8.

[38] Breen, *First To Fight*, pp. 231, 233.

[39] Annual Hist Sum, 1966, 2d Bn, 28th Inf, p. 6; Commander's Combat Note no. 1, 173d Abn Bde, p. 6. For its performance on 16 March, the 2d of the 503d Infantry received the Presidential Unit Citation. See General Order (GO) 40, DA, 21 Sep 67.

[40] Commander's Combat Note no. 1, 173d Abn Bde, p. 8; AAR, Opn SILVER CITY, 1st Bde, 1st Inf Div, 12 Apr 66, pp. 11, 14–15, box 1, 81/472, RG 338, NARA; Breen, *First To Fight*, p. 233.

9

Attrition and Pacification in Phu Yen

After Saigon, General Westmoreland made securing the populated coastal plain of I and II Corps his main objective for early 1966. The rice paddies of Phu Yen Province were particularly important to him. While the Communist main forces in II Corps drew their arms and equipment from the North, they obtained much of their food in Phu Yen's Tuy Hoa Valley. In fact, they had requisitioned so much of the valley's rice harvest in 1965 that the government had to import some six hundred tons of food per month to feed the territory's population. Aware that a rich harvest was once more about to come in, Westmoreland was determined to reverse the situation and deny the enemy sustenance. Colonel Timothy's 1st Brigade, 101st Airborne Division, drew the assignment.[1]

On the Coast

The Tuy Hoa Valley spanned twenty-one-hundred square kilometers of a triangular area, with thirty-five kilometers of the South China Sea coastline as its base. The north and south sides of the valley, enclosed by verdant mountains, converged at a point thirty-five kilometers inland. Bisecting the area was the Da Rang River, flowing east to the sea. The most important city in the area was Tuy Hoa, the province capital, which lay at the mouth of the river at the juncture of Highway 1 and Route 7B. Somewhere in the mountains within a twenty-kilometer radius of Tuy Hoa were three battalions of the *95th PAVN Regiment, 5th PAVN Division.*[2]

On 15 January Colonel Timothy launched Operation VAN BUREN, the first phase of the rice-protection campaign, by having Lt. Col. Henry E. Emerson's 2d Battalion, 502d Infantry, and a forward command group fly

---

[1] A. Terry Rambo, Jerry M. Tinker, and John D. LeNoir, *The Refugee Situation in Phu-Yen Province, Vietnam* (McLean, Va.: Human Sciences Research, 1967), pp. 59–60; ORLL, 1 Jan–30 Apr 66, 1st Bde, 101st Abn Div, 15 May 66, p. 1, Historians files, CMH; Sharp and Westmoreland, *Report*, pp. 113–14, 123.

[2] ORLL, 1 Jan–30 Apr 66, 1st Bde, 101st Abn Div, incl. 2, p. 1; Monthly OB Sum, CICV, 16–31 Mar 66, pt. 4, p. 4, Historians files, CMH.

The Tuy Hoa Valley

to the Tuy Hoa North airfield, some one hundred forty kilometers north of the brigade base camp at Phan Rang. Three days later Lt. Col. Melvin Garten's 2d Battalion, 327th Infantry, and brigade bulk supplies arrived on LSTs at Tuy Hoa port, leaving Lt. Col. Joseph B. Rogers' 1st Battalion, 327th Infantry, to hold Phan Rang. For the rest of the month the 2d of the 502d Infantry patrolled north of the Da Rang and the 2d of the 327th Infantry, with the South Korean 2d Marine Brigade, offered security to farmers south of the river. This arrangement continued until 31 January, when elements of the *95th Regiment* attacked the South Koreans. Although the marines repulsed the assault, they took heavy casualties. To give the battered marines a respite, the 1st Brigade's new commander, Brig. Gen. Willard Pearson, agreed to assume responsibility for their zone of operations south of the Da Rang, a commitment made easier by the arrival of Colonel Rogers' unit from Phan Rang in early February.[3]

When combat in earnest finally came to the Americans, Colonel Emerson's battalion precipitated it. On the morning of 6 February a platoon from Company B, 2d of the 502d, came under fire as it approached Canh Tanh 4, a hamlet about twenty kilometers southwest of Tuy Hoa. Hoping to turn the contact into something larger, the company commander, Capt. Thomas H. Taylor, sent a second platoon overland to block the enemy from the south and a third by air to the west to cut off pos-

---

[3] Annual Hist Sum, 1966, 2d Bn, 327th Inf, n.d., pp. 3–4, Historians files, CMH.

sible escape. Colonel Emerson completed the seal by moving Capt. Robert C. Murphy's Company C into open rice fields to the northwest.

Late in the afternoon the Americans attacked. When they reached to within fifty meters of the hamlet's outlying huts, the North Vietnamese opened fire, stopping the assault. Over the next several hours Emerson called in thirteen air strikes, but the Communists were solidly entrenched and could not be broken. The fight turned into a slow, deadly, hut-to-hut contest, which Emerson halted as darkness fell, believing that he had the enemy fixed in place. The next morning the Americans swept into Canh Tanh 4, only to discover that the North Vietnamese had escaped through a series of tunnels and paths leading off to the north. They left 39 bodies behind, and Emerson's men estimated that perhaps another 15 had been killed. The uniforms of the dead and the documents they contained identified the soldiers as members of the *95th Regiment's 5th Battalion*.[4]

While moving to Canh Tanh 4 on the sixth, Captain Murphy's Company C had come under fire from My Canh 2, a hamlet about two kilometers southeast of the battle, suffering 2 wounded. He had ignored the enemy position in order to proceed with his mission but had requested permission to investigate once the fight was over. Colonel Emerson agreed, setting the patrol for the following morning.[5]

Around 0900, 7 February, Captain Murphy approached My Canh 2 with two platoons. One attempted to enter the hamlet from the northeast, while the other circled around to the northwest to act as a blocking force. As the first platoon neared the settlement, it came under heavy fire from well-constructed bunkers. When Murphy's men returned fire, a second enemy force opened up from some fifty meters to their left, pinning them down. Murphy instructed the commander of the second platoon to come to the aid of the first, but when he and his men attacked, they too were brought to ground. Realizing that the enemy was present in strength, Murphy radioed Emerson for reinforcements, artillery support, and air strikes.

With Emerson's reserves committed elsewhere, the requested reinforcements came from Colonel Rogers' 1st of the 327th Infantry. Under the command of Rogers' executive officer, Major Hackworth, a relief force—Capt. Albert E. Hiser's Company B and 1st Lt. James A. Gardner's Tiger Force, a special reinforced battalion reconnaissance platoon—moved by helicopter north of My Canh 2. Hackworth's plan was for the Tiger Force to maneuver to Murphy's northern flank, while Hiser's men swung around to the south to set up behind the enemy. After tactical air and artillery preparation, the Tiger Force would hit the North Vietnamese. Hackworth assumed that they would break contact and run, only to get caught in the trap. As he recalled, "It was a neat, clean 'hammer and anvil,' right out of Fort Benning."[6]

---

[4] AAR, [Opn Van Buren], 2d Bn, 502d Inf, 12 Feb 66, p. 2, Historians files, CMH.

[5] Hackworth and Sherman, *About Face*, p. 501.

[6] Ibid., pp. 501–02 (quotation); Garland, ed., *Infantry in Vietnam*, p. 100; AAR, [Opn Van Buren], 2d Bn, 502d Inf, p. 3.

Whatever Hackworth's intentions, execution was far from perfect. Moving toward the sound of the guns, his men began arriving toward noon. Lieutenant Gardner chose to approach the hamlet through some tall grass, assuming the troops would remain hidden as they advanced. The grass, however, thinned out unexpectedly, leaving the Tiger Force exposed and, as Hackworth later described it, marching "straight across the open field in a perfect skirmish line, like Pickett's division at Gettysburg." The North Vietnamese held their fire until the Americans were in close and then let loose a volley that killed or wounded a number of Gardner's men. Undaunted, the survivors continued their advance, closing to engage in hand-to-hand combat. In the end, the assault cost Tiger Force 7 killed and 8 wounded.[7]

Recognizing that the enemy's decision to stay and fight had nullified the trap, Major Hackworth ordered Captain Hiser's Company B to attack from the south. In doing so, the men moved across an open field just as the Tiger Force had, but to even worse effect—19 killed and 20 wounded. Badly bloodied, the company broke off the assault and pulled back into a perimeter for the night.[8]

While Company B suffered its ordeal, the Tiger Force renewed its attack, only to be brought to ground by four machine guns as darkness approached. Hackworth, who as the senior officer present had taken command, believed that it was urgent to break the stalemate so that the Tiger Force could form a night perimeter. Radioing Gardner, he told the lieutenant to knock out the machine guns and to do it "now." The young lieutenant stuffed as many grenades as he could carry into his shirt and ran at the guns. In quick succession he destroyed the first, second, and third, but the gunner of the fourth cut him down. Gardner's men, now leaderless, remained pinned down.[9]

Learning of Lieutenant Gardner's death, Hackworth resorted to a simple expedient. Radioing the pinned-down platoon, he ordered the acting commander to use covering fire provided by artillery and nearby American units to lead his men in a dash across the open ground that separated them from Murphy's unit. The plan worked. The platoon made it to Company C's position without losing anyone.[10]

The next morning, after air and artillery strikes, the task force entered My Canh 2, only to find it deserted. Hackworth's men counted 63 enemy dead and retrieved some sixty discarded weapons, an indication that the toll may have been even higher. Hackworth's force lost 26 killed and 28 wounded. Undoubtedly, Murphy's company suffered

---

[7] Hackworth and Sherman, *About Face*, pp. 502–03 (quotation, p. 501).

[8] Ibid., p. 508.

[9] Ibid., p. 505. Official and unofficial accounts differ on the details of Lieutenant Gardner's actions, for which he received the Medal of Honor. See U.S. Congress, Senate, Committee on Veterans' Affairs, *Medal of Honor Recipients, 1863–1973*, 93d Cong., 1st Sess., 1973, pp. 847–48, and Garland, ed., *Infantry in Vietnam*, p. 100.

[10] Hackworth and Sherman, *About Face*, p. 506.

casualties as well, but they went unrecorded at the time. Evidence gathered on the battlefield indicated that the unit engaged was either the heavy weapons company or a reinforced rifle company of the *95th Regiment's 5th Battalion (see Map 13).*[11]

Over the next two weeks daily searches for North Vietnamese units continued, but no other large-scale battles occurred. By late February the 1st Brigade, 101st Airborne Division, had killed 282 North Vietnamese and captured 33. Air strikes accounted for another 66 enemy dead. American losses were 55 dead and 221 wounded.[12]

With the harvest drawing to a close, General Pearson decided to

A South Vietnamese soldier escorts villagers during VAN BUREN.

shift the focus of the 1st Brigade to the mountains along the northwest fringes of the Tuy Hoa Valley, where long-range patrols had detected elements of the *95th Regiment.* During this new phase of the campaign, Operation HARRISON, the 1st of the 327th Infantry, in conjunction with allied forces, would continue to secure the lowlands. The remainder of the brigade would hunt the enemy inland.

Operation HARRISON got under way on 26 February. Colonel Emerson's 2d of the 502d Infantry deployed by helicopter thirty kilometers northwest of Tuy Hoa, while Colonel Garten's 2d of the 327th Infantry took up positions ten kilometers southeast of Emerson. After several days of relatively unproductive patrolling, Pearson attempted to trap a North Vietnamese unit that was said to be near Tuy An, about twenty kilometers north of Tuy Hoa. Emerson's battalion flew to a landing zone north of the town; Garten advanced overland from the south. The pincer, however, failed to generate significant contact. The two battalions then scoured the region without notable result.[13]

The Americans soon got their first break not in the mountains but in the Tuy Hoa Valley itself, where Colonel Rogers' 1st of the 327th was providing security for the rice harvest. On 4 March an elderly Vietnamese man approached Rogers' forward command post, located a little over

---

[11] AAR, [Opn VAN BUREN], 2d Bn, 502d Inf, p. 3.

[12] Ibid., p. 4.

[13] AAR, Opn HARRISON, 2d Bn, 502d Inf, 1 Apr 66, pp. 2, 4, Historians files, CMH; ORLL, 1 Jan–30 Apr 66, 1st Bde, 101st Abn Div, p. 4.

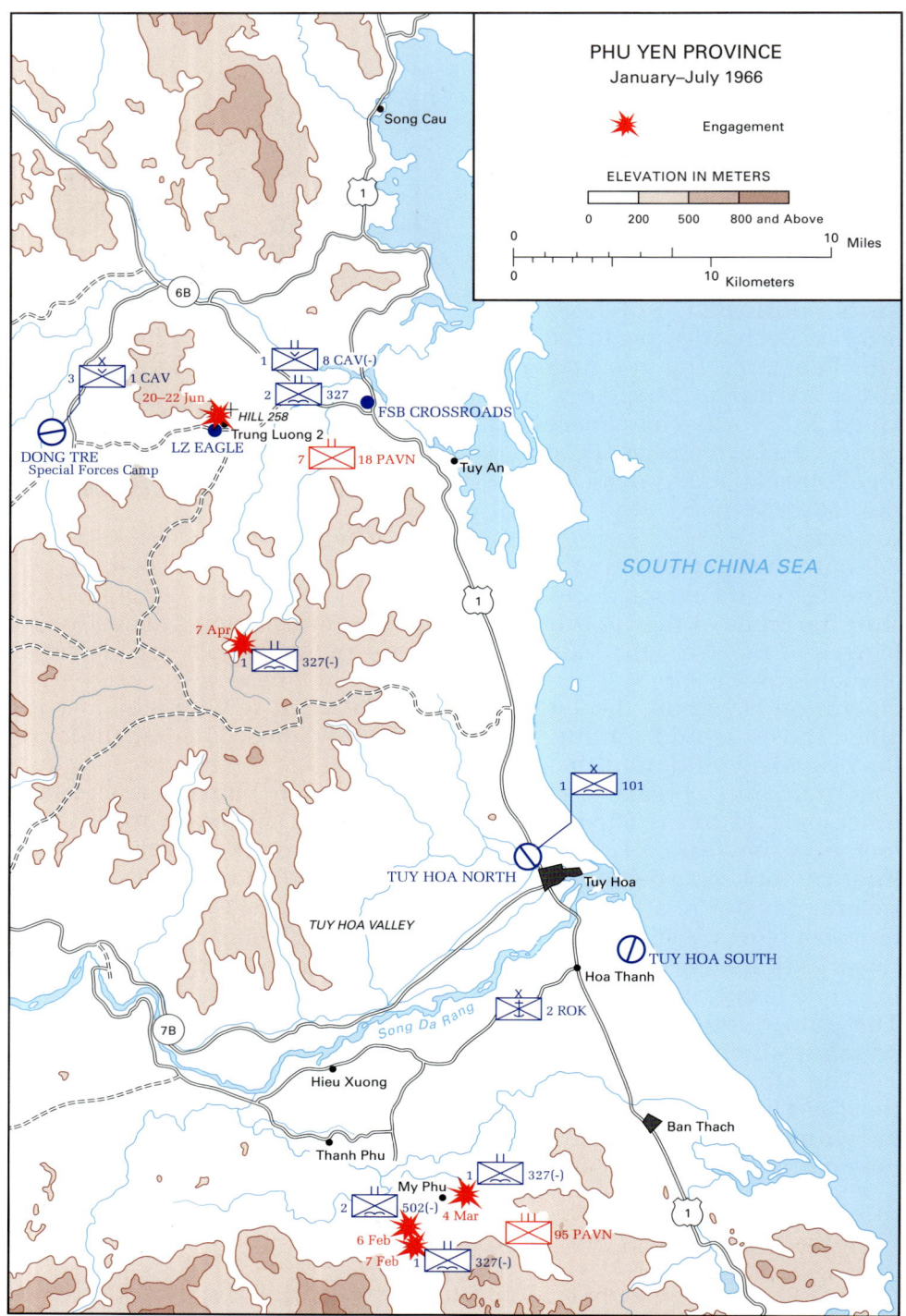

PHU YEN PROVINCE
January–July 1966

✷   Engagement

ELEVATION IN METERS

0   200   500   800 and Above

0   10   Miles

0   10   Kilometers

Song Cau

SOUTH CHINA SEA

1   8 CAV(-)

2   327

3   1 CAV
20–22 Jun

HILL 258
Trung Luong 2

FSB CROSSROADS

DONG TRE
Special Forces Camp

LZ EAGLE

7   18 PAVN

Tuy An

7 Apr

1   327(-)

1   101

TUY HOA NORTH   Tuy Hoa

TUY HOA SOUTH

Hoa Thanh

TUY HOA VALLEY

2 ROK

Song Da Rang

Hieu Xuong

Ban Thach

Thanh Phu

1   327(-)

My Phu

2   502(-)

4 Mar

6 Feb

95 PAVN

7 Feb   1   327(-)

MAP 13

A briefing for General Pearson on HARRISON *developments*

four kilometers south of the Da Rang and about sixteen kilometers south-west of Tuy Hoa, to tell the battalion intelligence officer that he had seen "men from the north" carrying "long stovepipes" in a direction that led toward the hamlet of Thanh Phu. Noting that Thanh Phu was about three kilometers southwest of his position, Rogers surmised that the "stovepipes" were actually mortars that the North Vietnamese intended to use to attack his headquarters. Rather than take any chances, he ordered two of his rifle companies operating southwest of Thanh Phu to move on separate axes toward the hamlet. Rogers accompanied Capt. Hal S. Eaton's Company A, and Major Hackworth moved with Captain Hiser's Company B.[14]

As the Americans pushed toward Thanh Phu that afternoon, Company B's route took it by the hamlet of My Phu, three kilometers north-east of My Canh 2. When the troops approached the settlement, they began to receive fire from well-prepared positions. At first, it seemed possible that the enemy had sprung a trap, but later Rogers learned from prisoners that the North Vietnamese themselves had been the ones surprised. Although Company B's troops took casualties, the way they

[14] Hackworth and Sherman, *About Face*, p. 516.

fought was in marked contrast to what they had done the month before at My Canh 2. Declining to assault strong emplacements, Hackworth allowed firepower to do the work. The result, he later wrote, was "enemy dead . . . strewn all over the hamlet."[15]

Captain Eaton's Company A was less fortunate. Arriving on the scene from a slightly different direction, it took up station on the side of the hamlet opposite Company B. Eaton then led his men in an attack across two dry rice paddies, suffering heavy casualties while failing to carry the enemy defenses. In the late afternoon Major Hackworth assumed command on the ground, while Colonel Rogers took to the air in his helicopter. The battle became "a slow, methodical, inch-by-inch" process, in which the Americans isolated "the enemy's dug-in positions and one by one destroy[ed] them." With the effort still incomplete at sunset, the Americans broke contact and established a night laager.[16]

Seeking to keep the enemy—later identified as the *95th Regiment's 4th Battalion*—bottled up during the night, Hackworth attempted an encirclement. But even by stretching his two companies thin, he lacked the men to do the job. Consequently, he positioned the Tiger Force to the south of My Phu and used artillery fire to plug the remaining gaps. Determined to escape, the North Vietnamese ran the gauntlet during the night, losing some 20 soldiers.[17]

The following morning the American task force searched the battlefield. The paratroopers retrieved the bodies of 72 North Vietnamese in Company B's area and another 37 in Company A's. Captains Eaton and Hiser estimated that their men had killed another 97. American casualties came to 8 killed and 11 wounded for Company B and 11 killed and 34 wounded for Company A. Those losses gave some weight to a later contention by Hackworth that Company B had learned critical lessons at My Canh 2 that the less experienced Company A had yet to absorb.[18]

The clash at My Phu led General Pearson to redirect his efforts south and southwest of Tuy Hoa. On 5 March Colonel Garten's 2d of the 327th relieved Colonel Rogers' 1st of the 327th so that it could move farther west. After a week in its new sector the battalion, by then commanded by Rogers' successor, Lt. Col. Walter E. Meinzen, moved east, where it operated north of Garten but south of the Da Rang. Meanwhile, on the sixth, Pearson shifted Emerson's troops from north of Tuy Hoa to Tuy Hoa South airfield, where they became the brigade reserve. On the night of the twelfth and thirteenth, however, the battalion returned to the field to exploit a B–52 strike scheduled for 0400

---

[15] Ibid., p. 517.

[16] Ibid., p. 518.

[17] Ibid., pp. 518–19.

[18] Ibid., pp. 516, 521; Sitrep no. 64, 1st Bn, 327th Inf, 4–5 Mar 66, p. 1, Historians files, CMH; ORLL, 1 Jan–30 Apr 66, 1st Bde, 101st Abn Div, p. 5 and incl. 2, p. 1.

southwest of Tuy Hoa. Emerson's men made a battalion-size air assault in the dark, an unusual maneuver under any circumstances, but found no enemy to fight at or near the strike. The unit carried out a similar mission in the same general area after another B–52 raid on the fifteenth, with the same result.[19]

General Westmoreland visited the brigade during those trying days. He took away an impression that the troops were performing well but that their officers were becoming frustrated at their inability to make the enemy fight. While being briefed, he was told, for example, that on one occasion the brigade had felt certain it had a North Vietnamese force surrounded. In that instance, the MACV commander noted, with an edge to his remark, "as usual, the slippery enemy got away."[20]

Having had no major encounters since 4 March and learning from prisoners that the *95th Regiment* had splintered into small bands and retreated into the mountains, General Pearson called a halt to HARRISON on the twenty-fifth. A more straightforward search and destroy operation than VAN BUREN, the effort had resulted in the death of 288 North Vietnamese, the largest number coming from the *95th's 4th Battalion*; the surrender of 35 more; the destruction or seizure of 185 individual and crew-served weapons; and the capture of large amounts of food, medical supplies, and ammunition. The cost to Pearson's 1st Brigade was 42 men killed, 234 wounded, and 2 missing.[21]

By late March much of the rice in the Tuy Hoa Valley had been harvested. To protect the remainder of the crop and deepen security in the valley, General Pearson inaugurated the final phase of the rice-protection campaign, Operation FILLMORE, on the twenty-sixth. Keeping one battalion on a rotating basis as a reserve force at Tuy Hoa South, he used his other two battalions to patrol the plain and bordering foothills. Then, in early April, he initiated a two-battalion block and sweep operation deep in the mountains northwest of Tuy Hoa. In this action a company from Colonel Meinzen's 1st of the 327th ousted a company-size force from bunkers on the seventh, killing 28 defenders. The battle brought the number of enemy troops killed up to that point in FILLMORE to 134, compared to 8 American dead. The action also confirmed American suspicions that the Communists had pulled away from the Tuy Hoa Valley. Based on this analysis and the continual need to juggle his forces to meet many different requirements, the I Field Force commander, General Larsen, drastically scaled down FILLMORE. On the eighth he transferred the bulk of the 1st Brigade out of the province to scour the bound-

---

[19] ORLL, 1 Jan–30 Apr 66, 1st Bde, 101st Abn Div, pp. 4–5; AAR, Opn HARRISON, 2d Bn, 502d Inf, pp. 6–8.

[20] Westmoreland Jnl, 22 Mar 66, Westmoreland History files, CMH.

[21] AAR, Opn HARRISON, 2d Bn, 502d Inf, incl. 1, p. 1; ORLL, 1 Jan–30 Apr 66, 1st Bde, 101st Abn Div, p. 5; Weekly Sum, 20–26 Mar 66, 1st Bde, 101st Abn Div, 27 Mar 66, box 10, 70A/4868, RG 319, NARA.

ary between II and III Corps, leaving only Colonel Garten's 2d of the 327th Infantry behind to assist the South Vietnamese and South Koreans in protecting the Tuy Hoa Valley.[22]

The Backcountry

For the next two months the men of the 2d of the 327th Infantry patrolled the Tuy Hoa Valley and the bordering ridges, mostly to the north and west of the city of Tuy Hoa. In mid-June, however, American intelligence received reports of a large North Vietnamese force in the Trung Luong Valley, about halfway between coastal Tuy An and the Dong Tre Special Forces camp in the mountains to the west. Unbeknownst to the Americans, the *18B PAVN Regiment* had just arrived there, joining the *5th Division* after a five-month trek from North Vietnam through Laos, Cambodia, and the western highlands. American suspicions deepened on the eighteenth, when an unidentified element estimated to be battalion in size overran a CIDG company operating out of Dong Tre. Concerned that the enemy might be massing to attack Dong Tre itself, I Field Force ordered the 2d of the 327th to investigate.[23]

The Trung Luong Valley and the surrounding countryside west of Tuy An were ideal for a Communist base camp. The area was close enough to the coastal lowlands to launch raids and foraging expeditions yet sufficiently remote to offer protection from allied counterattacks. Indeed, the region's steep jungle-covered mountains made it nearly inaccessible, even for heliborne troops. Finding the enemy and rooting him out of these mountain refuges promised to be difficult business.

On the morning of 19 June Lt. Col. Joseph E. Wasco, who had succeeded Colonel Garten as commander of the 2d of the 327th Infantry, air-assaulted two companies into the Trung Luong Valley. Company A landed in the mountains on the southeast side of the valley, while Company C deployed to a low-lying area on the northwest side. Fire support was provided by a battery of 105-mm. howitzers from the 2d Battalion, 320th Artillery, located at Firebase CROSSROADS near the junction of Highway 1 and Route 6B, roughly five kilometers from the valley's center. During the day Company A moved cautiously to the northwest, skirmishing lightly with the enemy before establishing a defensive perimeter two and a half kilometers southeast of the hamlet of Trung Luong 2 in the center of the valley. Company C also conducted a cautious search,

---

[22] Weekly Sum, 3–9 Apr 66, 1st Bde, 101st Abn Div, 10 Apr 66, box 10, 70A/4868, RG 319, NARA; AARs, Opn FILLMORE, 1st Bde, 101st Abn Div, 17 Aug 66, pp. 2–3, and 2d Bn, 502d Inf, 18 May 66, pp. 2–4, Historians files, CMH; Annual Hist Sum, 1966, 2d Bn, 327th Inf, pp. 11–14; ORLL, 1 Jan–30 Apr 66, 1st Bde, 101st Abn Div, p. 6.

[23] Annual Hist Sum, 1966, 2d Bn, 327th Inf, pp. 13–15; Rpt, 14th Mil Hist Det, 1st Cav Div (Ambl), 7 Mar 67, sub: Seven Month History and Briefing Data (April–October 1966), p. 97, Historians files, CMH.

briefly engaging a force of unknown size in midafternoon. It then encamped for the night about five hundred meters west of Trung Luong 2. Later in the evening a provisional force from the battalion's antitank and mortar platoons arrived to reinforce Company C. During the night small groups of enemy soldiers tried unsuccessfully to infiltrate the two American positions.

The operation changed dramatically the next day. Still uncertain about whether the North Vietnamese were in the valley in strength, Companies A and C continued their searches. Company A trekked northwest toward Trung Luong 2. As the troops approached, a reinforced North Vietnamese company lying in wait within the hamlet opened fire with automatic weapons, small arms, and mortars, wounding all of the company's officers except the commander. Stunned by the onslaught, the Americans scrambled for cover. Hoping to finish off the paratroopers, the North Vietnamese charged out of the hamlet. But they had miscalculated. The Americans fought hard, pushing the attackers back into the settlement and following them in. The deeper they penetrated, however, the more intense the enemy fire became and the more casualties they took. Finally, the company commander ordered a withdrawal. After retracing their steps and maneuvering to high ground about five hundred meters east of Trung Luong 2, the Americans established a defensive position. Company C also had a difficult day. Moving toward Hill 258, a high point about twelve hundred meters northwest of its overnight position, the unit took fire from an entrenched North Vietnamese company. Pinned down about eight hundred meters short of the hill, the company established a perimeter for the night.[24]

In the afternoon, with Companies A and C fully committed, Colonel Wasco's Company B air-assaulted into a "hot" landing zone northwest of Hill 258, losing 2 killed and 10 wounded. Once on the ground the company pushed toward the hill, but enemy gunners pinned it down before it could reach Company C. While air strikes and artillery sealed off both companies from counterattack, the Americans remained stalled. Wasco's casualties that day totaled 14 killed and 73 wounded. His companies claimed to have killed 11 enemy and possibly another 56.[25]

As the fight grew, General Larsen directed Col. Harold G. Moore, who had assumed command of the 3d Brigade, 1st Cavalry Division, in December, to take control of the operation, by now dubbed NATHAN HALE. Larsen also rushed in reinforcements. After deploying a second 105-mm. battery, this time from the 5th Battalion, 27th Artillery, to a position roughly two kilometers south of Firebase CROSSROADS, he committed the field force reserve, the 1st Battalion, 8th Cavalry. Under the command

[24] Annual Hist Sum, 1966, 2d Bn, 327th Inf, pp. 15–16.

[25] Ibid., p. 16; Rpt, 14th Mil Hist Det, 1st Cav Div, 7 Mar 67, sub: Seven Month History and Briefing Data (April–October 1966), p. 97.

of Lt. Col. Levin B. Broughton, the battalion flew from Kontum City to Tuy Hoa in C–130s. It deployed from there by helicopter, first to Dong Tre, where Colonel Moore had set up his command post, and then into the valley. Between 1915 and 2200 Colonel Broughton's Companies B and C arrived at Landing Zone AXE about six hundred meters north of Hill 258, which Wasco's Company B had managed by then to surround. At that point, enemy fire was dwindling, and the area around Hill 258 and Trung Luong 2 was growing quiet.[26]

The next morning, 21 June, with Colonel Broughton's Companies B and C providing covering fire, Colonel Wasco's Company B assaulted Hill 258, only to find that the enemy had abandoned the position during the night and left behind an abundance of equipment and a few dead. Meanwhile, Wasco's Companies A and C attacked Trung Luong 2 from east and west. As the pincer closed on the settlement, which extended for about eight hundred meters west to east, the defenders— later identified as belonging to the *18B Regiment*—opened fire. Although the two U.S. forces continued to make slow progress, enemy resistance kept them from linking up and stopped the advance. In the end, Company A withdrew to the eastern edge of the hamlet, where it formed a perimeter, and Company C pulled back to its position of the previous night. During the fighting the two companies, along with air strikes and artillery, had killed, by body count, at least 35 North Vietnamese at a cost of 6 of their own killed and 39 wounded.[27]

Just before dark Colonel Broughton's Companies B and C moved south from Hill 258 toward Trung Luong 2. Broughton's Company B joined Wasco's Company C west of the hamlet, where they established a new position called EAGLE. Broughton's Company C joined Wasco's Company A before both withdrew to A's location of the previous night. The action of the twenty-first convinced General Larsen to bring additional forces into NATHAN HALE. Accordingly, Lt. Col. Robert F. Litle's 2d Battalion, 7th Cavalry, deployed to Tuy Hoa that night to serve as the 3d Brigade's reserve.[28]

On 22 June, around 0540, the Americans at EAGLE received a rude shock, when North Vietnamese regulars launched a fierce attack. While mortar and automatic weapons fire pounded the U.S. perimeter, a company-size force charged the antitank platoon on the western edge. The commander of Company B called in air strikes and artillery, but by then the attackers were too close for heavy firepower to do much good.

[26] Rpt, 14th Mil Hist Det, 1st Cav Div, 7 Mar 67, sub: Seven Month History and Briefing Data (April–October 1966), p. 97.
[27] Annual Hist Sum, 1966, 1st Bn, 8th Cav, n.d., pp. 2–3; Intel Supp, Defense Intelligence Agency (DIA), Aug 66, sub: NVA Infiltration Into South Vietnam as of 9 August 1966, p. 3. Both in Historians files, CMH.
[28] Op Sum, Opn NATHAN HALE, MACV, Jul 66, p. 4, Historians files, CMH; Rpt, 14th Mil Hist Det, 1st Cav Div, 7 Mar 67, sub: Seven Month History and Briefing Data (April–October 1966), p. 97.

Over the next three hours the enemy, which probably consisted of the bulk of the *18B Regiment*'s *7th Battalion*, launched a series of assaults, penetrating the antitank platoon's sector and reaching other parts of the American line. Ultimately, the defenders held. Around 0900 the North Vietnamese pulled back, leaving snipers behind to protect their withdrawal.[29]

After the shooting died down, the Americans policed the battlefield. Just outside the antitank platoon's sector alone they counted 96 enemy dead and captured a small number of survivors, including the commander of the *7th*'s *2d Company*, Lt. Le Duc Thong, who reported that his entire company had been "annihilated." Around the rest of the perimeter the Americans found another 19 bodies. American losses were 12 killed and 17 wounded.[30]

NATHAN HALE continued to expand in the days that followed. On 26 June Maj. Gen. John Norton, who had assumed command of the 1st Cavalry Division in early May, augmented the American force with Col. John J. Hennessey's 1st Brigade. Initially, Colonel Hennessey commanded two battalions and an air troop from the division's cavalry squadron. By the twenty-eighth, however, he would have four full battalions at his disposal. With two brigades of his division in play, General Norton took command of the operation.

Although the additional American units increased the daily toll on the enemy, their presence did not produce the decisive battle that American commanders wanted. For example, on 26 June U.S. forces in the field killed 3 Communist soldiers, and on the twenty-seventh the two brigades dispatched 16. The addition of new battalions, however, did allow Norton to send units into the area immediately around Dong Tre, where intelligence reports had suggested other main forces might be present. But the effort produced little more than "sporadic light contact" because the North Vietnamese either had withdrawn from the area or were laying low. Effective at midnight on 1 July, Norton terminated NATHAN HALE.[31]

General Larsen believed that the operation had disrupted the enemy's buildup and had spoiled whatever plan he might have had to attack Dong Tre. Reported enemy losses were substantial: 450 North Vietnamese killed and another 300 estimated dead. Of equal importance was the conclusion, based upon prisoner interrogations and body counts, that the *2d Company, 7th Battalion, 18B Regiment*, had been virtually destroyed and that the rest of the battalion had lost possibly 50 percent of its

---

[29] Annual Hist Sums, 1966, 1st Bn, 8th Cav, pp. 2–3, and 2d Bn, 327th Inf, p. 17; Sykes, comp., *First Cavalry Division*, p. 44; ORLL, 1 May–31 Jul 66, 1st Cav Div (Ambl), 15 Aug 66, p. 12, box 12, 69A/702, RG 334, NARA.

[30] Annual Hist Sums, 1966, 1st Bn, 8th Cav, p. 3, and 2d Bn, 327th Inf, p. 17 (quoted word); Op Sum, Opn NATHAN HALE, MACV, Jul 66, p. 4; ORLL, 1 May–31 July 66, 1st Cav Div, p. 12.

[31] Rpt, 14th Mil Hist Det, 1st Cav Div, 7 Mar 67, sub: Seven Month History and Briefing Data (April–October 1966), pp. 94, 98–99 (quoted words, p. 98).

strength. The Americans suspected
that the regiment's other two battalions, the *8th* and *9th*, although
never linked formally with NATHAN
HALE, had also been involved and
had taken many casualties. General Westmoreland concluded that
the cavalry division had "seriously
reduced [the *18B Regiment*'s] . . . effectiveness for several months."[32]

Having bloodied the *18B*, General Larsen was loath to let it go.
Instead, he ordered General
Norton to launch his 1st and 3d
Brigades to hunt down and destroy
the regiment. The pursuit, Operation HENRY CLAY, began on 2 July
and eventually took elements of
the 1st Cavalry Division all the
way to the Cambodian border. But
the hunt was in vain, as the enemy
disappeared into the rugged high-

*A paratrooper protecting the
Tuy Hoa rice harvest*

lands with scarcely a trace. On 30 July Larsen called a halt to the pursuit
after the division had managed to kill just 35 North Vietnamese.[33]

The Security Picture

HENRY CLAY's lackluster outcome brought to a close what otherwise
had been a fairly good series of operations in Phu Yen Province. Over
the preceding seven months the Americans had wounded the *5th PAVN
Division* and driven it into the mountains away from the populated coast,
contributing to a rise in security. In addition, the rice-protection campaign had achieved some spectacular results. Compared with 1965, when
most of Tuy Hoa's crop had gone to the Communists, very little of the
1966 harvest fell into enemy hands, with the government taking in over
thirty thousand tons. The effects were immediate. By March enemy commanders in Phu Yen were forced to cut in half their soldiers' daily ra-

[32] Msg, CG, I FFV, 5051 to COMUSMACV, 29 Jun 66, box 6, 69A/702, RG 334, NARA;
Monthly Eval Rpt, MACV, Jun 66, p. 4, MHI; Rpt, 14th Mil Hist Det, 1st Cav Div, 7 Mar 67,
sub: Seven Month History and Briefing Data (April–October 1966), pp. 94, 99; Msg
(quotation), Westmoreland MAC 5740 to Sharp, 8 Jul 66, Westmoreland Message files, CMH.

[33] Msg, CG, I FFV, 5021 to CG, 1st Cav Div, 28 Jun 66, box 6, 69A/702, RG 334,
NARA; Op Sum, Opn HENRY CLAY, MACV, Jul 66, pp. 1–6, Historians files, CMH; Rpt,
14th Mil Hist Det, 1st Cav Div, 7 Mar 67, sub: Seven Month History and Briefing Data
(April–October 1966), pp. 101–03.

tion of seven hundred grams of rice, which caused a serious morale problem. At the same time, America's stock among the people rose, buoyed both by its military successes and the civic action programs of the 1st Brigade, 101st Airborne Division. The paratroopers distributed food and clothing to villagers, assisted in the government's effort to rebuild houses damaged during operations, and protected Army engineers assigned to repair roads and bridges. Army psychological warfare specialists helped South Vietnamese officials restore government authority, while medical personnel established the first dispensary in Tuy Hoa in many years, treating approximately one thousand patients per month.[34]

Tokens of friendship for Phu Yen orphans

Works such as these undoubtedly assisted the South Vietnamese pacification campaign in Phu Yen Province. Yet the government's efforts to consolidate its hold over the Tuy Hoa Valley generally lagged behind American military progress because of bureaucratic roadblocks and acute shortages of money, materiel, and manpower. Although captured documents indicated that allied dragnets had eliminated "entire VC village cadre" in some areas, many members of the Viet Cong underground had plainly survived. The absence of a permanent U.S. Agency for International Development public safety adviser in Phu Yen, and the fact that the province was able to recruit only half the number of men required to fill its Popular Forces, further impeded efforts to improve security. The departure of most of the 101st's 1st Brigade in early April had a similar effect. The move brought an immediate drop in public confidence and an increase in Viet Cong activity.[35]

But perhaps the most troubling feature of the war in Phu Yen was not that the government's victory was as yet incomplete but that its gains in securing the human and material resources of the Tuy Hoa Valley had

---

[34] ORLL, 1 Jan–30 Apr 66, 1st Bde, 101st Abn Div, p. 4; Special Joint Report on Revolutionary Development (RD), Phu Yen Province, 31 Mar 66, p. 2, RD files, CMH; Annual Hist Sum, 1966, 2d Bn, 327th Inf, pp. 11–15; Larry R. Lubenow, "Objective Rice," *Infantry* 56 (November/December 1966): 41–42.

[35] Special Joint RD Rpts, Phu Yen Province, 31 Mar 66, p. 2 (quoted words), 30 Apr 66, p. 1, 31 May 66, pp. 1–4, 30 Jun 66, p. 3, and 31 Jul 66, p. 1, RD files, CMH; Rambo et al., *Refugee Situation in Phu-Yen*, p. 114.

come at a high price. Partially by design and partially due to circumstances, Van Buren, and to a lesser extent the other allied operations, had created a large number of refugees. By mid-1966 Phu Yen's refugee population had risen to nearly sixty thousand or roughly 17 percent of the provincial population, with over half of these people having been displaced during the first six months of the year. In a small minority of cases, most notably in areas that were deemed excessively vulnerable to Communist activity, American and South Korean troops had forcibly evacuated people and destroyed their homes. In other cases the allies had merely encouraged people to leave, warning them of the risks of remaining in an area of active military operations while simultaneously holding out the prospect of peace and security in government-controlled enclaves. Many individuals needed no prompting and left their hamlets voluntarily, either to escape the fighting or the Viet Cong, whose interminable demands for food, labor, and recruits had begun to wear thin.[36]

Regardless of how they came to leave their homes, life for the refugees was hard. Whether inside the province's few formal camps (nine sheltering 2,963 families) or outside of them, living conditions were generally squalid. Government relief efforts were irregular and, with the exception of the harvest season, when American trucks and helicopters ferried people to and from the fields each day, unemployment and underemployment were high. American and South Vietnamese officials alike took solace from the fact that each refugee was one less person whom the Viet Cong could exploit, yet the large mass of relatively unproductive and destitute people also placed a serious strain on the province. Nor did the government succeed in converting the Viet Cong's loss to its gain, as it made little effort to develop the type of sustained programs that might have converted the refugees into active supporters of the Southern republic. The majority of Phu Yen's refugee population remained politically inert, representing neither a clear win nor a clear loss for the government.

Possibly the most revealing indicator of the state of pacification in Phu Yen by mid-1966 was the fate of the government's "Return to Village" campaign. Once the 1966 crop had been safely harvested, the government tried to convince displaced people to return to their villages in order to reduce the economic burdens created by the large refugee population. The program fizzled. Despite the hardships of refugee life, few were willing to return lest they fall victim to renewed fighting or Viet Cong exploitation. For all the statistics about rice harvested, villages secured, and numbers of people under government control, the people themselves knew that all was not yet well in Phu Yen Province.[37]

---

[36] Rambo et al., *Refugee Situation in Phu-Yen*, pp. 73–75.
[37] Ibid., pp. xii–xv, 30, 35–37, 52–54, 60, 72–74, 80–82; Briefing Folder, sub: Phu-Yen Province, 1966, p. 9, RD files, CMH; Lubenow, "Objective Rice," p. 42.

10

Testing in Binh Dinh

Although Phu Yen Province served as the principal granary for the enemy in II Corps, the stakes for the allies were far higher in Binh Dinh Province just to the north. The gateway to the Central Highlands along Highway 19 and the site of the allies' growing support complex at Qui Nhon port, the province held the key to the war in central South Vietnam. General Westmoreland would have to deal with Binh Dinh if he wanted to secure central and northern II Corps and the southern reaches of I Corps.

The situation that he faced in Binh Dinh was anything but ideal. Where the *5th PAVN Division* in Phu Yen had just two infantry regiments, the *3d PAVN Division* in Binh Dinh had three. Of those, the *12th PAVN Regiment* had infiltrated from the North in early 1965 and the *22d PAVN Regiment*, after a two-month trek, in September. The *2d PLAF Regiment*, however, more than filled the experience gap, for it had been fighting in the South since 1962. Adding to Westmoreland's burden was the fact that large parts of Binh Dinh had been insurgent redoubts for thirty years. The populace leaned heavily toward the Viet Cong, and the Communist underground was well developed. All that stood in the way of the enemy was the South Vietnamese 22d Infantry Division, which had been hit hard in recent fighting and seemed to be increasingly on the defensive.[1]

General Westmoreland instructed his field force commander, General Larsen, to take the situation in hand. He specified that Larsen should target the *12th PAVN Regiment* first because MACV had good intelligence on the unit's whereabouts. If the opportunity arose, however, Larsen was to go after any other enemy units that fell within his grasp.[2]

General Kinnard's 1st Cavalry Division received the assignment, but it was suffering from stress as 1966 began. Since arriving in Vietnam, the unit had sustained 342 killed, 860 wounded, and 9 missing—a good many of them in the Ia Drang Valley the past November. An additional 2,248 men had returned home because of sickness, reassignments, or service completion. Although 5,211 replacements more than made up

---

[1] Quarterly Cmd Rpt, 1 Oct–31 Dec 65, FFV, 14 Jan 66, p. 6, Historians files, CMH.
[2] ORLL, 1 Jan–30 Apr 66, I FFV, 15 May 66, incl. 7, Historians files, CMH.

the loss, close to 4,000 had arrived in December. The new men would have to learn how the division operated, and this would take time.[3]

Of more pressing concern was the state of the unit's helicopters in the aftermath of the Ia Drang, when division aviation had taken such a beating. Other units in Vietnam were also having difficulty at the time—the inevitable growing pains of the rapid buildup. The heavy artillery was short of barrels and breeches; the engineers lacked parts for their bulldozers; port units needed spare parts for their forklifts; and vehicles everywhere were deadlined from wear and tear. But because of the implications for the staying power of the airmobile division, helicopters were the big worry, so much so that, starting in January, General Johnson required weekly reports on how many of them were actually flying.

To increase readiness, Secretary McNamara inaugurated what became known as the Red Ball Express—taking the name from the famous road supply marathon in World War II France. Starting in early December, air shuttles directly responsive to MACV headquarters moved spare parts nonstop from Travis Air Force Base, near Oakland, California, to Tan Son Nhut. The effort paid particular attention to helicopters, and results came quickly. On 11 December one hundred eight of the 1st Cavalry Division's four hundred seventy-eight aircraft needed spare parts to fly; by 15 January the number had fallen to ninety-two. From then on, as the division returned to the fight, improvements proceeded apace.[4]

MASHER/WHITE WING

The main effort of the division's campaign in Binh Dinh would come on the Bong Son Plain and in the mountains and valleys that bordered it. The plain, a narrow strip of land starting just north of the town of Bong Son, ran northward along the coast into I Corps. Rarely more than twenty-five kilometers wide, it consisted of a series of small deltas, which often backed into gently rolling terraces some thirty to ninety meters in height, and, at irregular intervals, of a number of mountainous spurs from the highlands. These spurs created narrow river valleys with steep ridges that frequently provided hideouts for enemy units or housed enemy command, control, and logistical centers. The plain itself was bisected by the east–west Lai Giang River, which was in turn fed by two others—the An Lao, flowing from the northwest, and the Kim Son, flowing from the southwest. These two rivers formed isolated but fertile valleys west of the coastal plain. The climate in the region was governed by the northeast monsoon. The heaviest rains had usually ended

---

[3] Quarterly Cmd Rpt, 1 Oct–31 Dec 65, 1st Cav Div (Ambl), 10 Jan 66, p. 5, Historians files, CMH; Stanton, *Anatomy of a Division*, p. 65.
[4] Army Buildup Progress Rpt, 2 Mar 66, p. 49, CMH; Meyerson, "Logistics in the Vietnam Conflict," ch. 5, CMH.

by December, but a light steady drizzle—which the French had called *crachin* weather—and an occasional torrential downpour could be expected to occur through March. For division planners counting on gunships and fighter-bombers to help protect the ground troops, the weather was a real worry.[5]

The campaign in the Bong Son was initially code-named MASHER. But with President Johnson increasingly worried about the public's reaction to the deepening troop commitment, presidential adviser McGeorge Bundy asked that MACV refrain from choosing provocative titles for its operations. General Wheeler passed the request to General Westmoreland, citing MASHER as an example of what Bundy wanted to avoid and instructing him to select a name that would deprive "even the most biased person" of a theme for a public speech. Westmoreland complied, renaming MASHER—with just a touch of irony—WHITE WING. From then on, he made the naming of operations an important function of his staff.[6]

The 1st Cavalry Division broke the campaign into two parts. During the first, primarily a preparation and deception operation, a brigade-size task force would establish a temporary command and forward supply base at Phu Cat on Highway 1 south of the area of operations, secure the highway somewhat northward, and start patrolling around Phu Cat to convey the impression that the true target area was well away from the plain. During the second, division elements would move to Bong Son itself and launch a series of airmobile hammer-and-anvil operations around the plain and the adjacent valleys to flush the Viet Cong and North Vietnamese toward strong blocking positions. Kinnard assigned the mission to Colonel Moore's 3d Brigade, but if need be, he was ready to add a second brigade to MASHER/WHITE WING to intensify the pressure and pursuit.[7]

The morning of 25 January dawned cool and rainy at An Khe as the men of the 3d Brigade began their move to staging areas in eastern Binh Dinh. Two battalions—Lt. Col. Raymond L. Kampe's 1st of the 7th Cavalry and Lt. Col. Rutland D. Beard's 1st of the 12th Cavalry—went by road and air to Phu Cat, joined South Koreans in securing the airfield and support base, and carried out wide-ranging search and destroy actions nearby that met only light resistance. Meanwhile, Colonel McDade's 2d of the 7th Cavalry, with about 80 percent of its authorized strength and thus still not fully reconstituted after the fight at ALBANY, boarded a dozen C–123s at the An Khe airstrip for the short ride into Bong Son. Hard luck

[5] Rpt, Capt Bobby A. Ramsey, S–2, 52d Avn Bn, 31 Mar 65, sub: Enemy, Weather, and Terrain Analysis, p. 2; OPLAN 3A, II Corps/Military Region 2, Pleiku, Republic of Vietnam, 8 Jun 71, an. A, pp. 1–3. Both in Historians files, CMH.

[6] Hammond, *Military and the Media*, p. 229; Msg (quoted words), Wheeler JCS 460–66 to Westmoreland, 1 Feb 66, Historians files, CMH.

[7] AAR, Opn MASHER/WHITE WING, 1st Cav Div (Ambl), 28 Apr 66, pp. 2–5, 12, Historians files, CMH; John R. Galvin, *Air Assault: The Development of Airmobile Warfare* (New York: Hawthorn Books, 1969), pp. 299–301.

still dogged the battalion; forty-two riflemen and mortarmen from Company A were on a C–123 that, shortly after takeoff, crashed into a mountain slope, killing all aboard, including the crew. Though the rest of the battalion deployed without incident and then helicoptered north to Landing Zone Dog, where engineers started building an airstrip and digging in artillery, McDade's troubles in the Bong Son had just begun (*Map 14*).[8]

On paper, the hammer-and-anvil attack plan was not complicated. After 3d Brigade elements secured mountain positions west of the Bong Son and set up Firebases Brass and Steel, covering the northern and southern parts of the search area, McDade's battalion would push north from Landing Zone Dog and Colonel Ingram's 2d of the 12th Cavalry, also staging from Dog, would work its way south from the opposite end of the target zone. Meanwhile, with the South Vietnamese Airborne Brigade acting as an eastern blocking force along Highway 1, Colonel Kampe's 1st of the 7th Cavalry would air-assault onto the high ground to the west and push east toward McDade and Ingram. If enemy units were in the area, Colonel Moore would bring them to battle or destroy them as they fled.[9]

The plan began to unravel almost immediately. When the operation commenced on the morning of 28 January, low clouds, wind, and heavy rain prevented the movement of artillery to the northern firebase. Lacking supporting fire, Colonel Moore scrubbed Ingram's mission. In the meantime, enemy fire downed a Chinook helicopter at Landing Zone Papa north of Bong Son, and Kampe responded by sending a company to secure the crash site. When it too came under fire, he set aside his original mission—the attack east from the mountains—and moved his two other companies to Papa. By the time they arrived, however, the enemy had withdrawn. Kampe's units spent the night at the landing zone.[10]

Although Kampe was temporarily sidelined, McDade went ahead with the mission, directing his men to begin scouring the hamlets that started about two kilometers north of Dog and extended four kilometers farther up the plain. Captain Sugdinis' Company A, understrength at two rifle platoons because of the crash three days earlier, entered the area at Landing Zone 2 and pushed north through rice paddies. Captain Diduryk's Company B flew to Firebase Steel to secure it for an artillery battery. Captain Fesmire's Company C deployed by helicopter to the northern edge of the target in order to sweep to the southwest. The sandy plain where it set down, Landing Zone 4, seemed safe—a relatively open tract in the hamlet of Phung Du 2 with a graveyard in its midst and tall palm trees on three sides. Fesmire omitted the artillery preparation that normally preceded a landing.

---

[8] AAR, Opn Masher/White Wing, 1st Cav Div, incl. 1, p. 1.

[9] AAR, Opn Masher/White Wing (Eagle Claw), 3d Bde, 1st Cav Div (Ambl), 10 Mar 66, pp. 5–6, Historians files, CMH.

[10] Ibid., p. 7.

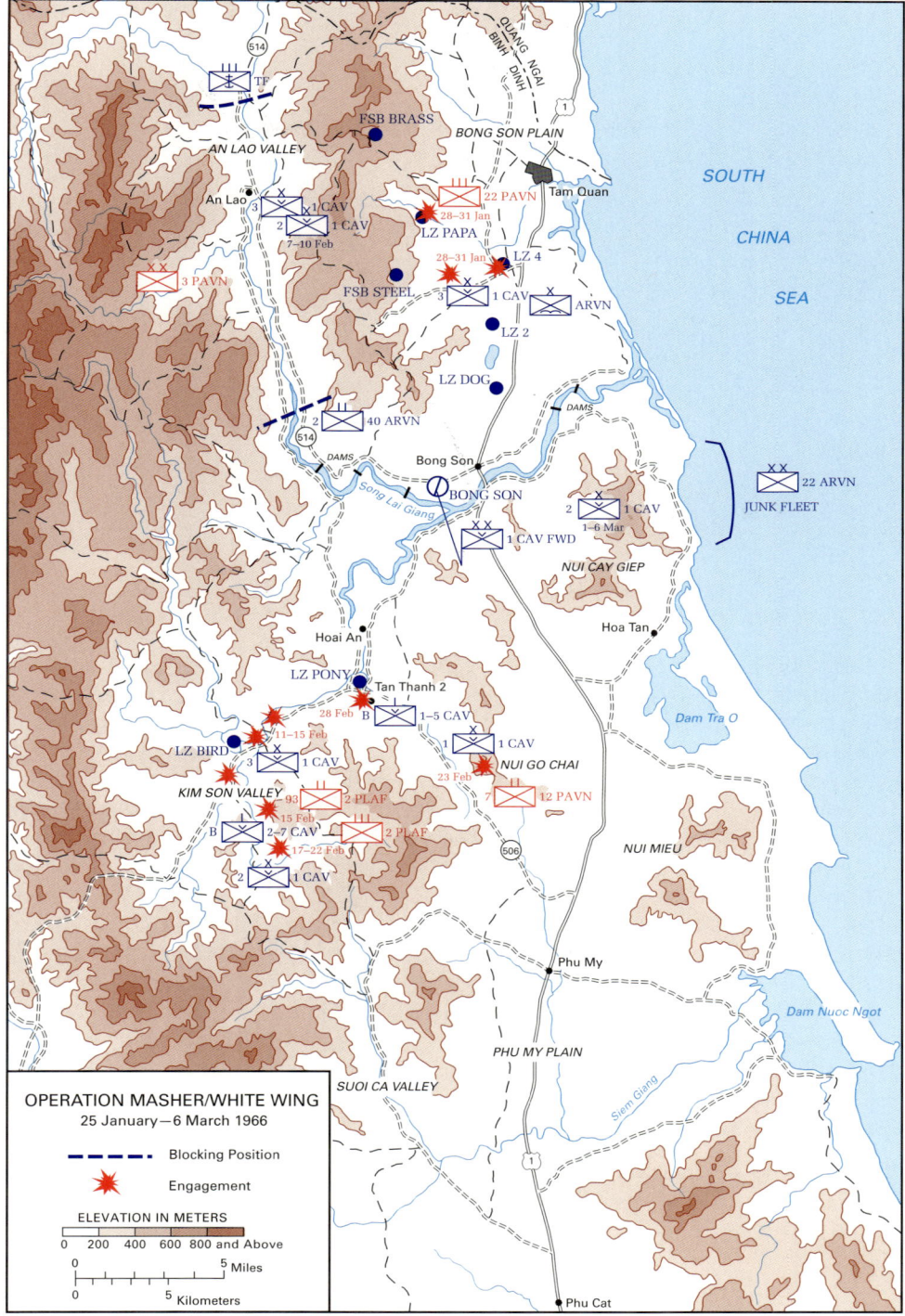

QUANG NGAI / BINH DINH

(514)

TF

FSB BRASS

AN LAO VALLEY

BONG SON PLAIN

Tam Quan

1

SOUTH

CHINA

SEA

An Lao

3 1 CAV

2 1 CAV
7-10 Feb

22 PAVN

LZ PAPA
28-31 Jan

3 PAVN

FSB STEEL

LZ 4
28-31 Jan

3 1 CAV

ARVN

LZ 2

LZ DOG

2 40 ARVN

514

DAMS

DAMS

Bong Son

DAMS

Song Lai Giang

BONG SON

1 CAV FWD

2 1 CAV
1-6 Mar

22 ARVN

JUNK FLEET

NUI CAY GIEP

Hoa Tan

Hoai An

LZ PONY

Tan Thanh 2

28 Feb

B 1-5 CAV

Dam Tra O

1 CAV

11-15 Feb

LZ BIRD

3 1 CAV

1 CAV

23 Feb

NUI GO CHAI

7 12 PAVN

KIM SON VALLEY

93 2 PLAF

15 Feb

B 2-7 CAV

2 PLAF

17-22 Feb

2 1 CAV

506

NUI MIEU

Phu My

Dam Nuoc Ngot

PHU MY PLAIN

Siem Giang

SUOI CA VALLEY

1

Phu Cat

OPERATION MASHER/WHITE WING
25 January – 6 March 1966

– – – – – Blocking Position

✸ Engagement

ELEVATION IN METERS

0 200 400 600 800 and Above

0 ————————— 5 Miles

0 ————————— 5 Kilometers

MAP 14

A battalion command post early in MASHER/WHITE WING

The first helicopter lift hit the ground at 0825, with no reaction from the enemy. When the second came ten minutes later, however, elements of an enemy battalion, entrenched in earthworks, palm groves, and bamboo thickets throughout the hamlet, poured mortar and machine gun fire into the landing zone. Fesmire's men had arrived seeking elements of the *12th Regiment*, but they were up against an altogether different unit—the *22d Regiment*'s *7th Battalion*, reinforced by a heavy weapons company.[11]

Fesmire waved the second flight away, expecting the troops to be dropped at an alternate landing zone a few hundred meters to the southwest. Instead, they ended up at four nearby but scattered locations. Returning ten minutes later with a third lift, the Hueys unloaded the men at a fifth site. By 0845 Company C was on the ground, but the unit was so fragmented and enemy fire so intense that the various parts found maneuver difficult and effective communication with one another impossible. Meanwhile, heavy rain impeded the provision of adequate air support, and the men were so dispersed that artillery was of little use. American casualties soon littered the hamlet ground.[12]

---

[11] AAR, Opn MASHER/WHITE WING, 1st Cav Div, incl. 3, pp. 1–2; Annual Hist Sum, 1 Jan–30 Jun 66, 2d Bn, 7th Cav, n.d., and AAR, Opn MASHER, 2d Bn, 7th Cav, 19 Feb 66, p. 2, Historians files, CMH; Interv, Broderick with Fesmire, 1982, ch. 2, pp. 35–38, Company Commanders in Vietnam, MHI.

[12] Interv, Broderick with Fesmire, 1982, ch. 2, pp. 36–37.

Troops of the 1st Cavalry Division advance on an enemy bunker near Bong Son.

As the day lengthened, Companies A and B became entangled in Company C's predicament. First, McDade ordered Sugdinis to reinforce Fesmire. But when Company A reached the southern edge of the landing zone, it likewise came under fire. Although the men formed a perimeter near a paddy dike, they were soon pinned down and never reached their goal.

Early in the afternoon McDade joined Company A, but to no effect. "Every time you raised your head, it was zap, zap, zap," he later commented. "The dirt really flew." Finally, six helicopters carrying reinforcements from Company B reached Landing Zone 4. But the effort generated so much enemy fire that all six were hit and two were driven off. Only Captain Diduryk and part of one platoon were able to land. They quickly found themselves in a cross fire.[13]

Rain fell in sheets that night, but as it did, the situation began to improve. Colonel McDade managed to pinpoint the fragments of Company C and succeeded in bringing in artillery support. Meanwhile, the darkness and poor weather gave Captain Fesmire the cover he needed to pull his unit together. As he prepared to settle in for the night, he received orders from McDade to move south, closer to the rest of the battalion. Under heavy fire, he completed the linkup at 0430.

---

[13] Terrence Maitland and Peter McInerney, *The Vietnam Experience: A Contagion of War* (Boston: Boston Publishing Co., 1983), p. 39.

Along with 20 wounded, his men carried with them the bodies of 8 killed.[14]

After dawn on the twenty-ninth the low overcast lifted, and tactical air support came to the rescue. Fighter-bombers pounded the area to McDade's north, detonating enemy ammunition and causing large fires. Soon after, McDade's companies, reinforced by Ingram's 2d of the 12th Cavalry, swept north to eliminate the last enemy from the hamlet. But the clearing operation took another day, and was completed only when elements of Kampe's 1st of the 7th Cavalry joined the sweep out of the landing zone.[15]

From then on, Colonel Moore's forces fought daily skirmishes and firefights, but combat tapered off. On 1 February Ingram's battalion swept west and Kampe's battalion continued its own searching. When neither effort proved productive, Moore shifted his troops to the west, northwest, and north. Once again, little action was forthcoming. With nothing more to gain, General Kinnard ordered an end to that phase of the operation, effective at 1200 on 4 February.[16]

The 3d Brigade had cleared elements of the *22d Regiment* from the coastal plain and had damaged enemy plans for a spring offensive, killing 566 North Vietnamese and Viet Cong. But the Americans lost 123 dead (including the 42 troops and 4 crew killed in the plane crash) and nearly 200 wounded. In addition, twenty-nine helicopters had been hit and two shot down on 28 January, prompting one aviator at Landing Zone 4 to write in his journal: "Hope not many more days like this!" These losses were telling; the Bong Son Plain had seemed more conducive to infantry operations than the territory west of Pleiku, where the division had battled in November. Instead of dense jungle, Moore's forces were now in an area that had ample landing zones as well as adequate roads and flat sandy ground that permitted easy access for troops on foot. In its own way, coastal Binh Dinh, with its deceptively open vistas, was proving to be a trial.[17]

As the number of contacts north of the Lai Giang dwindled, General Kinnard turned west to the An Lao Valley. According to American intelligence, the slender valley was an important center of activity for the Communists, laced with logistical and communications routes as well as rice caches and resupply points. Since the *3d Division* headquarters was also thought to be there, Kinnard considered the valley ripe for a two-brigade push.

---

[14] Ibid., pp. 39–40; AARs, Opn Masher/White Wing, 1st Cav Div, incl. 3, p. 6, and Opn Masher, 2d Bn, 7th Cav, p. 2; Interv, Broderick with Fesmire, ch. 2, pp. 37–38.

[15] AARs, Opn Masher/White Wing, 1st Cav Div, p. 14, and Opn Masher, 2d Bn, 7th Cav, pp. 2–3; AAR, Opns Masher and Eagle Claw, 1st Bn, 7th Cav, 22 Feb 66, p. 5, Historians files, CMH.

[16] AARs, Opn Masher/White Wing, 1st Cav Div, p. 14, and Opn Masher/White Wing (Eagle Claw), 3d Bde, 1st Cav Div, p. 9.

[17] AAR, Opn Masher/White Wing, 1st Cav Div, incl. 1, p. 1; Jnl, Lt Col Robert S. Kellar, CO, 229th Avn Bn, 28 Jan 66 (quoted words), Historians files, CMH.

Kinnard assigned Colonel Lynch's 2d Brigade and Colonel Moore's 3d Brigade to the mission. While U.S. Marines and soldiers from the South Vietnamese 40th Regiment, 22d Division, sealed the northern and southern exits of the valley, Lynch's and Moore's men landed on the high ground on 7 February and, from east and west, swept down the slopes to the valley floor. While scouring the An Lao, they succeeded in uncovering a remarkable system of trenches and fortifications and destroying large stores of rice and salt. But the enemy had evaporated. Since some forty-five hundred of the valley's inhabitants chose to leave under American escort rather than remain, the main forces were probably laying low. Communist rearguard forces suffered 11 killed; the Americans, 49 wounded, mostly from mines and booby traps.[18]

The next phase of MASHER/WHITE WING, a strike by the 3d Brigade at the Kim Son Valley southwest of Bong Son, was far more productive. The Kim Son, actually seven small valleys containing many streams and the fast-flowing Kim Son River, was an ideal enemy base that offered controlled entrances, well-positioned hiding places, and various escape routes. On 11 February Colonel Moore established ambush positions at each of the valley's exits and on the twelfth sent his remaining troops, backed by artillery fire, through the canyons as beaters to drive the enemy into the waiting Americans. The plan, while creative, failed to find much, so Moore reverted to scouring the valley with small unit patrols.[19]

Over the next few days the number of enemy dead slowly mounted as the result of over a dozen clashes with the Americans. One of the biggest began on the morning of 15 February, when a platoon from Company B, 2d of the 7th Cavalry, came under small-arms and mortar fire while patrolling about four kilometers southeast of Landing Zone BIRD, near the valley center. Captain Diduryk, the company commander, initially estimated that the opposing force was no larger than a reinforced platoon, but it soon became apparent that he had bumped into at least two companies occupying a three hundred-meter-long position running along a jungled streambank and up a hillside. Intelligence later identified the force as part of the *3d Division's 93d Battalion, 2d PLAF Regiment.*[20]

Fire from Company B's mortar platoon, from gunships and Skyraiders, and from artillery at Landing Zone BIRD pounded the insurgents. Then Diduryk's men attacked, yelling "like madmen." One pla-

[18] AAR, Opn MASHER/WHITE WING, 2d Bde, 1st Cav Div (Ambl), 16 Mar 66, p. 5, Historians files, CMH; AARs, Opn MASHER/WHITE WING, 1st Cav Div, pp. 9, 15, Opn MASHER/WHITE WING (EAGLE CLAW), 3d Bde, 1st Cav Div, p. 6, and Opn MASHER, 2d Bn, 7th Cav, p. 3.

[19] AAR, Opn MASHER/WHITE WING, 1st Cav Div, pp. 9, 15–16; Galvin, *Air Assault,* pp. 303–05.

[20] Rpt, Capt Myron F. Diduryk, Company Tactics Committee, Company Opns Dept, U.S. Army Infantry School, Fort Benning, Ga., n.d., sub: Rifle Company in Offensive Actions, pp. 4–9, copy in Historians files, CMH.

An A1–E Skyraider

toon fixed bayonets and charged the dug-in defenders across the stream.[21] A second pushed north to block an escape route, and a third stayed in reserve. Unnerved by the frontal assault, the Viet Cong retreated in disorder. Many stumbled into the open and were quickly killed. Those who survived fled to the north, where they came within range of the waiting platoon. A smaller group attempted to escape southward but came under fire from the reserve platoon, which took many prisoners, including *93d Battalion* commander Lt. Col. Dong Doan. A hardcore Communist who boasted to Colonel Moore that the Americans would never win, Doan inadvertently provided his interrogators with enough information to identify the locations of both his regiment and its headquarters. During the fight Diduryk and his men had killed 59 Viet Cong and possibly another 90. They lost 2 of their own.[22]

On 16 February General Kinnard decided to replace Colonel Moore's brigade with Col. Elvy B. Roberts' 1st Brigade. The next day, the 1st and 2d Battalions, 7th Cavalry, returned to An Khe, while Colonel Beard's 1st of the 12th remained behind to join its sister units—Colonel Mertel's

---

[21] Maitland and McInerney, *Contagion of War*, p. 47.

[22] AARs, Opn MASHER, 2d Bn, 7th Cav, p. 5, and Opn MASHER/WHITE WING (EAGLE CLAW), 3d Bde, 1st Cav Div, p. 9; Col Harold G. Moore, "Brigade Operations" (Address given at Association of United States Army Annual Meeting, Washington, D.C., October 1966), p. 4, copy in Historians files, CMH.

1st Battalion, 8th Cavalry, and Colonel Nix's 2d Battalion, 8th Cavalry. Together, the three battalions combed the area around Bird, but the enemy remained in hiding. Colonel Roberts' men soon grasped what the other participants in Masher/White Wing had already learned: The enemy fought only when he wished and sought to avoid contact otherwise, if only to escape the firepower available to the Americans.[23]

Frustrated, on 22 February Roberts changed the direction of the hunt, dispatching Beard's 1st of the 12th Cavalry to search Go Chai Mountain, a little less than fourteen kilometers east of Bird and almost seven kilometers west of Highway 1. During the afternoon of the twenty-third Beard's men met an estimated company of North Vietnamese, probably from the *12th Regiment*'s *7th Battalion*. They latched onto their opponents and maintained contact until dark, but then the enemy escaped.[24]

Operations in the area continued until the twenty-seventh, but when nothing more of substance occurred, Kinnard decided to abandon the Kim Son Valley. That evening he attached two battalions from Roberts' 1st Brigade to Lynch's 2d Brigade and returned the 1st's command group and Beard's battalion to An Khe. In all, the 1st Brigade had accounted for up to 160 enemy killed while losing 29 of its own men.[25]

While the 1st and 3d Brigades were patrolling the Kim Son Valley between 11 and 27 February, Colonel Lynch closed down operations north of the Lai Giang and transferred his command post to Landing Zone Pony just east of the valley. The move was triggered by Colonel Doan's revelation that the *2d PLAF Regiment* was operating in the mountains southeast of Pony, information that seemed to be confirmed when radio intercepts indicated the presence of a major enemy headquarters there.

On 16 February Lynch began a block and sweep of the suspected terrain. Lt. Col. Edward C. Meyer's 2d Battalion, 5th Cavalry, set up three blocking positions—Recoil, roughly six kilometers east of the Kim Son Valley; Joe, four kilometers southwest of Recoil; and Mike, just over two kilometers north of Recoil. The sweep force, Colonel Ackerson's 1st Battalion, 5th Cavalry, plus a battery of the 1st Battalion, 77th Artillery, helicoptered to Landing Zone Coil approximately six kilometers northeast of Recoil. Colonel Ingram's 2d of the 12th remained near Pony as a reserve.[26]

At 0630, on 17 February, the battery at Coil heralded the beginning of the sweep by pounding the area between Coil and Recoil. As the barrage lifted, two of Colonel Ackerson's companies stepped off toward

[23] AAR, Opn White Wing (Eagle Claw), 1st Bde, 1st Cav Div (Ambl), 4 Mar 66, p. 3, Historians files, CMH.

[24] Ibid., pp. 7–9.

[25] Ibid., 9–11; Memo, Maj Gen Harry W. O. Kinnard for 1st Cav Div Members, 11 Mar 66, Historians files, CMH.

[26] AAR, Opn Masher/White Wing, 1st Cav Div, p. 16; AAR, Opn Eagle Claw, 2d Bde, 1st Cav Div, 16 Mar 66, p. 2, box 2, 73/3330, RG 338, NARA; Galvin, *Air Assault*, p. 304.

Colonel Meyer's three blocking positions. One of Meyer's companies moved out to establish a fourth block east of RECOIL, but before the men had gone more than a kilometer they were engulfed by fire from upslope. Either they had run into an enemy fortification or the enemy had stumbled upon them while attempting to avoid Ackerson.[27]

After calling in air strikes and artillery, Colonel Meyer directed one of his rifle companies to reinforce, but on its way it became so heavily engaged that it could not advance. Meyer then committed his third rifle company, and Colonel Lynch ordered Ingram to send a company as well. In the end, the cumulative weight of the American ground attack and the artillery and air strikes drove the enemy from the heights. The Americans killed at least 127 Viet Cong—if not many more—and captured and destroyed three mortars, five recoilless rifles, and a quantity of ammunition, leading Lynch to conclude that he had crushed the *2d PLAF Regiment*'s heavy weapons battalion.[28]

In the days that followed, the 2d Brigade discovered that it had stirred up a hornet's nest. During the early afternoon of the eighteenth two platoons from Colonel Ackerson's 1st of the 5th Cavalry came under heavy fire while patrolling in one of the enemy's jungle strongholds. With the platoons pinned down, Ackerson reinforced with two rifle companies, but fire from earthworks cut them apart, and casualties were left where they fell. At the end of the day the Americans broke contact to retrieve their dead and wounded. The troops labeled the sector where the roughest fighting had taken place the "Iron Triangle," because of its shape.[29]

The fighting continued on the nineteenth. Company B of Ingram's 2d of the 12th joined Company C of Meyer's 2d of the 5th on a sweep southwest of the Iron Triangle. When one of the companies drew fire in the morning, the other attempted to turn the enemy's flank but ran into more Viet Cong. After breaking contact and calling in artillery and air strikes, the two companies attacked, killing 36 and forcing the remainder to withdraw. Ackerson's battalion, meanwhile, renewed its assault into the triangle, with two companies moving west while the third blocked. But the insurgents stood their ground, stalling the advance. At dark, Ackerson's men broke contact to remove their wounded.[30]

The next day, 20 February, Lynch ordered Ackerson to continue his attack. Following a morning artillery strike, one of the companies came under fire from a strongpoint no more than one hundred meters from the scene of the previous day's fighting. The Americans pulled back and called in artillery. In the afternoon one of Ingram's units fought a running battle that left 23 enemy dead before the Viet Cong withdrew.[31]

[27] Annual Hist Sum, 1966, 2d Bn, 5th Cav, n.d., p. 3, Historians files, CMH.
[28] AAR, Opn EAGLE CLAW, 2d Bde, 1st Cav Div, p. 3.
[29] Ibid., p. 4; AAR, Opn MASHER/WHITE WING, 1st Cav Div, p. 16.
[30] AAR, Opn MASHER/WHITE WING, 1st Cav Div, p. 17.
[31] AAR, Opn EAGLE CLAW, 2d Bde, 1st Cav Div, p. 4.

Circumstances were much the same on the twenty-first, attacks and counterthrusts by both sides. Meyer's and Ingram's battalions patrolled around their landing zones, while a platoon from one of Ackerson's companies probed the site of the previous day's combat. Once again, intense enemy fire forced the Americans to withdraw. Then, having arranged for air support, Lynch pulled all of his units out of the Iron Triangle. B–52s struck the site at midmorning and again in the afternoon. A tactical air mission then dropped three hundred tear gas grenades into the area. As evening approached, two of Ackerson's companies advanced toward the triangle but stopped before entering it when darkness fell. Artillery fired over seven hundred rounds into the redoubt, and an AC–47 gunship dropped illumination flares throughout the night. During the action a psychological operations team circled overhead in a loudspeaker plane, broadcasting the message that further resistance would be futile and dropping safe conduct passes.[32]

The next day, the twenty-second, Ackerson's men moved in to find bunkers, foxholes, and trenches, but no live enemy. Although 41 bodies remained at the site, blood trails, bloody bandages, and discarded weapons indicated that many more had been killed or wounded. Colonel Lynch insisted that the operation would have been even more successful if the two B–52 strikes had been timed more closely together. Instead, the delay between the first and the second bombing runs had prevented mopping up operations that might have kept more of the insurgents from escaping.[33]

During the fight in the Iron Triangle American ground and air forces had killed at least 313 Viet Cong soldiers and possibly 400 more. The Americans also estimated that the enemy had suffered some 900 wounded. Following the operation, one report observed, the entire valley floor reeked with the stench of Viet Cong dead. In addition to decimating the heavy weapons battalion of the *2d PLAF Regiment*, Colonel Lynch was certain that his units had inflicted heavy losses on the regiment's headquarters and its *93d* and *95th Battalions*. The cost to the 2d Brigade was 23 killed and 106 wounded.[34]

After the hectic pace in the Iron Triangle, Colonel Lynch's brigade rested for a few days before resuming operations. On 25 February Lynch returned to the hunt with two battalions. Over the next three days his men exchanged fire with small groups of enemy soldiers but failed to generate significant contacts. But an incident on the twenty-eighth struck a somber note. Early in the morning a patrol from Company B of Colonel Ackerson's 1st of the 5th Cavalry came under sniper fire less than two kilometers south of PONY. Unable to locate the position, the patrol members continued their advance.

---

[32] Ibid., p. 2; AAR, Opn MASHER/WHITE WING, 1st Cav Div, incl. 4, p. 2.

[33] AAR, Opn EAGLE CLAW, 2d Bde, 1st Cav Div, p. 4. On 26 February Ackerson's battalion and an engineer team returned to the Iron Triangle and blew up bunkers and other fortifications to prevent the enemy from using them. See ibid., pp. 6–7.

[34] Ibid., pp. 2, 7; AAR, Opn MASHER/WHITE WING, 1st Cav Div, pp. 11, 17.

Entering the hamlet of Tan Thanh 2, they met a hail of fire and suffered 4 wounded. As they pushed deeper into the settlement, automatic weapons opened up on them. They responded with grenades and small arms but soon came under attack on the right flank by fifteen to twenty Viet Cong, who killed 8 of them within minutes and wounded a number more. As the Americans scrambled for cover, the Communists emerged from hiding to strip the U.S. dead of their weapons. A relief force arrived a short while later, but by then the Viet Cong were gone.[35]

The final segment of MASHER/WHITE WING began on 1 March, with the 1st Cavalry Division returning to roughly where it had begun the operation at the end of January. Based on prisoner interrogations, American intelligence believed that the *12th PAVN Regiment*'s *6th Battalion* was operating in the Cay Giep Mountains. General Kinnard wanted to encircle and annihilate it. The South Vietnamese 22d Division surrounded the target area, deploying along the Lai Giang to the north, Highway 1 to the west, and the Tra O Marsh in the south, while the division's junk fleet patrolled the coast to prevent escape by sea. Colonel Lynch's 2d Brigade would conduct the attack.[36]

At 0730 General Kinnard unleashed an intense hour-long air, land, and sea bombardment of intended landing zones. When the firing stopped, the designated sweep force—Colonel Meyer's 2d of the 5th, Colonel Mertel's 1st of the 8th, and Lt. Col. John A. Hemphill's 2d of the 8th—came in over the mountains. But the troops, to their dismay, found that the bombardment had hardly dented the thick foliage, and the helicopters were unable to land. Eventually, additional air strikes opened holes in the jungle canopy wide enough to allow the men to reach the ground by scrambling down rope ladders suspended from the hovering helicopters. Once deployed, the three battalions, soon joined by Colonel Ackerson's 1st of the 5th, searched the area and found little, although a South Vietnamese unit near the Tra O Marsh killed about 50 enemy soldiers who were attempting to flee the dragnet. On the fourth, following word from South Vietnamese civilians that most of the North Vietnamese had left the area around the end of February, Kinnard decided that MASHER/WHITE WING had run its course and over the next two days returned Lynch's brigade to An Khe.[37]

MASHER/WHITE WING had dealt the *3d Division* a heavy blow. In forty-one days of campaigning the 1st Cavalry Division had killed more than 1,300 main force regulars, captured over 600 more, and received almost 500 defectors. In addition, Kinnard's men had seized or destroyed over

---

[35] Daily Jnl, 1st Bn, 5th Cav, 28 Feb 66, Historians files, CMH; AAR, Opn EAGLE CLAW, 2d Bde, 1st Cav Div, p. 6.

[36] AAR, Opn MASHER/WHITE WING, 1st Cav Div, p. 19.

[37] AAR, Opn BLACK HORSE, 2d Bde, 1st Cav Div, 16 Mar 66, pp. 2–4, Historians files, CMH; Rpt, 14th Mil Hist Det, 1st Cav Div (Ambl), 9 Jun 67, sub: Seven Month History and Briefing Data (September 1965–March 1966), pp. 26, 67, box 16, 74/053, RG 319, NARA.

two hundred individual and fifty-two crew-served weapons, large quantities of ammunition, many useful documents, and communications gear. Finally, the division had uncovered ninety-one tons of rice and fourteen tons of salt that were distributed to South Vietnamese refugees. All in all, MASHER/WHITE WING had dissolved any doubts that remained about the ability of the division to conduct sustained operations and to take the war to the enemy. But the price of progress was high: 228 Americans had died and 834 had been wounded. And Binh Dinh, which was still dotted with fortified villages and mountain hideouts, was not yet secure.[38]

DAVY CROCKETT

After spending most of March and April in the highlands conducting a series of spoiling attacks, the 1st Cavalry Division returned to Binh Dinh in May to resume operations against the *3d Division*. The move coincided with a change in leadership at An Khe. General Kinnard left the division to become the acting commander of I Field Force while General Larsen was on leave. He was succeeded by General Norton who, like Kinnard, had played an active role in developing the airmobile concept. The division was his reward for having headed U.S. Army, Vietnam, so ably during the first year of the buildup and for having demonstrated in that job an understanding of airmobile warfare logistical requirements.

General Norton's first operation, DAVY CROCKETT, was a reaction to intelligence pinpointing the *12th* and the *22d Regiments* around the town of Bong Son. By the time the effort began, however, most of the *12th Regiment* had slipped south of the Lai Giang, leaving only one of its battalions and the *22d Regiment* on the Bong Son Plain. Nevertheless, I Field Force analysts still believed that there were enough enemy units north of the river to justify an operation. If a battle failed to develop, Norton could shift his operations to the usually lucrative Kim Son Valley. To achieve surprise, U.S. commanders waited until shortly before the operation began to inform the South Vietnamese and then pretended to reverse the order of events by asserting that the attack in the Kim Son would come first (*see Map 15*).[39]

Colonel Moore and his 3d Brigade drew the mission, and he immediately laid a three-sided trap for the *22d Regiment*. On the morning of 4 May his two battalions, Lt. Col. Herman L. Wirth's 1st of the 7th Cavalry and Lt. Col. Robert F. Litle's 2d of the 7th Cavalry, air-assaulted west and

[38] AAR, Opn MASHER/WHITE WING, 1st Cav Div, p. 23, and incl. 1, p. 2; Periodic Intel Rpt, 1 Jan–30 Jun 66, MACV, 20 Aug 66 p. 10, MHI; AAR, Opn BLACK HORSE, 2d Bde, 1st Cav Div, p. 19; Rpt, 14th Mil Hist Det, 1st Cav Div, 9 Jun 67, sub: Seven Month History and Briefing Data (September 1965–March 1966), p. 67.

[39] AARs, Opn BEE BEE, 2d Bn, 7th Cav, 29 Apr 66, p. 2, and Opn DAVY CROCKETT, 3d Bde, 1st Cav Div (Ambl), 25 May 66, p. 2; ORLL, 1 May–31 Jul 66, I FFV, 25 Aug 66, incl. 8. All in Historians files, CMH.

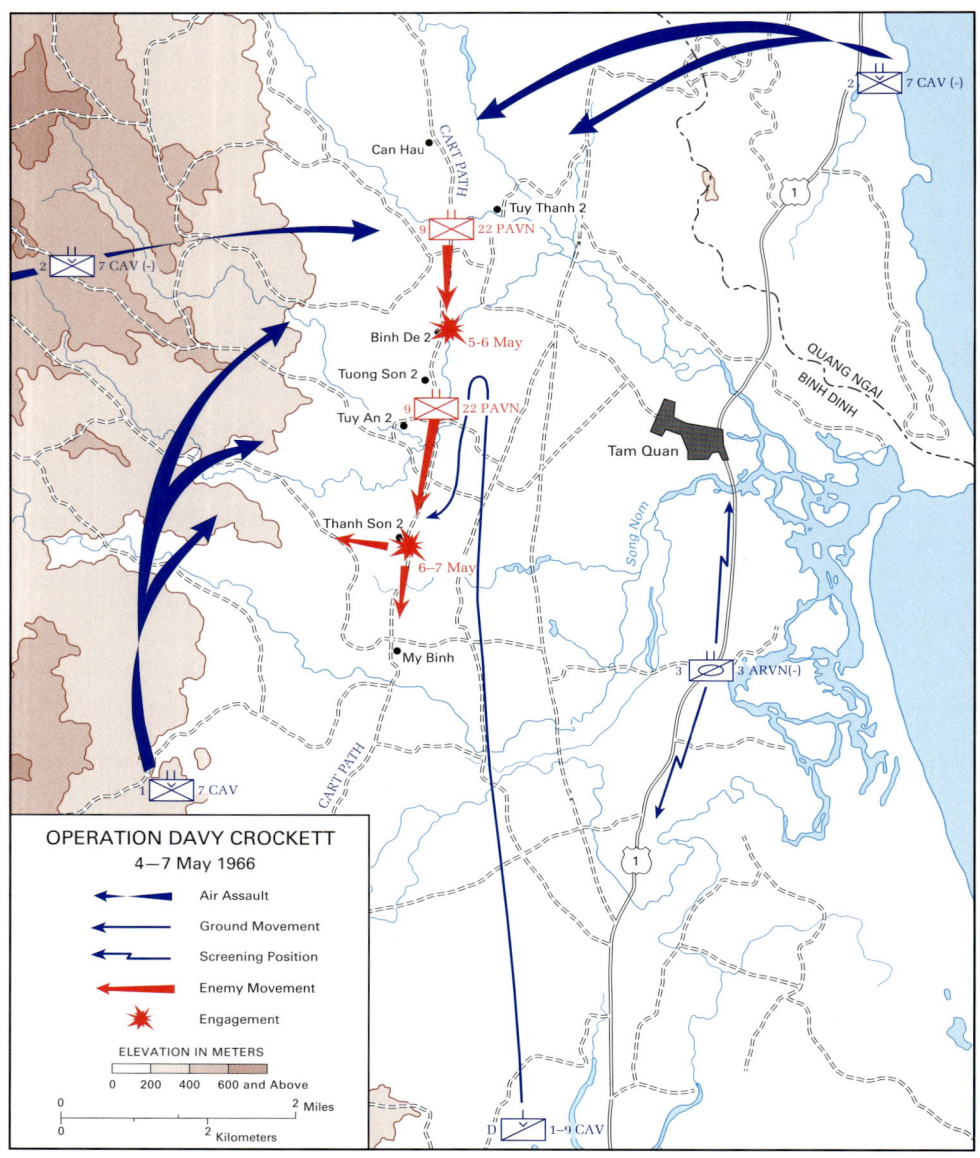

MAP 15

north of a cluster of hamlets where the *22d* was supposedly hiding, while a South Vietnamese force from the 3d Armored Cavalry Regiment established a defense line along Highway 1. With the snare set, Troop D from Lt. Col. James C. Smith's 1st of the 9th Cavalry, accompanied by South Vietnamese armor, attacked north to close the loop; the rest of the 1st of the 9th launched an aerial attack and pursuit from Landing Zone Dog. By the end of the first day the allies had killed 15 enemy soldiers and captured several prisoners who confirmed the presence of at least one large North Vietnamese unit in the area, later identified as the *22d Regiment's 9th Battalion.*[40]

The *9th Battalion* commander had no intention of standing and fighting on American terms. When he became aware of the 3d Brigade's arrival, he sideslipped his unit south using a cart path that paralleled Troop D's line of march. Unaware of the development, Moore's companies and the South Vietnamese scouted their sectors that day and then held in place overnight.

The next day, 5 May, Colonel Moore's two battalions carried out a series of air assaults and searches near their laagers, but by then the North Vietnamese were gone. Toward noon Litle's 2d of the 7th moved a short distance south to examine the hamlet of Tuy Thanh 2; Wirth's 1st of the 7th worked the same area as the previous day. Meanwhile, Troop D and the South Vietnamese contingent pushed north. At 1350 heavy automatic weapons opened up on them from the west, near Tuong Son 2. The volume of fire suggested that a large force was involved. As the fighting continued, it also became apparent that the enemy center of gravity was located not at Tuong Son 2 but at a point about five hundred meters to the north near the hamlet of Binh De 2.[41]

Moore planned to surround the position, keep the enemy there overnight with firepower, and then attack the next morning. In midafternoon he ordered Litle's men to set up blocks north and northwest of Binh De 2, and at sundown he sent Wirth's men to do likewise to the west. Throughout the night artillery and rocket fire laid down a continuous barrage over those areas not covered by the infantry. The artillery also targeted the cart path because it was a probable escape route. A later report claimed that the shelling killed 63 enemy troops; other estimates suggested that fatalities had run as high as 100. Yet when Moore's men launched their attack the next morning, the North Vietnamese were nowhere to be found. Since they had probably escaped to the south, Moore directed his brigade to pursue in that direction.[42]

An opportunity to reengage the *9th Battalion* presented itself almost immediately, when enemy fire downed one of Colonel Smith's helicopters about five kilometers south of Binh De 2. A second helicopter landed to secure the aircraft and rescue its crew, most of whom had been injured. Both helicopters quickly came under fire from the nearby hamlet of Thanh Son 2. Moore believed that he had found a major force, and he immedi-

---

[40] Op Sum, Opn DAVY CROCKETT, MACV, May 66, Historians files, CMH; AAR, Opn DAVY CROCKETT, 3d Bde, 1st Cav Div, p. 2.

[41] Rpt, 14th Mil Hist Det, 1st Cav Div, 7 Mar 67, sub: Seven Month History and Briefing Data (April–October 1966), p. 78, Historians files, CMH.

[42] Ibid.; AAR, Opn DAVY CROCKETT, 3d Bde, 1st Cav Div, p. 2; AARs, Opn DAVY CROCKETT, 1st Bn, 21st Arty, 21 May 66, pp. 2, 6, and 1st Bn, 7th Cav, 22 May 66, p. 1, and Rpt, 1st Cav Div (Ambl), Jun 66, sub: Operations in Vietnam, August 1965–May 1966, p. 25, Historians files, CMH.

ately set out to surround it, with Troop D approaching from the east and Litle's battalion air-assaulting to seal off the western and southern exits. At that point, Moore ordered Wirth to attack from the north, promising artillery and air support. The assault soon stalled, but F–4 Phantoms were on target. Twice during the afternoon groups of enemy soldiers—one estimated to number forty and the other sixty or more—rose from their trenches and foxholes in Thanh Son 2 and milled about in confusion, only to disappear in lethal clouds of smoke, flame, and metal shards.[43]

Although Moore had the battalion surrounded, he once again lacked enough troops to keep the noose tight. As darkness fell and a heavy rain set in, the North Vietnamese sneaked out of the trap in small groups. By the next morning Thanh Son 2 was virtually empty. There were, however, stragglers. Colonel Moore and his sergeant major personally captured the *9th Battalion* political officer, while American ambush parties and prowling Huey gunships pounced on several bands of regulars. In the end, while never verified, the *9th Battalion*'s losses during the fight were almost certainly substantial. The enemy commander himself and most of his officers perished in the engagement.[44]

Watching DAVY CROCKETT closely, General Norton reinforced the operation with Lt. Col. William B. Ray's 1st Battalion, 5th Cavalry. When the unit arrived at DOG on the morning of 7 May, Moore dispatched its companies to four landing zones in the far northern reaches of his operating area to search for the fleeing North Vietnamese. Between the ninth and eleventh Moore also continued to probe the countryside around Thanh Son 2 in hopes of generating another fight, but to no avail.[45]

Since the Communists seemed to be vacating the Bong Son Plain, Moore turned to his secondary target, the Kim Son Valley. Two of his battalions would act as "killer teams," while his remaining battalion and the division reconnaissance squadron would form lightly equipped, highly mobile "hunter teams." The hunters would search for the enemy and fix him in place; the killers would arrive to finish him off.[46]

Moore's artillery began to move into the valley on 11 May, after Litle's 2d of the 7th had secured sites for it at Landing Zones PONY and BIRD. Except for a company that stayed near PONY, most of Litle's men operated from BIRD, while the 1st of the 9th Cavalry reconnoitered the many

[43] AARs, Opn DAVY CROCKETT, 2d Bn, 7th Cav, 21 May 66, p. 3, and 1st Cav Div Arty, 27 May 66, p. 2, Historians files, CMH; AARs, Opn DAVY CROCKETT, 1st Bn, 7th Cav, p. 2, and 3d Bde, 1st Cav Div, pp. 6–7, and 1st Bn, 21st Arty, p. 2; Rpt, 1st Cav Div, Jun 66, sub: Operations in Vietnam, August 1965–May 1966, p. 26.

[44] Rpt, 1st Cav Div, Jun 66, sub: Operations in Vietnam, August 1965–May 1966, p. 26; AARs, Opn DAVY CROCKETT, 2d Bn, 7th Cav, p. 4, and 3d Bde, 1st Cav Div, p. 7, and 1st Bn, 7th Cav, p. 2; Interv, author with Lt Gen Harold G. Moore, 18 Feb 94, Historians files, CMH.

[45] Annual Hist Sum, 1966, 1st Bn, 5th Cav, n.d., box 1, 82/899, RG 338, NARA.

[46] ORLL, 1 May–31 Jul 66, 1st Cav Div (Ambl), 15 Aug 66, incl. 2, pp. 1–3, box 12, 69A/702, RG 334, NARA.

canyons. Wirth's 1st of the 7th and Ray's 1st of the 5th remained at DOG as killer forces, ready to react to any reported sightings.[47]

Over the next five days Moore's hunter teams prowled the Kim Son and Suoi Ca Valleys, engaging small groups of enemy soldiers. On only two occasions—on the eleventh, about eight kilometers northwest of PONY; and on the fourteenth, some fourteen kilometers southeast of BIRD—did they spot what appeared to be significant forces, but the killer teams were unable to intervene before darkness fell. On 16 May Moore terminated the operation.[48]

DAVY CROCKETT had peaked in its first few days, when Moore's brigade had virtually annihilated the *22d Regiment*'s *9th Battalion*. By the end of the operation the Americans had killed a total of 345 enemy soldiers and possibly another 192. American forces had lost 27 killed, 155 wounded, and 1 missing. The missing soldier moved to the killed column several months later, when allied forces recovered his body from a shallow grave. General Larsen attributed much of DAVY CROCKETT's success to the initial cover plan, which had deceived South Vietnamese and North Vietnamese alike.[49]

CRAZY HORSE

Operation CRAZY HORSE began on 16 May, the day DAVY CROCKETT ended. It took place south of the Kim Son Valley, in the mountainous jungles between the Vinh Thanh and Suoi Ca Valleys. A pass, referred to by the Americans as the Oregon Trail, distinguished the area and provided a partial reference point for planning. An obvious corridor for the enemy, it extended from the northwestern end of the Suoi Ca Valley into the center of the Vinh Thanh Valley. The weather during the period continued its transition from wet to dry, which meant that heavy showers and low ceilings often occurred during the late afternoon and early evening hours. Though the rainy season was ending and the skies were clearing, the humidity remained high and daily temperatures rose sometimes as high as 110 degrees Fahrenheit. While these conditions were bad for the soldier, they made for excellent flying weather.[50]

[47] AARs, Opn DAVY CROCKETT, 3d Bde, 1st Cav Div, p. 8, and 1st Bn, 7th Cav, p. 2, and 2d Bn, 7th Cav, p. 5.

[48] AARs, Opn DAVY CROCKETT, 3d Bde, 1st Cav Div, p. 8, and 2d Bn, 7th Cav, p. 6; Rpt, 14th Mil Hist Det, 1st Cav Div, 7 Mar 67, sub: Seven Month History and Briefing Data (April–October 1966), p. 80; Op Sum, Opn DAVY CROCKETT, MACV, May 66, p. 3.

[49] AAR, Opn DAVY CROCKETT, 3d Bde, 1st Cav Div, pp. 10–11; Rpt, 1st Cav Div, Jun 66, sub: Operations in Vietnam, August 1965–May 1966, pp. 26–27; ORLL, 1 May–31 Jul 66, I FFV, pp. 7–8; Interv, author with Col Gregory P. Dillon, former S–3, 3d Bde, 1st Cav Div, 2 Mar 94, Historians files, CMH.

[50] AAR, Opn CRAZY HORSE, 1st Bde, 1st Cav Div (Ambl), 15 Jun 66, p. 3, Historians files, CMH; Rpt, 14th Mil Hist Det, 1st Cav Div, 7 Mar 67, sub: Seven Month History and Briefing Data (April–October 1966), p. 84.

The level of enemy activity in the area had increased during the week before the operation. On 9 May a CIDG patrol had captured a soldier who told interrogators that his comrades intended to "liberate" the Vinh Thanh Valley in about two weeks. The meaning of the comment was open to interpretation, but the Special Forces camp in the valley was the most likely immediate target, with harassment of Highway 19 and the 1st Cavalry Division base at An Khe almost certainly in prospect. CIDG patrols began to make frequent contact with Communist forces in the days that followed. On the fifteenth one patrol ambushed the lead element of the *32d PLAF Artillery Battalion* about six kilometers east of the camp. The Montagnards killed 5 Viet Cong and captured a number of documents, one of which indicated that a major attack would take place in the area on the nineteenth, Ho Chi Minh's birthday.[51]

At the time, General Norton was planning other operations in Binh Dinh, Kontum, and Pleiku Provinces. But because of the unusual nature of recent intelligence, he decided to concentrate on the mountains east of the Vinh Thanh Valley. Exploratory probes would tell if his guess was correct. If the Communists were found in large numbers or if a main force attack occurred, he would insert two battalions to block and maintain contact. Two additional battalions would stand by, poised for commitment once the main axis of withdrawal could be determined. If the operation grew, it would be directed by the 1st Brigade's commander, Colonel Hennessey. Norton's willingness to commit up to five battalions to CRAZY HORSE indicated the high hopes he held for the effort (*see Map 16*).[52]

Norton launched the initial probe on 16 May, with Capt. Jean D. Coleman's Company B, 2d of the 8th Cavalry, deploying by helicopter to a rugged mountainous area about four kilometers east of the valley. Arriving at Landing Zone HEREFORD around 1100, the men climbed a jagged ridgeline and, three hours later, met the Viet Cong in prepared positions. One squad bounding forward was destroyed in a cross fire. But the Americans pushed on doggedly for two more hours, repeatedly overcoming additional strongpoints.

Viet Cong resistance became increasingly aggressive. At one point, U.S. soldiers watched as a tall Viet Cong officer—disdainful of the bullets flying around him—walked among his men, exhorting them to fight. Because of the intensity of the fire, the Americans decided that they were facing a battalion. Toward evening heavy rain fell, making maneuver in the jungle much more difficult and reinforcement practically impossible. But the Viet Cong, preferring horrendous weather, chose this time to attack, forcing the defenders into a tight perimeter under heavy machine gun fire.[53]

---

[51] AARs, Opn CRAZY HORSE, 1st Cav Div (Ambl), 10 Sep 66, p. 4, Historians files, CMH, and 1st Bde, 1st Cav Div, pp. 2–3 (quoted word, p. 2).

[52] Critique, Opn CRAZY HORSE, 1st Cav Div (Ambl), 27 Jun 66, p. 16, Historians files, CMH; AAR, Opn CRAZY HORSE, 1st Bde, 1st Cav Div, p. 6.

[53] AAR, Opn CRAZY HORSE, 1st Bde, 1st Cav Div, p. 3; Stanton, *Anatomy of a Division*, p. 79; Rpt, 1st Cav Div, Jun 66, sub: Operations in Vietnam, August 1965–May 1966, p. 29.

Reinforcements were badly needed. As the rain slackened, two companies from the 1st of the 12th Cavalry arrived. Company C secured HEREFORD, while Company A linked up with Coleman's men and strengthened the perimeter.

The Viet Cong, later identified as elements from the *2d PLAF Regiment*, probed the laager throughout the night, too close for tube artillery to come into play. In a downpour two gunships from the 2d of the 20th Artillery blunted one of the assaults. Then, early in the morning of the seventeenth the Viet Cong charged just as the Americans began a mad minute—firing every weapon as fast as they could. Many insurgents died instantly, although some managed to come within a few feet of the Americans before being killed. But a mad minute quickly consumes ammunition, and before long the defenders were running low. With fixed bayonets, the Americans waited to be overrun. Their luck held. The Viet Cong commander, unaware of his opponent's shortages and already suffering huge losses, withdrew. A short while later Company B carried its casualties down the ridge to HEREFORD and departed for An Khe. Company A also pulled out, but it remained at the landing zone with Company C.[54]

The fight convinced General Norton and Colonel Hennessey that a regiment from the *3d Division* was operating east of the Vinh Thanh Valley, with a second regiment possibly nearby. This offered a tempting target, so they decided to turn CRAZY HORSE into a large-scale multibattalion sweep. Under the new plan Hennessey would press the attack against the *2d Regiment*. Moving quickly into landing zones north and east of HEREFORD, his troops were to find the enemy and to pursue him "regardless of his direction of movement."[55]

Hennessey placed his forward command post at Landing Zone SAVOY in the Vinh Thanh Valley on 17 May, also the site of the Special Forces camp; brought in two battalions; and arranged for a third battalion to follow. Colonel Ray's 1st of the 5th Cavalry, the first battalion to arrive, helicoptered to HEREFORD to reinforce the two companies present. Assuming operational control of the landing zone, Ray had five rifle companies under his command in addition to his own Company D. Four of them immediately headed east to explore a ridge near the site of the previous day's fighting.[56]

The second battalion's entry onto the battlefield was more complicated. Assuming that the enemy was withdrawing to the east along the Oregon Trail rather than to the north, Hennessey decided to place Lt. Col. Otis C. Lynn's 2d of the 12th Cavalry about three kilometers

---

[54] 1st Cavalry Division (Airmobile), *1st Air Cavalry Division: Memoirs of the First Team, Vietnam, August 1965–December 1969* (Tokyo, Japan: Dai Nippon Printing, [1970]), p. 88.

[55] Critique, Opn CRAZY HORSE, 1st Cav Div, p. 3; Op Order no. 6617, p. 6 (quotation), Incl to AAR, Opn CRAZY HORSE, 1st Cav Div.

[56] Annual Hist Sum, 1966, 1st Bn, 5th Cav, p. 5.

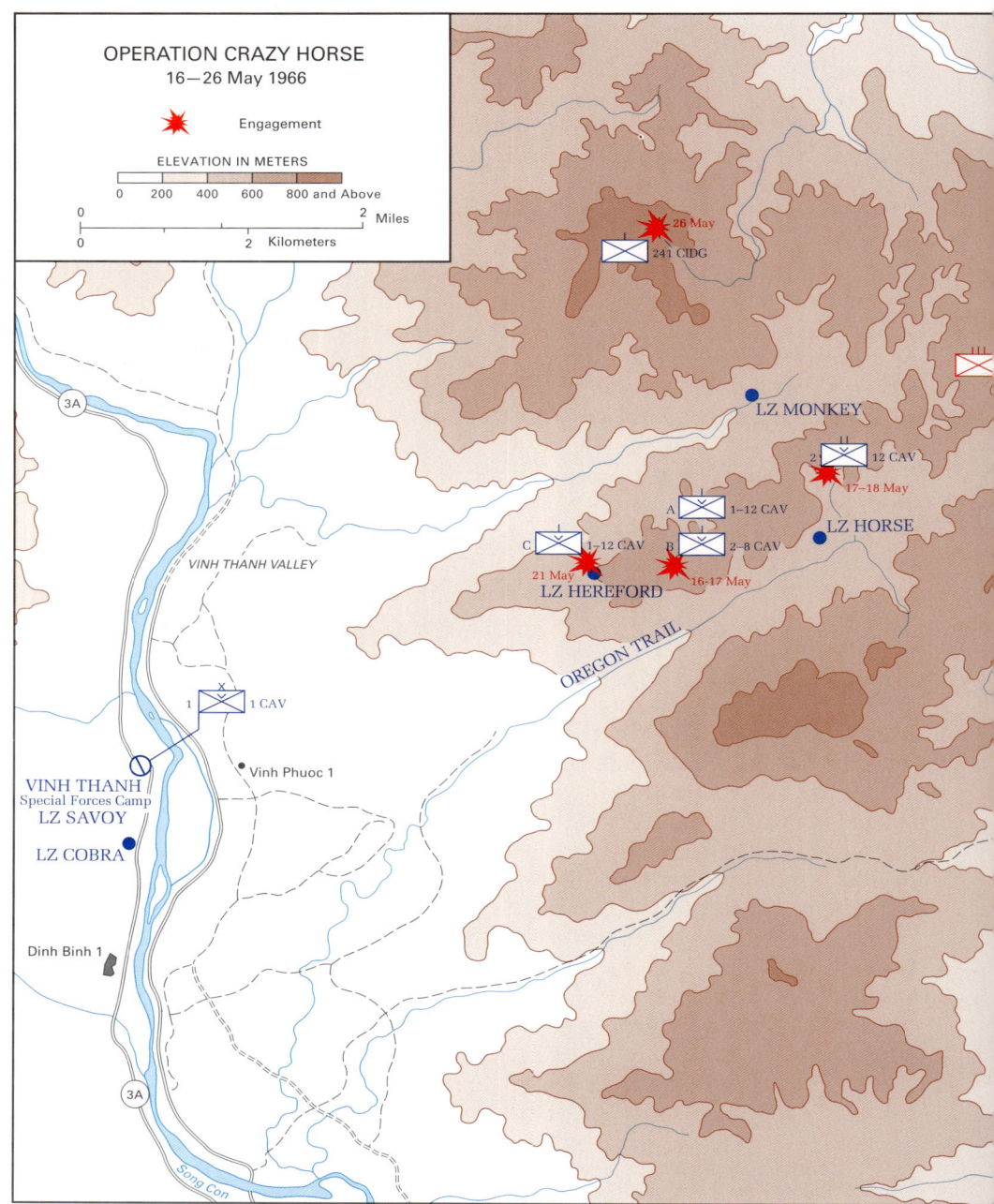

OPERATION CRAZY HORSE
16—26 May 1966

✸ Engagement

ELEVATION IN METERS

| 0 | 200 | 400 | 600 | 800 and Above |

0 ———————————————— 2 Miles

0 ———————————————— 2 Kilometers

241 CIDG — 26 May

LZ MONKEY

2 — 12 CAV — 17–18 May

A — 1–12 CAV

LZ HORSE

C — 1–12 CAV   B — 2–8 CAV

21 May   16-17 May

LZ HEREFORD

OREGON TRAIL

VINH THANH VALLEY

1   1 CAV

Vinh Phuoc 1

VINH THANH
Special Forces Camp
LZ SAVOY

LZ COBRA

Dinh Binh 1

Song Con

3A

3A

MAP 16

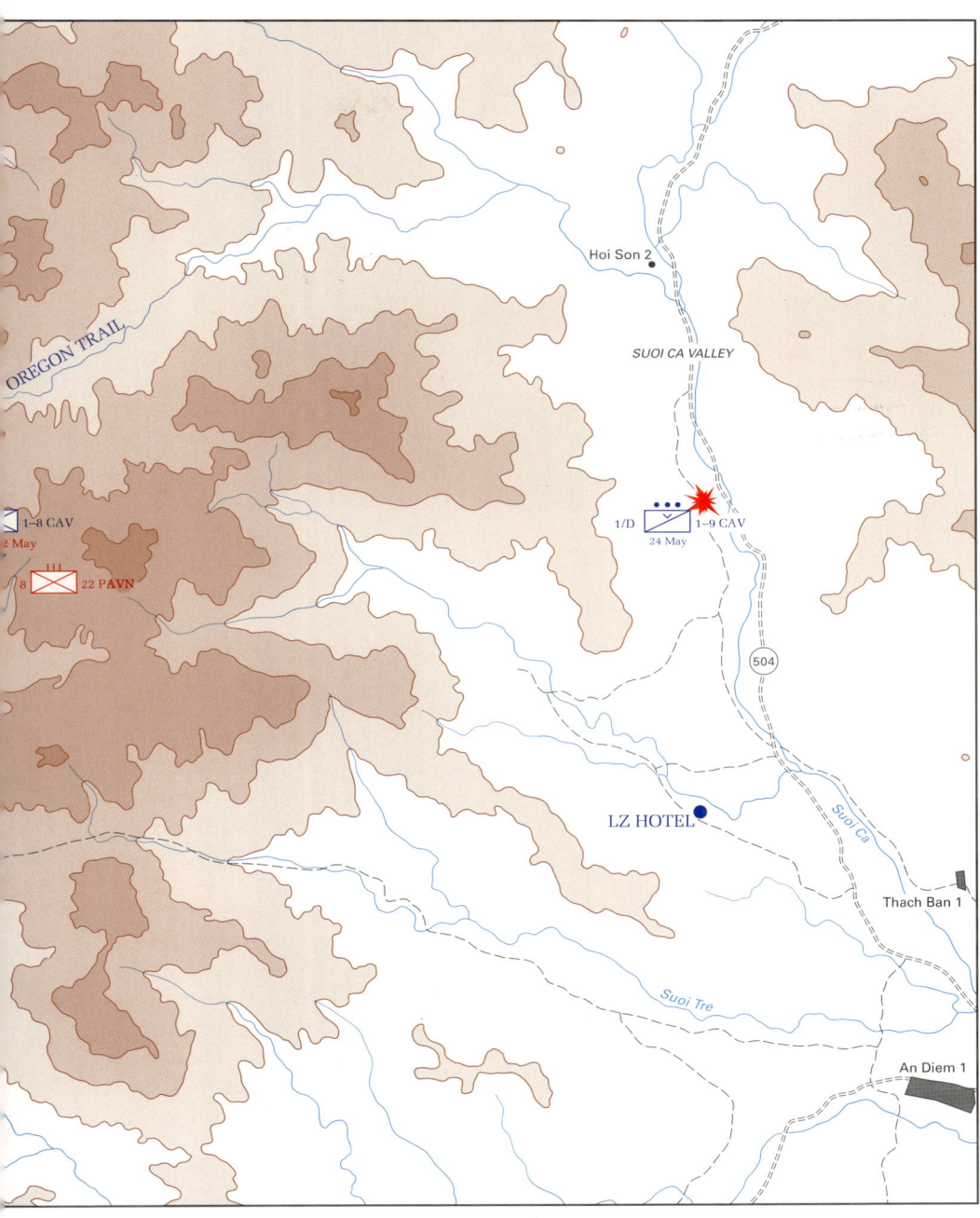

Hoi Son 2

SUOI CA VALLEY

OREGON TRAIL

1–8 CAV
2 May

8   22 PAVN

1/D   1–9 CAV
24 May

504

LZ HOTEL

Suoi Ca

Thach Ban 1

Suoi Tre

An Diem 1

*Artillerymen on a mountain near the Vinh Thanh Valley prepare
for action during* CRAZY HORSE.

east of HEREFORD. The plan hit a snag when the officers discovered that
the site they had selected for the insertion, Landing Zone HORSE, was
not large enough to take a helicopter. The battalion's reconnaissance
team and Army engineers had to rappel in to clear a space large enough
for the force to land. By 1600 Companies B and C were on the ground.
A sudden mortar attack, however, kept all but one of Company A's
platoons from landing. That unit, along with Colonel Lynn himself,
his command group, and his heavy weapons company, had no choice
but to turn back.[57]

The mortar barrage was a solitary event rather than the harbinger of
an attack, and the companies on the ground at HORSE soon began their
tasks. With Company C holding the landing zone, Company B and the
platoon from Company A headed north in search of the Communists.
After moving some five hundred meters, the Americans came under
intense automatic weapons fire from the crest of a hill. They assaulted
the position, but found the enemy heavily fortified in mutually supporting bunkers with overhead cover. Toward nightfall the troopers withdrew a short distance to establish a perimeter.

The next morning, 18 May, the company and platoon marched back
out to reestablish contact. They did not have to go far. A few hundred
meters northwest of HORSE, Company B suddenly came under heavy

[57] Annual Hist Sum, 1966, 2d Bn, 12th Cav, n.d., p. 20, Historians files, CMH.

224

fire from what seemed to be a company-size force. The troops responded in kind, and a spirited exchange developed. Around 1100 the platoon from Company A linked up with Company B, and the Americans called in air and artillery strikes. When the bombing and shelling stopped, the enemy withdrew with the troopers in pursuit. Later that afternoon the Communists moved into a line of bunkers some seven hundred meters from HORSE and turned to make a stand, stopping the Americans cold. More air strikes and artillery followed, but the Americans made no more headway. The enemy left after dark.[58]

Although inconclusive, the fight was of some consequence to Colonel Hennessey and his superiors. The enemy's tenacious defense of prepared positions near HORSE seemed to indicate that the region might be a major base area. To test that premise, Hennessey pulled additional troops into the operation. Late on the seventeenth the headquarters and heavy weapons companies from Colonel Beard's 1st of the 12th Cavalry had arrived at Landing Zone COBRA, just a kilometer south of Landing Zone SAVOY, leaving only one of his rifle companies as yet uncommitted back at An Khe. Then, on the evening of the eighteenth, all but one company of Colonel Hemphill's 2d of the 8th Cavalry reached SAVOY.[59]

Over the next few days the Americans trekked over heavily wooded and sharply ridged ground hunting for the enemy. Other than sniper fire, which slightly wounded Colonel Lynn, the troops moved unopposed. On the twentieth Colonel Broughton's 1st of the 8th Cavalry replaced Lynn's 2d of the 12th at HORSE. On the same day General Norton added Colonel Smith's 1st of the 9th Cavalry, minus its Troop A, to the operation.[60]

Two firefights broke out on 21 May, with mixed results for the Americans. The first came early in the morning, when Colonel Broughton's Companies B and C moved east of HORSE. Some three kilometers into the woods, with Company B in the lead, the Americans came under fire from what was later discovered to be the *22d Regiment's 8th Battalion*. The fight continued into the afternoon, and toward dusk the enemy withdrew about two hundred meters to the northwest. The Americans gave chase, only to find that the North Vietnamese had pulled into prepared hillside positions. The pitched battle continued until evening, but instead of establishing a perimeter for the night, the Americans stormed the bunkers in an unusual nighttime assault. When the fighting ended shortly after midnight, Broughton determined that his men had killed at least 60 soldiers and probably many more earlier. No one could say why the Communists stood and fought so tenaciously, but the 1st Brigade's intelligence officer later

---

[58] Ibid.; AAR, Opn CRAZY HORSE, 1st Bde, 1st Cav Div, p. 3.
[59] AAR, Opn CRAZY HORSE, 1st Bde, 1st Cav Div, pp. 3, 8–9.
[60] Ibid., p. 8; Annual Hist Sum, 1966, 2d Bn, 12th Cav, p. 20; AAR, Opn CRAZY HORSE, 1st Sqdn, 9th Cav, 28 Jul 66, p. 2, box 2, 73/3330, RG 338, NARA.

theorized that Broughton's men had met a rear guard that was buying time for the main body to escape.[61]

The second incident took place at HEREFORD, which by 21 May appeared to be a backwater because combat had drifted east. As the day began there were still two rifle companies at the landing zone, but by noon both had departed—one returning to An Khe, the other moving off to the west to patrol a ridge. The Weapons Platoon of Company C, 1st of the 12th, remained, its 81-mm. mortars supporting the infantry hacking through the thick jungle nearby. The platoon had no special protection and had not put out security, because everyone believed that the enemy was gone. Suddenly, in the midafternoon, the Communists proved otherwise, opening up on the base with 60-mm. mortars, rocket-propelled grenades, and machine guns. As the fire lifted, Viet Cong swarmed over the landing zone, killing 16 Americans, wounding 4 more, and driving the rest off the hill. One soldier was listed as missing. The 1st Brigade reacted immediately, two companies returning to HEREFORD and another landing five hundred meters to the northwest, but the attempt to trap the attackers failed. The enemy, carrying his dead, had vanished.[62]

The brigade pursued for the next two days, but by this time General Norton was beginning to have misgivings. The 1st Brigade was taking too many casualties, he later noted, and the jagged terrain and triple canopy jungle were hard on his men. Deciding that he no longer wanted his troops "to go banging around in the enemy's backyard," he overrode objections from Hennessey and drastically revised the operation. Hennessey would now pull his units out of the immediate area; an augmented American force would surround the battlefield, blocking all likely exits; and then air strikes and artillery would pound suspected concentrations within the circle. If the Communists stayed in place, they would suffer the effects of firepower. If they attempted to withdraw, they would come up against American or allied units blocking their way.[63]

It took three days before enough units were in place for the new offensive. Then, on 24 May, more than three battalions of artillery as well as tactical aircraft began their bombardment. That night the Americans put out some twenty-six platoon-size or smaller ambushes to intercept enemy efforts to escape. Around 2100 a column of fifteen soldiers walked into one such trap, set by a platoon from Troop D, 1st of the 9th Cavalry. The troopers detonated seven claymore mines, killing 10 and causing the rest to flee. Concerned that a larger force might be nearby, the platoon quickly returned to its landing zone, but nothing else happened. The episode turned out to be the sole high point in an otherwise unproductive night. General Norton cranked up the level of

[61] AAR, Opn CRAZY HORSE, 1st Bde, 1st Cav Div, pp. 3–4.

[62] Sykes, comp., *First Cavalry Division*, p. 43; AAR, Opn CRAZY HORSE, 1st Bde, 1st Cav Div, pp. 3, 12.

[63] Interv, author with Lt Gen John Norton, 8 Mar 94, Historians files, CMH.

firepower the next day by adding two B–52 strikes to the fighter-bomber sorties and artillery cannonade. The added firepower seemed to have little effect. Hennessey's forces patrolled during the day and laid more ambushes that night, without result.[64]

Four CIDG companies entered the operation on 26 May. Their job was to search inside the strike zone, while the American units maintained their seal. Led by Maj. Raymond L. George, who also commanded the American detachment at the An Khe Special Forces camp, the CIDG soldiers were accompanied by American artillery observers and engineers. Hennessey spread the four units into the central, northern, and eastern sectors of the target. Only one company made worthwhile contact. About two kilometers northwest of a landing zone named MONKEY, the 241st CIDG Company received fire from an estimated battalion. Having done what they set out to do, the troops attempted to break contact and pull back, but the Communists pursued. The company commander called for help, but soon canceled the request when the enemy withdrew. His men then evacuated their casualties and took up station at MONKEY.[65]

Late in the afternoon the 241st again came under fire and requested assistance. Company A, 1st of the 5th Cavalry, flew to the rescue and attempted to land some seven kilometers southwest of MONKEY. When heavy fire drove off the first helicopter, the company commander opted to land directly at MONKEY. The lead Huey managed to touch down safely, but the next one went down in a hail of bullets. Rather than try again, further reinforcement was delayed until the next morning. Luckily for the men on the ground, the enemy withdrew that evening.[66]

The abortive relief effort surfaced an important limitation of airmobile warfare in rugged mountains covered by double- and triple-canopy jungle. There were only a few natural landing zones in the jungle-clad hills, and they were usually not only small but also well known to the enemy. It took little time for North Vietnamese and Viet Cong commanders to realize the opportunities these clearings offered. They began to station troops at likely landing sites whenever U.S. troops were in the area. Wrong guesses would have little effect on the overall status of their forces, but a correct one could dramatically disrupt American operations. The landing zone at MONKEY illustrated the difficulties that the Americans faced. Col. Allen M. Burdette, the 1st Cavalry Division's 11th Aviation Group commander during CRAZY HORSE, described the site as an "all-time lemon, . . . a one-ship LZ with a 150-foot barrier [of thick trees] on the far end."[67]

---

[64] AARs, Opn CRAZY HORSE, 1st Bde, 1st Cav Div, pp. 13–14, and 1st Sqdn, 9th Cav, p. 5.

[65] Critique, Opn CRAZY HORSE, 1st Cav Div, p. 1; AAR, Opn CRAZY HORSE, 1st Bde, 1st Cav Div, p. 15.

[66] AAR, Opn CRAZY HORSE, 1st Bde, 1st Cav Div, p. 15.

[67] Critique, Opn CRAZY HORSE, 1st Cav Div, p. 10.

From 26 May through 1 June Colonel Hennessey's forces ringed the target area, the CIDG companies continued their search for the enemy, and air strikes and artillery pounded suspected emplacements. On the twenty-seventh Hennessey released the 241st CIDG Company to SAVOY, and the next day a battalion-size force from the South Vietnamese 22d Division assumed the duties of the 1st of the 9th Cavalry, which then resumed screening and reconnaissance. A South Korean battalion also joined Hennessey to serve as a blocking force. With these additions, CRAZY HORSE reached its peak strength: four U.S. Army battalions, a South Vietnamese battalion equivalent, a South Korean battalion, a provisional CIDG battalion, and a U.S. Army reconnaissance squadron. Nevertheless, the allied cordon remained porous, and it quickly became evident that most of the enemy had slipped away. Consequently, General Norton dismantled the encirclement at the end of May and reverted to mobile operations until 5 June, when he formally terminated CRAZY HORSE.[68]

Although impressed with his division's achievements, General Norton admitted that he and his men had at times courted disaster. There were some nights "when we weren't awfully sure what we could do" if all of the enemy troops in the area had massed in one place and attacked an American position. "We would have had some very hard times," he acknowledged, ". . . but we took those risks in order to . . . continue pressing the fight."[69]

The results, however, justified the risks, for despite the absence of any large battles, the heavy bombardment and occasional small clashes had taken their toll. The Americans had killed 350; the South Koreans, 123; and the CIDG troops, 34. Estimated enemy dead came to 381. In addition, the allies captured over forty tons of rice, ten tons of salt, one hundred thirteen individual and crew-served weapons, over twenty-seven thousand rounds of small-arms ammunition, and various other supplies. During the operation the Americans lost 83 killed; the South Koreans, 14; and the South Vietnamese, 8. In terms of the immediate goal of disrupting an enemy offensive in the Vinh Thanh Valley, the massive deployment of American troops seemed to have succeeded. The *2d PLAF Regiment* was badly damaged.[70]

But there was a broader outcome to CRAZY HORSE and the other Binh Dinh operations, for the 1st Cavalry Division's efforts, according to official reports, revived the pacification program in the contested province. By the spring American sweeps on the coastal plain had prompted Viet Cong to surrender in record numbers and prevented main forces from massing near population centers. Under the

[68] AAR, Opn CRAZY HORSE, 1st Bde, 1st Cav Div, pp. 4, 17–20.

[69] Critique, Opn CRAZY HORSE, 1st Cav Div, pp. 17–18.

[70] AARs, Opn CRAZY HORSE, 1st Cav Div, p. 9, and 1st Bde, 1st Cav Div, p. 22; Rpt, 14th Mil Hist Det, 1st Cav Div, 7 Mar 67, sub: Seven Month History and Briefing Data (April–October 1966), p. 89.

Refugees from MASHER/WHITE WING

division's protective umbrella, the government was also able to extend its presence into several previously contested areas, at least temporarily. Village self-defense groups were formed; the Popular Forces achieved nearly full strength by June, at least on paper; and the police increased their network of informers by 50 percent in the villages, producing new intelligence. The provincial economy also perked up during the winter, thanks in part to the presence of allied garrisons and their success in keeping portions of Highway 1 open for commerce during the day. Finally, allied military operations, most notably MASHER/WHITE WING, enabled the government to secure over 80 percent of Binh Dinh's winter rice harvest, adding to the Communists' supply troubles. The one negative aspect in what was an otherwise encouraging if still fragile political picture was Binh Dinh's swelling refugee population—approximately 120,000 people, more than any other province in South Vietnam. As in neighboring Phu Yen, the refugees represented a loss to the Communists, but until they could be returned to their homes to live peaceful, profitable lives they placed huge demands on Binh Dinh's still weak governmental apparatus, and they were becoming a public relations nightmare of the first order.[71]

Early in the Bong Son campaign a reporter from *Time* asked General Larsen if the effort represented the beginning of U.S. offensive operations. He responded pointedly that the answer was "No," that the United States was merely consolidating its position, and that it would be months before the Americans would be strong enough to take the war to the main forces in earnest.[72] As for what would happen to pacification once U.S. forces pulled out and went searching more systematically for enemy regulars, few were willing to say. The thinking at MACV was that the South Vietnamese would be able to step into the breach, take on the local forces, and weed out the still formidable underground. This was the hope, but few Americans were willing to take odds.

---

[71] Rpt, Adviser, Joint U.S. Public Affairs Office, MACV, to 1st Cav Div (Ambl), 31 Jan 66, sub: Binh Dinh; Rpt, United States Operations Mission (USOM), 28 Feb 66, sub: Binh Dinh; Special Joint RD Rpt, Binh Dinh Province, 31 Aug 66; Briefing, USOM, 1966, sub: Binh Dinh, p. 3; Rpt, Richard Kriegel, U.S. Agency for International Development (USAID) Representative, Binh Dinh Province, to Rpts Officer, Field Opns, USOM, 3 Aug 66, sub: Report for Month Ending 31 July 66, pp. 2, 6–7, 11–12, 14–15. All in RD files, CMH.

[72] MFR, Capt Michael T. Plummer, Larsen's Aide-de-Camp, 5 Feb 66, sub: Visit of Maj Gen Larsen to Pleiku and Bong Son, 5 Feb 66, p. 2, box 10, 70A/4868, RG 319, NARA.

11

Spoiling Operations on the High Plateau

While General Larsen concentrated his forces in the coastal lowlands during the spring, he could not ignore the less populated but strategically significant Central Highlands. After the bloody fighting in the Ia Drang the previous November, he believed that it was just a matter of time before Communist forces sortied across the border in strength and once again challenged allied positions in the western provinces. Already, intelligence findings were painting an ominous picture there, as General Man's *B3 Front* had grouped its forward command element and the three North Vietnamese regiments it controlled—the *32d*, *33d*, and *66th*—into a potentially formidable unit, the *1st PAVN Division*. Additional elements followed, among them the *24th* and *88th PAVN Regiments*, as the leadership in Hanoi easily matched the U.S. troop commitment.[1]

The best that General Larsen could counter with in the three highlands border provinces—Kontum, Pleiku, and Darlac—was the newly deployed 3d Brigade, 25th Infantry Division, at Pleiku City, still an untested force. He informed the brigade commander, Col. Everette A. Stoutner, that the 1st Cavalry Division would support him in an emergency but, because of its duties on the coast, would only be available for limited periods of time. To hold the line in the highlands, Colonel Stoutner would have to meet enemy threats as they arose. The spoiling attack would be his weapon of choice in the early months of 1966.[2]

The Highlands Brigade Enters Combat

Protected by the 1st Cavalry Division, the 3d Brigade settled into its encampment quickly and was ready by mid-January to undertake its first combat operation—a joint U.S.–South Vietnamese effort to secure Highway 19 from Qui Nhon to Pleiku. The work was routine, but it gave Colonel Stoutner's men a chance to gain practical experience in patrol-

---

[1] Periodic Intel Rpt, 1 Jan–30 Jun 66, MACV, 20 Aug 66, p. 6, MHI; *Western Highlands*, pp. 42–43, copy in CMH.

[2] Debriefing, Larsen, 31 Jul 67, p. 16, Senior Officer Debriefing Program, DA, Historians files, CMH.

ling, establishing ambushes, escorting convoys, and setting up perimeter defenses. On 22 January, shortly after the operation ended, General Westmoreland traveled to the brigade's base camp to welcome the unit. Although encouraging, he sounded a solemn note. The war would be long and hard, he told the troops. They would have to "work like hell and fight like tigers."[3]

Two weeks later General Larsen gave the 3d Brigade its second mission, Operation TAYLOR—a search and destroy expedition along the Krong Bolah River, about forty kilometers from the Cambodian border, where a North Vietnamese battalion reportedly was lurking. On 5 February, leaving Lt. Col. Edward F. Callanan's 1st Battalion, 35th Infantry, behind in reserve, Stoutner moved his other two battalions, Lt. Col. Gilbert Proctor's 1st of the 14th Infantry and Lt. Col. George A. Scott's 2d of the 35th Infantry, along with direct-support artillery, twenty kilometers northwest of Pleiku to the hamlet of Plei Mrong. The following day he sent Scott's battalion north along the east bank of the Krong Bolah, where it received harassing fire from the opposite side of the river. Proctor's battalion responded by helicoptering to the west bank in search of the offending units. After two more days of patrolling, Stoutner pulled the battalions back to Plei Mrong on the eighth, and shortly thereafter his entire brigade returned to Pleiku City. Except for a few minor skirmishes and several mortar attacks that killed 3 Americans and wounded 12, TAYLOR achieved little other than providing the new brigade with firsthand experience in conducting ground and airmobile operations in the rugged interior.[4]

General Larsen

The next assignment, Operation GARFIELD, took the 3d Brigade to Darlac Province, south of Pleiku. Standing some two hundred meters above sea

---

[3] AAR, Opn MATADOR, 1st Bde, 1st Cav Div (Ambl), 30 Jan 66, p. 4, Historians files, CMH; [Unit History], Jan 66–Jan 70, 3d Bde, 4th Inf Div, n.d., p. 6 (quoted words), box 1, 82/643, RG 338, NARA.

[4] ORLL, 1 Jan–30 Apr 66, 3d Bde, 25th Inf Div, 23 Jun 66, p. 6, box 5, 67A/5216, RG 319, NARA; ORLL, 1 Jan–30 Apr 66, I FFV, 15 May 66, incl. 7, Historians files, CMH; AAR, Opn TAYLOR, 3d Bde, 25th Inf Div, 31 Mar 66, p. 2, box 2, 82/655, RG 338, NARA.

level, much of the area consisted of rolling terrain, but rugged mountains up to twenty-five hundred meters in height and heavy jungle characterized its southern and southeastern portions. Since the dry season was under way, low humidity, warm temperatures, and prevailing winds from the east and northeast provided good campaigning weather.

The brigade was to search for North Vietnamese forces north and west of the province capital, Ban Me Thuot, in a large area bounded on the east by Highway 14, on the west by the Cambodian border, on the south by Ban Me Thuot, and on the north by the Darlac/Pleiku boundary. Although the brigade's intelligence officer suggested that a North Vietnamese battalion might be located about thirty kilometers north of Ban Me Thuot, intelligence on enemy activities in the region was sketchy at best. Whether or not the operation achieved its primary goal of flushing the enemy out of a long-standing safe haven, the hope was that it would generate the sort of intelligence that would lead to productive missions in the future.

Operation GARFIELD commenced on 25 February, when C–130s began a two-day round-the-clock airlift of the brigade from Pleiku to Ban Me Thuot East airfield, where Stoutner established his command post. The South Vietnamese 3d Battalion, 44th Regiment, 23d Infantry Division, provided security for the brigade headquarters, freeing Stoutner's maneuver elements for the hunt. From 28 February to 7 March his troops conducted numerous air assaults and saturation patrols, increasingly directing their attention to the area around the Mewal Plantation, a suspected infiltration way station about twenty kilometers north of Ban Me Thuot. Although sporadic firefights occurred, the largest force that Stoutner's men encountered was a squad.[5]

On 4 March General Larsen ordered Colonel Stoutner to shift his base of operations to Ban Brieng airfield, the site of a closed Special Forces camp fifty-five kilometers north of Ban Me Thuot and just west of Highway 14. After completing the move, Stoutner initiated a series of patrols between the eighth and fifteenth, mainly looking west of Ban Brieng along the boundary between Darlac and Pleiku Provinces. He was able to cover a great deal of ground this time because Larsen had made a number of Chinooks available to him to move his troops and artillery. Even so, one day was much like any another—air assaults into sterile landing zones, foot patrols into surrounding terrain, and no combat. The monotony was deceiving, however, because the enemy could appear unexpectedly. At 0320 on the eleventh one of Colonel Proctor's companies in a night laager received a pounding from between forty and sixty mortar rounds that wounded 11 men.[6]

---

[5] AAR, Opn GARFIELD, 3d Bde, 25th Inf Div, 19 Apr 66, pp. 7–8, box 2, 82/655, RG 338, NARA.

[6] Msg, CG, FFV, 1467 to CO, 3d Bde, 25th Inf Div, 4 Mar 66, box 5, 69A/702, RG 334, NARA.

Men of the 3d Brigade, 25th Infantry Division, load artillery on a Chinook during GARFIELD.

On 15 March Stoutner's brigade had its first taste of major combat. The previous evening Colonel Callanan's 1st of the 35th Infantry had settled in at a landing zone about thirteen kilometers northwest of Ban Brieng. During the night an enemy force fired forty to fifty mortar rounds at the perimeter, but the rounds fell short. The following morning Callanan ordered Company A to search in the direction from which the barrage had come. The 3d Platoon left on that mission at 0630, following the Ea Wy, a stream. Coming upon the mortaring site, the troops found a number of unfired rounds, a booklet with firing tables, and a history of the enemy unit's operations over the previous year. They spent the next three hours moving northwest along the stream. Around noon the platoon leader decided to return to base, but shortly afterward his point man discovered a wire and started to follow it to its source. When

234

he did, North Vietnamese troops who had been watching all along brought the platoon under fire.[7]

Although outnumbered, the Americans held their own against possibly two reinforced companies from a unit later identified as the *32d Regiment*. Within fifteen minutes a forward air controller brought in the first of what would become sixteen tactical air sorties over the afternoon. At 1315 the commander of Company A air-assaulted in with another platoon. The enemy chose that moment to launch an attack and inflicted casualties on the arriving troops. In the end, however, the North Vietnamese got the worst of it, as shells from the nearby 2d Battalion, 9th Artillery, continued to rain down upon them in between helicopter flights. A half hour after the arrival of the company commander, a third platoon landed. The company counterattacked, overrunning the strongpoint and pursuing the North Vietnamese as they fled to the west and south. Meanwhile, artillery and close-air support pounded likely avenues of escape along the Ea Wy, and Callanan sent his Company B about a thousand meters west to serve as a blocking force. The Americans then conducted a three-hour search, which resulted in 21 North Vietnamese killed. During the evening the two companies linked up near where the action had started and folded in behind a common perimeter to spend the night. In all, Callanan's men had suffered 11 killed and 27 wounded. Enemy casualties came to 36 known killed and possibly another 100 killed. The Americans captured twelve rifles and an American M79 grenade launcher.[8]

A second clash occurred a few days later. On 18 March Colonel Proctor's 1st of the 14th Infantry deployed some thirty kilometers northwest of Ban Brieng. After searching all day long, the battalion simulated a departure by helicopter, but only the command group and the artillery actually withdrew. During the night the three rifle companies that stayed behind moved out along different preselected routes, hoping that the North Vietnamese would think they had the area to themselves and would let down their guard. When nothing occurred the first night, the troops took cover during daylight and returned to the field when darkness fell. Once again nothing happened, but at 0745 on the twentieth Company C fought a North Vietnamese force for about forty-five minutes, killing 19 at a cost of 1 wounded.[9]

Over the next five days Stoutner's battalions continued their efforts. In a series of small firefights they accounted for 15 more enemy killed, losing 1 of their own. Stoutner finally terminated GARFIELD on 25 March. During the month-long operation the 3d Brigade, supported by air strikes and artillery, had tallied 122 enemy dead at a cost of 21 Americans killed.

---

[7] Memo, Brig Gen Glenn D. Walker, CG, 3d Bde, 25th Inf Div, for Headquarters (HQ), DA, 28 Sep 66, sub: Valorous Unit Award, box 1, 82/643, RG 338, NARA.

[8] Ibid.

[9] AAR, Opn GARFIELD, 3d Bde, 25th Inf Div, pp. 8–9.

Stoutner believed that he had also kept the North Vietnamese off balance, making it more difficult for them to prepare for operations during the coming rainy season (*Map 17*).[10]

The Airmobile Division Returns

In early March reliable reports received by American intelligence suggested that Communist forces would attack U.S. and South Vietnamese installations in western Pleiku Province when the monsoon season began. According to the reports, enemy commanders had conducted sand table exercises for assaults on the Special Forces camps at Plei Me and Duc Co and on the district headquarters at Thanh An. Later in the month intelligence analysts added that a North Vietnamese soldier captured in Darlac Province had revealed plans for large-scale attacks on South Vietnamese government positions in both Pleiku and Kontum Provinces.[11]

General Westmoreland took the information seriously. On 18 March, visiting I Field Force at Nha Trang, he told General Larsen that the *B3 Front* was building up stockpiles near targets slated for its monsoon offensive. He believed that the assaults would peak around 1 June. Prior to that time, he said, it was essential for U.S. forces to do everything they could to spoil the enemy's preparations. For if they failed to do so, the monsoon would inhibit American mobility and shield the North Vietnamese from the worst effects of American firepower. Taking Westmoreland at his word, Larsen laid out a series of four operations to thwart the enemy in the highlands. The 1st Cavalry Division shouldered the burden in three of these operations; the 3d Brigade, 25th Division, conducted the fourth.[12]

General Kinnard gave primary responsibility for the first operation, LINCOLN, to Colonel Hennessey's 1st Brigade. Lacking precise information on the whereabouts of the North Vietnamese, Hennessey decided to search suspected base areas around Duc Co, Plei Me, and Thanh An in hopes of developing a more accurate picture. His initial task force would consist of a forward headquarters, three infantry battalions, the division reconnaissance squadron, and his direct-support light artillery and a medium battery, as well as two units from Stoutner's 3d Brigade—Company B, 1st Battalion, 69th Armor, and Troop C, 3d Squadron, 4th Cavalry. The armor would protect the roads. Hennessey planned to employ one of the infantry battalions in each of the three target areas while establishing his forward command post at Landing Zone OASIS near Thanh An. Depending on how the situation developed, Kinnard

---

[10] Ibid., pp. 4, 6, 14.

[11] AAR, Opn LINCOLN/MOSBY I, 1st Cav Div (Ambl), n.d., p. 5; Intel Bull, DIA, 28 Mar 66, p. A2. Both in Historians files, CMH.

[12] Msg, CG, I FFV, 1818 to COMUSMACV, 18 Mar 66, sub: COMUSMACV Visit, box 2, 69A/702, RG 334, NARA.

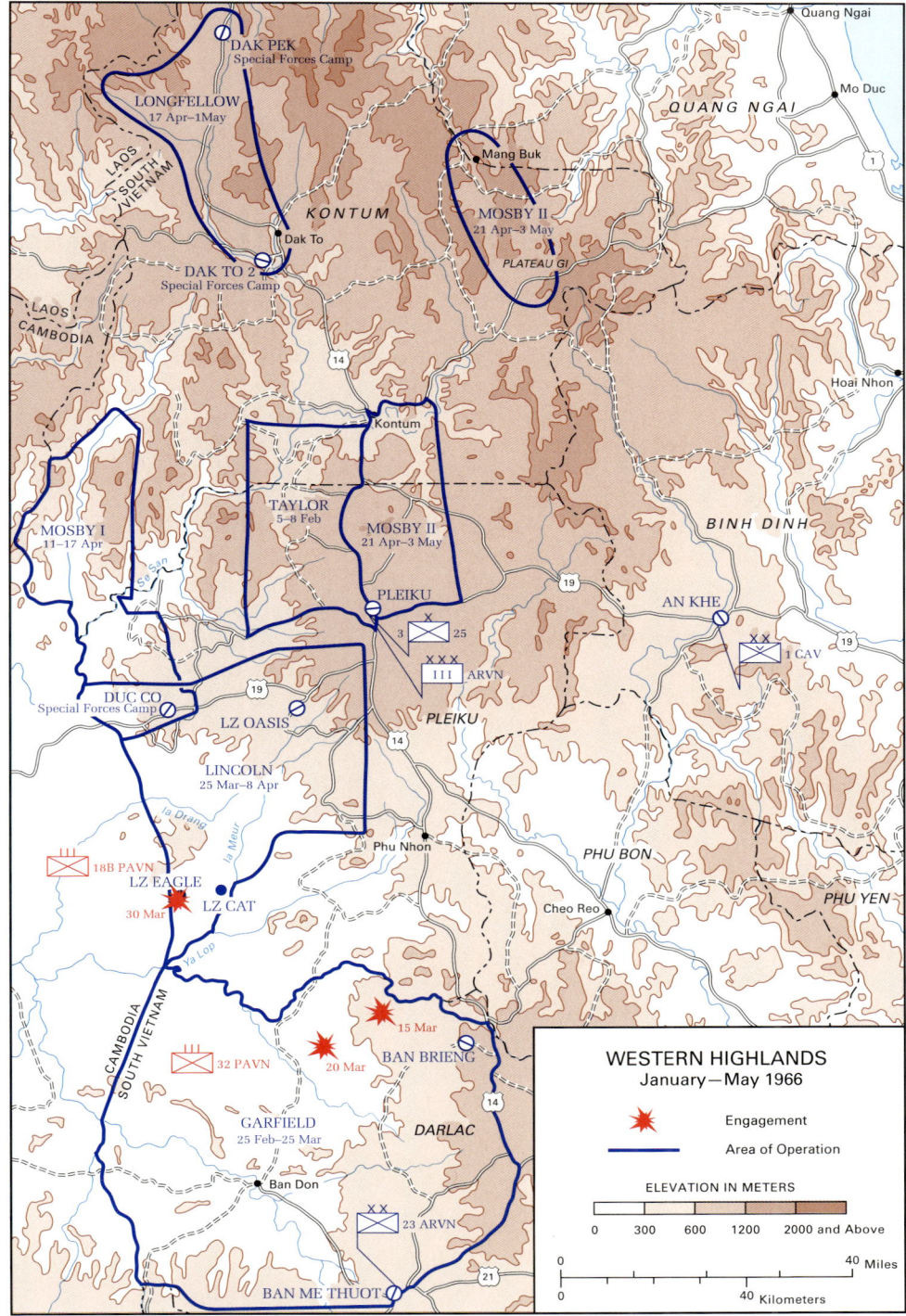

MAP 17

would decide at a later date on whether to continue the operation and commit a larger force.[13]

LINCOLN's area of operations was irregular in shape. It began about seven kilometers south of Pleiku City and extended west to the Cambodian border. The northern boundary lay a short distance north of Highway 19. The Lop and Meur Rivers, located south of the Chu Pong Massif, formed the southern boundary, running some twenty kilometers in a straight line from a point about ten kilometers east of the massif. Planners expected the weather to be fickle but not severe, with patchy ground fog on many mornings and occasional thunderstorms on some days, neither of which was expected to impede operations. The skies would be clear for much of the time, with unfavorable weather appearing only toward the end of the operational period. Daytime temperatures were of more concern, running in the mid-nineties. To avoid heat prostration while working the steep hills, the troops would have to drink a lot of water. South of the massif, the relatively flat terrain would be dry and fairly easy to traverse during April; but, once the rains began, it would become soggy, and heavy vegetation would begin to grow.[14]

Operation LINCOLN began on the morning of 25 March, when the tank company and the armored cavalry troop moved out to secure Highway 19 from the Mang Yang Pass westward through Pleiku City to OASIS. That completed, the brigade headquarters company, the 2d Battalion, 8th Cavalry, Battery B, 2d Battalion, 17th Artillery, and various support elements left An Khe for OASIS in a convoy of about four hundred fifty vehicles. Along the way, Company C, 2d of the 8th Cavalry, quit the convoy when it reached Pleiku City and headed north to a position called the TURKEY FARM, where the brigade had established a base for helicopter units supporting the operation. Company C would protect the aviation laager.

In the meantime, at 0715, Colonel Beard's 1st Battalion, 12th Cavalry, and the 2d Battalion, 19th Artillery, moved in C–130s from An Khe to the Special Forces camp at Duc Co. Soon after arriving, the infantry fanned out to the west and northwest. Also that morning Colonel Broughton's 1st Battalion, 8th Cavalry, flew to Landing Zone BEAR, a little more than ten kilometers southeast of Duc Co, and began its mission. As these units were deploying, Lt. Col. Robert M. Shoemaker's 1st Squadron, 9th Cavalry—minus Troop C, which was helping guard the TURKEY FARM—conducted search and screening operations throughout the area.[15]

---

[13] AARs, Opn LINCOLN, 1st Bde, 1st Cav Div (Ambl), 21 Apr 66, pp. 1, 6–7, and Div Arty, 1st Cav Div (Ambl), 22 Apr 66, p. 2, Historians files, CMH; AAR, Opn LINCOLN/ MOSBY I, 1st Cav Div, p. 9.

[14] AAR, Opn LINCOLN/MOSBY I, 1st Cav Div, p. 6; AAR, Opn LINCOLN III/MOSBY I, 3d Bde, 1st Cav Div (Ambl), 27 Apr 66, p. [2], Historians files, CMH.

[15] AAR, Opn LINCOLN, 1st Bde, 1st Cav Div, pp. 6–7; AAR, Opn LINCOLN, 1st Sqdn, 9th Cav, 1 May 66, p. 4, Historians files, CMH.

From 26 to 29 March Broughton's and Beard's battalions hunted for the North Vietnamese. The 1st of the 8th Cavalry ended up southwest of Duc Co near the border, sweeping almost to the Ia Drang on the twenty-eighth. The 1st of the 12th Cavalry also approached the border but west and north of Duc Co. Contact was limited to occasional exchanges of fire, with a few casualties on both sides. On the twenty-ninth Colonel Hennessey altered his lineup, substituting Colonel Hemphill's 2d of the 8th Cavalry for Colonel Beard's 1st of the 12th Cavalry, which became the brigade reserve at OASIS. He also replaced Company C, 2d of the 8th, at the TURKEY FARM with Company A, 1st of the 12th.

At first, Colonel Hennessey had intended to abandon the search near the border and to shift his forces eastward, but early in the afternoon of 30 March he changed his mind when helicopter scouts from Troop B, 1st of the 9th, spotted three enemy soldiers two kilometers from the border and five kilometers south of the Chu Pong Massif. The helicopters fired on the group, flushing some thirty from hiding. The soldiers scurried away. Hennessey ordered a rifle platoon to the site. He had hopes of seizing a prisoner or two who could provide information on the size of the force and its intentions.[16]

The platoon from Troop A, 1st of the 9th, twenty-eight strong, deployed in four Hueys to just south of where the scouts had seen the enemy troops. On the ground at 1530 three of its four squads, led by acting platoon leader Capt. John S. Sabine, moved northeast while the fourth held the landing zone. Intelligence later revealed that Sabine's men had landed in the midst of the *18B PAVN Regiment*, which had only recently arrived via the Ho Chi Minh Trail on its way south to Phu Yen Province to join the *5th PAVN Division*. The tired soldiers were resting at *Tram Giao Lien 17*, a communications-liaison station. Situated halfway between the larger military way stations, or *binh trams*, that provided movement control along the trail, many of these commo-liaison stations were on spurs that ran eastward into South Vietnam. The stations and the routes connecting them were vital to Hanoi's logistical pipeline, and most encroachments by American troops would be met with force.[17]

Within five minutes of landing Captain Sabine's men captured a North Vietnamese soldier, who told them that a thousand of his fellows were nearby. Hardly had he made the comment when enemy forces opened fire. Sabine fell in the initial volley, mortally wounded. As his three squads withdrew toward the landing zone, gunships from the 1st of the 9th covered their movement. When the Hueys ran out of ammu-

---

[16] AAR, Opn LINCOLN, 1st Bde, 1st Cav Div, pp. 7–13.

[17] AAR, Opn LINCOLN, 1st Sqdn, 9th Cav, p. 6; *Su Doan 325 (1954–1975)* [*325th Division (1954–1975)*], 2 vols. (Hanoi: Nha Xuat Ban Quan Doi Nhan Dan [People's Army Publishing House], 1981–86), 2:41, copy in CMH; Interv, author with Robert J. Destatte, 20 Oct 98, Historians files, CMH; Col. William E. LeGro, *Vietnam From Cease-Fire to Capitulation* (Washington, D.C.: U.S. Army Center of Military History, 1981), p. 38.

A binh tram on the Ho Chi Minh Trail

nition, the crews started blasting away with their sidearms rather than abandon the troops on the ground waiting to be rescued.

The extraction started at 1545. The first Huey lifted off without incident, but a second one, which included the captive, came under heavy fire and went down, killing the prisoner and injuring several others. The group was eventually rescued by another helicopter. That left fifteen troopers at the landing zone. Around 1615 a fourth helicopter arrived, but when the weight of the men proved too heavy for it to fly, three volunteered to stay behind. Fate was with them, for when the Huey finally took off, enemy troops concentrated their fire upon it and brought it down. All but one of the Americans on board and a Vietnamese interpreter died in the crash. A short time later, yet another helicopter landed and boarded the remaining three without further incident.[18]

Meanwhile, Colonel Hennessey ordered in Company A, 1st of the 12th Cavalry, from the TURKEY FARM. The unit landed unopposed at EAGLE, around five hundred meters from the original battle action, but the interlude did not last. Moving northeast and approaching to within some twenty meters of a tree line, the troops came under automatic weapons fire. According to one of the platoon leaders, 2d Lt. Daniel J. Kapica, enemy fire discipline and camouflage were remarkable. "We did not detect their presence until they opened fire at close range."[19]

[18] AAR, Opn LINCOLN, 1st Sqdn, 9th Cav, pp. 2, 6.
[19] AAR, Opn LINCOLN/MOSBY I, 1st Cav Div, incl. 4, p. 1.

Returning fire, the Americans managed to reach the tree line, where some fought hand to hand. Alerted that the company commander had been wounded and the executive officer killed, Lieutenant Kapica took charge. Facing imminent disaster, the lieutenant pulled the company back toward EAGLE while gunship fire covered his front and flanks. At 1930 a CH–47 attempted to extract Kapica's men, but it went down in a hail of fire. Convinced that any additional attempt at extraction would also fail, Hennessey instructed Kapica to form a perimeter. The lieutenant did so, centering on the downed Chinook. He had less than a hundred men left, ammunition was low, and the unit's water was nearly gone. At 0130, 31 March, American aircraft attempted to relieve the situation by making two passes over the position to drop ammunition and food. Neither delivery landed inside the perimeter, but the troops managed to retrieve the nearest supplies, which contained enough ammunition to withstand a sizeable attack.[20]

Although the North Vietnamese outside the perimeter conducted occasional probes, they mounted no major assault during the night, possibly because of the heavy fire support American commanders brought to bear. Huey gunships hammered the area throughout the night, expending some seventeen hundred 2.75-inch rockets. Meanwhile, Company A, 1st of the 8th Cavalry, deployed at 0105 and secured Landing Zone CAT about nine kilometers east of EAGLE. Battery A, 2d Battalion, 19th Artillery, followed a short while later and fired its first round in support of EAGLE at 0310. Air Force fighters were also present, flying five sorties before dawn.[21]

Faced with this onslaught, the North Vietnamese slipped away sometime during the early morning hours of the thirty-first. The troopers counted 197 enemy killed and estimated that another 217 might also have fallen. Their own casualties are unclear. Fourteen Americans perished in the crash of the Huey on the thirtieth and almost certainly more in the fighting.[22]

Combat at and around EAGLE triggered the movement of the rest of the 1st Brigade to positions south of the Chu Pong Massif. Colonel Beard's 1st of the 12th Cavalry took the lead, deploying to EAGLE on the morning of 31 March to search for any North Vietnamese that remained. Policing the area, the troops retrieved the enemy's dead and abandoned equipment and exchanged fire with small bands of stragglers. In the meantime, Hennessey's command post moved to CAT, where the rest of Broughton's 1st of the 8th Cavalry soon arrived to become the brigade reserve. By the end of the day Hemphill's 2d of the 8th Cavalry had also shifted south of the massif, taking up station about twenty-five

---

[20] Ibid., p. 12.

[21] Ibid., p. 2; AAR, Opn LINCOLN, 1st Bde, 1st Cav Div, p. 20.

[22] AAR, Opn LINCOLN, 1st Sqdn, 9th Cav, p. 1; Rpt, 14th Mil Hit Det, 1st Cav Div, 9 Jun 67, sub: Seven Month History and Briefing Data (September 1965–March 1966), p. 60, box 16, 74/053, RG 319, NARA.

hundred meters north of the Lop. Artillery elements entered the area to support the expanded effort.[23]

While Colonel Hennessey was repositioning his brigade, Generals Kinnard and Larsen were reevaluating the situation. Periodic intelligence reports since November had indicated the presence of a division-level command and the *32d, 33d,* and *66th Regiments* in the vicinity of the Chu Pong Massif. With the fight on 30 March evidence of increased enemy activity in the area, the two generals decided to seize the moment and expand the hunt with a larger force. On the thirty-first Larsen assigned Colonel Stoutner's 3d Brigade to LINCOLN, placing the 25th Division unit under the operational control of Kinnard's 1st Cavalry Division. At the same time, Kinnard assigned his own 3d Brigade under Colonel Moore to the operation. Their actions created a division-size force that combined Moore's and Hennessey's airmobile brigades with Stoutner's more traditional "heavy" brigade.

The new troops started to deploy on 31 March. By the end of the next day Stoutner's 3d Brigade, two battalions strong for the operation, had moved north by convoy from Ban Brieng to the region around Duc Co. The two battalions established their laagers about eighteen kilometers southwest and southeast of the Special Forces camp and just north of the Ia Drang, where they would be well positioned for forays into the territory around the massif. Meanwhile, Moore's 3d Brigade, also two battalions strong, established its forward command post at Plei Me.[24]

The three brigades began their work in earnest on 2 and 3 April by searching the jungle around the massif. Stoutner's 3d Brigade covered the area north of the mountain, Hennessey's 1st Brigade operated south, and Moore's 3d Brigade scoured the middle ground. Except for a brief clash between the 1st Brigade's 1st of the 12th Cavalry and a reinforced North Vietnamese company that produced some 15 enemy dead, their searches made little contact.[25]

The main event came on 4 April, when General Kinnard sent Hennessey's brigade off to the border to interdict likely escape routes and Stoutner's and Moore's against the Chu Pong Massif itself. Backed by lavish fire support, including medium and heavy tubes from I Field Force artillery, Stoutner's battalions attacked south onto the mountain and Moore's struck from the east. Throughout the day the four battalions traversed the massif, hunting for North Vietnamese. One battalion fought several fleeting skirmishes with small units, killing 7 of the enemy, but in general the searchers found no one to fight. The picture changed little on the fifth and sixth. Gunships from both the 1st Squad-

---

[23] AAR, Opn LINCOLN, 1st Bde, 1st Cav Div, pp. 13–14.

[24] AAR, Opn LINCOLN, 3d Bde, 25th Inf Div, 25 Apr 66, pp. 2–3, box 2, 82/655, RG 338, NARA; AAR, Opn LINCOLN III/MOSBY I, 3d Bde, 1st Cav Div, pp. [4–5].

[25] AARs, Opn LINCOLN, 3d Bde, 25th Inf Div, p. 2, and 1st Bde, 1st Cav Div, pp. 15–16; AAR, Opn LINCOLN III/MOSBY I, 3d Bde, 1st Cav Div, pp. [5–6].

ron, 9th Cavalry, and the 2d Battalion, 20th Artillery, fired upon small groups withdrawing toward Cambodia, but the large unit encounter that Kinnard had sought failed to develop. Consequently, on the seventh, Stoutner's 3d Brigade returned to Pleiku City. Hennessey's and Moore's brigades withdrew the next day, putting an end to the operation.[26]

After reviewing LINCOLN's objective, which was to anticipate and disrupt the Communists' preparations for rainy season operations, General Kinnard seemed satisfied with the effort. "I think," he concluded, "we . . . pushed their timetable back." That judgment, however, was purely subjective, for neither he nor MACV's intelligence analysts were particularly sure of what the timetable was. At the same time, the body count was impressive. Kinnard and his men claimed to have killed 477 soldiers and possibly another 232. Forty-three Americans lost their lives.[27]

With LINCOLN over, American commanders began to reconsider the significance of the Chu Pong to the enemy. Colonel Hennessey was especially convinced of its importance and strongly supported periodic return visits by battalion combat teams. As he told General Kinnard, "Just put them on the ground for maybe 3–4 days and let them operate with the Cav Troop, with perhaps an artillery battery and let them look around the area and stir [things] up a little bit." Kinnard filed the suggestions for future consideration.[28]

In his next operation, MOSBY I, General Kinnard sought to interdict North Vietnamese infiltration routes along the Cambodian border from Highway 19 to a point seventy kilometers north. Hennessey's 1st and Moore's 3d Brigades received the assignment. Preparations involved establishing a divisional forward command at Kontum City, as well as a temporary base camp at Plei Mrong, about twenty-five kilometers southwest of Kontum, for the 3d Brigade and another at OASIS for the 1st Brigade. Both brigades would work with CIDG companies, whose Montagnard members knew the terrain.

Active operations began the morning of 11 April, as the two brigades landed near the Cambodian border. The 3d Brigade's units patrolled the Dak Hodrai Valley. On the first day Colonel Kampe's 1st of the 7th Cavalry uncovered an abandoned 350-bed field hospital, and the next day patrols from Colonel McDade's 2d of the 7th Cavalry exchanged fire with small groups of enemy soldiers and also, by accident, with a CIDG company. By the thirteenth, however, because so little was happening, Kinnard returned the battalions to An Khe. Meanwhile, to the south, the 1st Brigade's units worked both sides of the Se San river. Their searches came up empty, and the troops withdrew on the seven-

---

[26] AAR, Opn LINCOLN/MOSBY I, 1st Cav Div, pp. 14–15.

[27] Ibid., p. 18; Critique, Opn LINCOLN, 1st Cav Div (Ambl), 3 May 66, p. 9 (quotation), Historians files, CMH.

[28] Critique, Opn LINCOLN, 1st Cav Div, pp. 2–3 (quotation), 9.

Punji stakes found in a hamlet during Mosby II

teenth. In all, the Americans had killed 3 or 4 of the enemy while losing 2 of their own.[29]

Operation Mosby II, which commenced on 20 April and ended on 3 May, followed the same approach as Lincoln and Mosby I, concentrating initially on a neighborhood east of Highway 14 and between the cities of Pleiku and Kontum. Intelligence reports indicated that enemy units and a political headquarters were in the area. The mission fell to General Kinnard's 2d Brigade, now commanded by Col. Marvin J. Berenzweig.[30]

On 20 and 21 April the 2d Brigade, which had guarded the division's base camp since mid-March, moved from An Khe to the area of operations by airplane, helicopter, and road. By the end of the day on the

---

[29] AAR, Opn Lincoln/Mosby I, 1st Cav Div, pp. 16–17; Rpt, 14th Mil Hist Det, 1st Cav Div, 9 Jun 67, sub: Seven Month History and Briefing Data (September 1965–March 1966), pp. 63–66; AAR, Opns Lincoln and Mosby, 1st Bn, 7th Cav, 19 Apr 66, pp. 2–3, Historians files, CMH.

[30] AAR, Opn Mosby II, 2d Bde, 1st Cav Div (Ambl), 29 May 66, pp. 1–5, Historians files, CMH; ORLL, 1 Jan–30 Apr 66, 1st Cav Div, p. 28, box 6, 67A/5216, RG 319, NARA.

twenty-first Colonel Berenzweig had established his command post near the town of Bien Ho and supporting helicopters had moved to the nearby TURKEY FARM. Meanwhile, his three battalions deployed to their assigned sectors to begin the search. The Americans captured a few suspected North Vietnamese soldiers and discovered small quantities of rice and ammunition but little else.

On the twenty-fifth the brigade moved deeper into its target zone. At first, all three battalions were to investigate an expanse about forty kilometers northeast of Bien Ho called Plateau Gi, a relatively inaccessible region of high peaks and valleys near the border of Kontum and Binh Dinh Provinces. However, Berenzweig soon sent one of the battalions to the hamlet of Mang Buk some thirty kilometers northwest of the plateau. None of these operations yielded any appreciable results, and by 3 May two of the battalions had returned to An Khe, concluding Operation MOSBY II. The third remained in the field to take part in another operation.[31]

The Americans suffered no combat deaths during MOSBY II, but 35 were wounded, two-thirds of them from injuries sustained when their boots were punctured by punji stakes—or sharpened bamboo sticks—that were fixed in camouflaged pits along trails. The troops may have killed 3 enemy soldiers, but because they found no bodies, they could not be sure. They did collect a strange assortment of equipment, weapons, and supplies when they explored one enemy camp—a ton of rice, canteens, pistol belts, bangalore torpedoes, field glasses, documents, and a spear.[32]

While the 1st Cavalry Division was busy with the two MOSBYS, the 3d Brigade, 25th Division, embarked on Operation LONGFELLOW. The purpose was twofold: to disrupt enemy activity in western Kontum Province north of MOSBY I, and to protect Army engineers repairing a stretch of Highway 14 running northward from the hamlet of Tan Canh, near Dak To, to the Special Forces camp at Dak Pek. Keeping one battalion back in reserve, the brigade's new commander, Brig. Gen. Glenn D. Walker, deployed his remaining two infantry battalions, artillery, and a CIDG company to Tan Canh on 15–16 April, with active operations beginning on the seventeenth, the last day of MOSBY I.[33]

Over the next two weeks company-size units searched predesignated sectors for signs of the enemy. After combing one sector, the companies would move to new search zones by foot, by truck, or by helicopters provided by the 52d Aviation Battalion. Although enemy units twice ambushed elements of the South Vietnamese 24th Special Tactical Zone that were working with the Americans, the 3d Brigade failed to gener-

---

[31] AAR, Opn MOSBY II, 2d Bde, 1st Cav Div, p. 4.
[32] Ibid., p. 11.
[33] AAR, Opn LONGFELLOW, 3d Bde, 25th Inf Div, 5 May 66, p. 7, box 2, 82/655, RG 338, NARA.

ate significant contacts. On 30 April, as soon as the engineers had completed their work on the highway, General Walker terminated the operation. By then, he and his men figured that they had killed 11 of the enemy at a cost of 3 of their own. They had also suffered 108 wounded, many to booby traps.[34]

By the time LONGFELLOW ended, the southwest monsoon season had begun, bringing with it daily showers and increasingly heavy cloud cover. This was the moment the North Vietnamese had been waiting for, when adverse weather conditions would conceal their movements, bog down allied vehicles, ground American helicopters, and minimize the effects of allied air power. Only time would tell if American spoiling operations had succeeded in disrupting the enemy's monsoon plans.

[34] Ibid., pp. 3–4, 9.

PART FOUR

The Tempo Quickens

12

New Momentum on the Coast

By the summer of 1966, after months of fighting on the defensive, General Westmoreland began urging his field commanders to step up the pace of the war. He had been awaiting this opportunity since returning from consultations with the president in February, when he had informed his combat and logistical planners that the wherewithal to wage the war aggressively would be developing somewhat slowly. He was still not completely free of the resources deficit that had plagued the command through the winter and spring. The lull in the deployment of maneuver battalions continued to hamper operations and was not likely to end until early September, when two new brigades and an armored cavalry regiment would enter battle. Nonetheless, as he surveyed his troop lists, the steady increases in artillery, helicopters, and air power, as well as improvements in theater logistics, created an atmosphere of expectancy at MACV headquarters—a patch of optimism not quite present before that the Americans might soon take charge of events and make real progress on the battlefield. The mobility and firepower gains were especially important to him. They would carry him safely through the fight until more infantry arrived.

Nowhere was this truer than in coastal II Corps, where Westmoreland prepared to push more deeply into the enemy's strongholds and to sever his supply lines. In May the 223d Aviation Battalion arrived at Qui Nhon, and in June Battery C, 6th Battalion, 16th Artillery, added its 155-mm. howitzers to the 1st Cavalry Division. Tactical air support also grew. A new air base had opened at Phan Rang in March, and by early spring it was home to a squadron of F–4 Phantoms and by summer to four squadrons of F–100s. In II Corps, and throughout the theater, sortie rates were on the rise, including B–52 ARC LIGHT strikes that were climbing from about three hundred per month when the year began to more than four hundred in July and August.[1]

One serious question mark for Westmoreland was the fighting proficiency of the South Korean forces entering the country. In April the

---

[1] ORLL, 1 Aug–31 Oct 66, I FFV, 30 Nov 66, p. 2, box 3, 73A/3330, RG 338, NARA; Schlight, *Years of the Offensive*, p. 257.

South Korean 26th Regimental Combat Team had joined the Capital Division at Qui Nhon, and four months later, in August, the South Korean 2d Marine Brigade deployed from Tuy Hoa north to Chu Lai, adding its three battalions to the U.S. Marines' fight in eastern I Corps. In September another full infantry division, the 9th (White Horse), arrived, taking up station in coastal II Corps, its mission to clear and hold contested territory and safeguard bases in Phu Yen, Khanh Hoa, and Ninh Thuan Provinces. On 15 August, in anticipation of the influx of new troops, the Saigon headquarters of the Republic of Korea Forces, Vietnam, established a field command at Nha Trang, just a few blocks from General Larsen's I Field Force headquarters. Under Lt. Gen. Chae Myung Shin, who had commanded the Capital Division, the new command would allow closer supervision of Korean units in I and II Corps and better liaison with the United States.[2]

From the outset command relationships between the Americans and Koreans had been complicated and had not improved with time. Although Generals Westmoreland and Chae had agreed in principle on close cooperation between their two forces, the Koreans insisted on being "a separate tactical entity and not under U.S. operational control." Accordingly, I Field Force issued directives to Korean units in the form of requests that the Koreans promised to honor as orders. In practice, the Koreans operated more or less independently in their own areas of responsibility and undertook offensives only when assured of substantial U.S. combat and logistical support.[3]

Phu Yen Again

The changing troop situation on the coast, although promising, did little to alter the mission of the unit responsible for Phu Yen Province—the 1st Brigade, 101st Airborne Division. Although satisfied with his unit's kills since January, when it had arrived to protect the rice harvest, General Pearson believed that he needed to acquire targets more efficiently and to react more quickly whenever the enemy appeared. He wanted his men to use small unit "semi-guerrilla tactics" that emphasized night operations and the aggressive employment of long-range reconnaissance patrols to find the Viet Cong and North Vietnamese. Once they had fixed them in their sights, Pearson said, his men would "throw

---

[2] Jack Shulimson, *U.S. Marines in Vietnam: An Expanding War, 1966* (Washington, D.C.: History and Museums Division, Headquarters, U.S. Marine Corps, 1982), p. 223; Cmd Fact Sheet, Free World Military Assistance Office, MACV, 10 Dec 66, sub: Republic of Korea Military Assistance to Republic of Vietnam, Historians files, CMH.

[3] Sharp and Westmoreland, *Report*, p. 224 (quotation); Lt. Gen. Stanley Robert Larsen and Brig. Gen. James Lawton Collins, Jr., *Allied Participation in Vietnam*, Vietnam Studies (Washington, D.C.: Department of the Army, 1975), pp. 134, 120–59. See also MACV History, 1966, pp. 86–92, CMH.

The port under construction at Vung Ro Bay

off the cloak of the guerrilla" and bring their firepower and mobility to bear. Then, after destroying their adversary, they would revert to guerrilla tactics, using stealthy stay-behind forces, and continue the hunt. He also decided to cut back on the use of artillery, especially harassment and interdiction fire, until profitable targets emerged.[4]

The test of General Pearson's ideas came during the 1st Brigade's two major operations in the summer and fall. The first, JOHN PAUL JONES, had three objectives and three phases. Phase I commenced on 21 July, when Pearson's men secured Vung Ro Pass and Highway 1 to protect engineer parties constructing a new port at Vung Ro Bay. MACV wanted the new facility to relieve some of the logistical strain on nearby Tuy Hoa, particularly when the northeast monsoon buffeted the coast. But by month's end Pearson was convinced that there were few enemy forces in the area, so he slipped most of the brigade northward to Tuy Hoa, freeing the South Korean 2d Marine Brigade for its shift into I Corps. His paratroopers would protect the next rice harvest in the Tuy Hoa Valley.[5]

---

[4] Critique, Opn SEWARD, 1st Bde, 101st Abn Div, 3 Nov 66, pp. 1 (quoted words), 9, 25; ORLL, 1 Aug–31 Oct 66, 1st Bde, 101st Abn Div, 12 Nov 66, p. 17. Both in Historians files, CMH.

[5] ORLL, 1 Aug–31 Oct 66, I FFV, p. 16; AAR, Opn JOHN PAUL JONES, 1st Bde, 101st Abn Div, 28 Sep 66, p. 3, Historians files, CMH.

Phase II of JOHN PAUL JONES began on 2 August, when B–52s hit the mountains west and southwest of the town of Song Cau about forty kilometers north of Tuy Hoa. Twenty minutes after the last explosion Lt. Col. Frank L. Dietrich's 2d Battalion, 502d Infantry, scoured the terrain but, finding no enemy, returned to base the next day. On the eighth more B–52s pounded suspected emplacements west of the Special Forces camp at Dong Tre. The smoke had not yet cleared when Lt. Col. Joseph E. Collins' 1st Battalion, 327th Infantry, helicoptered to the northern portion of the target area and swept south, meeting light resistance and capturing eight prisoners, including a captain from the *5th PAVN Division*. The prisoners confirmed that the *5th Division* headquarters was in Phu Yen and that the *18B* and *95th PAVN Regiments* were not far away. Combined with other intelligence, it appeared that a good-size formation of regulars had left the area in recent days and moved west.

Pearson believed that he could trap the North Vietnamese. On 9 August he ordered Colonel Dietrich's 2d of the 502d Infantry to leapfrog over the withdrawing enemy and work eastward toward Colonel Collins' 1st of the 327th. Neither unit found anyone to fight, so both returned to base on the fourteenth and fifteenth to prepare for Phase III (*Map 18*).[6]

At the beginning of Phase III General Pearson gained two additional battalions. On 16 August he took operational control of Lt. Col. Thomas H. Tackaberry's 2d Battalion, 8th Cavalry, and on 30 August of Lt. Col. Leonard A. Morley's 1st Battalion, 22d Infantry—the first unit of the 4th Infantry Division to arrive in Vietnam. Two battalions from the South Vietnamese 47th Regiment, 22d Infantry Division, also joined Pearson for a time, as did a mobile strike, or MIKE, force made up of CIDG troops under Special Forces command. As usual, the South Vietnamese were autonomous, but they coordinated with Pearson's forces and, for all practical purposes, acted according to his wishes.[7]

When reconnaissance platoons reported sighting enemy soldiers west of Dong Tre, General Pearson quickly sent in Colonel Tackaberry's men and his own 2d Battalion, 327th Infantry, under Colonel Wasco. Beginning on 17 August, they searched the adjacent Ky Lo Valley and the area around Dong Tre, but found little. Nine days later new intelligence placed main force troops in the mountains twelve to fifteen kilometers west of a site midway between Tuy An and Tuy Hoa. Pearson moved the two battalions from Dong Tre, with Tackaberry's maneuvering southeast toward Tuy Hoa and Wasco's searching to the southwest. South Vietnamese units already in the area formed blocking positions and a local

---

[6] AAR, Opn JOHN PAUL JONES, 1st Bde, 101st Abn Div, p. 5; Weekly Sums, 31 Jul–6 Aug and 14–20 Aug 66, 1st Bde, 101st Abn Div, 7 and 21 Aug 66, box 10, 70A/4868, RG 319, NARA.

[7] Col. Francis J. Kelly, *The U.S. Army Special Forces, 1961–1971*, Vietnam Studies (Washington, D.C.: Department of the Army, 1973), p. 54; Weekly Sum, 28 Aug–3 Sep 66, 1st Bde, 101st Abn Div, n.d., box 10, 70A/4868, RG 319, NARA.

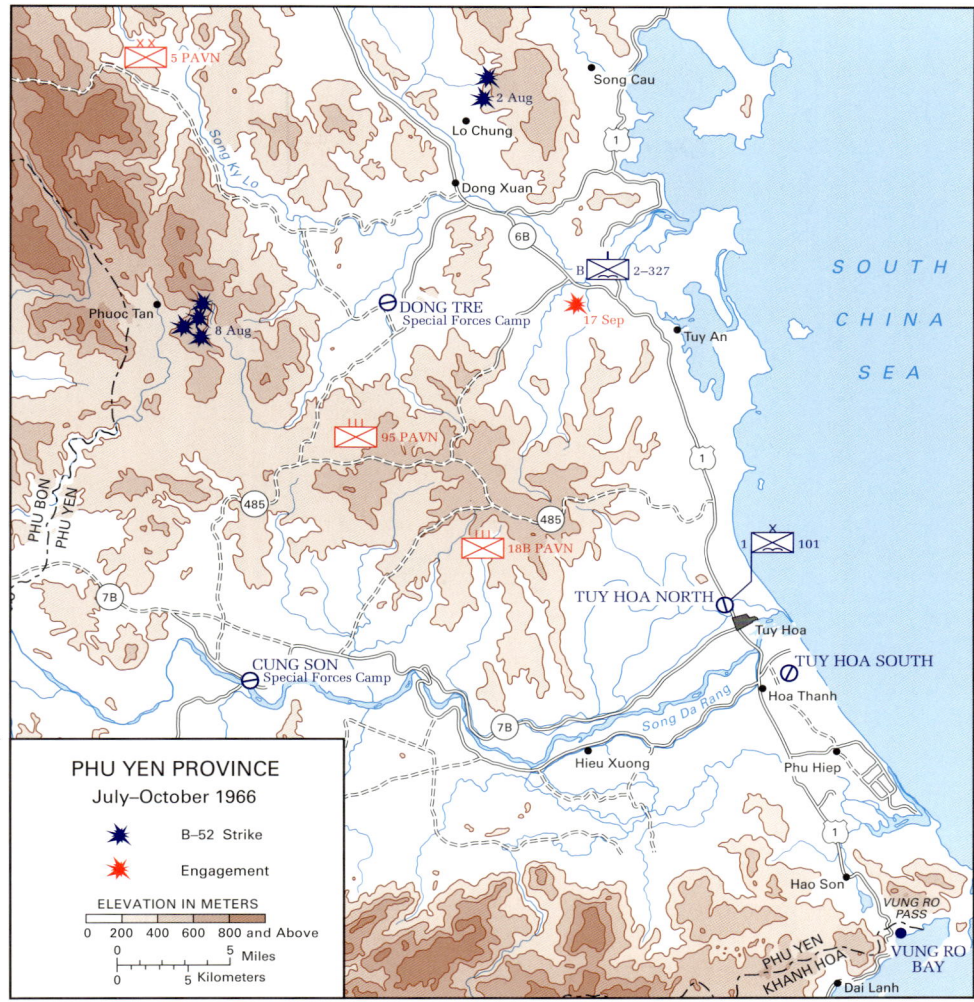

MAP 18

MIKE force formed a cordon to the south and southwest. Once again they found nothing. Frustrated by the lack of results, Pearson terminated JOHN PAUL JONES on 5 September.[8]

Despite his disappointment, Pearson's stay-behind tactics had resulted in enough small engagements during the operation to tally 209 enemy killed by body count and another 135 by estimate, many of latter from air strikes. American casualties totaled 23 killed and 132 wounded.

[8] Weekly Sum, 14–20 Aug 66, 1st Bde, 101st Abn Div; AAR, Opn JOHN PAUL JONES, 1st Bde, 101st Abn Div, p. 4.

Paratroopers guard Viet Cong suspects captured during SEWARD.

Pearson's techniques clearly showed that seeking out pitched battles was not the only way to fight in Vietnam.[9]

Pearson hoped for better results from his next campaign, Operation SEWARD, using the same maneuver battalions that had carried out JOHN PAUL JONES. This time he placed Wasco's 2d of the 327th Infantry north of Tuy An and a company of Collins' 1st of the 327th Infantry in the Hieu Xuong Valley southwest of Tuy Hoa. Morley's 1st of the 22d Infantry would secure the area between Vung Ro Bay and Tuy Hoa. Dietrich's 2d of the 502d Infantry would serve as a rapid-reaction force. Morley's and Dietrich's units would function as reserve forces, but they would also carry out operations west and northwest of Tuy Hoa.[10]

SEWARD began early on the morning of 5 September. The Americans knew the terrain from previous operations—dry flatlands, dotted with

[9] Annual Hist Sum, 1966, 2d Bn, 327th Inf, n.d., p. 21, Historians files, CMH; AAR, Opn JOHN PAUL JONES, 1st Bde, 101st Abn Div, p. 4.

[10] Op Sum, Opn SEWARD, MACV, Oct 66, p. 1, and AAR, Opn SEWARD, 1st Bde, 101st Abn Div, 6 Nov 66, p. 2 and incl. 2, tabs A, B, C, Historians files, CMH; ORLL, 1 Aug–31 Oct 66, I FFV, p. 11; MFR, MACV MACJ00, 3 Oct 66, sub: MACV Commanders' Conference, 28 August 1966, p. 31, Westmoreland History files, CMH.

rice paddies, giving way to jungle-clad hills and, near the coast, sand dunes and beaches. The sparsely vegetated lowlands offered extensive fields of fire but little cover and concealment. In the mountains the conditions were reversed. Rain would be a factor this time, since SEWARD was taking place during the transition from the dry to the wet season.[11]

The first eleven days were characterized by small encounters, producing scattered skirmishes and limited casualties on both sides. On 8 September, for example, Colonel Collins' 1st of the 327th Infantry battled a seven-man patrol from the *18B Regiment*, killing 4 and capturing 3. Maps taken from the prisoners revealed that the regiment intended to attack the hamlet of Tu Bong about twenty kilometers to the south, perhaps to raid a rice storage complex or to disrupt the area on the eve of national elections on the eleventh. In response, Colonel Dietrich's 2d of the 502d Infantry deployed to the hamlet on the tenth and remained there for almost a week, thwarting any attack that might have been planned. The unit returned to Tuy Hoa on the sixteenth, when the danger had passed.[12]

On 17 September Company B of Colonel Wasco's 2d of the 327th Infantry paid dearly for an instance of carelessness. For several days it had occupied a hill about ten kilometers northwest of Tuy An near Route 6B. Although the Viet Cong had probed the position more than once, the company commander had failed to shift his command post. Then on the seventeenth, around 0200, a hundred or so insurgents launched an all-out assault under cover of a driving rain. They knew exactly where to strike—grenades and satchel charges targeted the communications bunker while machine guns kept the defenders busy. Unable to call for reinforcements or fire support, the Americans fought back grimly but suffered 10 killed—including the company commander, his executive officer, and the artillery forward observer—and 12 wounded. Throughout the assault, crouched in ambush positions some eight hundred to twenty-five hundred meters away, the company's rifle platoons realized too late that the command post had come under attack. Only one managed to make it back in time to grapple with the attackers as they withdrew. Informed of what had happened, General Pearson knew that his brigade's standards had slipped. "When units are operating in a limited area," he noted in an after action report, "patterns of action must not be established." He recommended that in the future company command posts be relocated at least every forty-eight hours.[13]

Despite the setback, Pearson considered Operation SEWARD to be a success. By the third week in October the farmers around Tuy Hoa had

[11] AAR, Opn SEWARD, 1st Bde, 101st Abn Div, incl. 1, p. 1.

[12] Ibid., p. 3; Weekly Sum, 4–10 Sep 66, 1st Bde, 101st Abn Div, 11 Sep 66, box 10, 70A/4868, RG 319, NARA; Critique, Opn SEWARD, 1st Bde, 101st Abn Div, p. 2.

[13] Annual Hist Sum, 1966, 2d Bn, 327th Inf, p. 23; Op Sum, Opn SEWARD, MACV, Oct 66, p. 3; AAR, Opn SEWARD, 1st Bde, 101st Abn Div, p. 5 (quotation).

harvested almost 90 percent of their rice crop, about seventeen thousand metric tons, with little enemy interference. Collins' and Wasco's battalions withdrew from SEWARD on the nineteenth and twentieth. SEWARD itself ended at midnight on the twenty-fifth, when the last battalion in the operation, Dietrich's, also departed.[14]

The operation produced 239 enemy killed by body count, all from the *18B* and *95th Regiments* and the independent *307th PLAF Battalion*. American casualties were 27 killed and 169 wounded. In his critique of SEWARD General Pearson characterized the kill ratio of 9 to 1 as "excellent" and reiterated his tactics for future operations. As had been the case in JOHN PAUL JONES, he expected his battalion commanders to "find the elusive guerrilla and then destroy him by conventional means."[15]

Back to Binh Dinh—THAYER I

While Phu Yen was important, the neighboring province of Binh Dinh remained the heart of allied operations on the II Corps coast. And while destroying the main forces was crucial, pacification in this bastion of Communist sympathy was the real key to rooting out the insurgency. American forces had made some headway during MASHER/WHITE WING and follow-on operations earlier in the year, but this time their efforts would be different. Beginning in mid-September, elements of the 1st Cavalry Division carried out what became known as the Binh Dinh pacification campaign in the northeastern part of the province. With the *3d PAVN Division*'s threat much reduced, Lt. Gen. Stanley R. Larsen wanted the 1st Cavalry Division to become more involved in local security, especially in weeding out the enemy's shadow government. At the same time, the continued presence of the wounded but persistent *3d Division* in the coastal areas made clashes with it inevitable.[16]

On 21 August General Westmoreland visited Larsen at Nha Trang and made it clear that he wanted to see major operations under way in Binh Dinh before the monsoons started in November. Larsen and the 1st Cavalry Division's commander, General Norton, were already planning for just such a program, to be launched with Operation OLIVER WENDELL HOLMES. However, when the 1st Cavalry Division moved to Pleiku to join in heavy fighting there, the operation was postponed. Upon the division's return in early September, planning resumed for the by now renamed operation. Apparently, Westmoreland had expressed his

---

[14] Weekly Sums, 9–15 and 16–22 Oct 66, 1st Bde, 101st Abn Div, 16 and 23 Oct 66, box 10, 70A/4868, RG 319, NARA.

[15] Critique, Opn SEWARD, 1st Bde, 101st Abn Div, p. 25.

[16] The Binh Dinh pacification campaign included Operations THAYER I (13 September–1 October 1966), IRVING (2–24 October 1966), THAYER II (25 October 1966–12 February 1967), and PERSHING (11 February 1967–21 January 1968). See MFR, MACV MACJ00, 3 Oct 66, sub: MACV Commanders' Conference, 28 August 1966, p. 31.

dislike of the name OLIVER WENDELL HOLMES, so Larsen changed it to THAYER.[17]

The enemy was laying his own plans. When the 1st Cavalry Division had flown off to the highlands, the Communists had found time to rebuild and refit. By early September they were back to their old tactic of targeting South Vietnamese units and installations on the Bong Son Plain. At first, American commanders had unconfirmed rumors that the *3d PAVN Division*'s *2d PLAF Regiment* intended to strike the Special Forces camp in the Vinh Thanh Valley. Then on 7 September the *3d Division*'s *22d PAVN Regiment* struck all three bases of the South Vietnamese 40th Regiment, 22d Division, along Highway 1 north of the Lai Giang River. That same night a small force from the *2d PLAF Regiment* attacked two hamlets south of the river near Phu My, taking about twenty civilians prisoner. The next day two of its battalions ambushed a South Vietnamese convoy carrying two battalions of the 22d Division's 41st Regiment. There was now little doubt that a new U.S. offensive was needed.[18]

On 8 September General Norton put his plans into motion by issuing OPLAN 23–66. It called for division elements to deploy into northern Binh Dinh to uproot enemy base areas in the Kim Son Valley. They would also be prepared to join South Vietnamese and South Korean forces sweeping south to the Phu Cat Mountains closer to the coast. Initially, the effort was to unfold in three phases over a span of ninety days. But Norton subsequently organized the second and third phases into separate independent campaigns, Operations IRVING and THAYER II. The original operation became known as THAYER I (*see Map 19*).[19]

Preceded by two days of B–52 strikes on suspected enemy concentrations near the Kim Son Valley, THAYER I began on 13 September. Early in the morning two battalions from Col. Archie K. Hyle's 1st Brigade—Lt. Col. James T. Root's 1st Battalion, 12th Cavalry, and Colonel Tackaberry's 2d Battalion, 8th Cavalry—helicoptered unopposed to landing zones south and southeast of the valley. At the same time, two battalions from Colonel Berenzweig's 2d Brigade—Lt. Col. Robert H. Siegrist's 1st Battalion, 5th Cavalry, and Lt. Col. Jay A. Hatch's 2d Battalion, 12th Cavalry—landed to the north and northwest. Rain and mud delayed the movement of a fifth battalion, Lt. Col. William C. Louisell's 1st Battalion, 8th Cavalry, belonging to Colonel Hyle's brigade, but all units were in place by the end of the following day. By then, Colonel Smith's 1st Squadron, 9th Cavalry, had begun reconnaissance and screening flights.[20]

---

[17] ORLL, 1 Aug–31 Oct 66, I FFV, p. 17; Msg, CG, I FFV, A0525 to COMUSMACV, 21 Aug 66, sub: Visit of COMUSMACV, box 5, 69A/702, RG 334, NARA.

[18] AAR, Opn THAYER, 2d Bde, 1st Cav Div (Ambl), 28 Oct 66, pp. 3–4; CHECO Rpt, PACAF, 12 May 67, sub: Operations THAYER/IRVING, p. 19; AAR, Opns THAYER I and IRVING, 1st Cav Div (Ambl), 13 Jan 67, p. 5. All in Historians files, CMH.

[19] Rpt, 14th Mil Hist Det, 1st Cav Div (Ambl), 7 Mar 67, sub: Seven Month History and Briefing Data (April–October 1966), p. 113, Historians files, CMH.

[20] Ibid.; AAR, Opns THAYER I and IRVING, 1st Cav Div, p. 13.

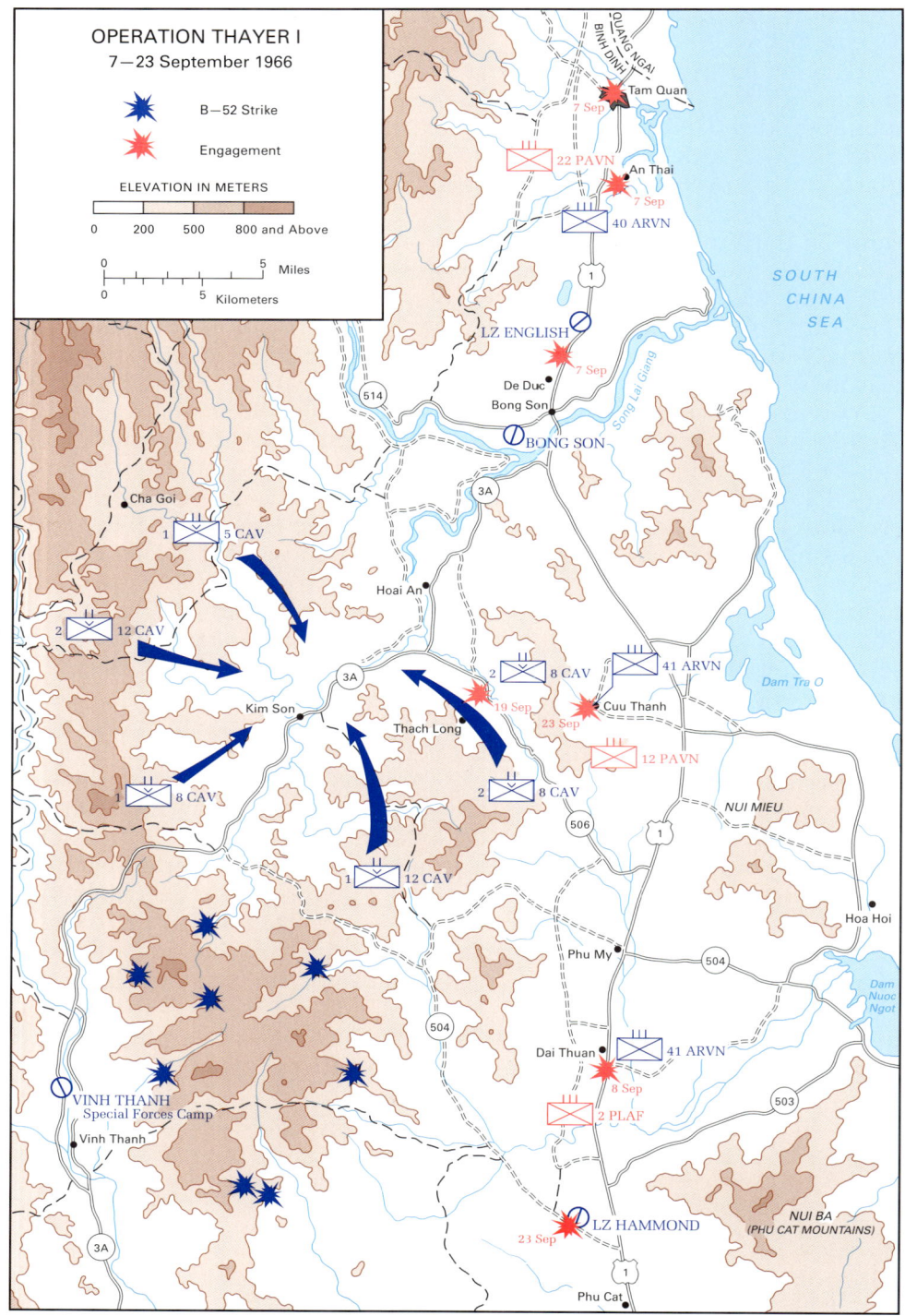

OPERATION THAYER I

7—23 September 1966

✦ B—52 Strike

✴ Engagement

ELEVATION IN METERS

0   200   500   800 and Above

0 — 5 Miles

0 — 5 Kilometers

QUANG NGAI

BINH DINH

Tam Quan

7 Sep

22 PAVN

An Thai

7 Sep

40 ARVN

1

SOUTH CHINA SEA

LZ ENGLISH

7 Sep

De Duc

Bong Son

Song Lai Giang

BONG SON

514

3A

Cha Goi

1   5 CAV

Hoai An

2   12 CAV

3A

2   8 CAV

41 ARVN

Dam Tra O

Kim Son

Thach Long

19 Sep

23 Sep

Cuu Thanh

12 PAVN

1   8 CAV

2   8 CAV

506

NUI MIEU

1   12 CAV

Hoa Hoi

Phu My

504

504

Dam Nuoc Ngot

Dai Thuan

41 ARVN

VINH THANH
Special Forces Camp

8 Sep

2 PLAF

503

Vinh Thanh

NUI BA
(PHU CAT MOUNTAINS)

LZ HAMMOND

23 Sep

3A

Phu Cat

1

MAP 19

Norton's forces formed a horseshoe on the high ground ringing the Kim Son canyons. Breaking down into company-size units, they swept the ridges as they descended toward the valley's floor. Each unit set up stay-behind ambushes and patrols to catch Viet Cong and North Vietnamese trying to sidestep the operation, and circling aircraft tried to prevent the enemy from escaping through the gaps that opened up as the Americans moved.[21]

As they advanced, the Americans encountered small groups of enemy soldiers and found caches of weapons and food, a hospital, an antipersonnel munitions factory, and bunkers. Most were located on the eastern and southern slopes of the hills in the 1st Brigade's zone. Clearly, the *3d Division* maintained substantial bases in the area, yet no main force units were there. Although the Americans scoured the valley's floor and searched along likely escape routes, they found few enemy to fight.[22]

One of the rare actions broke out on 19 September. Colonel Tackaberry's 2d of the 8th Cavalry pursued a group of enemy soldiers in a small valley that branched eastward from the northern end of the Kim Son along Route 506, called the 506 Valley by the Americans. After artillery and gunships chased them to ground, the battalion reconnaissance platoon joined the 2d Battalion and launched an attack that killed 15.[23]

The battle indicated that at least some enemy units had left the valley and were heading east. Colonel Berenzweig dispatched Siegrist's 1st of the 5th Cavalry to block a possible escape route and, newly added by Norton, the 2d Battalion, 5th Cavalry, under Lt. Col. Reginald T. Lombard, to the high ground east of where the last fight had taken place. Both units landed in the valley on the twentieth. They conducted company-size sweeps, but found no further trace of the Communists.[24]

Early on the morning of 23 September the enemy decided to fight. A few minutes after 0100 elements of the *2d PLAF Regiment*, probably the *95th Battalion* assisted by the regiment's two heavy weapons companies, attacked Landing Zone HAMMOND, the cavalry division's forward logistics and staging base located fifteen kilometers south of Phu My and thirty kilometers southeast of the Kim Son Valley. The Viet Cong hit the camp with a ten-minute mortar and recoilless rifle barrage, killing 1 American and wounding 32 while damaging seventeen aircraft. The Americans turned searchlights on the area and fired back with mortars, artillery, and recoilless rifles. But the Viet Cong slipped away to safety, aided by local guerrillas who guided the main force

---

[21] AAR, Opns THAYER I and IRVING, 1st Cav Div, p. 13.

[22] Rpt, 14th Mil Hist Det, 1st Cav Div, 7 Mar 67, sub: Seven Month History and Briefing Data (April–October 1966), pp. 113–14.

[23] AAR, Opns THAYER I and IRVING, 1st Cav Div, p. 16.

[24] Ibid., pp. 16–18; AAR, Opn THAYER, 2d Bde, 1st Cav Div, pp. 8, 18–20; Rpt, 14th Mil Hist Det, 1st Cav Div, 7 Mar 67, sub: Seven Month History and Briefing Data (April–October 1966), pp. 114, 120–21.

A C–123 Provider at HAMMOND

soldiers through fields of mines and booby traps that they had laid to kill Americans.[25]

That same morning another fight was brewing fourteen kilometers north of Phu My, when the *3d Division's 7th* and *8th Battalions, 12th PAVN Regiment*, attacked the South Vietnamese 41st Regiment's command post near Cuu Thanh. Supported by U.S. air strikes, the South Vietnamese drove the enemy off. More than 137 North Vietnamese died in the ill-fated assault, prompting General Westmoreland to congratulate the unit for its "spectacular victory."[26]

As usual in Binh Dinh, when the enemy had had enough, he withdrew into the mountains. Also as usual, the Americans tried to cut him off. General Norton assigned the task to the three battalions of Colonel Berenzweig's 2d Brigade and the better part of three other battalions already in the area. But other than a few scattered skirmishes, they found nothing. The North Vietnamese had slipped through gaps in the Ameri-

[25] AAR, Opn THAYER, 2d Bde, 1st Cav Div, p. 9; Rpt, 14th Mil Hist Det, 1st Cav Div, 7 Mar 67, sub: Seven Month History and Briefing Data (April–October 1966), p. 114 and incl. 2, p. 26-1.

[26] AARs, Opn THAYER, 2d Bde, 1st Cav Div, p. 9, and Opns THAYER I and IRVING, 1st Cav Div, p. 18; Unit Hist Rpt no. 5, 1st Cav Div (Ambl), n.d., sub: Operation IRVING, 2–24 October 1966, p. 9, box 1, 82/899, RG 338, NARA; Westmoreland Jnl, 8 Oct 66 (quoted words), Westmoreland History files, CMH.

can lines and into the Mieu Mountains, where they planned to lay low until the Americans lost interest and went away.[27]

The failure of Berenzweig's brigade to find the *12th Regiment's 7th* and *8th Battalions* convinced General Norton and his commanders that the units had slipped out of the American encirclement toward the east rather than the west. Believing that there still might be a chance to catch them, Norton sent Colonel Hyle's 1st Brigade into the mountains that separated Route 506 and its valley from Highway 1. By blocking and sweeping, American forces might be able to head off the retreating battalions. Positioned at the northern end of the 506 Valley, Colonel Tackaberry's 2d of the 8th Cavalry acted briefly as the division's reaction force. After negligible results, Hyle's men began to extend their blocking positions eastward onto the coastal plain and across Highway 1. By 29 September elements of Colonel Root's 1st of the 12th Cavalry and Colonel Louisell's 1st of the 8th Cavalry had assumed positions along a line that extended southwest toward Highway 1 from a point just north of the Mieu Mountains. From there, they could block enemy movement to the north or west.[28]

On 30 September and 1 October two battalions of Col. Charles D. Daniel's 3d Brigade augmented Colonel Hyle's forces. They were Lt. Col. Edward M. Markham's 1st Battalion, 7th Cavalry, and Lt. Col. Trevor W. Swett's 5th Battalion, 7th Cavalry. The battalions assumed positions just to the south along Highway 1. The arrival of Colonel Swett's unit from the United States at the end of August brought the 1st Cavalry Division up to nine battalions.[29]

Then new intelligence suggested that the *12th Regiment* headquarters might be found on the eastern slope of the 506 Valley. Tackaberry's 2d of the 8th Cavalry responded by conducting a two-company air assault into the area, but it came up with nothing. The information was either false or the enemy was once more avoiding contact. THAYER I officially ended shortly afterward, at midnight on 1 October. For over two weeks two cavalry brigades had searched, uncontested, through a large portion of the *3d Division's* base area in the Kim Son Valley and the surrounding mountains. They killed 231 enemy soldiers in scores of small unit skirmishes, more than half involving actions by the reconnaissance squadron's ground elements. During the operation the Americans lost 33 killed, 248 wounded, and 2 missing.[30]

Colonel Berenzweig looked beyond the body count in his appraisal of THAYER I. "Our violent and immediate destruction of those small groups who chose to resist had its psychological impacts," he wrote. Berenzweig also noted that the poor condition of the enemy's weapons

[27] AARs, Opns THAYER I and IRVING, 1st Cav Div, p. 18, and Opn THAYER, 2d Bde, 1st Cav Div, pp. 21–23.

[28] AAR, Opns THAYER I and IRVING, 1st Cav Div, p. 22.

[29] Ibid., pp. 20–21.

[30] Ibid., pp. 32, 40.

revealed the strain on his supply system, an indication of the long-term "invisible" effect of small engagements, hasty retreats, and the loss of caches and bases. Historically, unconventional wars had often been won by staying on the irregulars' track, pushing them, and capturing their camps and supplies.[31]

IRVING

The evidence seemed to back up General Norton's contention that the enemy was holed up in the mountains between Highway 1 and the coast. However, the area was so large that it would take a huge force to search it thoroughly. A combined allied force was the logical move, but that posed the old political problem of establishing a single command. Instead, General Larsen devised a three-pronged approach that allowed U.S., South Korean, and South Vietnamese forces to work independently while coordinating their activities.[32]

Operations of this sort had been under consideration for some time. On 24 July General Larsen had directed the commanders of the 1st Cavalry Division, the South Korean Capital Division, and the South Vietnamese 22d Division to begin planning for operations in the Phu Cat Mountains. His original concept called for three American battalions, two South Korean battalions, and two South Vietnamese battalions to converge on the region from the northeast, northwest, and south to root out the enemy. But by the end of September fresh intelligence pinpointing the *12th Regiment* in the area brought the proposed operation into sharper focus. Larsen increased the American force to two brigades, with five battalions. The South Vietnamese force would have three battalions, while the South Korean contingent would consist of five battalions under two regiments.[33]

The effort itself would take place in two phases. During Phase I each allied force would search its own area of operations. The South Koreans would lead off on 23 September with Operation MAENG HO 6, an attack into the Phu Cat Mountains from the south. The U.S. and South Vietnamese portions of the effort would begin on 2 October. The Americans, conducting Operation IRVING, would deploy from the north, northwest, west, and southwest into and south of the Mieu Mountains; the South Vietnamese would launch Operation DAI BANG 800, an advance from the west and southwest into the region's lowlands. During Phase II, which was primarily a South Korean action, allied forces would assist

[31] AAR, Opn THAYER, 2d Bde, 1st Cav Div, pp. 26–27.

[32] Unit Hist Rpt no. 6, 1st Cav Div (Ambl), 20 May 67, sub: Battle of Hoa Hoi, 2–3 October 1966, p. 5, Historians files, CMH.

[33] Msgs, CG, I FFV, 0118 to CG, 1st Inf Div, et al., 24 Jul 66, sub: Warning Order, and A0777 to Republic of Korea Forces, Vietnam, Field Cmd et al., 9 Sep 66, sub: Warning Order, box 5, 69A/702, RG 334, NARA.

the South Koreans as they incorporated the Phu Cat Mountains into their permanent tactical area of responsibility.[34]

During the American portion of the operation General Norton would command his 1st and 3d Brigades from Landing Zone HAMMOND. Colonel Siegrist's 1st of the 5th Cavalry—the division reserve—and Colonel Smith's 1st of the 9th Cavalry would come under his direct control. The three battalions in Colonel Hyle's 1st Brigade would deploy into the northern segment of the American sector, with Hyle overseeing them from Landing Zone UPLIFT. Two battalions of Colonel Daniel's 3d Brigade would share the southern segment, with Daniel controlling them from HAMMOND.

As dawn broke on 2 October, Norton's troops prepared for the start of IRVING at five different landing zones—four stretching from north of the Mieu Mountains to the town of Phu My in the south and another in the Kim Son Valley. Shouldering heavy packs, they shuffled toward waiting helicopters, and by 0700 the first Hueys were lifting off. The 1st Brigade deployed to three positions in the Mieu Mountains. Colonel Tackaberry's 2d of the 8th Cavalry fed four companies into one; Colonel Louisell's 1st of the 8th Cavalry sent three into the second; and the command group and a company of Colonel Root's 1st of the 12th Cavalry began to phase unopposed into the third. In the 3d Brigade's sector, Colonel Markham's 1st of the 7th Cavalry and Colonel Swett's 5th of the 7th Cavalry conducted air assaults into the lowlands to the east. Once on the ground, they cleared the areas around their landing zones and then swept toward the coast (*see Map 20*).[35]

Meanwhile, helicopters belonging to Lt. Col. George W. McIlwain's Troop A, 1st of the 9th Cavalry, departed HAMMOND just after 0700. Responsible for seeking out the enemy in the Nuoc Ngot Bay and Hung Lac Peninsula area on the South China Sea between the Mieu and Phu Cat Mountains and for maintaining surveillance over the coastline in the northern portion of the 1st Brigade's area of operations, they reached their target zones within minutes. By 0730 Colonel McIlwain had captured a local force soldier who admitted that North Vietnamese troops, tired and worn out, had arrived in the nearby hamlet of Hoa Hoi the previous night. Accompanied by two scout helicopters, McIlwain flew to the hamlet to investigate. As he passed over the settlement, soldiers poured out of the houses and blazed away at the helicopters. Still not sure what he faced, McIlwain called in his infantry platoon, the Blue Team, to have a look. By 0800 four eight-man squads were in the air, on their way to Hoa Hoi. Their leader, 1st Lt. Robert T. Lewis, learned in flight from McIlwain that his men would face what was thought to be a platoon of North Vietnamese regulars.[36]

---

[34] Msg, CG, I FFV, A1034 to COMUSMACV, 28 Sep 66, sub: Operation IRVING, box 5, 69A/702, RG 334, NARA.

[35] AAR, Opns THAYER I and IRVING, 1st Cav Div, pp. 22–31.

[36] Interv, author with Col Blake [formerly George W.] McIlwain, 22 Nov 95, Historians files, CMH; Unit Hist Rpt no. 6, 1st Cav Div, 20 May 67, sub: Battle of Hoa Hoi, 2–3 October 1966, p. 9.

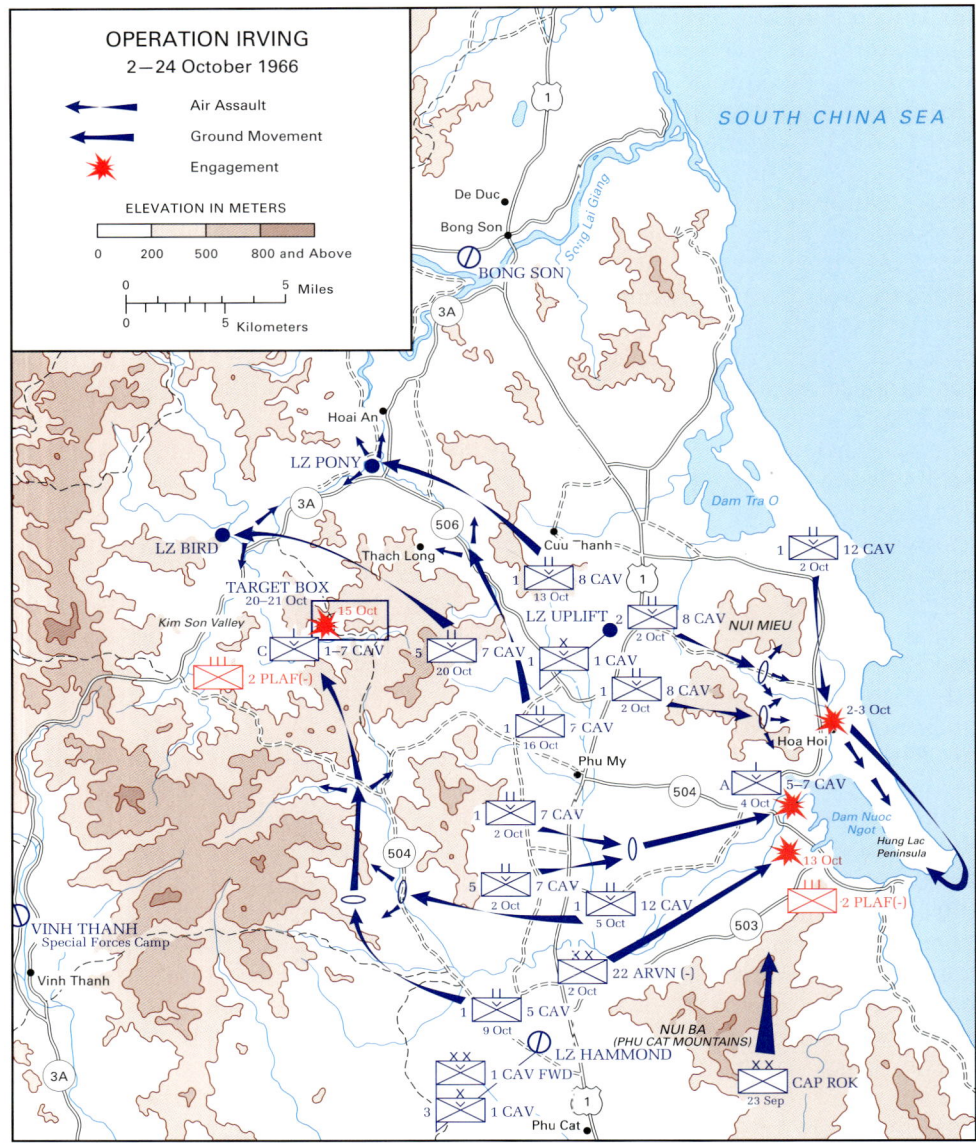

MAP 20

The hamlet that Colonel McIlwain was targeting, Hoa Hoi, belonged to a prosperous farming community about thirteen kilometers east of Phu My. A broad area of rice paddies lay to its immediate north, south, and west; sand dunes dotted with scrub cactus and the beaches of the South China Sea lay to its east. The sandy Hung Lac Peninsula stretched farther to the south, while, to the west, the Lach Moi River meandered in a north–south pattern toward the Nuoc Ngot Bay about two kilometers to the south. The river would swell into a broad shallow lake during the monsoon season, which usually began in the coastal lowlands during late October or November. Over the years the flooding had required the construction of a series of hedgerows, trenches, and dikes. Separating the rice paddies and parts of the hamlet into compartments, they served as ready-made, easily improved fortifications for the enemy. The hamlet's many palm-thatched huts and heavily foliated coconut palms also offered the Communists good cover and concealment. The open terrain outside Hoa Hoi, however, partly offset those advantages. Helicopters could deploy easily into these areas, and once American troops encircled the hamlet, the opposition would find it difficult to escape.[37]

About thirty minutes later the Hueys touched down on sand dunes fifty to one hundred thirty meters east of Hoa Hoi. The Blue Team advanced west toward the hamlet as gunships blocked routes of escape to the north, south, and west. The squad on the southern edge of the advance had covered barely twenty meters when machine gun fire killed a sergeant, the first American fatality of the day. North Vietnamese soldiers firing from concealed and protected emplacements soon had the entire platoon pinned down. Around 0920, with the assault going nowhere, McIlwain knew that his men were in trouble. Making another pass over the hamlet in his helicopter, he concluded that he was facing more than a platoon and radioed for help.[38]

Colonel Hyle reacted immediately. Already weighing his options if the enemy force at Hoa Hoi turned out to be dangerously large, he decided to reinforce as quickly as possible. Even though Colonel Tackaberry's 2d of the 8th Cavalry was operating just one kilometer from the fighting, Colonel Root wanted "a piece of the action," telling Hyle that "I could get there faster with my B Company. . . ."[39] Since Root already had twelve helicopters in the air carrying two platoons and the Company B command group, Hyle agreed. As a landing site Root selected the sand dunes east of the hamlet, where Capt. Frederick F. Mayer's Company B could relieve the Blue Team and then advance "to see what's what."[40] The remainder of Root's 1st of the 12th Cavalry would follow.

In the meantime, McIlwain's men began to withdraw amid an almost continuous hail of enemy fire. Supporting gunships assisted, but one squad refused to abandon a wounded medic and the bodies of two dead soldiers. In the end, McIlwain had to bring in his own helicopter

---

[37] Unit Hist Rpt no. 6, 1st Cav Div, 20 May 67, sub: Battle of Hoa Hoi, 2–3 October 1966, p. 2.

[38] Ibid., pp. 10–12.

[39] Ibid., p. 9.

[40] Interv, author with Col James T. Root, 27 Dec 95, Historians files, CMH.

to retrieve the wounded man. Another picked up the bodies as additional gunships raced overhead. Finally, all of the troopers reached the relative security of their landing zone, almost one hundred fifty meters away, but even then intense enemy fire delayed their final extraction until noon.[41]

While McIlwain continued his efforts, Root began his attack. Around 0945 he ordered Captain Mayer and the two platoons with him to deploy three hundred meters east of Hoa Hoi. Landing unopposed, the two platoons were on the ground by 1005. Ordering his 2d Platoon to the southwest side of Hoa Hoi to aid in the withdrawal of McIlwain's men, Mayer sent his 1st Platoon to establish a blocking position on the hamlet's northern edge. The block was easily done, but the platoon attempting to assist McIlwain came up against withering fire from troops in well-fortified trenches. After stopping for a moment to collect themselves, the Americans charged the North Vietnamese. Sweeping across the trench line, they forced the enemy back into the hamlet. By that time, approximately 1030, Captain Mayer's 3d Platoon and his weapons unit had arrived. Mayer deployed the 3d Platoon to reinforce the 2d.[42]

Now well aware that he had a large North Vietnamese force on his hands, Colonel Root decided to use his entire battalion to keep the enemy from slipping away. But time was short and his three rifle companies were not enough to encircle the hamlet, so he reorganized his troops for a hammer-and-anvil maneuver. Returning Captain Mayer's 1st Platoon to its parent unit east of Hoa Hoi, he positioned Capt. Thomas G. Fields' Company A to the south and southwest of the hamlet and Capt. Darrel G. Houston's Company C to the north. Once in place, Captain Houston's men could attack south into the pocket formed by Companies A and B on the other side of the settlement.[43]

Then at 1115 Colonel Hyle ordered Root to "stop the war." Hyle had received word that a psychological operations team orbiting Hoa Hoi in helicopters wanted to broadcast a message, calling upon civilians to leave the hamlet and the North Vietnamese to lay down their arms and surrender. About two hundred men, women, and children straggled out of the settlement in small groups, but the enemy refused to budge. Hyle's "stop the war" order, while it slowed the execution of Root's attack, saved the lives of many civilians.[44]

Colonel Root made his move at 1330, sending Company C to find the northernmost limit of the enemy's position. It would form the hammer; the other two companies were the anvils. An hour and a half later

[41] Unit Hist Rpt no. 6, 1st Cav Div, 20 May 67, sub: Battle of Hoa Hoi, 2–3 October 1966, pp. 12–13. See also AAR, Opns THAYER I and IRVING, 1st Cav Div, incl. 5, pp. 3–4.
[42] Unit Hist Rpt no. 6, 1st Cav Div, 20 May 67, sub: Battle of Hoa Hoi, 2–3 October 1966, p. 13.
[43] Interv, author with Root, 27 Dec 95.
[44] Ibid. (quoted words); Unit Hist Rpt no. 6, 1st Cav Div, 20 May 67, sub: Battle of Hoa Hoi, 2–3 October 1966, p. 18.

Captain Houston's Company C was ready to smash southward against the North Vietnamese, but the two anvils were still not in place. In fact, Captain Fields' Company A actually had to withdraw about one hundred meters, and Captain Mayer's Company B at one point had two platoons pinned down by machine gun fire. Gunships came to the rescue, laying down covering fire while the men consolidated their positions. Over the next three hours Company C moved southward, but also took fire and bogged down. Finally, with dusk approaching, Root decided to wait until the next day, and his men dug in for the night.[45]

Knowing that the North Vietnamese might slip out under the cover of darkness, Colonel Root requested reinforcements from Colonel Hyle, who gave him Companies A and C from Colonel Siegrist's 1st of the 5th Cavalry. Both units landed east of Hoa Hoi that evening and immediately moved up to tighten the seal. Root also arranged for constant shelling and illumination of the battle area. A 105-mm. artillery battery delivered 883 high-explosive rounds on the hamlet overnight. Illumination rounds initially came from another battery and then from an AC–47 Spooky gunship. As soon as they had exhausted their supply, Colonel Hyle made arrangements for U.S. Navy destroyers to fire illumination until dawn. Hoa Hoi and the surrounding countryside were transformed into "a dimly lit football field," making escape practically impossible. Many tried, but the Americans cut them down, killing 22.[46]

For the morning assault, Colonel Root laid on a block and sweep. From the northern edge of the hamlet Company C, 1st of the 12th Cavalry, and Company C, 1st of the 5th Cavalry, would attack south, the former scouring the main portion of the hamlet and the latter combing through rice paddies and sand dunes immediately to Hoa Hoi's east. Their drive would force the North Vietnamese either to stand and fight or to retreat into a deadly cross fire from the three blocking companies to the east, south, and west (*see Map 21*).[47]

The assault began at 0615. Houston's men rushed the hamlet and then dispersed into small groups to search the huts. For four hours they dashed in and out of homes, flushing out several groups of enemy soldiers in hand-to-hand fighting. When it was over, Root ordered a second sweep, this time from south to north. Company C, 1st of the 5th Cavalry, formed the block on the north, while Houston's Company C and elements of Mayer's Company B swept back through. They rooted out several more

[45] Unit Hist Rpt no. 6, 1st Cav Div, 20 May 67, sub: Battle of Hoa Hoi, 2–3 October 1966, pp. 18–24.

[46] Ibid., p. 26 (quoted words); Interv, author with Root, 27 Dec 95; Memo, Lt Col James T. Root, CO, 1st Bn, 12th Cav, for Maj Gen John Norton, CG, 1st Cav Div, 3 Oct 66, sub: Operations of 1st Battalion, 12th Cavalry, During Period 2–3 October 1966, Historians files, CMH.

[47] Interv, author with Root, 27 Dec 95; Unit Hist Rpt no. 6, 1st Cav Div, 20 May 67, sub: Battle of Hoa Hoi, 2–3 October 1966, p. 26.

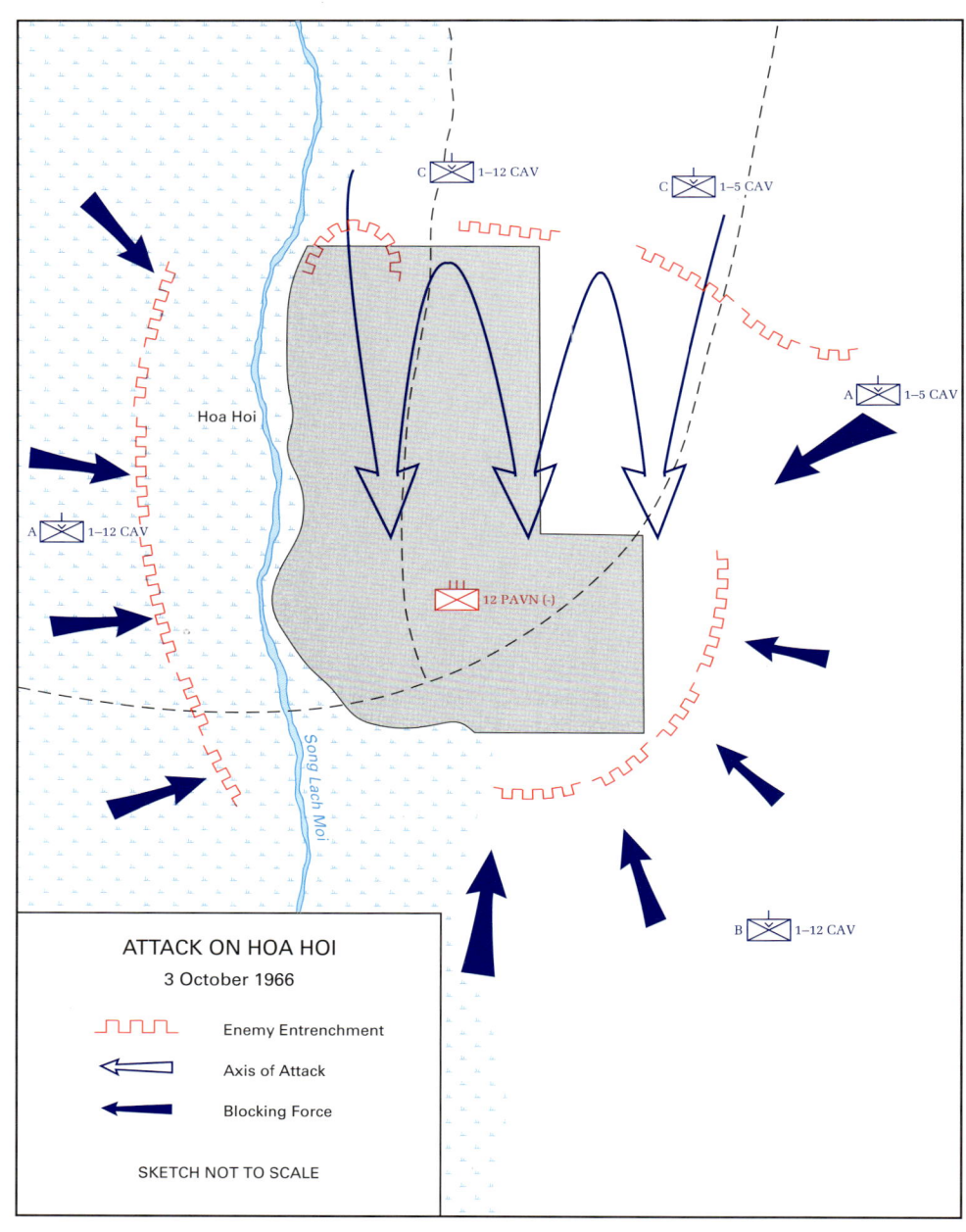

C ⊠ 1–12 CAV

C ⊠ 1–5 CAV

A ⊠ 1–5 CAV

Hoa Hoi

A ⊠ 1–12 CAV

12 PAVN (-)

Song Lach Moi

B ⊠ 1–12 CAV

ATTACK ON HOA HOI

3 October 1966

⊓⊔⊓⊔   Enemy Entrenchment

⟵   Axis of Attack

◄━   Blocking Force

SKETCH NOT TO SCALE

MAP 21

North Vietnamese soldiers and burned or demolished every building, haystack, and structure still standing. Root then directed Houston's company to conduct one more push through the devastation, but there was not much left to find. With the fighting over, Colonel Siegrist's two companies returned to their parent battalion, and Colonel Root's rifle companies departed to search southward toward Nuoc Ngot Bay.[48]

The battle at Hoa Hoi had been a bloody affair for the North Vietnamese. During the two-day engagement the Americans had fought some three hundred soldiers of the *3d Division*'s *12th Regiment* and had killed 233 of them—92 by Colonel McIlwain's Troop A, 1st of the 9th Cavalry, and the rest by Colonel Root's men. They had also taken 35 prisoners and had detained another 15 suspects. American forces had lost 6 killed, all on 2 October, and had suffered 32 wounded.[49]

The units in Operation IRVING continued searching for elements of the *3d Division* after the action at Hoa Hoi, but despite strenuous efforts no other American force found the enemy in a large concentration. On 2 October a troop from Colonel Smith's squadron had found 7 dead soldiers from the *2d PLAF Regiment* who had been killed by a B–52 strike north of the area of operations in the Cay Giep Mountains, confirming that at least part of the regiment had been there. Two days later Markham's 1st of the 7th Cavalry and Swett's 5th of the 7th Cavalry mounted parallel overland patrols in the lowlands south of the Mieu Mountains. In the process of securing a downed American helicopter just west of Nuoc Ngot Bay, Company A of Swett's battalion killed 30 enemy soldiers in a brief clash. On the same day Root swept the Hung Lac Peninsula, with one company working its way south and another its way north from the tip. The two met in the middle, without results. The following day Root's 1st of the 12th Cavalry, seeking to exploit a B–52 strike while protecting the rear of the operation, conducted an air assault into the Suoi Ca Valley west of Highway 1; other U.S. battalions, as well as South Vietnamese and South Korean forces, continued to search for the enemy east of the road. On the ninth Siegrist's battalion traded places with Root's weary troopers, who returned to HAMMOND to guard the installation and become the division reserve.[50]

The searches continued through 13 October, when the Americans shifted Louisell's 1st of the 8th Cavalry west to the Kim Son Valley in response to reports that the *2d PLAF Regiment* headquarters had moved

---

[48] AAR, Opns THAYER I and IRVING, 1st Cav Div, incl. 5, p. 10; Unit Hist Report no. 6, 1st Cav Div, 20 May 67, sub: Battle of Hoa Hoi, 2–3 October 1966, p. 28; Memo, Root for Norton, 3 Oct 66, sub: Operations of 1st Battalion, 12th Cavalry, During Period 2–3 October 1966.

[49] Memo, Root for Norton, 3 Oct 66, sub: Operations of 1st Battalion, 12th Cavalry, During Period 2–3 October 1966; Unit Hist Rpt no. 6, 1st Cav Div, 20 May 67, sub: Battle of Hoa Hoi, 2–3 October 1966, p. 30. Colonel Root's battalion and the two attached companies subsequently received a Presidential Unit Citation. See GO 47, DA, 12 Sep 68.

[50] Unit Hist Rpt no. 5, 1st Cav Div, n.d., sub: Operation IRVING, p. 16.

Men of the 1st Cavalry Division search a village during IRVING.

there. Louisell's troops found little. The only combat that day came about in rice lands east of Highway 1 in the South Vietnamese area of operations, where an airborne task force from the South Vietnamese 22d Division tangled with portions of the *2d Regiment*'s *95th Battalion* and was in danger of being overwhelmed. When the South Vietnamese requested assistance, gunships of the 2d Battalion, 20th Artillery, responded promptly. In the end, the South Vietnamese tallied 135 enemy dead and estimated that some 85 more had been killed by American helicopters.[51]

Over the next several days American battalions east and west of the highway mounted reconnaissances in force. Searching the hills west and north of the Suoi Ca Valley between 11 and 18 October, Siegrist's 1st of the 5th Cavalry discovered thirty-three caches containing rice, weapons, ammunition, medical supplies, and other equipment. The discoveries suggested that the unit had found a major center known to intelligence analysts as the Hoi Son Base Area. On the fifteenth one of Siegrist's companies operating in the Hoi Son found an enemy force later identified as the *52d Company, 95th Battalion, 2d PLAF Regiment*. During the fight, which lasted through the night and into the next day, the Americans killed 59 Viet Cong soldiers.[52]

[51] Ibid., pp. 19–20; AAR, Opns THAYER I and IRVING, 1st Cav Div, p. 27.
[52] Unit Hist Rpt no. 5, 1st Cav Div, n.d., sub: Operation IRVING, p. 20; AAR, Opns THAYER I and IRVING, 1st Cav Div, p. 28. See also Annual Hist Sum, 1966, 1st Bn, 5th Cav, n.d., pp. 8–9, box 1, 82/899, RG 338, NARA.

The engagement on the night of 15–16 October signified to American commanders that a substantial force—probably the *2d Regiment*—might well be lurking in the base area. As a result, General Norton moved Markham's 1st of the 7th Cavalry to the west of Highway 1 on the sixteenth, leaving Tackaberry's 2d of the 8th Cavalry and Swett's 5th of the 7th Cavalry to the east. Hoping to force the enemy to defend his redoubt, Norton had Markham's, Louisell's, and Siegrist's battalions block the exits, creating a roughly diamond-shaped pocket with the north–south and east–west points approximately sixteen kilometers apart. One of Siegrist's companies conducted the sweep. Once again, any insurgents who had been there escaped. The three-battalion force was not large enough to seal off the heavily forested mountainous terrain, especially when hindered by rainy weather. In numerous search and destroy missions over the next four days, the Americans found only supply caches.[53]

Still believing that the Viet Cong were nearby, General Norton expanded the search on 20 October by moving Swett's 5th of the 7th Cavalry directly to Landing Zone Bird in the Kim Son Valley. Swett then sent out company-size forces to hunt for the *2d Regiment*'s *95th Battalion*, while Smith's 1st of the 9th Cavalry conducted aerial searches southwest of the Suoi Ca Valley. The helicopter scouts spotted several small groups of enemy soldiers, but they were running westward and had no desire for a fight. When intelligence reports that day indicated that two Viet Cong battalions and a regimental headquarters might be in the same difficult terrain where Siegrist's men had fought portions of the *95th* a few days earlier, Norton decided not to send in ground forces. Instead, during the night he saturated a four- by two-kilometer area with artillery and air strikes; for over eight hours more than two thousand rounds of artillery struck the target zone along with three tons of Air Force bombs. Although three companies were supposed to sweep the area the next morning, heavy downpours and ground fog were imposing increasing restrictions on troop movements and aerial reconnaissance. Only one platoon entered the area, and its quick search revealed no enemy soldiers, living or dead. American forces continued searching in the Suoi Ca and Kim Son Valleys and to the east of Highway 1 until the twenty-third, but despite numerous signs that the enemy was lurking there, they were never able to generate significant contacts. At midnight, on 24 October, Norton terminated Irving and repositioned his forces deeper into the Kim Son Valley. The next phase of the campaign, Thayer II, was about to begin.[54]

General Norton would later write that the success of Irving had to be gauged in the context of the South Korean and South Vietnamese

---

[53] Rpt, 14th Mil Hist Det, 1st Cav Div, 7 Mar 67, sub: Seven Month History and Briefing Data (April–October 1966), p. 129; AAR, Opns Thayer I and Irving, 1st Cav Div, pp. 28–29.

[54] AAR, Opns Thayer I and Irving, 1st Cav Div, p. 30.

A revolutionary development team enters a hamlet.

operations that accompanied it, MAENG HO 6 and DAI BANG 800. In all, allied forces claimed to have killed a total of 2,063 Viet Cong and North Vietnamese and to have captured 1,409 more while losing 52 of their own men. Out of the total enemy dead, American forces accounted for 681 while suffering 19 killed, 6 at Hoa Hoi. The preponderance of enemy casualties came from the *7th* and *8th Battalions, 12th Regiment*, although the *2d PLAF Regiment*, especially its *95th Battalion*, was also hit hard.[55]

These heavy losses were only the beginning of the Communists' problems in Binh Dinh Province. During the summer the 1st Cavalry Division had also succeeded in uncovering and destroying many of their life-sustaining caches of food, ammunition, clothing, and medical supplies. Moreover, allied military police operations had damaged the enemy's underground severely in at least two of the province's districts, Phu My and Phu Cat. By the end of October revolutionary development, or pacification, teams had entered forty-seven of the fifty-six hamlets scheduled for pacification in the province's 1966 campaign plan.[56]

---

[55] Ibid., pp. 32–33, 40–41; ORLL, 1 Aug–31 Oct 66, I FFV, pp. 23, 25; CHECO Rpt, PACAF, 12 May 67, sub: Operations THAYER/IRVING, p. 52.

[56] Unit Hist Rpt no. 5, 1st Cav Div, n.d., sub: Operation IRVING, p. 24; AAR, Opns THAYER I and IRVING, 1st Cav Div, p. 40; Special Joint RD Rpt, Binh Dinh Province, 31 Oct 66, pp. 1, 4, RD files, CMH.

Viet Cong defectors enjoy a meal at a Chieu Hoi *center.*

The government's increased presence in the countryside yielded tangible results, as civilians provided the pacification teams with information that led to five successful strikes against Viet Cong cadres in September alone. By November 2,865 Viet Cong had turned themselves in under the government's *Chieu Hoi* amnesty program. The number far exceeded the province's goal of 1,500 for 1966. Although the Viet Cong still had great reserves of strength in Binh Dinh, the province advisory staff seemed to have cause to conclude that "the attitude of the people . . . appears to be swinging pro-GVN [government of Vietnam]."[57]

As was frequently the case, however, improved security came at a price—a new wave of refugees. One of the continuing ironies of the war was that operations undertaken to eliminate the enemy's presence among the population often generated more refugees than purely military search and destroy operations. Operation Irving alone produced approximately 40,000 refugees and 5,000 detainees, swelling the total number of refugees in the province to over 152,000—roughly 10 percent of South Vietnam's total refugee population. Inundated by a flood of newly displaced persons, allied relief agencies could do little more than provide emergency levels of food and shelter. Until these people could be resettled and gainfully employed in areas free of Viet Cong influence,

---

[57] Briefing, USAID, Nov 66, sub: Binh Dinh Province, p. 5, and Special Joint RD Rpt, Binh Dinh Province, 30 Sep 66, p. 1 (quotation), RD files, CMH.

the government's apparent gains in Binh Dinh Province could be counted as little more than tentative.[58]

[58] Special Joint RD Rpt, Binh Dinh Province, 30 Nov 66, p. 2, RD files, CMH; Briefing, USAID, Nov 66, sub: Binh Dinh Province, p. 4; AAR, Opns THAYER I and IRVING, 1st Cav Div, p. 44.

13

Raising the Stakes on the Border

Despite gains around Saigon and on the coastal plains of II Corps, the Americans had made only limited headway in the Central Highlands. The rugged peaks and valleys still masked crucial corridors carrying Hanoi's men, munitions, and supplies to South Vietnam. General Westmoreland had been making the same argument for the past year: If the enemy was allowed to use the highlands with impunity, he would have easy access to the heavily populated regions farther south and an easy avenue of retreat when defeated. Allied loss of the region would be "the first step in [the] total erosion of our posture in this country," the MACV commander concluded, and he intended to contest every invasion of the plateau.[1]

The opposing infantry strengths in the Central Highlands had been fairly settled as of Operations LINCOLN and LONGFELLOW, and would not change until the arrival of the 2d Brigade, 4th Infantry Division, at Pleiku City starting in July. But though the pipeline would not produce troops for several months, Westmoreland would not want for firepower once he went on the attack. Besides Phan Rang Air Base on the coast, Pleiku Air Base was also expanding, now home to A–1 Skyraiders, both American and South Vietnamese, and the latest in fixed-wing gunships. In addition, the arrival in June at Pleiku of the 52d Artillery Group and its 3d Battalion, 6th Artillery, boosted the fires that Westmoreland needed for his forward strategy.

To make good that strategy, South Korean and South Vietnamese elements would continue to secure installations along the coast while the 1st Cavalry Division scoured the lowlands and foothills for the enemy's main force units. Any threat that arose in the Central Highlands would be handled by the 3d Brigade, 25th Infantry Division, and, when available, the 1st Brigade, 101st Airborne Division. As North Vietnamese and Viet Cong regulars passed through the area, the Americans were to engage them when they appeared or—if too large to handle—to sound the alarm. In that case, the 1st Cavalry Division, the II Corps' swing division, would air-assault to the scene and into combat.

---

[1] Msg, Westmoreland MAC 11956 to Wheeler, 10 Dec 67, Westmoreland Message files, CMH.

Westmoreland believed that he had to be "more elusive" than the enemy and hoped that this forward-deployment approach would "keep him guessing, never let him get set. . . ."[2]

North to Kontum

The strategy would be tested immediately. In late May the enemy closed in on a Regional Forces outpost at Tou Morong, near Dak To, in northern Kontum Province. For several days mortar rounds and sniper fire kept the defenders pinned down, but soon the real intent of the North Vietnamese became apparent. Deserters revealed that the *88th PAVN Regiment* was across the border in Laos some thirty-five kilometers northwest of the outpost, while other intelligence placed units from the *24th PAVN Regiment* in the jungle to the north and southwest. Finally, a diary captured by American units reported that North Vietnamese forces were laying plans to fight a Dien Bien Phu–type of battle somewhere in the highlands, with the main axis of advance in Kontum Province. Although the diary contained no timetable, the weight of the information called for an American response.[3]

The response was named HAWTHORNE, and it would be conducted by General Pearson's 1st Brigade, 101st Airborne Division. As the planning took shape, General Kinnard, the acting commander of I Field Force, met with Pearson and Vinh Loc, the II Corps commander, on 28 May to discuss what forces to employ. At the time, Pearson had only one battalion at his temporary headquarters at Cheo Reo in Phu Bon Province, Colonel Meinzen's 1st Battalion, 327th Infantry; his other two were deployed elsewhere—Colonel Wasco's 2d Battalion, 327th Infantry, at Tuy Hoa and Colonel Emerson's 2d Battalion, 502d Infantry, at Pleiku, both under the command of I Field Force. Vinh Loc agreed to provide the operation's second and third battalions—the 1st Battalion, 42d Regiment, and the 21st Ranger Battalion, both assigned to the 24th Special Tactical Zone in Kontum Province.[4]

Pearson laid out a three-battalion attack to relieve Tou Morong. The South Vietnamese ranger battalion would helicopter some twelve to fif-

---

[2] Briefing, Asst CofS, J–3, MACV, for Preparedness Investigating Subcommittee, Senate Committee on Armed Services, 18 Oct 66, sub: Concept of Operations, vol. 1, p. 7, box 21, 69A/702, RG 334, NARA; MFR, MACV MACJ00, 20 Jun 66, sub: MACV Commanders' Conference, 5 June 1966, p. 9 (quoted words), Westmoreland History files, CMH.

[3] Statement of Maj Gen Willard Pearson, pp. 1–2, 5, Incl to Special Study, 22d Mil Hist Det, 1st Bde, 101st Abn Div, n.d., sub: The Battle of Tou Morong, RVN (Operation HAWTHORNE), 1st Brigade, 101st Airborne Division, 3–20 June 1966, in VNI 1, CMH (hereafter cited as HAWTHORNE Special Study); Willard Pearson, "Day-and-Night Battle in Relief of an Outpost," *Army* 17 (March 1967): 54.

[4] AAR, Opn HAWTHORNE, 1st Bde, 101st Abn Div, 22 Jul 66, p. 2; "Command Histories and Historical Sketches of RVNAF Divisions," January 1973, p. 31. Both in Historians files, CMH.

teen kilometers northwest of the base and the 1st of the 327th Infantry to the northeast. Once on the ground, they would converge on the installation. At the same time, the South Vietnamese infantry battalion would push overland from Dak To. Pearson believed that the enemy was on the north side of the base. With two battalions approaching from that direction, he said, "we would be able to attack him from the rear; and with the . . . [South Vietnamese] battalion coming up from the south, [then] moving east, we would have forces to his front." If the North Vietnamese failed to fight, the three forces would simply relieve the outpost.[5]

The plan agreed to, the 1st of the 327th Infantry deployed from Cheo Reo to Dak To 1. Much of the move was by air, with C–130s flying two hundred one sorties between 29 May and 3 June. The night before the operation began, Pearson made his executive officer, Major Hackworth, acting commander of the American battalion because Meinzen had become ill.[6]

Terrain and weather in the province held no surprises. Steep mountains, cloaked in jungle and heavy undergrowth, dominated the region. Highway 14 allowed reasonably easy north–south transportation, but otherwise troops on foot had to depend upon trails, many covered by the tangled jungle that made them invisible from the air. The southwest monsoon controlled the weather pattern. At this time of year low clouds and rain began daily in the late afternoon and sometimes lasted into the early hours of the next morning. Ground fog followed the early morning rain, providing concealment for the enemy and hampering air support for the Americans.[7]

Operation HAWTHORNE began on 2 June, with the South Vietnamese infantry battalion driving north along Highway 14 from Dak To. Some four kilometers up the road a company-size enemy force challenged the South Vietnamese, but after a short clash they continued on. That evening a small group from Major Hackworth's 1st of the 327th helicoptered about nine kilometers northeast of Tou Morong. The rest of his battalion flew in the following morning, just as the South Vietnamese ranger battalion arrived at its landing zone. All went according to plan, except that the South Vietnamese moved slower than expected. On the third, hoping to speed their advance, Pearson attached more firepower, deploying Battery B, 2d Battalion, 320th Artillery, to an old French fort known as Dak Pha on the Dak To–Tou Morong road. Company A, 2d Battalion, 502d Infantry, commanded by Capt. Walter R. Brown, was brought in to protect the guns (*see Map 22*).[8]

---

[5] Pearson Statement, pp. 2–3 (quoted words), Incl to HAWTHORNE Special Study; AAR, Opn HAWTHORNE, 1st Bde, 101st Abn Div, pp. 2–3.

[6] Hackworth and Sherman, *About Face*, p. 534; Statement of Maj John M. McDonald, S–3 [Opns], 1st Bn, 327th Inf, p. 1, Incl to HAWTHORNE Special Study.

[7] AAR, Opn HAWTHORNE, 1st Bde, 101st Abn Div, incl. 2, p. 1.

[8] Ibid., p. 3; Pearson Statement, p. 4, Incl to HAWTHORNE Special Study.

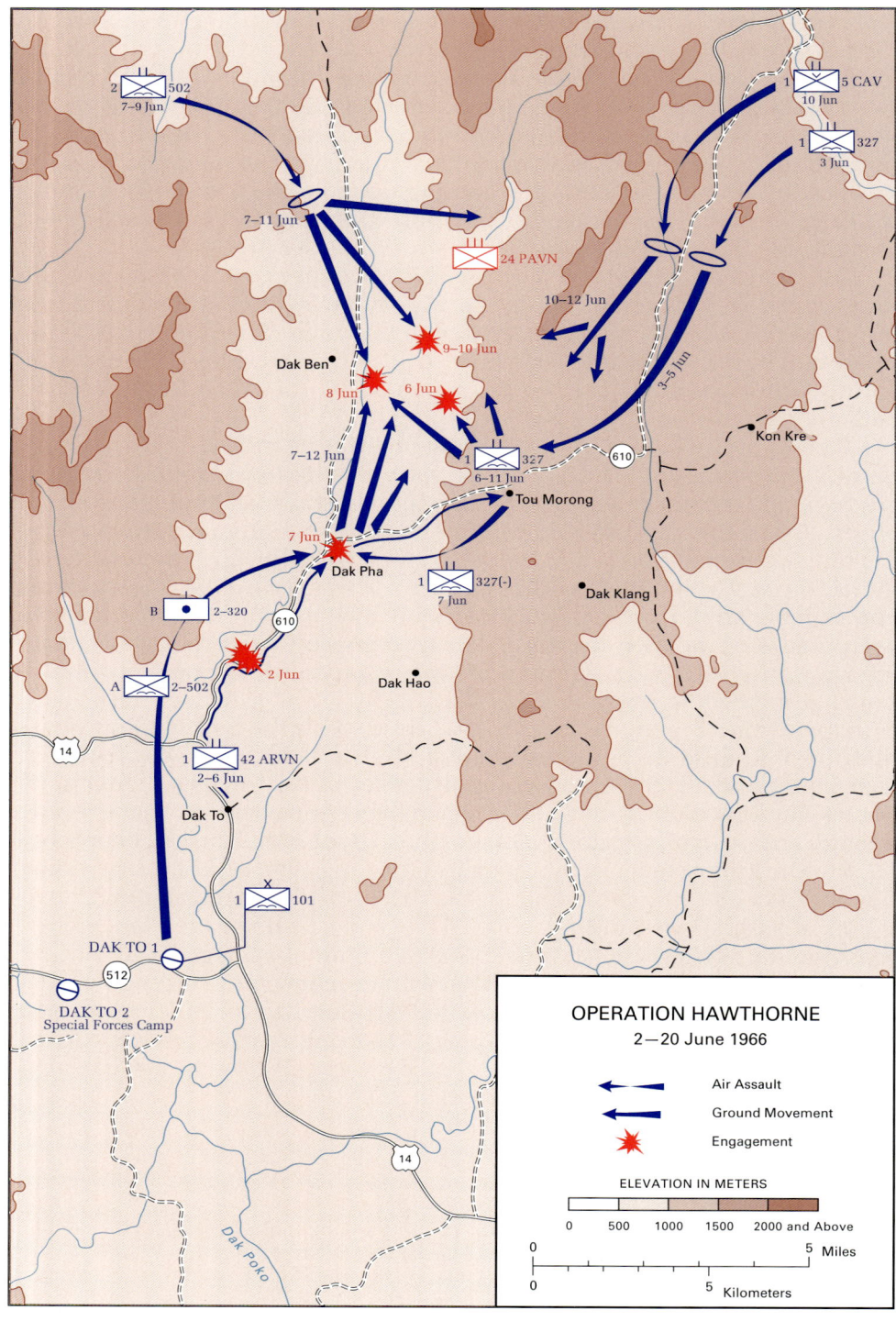

2 [XX] 502
7–9 Jun

1 [XX] 5 CAV
10 Jun

1 [XX] 327
3 Jun

7–11 Jun

24 PAVN

10–12 Jun

3–5 Jun

9–10 Jun

Dak Ben

8 Jun   6 Jun

Kon Kre

610

7–12 Jun

1 [XX] 327
6–11 Jun

7 Jun   Tou Morong

Dak Pha

1 [XX] 327(-)
7 Jun

Dak Klang

B [·] 2–320   2–320

610

A [XX] 2–502   2 Jun

Dak Hao

14

1 [XX] 42 ARVN
2–6 Jun

Dak To

1 [X] 101

DAK TO 1

512

DAK TO 2
Special Forces Camp

Dak Poko

14

OPERATION HAWTHORNE
2—20 June 1966

⟵⟶ Air Assault

⟵ Ground Movement

✳ Engagement

ELEVATION IN METERS

0   500   1000   1500   2000 and Above

0   5   Miles

0   5   Kilometers

MAP 22

The three battalions reached Tou Morong on 5 June, relieving the outpost. The next morning the South Vietnamese escorted the garrison back to Dak To. Because the North Vietnamese had chosen not to fight, General Pearson had to decide whether or not to continue HAWTHORNE. That afternoon his staff met with Hackworth at Tou Morong to assess the situation. Some favored leaving the area since the North Vietnamese were apparently gone, but Hackworth wanted to take a closer look. Although pessimistic about finding any of the regulars, Pearson gave Hackworth permission to search north, northwest, and west of Tou Morong but stipulated that if he failed to make contact with the enemy his battalion was to return to Dak To 1.[9]

Hackworth found a fight. That same afternoon one of his companies sweeping northwest of Tou Morong ran into a reinforced company. The Americans called in artillery, but a short round landed among Hackworth's men, killing 5 and wounding another 5. Although their aggressiveness was dampened, they attempted to keep the enemy in place through the night until the rest of the battalion arrived the next morning.[10]

But the first major engagement was at the Dak Pha firebase. The North Vietnamese had been harassing the base since it opened on 3 June. Then at 0200 on the seventh, under cover of a mortar bombardment, they probed the perimeter looking for weak points. Eight North Vietnamese died in the attack, as did 3 Americans. The full assault began around 0320, when an element later identified as part of the *24th Regiment* struck from the north, east, and west. The first wave came straight at the number six gun, the northernmost in the star-shaped fortress, pelting it with grenades and forcing the defenders to abandon it. At 0400 another attack came from the southwest, pushing part of the battery back toward the firebase's center, where a core perimeter had been established for just such an emergency. Minutes later the Americans counterattacked and drove the enemy back.[11]

About that time Battery B, 1st Battalion, 30th Artillery, near Dak To 1 opened fire in support of Dak Pha. The deadly barrage of 155-mm. shells, exploding just outside the firebase, drove the North Vietnamese away from the number six gun, and over the next several hours enemy machine gun and mortar fire dropped off significantly.[12]

The respite was only temporary. Just after dawn the action intensified, and at 0640 the Communists mounted yet another assault, again

---

[9] Hackworth and Sherman, *About Face*, p. 536; Pearson Statement, pp. 2, 5, 8, Incl to HAWTHORNE Special Study.

[10] McDonald Statement, p. 3, Incl to HAWTHORNE Special Study.

[11] Daily Jnl, 2d Bn, 320th Arty, 7 Jun 66; Sitrep no. 158, 1st Bde, 101st Abn Div, 7 Jun 66, p. 1; and Statement of Capt Larry W. Simpson, XO (Executive Officer), Btry B, 2d Bn, 320th Arty, pp. 1–3, Incls to HAWTHORNE Special Study. See also Hackworth and Sherman, *About Face*, p. 537.

[12] Daily Jnl, 2d Bn, 320th Arty, 7 Jun 66, and McDonald Statement, p. 4, Incls to HAWTHORNE Special Study.

American defenders at Dak Pha prepare for another attack by the North Vietnamese.

concentrating on the number six gun. Two squads overran it, forcing a withdrawal. This time, rather than counterattack, the Americans waited in their foxholes while round after round of artillery slammed the North Vietnamese for the next two hours. Gunships and air strikes followed until the attacks on Dak Pha ceased.[13]

The fighting was not yet over, however. Around 0730 Major Hackworth and his Companies B and C helicoptered from Tou Morong to the battle zone. On the ground at Dak Pha, Hackworth took command of Captain Brown's Company A defending the firebase and ordered it north toward the enemy's probable line of withdrawal. He sent Companies B and C along Brown's left flank to block any attempt to flee in that direction. By then, Hackworth's Company A and the battalion reconnaissance platoon, his Tiger Force, had also left Tou Morong and moved into the area. Hackworth now had three rifle companies and a reconnaissance unit maneuvering generally to the north. All signs suggested that the North Vietnamese were nearby but that they were withdrawing deeper into the mountainous jungle north of Tou Morong.[14]

At the brigade level, Pearson's main task on the morning of 7 June was getting more men into HAWTHORNE. At 0730 General Kinnard ap-

[13] McDonald Statement, p. 4, Incl to HAWTHORNE Special Study.
[14] Ibid., p. 5.

280

proved involving the rest of Colonel Emerson's 2d of the 502d Infantry now in reserve at Dak To 1. Pearson wanted to use it to help cut off the enemy's line of retreat. By 0920 Emerson's men had flown about ten kilometers north of Dak Pha. Emerson immediately deployed his two rifle companies, Company C screening to the south and Company B farther to the east.[15]

Maneuvering north, Hackworth's men believed they were chasing an enemy in disarray. "We thought we had the NVA moving in the open where they would be highly susceptible to our superior artillery and tactical air fire power," Maj. John M. McDonald, Hackworth's operations officer, later explained, "so we aggressively pursued."[16] Instead, the North Vietnamese had maintained most of their integrity as a fighting force and were conducting a systematic withdrawal. The Americans soon discovered this when the *24th Regiment* elements that they were pursuing pulled into a complex of well-prepared emplacements and readied themselves for what would be three days of heavy fighting for the U.S. brigade.[17]

The battle began with a series of firefights early on 8 June. One of the first involved Hackworth's Tiger Force. Now commanded by Capt. Lewis Higinbotham and accompanied by *Washington Post* correspondent Ward Just, the platoon had spent the preceding day following a recently used trail to the northwest and then to the north. The troops had found one abandoned camp after another but no enemy. "The jungle was utterly silent," Just later wrote, "the only movement an occasional exquisitely colored butterfly." As darkness fell, the unit dug in.[18]

The next morning, 8 June, the platoon continued its pursuit. Almost immediately the troops came upon another deserted camp, this one large enough to accommodate at least a battalion or possibly even a regiment. All was again quiet, but at 1315 the Americans walked into an ambush. At least two hundred North Vietnamese opened fire with small arms and grenades. Higinbotham's men dropped to the ground, returning fire as best they could, and then formed a hasty perimeter and called for artillery and air support. Incoming rounds whistled in, falling in a wide protective semicircle just beyond the Americans. Despite the artillery curtain, the North Vietnamese came on. Grenades fell closer to the perimeter and the hail of bullets became only thicker. Concerned that he might be overrun before reinforcements arrived, Higinbotham pulled in even tighter, but the move provided only temporary respite. "That

---

[15] Pearson, "Relief of an Outpost," p. 56; Hawthorne Special Study, tab K, an. A, p. 1.

[16] McDonald Statement, p. 5, Incl to Hawthorne Special Study.

[17] AAR, Opn Hawthorne, 1st Bn, 327th Inf, 27 Jun 66, p. 4, Incl to Hawthorne Special Study.

[18] Ward Just, "Ain't Nobody Been Walking This Trail But Charlie Cong," in *A Short History of the Vietnam War*, ed. Allan R. Millett (Bloomington: Indiana University Press, 1978), p. 75.

was when the awful fear set in," Just would write, "that . . . there was no way to stop them."[19]

Hackworth reacted immediately, sending his Company A and two platoons from Company C to reinforce. Racing overland toward the sound of the guns, the Company C troops ran into an enemy force. They were pinned down only momentarily, however, and by 1700 the two companies closed on the action. Higinbotham came up on the radio, while his men yelled and screamed in an attempt to guide their rescuers in. The North Vietnamese must not have liked the new odds because they continued their northward withdrawal. Higinbotham used the break to evacuate his dead and wounded and to bring in supplies. The Tiger Force suffered 5 killed and 17 wounded, a loss of nearly half its strength. Enemy losses went unreported.[20]

In the days that followed, Hackworth continued his search for the enemy. On 9 June Company C conducted an air assault to the northwest and Company B search and destroy missions just north of Dak Pha. Company A and the Tiger Force remained at the site of the 8 June engagement, under orders from Hackworth to police up the battlefield and to "see if you can't get a big body count."[21]

Meanwhile, to the north, Emerson's 2d of the 502d Infantry had achieved no significant contact during its first two days in the field, probably because Pearson had placed it too far north of the withdrawing enemy. It was, the general later admitted, "a tactical error of judgment. . . ."[22] However, on the third day, 9 June, Emerson's luck changed. While Brown's Company A rejoined him, securing the battalion command post, 1st Lt. Louis F. Sill's Company B swept east along multiple axes and Capt. William S. Carpenter's Company C moved south and east until it reached the boundary between Emerson's and Hackworth's battalions. Both companies soon found combat.[23]

After moving about a thousand meters, Lieutenant Sill's men were stopped cold by machine gun fire. Captain Carpenter also ran into North Vietnamese but was able to push on to high ground. At that point, with Hackworth on his way to help Company B, Carpenter was ordered to turn north and east and block the likely route of enemy withdrawal. Progress was slow through the tangled bamboo, so Carpenter formed

---

[19] Ibid., p. 79 (quotation); Daily Jnl, 1st Bn, 327th Inf, 8 Jun 66, Incl to HAWTHORNE Special Study.

[20] HAWTHORNE Special Study, tab G, pp. 3–4, and tab J, p. 4; Statement of Lt Col Edmond P. Abood, XO, 1st Bn, 327th Inf, pp. 4–5, and Daily Jnl, 1st Bn, 327th, 8 Jun 66, Incls to ibid.

[21] Daily Jnl, 1st Bn, 327th Inf, 9 Jun 66 (quoted words), Abood Statement, p. 5, and AAR, Opn HAWTHORNE, 1st Bn, 327th Inf, p. 4, Incls to HAWTHORNE Special Study.

[22] Pearson Statement, p. 6, Incl to HAWTHORNE Special Study.

[23] AAR, Opn HAWTHORNE, 2d Bn, 502d Inf, 7–11 Jun 66, an. A, pp. 1–2, and Statement of Capt William S. Carpenter, CO, Co C, 2d Bn, 502d Inf, pp. 1–2, Incls to HAWTHORNE Special Study.

his platoons into a single column, hoping to speed things up. His reconnaissance group took the lead, followed by the 1st Platoon, the company headquarters, the 3d Platoon, and finally the Weapons Platoon. Each element was about two hundred meters apart.[24]

As the column moved across a small ridge, the reconnaissance group heard voices about two hundred meters to the left. Carpenter ordered the unit to stop so that the rest of the column could catch up. He now had two options: detour slightly, thus avoiding the enemy and keeping on course; or advance up the ridge and go after the North Vietnamese. Carpenter chose to fight. He ordered his 1st Platoon to deploy in line and attack, while the other two platoons prepared to reinforce. If a fight developed, the 3d Platoon would join the 1st Platoon on its left and the Weapons Platoon would position itself to support either of them.[25]

At 1530 Carpenter was ready. The 1st Platoon's lead squad sneaked up on the voices—a group of ten to fifteen enemy soldiers, some washing in a stream and some cooking. The Americans opened fire, killing or wounding all of the surprised North Vietnamese, and then continued their advance. Within minutes other North Vietnamese converged on their comrades. At least two machine guns ahead and to the left of the Americans opened up, halting the 1st Platoon's attack. The 3d Platoon moved to within fifty meters of the unit's left, hoping to outflank the enemy, but also came under heavy fire and was pinned down.[26]

Fighting soon engulfed all of Carpenter's elements. Even the headquarters group and Weapons Platoon, far behind the main action, came under long-range machine gun fire. Of greater concern, however, was automatic weapons fire coming from a hill some two hundred meters to the east. Carpenter ordered the Weapons Platoon to silence it. The troopers had advanced only a third of the way up the slope before a wall of fire stopped them in their tracks.

The 3d Platoon's situation was grimmer. The enemy lobbed grenades, seeking to outflank the Americans. A bullet killed the platoon leader, and a grenade mortally wounded the platoon sergeant. Then one of the unit's squad leaders radioed Carpenter, frantically reporting that he was the only one alive and that the North Vietnamese were overrunning the position. After that brief transmission the radio went dead.[27]

Normally, artillery and air strikes probably would have turned the tide, but this time neither was effective. Thick vegetation made it difficult to adjust artillery fire and air strikes because the men could not see where the shells and bombs landed. They could target the strikes only by sound. Without effective fire support to keep the enemy at bay, the

---

[24] Carpenter Statement, p. 2, Incl to Hawthorne Special Study.

[25] AAR, Opn Hawthorne, 2d Bn, 502d Inf, an. A, pp. 2–6, and Sitrep no. 160, 1st Bde, 101st Abn Div, 9 Jun 66, pp. 1–3, Incls to Hawthorne Special Study.

[26] Carpenter Statement, p. 3, Incl to Hawthorne Special Study.

[27] Ibid., pp. 4–5.

attacks intensified, leaving Carpenter and his men in increasing danger of collapse. By 1615 the company was no longer functioning as a unit. Carpenter might have retreated, but the North Vietnamese seemed to be closing in on at least three sides, many of his men were wounded, and any 3d Platoon members hiding in the jungle would have been left behind.[28]

In desperation, Carpenter popped a smoke grenade and threw it just beyond the northern edge of his tiny perimeter, and then radioed a request for an air strike on the billowing smoke. An F–4 Phantom on station dropped two canisters of napalm around 1645. One tumbled some distance north of the Americans, hitting the enemy position; the other hit thirty to fifty meters from the first, closer to the American center. According to the company first sergeant, Sfc. Walter J. Sabalauski, the napalm "rolled among us and several yards to our front."[29] Carpenter remembered that the canister landed roughly between the Weapons and 1st Platoons, about fifteen meters forward of their positions. At least a dozen Americans were burned by the flames—one would later die. A medic reported that as the canister exploded "the world turned orange. . . . Hot and orange."[30] Later accounts would claim that Carpenter had specifically called for napalm, but the captain denied it, saying "I didn't know what type of armament the aircraft was carrying."[31]

But it was worse for the North Vietnamese. As the leader of the Weapons Platoon reported, "A lot of NVA got caught in it. . . . I saw NVA running up the ridge, on fire."[32] The napalm seemed to work. Staggering under the onslaught, enemy troops stopped firing for more than half an hour as they reorganized, allowing the Americans time to withdraw a short distance and establish a new perimeter. From there they held firm throughout the night, even though the enemy continued to probe.[33]

As the drama unfolded, American commanders to the rear were doing everything they could for Carpenter. Colonel Emerson ordered his remaining rifle companies to the rescue, with General Pearson directing Major Hackworth to provide what assistance he could. By 1710

---

[28] Ibid., p. 5; AAR, Opn Hawthorne, 2d Bn, 502d Inf, an. A, p. 5, Incl to Hawthorne Special Study; William Nack, "The Lonesome End," *Sports Illustrated* 79 (October 1993): 68.

[29] Carpenter Statement, pp. 5–6, and Statement of Sfc Walter J. Sabalauski, Co C, 2d Bn, 502d Inf, p. 1 (quoted words), Incls to Hawthorne Special Study.

[30] Carpenter Statement, p. 2, Incl to Hawthorne Special Study; Nack, "Lonesome End," p. 69 (medic quotation). See also S. L. A. Marshall, *Battles in the Monsoon: Campaigning in the Central Highlands, Vietnam, Summer 1966* (New York: William Morrow and Co., 1967), p. 374, and Ltr, Margaret O. Adams, Center for Electronic Records, NARA, to author, 17 Nov 93, Historians files, CMH.

[31] Carpenter Statement, p. 5, Incl to Hawthorne Special Study.

[32] Nack, "Lonesome End," p. 69.

[33] Sabalauski Statement, p. 1, and Carpenter Statement, p. 6, Incls to Hawthorne Special Study.

Emerson's Company B was less than three kilometers northeast of Carpenter when it met a North Vietnamese battalion. The two forces were locked in combat until midnight, making it doubtful that the company could reach Carpenter in time to help. Company A, 1st of the 327th, now under Emerson's command, was also en route, and it too found its way blocked. After three separate assaults failed to breach the enemy line, Capt. Benjamin L. Willis, the company commander, tried the flank but was unsuccessful. Out of options, Willis pulled his men into a night defense. Before dawn came, the North Vietnamese managed to kill 8 of Willis' men and wound 20 more.[34]

All was not lost, however. At 1715 Captain Brown's Company A, 2d of the 502d, operating less than two kilometers west of Carpenter, had begun the trek toward the battle. Throughout the night the troops moved to the southeast in a hard rain that started, then stopped, then started again. It was so dark that they had to hold hands at times to keep from being separated. When they came to within five hundred meters of the trapped company, they heard Vietnamese voices. Brown immediately radioed Carpenter, requesting a volley of fire so that he would know the company's exact position. His men then slipped through the enemy cordon, with the advance group reaching Carpenter at 2135 and the rest arriving shortly after midnight.

By then, members of Carpenter's 3d Platoon were also trickling in. To the startled but euphoric defenders, who had only hours earlier written them off as dead, they appeared like ghosts from the darkness; as it turned out, all but three had escaped. In fact, when Carpenter took a head count, he discovered that his casualties had not been as high as he had feared—3 killed, 34 wounded, and 3 missing.[35]

The willingness of the North Vietnamese to fight persuaded General Pearson to expand HAWTHORNE. As a first step he moved the South Vietnamese 1st Battalion, 42d Regiment, west of the action to block any escape that way. I Field Force then released a company from Colonel Wasco's 2d of the 327th Infantry to Pearson, which he attached to Colonel Emerson. At the direction of I Field Force General Norton's 1st Cavalry Division furnished Colonel Siegrist's 1st Battalion, 5th Cavalry, which Pearson placed east of the battle. With Hackworth's battalion attacking north and Emerson's attacking south, Pearson was convinced he had "a four way squeeze" on the North Vietnamese.[36]

But Pearson wanted to be sure that he hit the Communists hard, so on 10 June he requested a B–52 strike to soften the enemy up before his

---

[34] Hackworth and Sherman, *About Face*, p. 540; Abood Statement, p. 6, Incl to HAWTHORNE Special Study.

[35] Statement of Capt William C. Hookham, Plt Ldr, 1st Plt, Co A, 2d Bn, 502d Inf, pp. 3–4, plus Sabalauski Statement, p. 2, and Carpenter Statement, p. 6, Incls to HAWTHORNE Special Study. In the study see AAR, Opn HAWTHORNE, 2d Bn, 502d Inf, an. A, p. 6, for the official casualty total.

[36] Pearson Statement, p. 6, Incl to HAWTHORNE Special Study.

A B–52 Stratofortress on a mission over South Vietnam

men attacked. When the ARC LIGHT strike was approved for the thirteenth, Pearson told his battered companies to withdraw with their wounded at least three kilometers from the target zone, and to do so in a way that kept the North Vietnamese from becoming suspicious and disappearing.[37]

Although Carpenter's and Brown's companies could march out of the target box, removing their many wounded posed a problem. Carpenter wanted to evacuate them by helicopter, but when the Hueys tried to land enemy fire turned them away. The Americans would have to wait until nightfall, carrying the injured with them. In the face of more heavy fire helicopters managed to deliver enough litters for the wounded, but because the rain was so heavy, the night so dark, and the jungle so thick, the two company commanders called off the move until daybreak.

As the sun rose above the jungle on 11 June, the two companies began a seven-kilometer trek westward to a landing zone secured earlier by base camp troops. The Americans lost 1 soldier to a sniper during the move, but there was no other opposition. They arrived at the clearing shortly after 1100, boarded helicopters, and were clear of the landing zone by 1230. Throughout the next day they rested and refitted, and waited to return to the operation after the B–52 strike.[38]

[37] Ibid., pp. 6–7.
[38] Historian's Narrative, "The Battle of Tou Morong," p. 4, and Carpenter Statement, pp. 7–8, Incls to HAWTHORNE Special Study.

Meanwhile, General Pearson accelerated preparations for the B–52s. To make the enemy believe that the American companies were still in the area, he unfolded an elaborate artillery and air support plan to engage the North Vietnamese between 11 and 13 June. At the same time, elements from Hackworth's battalion aggressively patrolled, gradually slacking off as unit after unit quietly withdrew until only the Tiger Force was left. It would pull out early on 13 June, just hours before the air attack was to begin. Additionally, Pearson made certain that his blocking and exploiting forces were in position.[39]

The day of the strike dawned bright and clear—perfect weather for an Arc Light. At 0750 fighter-bombers swooped in and dropped nine hundred tear gas canisters into the target area. Pearson hoped that the riot agent would force the North Vietnamese out of their trenches and bunkers and into the open just before the B–52s dropped their loads. Thirty minutes later the B–52s arrived high overhead and unleashed their payload—six hundred forty-eight tons of iron bombs.[40]

As soon as the strike ended, the Americans followed up with a ground attack. Experience had shown that the enemy regrouped quickly after a strike and disappeared even before the dust had cleared, so Emerson and Hackworth began sending companies into the bombing zone right away. Their quick action produced good results. The stunned North Vietnamese milled about, reeling from the detonations. One of Emerson's companies rounded up a group of twenty. Others offered little resistance; those who did were quickly dispatched. Based on helicopter surveys of the area and interrogation of twenty-two prisoners, Pearson and his staff concluded that the bombs had killed at least 200 of the enemy and perhaps as many as 250. The Americans suffered no casualties that day.[41]

The strike had devastated the *24th Regiment*. Aggressive in firefights with American units between 6 and 12 June, the enemy now began to avoid combat, and Hawthorne increasingly became a mopping-up operation. Emerson's and Hackworth's battalions patrolled the same general areas as they had before the strike. The American and South Vietnamese battalions of the blocking force also joined the hunt. The four-battalion task force searched for the better part of a week, yet found almost nothing. On the twentieth General Pearson terminated the operation and pulled his brigade back to Dak To 1.[42]

---

[39] AAR, Opn Hawthorne, 1st Bde, 101st Abn Div, p. 4; Pearson Statement, pp. 7–8, and AAR, Opn Hawthorne, 1st Bn, 327th Inf, pp. 5–6, Incls to Hawthorne Special Study.

[40] Critique, Opn Hawthorne, 1st Bde, 101st Abn Div, 30 Jun 66, pp. 6, 18, Historians files, CMH; AAR, Opn Hawthorne, 1st Bde, 101st Abn Div, p. 4.

[41] Statement of Maj Harold P. Austin, S–2 [Intel], 1st Bde, 101st Abn Div, pp. 3, 6, plus Pearson Statement, p. 8, and Historian's Narrative, "Battle of Tou Morong," p. 5, Incls to Hawthorne Special Study. See also Pearson, "Relief of an Outpost," p. 57, and Critique, Opn Hawthorne, 1st Bde, 101st Abn Div, pp. 6, 14.

[42] AAR, Opn Hawthorne, 1st Bde, 101st Abn Div, p. 4; Pearson Statement, p. 8, Incl to Hawthorne Special Study.

Enemy captives from Hawthorne *with Marshal Ky*

In all, Pearson's forces took credit for eliminating 479 of the enemy and the Air Force tallied another 52. The estimated number of enemy dead was much higher. The ground forces claimed another 506 and the Air Force 209. That amounted to a combined body count of 1,246. If true, those figures meant that the 2,000-man *24th Regiment* had lost as much as 60 percent of its strength, enough to render it ineffective as a fighting unit. According to Pearson's intelligence officer, the *24th* did not participate in a substantial operation for most of the next year. American casualties came to 48 killed and 239 wounded—25 of the dead from Major Hackworth's 1st of the 327th Infantry and 16 from Colonel Emerson's 2d of the 502d Infantry.[43]

General Pearson believed that his task force had not only thwarted the enemy's designs on Tou Morong but also prevented the North Vietnamese from achieving other objectives in Kontum Province. Westmoreland agreed. He called Hawthorne "a classic spoiling attack" and held it up as the model of a successful operation.[44]

---

[43] Historian's Narrative, "Battle of Tou Morong," pp. 5–6, and Austin Statement, p. 3, Incls to Hawthorne Special Study; AAR, Opn Hawthorne, 1st Bde, 101st Abn Div, pp. 4–6; ORLL, 1 May–31 Jul 66, 1st Bde, 101st Abn Div, 13 Aug 66, incl. 2, p. 1, Historians files, CMH.

[44] AAR, Opn Hawthorne, 1st Bde, 101st Abn Div, incl. 2, pp. 2–3; Sharp and Westmoreland, *Report*, p. 126 (quoted words).

Pleiku Battles—Paul Revere I

The centerpiece campaign in the highlands during the spring and summer took place not in Kontum but in Pleiku Province. And Operation Paul Revere, which started as a small offensive to blunt a sortie of the *1st PAVN Division* from its Cambodian strongholds, soon escalated into a major contest for the western plateau. The trip wire initially was the 3d Brigade, 25th Division, under General Walker. He stepped off the operation on 10 May in response to sightings west of Duc Co and Plei Me, sliding two of his battalions toward the border. For more than a week they operated southwest of the brigade forward at Oasis and found almost nothing. But when they shifted their attention to the west around the Chu Pong Massif, the action picked up almost immediately.[45]

On the morning of 24 May, operating about ten kilometers southwest of its camp at Plei Djereng, a CIDG patrol ran into an enemy force estimated at two battalions. Two CIDG companies reinforced the patrol, and together they fought throughout the day. Toward evening they broke contact and moved to higher ground for the night. The Communists followed, digging in about three hundred meters to the west. Before dawn the next morning they attacked. The CIDG companies and their American advisers pulled back to Plei Djereng, with the North Vietnamese right behind. Two Special Forces troopers and 18 Montagnards died in the running firefight. Enemy mortars pounded Plei Djereng throughout the morning, killing 30 and wounding 54.[46]

General Walker immediately dispatched Lt. Col. Phillip R. Feir's 2d Battalion, 35th Infantry, to relieve pressure on the camp. His men searched south of Plei Djereng for two days. On the twenty-seventh Colonel Feir moved his command post, with its attached artillery, almost twenty kilometers south of the camp to Landing Zone Eleven Alfa. The next day Company B flew to Landing Zone Ten Alfa, about ten kilometers west of the command post. Enemy bullets greeted the helicopters as they dropped into the clearing, forcing them out after only sixty-three soldiers had dismounted. Over the next several hours the stranded Americans beat off attacks, opening the way for the rest of Company B as well as Company A, 1st of the 35th Infantry, to land. By early evening three hundred Americans were on the ground at Ten Alfa.

The Communists were determined to break the American foothold. Just past midnight, on 29 May, the *66th PAVN Regiment* launched a multibattalion assault on Ten Alfa. After fierce fighting throughout the night, the *66th* was repulsed. An attack on Feir's command post at Eleven Alfa by part of the *33d PAVN Regiment* was also turned away. At 0615

---

[45] ORLL, 1 May–31 Jul 66, 3d Bde, 25th Inf Div, 15 Aug 66, p. 1, box 1, 82/584, RG 338, NARA.

[46] Ibid., p. 12; Op Sum, Opn Paul Revere, MACV, Jul 66, p. 3, Historians files, CMH.

the Americans ventured outside TEN ALFA. They found about 80 enemy dead.[47]

The interlude was brief. As the troops pressed outward, they encountered more fire and were pushed back to the landing zone. Mortar rounds rained down, and the North Vietnamese again assaulted TEN ALFA. Once more the Americans fought them off. The North Vietnamese returned at midmorning, closing at times to within twenty meters of the defenders before they were forced back. By late morning the battle was over. Walker quickly reinforced TEN ALFA with the remainder of the 1st of the 35th Infantry under Lt. Col. Robert C. Kingston. The enemy had paid dearly, losing approximately 250 in the fighting (*Map 23*).[48]

Encouraged by his victory, Walker ordered his brigade to search west and south of TEN ALFA. Colonel Berenzweig's 2d Brigade, 1st Cavalry Division, joined the operation on 1 June, sending two battalions northwest of Duc Co to the banks of the Se San. Although the Americans spent eight days hunting, they found no North Vietnamese. Once again the enemy had apparently reached the safety of Cambodia. On the tenth the brigade reverted to the 1st Cavalry Division for an operation elsewhere.[49]

General Walker's task force continued its mission around TEN and ELEVEN ALFA, but the enemy had left the area. On 17 June Walker turned his attention back to the Chu Pong Massif, but only twice did the brigade meet North Vietnamese. On the twentieth elements of Colonel Feir's 2d of the 35th Infantry were searching near the border about ten kilometers north of the Chu Pong. In the jungle ahead they spotted small groups of enemy soldiers and called in mortar and artillery fire. At 1500 the battalion reconnaissance platoon chased four North Vietnamese across an open area, only to be pinned down by heavy fire. Other troops from Feir's battalion and from Troop C, 3d Squadron, 4th Cavalry, rescued the platoon, but 3 of Feir's men lost their lives and 14 were wounded.[50]

Four days later, on 24 June, Colonel Kingston's 1st of the 35th Infantry, which had replaced Feir's weary battalion on the twenty-second, approached the Cambodian border. At 1030 the battalion reconnaissance platoon took fire from what appeared to be a reinforced battalion. Going to ground, the troops called in air strikes and gunships, which drove off the North Vietnamese. The Americans pursued, only to run into more

---

[47] Memos, Brig Gen Glenn D. Walker, CG, 3d Bde, 25th Inf Div, for HQ DA, 17 and 31 Aug 66, subs: Distinguished Unit Citation [Co B, 2d Bn, 35th Inf, and Co A, 1st Bn, 35th Inf], box 1, 82/643, RG 338, NARA.

[48] Msg, MACV to National Mil Cmd Center, 25 Jun 66, Historians files, CMH; Memos, Walker for HQ DA, 17 and 31 Aug 66, subs: Distinguished Unit Citation [Co B, 2d Bn, 35th Inf, and Co A, 1st Bn, 35th Inf]; ORLL, 1 May–31 Jul 66, 3d Bde, 25th Inf Div, p. 13.

[49] AAR, Opns PAUL REVERE and HOOKER I, 2d Bde, 1st Cav Div, 9 Jul 66, p. 13, Historians files, CMH.

[50] Op Sum, Opn PAUL REVERE, MACV, Jul 66, p. 6.

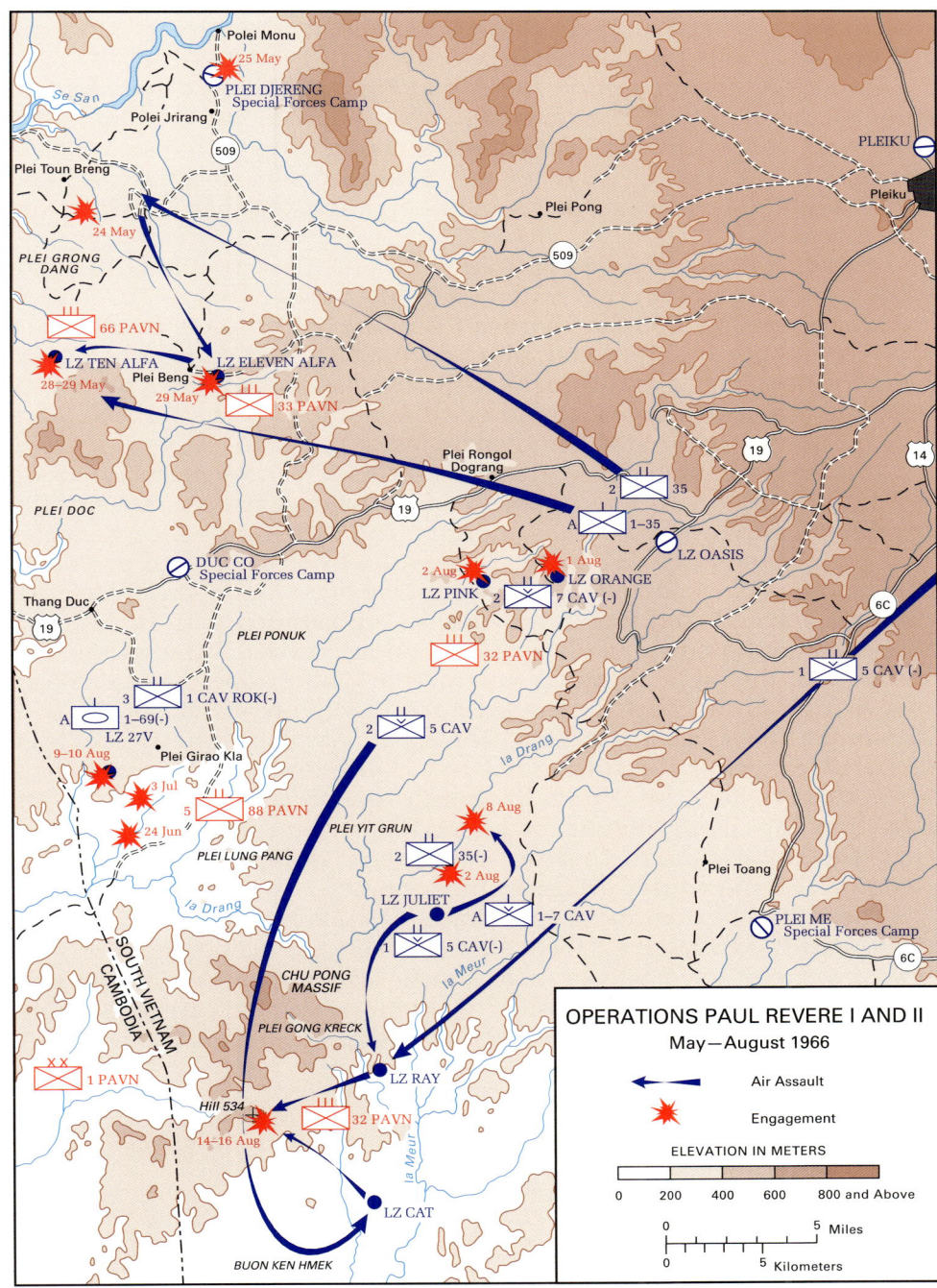

OPERATIONS PAUL REVERE I AND II
May–August 1966

Air Assault

Engagement

ELEVATION IN METERS

0   200   400   600   800 and Above

0   5   Miles

0   5   Kilometers

MAP 23

fire when they reached the border. Using what General Walker later described as a "suck-in tactic," the Communists had retreated to well-fortified positions from where they could fight the Americans.[51]

Colonel Kingston reinforced his platoon with the equivalent of two infantry companies and an armored cavalry troop, but the men made little headway. The North Vietnamese were fighting with their backs to the border, preventing encirclement. Kingston sent in air strikes and artillery, but the enemy stayed put until nightfall and then slipped away into Cambodia.[52]

Walker's men continued patrolling into the next month, with negligible results except for one action on 3 July. Colonel Kingston's battalion was operating along the border when one of Company B's platoons split in two to cover more territory. Each patrol had gone only a short distance when the North Vietnamese attacked and surrounded the southerly one. The platoon leader radioed the other for help, only to learn that it too was under attack and encircled.

Another Company B platoon and the brigade's armored cavalry troop went to the rescue. As they approached the beleaguered Americans, fire from small arms, machine guns, mortars, and rocket-propelled grenades opened up from three directions. The cavalry troop's armored personnel carriers moved ahead and, with the support of well-aimed artillery fire, punched through and linked up with the surrounded patrols. All units withdrew to the north, while artillery and air strikes pounded the area throughout the night. A sweep through the killing zone the next morning, 4 July, found that the enemy force, later identified as the *66th Regiment's 7th Battalion*, was gone. The North Vietnamese had lost at least 23 killed. American casualties came to 17 killed and 32 wounded.[53]

Five days later, on 9 July, the South Korean Capital Division's 3d Battalion, 1st Cavalry Regiment, joined Paul Revere, but it had less luck than the Americans in finding someone to fight. Walker's brigade remained on the border until the thirty-first.[54]

The situation was about to change. As July ended, intelligence reports indicated that the North Vietnamese were using the monsoon season's cloud cover and rains to shuffle old units and infiltrate new ones into South Vietnam. A North Vietnamese soldier, captured on the twenty-ninth, reported that his own regiment, the *66th*, was ensconced

[51] ORLL, 1 May–31 Jul 66, 3d Bde, 25th Inf Div, p. 16; MFR, MACV MACJ00, 17 Aug 66, sub: MACV Commanders' Conference, 24 July 1966, p. 26 (quoted words), Westmoreland History files, CMH.

[52] MFR, MACV MACJ00, 17 Aug 66, sub: MACV Commanders' Conference, 24 July 1966, p. 25; ORLL, 1 May–31 Jul 66, I FFV, 25 Aug 66, p. 9, Historians files, CMH; ORLL, 1 May–31 Jul 66, 3d Bde, 25th Inf Div, pp. 16–17; Op Sum, Opn Paul Revere, MACV, Jul 66, p. 6.

[53] *Western Highlands*, p. 49, copy in CMH; Op Sum, Opn Paul Revere, MACV, Jul 66, p. 7; ORLL, 1 May–31 Jul 66, 3d Bde, 25th Inf Div, p. 18.

[54] MACV History, 1966, p. 376, CMH.

about four kilometers east of the border on the northern slopes of the Chu Pong Massif and that a sister regiment, the *32d*, was about ten kilometers southwest of Oasis. General Larsen wasted no time. Concentrating infantry, armor, and the Koreans north and northeast of the massif, he enlarged General Walker's task force to six battalions by giving him control over the I Field Force reserve—Lt. Col. William M. Vaughn's 2d Battalion, 7th Cavalry—on the thirtieth. The next day Colonel Vaughn's Companies A and B air-assaulted to Landing Zone Orange, some seven kilometers southwest of Oasis, and began to search.[55]

The North Vietnamese found Vaughn first. Just after daybreak on 1 August mortars and grenades rained down on his command post at Orange, followed by three battalion-size ground attacks. The American perimeter held, aided by air strikes and an Air Force gunship. Confronted by the Spooky's wall of fire, the North Vietnamese withdrew to the northwest. They had killed 5 Americans and wounded 40 others, including Vaughn, who had to be replaced by the 1st Cavalry Division inspector general, Lt. Col. Robert D. Stevenson. After the battle, an American patrol found the bodies of 28 North Vietnamese dead and twelve weapons. Documents on the bodies indicated that the soldiers were from the *32d Regiment*.[56]

Paul Revere II

It now appeared that the enemy had begun a major offensive west of Pleiku City. The 1st Battalion, 69th Armor, under the command of Lt. Col. Ronald J. Fairfield, reported unusually heavy civilian traffic crossing Highway 19 from south to north, a good indicator of hostile activity. The Special Forces camp at Duc Co also reported a number of sightings of and encounters with enemy units. In response, General Larsen instructed General Norton to deploy his 3d Brigade to the battle area. That brigade, under Colonel Daniel, became part of the newly formed Task Force Walker. Three battalions came under Daniel's control: Colonel Markham's 1st Battalion, 7th Cavalry; Colonel Stevenson's 2d Battalion, 7th Cavalry; and Colonel Root's 1st Battalion, 12th Cavalry. At that point, Walker's two-brigade force contained eight battalions—seven infantry (six American, one South Korean) and one armor.[57]

Task Force Walker deployed from Oasis on 2 August, moving west toward the Cambodian border. Walker's battalions worked to the south-

---

[55] Westmoreland Jnl, 10 Aug 66, Westmoreland History files, CMH; ORLL, 1 May–31 Jul 66, 3d Bde, 25th Inf Div, p. 19. See also CHECO Rpt, PACAF, 27 Jul 67, sub: Operation Paul Revere/Sam Houston, p. 12; AAR, Opn Paul Revere II, 3d Bde, 25th Inf Div, 10 Sep 66, p. 4; and Annual Hist Sum, 1966, 2d Bn, 7th Cav. All in Historians files, CMH.

[56] AAR, Opn Paul Revere II, 3d Bde, 25th Inf Div, p. 9.

[57] Ibid., pp. 4, 10.

west and west, while Daniel's battalions hunted around the base camp. Fighting broke out almost immediately. Patrolling some fourteen kilometers west of Plei Me, Company A, 2d of the 35th Infantry, and elements from the battalion reconnaissance platoon encountered three North Vietnamese soldiers, killing 1 and pursuing the others to the northeast. Advancing thirteen hundred meters, they killed the second soldier and pressed on after the third. Around noon the odds changed. Suddenly the Americans found themselves up against a well-entrenched main force battalion, which was firing at them from all sides. Both the company commander and his first sergeant were killed, but the troops quickly returned fire and called in artillery, air strikes, and gunships. As the enemy took cover under the aerial onslaught, the Americans withdrew to the west. By midafternoon the North Vietnamese had all but disappeared.

But the battle was not over. After moving about nine hundred meters, the Americans established a perimeter in a clearing, and Company C, 2d of the 35th, joined them at dusk. They were just settling in when the North Vietnamese, now regrouped, began mortaring the laager. Forty minutes later the Americans heard them screaming and shouting, perhaps to nerve themselves for an attack. If that was their plan, they never got the chance because the noise gave away their positions, and artillery and air strikes soon found them. By morning the enemy regulars were gone.[58]

A second encounter on 2 August brought far different results. Early in the afternoon, following extensive air and artillery preparation, the 3d Platoon, Company A, from Colonel Stevenson's 2d of the 7th Cavalry, air-assaulted to Landing Zone PINK about four kilometers west of ORANGE. The move seemed routine and unopposed at first, but a reinforced company was concealed just beyond the ring of American fire. Maintaining impressive fire discipline, the North Vietnamese waited until the entire twenty-seven-man platoon was on the ground before attacking. Radio contact ended abruptly, and the company commander feared the worst. Helicopters lifted another Company A platoon to PINK an hour later in an attempt to reinforce, but heavy rain made it impossible to land. In the meantime, Colonel Daniel directed the commander of the 1st of the 12th Cavalry, Colonel Root, to move his Company B overland to the fight. Trekking in the heavy rain and slowed by thick mud, dense brush, and the possibility of an ambush, the company took more than three hours to march five kilometers. By then the rain had abated, permitting the remainder of Stevenson's Company A to land by helicopter just to the north.[59]

---

[58] Ibid., p. 10.

[59] Ibid., p. 11; ORLL, 1 May–31 Jul 66, 3d Bde, 25th Inf Div, p. 11; ORLL, 1 Aug–31 Oct 66, I FFV, 30 Nov 66, pp. 1, 18, box 3, 73A/3330, RG 338, NARA. See also Rpt, 14th Mil Hist Det, 1st Cav Div (Ambl), 7 Mar 67, sub: Seven Month History and Briefing Data (April–October 1966), p. 26; AAR, Opn PAUL REVERE II, 3d Bde, 1st Cav Div (Ambl), 5 Nov 66, p. 10. Both in Historians files, CMH.

Arriving around 1800, Colonel Root assumed command of U.S. forces on the scene, but he was too late. All was quiet; the Communists had gone. Later in the evening Colonel Stevenson's men found only a few survivors from the 3d Platoon. Too far apart to form a single perimeter, Companies A and B bedded down in separate positions north and south of the landing zone, but they kept in radio contact, relying on fire support for protection whenever the enemy probed them.

The next morning the two companies met with no resistance during a search of the area, an indication that the nighttime probes had probably been an effort by stay-behind forces to cover the withdrawal of a larger unit. The search revealed that the North Vietnamese had killed 18 Americans and wounded 6 at a cost of 12 of their own. Twenty of the 3d Platoon's weapons were missing, as were two radios. Two troopers and a South Vietnamese interpreter had come through unscathed.[60]

Although American commanders still had no clear picture of the Communists' intentions in western Pleiku Province, they had begun to identify North Vietnamese units in the area and to speculate on why they seemed so willing to stand and fight, if only temporarily. They knew, in addition to the *32d Regiment*, elements of which American units had encountered on 1 August, that the *33d* and *66th Regiments* were nearby and that the *88th Regiment* seemed to be standing in reserve in Cambodia. All of this led them to conclude that the North Vietnamese were planning attacks on the Special Forces camps at Duc Co and Plei Me, and perhaps even Pleiku City. But intelligence analysts differed as to the significance of the effort. Some contended that North Vietnamese commanders were desperate for a monsoon season victory; others argued that by mounting a new offensive in the highlands they hoped to draw U.S. forces away from Tuy Hoa and eastern Binh Dinh Province so that the Viet Cong could secure the critically important coastal rice harvest. A third hypothesis was that they planned to score a "major victory" in order to disrupt the South Vietnamese national elections in September.[61]

Whatever the Communists' motives, the buildup of the main forces in the highlands prompted General Larsen to make an important decision. Postponing the airmobile division's next operation on the coast, he reconfigured Paul Revere II as a 1st Cavalry Division operation. Effective at 1830 on 2 August, Task Force Walker was dissolved, and General Norton assumed control of both Colonel Daniel's 3d Brigade and General Walker's 3d Brigade, 25th Division.[62]

---

[60] AAR, Opn Paul Revere II, 3d Bde, 1st Cav Div, pp. 3, 10. For additional detail see ORLL, 1 Aug–31 Oct 66, I FFV, p. 18; Annual Hist Sum, 1966, 2d Bn, 7th Cav; ORLL, 1 May–31 Jul 66, 3d Bde, 25th Inf Div, p. 11; and AAR, Opn Paul Revere II, 1st Cav Div (Ambl), 25 Jan 67, p. 12, Historians files, CMH.

[61] AARs, Opn Paul Revere II, 3d Bde, 25th Inf Div, p. 4, and 1st Cav Div, pp. 5–6, 31 (quoted words); Rpt, 14th Mil Hist Det, 1st Cav Div, 7 Mar 67, sub: Seven Month History and Briefing Data (April–October 1966), p. 105.

[62] AAR, Opn Paul Revere II, 1st Cav Div, p. 11.

At first General Norton intended "to drive the two brigades down through the Ia Drang Valley," but bad weather hampered logistics and forced him to rethink the idea. In the end, "we simply followed our instincts to pursue contacts wherever we had them." Each of the two brigades was to search in carefully defined sectors in an area that extended north from the northern foothills of the Chu Pong Massif to Duc Co, west to the Cambodian border, and east to a line running south from Oasis. Walker would hunt to the west and south, while Daniel would operate in the northeast.[63]

Then new intelligence forced another modification. It now seemed more likely that the North Vietnamese would avoid combat and retreat toward Cambodia through the Ia Drang Valley and the Chu Pong Massif. Accordingly, General Norton decided that the time had come to bring a third brigade—Colonel Berenzweig's 2d of the 1st Cavalry Division—into the operation and to spread it around the massif in case enemy units were indeed withdrawing deeper into the mountains.[64]

The soundness of Norton's decision became apparent on 8 August, when the expanded search netted a main force unit. Early in the morning Berenzweig's two battalions—Colonel Markham's 1st of the 7th Cavalry and Colonel Lynn's 2d of the 12th Cavalry—deployed north and south of the massif. From Landing Zone Juliet Capt. Robert A. Wands' Company A, 1st of the 7th, began a probe just south of the Ia Drang. Following a trail near a supposedly abandoned enemy bunker complex, the lead platoon surprised a group of North Vietnamese soldiers, killing 3. The Americans pursued the survivors, but then ran into machine gun fire. Cut off from the rest of the company, the patrol fought its way back to safety, but the North Vietnamese—later identified as belonging to the *4th Battalion, 32d Regiment*—were close behind. They struck Wands' position with a human wave attack, threatening to overrun it. Wands was wounded in the fighting and had to be replaced by his executive officer, although before he went down he managed to call in fire support and reinforcements. Artillery fire poured in from Juliet, followed by fighter-bombers and gunships. They saved the day. By midafternoon, faced with a rain of steel, the enemy had withdrawn.[65]

Scouring the battlefield, the Americans found 15 enemy bodies. By the time the brigade, division, and field force headquarters had added their own estimates, the count had risen to 98. Whatever the actual figure, Wands' company paid a steep price—25 dead and 36 wounded.[66]

---

[63] Ibid.; MFR, MACV MACJ00, 3 Oct 66, sub: MACV Commanders' Conference, 28 August 1966, p. 41 (quotations), Westmoreland History files, CMH.

[64] AAR, Opn Paul Revere II, 2d Bde, 1st Cav Div (Ambl), 5 Sep 66, p. 4, Historians files, CMH.

[65] Ibid., p. 11; Annual Hist Sum, 1966, 1st Bn, 7th Cav, n.d., p. 23, and Op Sum, Opn Paul Revere II, MACV, Aug 66, pp. 1–2, Historians files, CMH; AAR, Opn Paul Revere II, 1st Cav Div, p. 14.

[66] AARs, Opn Paul Revere II, 1st Cav Div, p. 14, and 2d Bde, 1st Cav Div, p. 4; AAR, Opn Paul Revere II, 1st Bn, 7th Cav, 8 Sep 66, p. [3], Historians files, CMH; ORLL, 1

Although reinforcements arrived too late to help, they were not too late to pursue the withdrawing Communists. Two companies of Colonel Lynn's 2d of the 12th Cavalry were at the time in flight to a landing zone south of the massif. Diverted northward to relieve Wands, they landed near his perimeter on the afternoon of the eighth, where they came under Colonel Markham's control. About an hour later they were joined by two companies of Markham's 1st of the 7th Cavalry, and the chase was on. Artillery fired along likely escape routes, the rest of the 2d of the 12th blocked to the north, and 1st of the 9th Cavalry helicopters reconnoitered to the northeast, east, and southeast. But none of this had much effect. As darkness approached, Markham called off the pursuit and pulled his force into

South Korean soldiers on patrol

Wands' original position. The next day Markham's men continued the sweep, but the enemy was gone.[67]

On 9 August the North Vietnamese decided to fight again, this time in a different area against the South Korean 3d Battalion, 1st Cavalry Regiment. Having joined PAUL REVERE I a month earlier, the Koreans had established defensive positions just north of the massif. Under the operational control of the 3d Brigade, 25th Division, they had mounted almost daily patrols, but with no significant results. The battalion now occupied a position immediately to the east of the hamlet of Plei Girao Kla, about eight kilometers south of Duc Co. Its 9th Company was located about three kilometers farther to the southwest at Landing Zone 27V, only six kilometers from the Cambodian border, where it had been since 27 July. Each week the company had controlled a different tank platoon from the U.S. 1st of the 69th Armor. During the week

Aug–31 Oct 66, I FFV, p. 18; Rpt, 14th Mil Hist Det, 1st Cav Div, 7 Mar 67, sub: Seven Month History and Briefing Data (April–October 1966), p. 107; Annual Hist Sum, 1966, 1st Bn, 7th Cav, p. 24.

[67] Annual Hist Sum, 1966, 1st Bn, 7th Cav, p. 24; ORLL, 1 Aug–31 Oct 66, I FFV, p. 18; AARs, Opn PAUL REVERE II, 1st Bn, 7th Cav, p. [3], and 2d Bde, 1st Cav Div, pp. 11–12 and an. A.

beginning 5 August the 1st Platoon, Company A, was the one at hand.[68]

Roughly oblong in shape and surrounded by a trench two feet deep, Landing Zone 27V extended two hundred meters east–west and one hundred seventy meters north–south. The South Koreans had laid concertina wire some twenty meters outside of the trench line. Beyond that were trip flares and claymore mines. Interspersed among covered machine gun emplacements and trenches for the riflemen were the tank platoon's five M48A3 Pattons.[69]

The South Korean company had just returned from a two-day mission near the border. Before sunset on the ninth the company commander set up three listening posts about two hundred meters beyond the perimeter and, following standard Korean practice, placed 50 percent of the men inside the main laager on alert. Unlike the other nights, this one would not be quiet.

About an hour before midnight the southwest listening post reported sounds of digging. Five minutes later someone tripped a flare on the western side of the perimeter. Certain that an attack was in the offing, the company commander ordered all three listening posts inside the laager. The digging continued. One of the Pattons turned its searchlight on the noise and cut loose with one of its machine guns. Enemy soldiers in a tree line to the south fired back immediately, followed by mortars from the northwest. Three Americans outside their vehicles, including the platoon commander, were slightly wounded, but all reached their tanks safely. By now the defenders were on full alert.

As enemy fire increased, three Pattons sent antipersonnel rounds into the tree line to the south and the other two fired to the southwest. Two tanks were outfitted with searchlights, but during the night both searchlights were knocked out. For the rest of the night, artillery flares and Air Force flare ships provided illumination. Still, the attack intensified, prompting the South Korean company commander to call in fire support from his parent battalion nearby and from American batteries at Duc Co. One battery laid down fire within fifty meters of the allied position, another fired along the northern flank, a third aimed at the southern flank, and a fourth created a ring of fire about one kilometer beyond the perimeter. The 9th Company's own mortars concentrated their fire to the north.[70]

By 0130, 10 August, enemy fire had slowed, but the North Vietnamese were not finished. After a half-hour lull they attacked from the west, charg-

[68] AAR, Battle of 27V, 9–10 Aug 66, 1st Bn, 69th Armor, 8 Sep 66, p. 1, box 2, 81/376, RG 338, NARA.

[69] Memo, Brig Gen Glenn D. Walker, CG, 3d Bde, 25th Inf Div, for HQ DA, 3 Sep 66, sub: Distinguished Unit Citation [for South Korean 3d Bn, 1st Cav Regt], 3d Brigade Task Force, 25th Infantry Division, p. 1, box 1, 82/643, RG 338, NARA.

[70] Ibid., p. 2; AAR, Battle of 27V, 9–10 Aug 66, 1st Bn, 69th Armor, p. 2; ORLL, 1 May–31 Jul 66, 3d Bde, 25th Inf Div, p. 13.

ing to within fifty meters of the laager before being driven back by withering fire from the American tanks and South Korean machine guns. Over the next two hours they mounted two more assaults, this time from the north and south. A few of them came to within five meters of the allied position, and one actually penetrated the defensive wire before being bayoneted, but most were cut down or fell back. By 0600 the firing trailed off and then ceased altogether. When a combined American and South Korean tank-infantry team swept beyond the perimeter soon afterward, it encountered several wounded soldiers who fought to the end.[71]

The battle was a clear victory for firepower. Artillery from American and South Korean bases fired nearly nineteen hundred high-explosive rounds. Inside the laager the South Koreans expended fifteen hundred mortar rounds; the American tanks, twenty-four high-explosive and thirty-three 90-mm. canister rounds and nearly seventeen thousand machine gun rounds. All this resulted in at least 197 North Vietnamese killed, most from the *88th Regiment's 5th Battalion*. The South Koreans lost 7 men, the Americans none. Intelligence analysts later speculated that the assault might have been a diversionary move to distract attention from units escaping through the Ia Drang Valley–Chu Pong area.[72]

While the fighting at Landing Zone 27V was running its course, the rest of General Norton's force continued to search western Pleiku Province. Walker's 3d Brigade operated in the Duc Co area, Daniel's 3d Brigade patrolled in the Ia Drang Valley, and Berenzweig's 2d Brigade campaigned in the mountains and valleys south of the Chu Pong Massif. Although these units failed to find the enemy, interrogations of North Vietnamese prisoners and current intelligence seemed to suggest that Berenzweig's sector, south of the massif, held the most promise. Enemy units seeking to escape into Cambodia would have to pass through the area to reach the border.[73]

On 10 August Colonel Siegrist's 1st of the 5th Cavalry deployed from Juliet and the Turkey Farm to Landing Zone Ray, east of the massif, as a blocking force. The next day Colonel Lombard's 2d of the 5th Cavalry moved southeast of the massif to Landing Zone Cat, where Colonel Berenzweig located his command post. The two battalions searched the area over the next three days. When they began to encounter small groups of enemy soldiers moving toward Cambodia, U.S. commanders concluded that the North Vietnamese were indeed using the region as a thoroughfare. In one clash on the eleventh the Americans killed 9 soldiers from the

---

[71] [Unit History], 8 Mar 66–10 Apr 70, 1st Bn, 69th Armor, n.d., p. 13, box 2, 81/376, RG 338, NARA; Memo, Walker for HQ DA, 3 Sep 66, sub: Distinguished Unit Citation [for South Korean 3d Bn, 1st Cav Regt], 3d Brigade Task Force, 25th Infantry Division, p. 3; Op Sum, Opn Paul Revere II, MACV, Aug 66, p. 2.

[72] AAR, Battle of 27V, 9–10 Aug 66, 1st Bn, 69th Armor, incl. 2, p. 1; ORLL, 1 May–31 Jul 66, 3d Bde, 25th Inf Div, p. 14; AAR, Opn Paul Revere II, 3d Bde, 25th Inf Div, pp. 5, 14.

[73] AAR, Opn Paul Revere II, 1st Cav Div, p. 14.

66th Regiment and captured 2 others. Over the next two days they encountered several smaller groups; some fled, while others fought. Most of the soldiers who were captured belonged to the *32d Regiment*. One said that he and his comrades had not eaten in three days and that the *32d* was heading southwest toward a resupply base, a course that would carry the regiment directly through the 2d Brigade's sector.[74]

On 14 August Colonel Berenzweig's two battalions searched near Hill 534, on the southern slopes of the Chu Pong Massif about four kilometers from Cambodia. The hill became the reference point for much of the action over the next two days. Siegrist's 1st of the 5th Cavalry patrolled to its north; most of Lombard's 2d of the 5th Cavalry hunted to the southeast. Meanwhile, from a position named GEORGE about twenty-five hundred meters west of Hill 534, Capt. George D. Shea's Company A, 1st of the 5th, conducted a slow and cautious search eastward along a footpath through a valley north of the hill. Shea's men found a communications wire and followed it. They surprised a group of fifteen North Vietnamese soldiers, killing 2 and capturing 1 while the rest fled.[75]

The company continued along the footpath. At 1305 that afternoon, just before the path made a sharp turn to the north, the Americans ran headlong into what seemed to be a North Vietnamese company that opened fire from dug-in positions. Captain Shea called in artillery and air strikes and then pulled back. Shortly before 1500 he again met an enemy unit and called in more artillery and air support.[76]

A larger fight was brewing. Colonel Berenzweig had ordered Capt. William E. Taylor's Company B, 2d of the 5th Cavalry, searching two kilometers southeast of Shea, to move overland to reinforce the beleaguered company. After marching fifteen hundred meters to within a kilometer south of Shea, the unit stalled when it met an enemy force in a complex of well-camouflaged bunkers. Taylor called in air strikes and then moved his men into a perimeter. With evening approaching and the chance of linking up with Taylor before nightfall pretty slim, Shea also coiled in place. Throughout the night, air strikes and artillery protected the friendly laagers.[77]

The cavalry division had walked into a tempest. Although the size of the enemy force was not known at the time, it seemed large enough by the end of the day to justify a major American effort. Colonel Berenzweig decided to reposition his forces. Siegrist's battalion reserve, Capt. Donald

---

[74] AAR, Opn PAUL REVERE II, 2d Bde, 1st Cav Div, pp. 4–5; Annual Hist Sum, 1966, 1st Bn, 5th Cav, n.d., box 1, 82/899, RG 338, NARA.

[75] AARs, Opn PAUL REVERE II, 1st Cav Div, p. 17, and 2d Bde, 1st Cav Div, p. 14; AAR, Opn PAUL REVERE II, 1st Bn, 5th Cav, 26 Aug 66, p. [6], Historians files, CMH.

[76] AARs, Opn PAUL REVERE II, 1st Cav Div, p. 16, 1st Bn, 5th Cav, an. A, and 2d Bde, 1st Cav Div, p. 5.

[77] Edward Hymoff, *The First Air Cavalry Division, Vietnam* (New York: M. W. Lads Publishing Co., 1967), p. 97; AARs, Opn PAUL REVERE II, 1st Cav Div, p. 17, and 1st Bn, 5th Cav, p. [6].

R. Sims' Company C, 1st of the 5th Cavalry, moved fifteen hundred meters northeast of Hill 534; Colonel Lynn's 2d of the 12th Cavalry placed its Company C seven kilometers northwest of the hill. As these units completed their moves, Company A of Colonel Lombard's 2d of the 5th Cavalry, reinforced by the battalion reconnaissance platoon, formed a blocking force thirty-five hundred and fifty-five hundred meters southwest of 534, sealing off escape routes into Cambodia. Hopefully, firepower raining down on the North Vietnamese during the night would keep them in place until the Americans could attack the next day. If the North Vietnamese somehow eluded the encirclement and withdrew to the west toward Cambodia, they would still have to pass through or around the forces that stood between them and the border.[78]

When the fighting began the next day, 15 August, units under Siegrist's control met the enemy three times. The first to fight was Captain Taylor's Company B, 2d of the 5th. Moving from their overnight position to begin the hunt, the troops were pelted by mortar rounds around 0800 and then assaulted from the north and west. Taylor pulled his men back and called for fire support. He was on the radio when a mortar round burst nearby, killing him, his radio operator, and his first sergeant. An enlisted man picked up the radio and relayed orders and suggestions to platoon leaders from Lombard's operations officer, Maj. Wesley G. Jones. As the attack continued, the Americans began to run dangerously low on ammunition. Responding to pleas for more, two helicopters crisscrossed the jungle before finding the company and delivering what was needed.[79]

About an hour after Company B had started its fight, Captain Shea's company was also hit. While operating about five hundred meters northeast of Hill 534, his men began to receive heavy automatic weapons fire. Over the next two hours the two sides exchanged fire, but neither could gain an advantage over the other. Later in the morning the enemy pulled back.[80]

Fighting broke out at yet a third spot toward midafternoon. Colonel Siegrist had ordered Captain Sims' Company C to move southwest to relieve Company B. The platoons were closing in on the perimeter when machine gun fire forced them to take cover. With one platoon pinned down, Sims called in artillery fire and an air strike. Bombs landed between the two companies, forcing the enemy to withdraw and allowing the Americans to link up.[81]

At that point, Colonel Berenzweig threw another company into the fight, placing Company C, 2d of the 5th, under Siegrist. With the initial

---

[78] AARs, Opn PAUL REVERE II, 1st Cav Div, p. 5, 1st Bn, 5th Cav, an. A, and 2d Bde, 1st Cav Div, p. 14.

[79] AARs, Opn PAUL REVERE II, 2d Bde, 1st Cav Div, pp. 5, 15, and 1st Bn, 5th Cav, pp. [2–3], [6–7], and an. A; Hymoff, *First Air Cavalry Division*, pp. 98–99.

[80] AAR, Opn PAUL REVERE II, 1st Bn, 5th Cav, p. [6].

[81] Ibid., p. [2].

mission of assisting the reinforcement of Company B, the unit helicoptered to the western slopes of Hill 534 and pushed eastward. By late afternoon Siegrist had four companies on the slopes. The next morning, assuming that the enemy was still lurking around, the Americans launched a coordinated sweep of the area. Paced by artillery fire and air strikes and wielding flamethrowers and tear gas grenades, Siegrist's men moved methodically up Hill 534 from the south and then down the other side. They found nothing. Those North Vietnamese who had survived the fight had withdrawn in the night.

In policing the battlefield over the next two days, the troops uncovered living quarters, messing facilities, documents, graves, and scores of unburied bodies. The communications gear they found indicated the presence of at least a battalion and probably a regimental headquarters. Counting 126 enemy dead, they estimated that they had killed another 300, basing that judgment on "the volume of fire" U.S. forces had brought to bear. By comparison, 23 Americans died in the action and 27 more had been wounded. Colonel Berenzweig concluded that he and his men had disrupted an important way station that had been responsible for resting and refitting North Vietnamese forces for some time.[82]

Prisoner interrogations later revealed that Colonel Siegrist's force had fought all three battalions of the *32d Regiment*. Although there was no way to prove it at the time, Siegrist and the other American commanders believed that they had rendered the three units ineffective. Even so, Siegrist was convinced that no matter how much the Americans hurt the enemy, he would return to his old haunts as soon as they departed. To take advantage of this habit, he recommended a B–52 strike within forty days on a three- by one-kilometer rectangle, with Hill 534 at its center.[83]

While the action at Hill 534 progressed, Walker's brigade continued to search the northern sector, primarily to the west and south of Duc Co, and Daniel's brigade to the south in the Ia Drang Valley. Neither achieved significant results, though there was a modest battle on 17 August. Two companies, one from the 1st of the 69th Armor and the other from the 2d of the 35th Infantry, responded to an attack on CIDG elements west of Duc Co near Highway 19. The appearance of the tank-infantry force scattered the enemy.[84]

The dwindling number of sightings and clashes suggested that the North Vietnamese had withdrawn to their Cambodian sanctuaries. With no one to fight, General Norton saw no reason to keep a division-size force in the area. PAUL REVERE II began to wind down on 22 August, be-

---

[82] AARs, Opn PAUL REVERE II, 1st Cav Div, p. 18 (quoted words), 1st Bn, 5th Cav, p. [2], and 2d Bde, 1st Cav Div, p. 27.

[83] AAR, Opn PAUL REVERE II, 1st Bn, 5th Cav, pp. [6–8], [10–11]. See also AAR, Opn PAUL REVERE IV, 2d Bde, 1st Cav Div (Ambl), 25 Jan 67, p. 4, Historians files, CMH.

[84] AAR, Opn PAUL REVERE II, 1st Cav Div, pp. 20–21; ORLL, 1 Aug–31 Oct 66, I FFV, p. 19.

ginning with the withdrawal of the South Korean battalion. Three days later the cavalry units returned to An Khe or deployed elsewhere, and the operation came to an end.

In Norton's opinion, the three- to five-thousand soldiers committed by the *1st PAVN Division* had presented one of the finest targets that American forces had yet to find on the South Vietnamese battlefield. If the weather had been better, he asserted, the body count would have doubled. As it was, he felt that by killing 861 of the enemy with a loss of 90 Americans and 7 South Koreans, his forces had reduced the North Vietnamese to marginal effectiveness and had forced them back into Cambodia. The "marriage of the helicopter to conventional ground capabilities," he concluded, had allowed his division "to mass quickly when the enemy massed, to defeat his forces, and to conduct the pursuit of fleeing groups with devastating results."[85]

Norton's main criticism was that the reaction forces did too little when it came to hitting the enemy. A firm believer in the pile-on concept, he felt that too often his subordinate commanders were content with simply relieving pressure on beleaguered friendly units. "I know that's a big part of it," he said. "But we have reaction forces to exploit, cut off, chop-up, that's what I want to hear about. . . . When they [the Communists] concentrate, let's make the most of it. All of our reaction forces must be used with the consideration of being decisive." Still, Norton believed that overall, "we did damn well."[86]

---

[85] Critique, Opn Paul Revere II, 1st Cav Div (Ambl), 25 Oct 66, p. 8, Historians files, CMH; AAR, Opn Paul Revere II, 1st Cav Div, pp. 24–25, 31 (quotations).

[86] Critique, Opn Paul Revere II, 1st Cav Div, p. 8.

14

The 1st Division's War

While General Norton had been working out the architecture of air-mobile pursuit on the western border, General DePuy had been shaping the battle north of Saigon. For two years he had served at MACV headquarters as Westmoreland's operations officer and trusted confidant, shared with his chief a common view of the nature of the war, and was now prepared, given the limitations on the amount of infantry available in III Corps, to test new ways to step up his 1st Division's tempo. He explained his credo some months later after repeatedly grappling with his resources problem and the *B2 Front*, and it was not traditional U.S. Army maneuver warfare. "Find the enemy with the fewest possible men," he was quoted in a news magazine, "and . . . destroy him with the maximum amount of firepower."[1]

It would not be easy. Not until June would another corps-level battalion of artillery arrive in III Corps to augment his firepower, and no additional helicopters would be forthcoming until July. He could call on the 173d Airborne Brigade to help find and fix the Viet Cong, but that unit was busy with its own personnel issues as the 1st Battalion, Royal Australian Regiment, returned home at the end of June, replaced by the inexperienced 4th Battalion (Airborne), 503d Infantry.

While contending with these issues, General DePuy also faced an adversary of unusual tenacity, one who held his own controversial views on how best to conduct the war. General Thanh, as commander of *COSVN* and the *B2 Front*, had not been shy in advocating attrition and the big unit war. Even after the arrival of the American divisions, which had increased his casualties, he had pressed his views on Hanoi and won its support.

Thanh's troop lists had lengthened significantly as the year wore on. Besides his premier fighting unit, the *9th PLAF Division*, north of Saigon and the *5th PLAF Division* somewhere off to the east, the *7th PAVN Division* had recently infiltrated from North Vietnam while an elite phalanx, the *70th Guard Regiment*, now protected *COSVN* headquarters. All this was reinforced by the *U80 PLAF Artillery Regiment* with five battalions,

---

[1] *Newsweek*, 5 Dec 66, p. 53.

three in Tay Ninh Province and one each in Binh Long and Phuoc Tuy. On paper at least, given the battle strengths of the two opponents, General Thanh seemed more likely to go on the offensive than General DePuy.[2]

Toward the Rainy Season

In fact, General Westmoreland was betting on an offensive. Although he predicted that the main Communist effort would come in the highlands as the monsoons took hold, he also expected a fresh wave of attacks to the north and east of Saigon. Already, there were signs that supplies had been prepositioned during the dry winter months in preparation for battle. The only question to be settled at MACV and II Field Force headquarters was whether General Thanh would strike in May or during the summer.[3]

To counter the assaults in III Corps, General Seaman launched DePuy's 1st Division on a preemptive campaign. The first operation, ABILENE, took the hunt into Phuoc Tuy Province. DePuy's mission was to destroy prowling elements of the *274th* and *275th PLAF Regiments, 5th Division*, as well as any other forces encountered, along with their base camps and the May Tao Secret Zone off to the east. DePuy's 2d and 3d Brigades conducted the operation, along with the 1st Battalion, Royal Australian Regiment. For sixteen days, beginning on 29 March, they crisscrossed Phuoc Tuy in search of the Viet Cong but made only isolated contacts. The one exception was a fierce fight between soldiers from the 2d Battalion, 16th Infantry, and the *D800 Battalion* on the morning of 11 April. The Americans killed 41 of the enemy by body count and possibly 50 more. But the cost had been heavy: 35 Americans died during the close-quarter fighting, in part because effective firepower could not be brought to bear.[4]

Next the 1st Division turned to the mangrove swamps southeast of Saigon, the Rung Sat Special Zone. This dense tangle, although virtu-

[2] Monthly OB Sums, CICV, 16–31 Mar 66, ch. 4, p. 7, May 66, ch. 4, p. 8, and Jul 66, ch. 4, pp. 22–23, and Pringle, "NVA Strategy in the South," an. A, p. 8, Historians files, CMH; Intel Estimate no. 2, II FFV, 30 Nov 66, p. 16, box 2, 69A/729, RG 338, NARA; Periodic Intel Rpt, 1 Jul–31 Dec 66, MACV, 20 Jan 67, p. 35 and an. A, pp. 4, 11–12, MHI; *People's Army of Vietnam*, 2(bk.I,ch.3):54, copy in CMH.

[3] Monthly Eval Rpt, MACV, May 66, p. 2, MHI; Msg, Westmoreland MAC 4612 to Sharp, 5 Jun 66, Westmoreland Message files, CMH; II FFV, "Campaign Plan for the Southwest Monsoon Season, 1966, in III CTZ," 12 May 66, pp. 2–3, box 1, 69A/7350, RG 338, NARA.

[4] AAR, Opn ABILENE, 1st Inf Div, n.d., pp. 17–18, Historians files, CMH; AAR, Opn ABILENE, 2d Bde, 1st Inf Div, 26 Apr 66, p. 7, box 1, 81/471, RG 338, NARA; Rpt, 21 Feb 67, sub: Narrative—History of the Battle of Xa Cam My, pp. 3, 5, in VNI 97, CMH; Ltr, Maj Gen Jonathan O. Seaman to Brig Gen Randolf C. Dickens, Dep CG, John F. Kennedy Center for Special Warfare, Fort Bragg, N.C., 18 Apr 66, Corresp Vietnam (1966), Jonathan O. Seaman Papers, MHI.

General DePuy briefs Defense Department officials on ABILENE's *progress.*

ally uninhabited, was crucial to the capital's livelihood. As ships traveled from the South China Sea upriver to Saigon's wharves, they were vulnerable to hit-and-run attacks from Viet Cong concealed along the riverbanks. Army units had tried to clear the area in February, followed in March and early April by a U.S. Marine operation, JACKSTAY, but the Viet Cong had rebounded by mid-April and seemed to be rebuilding base camps and fortifications destroyed during the earlier initiatives. On 17 April the 1st Battalion, 18th Infantry, launched LEXINGTON III. For three weeks the battalion searched the swampland, only occasionally finding the Viet Cong. Then, LEXINGTON was suspended on 5 May, when General Seaman attached most of the battalion to Operation BIRMINGHAM in War Zone C. LEXINGTON resumed on the twenty-first, but the enemy remained elusive. On 9 June the operation ended. American forces had uncovered and destroyed a handful of small bases along with a number of sampans and some weapons, ammunition, and supplies. They killed 50 Viet Cong at a cost of 1 of their own.[5]

But most of DePuy's attention was turned northwest of Saigon, to War Zone C. Intelligence reported that two main force elements—the

[5] AAR, Opn LEXINGTON III, 1st Bn, 18th Inf, 20 Jun 66, pp. 4–8, box 1, 81/471, RG 338, NARA; Monthly Eval Rpt, II FFV, May 66, p. 3, Historians files, CMH; ORLL, 1 Jan–30 Apr 66, 1st Inf Div, n.d., p. 8, box 1, 81/472, RG 338, NARA; Annual Hist Sum, 1966, 1st Bn, 18th Inf, n.d., p. 3, box 5, 81/469, RG 338, NARA; Shulimson, *An Expanding War*, p. 301.

C230 and *C320 PLAF Battalions*, possibly belonging to the *70th Guard Regiment*—were ensconced in the huge enemy redoubt. DePuy sent two brigades after the insurgents. The 1st and the 3d began the effort, but after 7 May the 2d replaced the 1st. The South Vietnamese Army contributed an infantry battalion, three ranger battalions, and three airborne battalions, which operated east of the Americans with minimal coordination.[6]

Operation Birmingham began on 24 April. During the first days the Americans had only sporadic encounters with the enemy, but they uncovered a number of storage areas and base camps. On the twenty-seventh, in two fleeting engagements, a battalion of the 1st Brigade killed 3 Viet Cong and discovered several tons of supplies. That same day a battalion of the 3d Brigade found and destroyed a battalion-size base camp and several way stations for infiltrating troops (*see Map 24*).[7]

Three days later the Americans became involved in the most significant combat of the operation. On 30 April two battalions of Colonel Glotzbach's 1st Brigade swept north along the east bank of the Rach Cai Bac river, the border between South Vietnam and Cambodia. That morning the Americans began to take fire, both from across the river in Cambodia and from a hamlet named Lo Go on the Vietnamese side. Invoking its right of self-defense as specified by MACV's rules of engagement, Lt. Col. Richard L. Prillaman's 1st of the 2d Infantry turned its guns on the border and silenced the Viet Cong. That done, Prillaman's men and those from Lt. Col. William S. Hathaway's 2d of the 16th Infantry concentrated on the threat from Lo Go. Over the rest of the morning and into the afternoon the Americans advanced cautiously. Colonel Hathaway's Company A enveloped the insurgents' eastern flank, killing 8 and destroying company-size fortifications. Then, Colonel Prillaman's troops closed on Lo Go itself. Later identified as part of the *C230 Battalion*, the Viet Cong withdrew in midafteroon. In all, the Americans counted 54 enemy dead and estimated that they had killed another 100 at a cost of 6 of their own killed and 9 wounded.[8]

Birmingham lasted another two weeks as DePuy pushed deeper into War Zone C. He hoped to find *COSVN* headquarters itself, now thought to be hiding in the extreme northern reaches of Tay Ninh Province. But heavy rains soon turned northern Tay Ninh into a quagmire, and by then intriguing intelligence was summoning him back to Binh Long Prov-

---

[6] DePuy, *Oral History*, p. 140; ORLL, 1 May–31 Jul 66, 1st Inf Div, 15 Aug 66, p. 4, Historians files, CMH; AAR, Opn Birmingham, 3d Bde, 1st Inf Div, 15 Jun 66, pp. 2–3, box 1, 81/471, RG 338, NARA.

[7] AAR, Opn Birmingham, 1st Inf Div, n.d., p. 14, box 1, 81/471, RG 338, NARA.

[8] Ibid., pp. 5, 16, 38; AAR, Opn Birmingham, 1st Bde, 1st Inf Div, 24 May 66, p. 8, box 1, 81/471, RG 338, NARA; DePuy, *Oral History*, p. 141; Monthly Eval Rpt, II FFV, Apr 66, p. 3, Historians files, CMH; Ltr, Maj Gen William E. DePuy to Gen Harold K. Johnson, 13 May 66, William E. DePuy Papers, MHI.

ince, his unit's old haunt. There, the predicted monsoon offensive was about to begin in earnest.[9]

Thwarting the Offensive

MACV first learned of the enemy's intentions in late April, when deserters and prisoners told American interrogators that the *9th Division*'s *273d Regiment* was moving from War Zone D to War Zone C and that its *271st Regiment* would soon follow. Word also arrived that one or two North Vietnamese regiments might enter the Binh Long-Phuoc Long area as well.[10]

The picture grew clearer in May. Early in the month an enemy soldier's notebook revealed that his unit, the *9th Division*'s *272d Regiment*, would take part in a major offensive near the city of Loc Ninh in northern Binh Long Province. Around the same time, a CIDG unit patrolling about five kilometers southeast of Loc Ninh killed a Viet Cong officer who belonged to a reconnaissance unit from the *271st*. In his pockets were maps and a plan for multiple attacks against targets near Loc Ninh sometime before 10 May. The effort would involve four regiments: the three belonging to the *9th Division* and a fourth, the *101st PAVN Regiment*, which had recently infiltrated from North Vietnam.[11]

When 10 May passed with no attack, commanders at Loc Ninh breathed easier. However, one week later two separate South Vietnamese forces operating in the hills west of An Loc, the province capital, ran into two Viet Cong battalions. One came from the *273d Regiment*; the other may have been part of the *271st*. The encounters left little doubt that an enemy offensive was in the offing, so DePuy decided to blunt it before it began.[12]

DePuy called the operation EL PASO I, and he chose Colonel Brodbeck's 3d Brigade to carry it out. Three infantry battalions and supporting artillery moved to Loc Ninh on 19 and 20 May and immediately scoured the surrounding bush for Viet Cong. They found nothing, and on the morning of the twenty-fourth DePuy ordered the brigade to withdraw. Brodbeck considered the move inopportune. One of his battalions had been planning a sweep along the Cambodian border in areas where long-range

---

[9] MFR, MACV MACJ03, 1 May 66, sub: Planning Conference—Operation BIRMINGHAM, box 6, 69A/702, RG 334, NARA; AAR, Opn BIRMINGHAM, 2d Bde, 1st Inf Div, 7 Jun 66, p. 4, box 1, 81/471, RG 338, NARA; AARs, Opn BIRMINGHAM, 1st Inf Div, pp. 7–11, and 3d Bde, 1st Inf Div, p. 11.

[10] AAR, Opn EL PASO II/III, 1st Inf Div, n.d., p. 2, Historians files, CMH.

[11] Ibid.; Rpts, USARV, 5 Feb 70, sub: History of the 273 VC Regiment, July 1964–December 1969, p. 9, and Asst CofS, J–2, MACV, n.d., sub: 272 PLAF Regiment, p. 3, Historians files, CMH.

[12] Rpt, USARV, 5 Feb 70, sub: History of the 273 VC Regiment, July 1964–December 1969, pp. 9–10; ORLL, 1 May–31 Jul 66, 1st Inf Div, incl. 17, p. 1.

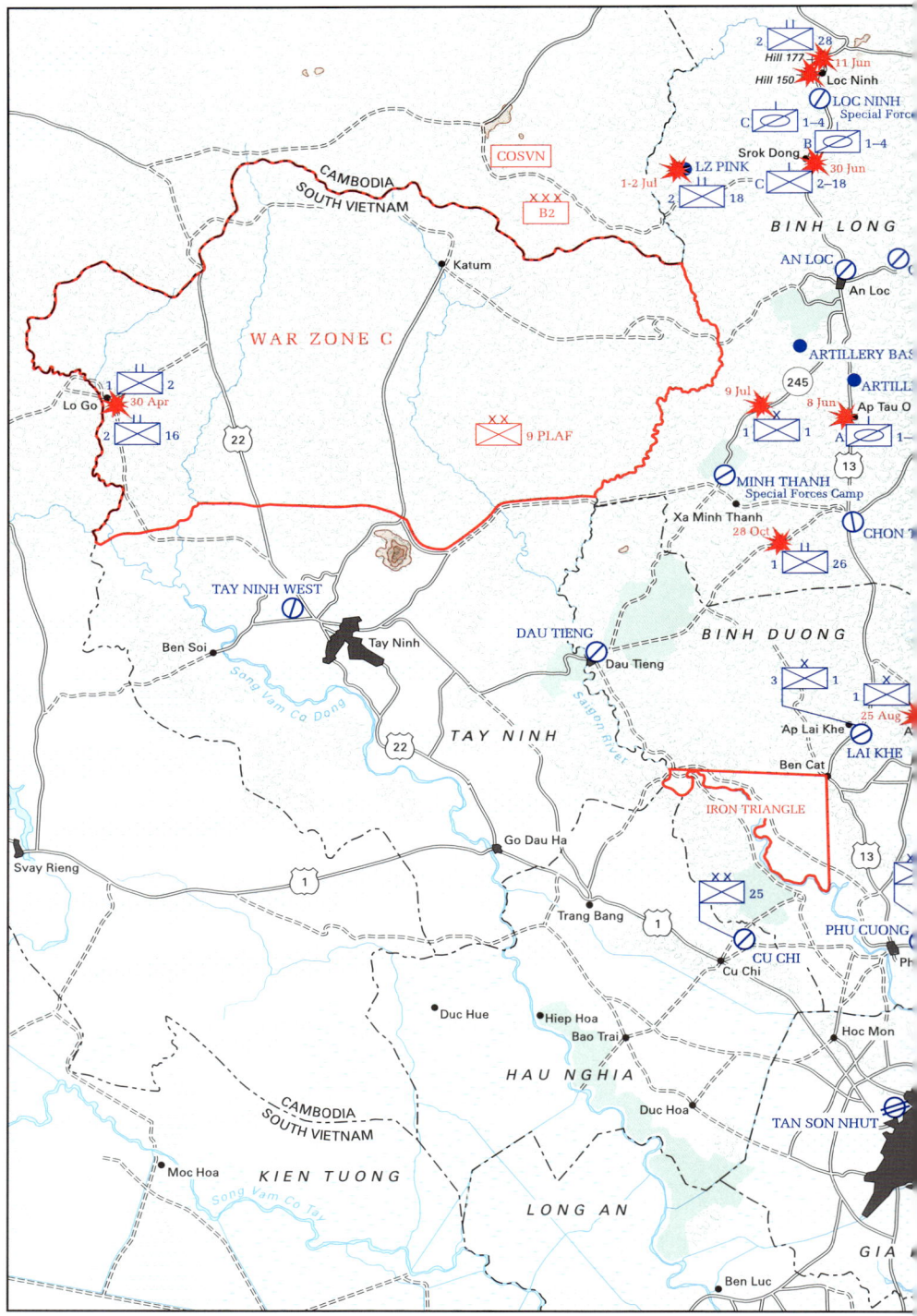

MAP 24

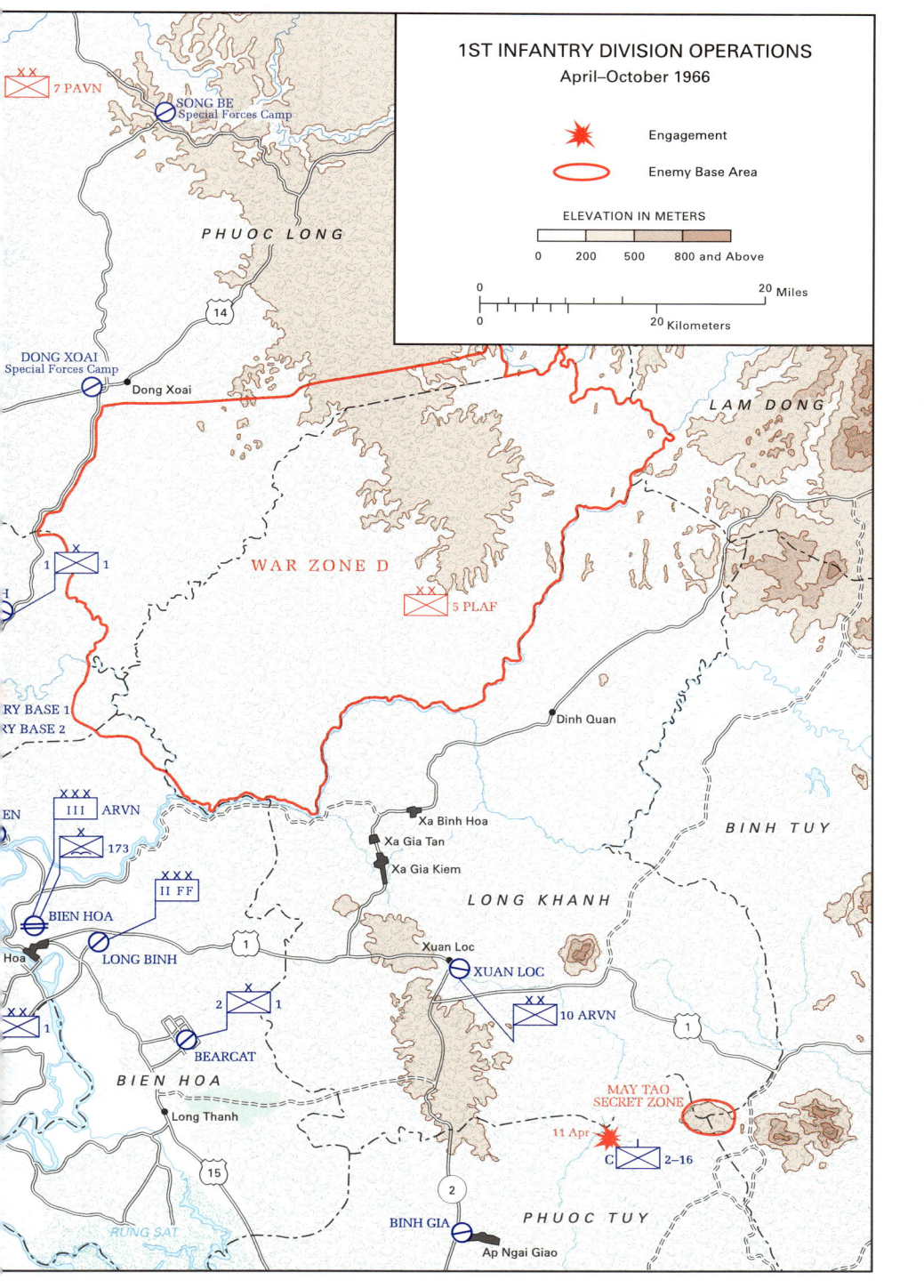

1ST INFANTRY DIVISION OPERATIONS
April–October 1966

✦ Engagement

⬭ Enemy Base Area

ELEVATION IN METERS

0   200   500   800 and Above

0   20 Miles

0   20 Kilometers

XX
7 PAVN

SONG BE
Special Forces Camp

PHUOC LONG

14

DONG XOAI
Special Forces Camp

Dong Xoai

LAM DONG

X
1   1

WAR ZONE D

XX
5 PLAF

RY BASE 1
RY BASE 2

Dinh Quan

BINH TUY

XXX
III ARVN

X
173

Xa Binh Hoa

Xa Gia Tan

Xa Gia Kiem

XXX
II FF

LONG KHANH

BIEN HOA

LONG BINH

Hoa

1

Xuan Loc

XUAN LOC

X
2   1

XX
10 ARVN

1

XX
1

BEARCAT

BIEN HOA

Long Thanh

MAY TAO
SECRET ZONE

15

11 Apr

C   2–16

2

BINH GIA

PHUOC TUY

RUNG SAT

Ap Ngai Giao

patrols had revealed an enemy presence. The Viet Cong might still be there.[13]

Within a week after EL PASO I DePuy's intelligence discovered that the enemy had postponed, rather than canceled, his attack on Loc Ninh, making it part of a broader campaign extending through mid-August. Under the new plan, the *9th Division*'s three regiments and, perhaps, several recently arrived North Vietnamese units as well would range as far west as Minh Thanh and as far east as Song Be, in Phuoc Long Province, in order to cut Highway 13 and attack the three most important towns in Binh Long Province: Loc Ninh, An Loc, and Chon Thanh. As the sole commercial artery that far north of Saigon, Highway 13 was an especially important target.[14]

On General Seaman's order, General DePuy launched Operation EL PASO II. Initially, the 1st Division's mission would be defensive: to secure and defend key installations in Binh Long and Phuoc Long Provinces. Then DePuy would attempt to locate and destroy the enemy before he could attack. Since Brodbeck's 3d Brigade was already there, it would make the first move. Between 2 and 8 June DePuy more than doubled Brodbeck's force, adding three infantry battalions and an armored cavalry troop. He acted just in time.[15]

To strengthen An Loc against attack, Brodbeck ordered Capt. Ralph M. Sturgis' Troop A, 1st Squadron, 4th Cavalry, to take up station near the town. The troop, with South Vietnamese soldiers attached, left Phu Loi early on the morning of 8 June with nine tanks and thirty-two other armored vehicles, including two flamethrower tracks. In the afternoon, as the three-kilometer-long column passed through the hamlet of Tau O, near a densely wooded area, the lead M48 was hit by either recoilless rifle fire or a mine. The crippled Patton stopped the column in its tracks.[16]

The fighting that followed was confused. Two of the three battalions of the *272d Regiment* were nearby, but they failed to coordinate their fire, instead bringing small arms, recoilless rifles, and mortars to bear at various points along the American column. Although some Americans would later suggest that "waves of [enemy] infantry assaulted the vehicles," what apparently happened was that small groups of Viet Cong would jump on an individual tank or armored personnel carrier in an attempt to plant charges that would destroy it.[17]

[13] AAR, Opn EL PASO I, 3d Bde, 1st Inf Div, 26 Jun 66, p. 9, Historians files, CMH; ORLL, 1 May–31 Jul 66, 1st Inf Div, p. 6.

[14] ORLL, 1 May–31 Jul 66, 1st Inf Div, incl. 17, p. 1. See also William E. DePuy, "Troop A at Ap Tau O," *Army* 36 (November 1986): 50.

[15] AAR, Opn EL PASO II/III, 1st Inf Div, p. 9; AAR, Opn EL PASO II, 3d Bde, 1st Inf Div, 20 Aug 66, p. 6, Historians files, CMH.

[16] ORLL, 1 May–31 Jul 66, 1st Inf Div, incl. 17, pp. 1–2; AAR, Opn EL PASO II/III, 1st Inf Div, pp. 11, 48.

[17] DePuy, "Troop A at Ap Tau O," p. 55; *9th Division*, p. 70, copy in CMH; AAR, Opn EL PASO II, 3d Bde, 1st Inf Div, p. 5 (quotation).

The vehicles that were spared in the first moments of the ambush wheeled into a perimeter. Over the course of the battle, which lasted nearly four hours, Captain Sturgis' men used all the firepower they could muster. In addition to their own guns, artillery from Loc Ninh and air strikes pounded the Viet Cong. The 2d Battalion, 18th Infantry, helicoptered from An Loc to the scene, setting down a few kilometers north of the action and maneuvering south to link up with the column. Elements of the South Vietnamese 5th Infantry Division also reinforced. By the time the 2d of the 18th Infantry reached the fighting, most of the enemy had withdrawn.[18]

The Americans found 105 Viet Cong dead and estimated that another 200 to 250 dead had been dragged away. In all, according to DePuy, allied forces had killed or wounded 90 percent of the *272d Regiment*'s *1st Battalion* and 50 percent of its *2d Battalion*. Its *3d Battalion*, somewhat south of the main action, escaped relatively unscathed. In return, the enemy had killed 14 Americans and 19 South Vietnamese.[19]

General DePuy later characterized the encounter as the *9th Division's* first big defeat. One hundred thirty-five Americans and South Vietnamese had handily stopped a force of some twelve hundred enemy regulars. Yet the performance of the commanders at the scene had not been flawless. It had taken them an hour to realize that they were probably up against an entire regiment. By concentrating only on the attacking units without taking into account the broader battlefield, they failed to make optimum use of their artillery and air strikes. This narrow focus allowed the Viet Cong the maneuvering room that they needed to escape.[20]

The battle did little to deter the Communists. Intelligence reports still placed all three regiments of the *9th Division* in the vicinity of Highway 13 and possibly in the Minh Thanh and Loc Ninh areas. Armed with this information, General DePuy expanded EL PASO II to nearly division-size. On 9 June he established a division forward command post at An Loc and brought his 1st Brigade, under Col. Sidney B. Berry, Jr., into the operation. Colonel Berry would hunt in a sector that stretched from Highway 13 west to Minh Thanh. From then on, except for a brief one-day interval, EL PASO II would be a reinforced two-brigade affair.[21]

Brodbeck's 3d Brigade kept the pressure on the insurgents near Loc Ninh. Early on the morning of 11 June Company A, 2d of the 28th Infan-

---

[18] CHECO Rpt, PACAF, 30 Nov 66, sub: Operation EL PASO, p. 4, copy in Historians files, CMH; AAR, Opn EL PASO II/III, 1st Inf Div, p. 49.

[19] Op Sum, Opn EL PASO II, MACV, May 66, pp. 3–4, Historians files, CMH; Annual Hist Sum, 1966, 1st Sqdn, 4th Cav, 7 May 67, p. 2, box 5, 81/469, RG 338, NARA; AAR, Opn EL PASO II, 3d Bde, 1st Inf Div, p. 5; ORLL, 1 May–31 Jul 66, 1st Inf Div, incl. 17, p. 2; *9th Division*, p. 70.

[20] AAR, Opn EL PASO II/III, 1st Inf Div, pp. 48–49; John M. Carland, "Double Ambush on Route 13," *Vietnam* 1 (Spring 1989): 42–49; DePuy, *Oral History*, p. 142.

[21] Rpt no. 6-075-1872-6, Asst CofS, J–2, MACV, 20 Jun 66, sub: VC Activities in Binh Duong Province, Historians files, CMH.

try, assisted by a CIDG platoon, began to clear a hamlet in a rubber plantation a few kilometers northwest of the town. Since morning fog would have delayed an air assault on the hamlet, the bulk of the force proceeded on foot. Within sight of the settlement the troops met scattered fire from what was later identified as the *273d's 1st Battalion*.

The fight lasted for ten hours and centered on two nearby hills, known by the elevations marked in meters on U.S. Army maps as Hills 150 and 177. When the enemy showed no sign of budging, the commander of the 2d of the 28th, Colonel Bowie, committed his Company C and called in artillery and air strikes. That afternoon the Americans launched two assaults against well-entrenched positions on the hills, which stood less than two kilometers apart.[22]

Company C and the battalion reconnaissance platoon stormed up Hill 177 from the west and the south beginning around 1430. As the Americans advanced, the Viet Cong lobbed mortar rounds and grenades and sprayed small-arms fire down the slopes. A vigorous counterattack followed, forcing twenty-four reconnaissance platoon members into a nearby trench. It was an unfortunate move. An enemy machine gun on one flank sprayed bullets down the trench line, killing 19. The company commander immediately sent in his reserve troops, who overran the insurgents at 1615 and hastened their withdrawal to the northwest. Air strikes herded the fleeing Viet Cong into range of American artillery, which further pounded them.[23]

The assault of Hill 150 was also difficult, though much less costly. While the reconnaissance platoon was dying on Hill 177, Company A tried twice to take Hill 150. Both attempts failed. After figuring out the enemy's likely escape route, Bowie placed a CIDG company astride it and committed his Company B, well rested and backed with plenty of fire support, to the action. Pitted against enemy soldiers who had been in combat since early morning, the Americans had little trouble. By 1630 the Viet Cong were on the run. They withdrew straight into the guns of the blocking unit and quickly disintegrated. Victorious, the Americans and their allies returned to Loc Ninh.[24]

It had been a bloody day. Colonel Brodbeck's men found 98 enemy bodies and estimated that they had killed another 150. If the estimate was anywhere close to accurate—and later interrogations of prisoners and plantation workers suggested that it was—Colonel Bowie's battalion had eliminated 50 percent or more of the *273d Regiment's 1st Battalion*, a good day's work in any war. In achieving that success, however, the Americans had paid dearly with 33 killed and another 33 wounded.[25]

---

[22] ORLL, 1 May–31 Jul 66, 1st Inf Div, pp. 12–13 and incl. 15, pp. 1–2.

[23] AAR, Opn EL PASO II/III, 1st Inf Div, p. 50; CHECO Rpt, PACAF, 30 Nov 66, sub: Operation EL PASO, p. 8.

[24] ORLL, 1 May–31 Jul 66, 1st Inf Div, incl. 15, p. 2.

[25] Ibid.

1st Division troops clear mines from a section of Highway 13.

If these engagements raised hopes for more opportunities to kill Viet Cong, the Americans were soon disappointed. Over the next week General DePuy's two brigades continued their patrols in the battle area but came up with little. Somewhat frustrated, DePuy and his commanders decided to cast their nets wider. On 18 June elements of the 1st Squadron, 4th Cavalry, conducted a "roadrunner" mission, sending a small group of armored vehicles along Highway 13 from An Loc south to Phu Loi to keep it free of mines and booby traps and the enemy off balance. That same day the 3d Brigade probed farther east near Quan Loi. Then, on the twentieth DePuy sent most of the 1st Brigade toward Dau Tieng and the Michelin Plantation, leaving its 1st of the 28th Infantry east of Highway 13 near Song Be. All the while, the 3d Brigade continued its work around Loc Ninh and An Loc.[26]

As EL PASO II progressed, the 1st Brigade found large supply caches along the Saigon River northwest of Dau Tieng—more than fifteen hundred tons of rice, twenty-five tons of salt, and some seventeen tons of dried fish—but no enemy troops. On the twenty-sixth DePuy attached the 1st of the 28th Infantry near Song Be to Brodbeck's 3d Brigade. Two days later the brigade's command post and some of its units moved to Song Be.[27]

[26] AAR, Opn EL PASO II/III, 1st Inf Div, pp. 13–22.
[27] Ibid., an. H.

Unit movements were not random. DePuy's commanders were operating almost exclusively in areas where radio direction finding equipment had revealed an enemy presence, and they depended on reconnaissance patrols and electronic intelligence to find the Viet Cong. The results, nonetheless, were meager. Despite all their efforts, the Americans seemed incapable—except for the occasional minor skirmish—of bringing the enemy to battle. Accordingly, DePuy decided to scale down the operation by withdrawing the 1st Brigade. The 3d Brigade continued its patrols around Song Be.[28]

On the morning of 30 June Troops B and C of Lt. Col. Leonard L. Lewane's 1st Squadron, 4th Cavalry, and Company C, 2d of the 18th Infantry, left An Loc for Loc Ninh. Their mission was to escort engineers to repair a damaged bridge at Cam Le, north of An Loc, and also to carry out a reconnaissance in force along portions of Highway 13 immediately north of the bridge. By 0910 the engineers had placed a temporary span next to the damaged one, allowing the vehicles to push north. Capt. Stephen M. Slattery's Troop C worked its way up the west side of the highway, while 1st Lt. James P. Flores' Troop B took the area to the east. Upon reaching Route 17, Captain Slattery's unit and two of Company C's rifle platoons turned left on the road and moved about fifteen hundred meters. After crossing a stream, the Americans dismounted and began looking for Viet Cong. Meanwhile, Lieutenant Flores' troop and the remaining rifle platoon, after a brief reconnaissance to the east on Route 17, returned to the highway and continued north.

The *271st Regiment* was waiting for them. Arrayed in an L-shaped ambush along the road, enemy positions extended almost two kilometers north of the intersection of Highway 13 and Route 17. Most of the Viet Cong were hiding along the west side of the highway behind stacks of logs, but a few also lay in wait east of the road. The *271st* initially had been ordered to attack Loc Ninh, but after 27 June the mission changed to "laying a mobile ambush" for any convoys.[29]

Around 0940, just as the lead elements of the column passed by rice paddies on each side of the road south of Srok Dong hamlet, mortars, recoilless rifles, machine guns, and small arms opened up from the north and northwest. Lieutenant Flores' lead units coiled and returned fire. His men organized a second hasty strongpoint at the intersection of Route 17 and Highway 13, but it also came under attack. Within thirty minutes all of Troop B's M48s were disabled, and Flores was in danger of being overrun. Flying overhead in his helicopter, Colonel Lewane diverted an air strike to Flores. Huey gunships followed, reaching the battle about fifteen minutes after the first shots were fired. Slattery's Troop C,

---

[28] Interv, John Albright with Lt Gen William E. DePuy, 3 Apr 71, p. 13, Historians files, CMH.

[29] DePuy, *Oral History*, p. 142; *9th Division*, p. 71 (quoted words).

which had mounted up when the shooting began, joined the force at the highway junction.

Colonel Lewane continued to monitor the situation from above, organizing additional fire support and reinforcements. Soon artillery strikes began and more jets arrived. Lewane established Highway 13 as the fire support coordination line—artillery would hit east of the highway and air strikes to the west. As the battle developed, he ordered Captain Slattery to the northern strongpoint. When Troop C arrived, Flores' men withdrew to the south, leaving their damaged vehicles behind. After replenishing their ammunition, they headed west along Route 17 to act as a blocking force.

By this time, about midday, the fire from the cavalry positions and from the Air Force, artillery, and gunships had apparently discouraged the Viet Cong, who began to withdraw. Reinforcements were also on their way. An element from the South Vietnamese 5th Division moved to the east of Troop B along Route 17, and a CIDG force took up blocking positions north of Srok Dong. The idea was that as the Viet Cong pulled out, they would be forced through a channel created by the Americans and their allies and be easier to find and destroy.

Just before noon Company A, 2d of the 18th Infantry, joined Slattery and began to deploy west. Shortly afterward, Company B and the battalion commander, Lt. Col. Herbert J. McChrystal, also arrived. With the Viet Cong on the run, Colonel McChrystal ordered his men to pursue—Company B pushing to the south, parallel to the highway, and Company A to the southwest. After moving about eight hundred meters, Company A ran into Viet Cong. When the Americans failed to dislodge them, McChrystal ordered Company C, which had fought alongside the cavalry troops during the day, to attack. The company did so at 1615, forcing the enemy to retreat.[30]

At that point, General DePuy recalled the 1st Brigade command to the operation and gave Colonel Berry operational control of all units involved at Srok Dong. Berry's job was to pursue the Viet Cong. On 1 July the 1st Brigade, assisted by units of the South Vietnamese 5th Division, searched the battlefield. After finding only a handful of dead enemy soldiers buried in shallow graves, Berry shifted his efforts to the west. Three infantry battalions pushed to the Cambodian border, hoping to catch the fleeing Viet Cong before they found sanctuary.

Meanwhile, the *9th Division*'s commander, Colonel Cam, was worried about the *271st Regiment*'s westward withdrawal. To cover the re-

[30] Above narrative on the Srok Dong action based on AAR, Opn EL PASO II/III, 1st Inf Div, p. 22 and an. A; ORLL, 1 May–31 Jul 66, 1st Inf Div, incl. 17, pp. 2–3; and Op Sum, Opn EL PASO II, MACV, Jul 66, pp. 5–6, Historians files, CMH. See also MFRs, 1st Sgt Anthony S. Moniz, Troop B, 1st Sqdn, 4th Cav, n.d., sub: Battle of Highway 13, 30 June 1966, and Capt Stephen M. Slattery, CO, Troop C, 1st Sqdn, 4th Cav, n.d., sub: Attached Infantry Action, 30 June 1966; Sitrep, 1st Inf Div, 1 Jul 66. All in Leonard L. Lewane Papers, Lexington, Va.

F–100 Super Sabres, armed with cluster bomb pods, head for a target.

treat, he ordered the *273d Regiment* to attack the American force that posed the greatest threat—Company A, 2d of the 18th Infantry, occupying an overnight position near the hamlet of Ta Thiet a few kilometers from the border.

The attack came just before dusk on 1 July, when Company A was hit by an estimated reinforced platoon. The fighting rapidly escalated. From his command post two kilometers to the northwest Colonel McChrystal organized a relief force, dispatching his reconnaissance platoon and then Company C. The move apparently prompted the Viet Cong to regroup. They broke off their assault around 2000.[31]

The lull lasted until 0545 the next morning, when the *273d* attacked Companies A and C with mortars and automatic weapons and followed up with ground assaults from several directions. McChrystal called for artillery and air support, but bad weather kept the planes away for more than an hour. Ground reinforcements were also sent, but they had to move cautiously, watching for enemy ambushes.

Eventually, retribution came from the air. Striking through the clouds with high explosives, napalm, and cluster bombs, F–100s from Bien Hoa laid down so much molten steel that the Viet Cong withdrew shortly

[31] Rpt, USARV, 5 Feb 70, sub: History of the 273 VC Regiment, July 1964–December 1969, p. 11; ORLL, 1 May–31 Jul 66, 1st Inf Div, incl. 17, p. 3; AAR, Opn EL PASO II/III, 1st Inf Div, an A., p. 7.

after 0900. Army records vary widely on the number of enemy killed, with the number for confirmed dead ranging from 21 to 98 and estimates running from 110 to 152. The 1st Division's casualties totaled 13 killed and 5 wounded. General DePuy credited the Air Force with saving the day by providing close and accurate support in difficult weather. Yet the *273d* also succeeded in its task, allowing the remnants of the *271st* to escape.[32]

The Battle of Minh Thanh Road

While units from the 1st Division continued to hunt the Viet Cong, General DePuy gave Colonel Berry a special assignment: trick the enemy into ambushing an American convoy that seemed to be vulnerable and, when he took the bait, destroy him. Berry decided that the best place to spring the surprise was along the Minh Thanh Road, or Route 245, a provincial artery that branched off from Highway 13 below An Loc and meandered to the southwest. Signal intelligence seemed to support his decision, placing a regimental-size command post just north of the road and seven kilometers west of the highway, with, presumably, a lot of troops nearby. "We had a fix" on the command post, DePuy recalled. The Viet Cong "were right there. They were obviously in an ambush position, either in it or moving into it."[33]

Berry decided to offer such a tempting target that an ambush would be inevitable. The deception plan would show that the 1st Division was sending a convoy of bulldozers and supply trucks, protected by a small armored cavalry contingent, from An Loc to Minh Thanh to repair the airfield there. In reality, the convoy—two cavalry troops, augmented by infantry—was formidable, as was the nearby reaction force—four infantry battalions ready to block or attack. The Americans would also set up two firebases within range, and the Air Force would have fighter-bombers poised to go on short notice. If the Viet Cong took the bait, they would bear the brunt of a lethal array.[34]

The plan unfolded beginning on 7 July. A three-battery mix of 105-mm., 155-mm., and 8-inch howitzers moved to Artillery Base I just west of Highway 13 and about six kilometers southwest of An Loc, while a battery of 105s formed Artillery Base II about eight kilometers south of

---

[32] Rpt, USARV, 5 Feb 70, sub: History of the 273 VC Regiment, July 1964–December 1969, p. 11; ORLL, 1 May–31 Jul 66, 1st Inf Div, p. 10 and incl. 17, p. 3; CHECO Rpt, PACAF, 30 Nov 66, sub: Operation EL PASO, pp. 15–19; AAR, Opn EL PASO II, 1st Bde, 1st Inf Div, 20 Aug 66, p. 7, Historians files, CMH; AAR, Opn EL PASO II/III, 1st Inf Div, p. 23; Annual Hist Sum, 1966, 2d Bn, 18th Inf, 28 Mar 67, p. 4, box 5, 81/469, RG 338, NARA.

[33] AAR, Opn EL PASO II/III, 1st Inf Div, an. C, p. 1; Interv, Albright with DePuy, 3 Apr 71, p. 47 (quoted words).

[34] AAR, Opn EL PASO II/III, 1st Inf Div, an. C, p. 1.

An Loc and just east of the highway. In the meantime, Lt. Col. Jack L. Conn's 2d Battalion, 2d Infantry, infiltrated in small groups to Minh Thanh, where it joined Maj. John C. Bard's 1st Battalion, 18th Infantry, and an artillery battery. On 8 July elements of Lt. Col. Robert Haldane's 1st Battalion, 28th Infantry, positioned themselves about twenty-five hundred meters east of Artillery Base I. The 1st Battalion, 16th Infantry, commanded by Lt. Col. Rufus G. Lazzell, stood ready at Quan Loi east of An Loc.

To lure the enemy to the convoy, General DePuy used a suspected enemy contact. Certain that a Viet Cong spy or sympathizer on the province chief's staff in Binh Long was leaking information on U.S. troop movements, DePuy made sure that the province chief and his entire staff heard the news that he planned to move construction equipment on 9 July to Minh Thanh airfield.[35]

With the stage set, it was time for the bait. Task Force DRAGOON, consisting of Capt. Nils P. Johannesen's Company B, 1st of the 2d Infantry, and Troops B and C, 1st of the 4th Cavalry, left An Loc airfield at 0700, 9 July. Captain Slattery's Troop C took the lead, while Capt. David S. Kelly's Troop B followed. Elements of Company B were interspersed throughout the column. Colonel Lewane, the task force commander, flew above the convoy in his helicopter.

As the convoy took the turn toward Minh Thanh, artillery pounded areas along the road where the Viet Cong might be lurking, jets streaked overhead dropping napalm, and gunships prowled both sides of the road. Troop C's tanks fired at right angles to the column's progress. This was a powerful war machine, not a weak convoy. But Viet Cong units were not known for their tactical flexibility. If they were preparing for an attack, it was unlikely that they would change their plans (*Map 25*).[36]

Around 1100 Captain Slattery's Troop C bumped into the base of an L-shaped ambush about four kilometers from the edge of the Minh Thanh Rubber Plantation. With Captain Kelly's Troop B close behind, Slattery moved up the L's stem, which lay to the north of the road. Most of the *272d Regiment* had deployed there, but a few Viet Cong were waiting to the south of the American advance, possibly to obscure the direction of the main attack. They had maintained remarkable discipline throughout the air and artillery attacks, waiting patiently until their targets were well within the killing zone.

At 1110 the Viet Cong made their move. Troop C's 1st Platoon, led by 2d Lt. John K. Lyons, spotted two small groups of insurgents sprinting across the road and fired on them. Enemy soldiers hidden along the road returned fire. In the minutes that followed, Lieutenant Lyons' men found themselves under crushing assault from automatic weapons, re-

---

[35] Ibid.; Interv, Lt Col Romie L. Brownlee and Lt Col William J. Mullen III with General William E. DePuy, 26 Mar 79, sec. 5, p. 31, Senior Officer Oral History Program, MHI.

[36] AAR, Opn EL PASO II/III, 1st Inf Div, an. C, p. 3; *9th Division*, p. 73.

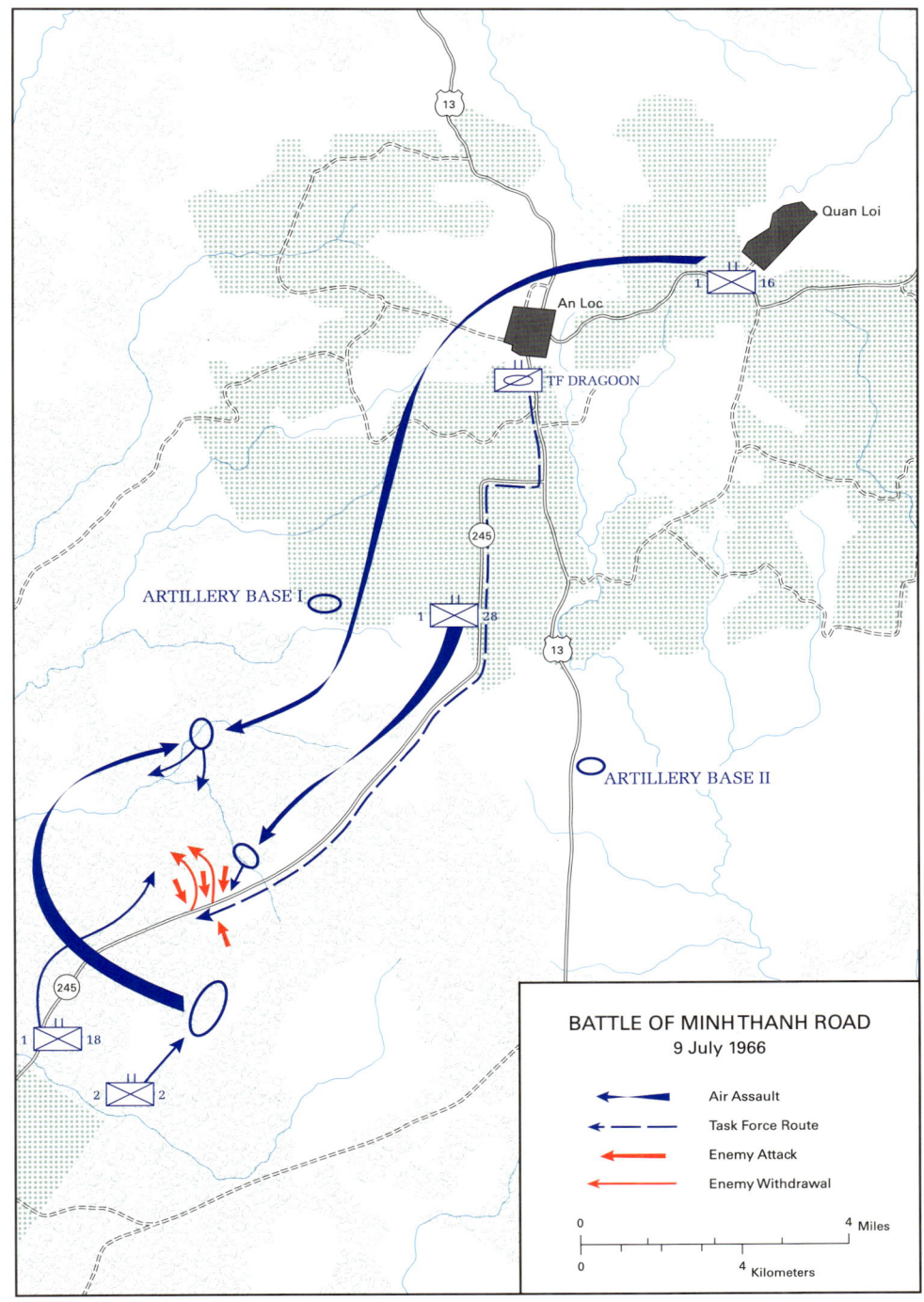

Quan Loi

13

An Loc

TF DRAGOON

1 II 16

245

ARTILLERY BASE I

1 II 28

13

ARTILLERY BASE II

245

1 II 18

2 II 2

BATTLE OF MINH THANH ROAD
9 July 1966

Air Assault
Task Force Route
Enemy Attack
Enemy Withdrawal

0   4 Miles

0   4 Kilometers

MAP 25

coilless rifles, and mortars. The enemy had taken the bait. Word went to Colonel Lewane: This was it.[37]

When the attack began, Slattery's and Kelly's tanks and armored personnel carriers immediately angled to alternate sides of the road in a herringbone formation. Directly behind Lyon's 1st Platoon, which had taken the brunt of the fire, and Slattery's command group, Troop C's 2d Platoon deployed its vehicles along each side of the road, forming a stable center for the column. With weapons aimed to the north and south, the platoon opened fire. Within minutes of the attack, American artillery and air strikes rained down north and south of the road. Huey gunships added their firepower, scouring the brush nearby and cutting off possible escape routes.[38]

The armor elements still did not know the exact direction of the enemy's attack. Slattery initially reported that most of the fire was coming from south of the road. After some moments, however, everyone realized that the threat lay to the north, so they concentrated their fire there. Meanwhile, Colonel Lewane ordered two platoons of Troop B forward to join Troop C, strengthening Slattery. By 1230 the Viet Cong realized that a successful assault would be impossible, and an hour later they were withdrawing.[39]

The battle was not yet over, however. Colonel Berry's infantry battalions were reinforcing the American column and moving to block the enemy's departure. Within the first few minutes of firing Berry had ordered Major Bard's 1st of the 18th Infantry to push north of the road, the likely avenue of escape. He also directed Colonel Conn's 2d of the 2d Infantry, operating near Minh Thanh, to shift south of the artery as a reserve. Dense jungle reduced progress to a crawl. Aware of the slow pace, and soon realizing that the Viet Cong would not withdraw southward, Berry had Conn's unit air-assault to the north.

As the firing tapered off, 1st Division forces tried to draw the enemy into another fight. Between 1210 and 1230 Colonel Haldane's 1st of the 28th helicoptered to a landing zone north of the action and then headed southwest. Viet Cong sniped at the Americans, but did not try to stop their progress.

Around 1330 air observers spotted large groups of insurgents moving northwest from the battlefield. Not all were fleeing, however, because a half hour later Haldane's men met a force of unknown size near the original ambush site. A two-hour firefight followed; then the enemy broke away. Haldane's men continued their sweep, moving to the outside edge of their fire support. Finding no Viet Cong, they turned back to hunt along the south side of the Minh Thanh Road. Again, they found nothing, so they settled into an overnight position just north of the road.

---

[37] Annual Hist Sum, 1966, 1st Sqdn, 4th Cav, p. 12.
[38] Ibid., pp. 13–14.
[39] AAR, Opn EL PASO II/III, 1st Inf Div, pp. 3–6.

A burned-out American armored personnel carrier, hit by recoilless rifle fire on the Minh Thanh Road, and a dead Viet Cong soldier

Major Bard's 1st of the 18th had better luck. Moving slowly through the choking undergrowth toward the battle area, the battalion ran into a small group of Viet Cong shortly before 1600. Bard called for artillery and then charged the hunkering insurgents, killing 12. But the fighting slowed the unit's movement into a blocking position, so Colonel Berry assigned another battalion to the task.[40]

The job went to Colonel Lazzell's 1st of the 16th, which air-assaulted north of the action and immediately maneuvered south. Dense jungle and occasional sniping by small groups of Viet Cong slowed Lazzell's progress, and it took him longer than expected to reach his destination. When an enemy bullet wounded him during the move, he was replaced by Lt. Col. George M. Wallace.

Colonel Conn's 2d of the 2d also had orders to help seal off the battlefield. His men, the last of whom did not arrive until 1755, formed a defense line near their landing zone. At the same time, Troops B and C joined a South Vietnamese armored personnel carrier troop and straddled the road where the original fighting had broken out. Despite the effort, the Americans were unable to prevent the Viet Cong from slipping through the net.[41]

[40] Ibid., p. 6.
[41] Ibid., p. 5.

The battle of Minh Thanh Road was over. General DePuy believed that he had inflicted another defeat on the *9th Division* and frustrated the monsoon offensive in northern III Corps. He also made much of the fact that, for once, the deceiver was deceived, stating: "I guess we took a lot of pleasure out of the fact that this was one of the few times that they did what we wanted them to do rather than us doing what they wanted us to do."[42] Colonel Berry agreed, noting that his troops had "accomplished exactly what was intended." They had lured the enemy into ambushing a hard-fighting target and had inflicted heavy damage with supporting fires and reaction forces.[43]

The 1st Division had killed 238 Viet Cong by body count and estimated that another 300 might have died and been carried away. In addition, it had captured or destroyed a substantial number of weapons and supplies. The enemy, in turn, had killed 25 Americans and wounded 113 and destroyed four armored personnel carriers, two helicopters, and a tank.[44]

In particular, Berry's four batteries of artillery plus air support had turned in a remarkable performance, in part because of the now typical 1st Division planning for their use that had gone into the preparations for the battle. By prior agreement, the Minh Thanh Road had been the fire support coordination line. During the fighting's first phases U.S. forces stayed mostly on the road, providing a clear line for the artillery and allowing the guns to bring their full power to bear. In addition, Air Force F–5 Freedom Fighters had flown over one hundred sorties, reinforced by carrier-based fighter-bombers. Tactical air support was continuing to prove essential to the survival of U.S. ground forces.[45]

Over the next few days the 1st Division continued its hunt for the *272d* and its sister regiments without success. All Viet Cong units involved in the fighting over the past four weeks were gone, recovering in nearby base areas. On 13 July General DePuy terminated EL PASO II, leaving a single brigade in the area to prevent the enemy from returning. Dubbed EL PASO III, the operation lasted until 3 September, with no significant results.

In statistical terms, EL PASO II produced a body count comparable to the 1st Cavalry Division's Pleiku and first Binh Dinh campaigns. In combination with a few other Army units and air power, DePuy's troops reported 825 enemy killed and estimated another 1,249 killed, mostly from the *9th Division*. In return, the division had lost 125 killed and 424 wounded.

---

[42] Interv, Brownlee and Mullen with DePuy, 26 Mar 79, sec. 5, p. 31.

[43] AAR, Opn EL PASO II, 1st Bde, 1st Inf Div, p. 16.

[44] AARs, Opn EL PASO II/III, 1st Inf Div, p. 48, and EL PASO II, 1st Bde, 1st Inf Div, incl. 5, p. 2. The enemy admitted losing 128 killed and 167 wounded. See *9th Division*, p. 180.

[45] AAR, Opn EL PASO II/III, 1st Inf Div, an. C, pp. 6–8; Annual Hist Sum, 1966, 1st Sqdn, 4th Cav, p. 13; CHECO Rpt, PACAF, 30 Nov 66, sub: Operation EL PASO, pp. 21–23.

Interrogations of captured soldiers indicated that during the operation the *9th Division* had sustained a 50-percent loss in combat effectiveness.[46]

North Vietnamese and Viet Cong commanders had a different view. A North Vietnamese analysis acknowledged that the *272d Regiment* had "suffered heavy losses" during the encounter, but blamed them mostly on the unit's "unsatisfactory organization of its withdrawal from the battlefield" rather than on American tactics and firepower.[47]

Whatever the reason, the enemy had been dealt a severe blow, and it would take some time to regroup. But the fight was far from over. DePuy had won partly because the Viet Cong had chosen to stand and fight. Next time, the Americans would have to find them.

Fighting the *Phu Loi Battalion*

As the southwest monsoon season reached its peak, General DePuy's campaigns accounted for nearly half of the theater's large unit operations during August and September. One of his objectives was to harry the enemy along Highway 13, as well as on other roads in Binh Long and Binh Duong Provinces. For the most part this worked—the Viet Cong did not contest the raids, except during Operation AMARILLO.[48]

The operation began in late August as a routine road security mission. Colonel Berry's 1st Brigade joined South Vietnamese regulars and Regional and Popular Forces in clearing Routes 1A and 16 from Phuoc Vinh, the brigade base camp, south to Di An, the division headquarters, and in providing protection for elements of the 1st Engineer Battalion, which were working on the roads. Berry's force consisted of Colonel Prillaman's 1st of the 2d Infantry, with the latter's executive officer, Maj. Richard D. Clark, in command during his absence; Lt. Col. Paul F. Gorman's 1st of the 26th Infantry; and Captain Slattery's Troop C, 1st of the 4th Cavalry. The force established two artillery bases a little more than thirty kilometers north of Di An: Artillery Base 1, at the hamlet of Bo La; and Artillery Base 2, about two kilometers to the south. Both were near Route 1A, allowing for easy resupply. Elements of the 1st Battalion, 5th Artillery, provided fire support.[49]

The topography and vegetation offered less than ideal operating conditions. Heavy underbrush cloaked the gently rolling countryside, limiting visibility to little more than twenty meters, and trees impeded

---

[46] AAR, Opn EL PASO II/III, 1st Inf Div, pp. 42, 48; ORLL, 1 May–31 Jul 66, 1st Inf Div, p. 3.

[47] *9th Division*, p. 74. See also AAR, Opn EL PASO II/III, 1st Inf Div, an. C, pp. 7–8; Combat Lessons Bull no. 6, USARV, 30 Apr 67, p. 3, Historians files, CMH.

[48] ORLL, 1 Aug–31 Oct 66, 1st Inf Div, n.d., pp. 4–7, Historians files, CMH.

[49] AAR, Opn AMARILLO, 1st Bde, 1st Inf Div, 18 Dec 66, pp. 1–2, Historians files, CMH; AAR, Opn AMARILLO, 1st Bn, 2d Inf, 11 Sep 66, pp. [1–2], Harry G. Summers Papers, Bowie, Md.

the movement of armor. On the other hand, the landscape offered good cover for enemy soldiers, who maintained myriad trails and fortifications in the area as well as platforms for observation and sniping.

Little happened during AMARILLO's first two days. On 23 August Major Clark's 1st of the 2d Infantry patrolled southward from Artillery Base 1, covering about eight kilometers. Colonel Gorman's 1st of the 26th Infantry, south of Clark, moved even farther south along Routes 1A and 16, securing the roads for future convoys.

During the evening of the twenty-fourth Capt. William J. Mullen III, commander of Company C, 1st of the 2d Infantry, sent out a fifteen-man patrol from Artillery Base 2. The men were to remain in the field overnight, looking and listening for Viet Cong. As darkness closed in, they settled about five kilometers west of the firebase.[50]

At dawn on the twenty-fifth the patrol moved east toward the firebase. The day turned out to be one of the few in August when rain did not fall, but the ground remained wet and soggy. Although the troops were unaware of it, they had begun their day inside a large enemy base area. They were about to find more Viet Cong than they might have thought possible (*Map 26*).[51]

The situation began to develop just after first light, when enemy soldiers—later identified as belonging to the crack *Phu Loi Battalion* and the separate local force *C62 Company*—attacked the patrol. After an initial exchange of fire, the Americans took cover in a nearby bunker and trench line and called for help. Immediately, Major Clark ordered the remainder of Captain Mullen's Company C and the 2d Platoon, Troop C, 1st of the 4th Cavalry, to the rescue. From Artillery Base 2 eighty-five men and seven armored personnel carriers headed out, led by a tank breaking trail. Captain Mullen directed the column's movement from a helicopter overhead.[52]

Meanwhile, the commander of the besieged patrol reported that insurgents had breached the trench line. With the Viet Cong threatening to overrun him, he called in artillery on his own position. The fire broke the momentum of the attack. No Americans were injured by the artillery, but the patrol had sustained 5 wounded and its machine guns were out of action. Still faced with what seemed by then to be a full enemy battalion, the surviving members separated. Nine of the men, led by Pfc. Dennis L. Peterson, hid together in an unoccupied bunker, while the others struck out on their own.[53]

[50] AAR, Opn AMARILLO, 1st Bde, 1st Inf Div, p. 5.
[51] Annual Hist Sum, 1966, 1st Bde, 1st Inf Div, 25 Mar 67, p. 2, box 5, 81/469, RG 338, NARA.
[52] Memo, Lt Col Richard L. Prillaman, CO, 1st Bn, 2d Inf, for 1st Inf Div Distribution, 3 Sep 66, sub: Journal Summary, 24–26 August 1966 (Operation AMARILLO), Summers Papers; Annual Hist Sum, 1966, 1st Sqdn, 4th Cav, p. 21.
[53] Memo, Prillaman for 1st Inf Div Distribution, 3 Sep 66, sub: Journal Summary, 24–26 August 1966 (Operation AMARILLO); Ltr, Col Sidney B. Berry, Jr., to Anne F. Berry, 28 Aug 66, Sidney B. Berry Papers, Arlington, Va.; Interv, Brownlee and Mullen with DePuy, 26 Mar 79, sec. 6, p. 16.

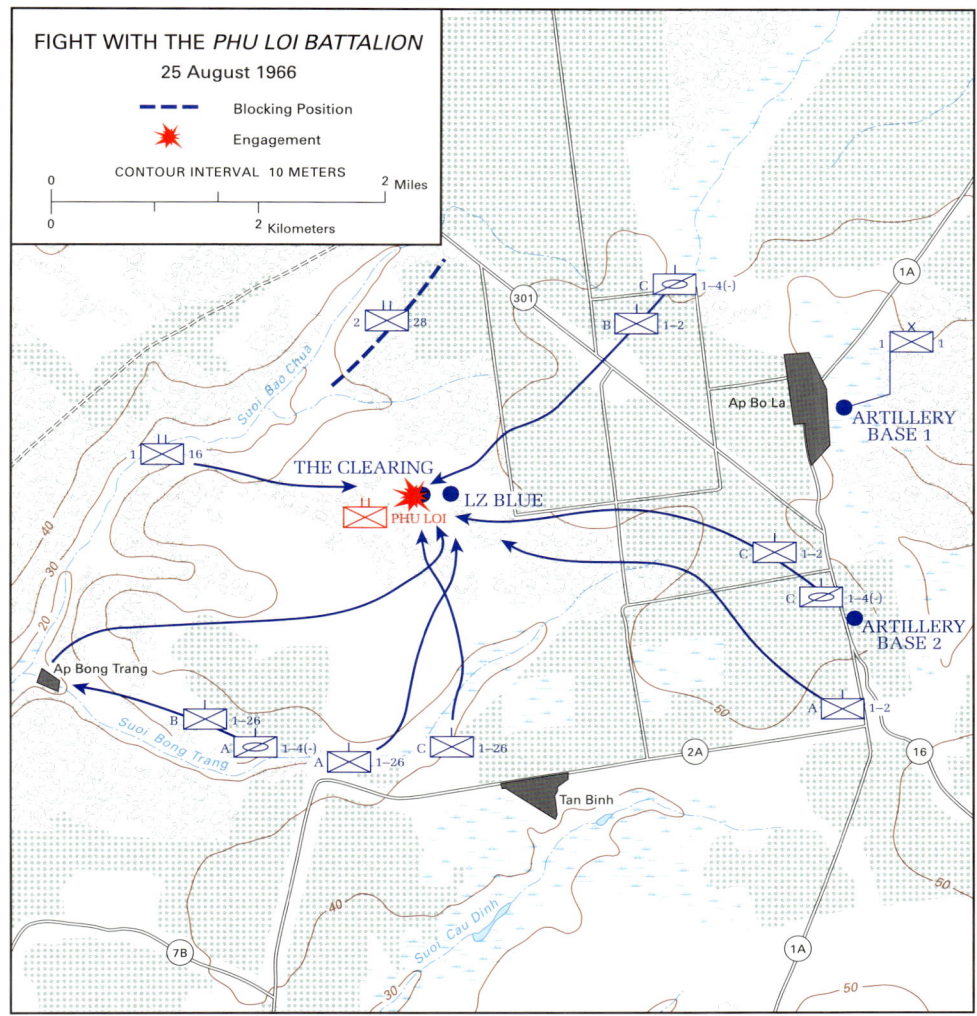

MAP 26

While the patrol struggled, Colonel Berry and General DePuy enlarged the relief force. Around 0830 Berry instructed Major Clark to detach his two other companies from road-clearing duties and move them in the direction of the battle. Colonel Gorman's 1st of the 26th Infantry received the same instruction—"move to the sound of the guns."[54] Berry also placed Gorman's Company C under Clark's control. Over the next two hours DePuy put two more battalions at Berry's disposal: Colonel

[54] Ltr, Berry to A. Berry, 28 Aug 66.

327

Wallace's 1st of the 16th Infantry and Lt. Col. Elmer D. Pendleton's 2d of the 28th Infantry. Both deployed from the airstrip at Lai Khe.[55]

While Colonel Berry and General DePuy shuffled units, Captain Mullen's relief column was already moving toward the beleaguered patrol. Around 0900 Mullen joined his command on the ground. A short while later, believing that his men were approaching the patrol but still unsure of its exact location, Mullen left a platoon at a small clearing to guard his rear and pushed the rest of his column deeper into the base camp. By then, his force had moved a little over four kilometers from Artillery Base 2.[56]

Then things began to go wrong. The tank leading Mullen's convoy and one of the M113s broke down and fell out of line. At almost that moment the Viet Cong attacked the security platoon in the clearing, inflicting heavy casualties. Receiving a frantic call for help, Mullen wheeled his vehicles around and raced toward the fight. But no sooner had the troops entered the clearing when they were pinned down by heavy fire.[57]

The clearing, which became the center of the action for the remainder of the day, was the perfect place for an ambush. Barely large enough for a single helicopter to land, it was surrounded by tall trees and clogged with thick underbrush and vines, nice cover for the Viet Cong. As the bullets flew, three of Mullen's M113 commanders were killed or wounded. As the leader of Troop C's 2d Platoon, Sgt. Wilbur J. Barrow, reported, "Every time we tried to get out, we were hit by mortars and hand grenades." As the commanders fell, Barrow continued, "privates were taking command of the tracks and calling me to ask for help. My answer to them was to pick up their wounded and take salt pills and drink water, and pray, pray, pray! There was no help for anyone."[58]

Mullen, who had taken cover in a small trench line at the clearing's northern edge, was more hopeful than the sergeant. Believing that his force could withstand the onslaught, he felt that this was an opportunity to hit the Viet Cong while they were massed and recommended that Major Clark delay any reinforcement until American firepower could be brought to bear all around. Clark rejected the advice, and Colonel Berry endorsed his decision. The commander of an infantry company under attack, Berry said later, hardly had the perspective to decide for or against a relief attempt.[59]

By noon that day, 25 August, the units that Berry had selected as a relief force were en route to Mullen. Company A, 1st of the 2d Infantry,

---

[55] AAR, Opn Amarillo, 1st Bde, 1st Inf Div, p. 6.

[56] Interv, author with Brig Gen William J. Mullen III, 24 Feb 94, Historians files, CMH. See also Interv, Brownlee and Mullen with DePuy, 26 Mar 79, sec. 6, pp. 16–17.

[57] Interv, Brownlee and Mullen with DePuy, 26 Mar 79, sec. 6, pp. 15, 17; Interv, author with Lt Gen Sidney B. Berry, Jr., 15 Mar 95, Historians files, CMH.

[58] Annual Hist Sum, 1966, 1st Sqdn, 4th Cav, pp. 21–22.

[59] Intervs, author with Mullen, 24 Feb 94, and with Berry, 15 Mar 95, plus Brownlee and Mullen with Depuy, 26 Mar 79, sec. 6, p. 17.

was about two kilometers away and maneuvering northwest toward the fight. Captain Johannesen's Company B, 1st of the 2d Infantry, and Captain Slattery's Troop C, 1st of the 4th Cavalry, had linked up two and a half kilometers northeast of the battle and were moving southwest. The force included part of the battalion command group—but not Major Clark, who was overhead in his helicopter. Company C, 1st of the 26th Infantry, was advancing north toward the action.[60]

As these reinforcements converged on Mullen, additional forces were preparing to pile on. Colonel Pendleton's 2d of the 28th Infantry moved eastward from Lai Khe, first on foot and then by helicopter, to occupy blocking positions directly north of the battle. Colonel Wallace's 1st of the 16th Infantry helicoptered about twenty-five hundred meters west of Mullen's clearing and pushed east. Meanwhile, Colonel Gorman, his command group, and Companies A and B, 1st of the 26th Infantry, had joined up with the armored personnel carriers of Troop A, 1st of the 4th Cavalry, and were preparing to enter the battle from the south. Thick jungle, soggy ground, and caution born of a certainty that the Viet Cong were nearby made progress slow.[61]

Around noon, after moving rapidly west across mostly open ground, Johannesen's Company B and Slattery's Troop C were slowed by dense jungle and formed up in a column. Since they had only the vaguest notion of where the embattled platoon was, they advanced toward the sound of circling helicopters. Close to 1300, after taking what Colonel Berry called "an interminable time," the two units neared the clearing. The infantrymen then separated from the mounted troops and began to sweep southwest toward Mullen against stiff opposition. Heavy automatic weapons fire from Viet Cong in the trees and incoming mortar fire pinned them down. When a grenade injured Johannesen, his intelligence officer, Capt. George M. Downs, replaced him. Company B made three unsuccessful attempts to break through, but with each try more and more men were wounded or became separated. Only fourteen made the last charge. By then, Captain Downs himself was wounded and almost everyone was exhausted. Clark's communications officer took charge.[62]

Slattery's cavalry troop found the going easier. Encountering almost continuous sniping, the troopers were well secured in their tanks and armored personnel carriers and made their way steadily through the

---

[60] Memo, Prillaman for 1st Inf Div Distribution, 3 Sep 66, sub: Journal Summary, 24–26 August 1966 (Operation AMARILLO); Daily Jnl, 1st Bde, 1st Inf Div, 25 Aug 66, Historians files, CMH.

[61] Annual Hist Sum, 1966, 1st Sqdn, 4th Cav, p. 18; Memo, Prillaman for 1st Inf Div Distribution, 3 Sep 66, sub: Journal Summary, 24–26 August 1966 (Operation AMARILLO).

[62] Ltr (quoted words), Berry to A. Berry, 28 Aug 66; Harry G. Summers, Jr., "Would You Believe . . . ?," p. 46, sidebar to Quentin L. Seitz, Jr., "Phu Loi Cornered," *Vietnam* 5 (April 1993): 42–49; Memo, Prillaman for 1st Inf Div Distribution, 3 Sep 66, sub: Journal Summary, 24–26 August 1966 (Operation AMARILLO); AARs, Opn AMARILLO, 1st Bn, 2d Inf, p. [3], and 1st Bde, 1st Inf Div, p. 7.

underbrush. As they neared the clearing, Slattery realized that Mullen's situation was precarious. Heavy enemy fire had downed an Air Force medevac helicopter in the clearing, making it impossible for other helicopters to land. But when Troop C broke through, the situation brightened. In order to keep the organization streamlined, Major Clark immediately put all units in or near the clearing under Mullen's command.[63]

Slattery and his men entered a scene of disarray. Wounded and dead littered the battleground, and some of the men had become separated from their superiors and were no longer firing their weapons. Slattery soon found Mullen and suggested that he remove the wounded to Landing Zone BLUE, which Slattery had established some four hundred meters to the east during his advance on the clearing. As preparations were made to move them, the 1st of the 2d's command group, minus Clark, arrived at BLUE, now secured by the battalion's Company A. Escorted by two platoons, the command group quickly made its way to the clearing. Mullen, though still in command, was no longer the senior officer present.[64]

Colonel Berry was not happy with the American performance. After hours of close-quarter combat, a cohesive perimeter did not exist. To make matters worse, as reinforcements from different battalions converged through the dense jungle, they were becoming intermingled and spread over a large area. Deciding that these problems were the result of a lack of central command and control, Berry ordered Major Clark to take charge on the ground.[65]

Clark's helicopter touched down at Landing Zone BLUE, followed shortly by Berry. As the officers reached the clearing, the continuing chaos confirmed the judgment that the situation required new leadership. They were talking over their plans when, suddenly, a bullet struck Clark in the head; Berry was unscathed. Slattery and a nearby soldier pulled the wounded man to cover and then moved him to an armored personnel carrier serving as an aid station. But the medics could do nothing. Clark was dead.[66]

With Major Clark gone, Colonel Berry took over. He would later describe the hours that followed as a time when he "ran around like a crazy man getting things moving." He ordered soldiers hiding in the thicket back into the fight. He then saw to the wounded by having the armored personnel carriers shuttle them back and forth between the clearing and Landing Zone BLUE. But, by taking command on the ground, Berry lost

[63] AAR, Opn AMARILLO, 1st Bde, 1st Inf Div, p. 6; Memo, Prillaman for 1st Inf Div Distribution, 3 Sep 66, sub: Journal Summary, 24–26 August 1966 (Operation AMARILLO); Annual Hist Sum, 1966, 1st Sqdn, 4th Cav, p. 18.

[64] Annual Hist Sum, 1966, 1st Sqdn, 4th Cav, pp. 19–20.

[65] Ltr, Berry to A. Berry, 28 Aug 66; Memo, Prillaman for 1st Inf Div Distribution, 3 Sep 66, sub: Journal Summary, 24–26 August 1966 (Operation AMARILLO).

[66] Interv, author with Berry, 15 Mar 95; Daily Jnl, 1st Bde, 1st Inf Div, 25 Aug 66; Ltr, Berry to A. Berry, 28 Aug 66.

the "big picture" and could no longer coordinate either the movement of his other battalions or the delivery of fire support. Those tasks now devolved upon his operations officer, Maj. John R. Galvin, orbiting above. Berry felt that he had no other choice. Faced with an emergency on the ground, his personal presence was needed to prevent disaster.[67]

While Colonel Berry was taking charge, his battalions were converging on the scene. By 1515 companies from Colonel Wallace's 1st of the 16th, moving from the west, had reached the edge of the battle. Various contingents from Colonel Gorman's 1st of the 26th were approaching from the south and southwest, and Colonel Pendleton's 2d of the 28th was completing its movement to blocking positions a few kilometers north of the clearing.[68]

The fight intensified during the afternoon. Elements of Gorman's 1st of the 26th Infantry overwhelmed a machine gun position, while his Company B joined the 3d Platoon, Troop A, 1st of the 4th Cavalry, in an assault on the enemy's east flank. Although meeting heavy resistance, the Americans punched into a network of bunkers and trenches. While his soldiers regrouped to penetrate deeper, Berry halted the assault and ordered Gorman to shift west to bolster the 1st of the 2d Infantry, which was "being chewed to pieces."[69] As Gorman moved, two companies of Colonel Wallace's 1st of the 16th Infantry swept through two Viet Cong camps just west of the clearing, but found only ammunition and clothing stored in tunnels, trenches, and bunkers. At 1600 they reached elements of the 1st of the 2d and 1st of the 26th. By then, the two had become so completely intermingled that determining which was responsible for what was practically impossible.[70]

Berry took further steps to ease the pressure on the 1st of the 2d Infantry by ordering Wallace's battalion to attack north. It would be a difficult maneuver. The 1st of the 16th Infantry had to turn ninety degrees in heavy jungle, with Company B on the left, Company A on the right, and Company C and the battalion command group in the rear.[71]

But an enemy assault preempted Wallace's attack. As the Americans moved into position, the right platoon of Capt. Peter S. Knight's Company A came under heavy fire from Viet Cong well entrenched in a deep bunker system immediately to the company's front. Hit with 57-mm. recoilless rifles, .50 caliber machine guns, grenade launchers, and small arms, Captain Knight ordered his troops to advance and committed his reserve platoon. As they closed with the enemy, Knight was killed lead-

---

[67] Ltr (quotation), Berry to A. Berry, 28 Aug 66; AAR, Opn AMARILLO, 1st Bde, 1st Inf Div, p. 18.

[68] AAR, Opn AMARILLO, 1st Bde, 1st Inf Div, pp. 7, 16.

[69] Summers, "Would You Believe . . . ?," p. 46.

[70] AAR, Opn AMARILLO, 1st Bde, 1st Inf Div, pp. 7, 16; Paul F. Gorman, "Daring DOBOL, 1966–1967: Part III of the Story of 1st Battalion, 26th Infantry Regiment," p. 33, copy in Historians files, CMH.

[71] ORLL, 1 Aug–31 Oct 66, 1st Inf Div, p. 7; Seitz, "Phu Loi Cornered," pp. 47–48.

ing an attack on a machine gun and all of his officers were wounded. Meanwhile, Company B began its push, moving forward almost two hundred meters against little resistance. Rather than disperse his forces too far, Colonel Wallace stopped the unit's forward movement. While it idled, awaiting developments, the enemy withdrew. The impetus for large-scale action on both sides seemed spent.[72]

As Wallace's fight petered out, the last of the American reinforcements began arriving at the clearing. Colonel Gorman rode in on an M48, and Colonel Berry climbed aboard to shake his hand. At that moment, Berry recalled, "a machine gun opened up on us, and we unceremoniously scrambled off the tank, dashed across the clearing, and jumped into the VC trench I was using as a CP." Shortly afterward, Berry placed Gorman in charge of all companies in contact with the insurgents and returned to his helicopter to resume control of the 1st Brigade. He had played an unusual role that day but was convinced that he had done the right thing: "I was at the critical place at the critical time, where the commander should be."[73]

As the sun set, the Americans prepared three night laagers. The 1st of the 2d Infantry, the 1st of the 26th Infantry, and a portion of the 1st of the 16th Infantry remained in the clearing, where they established a unified position under Colonel Gorman's command. The rest of Colonel Wallace's 1st of the 16th created a perimeter about four hundred meters to the north. Colonel Pendleton's 2d of the 28th Infantry stayed in its blocking positions still farther north. Throughout the night, artillery and a flare ship kept the battlefield illuminated.[74]

The next day, 26 August, started poorly. Colonel Berry called for an east-to-west napalm drop in the narrow slot between Gorman and Wallace, and the jets screamed overhead with their deadly payloads. The first thirteen canisters landed on target, but the fourteenth hit a tree and careened toward the waiting Americans. Burning jelly splattered across Colonel Gorman's command group, igniting a map in the colonel's hands. Despite the accident, Gorman requested that the bombing continue. The twenty-second canister fell short, killing 2 Americans and wounding 14. Deciding that his luck had run out, Berry called off further strikes.[75]

For the rest of the day Berry and his men concentrated on finding the Viet Cong. Gorman's battalion moved north against the fortified position that Wallace had been primed to attack the previous afternoon, but the area was empty. Meanwhile, Wallace's men moved east and then searched to the south. There they found the bodies of six members of

---

[72] Seitz, "Phu Loi Cornered," p. 48.

[73] Ltr (quotations), Berry to A. Berry, 28 Aug 66; Daily Jnl, 1st Bde, 1st Inf Div, 25 Aug 66.

[74] AAR, Opn AMARILLO, 1st Bde, 1st Inf Div, p. 8.

[75] Ltr, Berry to A. Berry, 28 Aug 66; Interv, Brownlee and Mullen with DePuy, 26 Mar 79, sec. 6, p. 18; AAR, Opn AMARILLO, 1st Bde, 1st Inf Div, p. 8; Seitz, "Phu Loi Cornered," p. 49.

Mullen's lost patrol. That was the bad news. The good news was that, on 26 August, the other nine who had taken refuge in the bunker made their way to Landing Zone BLUE, where they received a warm welcome. It was a last eventful moment in the operation. AMARILLO ended five days later, with no further action.[76]

During the nine-day operation the battle casualties were high on both sides. The Americans suffered 41 killed, 34 on 25 August. Berry's men accounted for 54 enemy dead and possibly another 92, with the Air Force adding 45 more by body count and possibly another 30. Shortly after the operation a South Vietnamese intelligence source reported that the enemy actually had lost 171 men: 101 from the *Phu Loi Battalion*, 60 from the *C62 Company*, and 10 laborers. Whichever figures were accurate, the Viet Cong had suffered severely. Out of a force estimated to be around five hundred men, either figure meant that the *Phu Loi Battalion* and the *C62 Company* were down to about half strength.[77]

In evaluating his brigade's performance during AMARILLO, Colonel Berry praised the aggressive patrolling of the 1st Battalion, 2d Infantry, which had generated the fight on 25 August. He claimed that as a result of the soldiers' efforts and performance, the brigade had been "victorious" in this "major battle" against the "elite *Phu Loi Battalion*."[78] Berry's assessment was, perhaps, too generous. The patrol's presence in the *Phu Loi Battalion*'s base camp, not its patrolling ability, triggered the fight. Indeed, a report penned by Colonel Prillaman characterized the fight as "essentially a meeting engagement in which neither side was prepared for or really wanted heavy contact." The isolation of Company C's patrol, he added, "forced us to fight, and the invasion of their base camp forced the Viet Cong to hold their positions in the face of a strong US effort."[79] Although still satisfied that his brigade won the day, Berry himself acknowledged many years later that "we ultimately committed about 3,000 American soldiers against about 500 Viet Cong. The VC had several advantages, principally well constructed, heavily fortified positions in jungle terrain they knew intimately. We thrashed our way almost blindly into the enemy's base camp and fought him on his home ground under conditions favorable to him."[80]

Retargeting the *9th Division*

After meeting the *Phu Loi Battalion*, and during the next two months, the 1st Division fought over old ground north of Saigon as it pressed on

---

[76] ORLL, 1 Aug–31 Oct 66, 1st Inf Div, p. 1; AAR, Opn AMARILLO, 1st Bde, 1st Inf Div, pp. 8–9; Ltr, Berry to A. Berry, 28 Aug 66.
[77] AAR, Opn AMARILLO, 1st Bde, 1st Inf Div, pp. 2, 12.
[78] Ibid., p. 15.
[79] AAR, Opn AMARILLO, 1st Bn, 2d Inf, p. [4].
[80] Ltr, Lt Gen Sidney B. Berry, Jr., to Brig Gen William J. Mullen III, 26 Dec 94, copy in Historians files, CMH.

with the search for its nemesis, the *9th Division*. One of its efforts was Operation Tulsa, which again returned the 1st and 3d Brigades to the mission area of Highway 13. From 9 to 16 October General DePuy used ten battalions of Americans and South Vietnamese to clear the big artery and bring the enemy division to battle. Starting on the twelfth, two large convoys traveled north, and for the first time since the end of El Paso II in August the highway was open to civilian traffic. For the South Vietnamese who used the highway that was certainly good news, but again there was every prospect that the Viet Cong would close it down when the Americans moved elsewhere.[81]

The larger hope of engaging the *9th Division* went unfulfilled. Lt. Gen. Jonathan O. Seaman wrote that he had "fully expected the Main Force units to make an effort to ambush the convoys—but the devils didn't even try. I guess they knew we were ready for them." Expressing the continuing frustration of American commanders, he concluded, "we are still having trouble picking a fight with the North Vietnamese and Main Force VC units in our zone of operations."[82]

After Tulsa, with the 3d Brigade returning to Lai Khe, Colonel Berry's 1st Brigade remained in the field to carry out a new operation, Shenandoah. DePuy planned to follow the approach employed so successfully in El Paso II at the Minh Thanh Road. First, the brigade would arrange for close air support and place rapid-reaction forces and firebases in the area of operations. Then it would send an armored column disguised as a small force on a reconnaissance mission along Highway 13 and later the Minh Thanh Road. If the enemy attacked, American firepower would respond quickly, and the reaction force would close in, either to attack or to block the escape of the ambushers. The 3d Brigade would be available to reinforce.[83]

On 18 October the 1st Brigade went into action, using Quan Loi as a base of operations. Over the next three days armored cavalry and other brigade elements moved north to Loc Ninh, hoping to provoke an attack. When the Viet Cong did not come out to fight, the Americans returned to Quan Loi. Colonel Berry shifted his attention to the southwest, where he set up his trap on the Minh Thanh Road. On 24 October, after a day's delay caused by heavy rains, brigade vehicles proceeded south from Quan Loi and then west to Minh Thanh. Once again, the Viet Cong did not take the bait.

That left the Minh Thanh Plantation. On 25 and 26 October Colonel Berry put units north and northwest of the plantation, but when they

---

[81] AAR, Opn Tulsa, 1st Inf Div, 26 Mar 67, pp. 1, 16, Historians files, CMH.

[82] Ibid., pp. 6–7, 16; Ltr (quotations), Lt Gen Jonathan O. Seaman to Ellsworth Gosling, 23 Oct 66, Seaman Papers, MHI.

[83] Op Sum, Opn Shenandoah, MACV, Nov 66, Historians files, CMH; AARs, Opn Shenandoah, 1st Inf Div, 26 Mar 67, pp. 10, 17, and 1st Bde, 1st Inf Div, 5 Jan 67, pp. 3–4, box 2, 81/471, RG 338, NARA.

Armor in herringbone formation during Shenandoah

found nothing, he shifted them to the south. Two days later Berry found something to fight, when his brigade bumped into a main force unit—later identified as the *272d Regiment's 3d Battalion*. He immediately sent Colonel Gorman's 1st of the 26th Infantry to scour the area. Lt. Col. Jack G. Whitted's 1st of the 28th Infantry, meanwhile, was to search three or four kilometers farther east, close to where intelligence reports had placed the enemy battalion earlier.[84]

Gorman's men found the Viet Cong first. While patrolling through the brush, a platoon from Company B heard voices approaching. Settling into a hasty ambush, the Americans opened up with a long volley of automatic fire and 4 or 5 Viet Cong went down. The rest of the enemy column withdrew but ran into another platoon from Company B, and a second firefight broke out. Shortly afterward, an air strike pounded the Viet Cong.[85]

Berry was convinced that he had found a major unit, and he intended to surround and destroy it. Two more battalions were thrown into the operation. Colonel Pendleton's 2d of the 28th Infantry helicoptered a few kilometers west of the fight; Lt. Col. Lewis R. Bauman's 2d of the

[84] Rpt, 17th Mil Hist Det, 1st Inf Div, n.d., sub: The Battle of Cam Xe, 28–29 October 1966, p. 1, and Memo, 2d Lt E. J. Heacock, Asst Adj Gen, 1st Inf Div, for 1st Inf Div Soldier, 12 Nov 66, sub: The Enemy Situation, in VNI 108, CMH.

[85] Memo, Lt Col Paul F. Gorman, G–3, 1st Inf Div, for G–2, 1st Inf Div, 17 Dec 66, sub: Battle of Cam Xe (28–29 October 1966), pp. 1–3, in VNI 108, CMH.

18th Infantry air-assaulted along a stream, the Da Keu, on the south and headed northeast. The other two battalions also spent the late afternoon moving into position—the 1st of the 26th to the north and the 1st of the 28th to the east. Satisfied that he had the Viet Cong surrounded with four battalions and that he had covered the gaps with artillery, Berry held off ordering a ground attack.[86]

Instead, beginning about 1745, shells and bombs pummeled the suspected emplacements. The pounding continued all night, with the Air Force flying seventy sorties and the artillery firing some two thousand rounds. Berry's trap, however, was not airtight because at some point during the night the insurgents slipped away to the southwest, using a route that ran between Pendleton and Bauman.[87]

The next day, 29 October, General DePuy assumed command of the operation. Bringing in Col. Sidney M. Marks and his 3d Brigade headquarters, he gave him Bauman's and Pendleton's battalions and sent them to head off the Viet Cong. They deployed by helicopter twenty-five kilometers south of Minh Thanh and then patrolled along probable withdrawal routes throughout the day. Their efforts were not productive, and Pendleton's battalion returned to Lai Khe. Meanwhile, under Colonel Berry's command, Whitted's battalion swept through the previous day's target area and Gorman's moved south to block. Although the two battalions took a few prisoners, they mostly encountered abandoned base camps. Scattered around the battlefield were more than 60 enemy bodies, which, when added to the tally from the previous day, brought the body count to 74. Air and artillery fire were apparently responsible for most of the casualties. The Americans suffered 5 killed.[88]

Although DePuy considered SHENANDOAH a limited success, it was clear that the *9th Division* was refusing battle and the certainty of being on the receiving end of American firepower. What the U.S. command did not know was that most of the *9th* had pulled back into War Zone C in Tay Ninh Province, but not with any intention of laying low. Already, General Thanh was readying plans for a new offensive against the Americans. This time, however, the target would be carefully chosen, not the well tested 1st Division and its aggressive commander, General DePuy, but a newly arrived U.S. infantry brigade near Tay Ninh City that had yet to be bloodied. The main force war in III Corps was about to grow.

---

[86] Interv, Brownlee and Mullen with DePuy, 26 Mar 79, sec. 6, p. 4.

[87] AARs, Opn SHENANDOAH, 1st Bde, 1st Inf Div, pp. 5, 9, and 1st Inf Div, p. 10; Memo, Heacock for 1st Inf Div Soldier, 12 Nov 66, sub: The Enemy Situation; Rpt, 17th Mil Hist Det, 1st Inf Div, n.d., sub: The Battle of Cam Xe, 28–29 October 1966, p. 3.

[88] Rpt, 17th Mil Hist Det, 1st Inf Div, n.d., sub: The Battle of Cam Xe, 28–29 October 1966, p. 3; AAR, Opn SHENANDOAH, 1st Bde, 1st Inf Div, p. 9.

15

The 25th Division's War

While the 1st Division waged a running battle with some of the best enemy units north of Saigon, the 25th Division off to the west fought a different kind of war. When the 25th's commander, General Weyand, reached Cu Chi in March, he had no reservations about undertaking conventional search and destroy operations to clear out resistance around his bases and along the highways. From the beginning, however, he was skeptical of pursuit operations deep into the countryside, doubting that the chase of the main forces from place to place would have a permanent effect on the Communist underground or do much to enlarge the security zone west of the capital. The outgrowth of this skepticism was his pacification approach to the war. It combined military operations with police and civic action programs to provide security for the local inhabitants and other reasons for supporting the Saigon government.[1]

Weyand's view of the war was shaped by several factors. The war was not the same throughout the theater, and there was no single way to fight it. He took seriously President Johnson's admonition at Honolulu in February to make the "other war"—pacification—a primary goal of the American effort. He also saw what pacification, consistently applied, could accomplish. In I Corps the U.S. Marines, longtime proponents of the small wars philosophy, were sending squad-size teams into villages to work with the Popular Forces and ensure that civic action efforts were more than just one-shot affairs. For Weyand, the Communists' tenacious hold on the rural population, not the main force threat, gave them their strength. As he later commented, "No single element of the enemy's organization . . . , if attacked alone, would cause the collapse of his force structure or the reduction of his will to resist." Furthermore, he continued, the destruction of a large Viet Cong force would probably have little effect on the enemy's control of a populated area—the ultimate objective of U.S. operations. In fact, expending too much time and effort on the main force war reduced the pressure American

---

[1] Frederick C. Weyand, "Winning the People in Hau Nghia Province," *Army* 17 (January 1967): 52–55.

*General Weyand (right) demonstrates a Viet Cong land mine to
Deputy Secretary of Defense Cyrus R. Vance and others.*

units could exert on the remainder of the Viet Cong apparatus that bore
so directly upon the South Vietnamese people. What was needed,
Weyand concluded, was a balanced approach "against the entire enemy
system from hamlet level to Hanoi" rather than one that concentrated
only on the regular forces. The results of Weyand's thinking were plain
to see in the way he fought in Hau Nghia and Long An Provinces.[2]

The Struggle for Hau Nghia

Flat, low lying, and heavily populated, Hau Nghia Province was strategically significant to both sides. The Communists used the province
to link their forces in the Mekong Delta with their command-and-con-

[2] Debriefing, Weyand, 15 Jul 68, pp. 3–4 (quotations, p. 3), Senior Officer Debriefing
Program, DA, Historians files, CMH.

trol and logistical bases in Tay Ninh Province and Cambodia. Hau Nghia also provided a major avenue of approach to Saigon along Highway 1, which ran from Saigon to enemy sanctuaries on the Cambodian border. To keep pressure on the capital, the *B2 Front*'s *Military Region 4* maintained several strongholds in the province. The most important of these were the Plain of Reeds, a vast swampland that comprised the western half of Hau Nghia Province, and the Boi Loi Woods, the Ho Bo Woods, and the Filhol Rubber Plantation, a succession of heavily forested areas that ran along the province's northern border.

In the spring of 1966 Hau Nghia was a dangerous place for the South Vietnamese government. According to MACV statistics, the province controlled no more than ten out of one hundred thirty-one hamlets. In fact, the Viet Cong ruled hamlets extending right to the outskirts of Bao Trai, the provincial capital, and many of them had not seen a government official in more than three years. The people were openly hostile to South Vietnamese troops and their American advisers, and travel on all but the main roads was hazardous day or night. South Vietnamese units in the province rarely ventured from their garrisons, and then only at great risk.[3]

For the most part, Communist strength in Hau Nghia rested upon numerous small bands of guerrillas. North Vietnamese formations were not present, the only main force units being three understrength battalions of the *165A PLAF Regiment*. Hau Nghia also lacked local force battalions, although four were based in neighboring provinces and occasionally entered Hau Nghia. Each district, village, and hamlet, however, maintained a contingent of guerrillas to enforce Communist Party edicts, to mine roads, and to harass government officials, troops, and installations. Collectively, these guerrillas represented the equivalent of six battalions, vastly outnumbering the government's Regional and Popular Forces. Because the Communists so dominated the countryside, the Regional and Popular Forces were unable to find willing recruits.[4]

Backing Saigon's local forces in Hau Nghia before the arrival of the U.S. 25th Division were the National Police and the South Vietnamese 25th Infantry Division. The police were widely despised by the population; the 25th—one of the worst divisions in the South Vietnamese Army—was poorly trained, ill led, and demoralized. The troops never ventured far from their bases and the major roads that linked them, in part because Premier Ky had ordered the 25th Division to keep the vast majority of its men in their barracks at all times so that they could return to the nation's capital at a moment's notice to thwart attempted coups.[5]

---

[3] Briefing, CG, 25th Inf Div, for Preparedness Investigating Subcommittee, Senate Committee on Armed Services, 23 Oct 66, vol. 3, incl. 2, pp. 3–4, box 16, 70A/782, RG 334, NARA.

[4] Eric M. Bergerud, *The Dynamics of Defeat: The Vietnam War in Hau Nghia Province* (Boulder, Colo.: Westview Press, 1991), pp. 93–94.

[5] Ibid., pp. 102–03.

Given the nature of the situation west of Saigon, and his limited resources and other constraints, General Weyand was almost bound to settle on different fighting methods than General DePuy's. Because main force units were more common in the 1st Division's sector, DePuy's primary mission was to eliminate their threat to the capital. Weyand did not disagree with this emphasis, but in Hau Nghia, with few enemy regulars to fight, he was able to focus more on pacification support. A shortage of U.S. troops also influenced Weyand's battle plans. In the spring of 1966 he had only his 1st and 2d Brigades, but in April General Westmoreland took the rest of the 1st Battalion, 69th Armor, and sent it north to the Central Highlands, leaving Weyand even more shorthanded. The monsoon season, which complicated large-scale operations in Hau Nghia between May and October, and Westmoreland's orders to improve the performance of the South Vietnamese through increased assistance and "buddy" operations with their 25th Division further shaped Weyand's approach to the war in the province.[6]

Weyand's first major offensive was CIRCLE PINES—a reinforced brigade-size search and destroy operation whose results helped crystallize his uneasiness with large-scale attacks. The target was the *165A Regiment*, and the area of operations was the Filhol Plantation just west of the Saigon River, about thirty kilometers from the capital city, and the Ho Bo Woods northwest of the plantation. The region was flat, barely above sea level, and was covered with rubber trees, underbrush, and bamboo hedgerows—good concealment for the guerrillas. In addition, the Viet Cong had improved the area by constructing tunnels, bunkers, and trenches to form an excellent network of defensive positions and evacuation routes.[7]

CIRCLE PINES began on the morning of 29 March. Over the next ten days four battalions combed their assigned sectors, hoping to push the Viet Cong up against U.S. blocking forces. Although the Americans found and destroyed enemy supplies, the Viet Cong decided in general not to fight. The one exception was an enemy attack on 5 April against a company-size overnight position about fifteen kilometers north of Cu Chi. Artillery helped beat back the assault, but when reinforcements arrived within the hour, the Viet Cong were gone. Two days later CIRCLE PINES came to a close. In the ten days of searching and skirmishing the Americans killed 170 of the enemy by body count at a cost of 30 dead and 195 wounded. But more important, and somewhat discouraging from the standpoint of achieving lasting security, the Americans immediately left the battle area after the operation ended (*Map 27*).[8]

The next effort, Operation MAILI, proceeded more to General Weyand's liking. During MAILI Lt. Col. Harley F. Mooney's 1st Battalion, 27th Infan-

---

[6] Ibid., p. 148; Clarke, *Final Years*, pp. 184–86.

[7] ORLL, 1 Jan–30 Apr 66, 25th Inf Div, n.d., app. 5, p. 2, box 8A, 67A/5293, RG 319, NARA.

[8] Ibid., app. 5, pp. 2, 8.

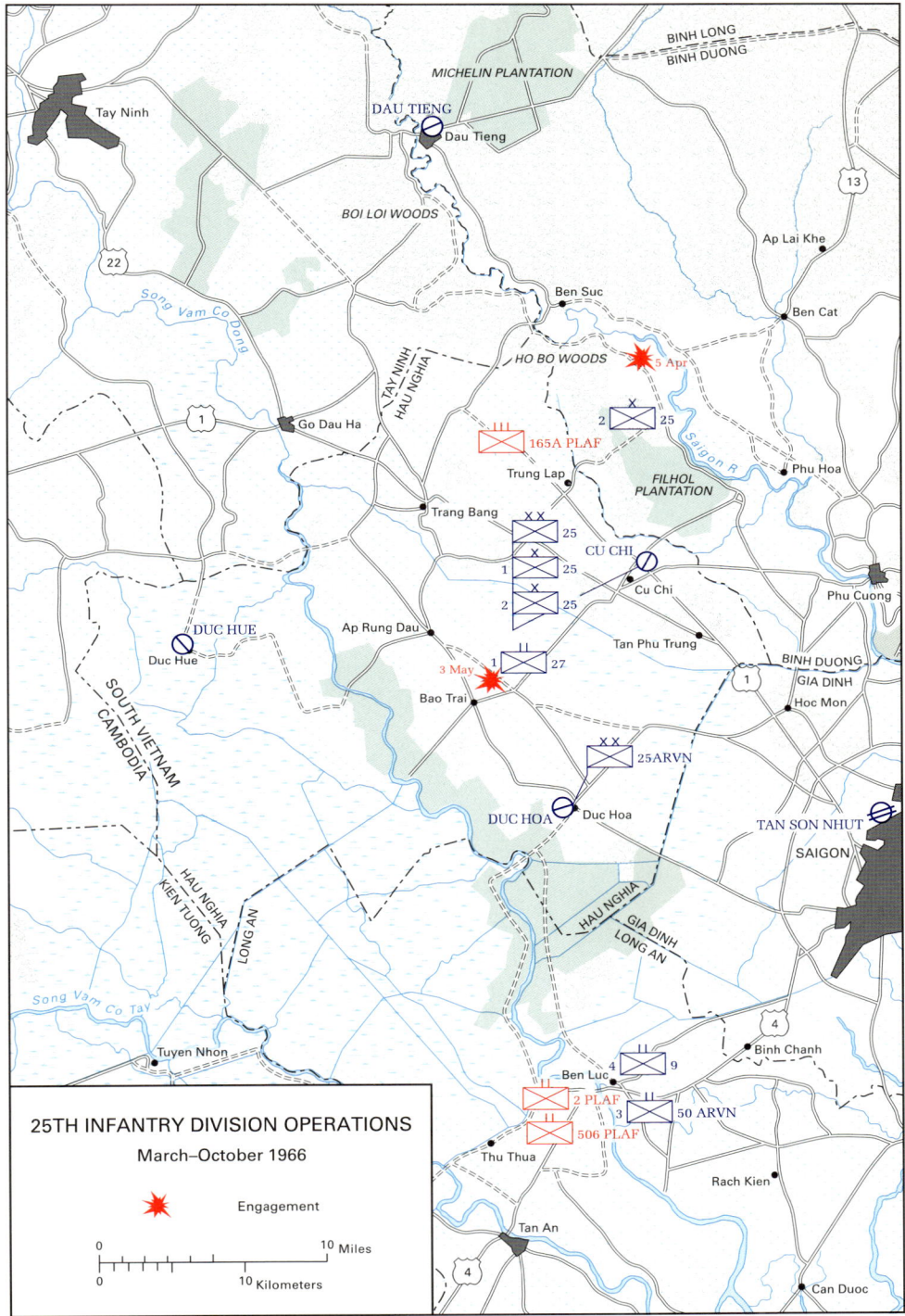

25TH INFANTRY DIVISION OPERATIONS

March–October 1966

✴ Engagement

0 —— 10 Miles

0 —— 10 Kilometers

MAP 27

Go Team members check credentials of farmers in Hau Nghia Province.

try, went after the Viet Cong around Bao Trai about thirty-five kilometers west of Saigon. Over the past few months the enemy had succeeded in driving South Vietnamese forces from the area, and Colonel Mooney's mission was to even the score. On 27 April he established a battalion command post northeast of Bao Trai and then conducted air assaults, search and destroy operations, patrols, and ambushes. He complemented his military activities with extensive civic action measures to underscore the benefits the allied side could offer the population.

What distinguished MAILI from many predecessor operations in III Corps was the degree to which American and South Vietnamese forces cooperated to achieve the operation's pacification goals. Colonel Mooney and his staff met daily with an officer from the South Vietnamese unit involved, the 25th Division's 49th Regiment, as well as with the province and district/sector chiefs and their American advisers. The group critiqued that day's actions and discussed plans for the next. This approach cemented close working relationships between the allies.[9]

Mooney divided the area of operations into sectors, which followed hamlet boundaries. Each day he selected one sector to be cleared of Viet Cong in order to provide security for a South Vietnamese "Go Team," consisting of National Police, psychological operations troops, intelli-

[9] ORLL, 1 May–31 Jul 66, 25th Inf Div, 3 Aug 66, app. 2, pp. 2, 11, and app. 14, pp. 5, 10–11, Historians files, CMH.

342

gence specialists, and medical personnel. The police searched each house and checked the credentials of the residents; the psychological operations team, equipped with bullhorns and leaflets, informed the people of various South Vietnamese government aid programs available to them; the intelligence team attempted to identify members of the Viet Cong underground and to recruit agents; and the medical group offered to treat the area's sick and infirm. An American officer and a noncommissioned officer from the province advisory team provided liaison between the Vietnamese and U.S. platoon and company commanders.

Of all the techniques employed to engage the enemy during the operation, nighttime ambushes were the most successful. From the beginning, American and South Vietnamese companies assisted one another in laying down squad-size ambushes. The one significant action occurred early on the morning of 3 May, when from fifty to seventy-five Viet Cong—believed to consist of one local force and two main force platoons—assaulted one of the ambush positions. Mooney's men drove off the attackers but fifteen minutes later were hit again, this time from three sides. After calling in artillery support, they repulsed the second assault, and reinforcements arrived soon afterward. The Americans suffered 5 killed and 5 wounded, while the Viet Cong left behind 31 dead. No other major contacts took place during the remainder of the operation, which ended on 12 May. In the few small engagements that preceded and followed the one large action, the allies killed another 16 insurgents, losing none of their own.[10]

Within days of Maili's end, the 25th Division mounted Operation Wahiawa. Intelligence suggested that the *165A Regiment*'s headquarters and its *1st Battalion*, as well as supply depots and an important commoliaison station, could be found in an area thirty to sixty kilometers northwest of Saigon that encompassed the Filhol Plantation, the Ho Bo Woods, and the Boi Loi Woods. Since the target zone was relatively close to the division's main base at Cu Chi, General Weyand committed all six of his battalions to the operation. For twelve days, starting on 16 May, the division's units moved from objective to objective with almost no resistance, although on occasion they ran into sniper fire, land mines, and booby traps. In the end, the Americans found and destroyed large caches of supplies and killed 157 of the enemy.[11]

The 25th Division conducted three area pacification operations in June and July. The shortest lasted three weeks and the others four. Lt. Col. John M. Shultz's 2d Battalion, 14th Infantry, conducted Fort Smith between 3 June and 3 July in Trang Bang District; Lt. Col. Boyd T. Bashore's 2d Battalion, 27th Infantry, carried out Fresno from 13 June to 14 July in an area west of Bao Trai; and Colonel Mooney's 1st of the 27th

---

[10] Ibid., app. 2, pp. 6, 9–11, and app. 14, pp. 4–5.
[11] AARs, Opn Wahiawa, 2d Bde, 25th Inf Div, 21 Jun 66, box 3, 81/426, and 1st Bn (Mech), 5th Inf, 10 Jun 66, box 2, 81/434, RG 338, NARA.

Infantry implemented SANTA FE between 13 June and 4 July in Duc Hoa District. During these efforts the units involved applied the control techniques employed in Operation MAILI—hamlet searches, day-and-night ambushes, and small unit patrols, often conducted with South Vietnamese military and paramilitary units on a buddy basis—to clear their assigned sectors of Viet Cong.

General Weyand believed that he was well on the way to suppressing the enemy in Hau Nghia Province, but there was still much work to be done. Beginning on 22 July, Operation KOKOHEAD targeted enemy base areas just east of the Saigon River. Using a mechanized infantry battalion and a reinforced artillery battalion in conjunction with South Vietnamese forces, Col. Thomas M. Tarpley's 2d Brigade scoured the countryside for signs of either local or main force units and called in B–52 strikes to collapse the tunnels and underground fortifications that honeycombed the area. Following one of the raids, the troops scouted a target box and captured an enemy soldier, who disclosed the location of his unit's headquarters. Guided by the information, they uncovered a large tunnel complex, with concrete walls, containing weapons and supplies. Once emptied, the tunnels were destroyed. By the end of the operation on 6 August the Americans had killed 11 of the enemy by body count and possibly another 174, with 31 more attributed to the supporting air strikes.[12]

Despite what seemed to be meager results, Weyand emphasized that the primary objective of these operations was pacification—not the destruction of the main forces. He added that no one should expect "spectacular results or large VC losses" because pacification was intended primarily to win over the local population by enhancing security.[13]

During September the 25th Division began four larger operations, three in Hau Nghia and one in Long An Province. Two of them, KAHILI and KAMUELA, produced little in the way of combat. KAHILI, which began on 17 September and ended on 14 November, was a search and destroy operation conducted by Col. William B. Sandlin's 1st Brigade. Colonel Sandlin initially concentrated on the Filhol Plantation and then extended the patrolling east of the Saigon River, where a major infiltration corridor ran. The main American unit in the operation, the 4th Battalion, 23d Infantry, worked with a battalion of the South Vietnamese 7th Regiment, 5th Infantry Division, teaming up for air assaults, ambushes, hammer and anvil operations, and patrols. In a series of small firefights the allies killed 37 of the enemy by body count and possibly another 165.[14]

KAMUELA, which began on 20 September and ended on 4 October, was also a search and destroy operation, this time along the western

---

[12] ORLL, 1 Aug–31 Oct 66, 25th Inf Div, 18 Nov 66, p. 1, Historians files, CMH.

[13] ORLL, 1 May–31 Jul 66, 25th Inf Div, p. 46.

[14] Op Sum, Opn KAHILI, MACV, Nov 66, pp. 2–8, Historians files, CMH; ORLL, 1 Nov 66–31 Jan 67, 25th Inf Div, 20 Feb 67, p. 2, box 5, 68A/75, RG 319, NARA; ORLL, 1 Aug–31 Oct 66, 25th Inf Div, p. 4.

A warehouse in Hau Nghia filled with enemy rice

edge of the Boi Loi Woods a few kilometers south of Dau Tieng. The 2d of the 14th Infantry did the hunting, initially without much luck. Then on 26 September, acting on intelligence supplied by a defector, the troops found seven supply stockpiles containing almost three hundred tons of rice. Since the Americans could not continue the operation and guard the rice, they halted the search until the following day, when a battalion from the 1st Division arrived to secure the cache. The two units oversaw the removal of nearly half the supply to Dau Tieng, for distribution to the South Vietnamese, and subsequently destroyed the rest. The operation continued for four more days, again without finding the enemy.[15]

Operation Sunset Beach began on 2 September and ended on 11 October. During this period Colonel Tarpley's 2d Brigade ranged freely across eastern and northern Hau Nghia and into southeastern Tay Ninh and southwestern Binh Duong Provinces in an attempt to find and destroy enemy forces and to interdict their lines of communication. Initially, the 1st and 2d Battalions, 27th Infantry, worked with South Vietnamese units to throw the Communists off balance so that they would be unable to disrupt the South Vietnamese national elections scheduled for 11 September. To that end, the Americans and their allies conducted a series of air and ground assaults near population centers and polling places.

---

[15] ORLL, 1 Aug–31 Oct 66, 25th Inf Div, pp. 4–5.

A few days before the election the American units pulled back from the polling places to demonstrate that they were not interfering in South Vietnam's internal affairs. On 20 September the 1st Battalion (Mechanized), 5th Infantry, joined the operation to cover the northern section of the target area. Beginning a search in the Boi Loi Woods, the troops found and destroyed supplies and fortifications but discovered no one to fight except small bands of guerrillas.[16]

On 6 September the 2d of the 27th Infantry held a county fair in the hamlet of Rung Dau, about ten kilometers south of Trang Bang. Some five hundred South Vietnamese attended. At the fair a MEDCAP team, composed of brigade and battalion surgeons, provided outpatient care for the inhabitants. The 2d Brigade also contributed clothing, candy, baseball equipment, and volleyballs to a children's festival at the hamlet of Tan Phu Trung, about seven kilometers southeast of Cu Chi; presented a brickmaking machine to the same hamlet; and delivered scrap timber to build quarters for the Popular Forces at the Trung Lap outpost, ten kilometers east of Trang Bang. Additionally, under a program called "Helping Hands," the brigade distributed clothing, food, pencils, tablets, and crayons to over forty-one hundred villagers and their children. As later claimed in a brigade report, civic action programs, such as the ones conducted during SUNSET BEACH, helped gain the friendship and trust of the local populace.[17]

The operation continued for a few more days. Small unidentified Viet Cong units killed 29 Americans and wounded 194. In turn, Colonel Tarpley's brigade reported 80 enemy killed by body count and possibly an additional 135. American aircraft supporting the operation accounted for another 6. A II Field Force analysis struck a positive note about the operation shortly before it ended, asserting that "this prolonged operation is adversely affecting local Viet Cong morale, reducing his aggressiveness, and increasing GVN influence in Hau Nghia Province." A later report emphasized the twenty-two buddy operations during SUNSET BEACH, claiming that the South Vietnamese who participated had gained not only more confidence in their military skills but also the respect of the local inhabitants.[18]

To Long An and Back

The last of the September operations took place in the Mekong Delta south of Saigon, the country's most fertile and populous territory and a cradle of the insurgency. For months Westmoreland, worried about a

---

[16] AAR, Opn SUNSET BEACH, 2d Bde, 25th Inf Div, 7 Nov 66, pp. 5–6, 10, 17, box 3, 81/426, RG 338, NARA.

[17] Ibid., pp. 24–26; Neel, *Medical Support*, p. 164; Bergerud, *Dynamics of Defeat*, pp. 165, 173.

[18] AAR, Opn SUNSET BEACH, 2d Bde, 25th Inf Div, p. 27; Monthly Eval Rpts, II FFV, Sep 66, p. 4 (quotation), and Oct 66, p. 4, Historians files, CMH.

lack of progress there, had been trying to send infantry to the delta's
Long An Province, only to run into opposition from the U.S. Embassy
and the Saigon government. Ambassador Lodge led the skeptics,
believing that American operations would alienate Long An's population and that heavy fighting and increased firepower would dampen
the rice-bowl economy that helped to feed Saigon. He was also concerned that American ground troops would take over the fighting from
the local forces as they had elsewhere, changing the whole character of
the struggle in the delta and thus postponing the day when the South
Vietnamese could stand on their own. All of this became moot, however, when the level of Viet Cong activity rose alarmingly in August
and September and civilian officials changed their minds and asked for
U.S. assistance. General Weyand, who drew the assignment, felt that he
could safely commit one battalion to the threatened province, and he
overcame Lodge's objections by promising to subordinate military operations to the broader needs of pacification. Weyand's operation, code-
named LANIKAI, became a litmus test to determine how the people of
Long An would react to U.S. forces.[19]

Different battalions rotated into and out of the operation as it progressed. Weyand assigned the mission to Colonel Sandlin's 1st Brigade, and Sandlin chose Lt. Col. Shepherd A. Booth, Jr.'s 4th Battalion,
9th Infantry, to go in first. Booth's battalion conducted what came to
be known as LANIKAI I from mid-September until 5 November, after
which other battalions took charge of the operation that continued into
1967.[20]

The 4th of the 9th Infantry had a laundry list of missions to perform.
It was to initiate search and destroy operations against enemy units and
base camps, conduct buddy operations with South Vietnamese forces,
and support pacification. Rather than merely cooperate and coordinate
with the South Vietnamese, Colonel Booth was to take operational control of the unit working with his troops—the South Vietnamese 3d
Battalion, 50th Regiment, 25th Division—and in the process record whatever lessons he and his officers could draw from their efforts. These
lessons would not only assist other U.S. units pursuing parallel missions elsewhere but also help MACV to determine whether American
forces could, in fact, function in heavily populated rural locales without
disrupting the traditional cycle of everyday life. Since LANIKAI's objectives were quite different from the standard infantry operation, Weyand
instructed Booth to hold a special briefing for his men to emphasize the
unusual circumstances under which they would operate.[21]

[19] Hunt, *Pacification*, pp. 50–52; Action Memos 120 and 122, Mission Council, 15
and 20 Sep 66, sub: Minutes of the Mission Council Meetings, September 12 and 17,
1966, p. 6 and pp. 1–2, Historians files, CMH.
[20] AAR, Opn LANIKAI, 4th Bn, 9th Inf, 30 Nov 66, p. 1, box 5, 68A/75, RG 319, NARA.
[21] Ibid., pp. 5–6. See also Action Memo 122, Mission Council, 20 Sep 66, sub: Minutes
of the Mission Council Meeting, September 17, 1966, pp. 4–5.

Weyand and his staff decided to begin LANIKAI as soon as possible after the national election. On 14 September Colonel Booth's command group moved to the Long An town of Ben Luc, about thirty-five kilometers due south of Cu Chi. Most of the battalion followed the next day. As the convoy pulled into Ben Luc, a crowd of two thousand Vietnamese greeted the Americans. During a short ceremony the district chief welcomed the battalion and gave Booth a bloodstained Viet Cong flag mounted on a plaque; in return, Booth made the district chief an honorary member of the battalion. Because Ben Luc turned out to be too small to accommodate all three of Booth's rifle companies, he decided to rotate the units. Two companies would stay at Ben Luc, while the third would remain in reserve at Cu Chi.[22]

The battalion expected significant Viet Cong opposition. According to available intelligence, the enemy appeared to maintain a heavy presence in the area: the *506th Local Force* and the *2d Independent Battalions*, each with four hundred to five hundred men; seven independent Viet Cong companies, each with up to two hundred men; a heavy weapons company of unknown strength; and an unknown number of guerrillas.

Terrain and weather also posed challenges for the Americans. Long An was extremely flat, with no discernable terrain features, and was crisscrossed with rivers, canals, and irrigation ditches that provided excellent mobility for Viet Cong traveling in small boats. Additionally, the southwest monsoon was in full swing. The days were cloud covered, and heavy and frequent rainstorms made movement by foot impossible in many areas and extremely fatiguing in nearly all others. Water was knee to chest high in the rice paddies, mines and booby traps made walking on the dikes hazardous, and mud and thick vegetation on the riverbanks made marching insuperably difficult for any distance. Troops often had to be ferried to target zones by helicopter or in the boats of the South Vietnamese Navy's 24th and 28th River Assault Groups.

The work was varied. On 29 September Booth's Company B, a squad from the South Vietnamese battalion, and members of a Go Team helicoptered to the hamlet of Xom Dong. Landing unopposed, the troops surrounded the settlement and began a systematic check of the inhabitants' credentials. When eighteen suspected Viet Cong were flushed out, all were immediately evacuated to Ben Luc for interrogation. In another hamlet a civil affairs team gave cakes, lanterns, and candles to one hundred thirty-five school children.

During LANIKAI Booth's troops applied the full range of American pacification techniques. They distributed clothes, food, and other gifts at children's festivals, provided pamphlets to explain America's goals in Vietnam, delivered sanitation kits to orphanages, and handed out educational kits to schools. A psychological operations team made

[22] AAR, Opn LANIKAI, 4th Bn, 9th Inf, pp. 11, 13, 16, 19.

25th Division troops wade through the mangrove south of Ben Luc.

extensive airdrops of leaflets, designed to persuade enemy soldiers to surrender through the *Chieu Hoi* program. On 3 November, while a MEDCAP team treated nearly twelve hundred patients in the hamlet of Ben Nhut and passed out soap and toothpaste, the psychological operations team air-dropped three hundred thousand propaganda leaflets.[23]

Two days later Booth's 4th of the 9th Infantry returned to Cu Chi, ending LANIKAI I, and the 4th of the 23d Infantry took over the mission. By the standards of the usual search and destroy operation the 26 enemy killed during the operation seemed a paltry haul. Nevertheless, Colonel Booth maintained that LANIKAI I had achieved much and that the campaign had wide significance for the American war effort. Starting with the assumption that body counts had little bearing on the success of a pacification-oriented operation, he based the success of his task force on three criteria: how much the South Vietnamese Army and the Regional and Popular Forces improved through their association with the Americans; how much the local populace, after close exposure to the Americans, looked upon them favorably; and how quickly American and South Vietnamese forces were able to exploit hard intelligence gained during the operation. Admitting candidly that pacification was "complex, delicate, and often exasperating," Booth insisted that opera-

[23] Ibid., pp. 2–5, 19, 37, 52.

tions such as LANIKAI I, while "neither dramatic or immediately impressive," offered "a fruitful approach and holds more prospect of enduring results in certain geographical areas than other methods practiced for the elimination of the VC infrastructure."[24]

Not everyone in the division believed in pacification. Booth's successor in LANIKAI, Lt. Col. Louis J. North of the 4th of the 23d Infantry, found the process of leaflet drops and MEDCAP support not only tedious but unproductive, with little to show for the time and effort invested.[25]

While LANIKAI I was under way in Long An, Colonel Tarpley launched a new effort, Operation KAILUA, in Hau Nghia Province. Starting on 14 October, his 2d Brigade and the South Vietnamese 49th Regiment, 25th Division, targeted the northern part of the province, conducting small unit searches, buddy operations, and hamlet medical efforts. They also introduced two programs aimed at disrupting the enemy's movement of men and supplies: CHECKMATE, under which the Americans and South Vietnamese established random checkpoints along major roads; and BUSHMASTER, a system under which night ambushes targeted the lines of communication.[26]

All of the 25th Division's operations were facilitated by the existence of two joint operations and intelligence centers, one at Bao Trai and the other at Trang Bang. Initially established during Operation MAILI, the centers provided a forum for American and South Vietnamese commanders to pool information. Prior to their establishment, information gathered by a South Vietnamese source in Hau Nghia had to travel all the way up the South Vietnamese chain of command to III Corps headquarters before being sent to II Field Force headquarters, which in turn would send the information back down the American chain to a tactical unit in Hau Nghia for action. This process often took several days to complete, by which time the data was too old to be of value. By sharing information directly with each other at the local level through the joint operations and intelligence centers, American and South Vietnamese commanders were able to act on information generated by their counterparts with much greater speed and effectiveness. During Operation KAILUA information provided through the joint centers led U.S. and South Vietnamese units to initiate over twenty operations, many of which resulted in contact. No large battles occurred, but the forces involved in small unit day-to-day actions reported 67 of the enemy killed by body count and possibly another 175. Security in northern Hau Nghia seemed to improve.[27]

---

[24] Ibid., pp. 55–57 (quotations, p. 56); AAR, Opn LANIKAI [II], 4th Bn, 23d Inf, 18 Dec 66, p. 3, box 5, 68A/75, RG 319, NARA.

[25] AAR, Opn LANIKAI [II], 4th Bn, 23d Inf, p. 14.

[26] ORLLs, 1 Aug–31 Oct 66, 25th Inf Div, p. 5, and 1 Nov 66–31 Jan 67, 25th Inf Div, pp. 2–3.

[27] Interv, author with Maj Gen Harley F. Mooney, 15 Oct 98, Historians files, CMH; Action Memo 122, Mission Council, 20 Sep 66, sub: Minutes of the Mission Council Meeting, September 17, 1966, p. 3.

An Overview

But how much did security improve in 1966? Ambassador Lodge thought the gains significant, at least in Hau Nghia, for he told President Johnson that "we are winning" thanks to General Weyand's visionary support for pacification. Indeed, the statistics were impressive. In August Lodge reported that the government had gained control over 53 percent of Hau Nghia's population, up from only 20 percent at the start of the year. Between January and October the 25th Division had handed out food and clothing to fifty-six thousand people, provided free medical care to more than fifty-four thousand, and had hosted parties for over four thousand children. It had distributed millions of propaganda leaflets, engaged in over three hundred construction projects, and directly supported pacification in hundreds of other ways. Encouraged and assisted by the Americans, the South Vietnamese government's moribund institutions became more active and its forces more aggressive, undertaking more operations and demonstrating greater skill. During the second half of the year the Regional and Popular Forces had succeeded in recruiting over eleven hundred new members in Hau Nghia, while in October the revolutionary development cadre program in the province had grown from three to five groups and had achieved 75 percent of its goals in the hamlets in which it was operating. The 25th Division found similar good news in Long An, albeit on a lesser scale given the short time in which division elements had operated there.[28]

Yet, like the statistics in the big unit war, the tallies of villages and hamlets secured, civilians fed, and children inoculated were unreliable indicators of progress. In September the American senior adviser in Hau Nghia Province, Lt. Col. Andrew M. Rutherford, openly doubted whether the revolutionary development cadres had truly achieved 75 percent of their goals, noting that the cadres never stayed overnight in their assigned hamlets and were doing little to improve hamlet security or win popular support for the government. He likewise rated American county fair operations, in which the 25th Division used band music during lunches hosted by district chiefs to ameliorate the unpleasantness of hamlet screenings, as "ham-handed and clumsy attempts to win over the people" that were "little understood by the inhabitants."[29]

Although the number of enemy big unit operations and mortar attacks declined precipitously in Hau Nghia, the number of small-scale assaults, ambushes, mining incidents, and assassinations had increased slightly during 1966 despite allied pacification efforts. A similar trend existed in Long An, where American embassy officials disputed the 25th

[28] Msg (quoted words), Saigon 3429 to State, 13 Aug 66, Historians files, CMH; ORLL, 1 Aug–31 Oct 66, 25th Inf Div, pp. 20–22; Bergerud, *Dynamics of Defeat*, p. 159; Special Joint RD Rpt, Hau Nghia Province, 30 Sep 66, p. 1, RD files, CMH.

[29] Bergerud, *Dynamics of Defeat*, p. 153 (first quotation); Special Joint RD Rpts, Hau Nghia Province, 31 Jul 66, p. 1 (second quotation), and 30 Sep 66, p. 4, RD files, CMH.

Division's claims of increased security by arguing that the number of enemy soldiers operating in the province since the division's arrival had actually grown from thirty-two hundred to six thousand. Despite some improvements, the South Vietnamese 25th Division retained its reputation as being one of the worst outfits in the South Vietnamese Army, the Viet Cong underground remained largely intact, and nighttime travel along the roads of Hau Nghia and Long An continued to be dangerous. Moreover, given the mediocre performance of South Vietnamese officials in reasserting government authority and winning support in the countryside, any measurable progress had been gained largely through military action. Even the American ambassador had to admit that much had to be done and that progress would continue only if U.S. combat units remained in place.

Unfortunately, limited manpower proved to be just as much a hindrance in pacification as it was in the main force war. General Weyand's strong commitment notwithstanding, only 25 percent of his operations were dedicated to pacification support while he concentrated on eliminating the main forces and their bases. Even if he had the luxury of focusing totally on the local guerrillas, he hardly had enough men for the job; according to his estimate, an infantry battalion could only control a circular area some twelve kilometers in diameter. With just six infantry battalions, he was in no position to expand his hold over territory. Against an enemy who had been entrenched in the countryside for over thirty years, Weyand had barely begun to impose the type of security necessary for success.[30]

The two philosophies of war in Vietnam—main force combat and pacification—were in clear contention in the countryside surrounding Saigon. To the north and northwest main force regiments roamed the tangled jungles near Cambodia, a serious problem for both American and South Vietnamese units. In the delta and in many other rural areas farther from the sanctuaries in Cambodia local forces and guerrillas were the primary threat. This did not make the security situation there any better; in many of the regions, such as Long An, Communist control was almost total. But, as the 25th Division's experience illustrated, while it was difficult to force the guerrillas into a fight, the allies had to show the population that they were willing and able to maintain security over the long run. Clearly, both pacification and search and destroy had their role in the war. The problem was that the Americans could not do both. A lack of troops forced them to shift from place to place in search of the enemy, ensuring that security would be only temporary, which is precisely what happened in Hau Nghia

---

[30] Briefing, CG, 25th Inf Div, for Preparedness Investigating Subcommittee, Senate Committee on Armed Services, 23 Oct 66, vol. 3, incl. 2, p. 8; Hunt, *Pacification*, p. 52; Bergerud, *Dynamics of Defeat*, pp. 161–62; Msg, Saigon 3429 to State, 13 Aug 66; ORLL, 1 May–31 Jul 66, 25th Inf Div, app. 14, p. 2.

Province. Operation KAILUA was three weeks old when the South Vietnamese had to assume control because the 25th Division had been ordered to Tay Ninh Province to support Operation ATTLEBORO, launched against an ominous main force threat. The guerrillas in Hau Nghia had been waiting for this. They moved quickly to fill the vacuum when the Americans departed.

16

Summing Up

By the end of October 1966 the U.S. armed forces had fought in South Vietnam for almost eighteen months. Between May and December 1965 they had succeeded in achieving the objectives of the emergency phase of the war, assuring the immediate survival of the South Vietnamese nation. Then, through the autumn of 1966 they had attempted to take the war to the enemy and foil his efforts to regain the initiative while continuing their troop buildup and establishing bases and other installations. The number of U.S. military personnel in the theater grew in the process, from 184,313 at the beginning of 1966 to 351,572 at the end of October. Over the same period the number of U.S. Army troops increased from 116,755 to 221,067. As 1966 drew to a close, U.S. forces were poised to take the offensive, a step that General Westmoreland believed would lead to eventual victory. "We now have three consecutive large scale operations planned starting after the first of the year," he wrote in December. "This is the first time I have had enough troops to engage in such an ambitious program. Hopefully, they will achieve great success."[1]

Operational Developments

The U.S. experience in South Vietnam during 1965 and 1966 was at the root of Westmoreland's judgment, for he and his commanders had come to believe that they had a grip on what they had to do to win. Having started with a list of ideas and techniques of what the war would entail, they had validated some while eliminating others. They also had the power of American technology to back them.

Over the past months the search and destroy operation had become the chief means employed by American ground forces. The operation invariably took place in Communist-dominated territory and was "aimed at neutralizing the enemy's main forces and destroying his supply and operational bases." General Westmoreland phrased it tactfully as a re-

---

[1] Westmoreland Jnl, 13 Dec 66, Westmoreland History files, CMH.

statement of the infantry's traditional mission of finding, fixing, fighting, and finishing the enemy. But at its core were a rawness and a vigor that appealed deeply to the American soldier, who was impatient with delay and who viewed war as the wreaking of total chaos upon one's adversary. Although U.S. commanders used other methods, such as clear and hold, search and destroy remained their tactic of choice. It would, Westmoreland believed, eventually inflict enough unacceptable losses in men and materiel on the Viet Cong and North Vietnamese to force them to settle up on terms favorable to the United States and its allies.[2]

Whatever the hopes of senior American commanders, the allied contingent in South Vietnam was essentially on the defensive through much of 1966. No matter how the goals for such operations as MASHER/WHITE WING, PAUL REVERE, and EL PASO were phrased, the Americans were in a buildup mode. The brigades and divisions that were present had to concentrate upon providing security either for units that would follow or for those that were involved in opening roads, improving ports, building air bases and other installations, and in general laying down the support structure that the U.S. Army required. If search and destroy was the preferred tactic for large unit American operations during 1965 and 1966, the end most often served was that of keeping the Communists at bay by thwarting their attempts to mass for attacks, by demolishing their supply caches and base camps, by cutting their lines of infiltration into the South, and by spoiling their plans to seize important harvests.[3]

Westmoreland would later contend that those operations had disrupted the enemy's plans, kept him off balance, and induced high casualties among his troops. That may have been the case, but the situation was hardly clear cut, for the enemy usually controlled the tempo of the fighting and thus the rate at which he suffered casualties. Whether an engagement pitted a small American patrol against a few guerrillas or an American battalion against a main force unit, the enemy usually decided when to fight and when to withdraw. Beyond that, the American soldier normally fought from the tactical defensive even if he was supposedly on the offensive. On numerous occasions an American company, battalion, or brigade would enter an area suspected of harboring enemy units and find signs of them but no soldiers. Then the Viet Cong or North Vietnamese would attack, sometimes before, sometimes after the American unit had established a defensive position. Regardless of when the assault occurred, the Americans would almost always wind up fighting back from within a 360-degree perimeter. In describing the 1st Cavalry Division's battle at Landing Zone X-RAY in November 1965, an intelligence officer observed that the cavalry battalion "attacked" by

---

[2] MACV History, 1965, p. 161 (quotation), CMH; Westmoreland, *A Soldier Reports*, p. 83.
[3] Davidson, *Vietnam at War*, p. 350.

moving toward a known enemy stronghold near the Cambodian border. The North Vietnamese then "defended" the area by "attacking" the American unit at the foot of the Chu Pong Massif, at which time the offensively minded Americans went on the "defensive."[4]

Complicating matters even further was the fact that commanders could view the war in 1965 and 1966 from a number of perspectives. From one angle, it was an area war involving not only North and South Vietnam but also Laos and Cambodia. From another, it constituted a range of simultaneous conflicts that ran in stages, from a classic small unit/guerrilla contest at one end to a conventional large unit/main force war on the other. And intermingled was the contest to win the allegiance of the South Vietnamese people, the pacification war.

The burdens involved in coordinating the various efforts were clearly apparent in Westmoreland's concept of operations. The general felt obliged to commit most of his American and third-country forces to the large unit war because, as he later wrote, "the enemy had committed big units and I ignored them at my peril."[5] But in the process he had to pay attention to the counterinsurgency struggle and the pacification campaign, as well as remain sensitive to South Vietnamese and American politics. In the end, Westmoreland pulled it all together by saying that the big unit war was a way station along the path to President Johnson's political objective: a secure, pacified South Vietnam. Without military security, none of the other political, social, and economic programs sponsored by Saigon and Washington would make much headway. In that respect, how he waged the war would change with the nature of the threat and how the situation was developing.

In pursuing the war, the frequency of both small and large unit combat proved to be considerably less than what Westmoreland's commanders wanted because of the difficulty in finding and fighting the enemy. Looking back on his experience as the 1st Infantry Division commander, General DePuy remarked, "I guess I was surprised . . . about the difficulty we had in finding the VC. We hit more dry holes than I thought we were going to hit. They were more elusive than I had expected."[6] The U.S. and South Vietnamese systems for collecting, analyzing, and distributing intelligence improved over time, making dry holes less frequent. Even so, the accuracy and timeliness of the information on the enemy developed by allied analysts would never be wholly satisfactory to officers in the field, such as General DePuy, whose troops lived or died on the basis of the intelligence their commanders received.

Just as inadequate intelligence had its impact on the Army's performance, so too did a lack of sufficient combat forces. Westmoreland later

---

[4] Ltr, Maj John Pritchard, Asst S–2, 3d Bde, 1st Cav Div, to Capt John A. Cash, [1967], box 16, 74/053, RG 319, NARA.

[5] Westmoreland, *A Soldier Reports*, p. 149.

[6] DePuy, *Oral History*, p. 160.

observed that "the cordons erected when the enemy was found were sieve-like, and the enemy often escaped . . . because neither Americans nor South Vietnamese possessed overwhelming numbers."[7] The unfamiliarity of American commanders with the difficult terrain further diminished the odds of finding and surrounding the opposition.

Westmoreland's commanders responded by modifying their tactics. Believing that the Viet Cong and North Vietnamese were more likely to assault a small or poorly defended force rather than a large well-positioned one, they broke down their units into platoon- and company-size patrols to lure them into attacking. The risks were justified if the Communists took the bait, because reinforcing units could then pile on. The approach generated some successes, but it also had drawbacks. On several occasions the unit that served as bait took heavy casualties when reinforcements and fire support were delayed. In another effort to generate combat, commanders ran what appeared to be lightly defended convoys down roads in hopes of inducing the enemy to attack. The tactic worked in the case of the Minh Thanh Road encounter during Operation EL PASO II, but subsequent attempts failed.

Army maneuver elements supported the pacification effort directly and indirectly in 1966. In such operations as the 25th Infantry Division's LANIKAI commanders assigned an American unit, usually an infantry battalion, to work with South Vietnamese Army, police, and government authorities in cordon and search, medical and dental, propaganda, and entertainment activities in a specific hamlet or group of hamlets. These operations often led to the identification and capture of enemy soldiers on leave, members of the Communist underground, or South Vietnamese military deserters, and it was hoped that the entertainment and medical care would incline the local inhabitants more favorably toward the central government. In I Corps the U.S. Marines engaged in similar efforts. Although the 25th Division became associated with pacification support more than most Army units, all divisions and separate brigades in 1965 and 1966 participated in these activities to a greater or lesser degree, particularly the units charged with protecting base camps.

Pacification operations contributed directly to attrition when they resulted in the killing or capture of local force soldiers and guerrillas. Conversely, U.S. Army units in search and destroy operations sustained pacification by driving enemy units out of populated territory, where they obtained supplies and recruits, to less hospitable mountain and jungle areas. A forced withdrawal by the *3d PAVN Division* in the 1st Cavalry Division's Operations THAYER I and IRVING gave South Vietnamese authorities the chance to reestablish local administration and to win the inhabitants over to the Saigon government. In these cases, however, the assigned government officials were often less than diligent in pro-

---

[7] Westmoreland, *A Soldier Reports*, p. 152.

viding the social, economic, and political services and reforms that were necessary to do the job.

Fire support, whether delivered by tube artillery, helicopter gunships, or the Navy and Air Force, often provided infantry units with the critical margin they needed for success and even survival. When enemy tactics or bad weather prevented the application of fire support, as occurred at Landing Zone ALBANY in November 1965 and at Landing Zone PINK during PAUL REVERE II in August 1966, the results could be catastrophic for the American unit. Such disasters were rare, but when they happened they made clear the need for the lavish fire support that technology provided; without it, the U.S. Army's troops were about evenly matched with the enemy's well-trained regulars. Westmoreland had no doubts. "Our major advantage in war," he told his commanders, "lies in our superior firepower."[8]

The level of fire support available to the American soldier and his allies grew rapidly as the ground war developed in 1965 and 1966. Carrier-based aircraft, Navy warships offshore, Air Force planes stationed in South Vietnam or elsewhere, artillery batteries deployable around the battlefield, and helicopter gunships—they all supplied fire when called upon. Given the profusion of sources, the question for commanders became not whether they could get help but how they could use what they had most efficiently. The 1st Division's battles at Nha Mat in December 1965 and on the Minh Thanh Road in July 1966 provide examples of effective response. Using roads or other clearly defined terrain features to create fire coordination lines, American forces laid down powerful fields of fire that took a heavy toll of the enemy.

The amount of firepower expended in 1966 in support of the ground forces in combat represented only a small percentage of the total applied. About a third of the bomb tonnage and artillery rounds was directed against targets discovered by maneuvering units or patrols. The rest, harassment and interdiction fire, went against targets where the enemy might or could have been. The contrast is even more striking when naval and Air Force fires are stripped away and the Army's artillery is viewed by itself. In 1966 Army artillery fired 15 percent of its rounds in support of troops in combat and the remainder as harassment and interdiction. General Seaman agreed that the tactic was "overdone in many cases because we were firing into the wild blue yonder, [and] not exactly sure what was there."[9] General Johnson had deeper reservations. "We got into a firepower war," he said in 1973, ". . . where firepower was not really effective. Ammunition costs were simply astro-

---

[8] Briefing, Gen William C. Westmoreland, 25 May 68, sub: Lessons in Strategy, p. 8, Westmoreland History files, CMH.

[9] Thomas C. Thayer, ed., "A Systems Analysis View of the Vietnam War, 1965–1972," vol. 4, "Allied Ground and Naval Operations," pp. 207–08, CMH; Interv, John Albright with Lt Gen Jonathan O. Seaman, 4 Nov 70, p. 12 (quotation), Historians files, CMH.

nomical, and when we first began to examine where our artillery ammunition went, we found something in the neighborhood of 85% of it was unobserved fire, which was a rather staggering volume. I don't know what good it was doing."[10] Still, harassment and interdiction fire represented a high degree of security to a unit that had pulled into a perimeter after a long, hard day of combat.

The relationship between fire and maneuver in combat operations changed as the ground war evolved during 1965 and 1966. On the basis of its experience in World War II the Army entered the Vietnam War assuming that "firepower and maneuver were the fundamental elements of combat." Under that theory, the application of firepower preceded attacks in order to permit the infantry and armor to take objectives without suffering heavy casualties.[11] As the Vietnam War developed, General DePuy came to a different conclusion. Reflecting on his own experience as an infantry commander in World War II, he decided that his unit's most significant contribution to victory in Europe had been its support for the artillery. "My battalion," he recalled, "was the means by which Field Artillery forward observers were moved to the next piece of high ground. Once you had a forward observer on a piece of ground, he could call up five to ten battalions of artillery and that meant you had moved combat power to the next observation point." In a ground war "what you're trying to do . . . [is] move combat power forward to destroy the enemy, and the combat power that you are moving forward has been . . . mostly artillery."[12]

DePuy's generalizing "infuriated the Infantry School," as he himself admitted, but the approach it outlined was well suited to the kind of war the United States was fighting in Vietnam. Up against an elusive opponent and fighting on terrain that often favored the Viet Cong and North Vietnamese, commanders expanded the role of firepower, transforming it from an effort to soften a target in preparation for a final infantry assault to an outright attempt to eradicate all resistance.[13] Thus, an infantry assault on an enemy position became a last-chance choice, one that would likely produce unacceptably high friendly casualties while failing to generate the level of enemy losses desired by the American command.

One of General DePuy's brigade commanders, Colonel Berry, explained the approach in 1968. "Commanders at all levels," he wrote, "should seek the enemy with minimum forces and then use maneuver

[10] Interv, Lt Col James B. Agnew with Gen Harold K. Johnson, 21 May 74, sec. 15, p. 20, Senior Officer Oral History Program, MHI.
[11] Boyd L. Dastrup, *King of Battle: A Branch History of the U.S. Army's Field Artillery* (Fort Monroe, Va.: Office of the Command Historian, United States Army Training and Doctrine Command, 1992), p. 226.
[12] DePuy, *Oral History*, pp. 86–87.
[13] Ibid., p. 86 (quoted words); Lt. Gen. John H. Hay, Jr., *Tactical and Materiel Innovations*, Vietnam Studies (Washington, D.C.: Department of the Army, 1974), p. 180.

units to block the enemy's withdrawal and supporting firepower to destroy him. They should seek to avoid heavy infantry attack on, or entanglement in, enemy fortified positions. The key to success . . . is the massive use of supporting firepower."[14] Berry emphasized that the unit locating the enemy should not hesitate to break contact and withdraw far enough to permit free, uninhibited employment of supporting fires. Afterward, the unit could push small elements forward to survey the situation, continue the search, or bring in new supporting fires. The degree to which artillery actually finished off the Viet Cong and North Vietnamese in a given instance frequently proved difficult to ascertain because of their skill at withdrawing from battle and removing their dead and wounded. Still, by the middle of 1966 the levying of firepower on enemy positions had become "the dominant characteristic of American [ground] operations."[15]

The helicopter also came into its own during the period, but especially in 1966. Adding a vertical element to ground combat, it distinguished the Vietnam War from all previous conflicts. As the indispensable instrument of airmobile warfare, the helicopter, in the usage of a later military generation, was a "force multiplier," making it possible to reinforce a sister unit in combat miles away. As a troop carrier, it moved soldiers to and around the battlefield; as a resupply vehicle, it brought ammunition, food, and other supplies to a platoon or company in need; as a utility vehicle, it moved artillery units to appropriate locations with great promptness; and as an ambulance, it evacuated the wounded rapidly to fully equipped hospitals in the rear area. At the same time, helicopter gunships supported the infantry with fire in a focused way that neither artillery nor fixed-wing air strikes could equal. For General Westmoreland and others, the helicopter was "the greatest breakthrough in tactical mobility since the first time a doughboy went into battle aboard an armed vehicle."[16]

But if the helicopter endowed troops in the field with advantages, it also had drawbacks. Its limited ability to fly at night and in poor weather lessened its impact, as did an inability to carry a standard load of men or cargo in the thin air of South Vietnam's Central Highlands and similar elevations. In addition, there never seemed to be enough helicopters during battle. The machine's popularity with commanders, and the fact that it was the only means of taking the war to the enemy on many occasions, resulted in too great a demand chasing too small a supply.

---

[14] Sidney B. Berry, Jr., "Observations of a Brigade Commander," Part 1, *Military Review* 48 (January 1968): 17.

[15] Robert A. Doughty, *The Evolution of US Army Tactical Doctrine, 1946–1976* (Fort Leavenworth, Kans.: Combat Studies Institute, U.S. Army Command and General Staff College, 1979), p. 38.

[16] General William C. Westmoreland, "[Honoring Army Aviators]" (Address given at Army Aviation Association of America Annual Meeting, Washington, D.C., November 1, 1968), p. 1, Historians files, CMH.

The 1st Cavalry Division was unique in possessing, as an organic part of its force structure, enough helicopters to carry out almost any operation assigned. Still, the division did at times stretch itself thin—for example, in November 1965, when it had only sixteen helicopters available to lift the 1st Battalion, 7th Cavalry, into Landing Zone X-Ray. Although the Department of the Army committed itself to create another airmobile division, it would not do so until 1969. Chronic deficiencies in spare parts and in the number of aviators, as well as the large fuel requirements and the high maintenance overhead, contributed to this delay.

The helicopter may also have taken an unanticipated toll on the will and morale of the soldier. Despite all of its obvious benefits, the aircraft moved the soldier so rapidly from the rear to the field that it eliminated a critical period in which the soldier of the past had prepared himself mentally for battle. "Men entering combat," General Johnson explained, needed time "to build themselves up psychologically" as the moment to go into battle approached, but in Vietnam that preparatory period practically disappeared because of the helicopter. Units not engaged in combat became rapid-reaction forces that could be deployed on short notice. "An individual could be playing volleyball in base camp when a call came for assistance," Johnson said, and "an hour later, through the use of the helicopter, . . . [he was] engaged in violent combat." Such "rapid and traumatic changes" could be endured only to a certain point.[17] Johnson believed that the twelve-month tour of duty eased the tension, to a degree, by limiting the number of times soldiers could participate in combat air assaults. Even so, if he was right, the very rapidity with which the helicopter could thrust a soldier into combat might have diminished his effectiveness.

Did the helicopter's promise to increase the operational and the tactical mobility of American maneuver units bear out in Vietnam? Freed from what General Kinnard termed the "tyranny of terrain," were American commanders able to deliver forces to the battlefield from any point on the compass and then to shift them according to the demands of an engagement? Only the first part of this promise was realized in 1965–66. Commanders readily sent troops to various parts of the battlefield to block, assault, flank, and envelop the enemy. After a time, however, the enemy caught on to the tactic and began to identify likely landing zones and to assign forces to lie in wait to attack the incoming troops at their moment of greatest vulnerability—when they were deploying from their helicopters. Once the troops had landed, moreover, U.S. commanders, worried about the helicopter's vulnerability, were rarely willing to use it to move forces around an active battlefield, even though the helicopter's ability to do just that had been one of the arguments justi-

---

[17] Gen Johnson's Critique of "Department of the Army: The Buildup, 1965–1967," p. 9, Historians files, CMH.

fying an airmobile division. As a result, once on the ground, American forces in the jungles, rice paddies, and mountains of South Vietnam were often less mobile than their Viet Cong or North Vietnamese opponents. Despite these disadvantages, the helicopter represented an essential element of the American war effort. Westmoreland in 1968 posed the question, "What would we do without helicopters?" His answer was simple. "We could not do the same job. We are a three-dimensional Army, and every unit in Vietnam depends greatly on airmobility."[18]

Benchmarks

The conflict in South Vietnam in 1965 and 1966 was truly Westmoreland's war. "I . . . had a carte blanche," the general stated unequivocally in 1969, in "devising and pursuing tactics and battlefield strategy of the war." President Johnson "never tried to tell me how to run the war. . . . He deferred to my judgment, and he let me run the war . . . as I saw fit. He backed me and supported me without exception."[19] In late 1965 attrition emerged as the guiding principle for American combat operations. American policy required the establishment of a stable, independent, viable, and non-Communist South Vietnam. Seeing the enemy units in South Vietnam as the major military obstacle to achieving that goal, Westmoreland made "the destruction of the main force units" his "ultimate military objective."[20] He maintained that the president and his senior advisers had endorsed this approach in early 1966, when they adopted, among other objectives, the goal of killing or wounding at least as many soldiers during the year as the other side could infiltrate or recruit. By doing so the allies could reach what the MACV commander called the "crossover point," the level at which the enemy's losses would exceed his gains and his strength would begin to decay.[21] Westmoreland's senior commanders understood the approach and the imperatives it entailed. As General Larsen observed, U.S. forces had to "destroy the [North Vietnamese regulars] . . . first, destroy the hard core [Viet Cong] next, and finally root out the [Communist] infrastructure. Only after that could an effective pacification effort begin."[22]

[18] Westmoreland, "[Honoring Army Aviators]," p. 6.
[19] Interv, Dorothy Pierce McSweeny with Gen William C. Westmoreland, 8 Feb 69, pp. 12–13, Oral History Collection, AC77–32, LBJL.
[20] Sharp and Westmoreland, *Report*, p. 6; Briefing, Westmoreland, 25 May 68, sub: Lessons in Strategy, p. 3 (quotation).
[21] Westmoreland, *A Soldier Reports*, p. 161; Memo, John T. McNaughton, Asst Sec Def, International Security Affairs, for Sec Def, 10 Feb 66, sub: 1966 Program To Increase the Effectiveness of Military Operations and Anticipated Results Thereof, p. 2, file MCNTN VII—Late Vietnam (2) Tab K, box 3, Paul C. Warnke Papers, LBJL.
[22] Debriefing, Larsen, 31 Jul 67, an. B, pp. 1–2, Senior Officer Debriefing Program, DA, Historians files, CMH.

Westmoreland later came under criticism for adopting this approach.[23] In reply, he raised a stark question: Given the geographical constraints imposed by President Johnson and the limit on the number of American troops available to him, "what alternative was there?"[24] Acknowledging that attrition had been "a strategy in disrepute" since World War I, he nonetheless argued that, "for all the horrendous cost, it eventually worked."[25] He thought that "a long-term grinding machine" would work in Vietnam as well.[26]

In measuring success, American military and civilian authorities considered the body count critical. By the time General Westmoreland took charge of the war, the indices for measuring progress were already in place, deeply rooted in the statistical methodology advanced by Secretary of Defense McNamara.[27] McNamara believed that "things you can count, you ought to count." Westmoreland, with less enthusiasm, noted that although "statistics were . . . an imperfect gauge of progress, . . . in the absence of conventional front lines, how else to measure it?"[28] Both assumed that the figures arriving on their desks were reasonably accurate and maintained, in McNamara's words, that as "a measurement of the adversary's manpower losses" the body count would allow U.S. analysts to know when they had reached Westmoreland's crossover point.[29] Other American officials and generals in South Vietnam were less at ease with the body count as the key indicator of progress, but most took a line of least resistance because, as DePuy put it, "there didn't seem to be any other way to keep track of progress."[30]

The numbers themselves were revealing. On 1 January 1966 MACV estimated the strength of enemy forces in South Vietnam, including main force units, local forces, guerrillas, and political cadre, to be approximately 240,000. By the end of October, despite the Americans and their allies having killed some 48,000 soldiers during ten months, the MACV

---

[23] Krepinevich, *The Army and Vietnam*, pp. 164–68, 260; Bruce Palmer, Jr., *The 25-Year War: America's Military Role in Vietnam* (Lexington: University Press of Kentucky, 1984), pp. 178–79; and Harry G. Summers, Jr., *On Strategy: A Critical Analysis of the Vietnam War* (Novato, Calif.: Presidio Press, 1982), pp. 86–88.

[24] Westmoreland, *A Soldier Reports*, p. 153.

[25] Westmoreland, "Military War of Attrition," in *Lessons of Vietnam*, pp. 65–66.

[26] Interv, Charles B. MacDonald with Gen William C. Westmoreland, 12 Mar 73, Historians files, CMH.

[27] Briefing, Asst CofS, J–2, MACV, for Preparedness Investigating Subcommittee, Senate Committee on Armed Services, 18 Oct 66, sub: Intelligence Estimate, incls. D and G, vol. 1, box 21, 69A/702, RG 334, NARA. For an example of earlier use of the body count, see Memo, Thomas L. Hughes, Bureau of Intel and Research, for Sec [State], 22 Oct 63, sub: Statistics on the War Effort in South Vietnam Show Unfavorable Trends, in *U.S.-Vietnam Relations*, 12:V.B.4(bk.II):579–82.

[28] McNamara, *In Retrospect*, p. 238, and Westmoreland, *A Soldier Reports*, p. 273.

[29] McNamara, *In Retrospect*, p. 238.

[30] DePuy, *Oral History*, p. 162.

TABLE—KILLED IN ACTION STATISTICS, JANUARY–OCTOBER 1966

Month	Enemy	American	South Vietnamese
January	2,934	285	792
February	4,964	420	1,009
March	5,842	430	928
April	3,644	288	945
May	4,384	449	961
June	5,310	482	1,185
July	5,359	356	1,006
August	5,511	369	914
September	4,582	351	803
October	5,534	250	357
Total	48,064	3,680	8,900

Source: Monthly Eval Rpts, MACV, Jan–Oct 66, MHI; Table 52 in Southeast Asia Statistical Sum, Office Asst Sec Def (Comptroller), 3 Dec 73, Historians files, CMH.

strength estimate had grown to 271,000 (*Table*). This represented a net gain of some 31,000, which implied that in this ten-month period the Communists had added just under 80,000 men to their forces by infiltration and recruitment.[31] While part of the increase was almost certainly the result of improved intelligence on enemy units already present at the beginning of the year, the final estimates indicated that Westmoreland was still far from his objective of inflicting losses at a higher rate than possible for the other side to replace. Addressing this body of statistics, Secretary McNamara concluded in a 17 November draft memorandum for the president that "we have no prospects of attriting the enemy force at a rate equal to or greater than his capability to infiltrate and recruit."[32] Westmoreland, however, did not then or later modify his own belief that attrition represented a viable approach for which he saw no alternative.

One analyst of the war, Brig. Gen. Douglas Kinnard, would write later that the body count could be taken to mean almost whatever anyone wanted. What was important, he contended, was the will of each participant to fight on without wavering, whatever the losses he sustained. General DePuy said much the same thing in 1979. "My biggest surprise," he reflected, "and this was a surprise in which I have lots of

[31] Monthly Eval Rpts, MACV, Jan–Oct 66, by month, pp. 55, 52, 3, 51, 61, 73, 72, 74, 81, 76; Periodic Intel Rpts, 1 Jan–30 Jun 66, MACV, 20 Aug 66, p. 9, and Oct 66, MACV, 20 Nov 66, p. 9. All in MHI.
[32] *Pentagon Papers* (Gravel), 4:370.

company, was that the North Vietnamese and Viet Cong would continue the war despite the punishment they were taking. I really thought that the kind of pressure they were under would cause them to perhaps knock off the war for awhile, as a minimum, or even give up and go back north. But I was completely wrong on that."[33]

In assessing progress region by region, MACV had fairly good indications of its success in coaxing the main forces out of their usual operating areas, where established sources of supplies and recruits sustained them, into less hospitable territory. In the western highlands the *B3 Front* carefully husbanded its units well into 1966, keeping them either in Cambodia and Laos or in isolated redoubts in Kontum and Pleiku Provinces. The *Front* commander, General Man, after seeing his forces hit hard in the Pleiku campaign in late 1965, ordered them into Cambodia to refit and recuperate. They emerged only occasionally to fight the Americans over the next several months—during the PAUL REVERE operations in Pleiku Province and during HAWTHORNE in Kontum. This reluctance of the enemy to operate on the high plateau allowed the Americans to station, for part of the year, a relatively small body, the 3d Brigade, 25th Division, to conduct an economy-of-force mission there.

In II Corps' coastal provinces U.S. and allied forces, beginning with Operation MASHER/WHITE WING, gradually ground down the three regiments of the *3d PAVN Division* in Binh Dinh and the two regiments of the *5th PAVN Division* in Phu Yen and compelled their withdrawal, at least temporarily. As South Korean forces assumed responsibility for securing more of the lowlands, the Americans became available for additional spoiling operations against enemy formations. In Operations DAVY CROCKETT and CRAZY HORSE in May the 1st Cavalry Division fought elements of the *3d Division* again and hit them hard. The 1st Brigade, 101st Airborne Division, later joined by the cavalry division, did the same in June, when it fought the *5th Division's 18B Regiment* in NATHAN HALE. Later efforts continued the harrying of these main force units. In Binh Dinh Province Operations THAYER I and IRVING allowed the cavalry division and American allies to embark on a general province-wide pacification campaign, which would continue into early 1968. In Phu Yen Province various American units, with South Vietnamese and South Korean support, conducted search and destroy operations, using quasi-guerrilla tactics to bring the enemy to battle.

In III Corps American methods and objectives remained essentially the same as those in II Corps, qualified by the requirement that the capital, Saigon, be protected at all costs. Until August 1966, when fresh troops began to arrive, the 1st Division, two brigades of the 25th Division, and the 173d Airborne Brigade carried out the combat mission in III Corps.

---

[33] Kinnard, *War Managers*, p. 74; DePuy, *Oral History*, p. 160 (quotation).

From a series of base camps that increasingly formed a defensive arc around the capital city, the divisions and brigade conducted many large unit operations, from MARAUDER and CRIMP in January to BIRMINGHAM in April and May. Although General Westmoreland could not say with absolute certainty that his forces had secured Saigon, he was satisfied that spoiling operations in the early months of 1966 had basically accomplished that goal. As a result, he allowed units belonging to II Field Force to begin moving farther afield. The *9th PLAF Division* operating mostly north of Saigon, the *5th PLAF Division* working east of the city, and a host of other main and local force units represented the Americans' most significant operational targets. The two high-level command-and-control headquarters, *COSVN* and the *B2 Front*, generally thought to be northwest of Saigon in War Zone C or across the border in Cambodia, also received a good deal of attention.

General Westmoreland had believed that the Communists would initiate a concerted effort against American and allied troops in the Saigon region during the southwest monsoon season, which began in May. For that reason, he directed his senior commanders to carry out spoiling operations before and during the rainy season to keep the enemy off balance. Launching Operation EL PASO II and conducting a series of attacks north of Saigon that culminated in the battle of the Minh Thanh Road, Westmoreland, Seaman, and DePuy all believed by early July that they had broken the back of the offensive. The Viet Cong's apparent retreat into distant strongholds did nothing to disabuse Westmoreland of this belief.

Looking back, it seems clear that U.S. operational efforts in 1966 had damaged the main forces and curtailed their activities. In II Corps the Americans had stemmed the Communists' advances in the highlands while starting to neutralize their sources of manpower on the coast. In III Corps the Americans had stifled various enemy initiatives. Although Westmoreland recognized that these accomplishments were hardly absolute, they were still encouraging enough to confirm his belief that the search and destroy approach was working. Officials in Washington, even those privy to McNamara's analysis of the casualty figures, generally accepted Westmoreland's view. And so Westmoreland's analysis became the basis for continued action. Emboldened by his progress in 1966 and secure in the belief that he had found a formula for victory, Westmoreland in early September told General Johnson that "my future strategy is to continue to carry the fight to the enemy but with a greater tempo and mass."[34]

Westmoreland made such declarations with full knowledge of the opponent he faced. In a sober late-October appraisal of Communist capabilities and intentions, he asserted that the enemy had

---

[34] Msg, Westmoreland MAC 7745 to Gen Johnson, 6 Sep 66, sub: Airborne Capability in Vietnam, Westmoreland Message files, CMH.

embarked on a war of attrition involving protracted guerrilla warfare supported by large formations of conventional troops operating from base areas and sanctuaries in difficult terrain and neutral countries. His purpose is to create a state of mind in our troop units and at home that is characterized by insecurity and futility. There is no current evidence that he will change his strategy or tactics. He believes that his will and resolve are greater than ours. He expects that he will be the victor in a war of attrition in which our interest will eventually wane.[35]

Yet the MACV commander remained optimistic about the future of America's ground war. To his mind, for every strength the Communists possessed the Americans possessed a greater one. In time, the United States and its allies would prevail.

[35] MFR, Westmoreland, 23 Oct 66, sub: Assessment of the Situation in South Vietnam, October 1966, p. 3, Paul Miles Papers, MHI.

Bibliographical Note

Unpublished Sources

Two types of Army documents proved to be essential in the writing of *Stemming the Tide*: the periodic reports of divisions and separate brigades, and the combat after action reports prepared by or for units involved in operations. Since these accounts sometimes magnified success and minimized failure, researchers should treat them cautiously and, whenever possible, use them in conjunction with other records—for example, daily situation reports, daily journals, intelligence summaries and reports, and unit annual histories—to achieve a balanced understanding of the Army's performance and accomplishments in South Vietnam.

The periodic report, called the quarterly command report until the end of 1965, became in 1966 the operational report–lessons learned, or ORLL. However named, the report usually recorded a unit's activity over a three-month span, organized into sections on intelligence, operations, training, logistics, lessons learned, and other topics. It was supplemented by such inclosures as accounts of combat, statistics, maps, lists of commanders' names, and other subjects. The ORLL is useful for producing a general narrative of the unit's activities and for understanding much of the larger context of any particular operation. It fails, however, to provide sufficient detail on the individual operations and combat actions. For this, the researcher must turn to the combat after action report, or AAR.

Although an AAR was not produced for every combat operation, one was written for those deemed to be significant. The word *significant* had specific meaning to the staff of a unit preparing the report. In the 1st Cavalry Division a significant operation occurred if the enemy body count was high, if a maneuver element larger than a reinforced company carried out a separate operation, or if the tactical unit committed notable errors in the operation's planning or execution. In all of these cases an AAR had to be written. Accounts also had to be rendered in three other instances: if forces from a friendly nation or nations participated in an operation, if combat occurred as a result of enemy initiative, and if higher headquarters requested a report. The virtue of the AARs, beyond the obvious one of recordkeeping, was the resulting information—the valuable lessons—on which the Army could base future doctrine, tactics, techniques, and possible corrective action.

Typically, the staff of the commander responsible for carrying out an operation drafted the after action report, although on occasion special Army teams—military history detachments—did so. The larger the operation the more likely that not one but several AARs were forthcoming. In a division-size action the individual battalions involved often prepared accounts, and the brigades and the division did so as a matter of course. In addition, combat support units, such as engineer elements, might themselves produce an after action report. Each account of the operation usually followed an established outline with fifteen topical headings, the most important being intelligence, mission, concept of operation, execution, results, and commander's analysis or comments. The section with the commander's comments on the operation became the Army's first-level interpretation of the action and its significance.

Other sources have been exploited in preparing this volume. Interviews have proved valuable for fleshing out the narrative with detail about people and events missing from more formal reports, thus providing much needed contextual information. Personal accounts or memoirs have been used to fill gaps and, like the interviews, to add a human dimension often missing from official records. For background and insight into the higher conduct of the war, the MACV commander's backchannel messages and his journal, sundry American Embassy reports, foreign policy documentary collections, *The Pentagon Papers*, and material in President Johnson's papers were examined.

National Archives and Records Administration

Most of the Vietnam War documents cited in this volume are in the custody of the National Archives and Records Administration (NARA). The operational records are housed at its facility in College Park, Maryland, while the national security files and other White House–level material are located at NARA's Lyndon Baines Johnson Library in Austin, Texas.

At the College Park facility three record groups—Record Group (RG) 334, Records of Interservice Agencies; RG 338, Records of U.S. Army Commands; and RG 319, Records of the Army Staff—were used to research this volume. Together, they contained most of the ORLLs, AARs, daily journals, situation reports, intelligence summaries, and annual histories essential to the study of the war. After the manuscript was completed, however, NARA transferred the Vietnam War material in RGs 334 and 338, about thirty thousand linear feet, to a newly created record group—RG 472, Records of the U.S. Forces in Southeast Asia, 1950–1975. Because the citations in this volume reflect RGs 334 and 338, researchers should rely on the archivists at NARA to locate the documents in RG 472.

At the Johnson Library much of the material focuses on the formation and implementation of Vietnam War policy and strategy. However, certain items in the national security files on the war—for example, memoranda drafted by McGeorge Bundy, Robert S. McNamara, and other senior advisers to President Johnson—should be examined by researchers seeking to grasp the conflict's larger context. The library also contains the original set of the William C. Westmoreland Papers and an oral history collection. In the latter, Dorothy Pierce McSweeny's interview with General Westmoreland (8 Feb 69) was most helpful.

U.S. Army Center of Military History

At the U.S. Army Center of Military History (CMH) in Washington, D.C., three sets of Vietnam War records are noteworthy: a photocopied collection of the Westmoreland Papers, including his backchannel messages and journal, as well as additional material relevant to his work as the MACV commander; the Vietnam Interview Collection, consisting of reports prepared in theater by Army historians or by units themselves and based on interviews and documents; and the Vietnam Interview Tape Collection, containing tape-recorded interviews—some transcribed, some not—with participants in operations. Attached to both interview collections are supporting documents, such as after action reports, combat narratives, and daily journals.

Other useful CMH holdings are the copies of MACV's "Command History" for the years 1964 to 1966 and, in the Historians files collection, various AARs, ORLLs, and a number of long and short interviews.

To clarify the official record regarding specific operations or engagements, the following key participants were interviewed by telephone: Lt. Gen. Sidney B. Berry, Jr., Commander, 1st Brigade, 1st Infantry Division (15 Mar 95); Col. Kyle W. Bowie, Commander, 2d Battalion, 28th Infantry, 1st Infantry Division (11 Mar 99); Col. Gregory Dillon, S–3, 1st Battalion, 7th Cavalry, 1st Cavalry Division (2 Mar 94); Maj. Gen. John A. Hemphill, G–3 Forward, 1st Cavalry Division (23 Aug 96); Col. John D. Herren, Commander, Company B, 1st Battalion, 7th Cavalry, 1st Cavalry Division (6 Jul 95); Lt. Gen. Richard T. Knowles, Assistant Division Commander (Operations), 1st Cavalry Division (20 Aug 96); Col. Blake [George W.] McIlwain, Commander, Troop A, 1st Squadron, 9th Cavalry, 1st Cavalry Division (22 Nov 95); Maj. Gen. Harley F. Mooney, 2d Battalion, 27th Infantry, 25th Infantry Division (15 Oct 98); Lt. Gen. Harold G. Moore, Commander, 1st Battalion, 7th Cavalry, 1st Cavalry Division (18 Feb, 1 and 19 Jun 95, 19 Aug 96, and 7 Jul 98); Brig. Gen. William J. Mullen III, Commander, Company C, 1st Battalion, 2d Infantry, 1st Infantry Division (24 Feb 94); Lt. Gen. John Norton, Commanding General, 1st Cavalry Division (8 Mar 94); Col. James T. Root, Commander, 1st Battalion, 12th Cavalry, 1st Cavalry Division (27 Dec 95);

Brig. Gen. George M. Shuffer, Commander, 2d Battalion, 2d Infantry, 1st Infantry Division (25 Jun 98); Col. Robert B. Tully, Commander, 2d Battalion, 5th Cavalry, 1st Cavalry Division (19 Jun 95); and Maj. Gen. Ellis W. Williamson, Commanding General, 173d Airborne Brigade (22 Jan 93, 2 Jun 98, and 17 Jul 98). Senior analyst Robert J. Destatte of the Defense Prisoner of War and Missing Personnel Office (20 Oct 98), journalist Joseph L. Galloway (7 Jul 98), and General Tran Van Tra of the People's Army of Vietnam (23 Nov 90) were also interviewed.

The longer interviews cited include John Albright's interviews with Lt. Gen. William E. DePuy, J–3, MACV, and Commanding General, 1st Infantry Division (3 Apr 71), and with Lt. Gen. Jonathan O. Seaman, Commanding General, 1st Infantry Division and II Field Force, Vietnam (10 Sep and 4 Nov 70); Charles B. MacDonald's and Charles von Luttichau's with General Harold K. Johnson, Army Chief of Staff (20 Nov 70); Charles MacDonald's with General William C. Westmoreland (12 Mar 73); and Allan W. Sandstrum's with Lt. Gen. Stanley R. Larsen, Commanding General, Field Force, Vietnam, and I Field Force, Vietnam (6 Dec 68).

U.S. Army Military History Institute

During and after the war the U.S. Army Military History Institute (MHI) at Carlisle Barracks, Pennsylvania, received a large quantity of documents from the American military in South Vietnam, ranging from the tactical and operational (AARs and ORLLs) to the high-level conduct of the war (including MACV's monthly evaluations of the war, periodic intelligence reports, and other studies and reports). In most but not all instances these documents duplicate material in the National Archives. The institute also holds the personal papers of many senior Army officers, especially those of Generals DePuy and Seaman. DePuy's and Seaman's papers contain official reports and memoranda, as well as their personal correspondence with colleagues in the Army and friends and relatives at home, in which researchers will find comments on operations, on the enemy, on the nature of the war, on U.S. objectives and their attainment, and on other topics important to the prosecution of the war. Finally, a large collection of interviews of not only general officers but also battalion and company commanders who served in South Vietnam are also housed at MHI, most of which are available to the public.

Private Papers

Many collections of papers significant to understanding the Army's combat operations in South Vietnam in 1965–66 remain in private hands. Six such collections are those of retired Lt. Gen. Sidney B. Berry, Jr., Lt. Gen. Harold G. Moore, Maj. Gen. Ellis W. Williamson, Col. Leonard L.

Lewane, Col. Harry G. Summers, Jr., and Capt. Stephen M. Slattery, each of whom generously shared items in his papers as well as his experiences of the war.

Published Sources

Socialist Republic of Vietnam Histories

Researchers can experience the war from the enemy's perspective, and find much that is useful and provocative, in the official histories published in Hanoi. The accounts of North Vietnamese and Viet Cong units and campaigns seem reliable when addressing such topics as campaign objectives, order of battle, and movement of troops; however, they tend to be untrustworthy when describing the damage inflicted in battle against the Americans—for example, the number of soldiers killed and aircraft and ground vehicles destroyed.

Four of these histories have been used as sources for this work. Obtained and translated, either wholly or partially, under the auspices of the Center of Military History, they are:

Lich Su Quan Doi Nhan Dan Viet Nam [*History of the People's Army of Vietnam*]. 2 vols. Hanoi: Nha Xuat Ban Quan Doi Nhan Dan [People's Army Publishing House], 1974–90.

Luc Luong Vu Trang Nhan Dan Tay Nguyen Trong Khang Chien Chong My Cuu Nuoc [*The People's Armed Forces of the Western Highlands During the War of National Salvation Against the Americans*]. Hanoi: Nha Xuat Ban Quan Doi Nhan Dan [People's Army Publishing House], 1980.

Su Doan 9 [*9th Division*]. Hanoi: Nha Xuat Ban Quan Doi Nhan Dan [People's Army Publishing House], 1990.

Su Doan 325 (1954–1975) [*325th Division (1954–1975)*]. 2 vols. Hanoi: Nha Xuat Ban Quan Doi Nhan Dan [People's Army Publishing House], 1981–86.

The histories and translations may be used by researchers who visit the Center.

Captured enemy documents also offer insights into the implementation and effect of U.S. Army operations. Such documents exist in the thousands in a microform collection at the National Archives. Although a number of these documents are cited, exploiting them fully was and continues to be difficult because so few have been translated and because the automated finding aid to the collection can no longer be read.

Primary Publications

Foreign Relations of the United States, 1964–1968. Vol. 2. *Vietnam, January–June 1965*. Washington, D.C.: Government Printing Office, 1996.

The Pentagon Papers: The Defense Department History of United States Decisionmaking on Vietnam. Senator Gravel Edition, 4 vols. Boston: Beacon Press, 1971.

Public Papers of the Presidents of the United States: Lyndon B. Johnson, Containing the Public Messages, Speeches, and Statements of the President, 1963–64. 2 vols. Washington, D.C.: Government Printing Office, 1965.

Public Papers of the Presidents of the United States: Lyndon B. Johnson, Containing the Public Messages, Speeches, and Statements of the President, 1965. 2 vols. Washington, D.C.: Government Printing Office, 1966.

Stanton, Shelby L. *Vietnam Order of Battle*. New York: Galahad Books, 1986.

U.S. Congress, Senate, Committee on Veterans' Affairs. *Medal of Honor Recipients, 1863–1973*. 93d Cong., 1st Sess., 1973.

"United States and South Vietnamese Forces Launch Retaliatory Attacks Against North Viet-Nam." *Department of State Bulletin*, 22 Feb 65, p. 238.

United States–Vietnam Relations, 1954–1967: Study Prepared by Department of Defense. 12 vols. Washington, D.C.: Government Printing Office, 1971.

U.S. Department of Defense Official Histories

Bowers, Ray L. *Tactical Airlift*. United States Air Force in Southeast Asia. Washington, D.C.: Office of Air Force History, United States Air Force, 1983.

Clarke, Jeffrey J. *Advice and Support: The Final Years, 1965–1973*. United States Army in Vietnam. Washington, D.C.: U.S. Army Center of Military History, 1988.

Dastrup, Boyd L. *King of Battle: A Branch History of the U.S. Army's Field Artillery*. Fort Monroe, Va.: Office of the Command Historian, United States Army Training and Doctrine Command, 1992.

Hammond, William M. *Public Affairs: The Military and the Media, 1962–1968*. United States Army in Vietnam. Washington, D.C.: U.S. Army Center of Military History, 1988.

Marolda, Edward J., and Fitzgerald, Oscar P. *From Military Assistance to Combat, 1959–1965*. United States Navy and the Vietnam Conflict. Washington, D.C.: Naval Historical Center, Department of the Navy, 1986.

Sbrega, John J. "Southeast Asia." In *Case Studies in the Development of Close Air Support*, edited by Benjamin Franklin Cooling, pp. 411–90. Washington, D.C.: Office of Air Force History, United States Air Force, 1990.

Schlight, John. *The War in South Vietnam: The Years of the Offensive, 1965–1968*. United States Air Force in Southeast Asia. Washington, D.C.: Office of Air Force History, United States Air Force, 1988.

Shulimson, Jack. *U.S. Marines in Vietnam: An Expanding War, 1966*. Washington, D.C.: History and Museums Division, Headquarters, U.S. Marine Corps, 1982.

Shulimson, Jack, and Johnson, Maj. Charles M. *U.S. Marines in Vietnam: The Landing and the Buildup, 1965*. Washington, D.C.: History and Museums Division, Headquarters, U.S. Marine Corps, 1978.

Memoirs, Firsthand Accounts, and Special Studies

Beckwith, Charlie A., and Knox, Donald. *Delta Force*. New York: Harcourt Brace Jovanovich, 1983.

Cash, John A. "Fight at Ia Drang, 14–16 November 1965." In *Seven Firefights in Vietnam* by John A. Cash, John Albright, and Allan W. Sandstrum, pp. 3–40. Washington, D.C.: Office of the Chief of Military History, United States Army, 1970.

Clodfelter, Michael. *Mad Minutes and Vietnam Months: A Soldier's Memoir*. New York: Zebra Books, 1988.

Eckhardt, Maj. Gen. George S. *Command and Control, 1950–1969*. Vietnam Studies. Washington, D.C.: Department of the Army, 1974.

Giap, Vo Nguyen. *People's War, People's Army*. New York: Frederick A. Praeger, 1962.

Hackworth, David H., and Sherman, Julie. *About Face: The Odyssey of an American Soldier*. New York: Simon and Schuster, 1989.

Hay, Lt. Gen. John H., Jr. *Tactical and Materiel Innovations.* Vietnam Studies. Washington, D.C.: Department of the Army, 1974.

Hutchens, James M. *Beyond Combat.* Chicago: Moody Press, 1968.

Johnson, Lyndon Baines. *The Vantage Point: Perspectives of the Presidency, 1963–1969.* New York: Holt, Rinehart and Winston, 1971.

Kelly, Col. Francis J. *The U.S. Army Special Forces, 1961–1971.* Vietnam Studies. Washington, D.C.: Department of the Army, 1973.

Larsen, Lt. Gen. Stanley Robert, and Collins, Brig. Gen. James Lawton, Jr. *Allied Participation in Vietnam.* Vietnam Studies. Washington, D.C.: Department of the Army, 1975.

McChristian, Maj. Gen. Joseph A. *The Role of Military Intelligence, 1965–1967.* Vietnam Studies. Washington, D.C.: Department of the Army, 1974.

McNamara, Robert S., with VanDeMark, Brian. *In Retrospect: The Tragedy and Lessons of Vietnam.* New York: Times Books, Random House, 1995.

Mao Tse-tung. *On Protracted War.* Peking: Foreign Languages Press, 1967.

Mason, Robert. *Chickenhawk.* New York: Viking Press, 1983.

Mertel, Kenneth D. *Year of the Horse—Vietnam: 1st Air Cavalry in the Highlands.* New York: Exposition Press, 1968.

Moore, Harold G., and Galloway, Joseph L. *We Were Soldiers Once . . . and Young. Ia Drang: The Battle That Changed the War in Vietnam.* New York: Random House, 1992.

Neel, Maj. Gen. Spurgeon. *Medical Support of the U.S. Army in Vietnam, 1965–1970.* Vietnam Studies. Washington, D.C.: Department of the Army, 1973.

Operation Cedar Falls: I Corps Battle Analysis Conference, 13–14 September 1988. Fort Lewis, Wash.: History Office, 1988.

Ploger, Maj. Gen. Robert R. *U.S. Army Engineers, 1965–1970.* Vietnam Studies. Washington, D.C.: Department of the Army, 1974.

Sharp, U. S. Grant. *Strategy for Defeat: Vietnam in Retrospect.* San Rafael, Calif.: Presidio Press, 1978.

Sharp, Admiral U. S. G., and Westmoreland, General William C. *Report on the War in Vietnam (as of 30 June 1968).* Washington, D.C.: Government Printing Office, 1969.

Starry, General Donn A. *Mounted Combat in Vietnam.* Vietnam Studies. Washington, D.C.: Department of the Army, 1978.

Smith, Jack P. "Death in the Ia Drang Valley." *Saturday Evening Post,* 28 Jan 67, pp. 80–85.

Summers, Harry G., Jr. "Would You Believe . . . ?," p. 46. Sidebar to Seitz, Quentin L., Jr. "Phu Loi Cornered." *Vietnam* 5 (April 1993): 42–49.

Tho, Brig. Gen. Tranh Dinh. *Pacification.* Indochina Monographs. Washington, D.C.: U.S. Army Center of Military History, 1980.

Tully, Walter B. "Company B," *Armor* 76 (September/October 1967): 13–19.

Westmoreland, William C. *A Soldier Reports.* Garden City, N.Y.: Doubleday and Co., 1976.

Oral Histories

Brennan, Matthew, ed. *Headhunters: Stories From the 1st Squadron, 9th Cavalry, in Vietnam, 1965–1971.* Novato, Calif.: Presidio Press, 1987.

DePuy, General William E. *Changing an Army: An Oral History of General William E. DePuy, USA Retired.* Interviewed by Romie L. Brownlee and William J. Mullen III. [Carlisle Barracks], Pa., and Washington, D.C.: U.S. Army Military History Institute and U.S. Army Center of Military History, 1988.

Cochran, Alexander S., Jr., with Kinnard, Harry W. O. "First Strike at River Drang." *Military History* 1 (October 1984): 44–51.

Maurer, Harry, comp. *Strange Ground: An Oral History of Americans in Vietnam, 1945–1975.* New York: Avon Books, 1989.

Secondary Publications

Bergerud, Eric M. *The Dynamics of Defeat: The Vietnam War in Hau Nghia Province*. Boulder, Colo.: Westview Press, 1991.

Berry, Sidney B., Jr. "Observations of a Brigade Commander," Part 1. *Military Review* 48 (January 1968): 3–21.

Breen, Bob. *First To Fight: Australian Diggers, N.Z. Kiwis and U.S. Paratroopers in Vietnam, 1965–66*. Sydney, Australia: Allen and Unwin, 1988.

Carland, John M. "Double Ambush on Route 13." *Vietnam* 1 (Spring 1989): 42–49.

Cochran, Alexander S., Jr. "American Planning for Ground Combat in Vietnam, 1952–1965." *Parameters* 14 (Summer 1984): 63–69.

Coleman, J. D. *Pleiku: The Dawn of Helicopter Warfare in Vietnam*. New York: St. Martin's Press, 1988.

Davidson, Phillip B. *Secrets of the Vietnam War*. Novato, Calif.: Presidio Press, 1990.

———. *Vietnam at War: The History, 1946–1975*. Novato, Calif.: Presidio Press, 1988.

DePuy, William E. "Troop A at Ap Tau O." *Army* 36 (November 1986): 50–60.

Doughty, Robert A. *The Evolution of US Army Tactical Doctrine, 1946–1976*. Fort Leavenworth, Kans.: Combat Studies Institute, U.S. Army Command and General Staff College, 1979.

1st Cavalry Division (Airmobile). *1st Air Cavalry Division: Memoirs of the First Team, Vietnam, August 1965–December 1969*. Tokyo, Japan: Dai Nippon Printing, [1970].

Galvin, John R. *Air Assault: The Development of Airmobile Warfare*. New York: Hawthorn Books, 1969.

Garland, Albert N., ed. *Infantry in Vietnam*. Fort Benning, Ga.: Infantry Magazine, 1967.

Gelb, Leslie H., and Betts, Richard K. *The Irony of Vietnam: The System Worked*. Washington, D.C.: Brookings Institution, 1979.

"The Gallup Poll: Less Than 40% of People Follow Vietnam Events." *Washington Post*, 27 May 64.

Hallin, Daniel. *The Uncensored War: The Media and Vietnam*. New York: Oxford University Press, 1986.

Harris, Louis. *The Anguish of Change*. New York: W. W. Norton, 1973.

Herring, George C. *America's Longest War: The United States and Vietnam, 1950–1975*. 3d rev. ed. New York: McGraw-Hill, 1996.

———. "The 1st Cavalry and the Ia Drang Valley, 18 October–24 November 1965." In *America's First Battles, 1776–1965*, edited by Charles E. Heller and William A. Stofft, pp. 300–26. Lawrence: University Press of Kansas, 1986.

Hunt, Richard A. *Pacification: The American Struggle for Vietnam's Hearts and Minds*. Boulder, Colo.: Westview Press, 1995.

Hymoff, Edward. *The First Air Cavalry Division, Vietnam*. New York: M. W. Lads Publishing Co., 1967.

Just, Ward. "Ain't Nobody Been Walking This Trail but Charlie Cong." In *A Short History of the Vietnam War*, edited by Allan R. Millett, pp. 73–80. Bloomington: Indiana University Press, 1978.

Kinnard, Douglas. *The War Managers*. Hanover, N.H.: University Press of New England, 1977.

Kinnard, Harry W. O. "A Victory in the Ia Drang: The Triumph of a Concept." *Army* 17 (September 1967): 71–91.

Krepinevich, Andrew F., Jr. *The Army and Vietnam*. Baltimore: Johns Hopkins University Press, 1986.

Lubenow, Larry R. "Objective Rice." *Infantry* 56 (November/December 1966): 41–42.

McNeill, Ian. *To Long Tan: The Australian Army and the Vietnam War, 1950–1966*. St. Leonards, New South Wales, Australia: Allen and Unwin in association with the Australian War Memorial, 1993.

Maitland, Terrence, and McInerney, Peter. *The Vietnam Experience: A Contagion of War*. Boston: Boston Publishing Co., 1983.

Mangold, Tom, and Penygate, John. *The Tunnels of Cu Chi*. New York: Random House, 1985.

Marshall, S. L. A. *Battles in the Monsoon: Campaigning in the Central Highlands, Vietnam, Summer 1966*. New York: William Morrow and Co., 1967.

Meyerson, Joel D. "War Plans and Politics: Origins of the American Base of Supply in Vietnam." In *Feeding Mars: Logistics in Western Warfare From the Middle Ages to the Present*, edited by John A. Lynn, pp. 281–87. Boulder, Colo.: Westview Press, 1993.

Moore, Harold G., and Galloway, Joseph L. "Death in the Tall Grass." *U.S. News & World Report*, 12 Oct 92, pp. 50–58.

Nack, William. "The Lonesome End." *Sports Illustrated* 79 (October 1993): 64–75.

Olson, James S., and Roberts, Randy. *Where the Dominos Fell: America and Vietnam, 1945–1995*. New York: St. Martin's Press, 1996.

Palmer, Bruce, Jr. *The 25-Year War: America's Military Role in Vietnam*. Lexington: University Press of Kentucky, 1984.

Pearson, Willard. "Day-and-Night Battle in Relief of an Outpost." *Army* 17 (March 1967): 54–58.

Rambo, A. Terry; Tinker, Jerry M.; and LeNoir, John D. *The Refugee Situation in Phu-Yen Province, Vietnam*. McLean, Va.: Human Sciences Research, 1967.

Seitz, Quentin L., Jr. "Phu Loi Cornered." *Vietnam* 5 (April 1993): 42–49.

Shuffer, George M., Jr. "Finish Them With Firepower." *Military Review* 47 (December 1967): 11–15.

Stanton, Shelby L. *Anatomy of a Division: The 1st Cav in Vietnam*. Novato, Calif.: Presidio Press, 1987.

Summers, Harry G., Jr. *On Strategy: A Critical Analysis of the Vietnam War*. Novato, Calif.: Presidio Press, 1982.

Sykes, Charles S., comp. *Interim Report of Operations: First Cavalry Division, July 1965 to December 1966*. Albuquerque, N.Mex.: 1st Cavalry Division Association, n.d.

Tourison, Sedgewick D. Jr., *Talking With Victor Charlie: An Interrogator's Story.* New York: Ivy Books, 1991.

Triplett, William. "Chaos in the Ia Drang." *Veteran* 6 (October 1968): 18–22.

Turley, William S. "Order of Battle of PAVN and PLAF." In *Encyclopedia of the Vietnam War*, edited by Stanley I. Kutler, pp. 385–402. New York: Charles Scribner's Sons, 1996.

Vinh Loc. *Why Plei Me?* Pleiku, 1966.

Westmoreland, William C. "A Military War of Attrition." In *The Lessons of Vietnam*, edited by W. Scott Thompson and Donaldson D. Frizzell, pp. 57–71. New York: Crane, Russak and Co., 1977.

Weyand, Frederick C. "Winning the People in Hau Nghia Province." *Army* 17 (January 1967): 52–55.

Map Symbols/Terms

Military Units

Function

Airborne Infantry . . . .

Airmobile Infantry . . . .

Armor . . . .

Armored Cavalry . . . .

Cavalry (Aerial Reconnaissance) . . . .

Field Artillery . . . .

Infantry . . . .

Marine Infantry . . . .

Size

Platoon . . . . • • •
Battery, Company, or Cavalry Troop I
Battalion or Cavalry Squadron II
Regiment III
Brigade X
Division . . . . X X
Corps . . . . X X X

Examples

Company C, 1st Battalion, 18th Infantry . . . . C ⊠ 1-18

2d Battalion, 35th Infantry . . . . 2 ⊠ 35

1st Brigade, 101st Airborne Division . . . . 1 ⊠ 101

Headquarters, 1st Cavalry Division (Airmobile) . . ⊠ 1 CAV

Culture Feature

Airfield . . . . ⊖

Air Base . . . . ⊜

Geographic Terms

Ap	Hamlet
Chu	Mountain
Dak	Stream
Dam	Bay, lake
Ia	River
Nui	Mountain, ridge
Prek	Stream
Se	River
Song	River
Suoi	Stream
Xa	Village
Ya	Stream

Abbreviations and Acronyms

ARVN	Army of the Republic of Vietnam
CAV	Cavalry
CIDG	Civilian Irregular Defense Group
COSVN	*Central Office for South Vietnam*
CTZ	Corps Tactical Zone
FF	Field Force
FSB	Fire Support Base, Firebase
FWD	Forward
LZ	Landing Zone
MR	*Military Region*
PAVN	*People's Army of Vietnam*
PLAF	*People's Liberation Armed Forces*
RAR	Royal Australian Regiment
RCN	Reconnaissance
ROK	Republic of Korea
SF	Special Forces
TF	Task Force

Index

ISBN 0-16-050198-9

9 780160 501982

90000

PIN : 076472–000